YOOKOSO!

ようこそ

YOOKOSO!

An Invitation to Contemporary Japanese

Yasu-Hiko Tohsaku
University of California, San Diego

McGraw-Hill, Inc.
New York St. Louis San Francisco Auckland Bogotá Caracas
Lisbon London Madrid Mexico City Milan Montreal New Delhi
San Juan Singapore Sydney Tokyo Toronto

This is an EBI book.

Yookoso! An Invitation to Contemporary Japanese

This book is printed on acid-free paper.

6 7 8 9 0 VNH VNH 9 0 9 8 7 6 5

ISBN 0-07-072291-9

Library of Congress Cataloging-in-Publication Data

Tohsaku, Yasu-Hiko.
Yookoso! : an invitation to contemporary Japanese / Yasu-Hiko Tohsaku.
p. cm.
Includes index.
ISBN: 0-07-072291-9
1. Japanese language—Textbooks for foreign speakers—English.
2. College readers. I. Title.
PL539.5.E5T64 1993
495.6'82421—dc20 93-7948
CIP

Sponsoring editor: Thalia Dorwick
Development editors: Karen Sandness and Pamela Pasti
Editing supervisors: Christina Dekker and Celine-Marie Pascale
Production supervisor: Tanya Nigh
Designer: Adriane Bosworth
Illustrators: Akiko Shurtleff and Rick Hackney
Cover designer: Francis Owens
Cover art by: Sally Vitsky
Photo researcher: Stephen Forsling
Compositors: Mitaka and GTS Graphics
Printer and binder: Von Hoffman Press
Cover color separator and printer: New England Book Components

Grateful acknowledgment is made for use of the following:

Photographs: *Page 1* © Hideaki Omura/Camera Tokyo Service; *33* © Burbank/The Image Works; *34* © Fujifotos/The Image Works; *55* © Fujifotos/The Image Works; *61* © Sonia Katchian/Photo Shuttle: Japan; *97* © Sonia Katchian/Photo Shuttle: Japan; *99* © Fujifotos/The Image Works; *103* © Charles Gupton/Stock, Boston; *107* © Fujifotos/The Image Works;

(*Continued on page 548*)

Contents

Linguistic Notes and Communication Notes are not listed here.

Topics / Vocabulary	Grammar

REVIEW CHAPTER 1 210

CHAPTER 4: WEATHER AND CLIMATE 217

CHAPTER 5: HOBBIES AND LEISURE ACTIVITIES 280

Topics / Vocabulary	Grammar

CHAPTER 6: FOOD 350

CHAPTER 7: SHOPPING 414

REVIEW CHAPTER 2

APPENDICES 489

To the Instructor

Welcome to *Yookoso! An Invitation to Contemporary Japanese*, a complete package of instructional materials for beginning Japanese. *Yookoso!* has been developed according to two basic premises: (1) Proficient communication is the goal of foreign language instruction; and (2) language's primary function is to allow people to communicate, interact, and negotiate meaning. These materials provide a starting point for oral and written activities and help students develop proficiency in the four language skills of listening, speaking, reading, and writing, as well as in developing cultural awareness. By promoting free interaction in the classroom, *Yookoso!* also helps students enjoy learning Japanese.

The *Yookoso!* materials and approach have been extensively class-tested with beginning students of Japanese. In our experience, students' proficiency in Japanese develops far better and faster with this approach, in which grammar is one of the tools for developing language proficiency, than with materials in which grammar is the focal point. The *Yookoso!* materials do not ignore grammar; rather, they integrate grammar in a different and, we hope, more useful way. Overall, the flexible framework of the *Yookoso!* materials can accommodate various approaches to language teaching and different learning styles.

Objectives of the *Yookoso!* Program

The objectives of these materials are the following:

- to teach the listening skills needed to understand a basic core of topics relevant to everyday life and the students' interests
- to teach the oral skills needed to talk about these topics and to function in basic everyday situations in Japanese
- to teach skimming, scanning, and intensive reading skills
- to teach basic writing skills, including descriptions and some functional writing tasks, such as letter writing

- to provide grammar explanations that help students acquire functional skills more readily
- to provide sociocultural information useful to beginning-level Japanese language students

Components

There are two major student components in the *Yookoso!* program:* a main text and a combined workbook and laboratory manual. The main text contains three preliminary chapters in Getting Started and seven main chapters. All chapters are organized according to topics essential to communication at the beginning level, and they include numerous cultural, linguistic, and grammar notes that help put language learning into context.

The workbook/laboratory manual includes listening comprehension activities, **kanji** exercises, and writing activities.

In addition to the main textbook and the combined workbook/laboratory manual, the *Yookoso!* package includes an instructor's manual, an audiotape program, a video program, and a computer program. Using these materials greatly enhances the effectiveness of the textbook.

- The *Instructor's Manual* includes a general introduction to the communicative approach to language teaching and learning, general guidelines for using this textbook, a sample lesson plan and syllabus, sample semester and quarter schedules; suggestions for using and expanding the text materials, additional exercises, models for vocabulary introduction and expansion, other teaching hints and techniques, sample tests and quizzes, listening comprehension materials, and scripts for the Listening Comprehension section of each chapter and the Situations section of the Review chapters. A transcript of the listening comprehension activities from the audio program is also included.
- The *Audiocassette Program* includes recorded oral texts from the textbook and the workbook/laboratory manual. (It may be used by students in a language laboratory or purchased by them to use at home.)
- The *Video Program* includes some situations and dialogues presented in the textbook and others related to chapter topics. The majority of segments were shot in Japan and include a variety of interactions in natural settings.
- The *Computer Program*, based on the Hypercard program for Macintosh computers, is designed so that students can review **hiragana**, **katakana**, **kanji**, vocabulary, and grammar outside of class.

*A follow-up to *Yookoso!*, appropriate for intermediate students, is planned for 1994. Please consult the publisher for information about it.

Organization of the Textbook

Getting Started

Yookoso! begins with three preliminary chapters called Getting Started. These chapters are a functional introduction to the Japanese language. In them, students learn to express themselves in a variety of situations without formally studying grammar. At the same time, they learn to read and write **hiragana** and **katakana** and are introduced to the basic concepts and uses of **kanji**. Getting Started also explains the organization of the main chapters.

Chapters 1–7

Chapters 1 through 7 are organized as follows:

Opening page, with chapter objectives and a photo
Vocabulary and oral activities
Grammar and exercises
Active vocabulary and **kanji** for the chapter
Reading and writing activities
Language functions and situations
Listening comprehension practice

- The *opening page* of each chapter lists the topics, categories of vocabulary, grammatical structures, language functions, and situations that students will study in the chapter. In addition, it contains a photo related to the theme of the chapter, which can be used as a starting point for oral activities or class discussion.
- The *Vocabulary and Oral Activities* section is intended for vocabulary building and oral communication practice in the classroom. Activities in this section are designed so that students can build up their knowledge of vocabulary and grammar and practice using them in natural communicative situations, in an integrated fashion. Some activities start with (勉) Grammar (number), which provides a cross reference to the relevant sections of Grammar and Exercises.
- The *Grammar and Exercises* section includes concise explanations of grammar with examples and short exercises. This section is closely linked to other parts of the text, including the Vocabulary and Oral Activities section, and the exercises may be done either orally or in writing. In most cases, these series of exercises begin with mechanical drills and proceed through contextualized exercises to creative, free-answer sequences. Answers to most of the exercises are given in Appendix 8 of the textbook so that students can check their responses on their own. The separation of Grammar and Exercises from the other sections of the chapter makes it possible to accommodate deductive, inductive, or eclectic approaches to teaching grammar in the classroom.
- The *Active Vocabulary and **Kanji*** are reference lists of all the new vocabulary and **kanji** that have been introduced for active learning. Students can use these lists for reference and review. The **kanji** in each chapter are selected for their connec-

tion to chapter themes and for their high frequency in materials written for adult readers of Japanese. *Yookoso!* includes about 380 characters in Volumes One and Two that are presented as active **kanji**, those which students are required to learn to write.

- The *Reading and Writing Activities* section contains two sets of reading materials and writing assignments. Most of the reading selections are semiauthentic and related to a chapter theme; they are based on a variety of authentic materials, such as magazine articles, personal messages, and advertisements. All reading selections are preceded by activities to facilitate students' comprehension of the content and help them develop good reading strategies. Post-reading activities are mostly comprehension-oriented; in some cases, they encourage students to apply their reading skills to other related materials. Some writing exercises are extensions of the preceding reading activities, in that students write a response to the content of the reading selection or write a similar passage on their own. Other writing exercises encourage students to write about their own lives and ideas by using the vocabulary and grammatical structures they have learned in the chapter.
- In the *Language Functions and Situations* section, students learn how to express themselves in specific real-life situations. Students first study dialogues that illustrate functional language and situations related to chapter themes. Then they practice interacting in role plays enabling them to engage in real communication in meaningful contexts.
- In the *Listening Comprehension Activities* section, students practice comprehending the general content of rather lengthy conversations or narratives related to chapter themes. This section includes training in listening for meaning and tasks to perform based on the listening. It can also serve as the basis for a variety of interactive oral activities in class. A cassette with the listening comprehension selections is part of the Audiocassette Program; a transcript of the selections appears in the Instructor's Manual.

Additional Features

- *Boxed notes* are provided at logical points throughout the text to present helpful information and hints for students. There are four types: Culture Notes, Communication Notes, Grammar Notes, and Linguistic Notes. *Culture Notes* provide information on Japanese culture that is important or pertinent for understanding vocabulary and facilitating oral or written activities. *Communication Notes* provide information useful for communicating smoothly in a variety of real-life situations. *Grammar Notes* present brief information on grammar that is helpful for conducting oral activities or understanding reading materials. *Linguistic Notes* highlight certain characteristics of the Japanese language in a way that benefits beginning-level Japanese language students.
- *Study hints* provide advice about how to acquire language skills: how to learn vocabulary, **kanji**, verb conjugations, and so forth.
- *Marginal notes* provide brief references to previously presented grammar, offer sociolinguistic information, and so on.

- *Realia*, *photos*, and *line drawings* make the text more appealing to students so that they will seek out more information on the Japanese people and culture. Some of them may serve as a starting point for oral and written activities, while others are intended to expose students to real culture; others are simply decorative. The authentic realia enriches the learning environment by giving students opportunities to work with real-life materials and develop effective strategies for reading them. Students should be made aware that they need not try to understand everything presented in the realia.
- The *Review* sections follow Chapter 3 and Chapter 7. They include oral activities, interviews, listening activities, roleplay, and cultural readings, along with personal narratives called This Is My Life. These sections combine, recycle, and review vocabulary, grammar, and language functions presented in previous chapters.

The Cast of Characters

The same set of characters appears repeatedly throughout the text. The three main characters are students from North America studying Japanese language and culture at the University of Tokyo. Their classmates, professors, homestay family members, neighbors, and friends interact with them. These people reappear in dialogues, grammar examples, reading materials, and listening comprehension activities. We believe that the use of these characters clarifies the social relationships that are a key factor in determining speech style and the use of honorifics in Japanese. In order to keep the structure of the textbook flexible we have avoided using a "story line" concept.

Orthography

Students are expected to master the reading and writing of **hiragana** and **katakana** while working with Getting Started. All texts in Getting Started are presented in a style of romanization that combines the Hepburn system and the Government Ordinance System. When representing Japanese place and personal names commonly known among English speakers, however, we may use their familiar romanized spellings.

The author believes that students can best learn to read Japanese by being exposed as much as possible to normal Japanese writing from the early stages of their study of the language. For this reason, romanization is limited to Getting Started, and from Chapter 1 on every attempt is made to present materials that are as orthographically natural as possible. The materials students use for oral and reading activities are written just as native speakers of Japanese would write them. **Hurigana** accompanies a **kanji** in the chapter in which it is first presented and also in the following chapter. Thereafter, no **hurigana** are provided for that **kanji**.

The materials in the Grammar Exercises also follow this principle, but students need not use **kanji** that have not yet been presented for active learning, and they may write these words in **hiragana**.

Organization of Workbook/Laboratory Manual

The accompanying workbook/laboratory manual consists of three sections:

Listening Activities (coordinated with audiocassette tapes)
Kanji Exercises
Writing Activities

- The *Listening* and *Writing Activities* sections, intended to help students review the grammar, vocabulary, and language functions presented in the main text, are organized along the same line as the Vocabulary and Oral Activities section of the main text. The Listening Activities section is designed to develop listening comprehension abilities through dialogues, interviews, and narratives. The Writing Activities section provides additional vocabulary and grammar practice through a variety of means, from controlled, mechanical exercises to creative, free-response activities. Several activities in these sections are realia-based, and many of them can also be used for speaking practice.
- The *Kanji Exercises* section for each chapter consists of a list of newly introduced **kanji**, including the pronunciations, meanings, examples of use, and stroke order, followed by exercises. This section also includes some interesting and useful notes about **kanji** and the writing systems of Japanese (for example, the radicals, the principles of stroke order).

Methodology

This textbook has been developed based on the results of recent research into second language acquisition and language pedagogy. All activities and exercises have been designed so that students develop proficiency in Japanese rather than simply acquiring grammatical knowledge.

- The main purpose of this text is to teach students how to use language in real-life situations for different communicative purposes. Since activities involving interaction promote communication abilities, the textbook includes a variety of activities that serve as starting points for communicative interaction in the classroom.
- The role of grammar in language learning is less important than previously believed. The study of grammar is neither a sufficient nor a necessary condition for learning to communicate, and it is best learned through self-study outside of class. For this reason, grammar is presented in simple terms and via charts whenever possible. Easily understood explanations, abundant examples, and sample answers to exercises (provided at the end of the textbook) make it possible for students to study grammar on their own. Thus, instructors can devote precious class time to more meaningful communicative, interactive activities.

- In each chapter, all activities are related to the main theme, and students can practice listening, speaking, reading, and writing about this theme in an integrated way.
- Topics selected for the textbook are all relevant to college students' lives and interests. Topic-based organization presents meaningful contexts for language learning and raises students' motivation for learning the language.
- For successful language acquisition, learners must be exposed to meaningful input. Activities throughout the text are designed to encourage instructors and students to engage in meaningful interactions.
- The acquisition of vocabulary is of great importance for achieving proficiency, especially at the early stage of language learning. For this reason, a large number of vocabulary items is presented throughout the text.
- Language acquisition takes place when learners are trying to comprehend conveyed messages. Also, students must be able to comprehend before they can produce. Thus priority is given to the development of comprehension abilities over production abilities. In order to facilitate students' language acquisition, the activities are carefully sequenced from comprehension activities to simple production activities to creative, personalized production activities. Total Physical Response (TPR) has been proven to be an effective technique in helping beginning-level language students develop their comprehension abilities. For this reason, TPR will be used to introduce new vocabulary and expressions in *Getting Started.*
- Reintroduction of vocabulary, grammar, and language functions at regular intervals facilitates the development of students' proficiency. The cyclical organization of this textbook helps students review materials consistently and repeatedly.
- Group work encourages interaction and communication. For this reason, this textbook includes a variety of pair work, small-group work, and interviews, during which students can practice using language in a stress-free, nonthreatening atmosphere.

Acknowledgments

The author would like to acknowledge the following colleagues, friends, and students, all of whom have provided valuable feedback.

First of all, I would like to express my sincere appreciation to those who reviewed an earlier version of this text. Reviews are invaluable in the formulation of ideas. The appearance of the names of these reviewers does not necessarily constitute their endorsement of the text or its methodology.

Carl Falsgraf (University of Oregon), Michiko Hiramatsu (Foothill College, Foothill, California), Miyako Iwami (AJALT, Tokyo, Japan), Mitsuyoshi Kaji (AJALT, Tokyo, Japan), Hiroko Kataoka (University of Oregon), Toshiko Kishimoto (Clemson University), Akemi Kurokawa (University of California, Irvine), Haruko Matsui (AJALT, Tokyo, Japan), Keiji Matsumoto (California State University, Fullerton), Keiko Nishio (AJALT, Tokyo, Japan), Noriko Omae (Capilano College and Simon

Fraser University, British Columbia, Canada), Peter Patrikis (Consortium of Language Learning and Teaching), Yoko Pusavat (California State University, Long Beach), John Treat (University of Washington), Eri Yasuhara (California State University, Los Angeles), Toshiko Yokota (University of California, Irvine)

I thank the following colleagues for helping me class-test this textbook: Carl Falsgraf (University of Oregon), Sachiko Fuji (formerly at the University of California, Irvine), Mizue Funakoshi-Clark (Indiana State University), Miyoko Hamanaka (Mesa College), Hifumi Ito (University of California, San Diego), Noriko Kameda (Mira Costa College), Hiroko Kataoka (University of Oregon), Akemi Kurokawa (University of California, Irvine), Naoki Takei (Tokyo University of Foreign Studies), Yumiko Shiotani (University of Oregon), and Toshiko Yokota (University of California, Irvine).

I also would like to express my gratitude to Teruhiro Ishiguro, Joe Kess, Yuki Kuroda, Leonard Newmark, Marianne McDonald, Sanford Schane, and Jan Walls for their encouragement.

Many people at McGraw-Hill and their associates deserve my appreciation for their irreplaceable support and hard work in editing and producing this textbook: Laura Jones, Karen Judd, Kathy Melee, Tanya Nigh, Leda Ortega, Francis Owens, Celine-Marie Pascale, Mary Pasti, Pamela Pasti, Christina Dekker, Karen Sandness, Yoko Shioiri-Clark, Margaret Metz, Akiko Shurtleff, Stephen Forsling, Anita Wagner, Shinji Ichiba, Sally Vitsky, Edie Williams, Linda McPhee and Tomoko Gorgon. I owe a lot to artist Rick Hackney for his splendid illustrations. I also appreciate the help of Chieko Altherr, Yutaka Kunitake, and Masuhiro Nomura, who checked the linguistic accuracy and cultural authenticity of the text and provided other editorial assistance.

This project could not have been completed without the assistance, support, and encouragement of the following people at the University of California, San Diego: Bob Barker, Sheri Brusch, Jane Geddes, Sherman George, Peter Gourevitch, Linda Jones, Linda Murphy, Eric Nelson, and Jeff Winkler.

I would like to thank my wife, Carol, for always being beside me and inspiring me to write this textbook. And all my love to Umechiyo and Takechiyo, who are really what it's all about.

And finally, a very, very special thanks to Thalia Dorwick, who guided me throughout the development of this textbook, paying close attention to every detail and tirelessly providing me with advice and assistance. Her editorial leadership and talents made all the difference. She is a gem!

* * * *

My first attempt to write a Japanese language textbook within the framework of a communicative approach started about ten years ago when I read Tracy Terrell's papers on the Natural Approach. Later, I had the chance to work closely with Tracy on the same campus and to talk with him about language teaching. Many of his insights and enlightening ideas gave shape to this textbook. I dedicate this volume to the memory of Tracy Terrell. He will live in my heart and thoughts forever.

To the Student

Yookoso means *welcome* in Japanese, and we are delighted to welcome you to this program for learning contemporary Japanese. The main objective of this text is to provide you with opportunities to develop four communicative language skills in Japanese: listening, speaking, reading, and writing. You will also learn about Japanese culture in general and about features of Japanese culture that influence the use of the language in daily life.

With the *Yookoso!* approach, you will not only *learn about* the language by reading or hearing explanations of grammar, usage, and culture but also *acquire competence in using* the language through practical experience in communication. *Yookoso!* is designed so that you will have ample opportunities both to *acquire* the Japanese language experientially and *learn about* it consciously.

Yookoso!: An Invitation to Contemporary Japanese (the main textbook) and *Yookoso!: Workbook and Laboratory Manual* (the workbook) have different purposes. The main textbook, for use in the classroom, contains many activities that allow you to interact with your instructor and classmates. The workbook allows you to work on listening comprehension skills through practice with tapes and to do written exercises that reinforce the material introduced in class.

Chapters 1 Through 7

The main part of the text consists of seven regular chapters and two review chapters. Each regular chapter contains **Vocabulary and Oral Activities, Grammar and Exercises, Vocabulary, Kanji, Reading and Writing, Language Functions and Situations**, and **Listening Comprehension** sections, all centered on the thematic topic of that chapter.

Vocabulary and Oral Activities

The objective of this section is to provide you with opportunities to hear and speak everyday Japanese. While learning new vocabulary, expressions, and structures, you will practice using them in communicative contexts.

Vocabulary is presented in two ways. Those words presented in the **Vocabulary** boxes are considered essential for you to acquire so that you can survive in everyday situations and carry out daily activities. Words in the **Vocabulary Library** boxes allow you to express yourself more fully during classroom activities, and you need to learn only the ones that are relevant to your personal situation.

Some oral activities are designed so that you will learn how to use grammatical structures in communicative contexts. Those activities are preceded by the symbol (勉) along with the numbers for relevant **Grammar and Exercises** sections (the kanji in the circle means *study*). Depending on your learning style, you may want to read the grammar explanations and do the grammar exercises before doing the associated oral activities. On the other hand, you may want to plunge right into the oral activities, trying to infer the underlying structures as you practice speaking, and then check your understanding by reading the **Grammar and Exercises** section later. Whichever approach you prefer, the **Vocabulary and Oral Activities** section forms the core of each chapter, giving you opportunities to practice communicating in Japanese.

Grammar and Exercises

This part presents an explanation of the new grammatical structures followed by written exercises. You are not expected to learn all of the rules. Just read the explanations carefully and look at the examples to see how the rules work. Then verify your understanding by doing the written exercises. Be aware, however, that simply learning grammar won't make you a fluent speaker of the language, because when you speak you don't have time to choose and apply grammatical rules in a conscious manner. You will learn how grammatical rules are used in written materials and practice using some grammatical structures in writing in the **Reading and Writing** section.

Vocabulary

This section lists active new vocabulary organized by topics or categories, for your reference and review. Each new word or phrase is presented in **hiragana** or **katakana** (two of the three writing systems used in Japanese) in the first column of the vocabulary box. The **kanji form** (the third writing system), if there is one, appears in the second column. The third column gives the English equivalent of the word or phrase.

Kanji

You will learn how to read and write approximately 25 **kanji** in each chapter. The **Kanji** section in the middle of each chapter lists these active **kanji** simply for reference purposes, while the workbook explains their use and provides practice materials.

Reading and Writing

You and your classmates have come to the study of Japanese with various goals. Some of you may want nothing more than to read signs and menus when traveling in Japan, while others may hope to read Japanese literature in the original someday. You may never write anything more complicated than a brief personal letter, or you may write sophisticated research reports while studying at a Japanese university or working at a Japanese company. Whatever your ambition is, this section will help you build a foundation for developing reading and writing abilities in Japanese.

The reading materials chosen for each **Reading and Writing** section are related to the chapter's theme, and most of them are similar to the actual materials that native speakers of Japanese read in their everyday life. Your objective in most of these reading activities is to understand the overall meaning of the selection or to look for some specific information in it. You are not expected to understand every word and every grammatical structure. You may find some words and structures that you have not studied, but you may skip over them, as long as they are not necessary for understanding the main meaning. The meanings of essential but unfamiliar words are given in side notes, but you do not have to memorize them.

Writing activities are also related to the theme of the chapter. You will practice writing a variety of things by using the vocabulary and grammatical structures that you have been learning. In many cases, the preceding reading selection will serve as a model or a springboard for your own writing.

Language Functions and Situations

This section provides you with opportunities to practice using Japanese in real-life situations through role playing and other creative activities. In addition, you will learn a variety of useful expressions that will help you communicate smoothly with native speakers even with limited vocabulary and structures. You will also find hints for turning your interactions with native speakers into opportunities for extra language learning.

Listening Comprehension

The first step toward the acquisition of a foreign language is to develop a good listening comprehension ability. For this reason, the final section of each chapter is a set of listening activities in which you will check your comprehension of the vocabulary, expressions, and structures you have learned in the chapter. As you develop your ability to understand spoken Japanese, you will find that your ability to produce spoken Japanese also improves.

Review Chapters

When you study a foreign language, it is important for you to review and use previously studied items constantly and repeatedly. The **review chapters**, which appear after Chapter 3 and Chapter 7, give you opportunities to review vocabulary and structures and to synthesize and use them in different contexts. In addition, you will learn more about Japan and the Japanese people through the **Culture Reading** and **This Is My Life** reading selections.

Writing Systems

Because it is essential for you to be exposed to natural Japanese writing as early as possible, this textbook uses romanization (the familiar Latin alphabet) only in the preliminary **Getting Started** section. Unlike other beginning-level textbooks, it follows the standard Japanese convention of not using spaces between words. The *Yookoso!* approach may be difficult in the beginning, but it will help you acquire greater facility in reading authentic Japanese materials than do approaches that present unnatural writing at the beginning stages.

The best way to learn **kanji** is to have extensive and constant exposure to them. It is important for you to learn **kanji** in actual contexts rather than memorizing them one by one, so most materials in the book are written in standard Japanese style, including **kanji** that have not yet been introduced for active acquisition. The pronunciations of these unfamiliar **kanji** are indicated by **hurigana**, small **hiragana** written above them, so that you can identify them and recall their meanings.

While reading the questions in the grammar exercises, you will have further opportunities to see **kanji** in their natural contexts. When you write the grammar exercises, however, don't force yourself to write the unfamiliar **kanji**. Because **kanji** must be written following a strict stroke order, imitating the printed form without knowing the correct stroke order can lead to bad writing habits, so just write the words represented by nonactive **kanji** in **hiragana**, using the **hurigana** as a guide.

Getting to Know the Characters

Throughout the *Yookoso!* text, you will read and talk about a group of characters who appear repeatedly in oral activities, grammar exercises, and reading materials.

You will meet three main characters: two American students, John Kawamura and Linda Brown, and one Canadian student, Heather Gibson. All of them are currently studying at the University of Tokyo. Their academic majors are different, but they know one another through Professor Toshiko Yokoi's Japanese culture class.

You will also meet six of their classmates. Masao Hayashi, Hitomi Machida, and Takeshi Mimura are Japanese, while Henry Curtis and Mei Lin Chin are American and Chinese, respectively.

John Kawamura lives with his host family, the Yamaguchis. You will meet Kenji Yamaguchi, Yuriko Yamaguchi, Daisuke Yamaguchi, and Satomi Yamaguchi.

Linda Brown lives in an apartment in the Nakano area of Tokyo. You will meet her landlords, Kunio and Yoshiko Sano. Yooichi Takada and Yayoi Murayama are Linda's next-door neighbors. Both Takada and Murayama are company employees living alone. Sayuri Yamamoto works at a coffee shop across the street from Linda's apartment and is a good friend of hers.

Professor Kiyoshi Oono is a professor at the University of Tokyo and John's advisor.

Before Starting **Getting Started**

The main text begins with a section called **Getting Started**. By the end of it, you will have (1) developed some ability to comprehend spoken Japanese, (2) learned to recognize several classroom expressions that will allow your instructor to conduct the class sessions in Japanese as much as possible, (3) practiced expressing some basic ideas without studying grammar, and (4) come to understand the basics of Japanese pronunciation and accentuation. You will also master **hiragana** and **katakana** and learn how Chinese characters or **kanji** fit into the writing system.

The first step toward developing Japanese language proficiency is to develop your listening comprehension ability. Thus your instructor will use Japanese in class as much as possible, including words and phrases to which you have not yet been officially introduced. To understand the gist of what someone says, you need not understand every word. Try to concentrate on the key words only. For example, if your instructor is talking about what time he or she gets up in the morning, try to catch the words related to numbers, so you can guess the time. Also, pay a great deal of attention to your instructor's body language, gestures, and facial expressions.

Another important thing to note is that you need not know the underlying grammar rules to understand most of your instructor's message. While working with **Getting Started**, you won't study any formal explanations of grammar. As the course progresses, you will be amazed at how much you can understand and express without studying grammar at all, merely by immersing yourself in the language, guessing, and using a variety of clues. You will even find that you can figure out some of the grammatical rules of Japanese on your own while working with **Getting Started**.

The more vocabulary you learn, the more you can understand and the more ideas you can express. In the **Getting Started** section you will learn basic words that will become the basis for future comprehension and acquisition activities in class. The more you hear them and the more you use them, the sooner you will acquire correct pronunciation. These basic words, along with some basic expressions, are listed at the end of **Getting Started** for your review and reference.

In this section, you will do several different types of classroom activities: dialogues, role plays, description, and TPR (Total Physical Response).

You will need to practice the dialogues until you can act them out easily and fluently. It is perfectly natural to make mistakes, speak haltingly, and produce incomplete sentences at the beginning, so don't worry about it. Just relax, keep practicing, and have fun with the class activities. Then you will be ready to do the simple role plays presented in **Getting Started**.

In TPR activities, your instructor will give you a command, which he or she will then either act out or ask a Japanese-speaking assistant to act out. Your instructor will then have you act out the command on your own. You will be surprised at how much vocabulary you can learn by this method and how much complicated speech you can come to understand without receiving any formal instruction in grammar. Above all, TPR is fun.

While you are working on these classroom activities, you will learn **hiragana** and **katakana**, which are introduced in Parts One and Two of **Getting Started**. Your instructor will explain how to write each **hiragana** and **katakana** symbol, and then you will practice recognizing and writing them in your workbook.

Throughout your study of Japanese, be sure to consult your instructor if you have difficulty with any aspect of spoken or written Japanese. Foreign language instructors appreciate students who take responsibility for their own learning by asking questions.

With all this in mind, let's get started.

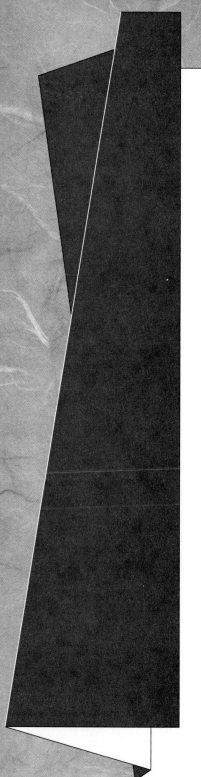

Getting Started

In **Getting Started** you will learn how to handle several everyday situations while getting acquainted with spoken Japanese. In addition, you will learn **hiragana** and **katakana**, two writing systems used in Japanese and used throughout the book. The listening skills you develop during these first days of class and your mastery of the writing basics will form an important foundation for enhancing your language skills in later chapters.

Oral Activities

- Meeting others and introducing yourself
- Everyday greetings
- Asking what something is
- Classroom expressions
- Numbers up to 20
- Asking and giving telephone numbers
- Asking and telling time
- Talking about likes and dislikes
- Asking location
- Numbers up to 9,999
- Asking about existence
- Asking about price
- Talking about daily activities

Writing

- The Japanese writing system
- **Hiragana**
- **Katakana**
- Introduction to **Kanji**

Part One

Meeting Others and Introducing Yourself

Dialogue 1

KAWAMURA: Hajimemashite.
BURAUN: Hajimemashite.
KAWAMURA: Kawamura desu.
BURAUN: Buraun desu.
KAWAMURA: Doozo yoroshiku.
BURAUN: Doozo yoroshiku.

Hajimemashite (*literally, it's the first time we meet*) and **doozo yoroshiku** (*lit., please regard me favorably*) are set phrases. **Desu** corresponds to the verb *to be* (*am, are, is,* etc., depending on context).

Using **Dialogue 1** as a model, introduce yourself to several classmates.

Dialogue 2

BURAUN: Sumimasen. Chin-san desu ka.
CHIN: Hai, soo desu.
BURAUN: Buraun desu. Hajimemashite. Doozo yoroshiku.
CHIN: Chin desu. Hajimemashite. Doozo yoroshiku.

Sumimasen is an expression of apology, corresponding to the English *I'm sorry* or *excuse me*. It is also frequently used to attract someone's attention or to express appreciation (in the latter case *thank you* is a closer English equivalent). To form a simple yes/no question in Japanese, add **ka** to the end of a statement. **Ka** takes the place of a question mark.

Dialogue 1 KAWAMURA: How do you do? BROWN: How do you do? KAWAMURA: I am Kawamura. BROWN: I am Brown. KAWAMURA: It's nice to meet you. BROWN: It's nice to meet you.

Dialogue 2 BROWN: Excuse me. Are you Ms. Chin? CHIN: Yes, I am. (*lit., Yes, that's right.*) BROWN: I am Brown. How do you do. It's nice to meet you. CHIN: I am Chin. How do you do? It's nice to meet you.

文化ノート

Culture Note: Japanese Names

When Japanese give their full names, they say their family name first and given name last (Japanese do not have middle names). Japanese typically introduce themselves with their family name alone and address others by family name followed by a respectful title. For now, the only titles you need to know are **-san** (*Mr./Ms.*) for your friends or classmates and **-sensee** (*Professor*) for your instructor. Never attach these titles to your own name.

Practice **Dialogue 2** with several classmates, using your own names.

Dialogue 3

KAWAMURA: Sumimasen. Hayashi-san desu ka.
TANAKA: Iie.
KAWAMURA: Shitsuree shimashita.
TANAKA: Iie.

Practice **Dialogue 3** with several classmates, substituting other names for Hayashi.

Dialogue 4

BURAUN: Hajimemashite. Buraun desu. O-namae wa?
CHIN: Chin desu. Hajimemashite.

コミュニケーション・ノート

Communication Note: Informal Questions

Notice that the question **O-namae wa?** does not end in **ka**. In formal Japanese, questions end in **ka**, but in an informal, colloquial style of speech questions are often abbreviated. **O-namae wa?** is short for **O-namae wa nan desu ka** (*lit., As for your name, what is it?*). A very literal translation of **Dialogue 4** follows.

BURAUN:	O-namae wa?	*Your name?*
CHIN:	Chin desu.	*Is Chin.*

Dialogue 3 KAWAMURA: Excuse me. Are you Mr. Hayashi? TANAKA: No. KAWAMURA: Excuse me. (*lit.,* I committted a rudeness.) TANAKA: Not at all.

Dialogue 4 BROWN: How do you do? I am Brown. May I have your name? CHIN: I am Chin. How do you do?

Notice how Brown began the sentence and Chin finished it. This is very common in Japanese conversation. You must be an active listener when speaking Japanese.

Dialogue 5

BURAUN: Hajimemashite, Tookyoo Daigaku no Buraun desu.
TAKADA: Hajimemashite, Sonii no Takada desu.
BURAUN: Kore, watashi no meeshi desu.
TAKADA: Doomo arigatoo gozaimasu.
Kore, watashi no meeshi desu.
BURAUN: Doomo arigatoo gozaimasu.

You may also hand your name card in silence while bowing slightly.

When you introduce yourself in Japan, it is common to state your affiliation. Japanese tend to identify strongly with the group they belong to (their "in-group") and to judge affiliation and rank as more important than an individual's personality or ability. Stating affiliation also helps get a conversation going by giving your conversational partner something to ask you more about. To clarify your affiliation, say

(*Company/School*) no (*family name*) desu.	*I am* (*name*) *of* (*institution*).
Tookyoo Daigaku no Kawamura desu.	*I am Kawamura of the University of Tokyo.*

文化ノート

Culture Note: Name Cards

Name cards, or business cards (**meeshi**), play an important role in Japan because they contain the following pieces of information essential to developing a relationship.

- company or school affiliation
- rank in the company or school
- the Chinese characters used to write a person's full name
- address and telephone/fax numbers

Without referring to a name card, even native speakers of Japanese are often unable to write a person's name in Chinese characters. Other information on the card helps you know what level of speech is appropriate for you to use with that person. (You'll learn later about the different levels of Japanese speech, such as polite, honorific, and humble.) To choose the appropriate level of speech, you need to know the other

Dialogue 5 BROWN: How do you do? I am Brown of the University of Tokyo. TAKADA: How do you do? I am Takada of Sony. BROWN: This is my name card. TAKADA: Thank you very much. This is my name card. BROWN: Thank you very much.

person's status in relation to yourself. Status is determined by such factors as affiliation, rank and age.

When exchanging name cards, remember that a person's name card represents him or her. Thus, receive a name card respectfully with both hands extended and a simultaneous bow. Examine it carefully for a few moments. If you are sitting at a table, place it in front of you for easy reference. Never put it in your back pocket. Place it in a suit pocket, a purse, or, best of all, a name card holder (**meeshi-ire**). When presenting your own name card, make sure that it faces the other person for easy reading.

Name cards may be typeset so that the words run vertically or horizontally, depending on the company's or individual's preference. Sometimes a person's photo will be included on the card. Many Japanese, especially those who come into frequent contact with non-Japanese, have an English translation printed on the reverse side of the card.

山村商事
営業部
部長 山口健次
〒120 東京都千代田区三番町
二ー六ー七山村ビル
TEL 〇三ー三三三四ー四五六一

Now make yourself an English name card. Practice **Dialogue 5** with your classmates, using your name card. Be sure to offer and receive the name cards properly.

東京大学工学部三年
ジョン・カワムラ

〒118 東京都文京区本郷三丁目2-11
TEL (03)3212-2118

コミュニケーション・ノート

Communication Note: Expressing Gratitude

Japanese express gratitude and apologize frequently as ways of maintaining harmonious relationships. Among the many ways to express gratitude in Japanese, the following are very common expressions, listed from formal to informal.

Doomo arigatoo gozaimasu.
Arigatoo gozaimasu.
Doomo arigatoo.
Sumimasen (deshita).
Arigatoo.
Doomo.

Among these, **doomo** (*lit., very*) is commonly used in everyday conversation when speaking to social equals or subordinates. Among students, **sankyuu** (from English *thank you*) is also used. When someone expresses gratitude and you would like to say *you're welcome*, say **doo itashimashite**.

Everyday Greetings

Dialogue 6

Linda Brown sees Professor Yokoi in the morning.

BURAUN: Yokoi-sensee, ohayoo gozaimasu.
YOKOI: Aa, Buraun-san, ohayoo.
BURAUN: Ii o-tenki desu ne.
YOKOI: Ee, soo desu ne.

Vocabulary: Common Greetings and Leave-Takings

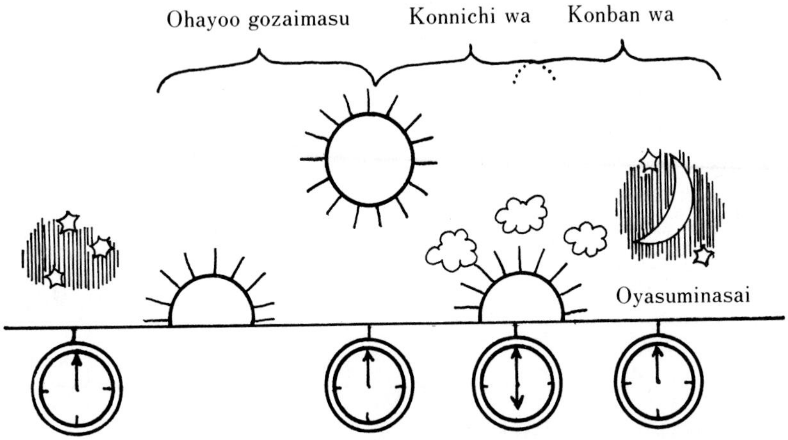

Greetings

Ohayoo gozaimasu.	Good morning. (*formal*)
Ohayoo.	Good morning. (*informal*)
Konnichi wa.	Good afternoon.
Konban wa.	Good evening.
Ogenki desu ka.	How are you?
Ee, genki desu.	(Yes,) I am fine.
Okagesama de, genki desu.	Thanks to you, I'm fine.
Ee, okagesama de.	(Yes,) thanks to you . . . (I'm fine). (*informal*)
Shibaraku desu ne.	I haven't seen you for a long time.
Ohisashiburi desu ne.	I haven't seen you for a long time.

Dialogue 6 BROWN: Professor Yokoi, good morning. YOKOI: Ah, Ms. Brown, good morning. BROWN: It's fine weather, isn't it? YOKOI: Yes, it is.

Leave-Takings

Shitsuree shimasu.	Goodbye. (*lit.*, Excuse me.)
Ja (*or* **Dewa**)**, mata.**	See you later (*lit.*, again).
Ja (*or* **Dewa**)**.**	See you. (*very informal*)
Sayo(o)nara.	Goodbye.
Oyasuminasai.	Good night. (*informal*)

コミュニケーション・ノート

Communication Note: Greetings

In America, *How are you?* is not an inquiry about your health as much as an idiomatic way of saying *Hello!* In Japan, commenting on the weather serves much the same function. If someone greets you with **Ii o-tenki desu ne**, do not feel compelled to give your opinion on the matter. Just be agreeable: **Soo desu ne** (*Yes, it is, isn't it?*).

So what about **O-genki desu ka?** This *How are you?* really means *How have you been lately?*, so don't say it to anyone you have seen recently. If you haven't seen someone for some time, or if you are sincerely concerned about his/her health, **O-genki desu ka** is appropriate. The proper response when asked **O-genki desu ka** is **Okagesama de** (*lit., Thanks to you*). The implication is that the questioner's concern has contributed to your physical and spiritual health.

Also, be careful with **Sayo(o)nara**. It has a sense of finality, so avoid saying it to someone you expect to see later in the day or in a couple of days. In this case, you have to say **Dewa mata** or **Ja mata**.

Activity 1

How would you respond to the following greetings and phrases?

1. Konnichi wa.
2. O-genki desu ka.
3. Ja, mata.
4. Konban wa.
5. Arigatoo gozaimasu.
6. Hajimemashite.
7. Shibaraku desu ne.
8. Ohayoo gozaimasu.
9. Ii o-tenki desu ne.
10. Oyasuminasai.

Activity 2

Practice the following situations with your classmates.

1. It's 8:00 A.M. on a fine day and you see one of your friends, Mr. Sawai. Greet him.
2. It's 2:00 P.M. You see Ms. Koike after a long absence. Greet her and ask about her health.
3. It's 6:00 P.M. on an evening when it's raining cats and dogs. You see your neighbor Ms. Maruyama. Greet her.
   Useful expression: Hidoi ame desu ne. (*It's a terrible rain, isn't it?*)
4. It's 10:00 P.M. You see your friend Mr. Kawai, who is on his way home from work. Greet him.

Activity 3

Turn to the classmate sitting next to you and do the following.

- Greet him or her appropriately.
- Ask how he or she is.
- Find out his or her name.
- Give a book to him or her.

Useful Expression: Doozo. (*Please* [*accept this*].) *or* (*Here you are.*)

Asking What Something Is

In Japan, you may encounter many things you have never seen before. Here's how to ask people what things are.

Dialogue 7

At a restaurant

CHIN: Sumimasen. Are wa nan desu ka.
UEITORESU: Soba desu.
CHIN: Nihon ryoori desu ka.
UEITORESU: Hai, soo desu.
CHIN: Jaa, are o onegai shimasu.

Dialogue 7 CHIN: Excuse me. What's that? WAITRESS: That is soba. CHIN: Is it Japanese food? WAITRESS: Yes, it is. CHIN: Well, then, I would like some.

Activity 4

With a classmate, take the roles of a foreign student who is in Japan for the first time and a waiter or waitress in a restaurant. When the student asks what a certain dish is, the waiter or waitress will respond using the answer in the first column. The student will then ask for more information, as indicated in the second column. Finally, the waiter or waitress must decide which of the following ways to end the exchange.

	Hai, soo desu.	*Yes, it is.*
or	Iie, chigaimasu. _____ desu.	*No, it's not. It's _____.*

	WAITER/WAITRESS	STUDENT
1.	sushi	Nihon ryoori (*Japanese food*) desu ka.
2.	marugariita	O-sake (*alcoholic beverage*) desu ka.
3.	tenpura	Amerika ryoori desu ka.
4.	kiui	Yasai (*vegetable*) desu ka.

Useful word: kudamono (*fruit*)

Classroom Expressions

Useful Vocabulary: Classroom Expressions

Here are some useful expressions that you will hear and use frequently in class. Learn to understand your instructor's commands and to make the appropriate responses. Other useful expressions, which you will learn gradually as you hear them repeated, are presented in **Vocabulary Library: More Classroom Expressions**.

Student

Practice saying these aloud.

Shitsumon ga arimasu.	I have a question.
Moo ichido onegai shimasu.	Please say that again.
Wakarimasen.	I don't understand.
Wakarimashita.	I understood.
Chotto matte kudasai.	Please wait a moment.
Book **wa Nihongo de nan to iimasu ka.**	How do you say *book* in Japanese?

Instructor

Hon o tojite kudasai.	Please close your book.
Hon o akete kudasai.	Please open your book.
Hon o mite kudasai.	Please look at your book.
Hon o minai de kudasai.	Please don't look at your book.
Kiite (ite) kudasai.	Please listen.
Mite kudasai.	Please look at (me, it, this).
Itte kudasai.	Please say it.
Nihongo de itte kudasai.	Please say it in Japanese.
Kurikaeshite kudasai.	Please repeat.
Kaite kudasai.	Please write.
Renshuu shite kudasai.	Please practice.
Pea o tsukutte kudasai.	Pair off with a classmate.
Nooto o dashite kudasai.	Please take out your notebook.
Nooto ni kaite kudasai.	Please write in your notebook.
Nani mo kakanai de kudasai.	Please don't write anything down.
Wakarimasu ka.	Do you understand?
—**Hai, wakarimasu.**	—Yes, I understand.
—**Iie, wakarimasen.**	—No, I don't understand.
Shitsumon ga arimasu ka.	Do you have any questions?
—**Hai, arimasu.**	—Yes, I do.
—**Iie, arimasen.**	—No, I don't.

Vocabulary Library

More Classroom Expressions

Hajimemashoo.	Let's begin.
Moo ichido.	Once again, please.
Minasan, issho ni.	Everyone (do it) together.
Ii desu ka.	Is that all right?
Ii desu ne.	That's fine.
Yoku dekimashita.	Well done.
Yoshuu shite (kite) kudasai.	Please prepare (for next time).
Dewa mata kono tsugi.	See you next time.

Activity 5

Follow your instructor's commands.

1. Hon o akete kudasai.
2. Tatte kudasai.
3. Suwatte kudasai.
4. Doa o akete kudasai.
5. Nooto o tojite kudasai.
6. Aruite kudasai.
7. Hashitte kudasai.
8. Kokuban o mite kudasai.

a. b.

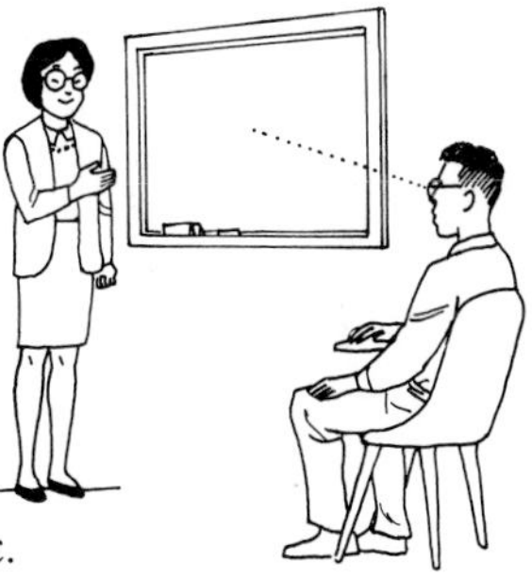

c.

d.

e.

f.

g.

h.

In the Classroom

文法ノート

Grammar Note: Japanese Nouns

Japanese nouns do not have different singular and plural forms. One word means both book and books; person and people; idea and ideas. Context determines which is meant. Later you will learn how to specify a specific number of items in cases where you need to make a plural/singular distinction. Remember that, although their English equivalents are given in the singular, Japanese nouns in vocabulary lists throughout this book assume the plural too, unless otherwise stated. Note, too, that unlike nouns in such Romance languages as Spanish and French, Japanese nouns have no gender (i.e., masculine or feminine).

The Japanese Writing System (1)

Modern Japanese is written by combining three different writing systems: **hiragana**, **katakana**, and **kanji**. **Hiragana** and **katakana**, like the Roman alphabet, are composed of symbols that represent sounds. **Kanji**, or Chinese characters, are ideographs that represent sound and meaning. You will study **hiragana** and **katakana** in **Getting Started** and **kanji** in subsequent chapters. The textbook introduces only the basics of these writing systems; you will need to complete the extensive exercises in the workbook to master them.

言語ノート

Linguistic Note: The Origins of *Hiragana* and *Katakana*

Chinese characters (**kanji**) were imported to Japan around the fifth century A.D., before which time Japan had no writing system. The use of **kanji** to transcribe the Japanese language was inconvenient, to say the least, because **kanji** were designed to transcribe a completely different language. To remedy this problem, **hiragana** symbols were created by simplifying **kanji**.

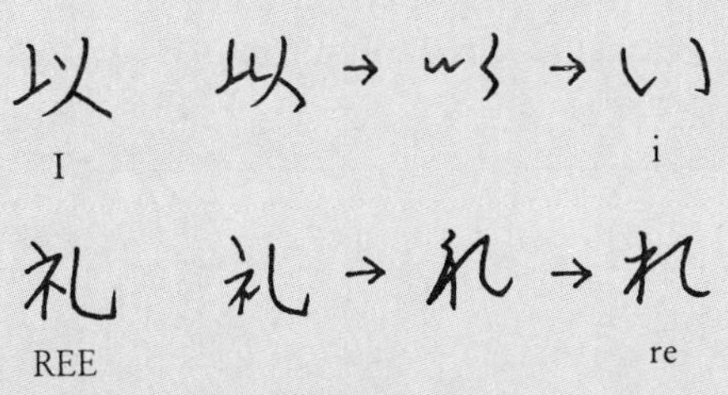

Katakana was originally created by Japanese priests to annotate Buddhist books written in **kanji**. **Katakana** symbols were created from parts of **kanji**.

Hiragana and **katakana** are called *syllabaries*, which means each letter represents one syllable (a vowel, a consonant, or a consonant + vowel). Native speakers of Japanese spell words in terms of syllables and describe a word's length in terms of the number of syllables it contains. For example, **sushi** is a two-syllable word (**su-shi**), **Honda** is a three-syllable word (**Ho-n-da**), and **Tookyoo** (*Tokyo*) is a four-syllable word (**To-o-kyo-o**). Each syllable is held for one beat, so **Tookyoo** (four syllables) takes twice as long to say as **sushi** (two syllables).

With the 46 basic symbols of the **hiragana** or **katakana** syllabary and two diacritical marks, you can transcribe all standard Japanese sounds. In theory you could write Japanese using just **hiragana** or **katakana**, but in practice the result would be too hard to read and understand.

Because the use of **katakana** is restricted primarily to transcribing foreign loanwords (e.g., **hottodoggu** from English *hotdog*) and onomatopoeic words (e.g., **zaa zaa**, meaning [*raining*] *cats and dogs*), you will learn **hiragana** first.

言語ノート

Linguistic Note: Romanization

Romanization is the transcription of Japanese using **rooma-ji** (*lit., Roman letters*), or the English alphabet. In Japan the only words you see written in **rooma-ji** are station names (for the sake of foreigners), trademarks, ad catchphrases, and the like. In this textbook, romanization is used only in **Getting Started** as an aid for the beginning student. By the end of **Getting Started** you should have a good working knowledge of **hiragana** and **katakana**, for thereafter you will read only authentic Japanese writing. The romanization system used in this book is a combination of two standard systems (Hepburn and the Cabinet Ordinance system); the result is a written representation of Japanese that most closely approximates the authentic sounds to an English speaker.

Hiragana

Here is the basic **hiragana** syllabary chart. Under each symbol is the romanization used in this book to remind you of the Japanese pronunciation. Remember, you must listen closely to your instructor and the tapes to learn true native pronunciation.

あ	い	う	え	お
a	i	u	e	o
か	き	く	け	こ
ka	ki	ku	ke	ko
さ	し	す	せ	そ
sa	shi	su	se	so

た	ち	つ	て	と
ta	chi	tsu	te	to
な	に	ぬ	ね	の
na	ni	nu	ne	no
は	ひ	ふ	へ	ほ
ha	hi	hu	he	ho
ま	み	む	め	も
ma	mi	mu	me	mo
や		ゆ		よ
ya		yu		yo
ら	り	る	れ	ろ
ra	ri	ru	re	ro
わ				を
wa				o
ん				
n				

を falls on the **w** line because historically it was pronounced **wo**.

The addition of two diacritical marks adds twenty-five more sounds (see below) to the basic **hiragana** chart. The ゛ (called **dakuten**) turns the unvoiced consonants (**k, s, t,** and **h**) into voiced consonants (**g, z/j, d/j,** and **b,** respectively). The ° (**han-dakuten**) changes **h** to **p**.

が	ぎ	ぐ	げ	ご
ga	gi	gu	ge	go
ざ	じ	ず	ぜ	ぞ
za	ji	zu	ze	zo
だ	ぢ	づ	で	ど
da	ji	zu	de	do
ば	び	ぶ	べ	ぼ
ba	bi	bu	be	bo
ぱ	ぴ	ぷ	ぺ	ぽ
pa	pi	pu	pe	po

By writing や (**ya**), ゆ (**yu**), or よ (**yo**) small after symbols ending in the vowel **i**, you can transcribe the following sounds. Each syllable is composed of a **consonant** + **y** +**a, u,** or **o**. (In horizontal writing the small symbols are written lower down than the regular-size ones; in vertical writing they are written somewhat to the right.)

きゃ kya	きゅ kyu	きょ kyo
しゃ sha	しゅ shu	しょ sho
ちゃ cha	ちゅ chu	ちょ cho
にゃ nya	にゅ nyu	にょ nyo
ひゃ hya	ひゅ hyu	ひょ hyo
みゃ mya	みゅ myu	みょ myo
りゃ rya	りゅ ryu	りょ ryo
ぎゃ gya	ぎゅ gyu	ぎょ gyo
じゃ ja	じゅ ju	じょ jo
びゃ bya	びゅ byu	びょ byo
ぴゃ pya	ぴゅ pyu	ぴょ pyo

言語ノート

Linguistic Note: a-i-u-e-o Order

In Japanese dictionaries, words are listed in the same order as the basic **hiragana** syllabary chart: **a, i, u, e, o, ka, ki, ku, ke, ko, sa, shi,** and so on. You could call this Japanese alphabetical order. Because you cannot use a Japanese dictionary without it, it is important for you to learn the order of the **hiragana** symbols. In addition, knowing the **hiragana** syllabary makes it easier to remember Japanese verb conjugations. By the way, listings in address books, encyclopedias, and the **Japanese-English Glossary** at the end of this book are ordered in the same way. Other basic rules of **a-i-u-e-o** order include: voiced symbols follow the corresponding unvoiced symbols, and **hiragana** precedes **katakana**. Telephone directory entries are also listed in **a-i-u-e-o** order, but when names are homonyms, other rules governing **kanji** order come into play.

The first line of **hiragana** consists of five symbols representing the five Japanese vowels.

あ	*a*	pronounced roughly as in English *father*, but the mouth is not so wide open as in English
い	*i*	as in English *see*, but shorter in length
う	*u*	as in English *doodle*, but it is short and does not require lip-rounding
え	*e*	as in English *egg*, but the mouth is not open so wide
お	*o*	as in English *comb*, but it does not require so much lip-rounding

The rest of the symbols (except ん **n** and を **o**) consist of a consonant or a semi-vowel (i.e., **y** or **w**) followed by one of the five vowels. Most Japanese consonants are easy to pronounce for English speakers, but note the following differences.

sh in し	as in *she*, but less lip-rounding
ch in ち	as in *cheese*, but with no lip-rounding
ts in つ	as in *cats*
h in は、へ、ほ	is similar to English *h*
h in ひ	as in *he*, but with friction as the air is expelled
h in ふ	articulated by bringing both lips close together without any rounding and then forcing air out between them
r in ら	Japanese *r*, similar to the *t/d in water* or *rider*, is articulated by tapping the tip of the tongue very quickly against the gum just behind the upper teeth.
w in わ	as in English *we*, but with less tension
g in が	as in *gate*, but some speakers pronounce this sound like *ng* in *sing* when it occurs in the middle of a word
j in じ、ぢ	as in English *jeep*

Some Japanese pronounce ひ **hi** like English **he** but shorter and with no friction.

Syllabic Nasal

ん (**n**) represents a nasal sound with the length of one full syllable. The actual sound represented by this symbol depends on the context. Before [m], [p], or [b], it is pronounced [m]; before [s], [sh], [t], [ts], [ch], [n], [r], [z], [d], or [j], it is pronounced [n]; and before vowels, before [k], [y], [w], [g], or [ng], or at the end of a word, it is pronounced [ng]. In **Getting Started**, however, ん is represented **n** irrespective of where it appears.

enpitsu	えんぴつ	*pencil*
kanji	かんじ	*Chinese character*
Nihongo	にほんご	*Japanese language*
hon	ほん	*book*
kin'en	きんえん	*no smoking*
Cf. kinen	きねん	*commemoration*

Note that ん can never begin a word.

Double Vowels

When two of the same vowel come together in sequence, hold the sound twice as long as for a single vowel. In writing, these double vowels are transcribed by adding a corresponding single vowel symbol.

obasan	おばさん	*aunt*
obaasan	おばあさん	*grandmother*
ie	いえ	*house*
iie	いいえ	*no*
suugaku	すうがく	*math*

A double vowel sound **ee** is in most cases written by adding い (**i**).

eega	えいが	*movie*

There are a few exceptions in which え (**e**) is added.

oneesan	おねえさん	*older sister*
ee	ええ	*yes*

A long vowel **oo** is in most cases written by adding う (**u**).

otoosan	おとうさん	*father*

There are several exceptions in which お (**o**) is added.

ooi	おおい	*many*
tooi	とおい	*far*
too	とお	*ten*

Double Consonants

Double consonants (**pp, kk,** etc.) are written with a small っ (**tsu**), which doubles the sound it precedes.

kita	きた	*north*
kitta	きった	*(I) cut*
kako	かこ	*past*
kakko	かっこ	*parenthesis*

However, double **nn** is written with ん (**n**).

hone	ほね	*bone*
honne	ほんね	*true intention*

Linguistic Note: Japanese Accent

Japanese has pitch accent, which is very different from the stress accent in English. In English, accented syllables are pronounced louder than non-accented syllables. In Japanese, accented syllables are pronounced at a higher pitch than other syllables. In English, only one sound (or syllable) can be primarily accented, while in Japanese more than one syllable in a word can be accented and pronounced at the same pitch. Generally speaking, Japanese has only two pitches — high and low.

ichi (*one*) yon (*four*)
kokoro (*heart*) toomorokoshi (*corn*)

Here, a bar (¯) over a syllable means the syllable is pronounced with high pitch; a syllable with no bar is pronounced with low pitch. ¬ indicates a fall in pitch — i.e., the preceding syllable is the last high-pitched syllable in the word. Thus, **ichi** has the accent pattern low-high, while **yon** has the accent pattern high-low. In **kokoro**, the pitch rises after the first syllable and falls after the second syllable for a low-high-low pattern. In **toomorokoshi**, the pitch rises after the first syllable and falls after the third syllable. Sometimes pitch is the only way (other than context) to distinguish between two homonyms in spoken Japanese, for example,

hashi (*bridge*) hashi (*chopsticks*)
hana (*flower*) hana (*nose*)

Both **hana** (*flower*) and **hana** (*nose*) have the same pitch pattern (low-high) when they are pronounced independently. However, there is a fall in pitch after **na** in **hana** (*flower*). This means that when a particle follows the word, the particle is pronounced with low pitch. On the other hand, the particle following **hana** (*nose*) is pronounced with high pitch.

hana ga ookii (*The flower is big*) hana ga ookii (*The nose is big*)

Nevertheless, the primary function of Japanese accentuation is to show the unity of words in a phrase more than to distinguish between the meanings of homonyms. For this reason, no accent is indicated in the vocabulary lists in this textbook. Just listen to your instructor and the tape very carefully and try your best to mimic them. Rather than pay too much attention to the accent pattern of each word, you should accurately articulate the overall intonation of the sentence in order to communicate effectively in Japanese.

Part Two

Numbers Up to 20

Here's how to count to 20.

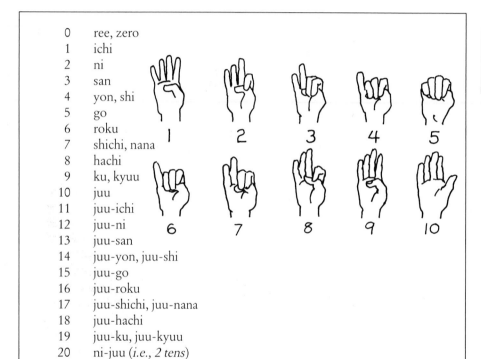

0	ree, zero
1	ichi
2	ni
3	san
4	yon, shi
5	go
6	roku
7	shichi, nana
8	hachi
9	ku, kyuu
10	juu
11	juu-ichi
12	juu-ni
13	juu-san
14	juu-yon, juu-shi
15	juu-go
16	juu-roku
17	juu-shichi, juu-nana
18	juu-hachi
19	juu-ku, juu-kyuu
20	ni-juu (*i.e., 2 tens*)

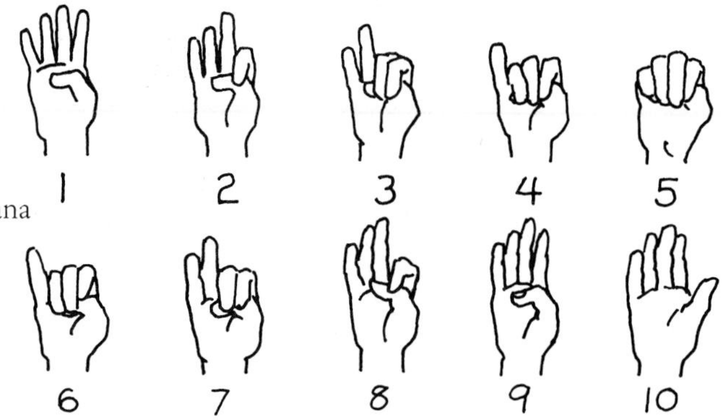

There are two different ways to say *zero*, *four*, *seven*, and *nine*. Listen to native speakers to learn which pronunciations are preferred in which contexts.

Activity 1

What number(s) between 0 and 20 do you associate with the following? Answer in Japanese.

1. baseball
2. unlucky
3. twin
4. rainbow
5. rectangle
6. a week
7. a watch
8. fingers
9. lucky
10. circle

Activity 2

These mathematical symbols are read as follows.

$+$	tasu	$-$	hiku	$\times$	kakeru	$\div$	waru	$=$	wa

Examples:

$4 + 5 = 9 \rightarrow$ yon tasu go wa kyuu
$20 - 8 = 12 \rightarrow$ ni-juu hiku hachi wa juu-ni
$2 \times 4 = 8 \rightarrow$ ni kakeru yon wa hachi
$6 \div 3 = 2 \rightarrow$ roku waru san wa ni

Say the following in Japanese.

1. $1 + 1 = 2$	6. $2 + 1 = 3$	11. $2 + 3 = 5$	16. $4 + 6 = 10$
2. $5 + 3 = 8$	7. $3 + 6 = 9$	12. $10 - 2 = 8$	17. $7 + 1 = 8$
3. $9 - 5 = 4$	8. $4 - 3 = 1$	13. $2 \times 3 = 6$	18. $6 \times 3 = 18$
4. $4 \times 5 = 20$	9. $3 \times 3 = 9$	14. $9 \div 3 = 3$	19. $12 \div 6 = 2$
5. $18 \div 2 = 9$	10. $10 \div 5 = 2$	15. $16 \div 4 = 4$	20. $5 \div 1 = 5$

Read these equations, filling in the correct answer.

1. $2 + 4 = ?$	3. $9 + 6 = ?$	5. $16 - 8 = ?$	7. $13 - 10 = ?$
2. $20 \div 5 = ?$	4. $15 \div 3 = ?$	6. $3 \times 5 = ?$	8. $2 \times 7 + 3 = ?$

Asking and Giving Telephone Numbers

Dialogue 1

BURAUN: Machida-san no denwa bangoo wa?
MACHIDA: 675-8941 desu.
BURAUN: 675-8941 desu ne.
MACHIDA: Hai, soo desu.

The particle **no** in **Machida-san no denwa bangoo** denotes possession and roughly corresponds to English *of.*

You can ask for a telephone number by saying

(*Place or person*) no denwa bangoo wa?	*What is _____'s telephone number?*

Practice **Dialogue 1** with several classmates, substituting your real names and telephone numbers.

Dialogue 1 BROWN: Ms. Machida, what is your telephone number? MACHIDA: It's 675-8941. BROWN: 675-8941, right? MACHIDA: Yes, that's right.

新宿区（０３）

132

か

カキ（スナック） .... 3018-3252 歌舞伎 3-12-1
柿（酒場） .... 3099-5698 歌舞伎 1-12-4
柿沢食堂 .... 3295-9532 若葉 2-19-6
川村ガラス製品 .... 3109-3214 新宿 2-1-15
河本会計事務所 .... 3388-2393 高田馬場 1-7
かんかん（スナック） 3211-3997 西新宿 5-13
カンカン 3902-5342 新宿1-34-11
神田歯科 3210-2062 若葉3-5-3
甘味堂（和菓子） .... 3790-1937 西新宿 14-5

新宿区（０３）

178

た

タカラファッション .... 3354-5580 新宿 2-17
タカラ部品(株)新宿寮 .. 3958-0382 新宿 2-9
タカラ部品(株)四谷寮 .. 3207-1089 内藤 2-11-3
タキ（健康食品） .... 3390-4096 神楽坂 1-15
タキオン(株)(貿易) .... 3956-4092 歌舞伎 5-11
タキオン(株) .... 3801-3492 四谷 3-11-9
タキオン研究所(株) ...... 3109-9482 若葉 3-14-3
タキカワ(株)(不動産) ... 3840-4023 荒木 2-17-1
.... 3109-4398
.... 3305-8302
.... 3098-2496
タキガミピアノ運送 .... 3192-4048 大久保 2-17
タキガミピアノ .... 3946-4721 新宿 2-16-3
タキ工房(株) .... 3956-4501 神楽坂 2-17-1
タキノ写真館 .... 3956-4501 四谷 1-4-4
タクインシュアランス 3634-4920 新宿 3-11-4
（保険代理業）
タクシーローン .... 3459-4502 西新宿 2-17-1
サービス
タクショ秘書センター 3956-4501 神楽坂 1-21-3
タクト(株) .... 3309-5082 神楽坂 4-9
タクトアトラス(株) ...... 3984-6021 新宿 1-3-14
タクトエンジニア .... 3209-5098 四谷 2-7-9
リング(有)
タクトシステム(株) ...... 3109-3842 西早稲田 1-12
.... 3871-3947
.... 3055-9283
.... 3045-4901
タクマ汎用機械(株) ...... 3101-9384 高田馬場 17-1
東京支社 .... 3893-2008 若葉 2-21-8
タクミ技研(株) .... 3058-5602 河田 3-11-7
タクミ商事 .... 3122-0983 歌舞伎 1-13-1
（電気商）
タクミ設計(有) .... 3106-9482 神楽坂 2-18
.... 3106-7724
.... 3106-2048
タグドーナッツ .... 3209-0348 歌舞伎 1-5-12
（ファーストフード）
タケイカメラ(株) .... 3059-3394 四谷 3-19-7

たけうち（料理） .... 3195-7834 新宿 2-11-7
たけひ美術 .... 3208-0982 四谷 3-17-4
たけもと .... 3209-4953 神楽坂 2-9-1
たこ福（割ぽう） .... 3094-5028 西新宿 1-17
.... 3058-1785 歌舞伎 3-1-2
たこぽん .... 3395-1988 歌舞伎 5-1
（お好み焼き） .... 5372-0781 西新宿 1-13-1
たしろ（スナック） .... 3354-0536 西早稲田 2-1
たじ馬（酒場） .... 3354-6418 西新宿 2-3-7
たち川（弁当持帰り） 3360-2679 神楽坂 3-11
たち吉(株)（陶器） ...... 3200-8191 中落合 5-11
新宿小田急店 .... 3200-3352 西新宿 1-7
新宿京王店 .... 3200-9452 西新宿 5-11
新宿京王店A、E 3203-4543
たちそば司 .... 3373-4218 四谷 2-11
たちぬい企画(有) .... 3472-8102 西新宿 3-1
たちばな（製菓） .... 3387-8356 大久保 1-12
たちばな社 .... 3772-6468 神楽坂 2-3
たつ川 .... 3110-4431 內元 2-9-3
たっちゃん（食堂） .... 3378-1515 新宿 5-1
たつみ .... 3936-0961 百人 1-4-4
たつみ鮨 .... 3964-5564 市谷柳 3-4
たつみや菓子店 .... 3732-3906 若松 2-1-1
たつ巳観光トラベル .... 3824-1051 神楽坂 3-21-3
サービス
たつ美や（うなぎ） .... 3119-9345 神楽坂 2-9
たつ屋(株) .... 3209-6041 余丁 1-3-1
（牛どん店）
たつ屋(株)新大久保店 .. 3209-3095 大久保 2-2-9
（牛どん店）
たなか美容室 .... 3090-4363 弁天 1-2
たぬき（お好焼） .... 3777-4653 北新宿 13-9
たぬき .... 3101-4954 舟 17-1
たぬき（焼鳥） .... 3813-2928 若葉 1-8
たぬき（焼鳥） .... 3737-4600 河田 4-7
たぬき亭（酒場） .... 3109-0943 北新宿 1-13-1
たべのみや写楽 .... 3371-7682 荒木 2-18
たまがわ編集室 .... 3209-5508 歌舞伎 3-3-12
たま川（うなぎ料理） 3492-4494 四谷 3-2-7

田矢クリーニング .... 3720-8027 北新宿 2-17-7
田谷税務会計事務所 .... 3842-8092 山吹 3-17-4
田谷不動産 .... 3209-3603 百人 2-9-1
田屋ナカニシ新宿店 .... 3113-0728 北 1-17
（洋品店）
田屋ワイシャツ店 .... 3724-6918 赤城下 3-1-2
田山勝久法律事務所 .... 3014-1673 西落合 3-11
田んぼ（郷土料理） .... 3698-5573 新宿 2-10-2
.... 3204-7387 下落合 2-9
多かせ（お好焼） .... 3944-7729 新宿 2-14-3
多華（中華料理） .... 3093-2242 神楽坂 3-15
多賀建設(株) .... 3734-3730 北新宿 5-1
多賀製作所(株) .... 3634-2956 北新宿 5-4
（工作機械）
多賀屋（運送） .... 3241-4003 荒木 2-17-1
多賀谷製作所 .... 3009-4211 四谷 3-11-9
（非鉄金属製練）
多希（パブビストロ） 3705-2252 山吹 1-3-1
多紀（酒場） .... 3007-3336 市谷柳 2-17
多田オフセット印刷 .... 3373-2028 愛住 1-4
多田特許事務所 .... 3140-9000 市谷柳 2-3
多津美（たばこ） .... 3016-3533 神楽坂 2-4-1
多名香（スナック） .... 3270-4984 舟 4-4
多奈加（酒場） .... 3436-7710 新宿 3-13-5
多奈加屋丹芭鈴 .... 3029-3312 北新宿 2-11-1
多奈何すし .... 3205-7731 神楽坂 1-11-3
.... 3205-9912 神楽坂 5-9-5
多奈辺（日本料理） .... 3774-3311 新宿 5-1-14
多満（弁当） .... 3209-2048 四谷 2-5-7
多満川（料亭） .... 3035-1089 西早稲田 5-16
.... 3035-7140
多摩印刷(株) .... 3057-5513 余丁 2-1
多摩運送(株)都内 .... 3063-7301 西新宿 2-7-9
センター
多摩授産所 .... 3205-5504 高田馬場 3-1
.... 3205-6801
.... 3205-7702
多摩製版(有) .... 3275-1143 南元 1-13-1
多摩旅館 .... 3107-9284 百人 2-18

文化ノート

Culture Note: Telephone Numbers in Japan

Telephone numbers in Japan are usually four-digit numbers preceded by a one- to four-digit prefix, like 3521-0987 or 890-2134. When reading a telephone number, many people use **no** to indicate a hyphen and to separate the area code from the number. Japanese area codes start with 0 and have at least two digits. For example, the area code of Tokyo is 03, and that of Sapporo, 011.

コミュニケーション・ノート

Communication Note: Sentence-Final Particle *ne*

The sentence-final particle **ne**, as in **675-8941 desu ne**, is ubiquitous in Japanese. When said with a high or rising intonation **ne**(**e**) is used to ask for someone's agreement (*don't you think?*), to confirm that your knowledge is correct (*that's right, isn't it?*), and to check that the listener is following you (*you see?*). When said with a falling intonation and extended to **nee**, the particle indicates your agreement with the listener or your hesitation. **Ne**(**e**) is just one of a variety of sentence-final particles that reveal the speaker's emotion and introduce subtle shades of meaning to an utterance.

Dialogue 2

Practice this variation of **Dialogue 1**, substituting the names and places in the address book for those underlined in the dialogue.

BURAUN: Yokoi-sensee no denwa bangoo wa?
KAWAMURA: (0134) 76-9328 desu.
BURAUN: (0134) 67-9328 desu ne.
KAWAMURA: Iie, soo ja arimasen. (0134) 76-9328 desu.

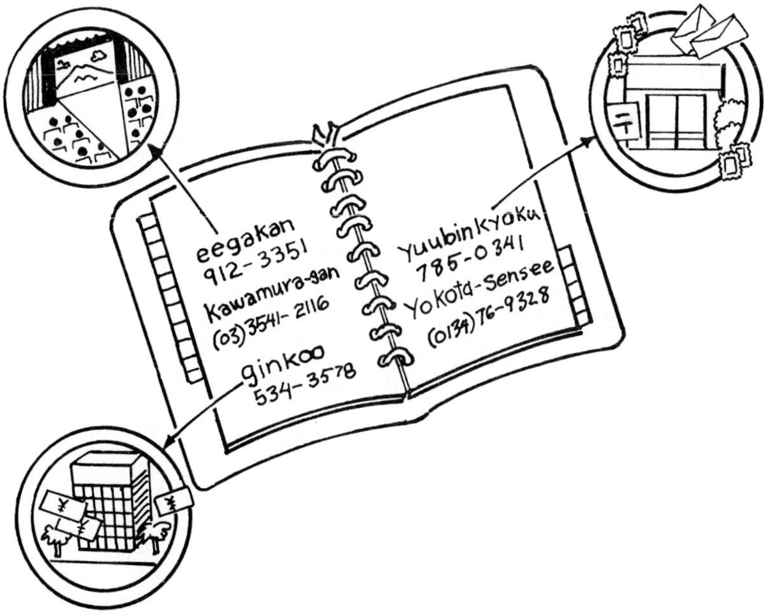

Dialogue 2 BROWN: What is Professor Yokoi's telephone number? KAWAMURA: It's 0134-76-9328. BROWN: It's 0134-67-9328, right? KAWAMURA: No, that's not right. It's 0134-76-9328.

Asking and Telling Time

Dialogue 3

KAWAMURA: Sumimasen. Ima nan-ji desu ka.
HAYASHI: Hachi-ji desu.
KAWAMURA: Soo desu ka. Arigatoo gozaimasu.
HAYASHI: Doo itashimashite.

Practice **Dialogue 3** by changing the underlined part.

Telling Time

To tell time, add -**ji** (*o'clock*) to the appropriate numeral.

ichi-ji	shichi-ji (*some people say* nana-ji)
ni-ji	hachi-ji
san-ji	ku-ji (*not* kyuu-ji)
yo-ji (*not* yon-ji *or* shi-ji)	juu-ji
go-ji	juu-ichi-ji
roku-ji	juu-ni-ji
ni-ji han	*2:30* (**han** means *half*)
Nan-ji desu ka.	*What time is it?*
Ni-ji han desu.	*It's 2:30.*

Nana-ji is commonly used in announcements at train stations and airports because *shichi-ji* can easily be confused with *ichi-ji* in a noisy environment.

Activity 3

Ima nan-ji desu ka. —_____-ji desu.

Practice this short dialogue, substituting the times that follow.

Dialogue 3 KAWAMURA: Excuse me. What time is it now? HAYASHI: It's eight o'clock. KAWAMURA: I see. Thank you very much. HAYASHI: You are welcome.

Dialogue 4

GIBUSON: Ima nan-ji desu ka.
MIMURA: Juu-ji desu.
GIBUSON: Shikago wa ima nan-ji desu ka.
MIMURA: Eeto, Shichi-ji desu.
GIBUSON: Gozen Shichi-ji desu ka.
MIMURA: Hai, soo desu. Amerika wa ima asa desu.

Eeto, an interjection resembling *uh*, is used as a speech filler.

Vocabulary: Time of Day

gozen	A.M.	**asa**	morning
gogo	P.M.	**hiru**	noon, around noontime
		yuugata	evening
		yoru	night

Practice **Dialogue 4** with several classmates, substituting the following place names.

Rosanzerusu
Rio de Janeiro (Burajiru)
Kairo (Ejiputo)
Shidonii (Oosutoraria)
Toronto (Kanada)
Tookyoo
Atoranta
Pari (Huransu)
Bankoku (Tai)
Nyuu Yooku
Akapuruko (Mekishiko)

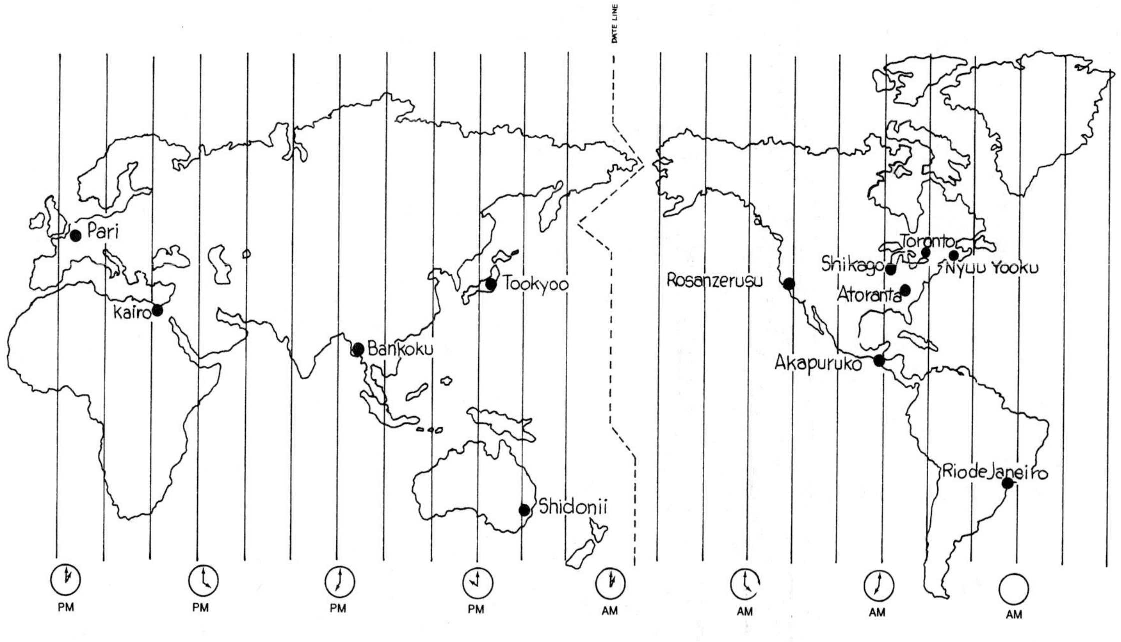

Dialogue 4 GIBSON: What time is it now? MIMURA: It's six o'clock. GIBSON: What time is it now in Chicago? MIMURA: Uh . . . it's ten o'clock. GIBSON: Do you mean 10 A.M.? (*lit.*, Is it 10 A.M.?) MIMURA: That's right. It's morning in the States now.

Dialogue 5

KAWAMURA: Ima nan-ji desu ka.
CHIN: Eeto, ni-ji desu.
KAWAMURA: Miitingu no jikan desu ne.
CHIN: Ee, soo desu ne.

Practice **Dialogue 5** substituting times and activities from John Kawamura's schedule below.

JOHN'S SCHEDULE

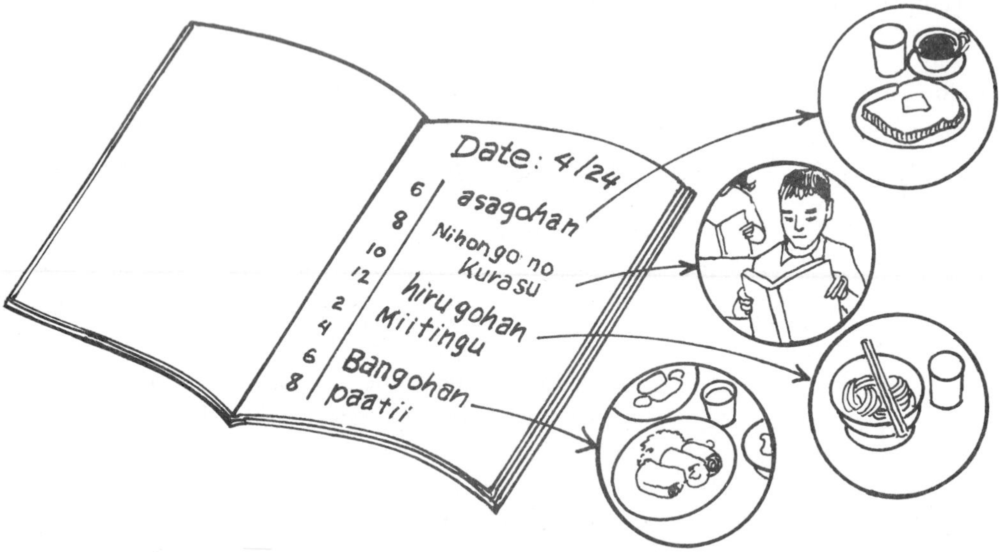

Activity 4

Referring to John's schedule, ask a classmate what time each activity occurs. An example follows.

S1: Nihongo no kurasu wa nan-ji desu ka.
S2: Gozen ku-ji desu.

Now ask a classmate about his or her schedule, making up your own questions.

Dialogue 5 KAWAMURA: What time is it now? CHIN: Uh . . . it's two o'clock. KAWAMURA: It's time for the meeting, isn't it? CHIN: Yes, it is.

Activity 4 Example S1: What time is Japanese class? S2: It is at 9:00 A.M.

Vocabulary Library

Daily Activities

asagohan	breakfast	**eega**	movie
hirugohan	lunch	**paatii**	party
bangohan	dinner, supper	**kaimono/shoppingu**	shopping
kurasu	class	**sanpo**	a walk, walking
Nihongo no kurasu	Japanese language class	**undoo**	(physical) exercise
miitingu	meeting	**benkyoo**	study, studying
deeto	date		

Talking About Likes and Dislikes

Dialogue 6

John Kawamura and a classmate, Hitomi Machida, are talking in a cafeteria.

KAWAMURA: Machida-san wa sakana ga suki desu ka.
MACHIDA: Ee, toku ni sashimi ga suki desu.
KAWAMURA: Watashi wa sashimi ga kirai desu.
MACHIDA: Hontoo desu ka.

コミュニケーション・ノート

Communication Note: Talking About Likes and Dislikes

Use the following sentence structures to express likes and dislikes.

_____ ga suki desu.	*I (you, he, she, we, they, etc.) like _____.*
_____ ga kirai desu.	*I (you, etc.) dislike _____.*
_____ ga suki ja arimasen.	*I (you, etc.) don't like _____.*

To ask if someone likes something, say

_____ ga suki desu ka.	*Do (you, etc.) like _____?*

Dialogue 6 KAWAMURA: Do you like fish, Ms. Machida? MACHIDA: Yes. I especially like raw fish. KAWAMURA: I dislike raw fish. MACHIDA: Really! (*lit.,* Is that true?)

Activity 5

Ask a classmate whether he or she likes the following things.

Examples

> Nihongo no kurasu ga suki desu ka. → Hai, suki desu.
> Paatii ga suki desu ka. → Iie, suki ja arimasen.

1. yasai (*vegetable*[*s*]), niku (*meat*), sakana, burokkorii, piza, aisu kuriimu
2. Nihon ryoori (*Japanese food*), Itaria ryoori, Huransu ryoori
3. koohii (*coffee*), aisu tii, koora, juusu
4. biiru, wain, kakuteru, uisukii
5. huttobooru, sakkaa, tenisu, supootsu
6. bokushingu, sukii, suiee (*swimming*)
7. eega (*movies*), sanpo (*walking*), undoo (*exercise*), benkyoo, paatii
8. jazu, rokku, kurashikku (*classical music*)
9. Madonna, Juria Robaatsu, Maikeru Jakuson

言語ノート

Linguistic Note: Devoiced Vowels

When Japanese vowels [i] and [u] fall between voiceless consonants (i.e., [k], [s], [sh], [t], [ch], [ts], [h], and [p]) or when one of these vowels, preceded by a voiceless consonant, ends a word, the vowel is whispered. Vowels are normally pronounced by vibrating the vocal chords, but no vibration of the vocal chords accompanies pronunciation of these whispered, or devoiced, vowels. Here are some examples of devoiced vowels. (The devoiced vowels are those underlined in the romanization.)

くつ	**kutsu**	*shoe*
すし	**sushi**	*sushi*
えんぴつ	**enpitsu**	*pencil*
スペイン	**Supein**	*Spain*
ふたり	**hutari**	*two people*
あのひとはやまぐちさんです。	**Ano hito wa Yamaguchi-san desu.**	*That person is Mr. Yamaguchi.*

In standard, everyday Japanese spoken at a normal or fast speed, the devoicing of vowels occurs naturally in the aforementioned contexts. However, when people enunciate words slowly or emphatically or when they are nervous when speaking, devoicing may not take place. Also, some dialects may not use devoiced vowels.

The Japanese Writing System (2)

Katakana

The second syllabary used in writing Japanese is very similar to **hiragana**. The forty - six symbols represent the same sounds and many even resemble their **hiragana** counterparts. The differences are in appearance — **katakana** is more angular compared to the flowing lines of **hiragana** — and in use. Generally speaking, the use of **katakana** is restricted to loanwords, onomatopoeic words, and words the writer wishes to emphasize.

Over the centuries the Japanese language has borrowed many foreign words from Chinese and Western languages (especially English, French, and German). In transcribing Western loanwords, the Japanese usually try to replicate the foreign pronunciation with **katakana**. Thus, *Porsche* becomes ポルシェ (**porushe**). Because foreign loanwords give an impression of sophistication and modernity, you will find they're used frequently in fashion magazines and advertisements and among young urbanites, even when a perfectly good native Japanese word exists.

Included in the category of onomatopoeic words written with **katakana** are words expressing natural sounds (*meow, bang,* etc.) and those expressing manner (*twinkle, zigzag,* etc.). There are so many **katakana** words in Japanese that entire dictionaries are devoted just to foreign loanwords and to onomatopoeic words.

Here is the basic **katakana** syllabary.

ア a	イ i	ウ u	エ e	オ o
カ ka	キ ki	ク ku	ケ ke	コ ko
サ sa	シ shi	ス su	セ se	ソ so
タ ta	チ chi	ツ tsu	テ te	ト to
ナ na	ニ ni	ヌ nu	ネ ne	ノ no
ハ ha	ヒ hi	フ hu	ヘ he	ホ ho
マ ma	ミ mi	ム mu	メ me	モ mo
ヤ ya		ユ yu		ヨ yo

ラ	リ	ル	レ	ロ
ra	ri	ru	re	ro
ワ				ヲ
wa				o
ン				
n				

Use the diacritical marks ﾞ and ﾟ, just as you do in **hiragana**.

ガ	ギ	グ	ゲ	ゴ
ga	gi	gu	ge	go
ザ	ジ	ズ	ゼ	ゾ
za	ji	zu	ze	zo
ダ	ヂ	ヅ	デ	ド
da	ji	zu	de	do
バ	ビ	ブ	ベ	ボ
ba	bi	bu	be	bo
パ	ピ	プ	ペ	ポ
pa	pi	pu	pe	po

Similarly, add small ヤ (**ya**), ユ (**yu**), and ヨ (**yo**) just as in **hiragana**.

キャ	キュ	キョ
kya	kyu	kyo
シャ	シュ	ショ
sha	shu	sho
チャ	チュ	チョ
cha	chu	cho
ニャ	ニュ	ニョ
nya	nyu	nyo
ヒャ	ヒュ	ヒョ
hya	hyu	hyo
ミャ	ミュ	ミョ
mya	myu	myo
リャ	リュ	リョ
rya	ryu	ryo
ギャ	ギュ	ギョ
gya	gyu	gyo
ジャ	ジュ	ジョ
ja	ju	jo

ビャ	ビュ	ビョ
bya	byu	byo
ピャ	ピュ	ピョ
pya	pyu	pyo

Double Vowels

In **katakana**, double vowels are written with the vowel extender symbol ー (**choo-on kigoo**).

aato	アート	*art*
kii	キー	*key*
suutsu	スーツ	*suit*
sukeeto	スケート	*skate, skating*
nooto	ノート	*notebook*

When written vertically, the extender symbol is written 丨.

Double Consonants

As in **hiragana**, double consonants are written with a small ッ (**tsu**) that doubles the following consonant.

katto	カット	*cut*
beddo	ベッド	(*Western-style*) *bed*

In **katakana** you can use a small vowel symbol in combination with other symbols to create sounds that Japanese originally didn't have—that is, the foreign sounds introduced with loanwords.

ウィ	wi	ウィンター	wintaa	*winter*
ウェ	we	ウェーター	weetaa	*waiter*
ウォ	wo	ウォーター	wootaa	*water*
シェ	she	シェーカー	sheekaa	*shaker*
チェ	che	チェーン	cheen	*chain*
ツァ	tsa	ツァー	tsaa	*tsar*
ツィ	tsi	ツィーグラー	tsiiguraa	*Ziegler* (German)
ツェ	tse	ツェッペリン	tsepperin	*Zeppelin* (German)
ツォ	tso	ツォイス	tsoisu	*Zeus* (German)
ティ	ti	ティー	tii	*tea*
トゥ	tu	トゥエンティー	tuentii	*twenty*
ヒェ	hye	ヒェー	hyee	(screaming sound)
ファ	fa	ファッション	fasshon	*fashion*
フィ	fi	フィルム	firumu	*film*
フェ	fe	フェリー	ferii	*ferryboat*
フォ	fo	フォーム	foomu	*form*
ジェ	je	ジェット	jetto	*jet*
ディ	di	ディーゼル	diizeru	*diesel*
デュ	dyu	プロデューサー	purodyuusaa	*producer*

ドゥ	du	ドゥー	duu	*do (it yourself)*
クァ	kwa	クァトロ	kwatoro	*cuatro* (Spanish)
クォ	kwo	クォーター	kwootaa	*quarter*
ヴァ	va	ヴァイオリン	vaiorin	*violin*
ヴィ	vi	ヴィオラ	viora	*viola*
ヴェ	ve	ベートーヴェン	Beetooven	*Beethoven*
ヴォ	vo	ヴォリューム	voryuumu	*volume*

Some Japanese transcribe the foreign sound [v] as ヴ, while most simply use バ、ビ、ブ、ベ、 or ボ, which represent the more usual Japanese pronunciation. Note that the **katakana** spelling of foreign loanwords may differ from Japanese to Japanese, depending on each speaker's pronunciation.

言語ノート

Linguistic Note: *Katakana Kuizu*

According to one survey, about 5 percent of the vocabulary listed in a medium-size Japanese dictionary for use of native speakers are **katakana** words, that is, loanwords from Western languages. (These **katakana** loanwords are usually called **gairaigo**.) In fact, more and more **gairaigo** are used every day in Japan, reflecting the increasing interaction of Japanese people with foreigners and foreign countries. A Japanese life is full of **gairaigo**. Let's take a look at one typical young Japanese urbanite, Mr. Kimura. Can you guess what each **katakana** word means? (Answers are in **Appendix 8**.)

Mr. Kimura lives in an **apaato** in the suburbs of Tokyo. He gets up with the noisy sound of an **araamu kurokku**. He shaves with a **sheebaa** and brushes his teeth with a **ha-burashi**. He eats **toosuto** with **bataa** and drinks **koohii** for breakfast. He goes to work in his **ootomachikku kaa** with **kaa sutereo**, **san ruuhu**, and **eakon**. On the way to his company, he listens to **kasetto teepu** of **popyuraa myuujikku**. He arrives at the **biru** of his company at 8:45 A.M. From **andaaguraundo paakingu** he goes to his **ofisu** by **erebeetaa**. Between 12 NOON and 1 P.M. is his **ranchi taimu**. He eats lunch at a nearby **resutoran**. He likes **karee raisu**. After lunch, he goes to the **koohii shoppu** and has **remon tii**. After work, he has a **deeto** with his **fianse**, who is a **konpyuuta puroguramaa** at the same company. He plans to marry her, so he gave her an **engeeji ringu** last month. After eating **dinaa** at a **Huransu resutoran**, they go for a **doraibu** to the top of a mountain. From there, they can see the beautiful **neon** of the city. After returning home from his **deeto**, Mr. Kimura drinks **uisukii**. He takes a **shawaa**. He goes to **beddo** around midnight.

DRINKS
お 飲 物

ブレンドコーヒー ……………………… ¥400
YōKōのオリジナルの香りをお楽しみください。

アメリカンコーヒー……………………… ¥400
一日に何回も飲む人のコーヒーです。

カフェオレ(Hot or Ice)……………… ¥600
ミルクとコーヒー2つの味の調和をお楽しみください。

カフェウィンナー………………………… ¥600
生クリームとコーヒーの2つの味を一度に味わってください。

カフェカプチーノ ……………………… ¥650
シナモンの香りをお楽しみください。

エスプレッソコーヒー ………………… ¥600
コクと香りの世界がお楽しみいただけます。

アイリッシュコーヒー………………… ¥800
アイリッシュウイスキーの入った大人のコーヒーです。

レモンティー…………………………… ¥400
ダージリン葉を使用した香り高い紅茶です。

ロイヤルティー ……………………… ¥600
本格派の紅茶。

ロシアンティー ……………………… ¥600
ジャムの甘さと紅茶の香りを楽しんでください。

フレーバーティー(アールグレ・アップル
・ストロベリー)……………………… ¥500
飲むほどに味のある紅茶です。

ミルク(Hot or Ice)………………… ¥600

100パーセントFresh Juiceです。

オレンジジュース……………………… ¥750

グレープフルーツジュース…………… ¥800

グレープジュース……………………… ¥800

アップルジュース …………………… ¥650

レモンジュース ……………………… ¥750
サンキストレモンを絞った生の味です。

FOODS
お 食 事

サンドイッチはイギリスパンです。

ヒレカツサンドイッチ………………… ¥1,200
カツの厚みとイギリスパンの調和した力作です。

フィンガーサンドイッチ……………… ¥1,000
女性にやさしい一口タイプのサンドイッチです。

アメリカンクラブハウスサンドイッチ…. ¥1,500
ボリュームタップリのアメリカ風サンドイッチです。

ハンバーグサンドイッチ …………… ¥1,000
牛肉と玉子だけのYōKō自満のサンドイッチです。

ワッフル……………………………… ¥1,000
YōKōのオリジナルの味をお楽しみください。

A LA CARTE
アラカルト

フルーツ(季節ごとに変わります)….. ¥1,000
四季のバラエティーに富んだメニューです。

フルーツクリームヨーグルト ………… ¥800
アイスクリームとフルーツを添えたヨーグルトです。

ヨーグルトドリンク…………………… ¥700
ヘルシー志向の人に最適な飲物です。

ココア………………………………… ¥800
ヨーロッパスタイルのやさしい飲物です。

ペリグリーノ………………………… ¥500
イタリア産自然炭酸水です。

ビール(小ビン)……………………… ¥600

café-terrasse
yōkō
燿光

Koohii shoppu

Part Three

Asking Location

Hai, kasa wa sankai desu.

Dialogue 1

At a department store

KAWAMURA: Sumimasen. Kasa wa doko desu ka.
TEN-IN: Hai, kasa wa san-kai desu.
KAWAMURA: A, soo desu ka. Arigatoo gozaimasu.
TEN-IN: (*bows*)

One way to ask the location of something is to say

_____ wa doko desu ka. *Where is _____?*

To indicate the location of something, say

_____ wa (*place*) desu. _____ *is at/on* (*place*).

Use the counter suffix **-kai** to name floors of a building. Add **chika** (*underground*) before the number to indicate a basement level. For example, **chika san-kai** (often written as **B3** in Japan) is three stories underground.

Counter suffixes are attached at the end of a number to describe what sort of thing is counted. You'll learn more about counters in **Grammar 9.3** and **9.4** in Chapter 2.

Dialogue 1 KAWAMURA: Excuse me. Where are the umbrellas? CLERK: (Yes.) They are on the third floor. KAWAMURA: Oh, I see. (*lit.*, Oh, is that right?) Thank you. CLERK: (bows)

Floors of a Building

B1	chika ik-kai	6th	rok-kai
1st	ik-kai	7th	nana-kai
2nd	ni-kai	8th	hachi-kai (*or* hak-kai)
3rd	san-kai	9th	kyuu-kai
4th	yon-kai	10th	juk-kai (*or* jik-kai)
5th	go-kai	11th	juu-ik-kai

An alternate pronunciation for 3rd floor is **san-gai**.

Activity 1

Ask a classmate where the following items are, using **Dialogue 1** as a model.

1. kamera
2. seetaa
3. kutsushita
4. doresu
5. kagu
6. tokee
7. shatsu
8. hon
9. bunboogu
10. teeburu

Dialogue 2

BURAUN: Kawamura-san no uchi wa doko desu ka.
KAWAMURA: Setagaya desu.
BURAUN: Chotto tooi desu ne.
KAWAMURA: Ee.

Practice **Dialogue 2** using the following map to find substitutions for the underlined parts.

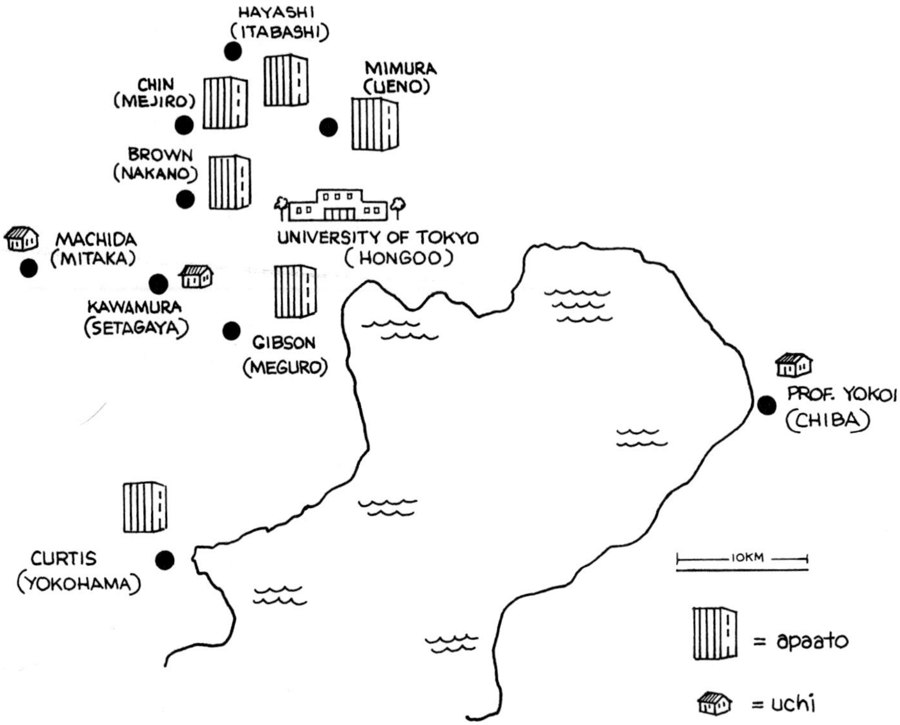

Dialogue 2 BROWN: Where is your house, Mr. Kawamura? KAWAMURA: It's in Setagaya. BROWN: That's a bit far, isn't it? KAWAMURA: Yes.

Now ask a classmate where his or her house or apartment is. Do you think it is close to or far from your school?

Useful Words

uchi	*house, home* (informal)
apaato	*apartment*
ryoo	*dormitory*
daigaku	*university*
(Totemo) chikai desu.	*It's (very) close.*
(Totemo) tooi desu.	*It's (very) far.*

Numbers Up to 9,999

Large Numbers

21	ni-juu-ichi	400	yon-hyaku
29	ni-juu-kyu, ni-juu-ku	500	go-hyaku
30	san-juu	600	rop-pyaku
40	yon-juu	700	nana-hyaku
50	go-juu	800	hap-pyaku
60	roku-juu	900	kyuu-hyaku
70	nana-juu, shichi-juu	996	kyuu-hyaku-kyuu-juu-roku
80	hachi-juu	1,000	sen
90	kyuu-juu	2,000	ni-sen
99	kyuu-juu-kyuu, kyuu-juu-ku	3,000	san-zen
100	hyaku	4,000	yon-sen
101	hyaku-ichi	5,000	go-sen
110	hyaku-juu	6,000	roku-sen
153	hyaku-go-juu-san	7,000	nana-sen
200	ni-hyuaku	8,000	has-sen
300	san-byaku	9,000	kyuu-sen

9,990	kyuu-sen-kyuu-hyaku-kyuu-juu
9,999	kyuu-sen-kyuu-hyaku-kyuu-juu-kyuu (-ku)

Activity 2

Read these numbers aloud.

1. 34
2. 66
3. 87
4. 108
5. 196
6. 459
7. 555
8. 803
9. 1,001
10. 1,562
11. 2,073
12. 5,555
13. 8,906
14. 9,713

Activity 3

More math problems.

Do you remember?
+ tasu, − hiku, × kakeru,
÷ waru, = wa

1. 30 + 53 = ?
2. 60 + 105 = ?
3. 345 + 80 = ?
4. 2,001 + 458 = ?
5. 6,000 − 2,000 = ?
6. 8,900 − 350 = ?
7. 9,999 − 1,111 = ?
8. 590 − 180 = ?
9. 50 × 40 = ?
10. 7 × 111 = ?
11. 80 × 30 = ?
12. 100 × 8 = ?
13. 5,000 ÷ 25 = ?
14. 8,888 ÷ 4 = ?
15. 600 ÷ 30 = ?
16. 440 ÷ 8 = ?

Asking About Existence

Dialogue 3

At the student cafeteria of the University of Tokyo

KAWAMURA: Sumimasen. Supagetti wa arimasu ka.
UEITORESU: Sumimasen ga, chotto . . .
KAWAMURA: Ja, hanbaagaa wa arimasu ka.
UEITORESU: Hai, arimasu.
KAWAMURA: Ja, hanbaagaa o onegai shimasu.
UEITORESU: Hai, 220-en desu.

Arimasu is a verb meaning *to exist* or *to have*. To ask whether something exists, say

_____ wa arimasu ka. *Is there (Do you have) _____?*

Dialogue 3 KAWAMURA: Excuse me. Do you have spaghetti? WAITRESS: I'm sorry, but . . . KAWAMURA: Then, do you have hamburgers? WAITRESS: Yes, we do. KAWAMURA: Then, I would like a hamburger. WAITRESS: Certainly. (*lit.*, Yes.) That's 220 yen.

コミュニケーション・ノート

Communication Note: Saying No (Without Saying No)

Sumimasen ga, chotto . . . (**Dialogue 3**) literally means *I am sorry, but a little bit. . . .* In Japan it is considered clumsy and impolite to say no directly. For example, in this case, to say **Iie, arimasen** (*No, we don't have any*) would be grammatically correct but socially inappropriate. There are a number of ways to indicate a negative answer indirectly. **Sumimasen ga, chotto . . .** or just **Chotto . . .** said with a trailing intonation is one of these strategies.

Now practice **Dialogue 3**, using the following menu.

Tookyoo Daigaku Kafeteria menyuu

supagetti	urikire	**Nomimono**	
piza	urikire	koora	¥100
suteeki	¥1100	juusu	¥180
sushi	urikire	aisu miruku	urikire
omuretsu	¥470	aisu tii	¥120
raamen	¥400	koohi	¥150
Hanbaagaa		**Saido Oodaa**	
hanbaagaa	¥220	hurenchi hurai	¥90
chiizu baagaa	¥330	onion ringu	¥170
daburu baagaa	¥420	suupu	¥150
janbo baagaa	¥510	sarada	¥230
chikin baagaa	urikire		
fisshu baagaa	¥350		

Asking About Price

Dialogue 4

BURAUN: Sumimasen. Chiizu baagaa wa arimasu ka.
UEITORESU: Hai, arimasu.
BURAUN: Ikura desu ka.
UEITORESU: 330-en desu.
BURAUN: Jaa, chiizu baagaa to koohii o onegai-shimasu.
UEITORESU: Arigatoo gozaimasu. 480-en desu.

To is a particle meaning *and*. It can connect two or more nouns to express such meaning as *A and B* and *A, B, and C*.

Dialogue 4 BROWN: Excuse me. Do you have cheeseburgers? WAITRESS: Yes, we do. BROWN: How much are they? WAITRESS: 330 yen. BROWN: Well then, please give me a cheeseburger and coffee. WAITRESS: Thank you. That will be 480 yen.

コミュニケーション・ノート

Communication Note: Asking Price

The most common way to ask how much something costs is to say **Ikura desu ka**.

> Kore wa ikura desu ka. (*How much is this?*) —3000-en desu.
> Kono tokee wa ikura desu ka. (*How much is this watch?*) —9500-en desu.

Dialogue 5

KAWAMURA: Fisshu baagaa wa arimasu ka.
UEITORESU: Hai, arimasu.
KAWAMURA: Ikura desu ka.
UEITORESU: 350-en desu.
KAWAMURA: Ja, fisshu baagaa o onegai shimasu.
UEITORESU: Nomimono wa ikaga desu ka.
KAWAMURA: Kekkoo desu.

. . . **Wa ikaga desu ka** is ommonly used to make a suggestion.

コミュニケーション・ノート

Communication Note: *Kekkoo desu*

Kekkoo desu can mean *it's fine* or *no, thank you*, depending on the context. In **Dialogue 5**, **kekkoo desu** means *no, thank you*, while in the following exchange, it means *it's fine*.

Kore de ii desu ka. —Ee, kekkoo desu.	*Is this OK?* —*Yes, it's fine.*

Activity 4

Pair up with a classmate and practice ordering at a **kissaten**. **Kissaten** are coffeeshops where people go to talk or rendezvous with friends or business contacts, to relax, to eat, or just plain to kill time. Order from the cafeteria menu on page 33.

Dialogue 5 KAWAMURA: Do you have fish burgers? WAITRESS: Yes, we do. KAWAMURA: How much are they? WAITRESS: 350 yen. KAWAMURA: Well then, I would like a fish burger. WAITRESS: How about something to drink? KAWAMURA: No, thank you.

Talking About Daily Activities

Dialogue 6

Masao Hayashi and Linda Brown are talking.

HAYASHI: Buraun-san wa nan-ji ni okimasu ka.
BURAUN: Go-ji desu.
HAYASHI: Waa, hayai desu ne.
BURAUN: Hayashi-san wa.
HAYASHI: Ku-ji desu.

Activity 5

First, listen to your teacher or tape while looking at the following schedule.

JOHN KAWAMURA'S DAY

6:00 A.M.	okimasu (*he gets up*)
7:00 A.M.	asagohan o tabemasu (*he eats breakfast*)
8:00 A.M.	gakkoo e ikimasu (*he goes to school*)
12:00 NOON	hirugohan o tabemasu (*he eats lunch*)
1:00 P.M.	koohii o nomimasu (*he drinks coffee*)
3:00 P.M.	toshokan e ikimasu (*he goes to the library*)
7:00 P.M.	bangohan o tabemasu (*he eats dinner*)
8:00 P.M.	terebi o mimasu (*he watches TV*)
9:00 P.M.	hon o yomimasu (*he reads a book*)
12:00 P.M.	nemasu (*he goes to sleep*)

Vocabulary Library

Daily Activities

	(*I, you, he, she, we, they, etc.*)
okimasu	. . . get up
asagohan o tabemasu	. . . eat breakfast
hirugohan, bangohan	
gakkoo e ikimasu	. . . go to school
kurasu, toshokan (library), **shigoto** (work)	
o-cha o nomimasu	. . . drink tea
koohii, wain, koocha (black tea)	

There is no subject-verb agreement in Japanese.

Dialogue 6 HAYASHI: What time do you get up, Ms. Brown? BROWN: Five o'clock. HAYASHI: Wow, that's early. BROWN: How about you, Mr. Hayashi? HAYASHI: (I get up at) Nine o'clock.

	(*I, you, he, she, we, they, etc.*)
uchi e kaerimasu	. . . go back home
undoo o shimasu	. . . do exercise
jogingu, earobikusu	
terebi o mimasu	. . . watch TV
eega (movie), **dorama, nyuusu**	
hon o yomimasu	. . . read a book
shinbun (newspaper), **zasshi** (magazine)	
ongaku o kikimasu	. . . listen to music
rajio (radio), **sutereo** (stereo)	
Nihongo o benkyoo shimasu	. . . study Japanese
suugaku (math), **Huransugo** (French)	
nemasu	. . . go to sleep/bed

Now answer the following questions in Japanese.

Example

mainichi *every day*

Kawamura-san wa mainichi nan-ji ni okimasu ka. → Gozen roku-ji desu. (*What time does Mr. Kawamura get up every day?*)

1. Nan-ji ni asagohan o tabemasu ka.
2. Nan-ji ni gakkoo e ikimasu ka.
3. Nan-ji ni hirugohan o tabemasu ka.
4. Nan-ji ni toshokan e ikimasu ka.
5. Nan-ji ni bangohan o tabemasu ka.
6. Nan-ji ni hon o yomimasu ka.
7. Kawamura-san wa mainichi nan-ji ni nemasu ka.

More Time Expressions

2:05	ni-ji go-hun	2:35	ni-ji san-juu-go-hun
2:10	ni-ji jup-pun ni-ji jip-pun	2:40	ni-ji yon-jup-pun ni-ji yon-jip-pun
2:15	ni-ji juu-go-hun	2:45	ni-ji yon-juu-go-hun
2:20	ni-ji ni-jup-pun ni-ji ni-jip-pun	2:50	ni-ji go-jup-pun ni-ji go-jip-pun
2:25	ni-ji ni-juu-go-hun	2:55	ni-ji go-juu-go-hun
2:30	ni-ji han ni-ji san-jup-pun ni-ji san-jip-pun		

コミュニケーション・ノート

Communication Note: Telling Time Politely

Japanese people think it is more polite to express themselves vaguely rather than clearly and directly. This tendency extends to unexpected areas like telling time. When you would like to tell time politely or give an approximate time, use **goro** (*about*).

Nan-ji ni uchi o demasu ka. —Hachi-ji goro demasu.	*What time do you leave home? —I leave about 8:00.*
Ni-ji goro ikimasu.	*I'll go at 2:00 (lit., at about 2:00).*

Don't be fooled by the use of **goro**. Japanese tend to be extremely punctual and expect the same of others.

Activity 6

Let's talk about your daily schedule.

1. Anata wa mainichi nan-ji ni okimasu ka.
2. Nan-ji ni uchi o demasu ka.
3. Nan-ji ni uchi e kaerimasu ka.
4. Nan-ji ni bangohan o tabemasu ka.
5. Yoku (*often*) terebi o mimasu ka.
6. Yoku hon o yomimasu ka.
7. Yoku ongaku o kikimasu ka.
8. Nan-ji ni nemasu ka.

Vocabulary Library

More Daily Activities

	(*I, you, he, she, we, they, etc.*)
tegami o kakimasu	. . . write a letter
deeto (o) shimasu	. . . have/go on a date
yakyuu o shimasu	. . . play baseball
kaimono ni ikimasu	. . . go shopping
ichi-nichi-juu nemasu	. . . sleep all day
tomodachi ni aimasu	. . . see/meet a friend
tomodachi to hanashimasu	. . . talk with a friend
Nihongo o renshuu shimasu	. . . practice Japanese
denwa (o) shimasu	. . . make a phone call

文法ノート

Grammar Note: Basic Sentence Structure of Japanese

You may have already noticed that the sentence structure of Japanese is different from that of English. In English, the basic sentence structure is Subject-Verb-Object (e.g., *I watch TV*). In Japanese the basic structure is Subject-Object-Verb (**watashi wa terebi o mimasu**). Thus, Japanese verbs (e.g., **mimasu, okimasu**) come toward the end of a sentence.

In English, you can tell whether a noun is a subject or an object by its position in the sentence. If a noun comes at the beginning of a sentence, it is the subject. If it comes after a verb, it is an object. In Japanese, both the subject noun and object noun come before a verb. The roles of the nouns are differentiated by the use of particles (small words) that follow the word they mark. Notice, for instance, that the particle **o** marks the direct object. In **bangohan o tabemasu** (*I eat supper*), **o** marks **bangohan** as the object of the verb **tabemasu**. You will study particles in more detail later.

The Japanese Writing System (3)

As you now know, to write modern Japanese you need to use a combination of **kanji** (*Chinese characters*), **hiragana**, and **katakana**. The general rules of each script's use can be summarized as follows.

1. **Kanji** are usually used to represent such content words as nouns, adjective roots, adverbs, and verb roots.
2. **Hiragana** is used to represent, in most cases, such functional words as particles, verb and adjective conjugational endings.
3. **Katakana** is used to represent loanwords from Western languages and onomatopoeic words.

For instance,

兄	は	フランス	から	帰	りました
kanji	hiragana	katakana	hiragana	kanji	hiragana

兄	*brother* (noun)
は	(topic particle [functional word])
フランス	*France* (loanword)
から	*from* (functional word)
帰	*to return* (verb root)
りました	past, polite form (verb conjugational ending)

By the way, the only exception to writing with all three scripts is children's books (because young children have not studied many **kanji, hiragana** is used in place of **kanji**).

Some Notes on the Writing of Functional Words

Japanese use several particles (small words) to indicate grammatical functions. They are written in **hiragana**, but you must be careful about how to write some of them.

- Topic particle (indicating the topic of a sentence) **wa** is written は.
- Direction particle (indicating the direction of movement) **e** is written へ.
- Direct object particle (indicating the direct object of a verb) **o** is written を.

はやしさんはまいにちカフェテリアへいきます。
Mr. Hayashi goes to the cafeteria every day.
ブラウンさんはまいあさジョギングをします。
Ms. Brown jogs (lit., does jogging) every morning.

言語ノート

Linguistic Note: Word Space and Punctuation

In Japanese writing, no space is used between words. An exception is books and other written materials for young children; because they are written entirely in **hiragana** and **katakana**, they need word spaces to make them readable. The concept of a word space didn't develop in written Japanese due to the influence of Chinese writing, which does not use space between words, and because word boundaries are quite clear when **hiragana**, **katakana**, and **kanji** are intermixed. In fact, in many cases the changes in script in a sentence coincide with word boundaries.

Similarly, the co-use of the three orthographies makes it possible for readers to easily tell where a clause or sentence ends. For this reason, a punctuation system was not developed until about fifty years ago. In modern Japanese, the following punctuation marks are used.

。	**maru**	period	・	**nakaten**	midpoint
、	**ten**	comma	…	**santen riidaa**	ellipsis points
「 」	**kagikakko**	quotation marks			

The Japanese period is used to end a sentence, but the usage of the Japanese comma is not clear-cut. It resembles the English comma, but writers vary in how they use it. The quotation marks are used to set off quoted speech, titles of works (books, movies, etc.), and words the writer wishes to emphasize (somewhat as English writers underline words). The midpoint separates the individual words of **katakana** loanwords (e.g., トレーニング・センター), including personal names (the midpoint occurs between the first and last name; e.g., リンダ・ブラウン), or connects two nouns with the meaning *and*. Finally, as in English, Japanese ellipsis points are used to indicate missing words. You will also occasionally see question marks and exclamation points, both borrowed from Western languages.

Introduction to Kanji

Japan's Ministry of Education requires Japanese grade schools to teach 1,006 **kanji** from grades one through six. These **kanji** are called **kyooiku kanji** (*educational Chinese characters*). By the time they graduate from high school, Japanese are expected to know a total of 1,945 **kanji**. These 1,945 **kanji** are called **jooyoo kanji** (*Chinese characters for everyday use*). Not only must students be taught these **kanji**, but the Ministry of Education also recommends that newspapers and magazines use only **jooyoo kanji** plus about 200 other characters used in people's names (or else provide the pronunciation for the unsanctioned **kanji**). Generally, Japanese know more than these required **kanji**. In **Yookoso! Volume I**, you will learn approximately 180 **kanji**, some of which are **kyooiku kanji** and some, **jooyoo kanji**. You will also be exposed to many more in the readings and vocabulary listings.

Kanji represent both sound and meaning. Most characters have more than one sound, or reading. Centuries ago, when **kanji** were originally borrowed from Chinese for use in transcribing spoken Japanese, their Chinese pronunciations came with them. These Chinese readings are called **on-yomi** (**on**-*readings*). When Chinese characters were used to write native Japanese concepts or words, the native Japanese pronunciations were also assigned to the characters. These native Japanese readings are called **kun-yomi** (**kun**-*readings*). For historical reasons, many **kanji** have more than one **on**-reading and more than one **kun**-reading. How do you know which reading applies? The answer is context. For instance, the character 人 meaning *person* is read **hito** in the phrase あの人 (*that person*), while it is read **jin** in the word アメリカ人 (*American*). **Hito** is the **kun-yomi**, and **jin** is the **on-yomi**. The more you practice reading Japanese, the more quickly and intuitively you will be able to choose the correct reading.

言語ノート

Linguistic Note: *Hurigana*

Because one **kanji** may have several different pronunciations (e.g., some twenty for the character 生), it can be difficult even for the native Japanese speaker to remember all of them. For rarely occurring pronunciations and for rarely used **kanji** (those not included in the standard 1,945), the remedy is **hurigana**. These tiny **hiragana** or **katakana** written above the character (or to the right in vertical writing) provide the correct reading. You will see many **hurigana** in children's books, books dealing with difficult subjects, and textbooks for Japanese language students. In this book, **hurigana** are provided for characters you haven't studied yet and for those you have just learned. In other words, if a character has no **hurigana**, you are supposed to know it. Here is a sample of what it looks like.

佐野さん御夫婦はわたしのアパートの管理人です。

山本さんの勤める喫茶店は中野の住宅街にあります。

Vocabulary

This is a list of words that you have used or heard in **Getting Started**. Before beginning **Chapter 1**, make sure that you know the words listed under the first seven categories: **Greetings and Polite Expressions, Questions, Classroom, Numbers, Time Expressions, Commands,** and **Other Useful Words**. These are considered active vocabulary, which means you will need to be able to use them in later chapters.

For your reading practice this list is rendered in **hiragana** and **katakana**, but in authentic writing, Chinese characters would be used in many words.

Greetings and Polite Expressions

Arigatoo.	ありがとう。	Thank you.
Arigatoo gozaimasu.	ありがとうございます。	Thank you. (*formal*)
Chotto.	ちょっと。	Well (no) . . . (*lit.*, A little . . .)
Doo itashimashite.	どういたしまして。	You are welcome.
Doomo arigatoo gozaimasu.	どうもありがとうございます。	Thank you very much. (*most formal*)
Doomo arigatoo.	どうもありがとう。	Thank you very much.
Doomo.	どうも。	Thanks. (*very informal*)
Doozo yoroshiku.	どうぞよろしく。	Nice meeting you.
Genki desu.	げんきです。	I am fine.
Hajimemashite.	はじめまして。	How do you do?
Ja (dewa) mata.	じゃ（では）また。	See you.
Ja (dewa).	じゃ（では）。	See you.
Kekkoo desu.	けっこうです。	No, thanks.
Konban wa.	こんばんは。	Good evening.
Konnichi wa.	こんにちは。	Good afternoon.
. . . o kudasai.	…をください。	Please give me . . .
O-genki desu ka.	おげんきですか。	How are you?
Ohayoo.	おはよう。	Good morning. (*informal*)
Ohayoo gozaimasu.	おはようございます。	Good morning. (*formal*)
Ohisashiburi desu ne.	おひさしぶりですね。	I haven't seen you for a long time.
Okagesama de genki desu.	おかげさまでげんきです。	Thanks to you, I am fine.
Onegai shimasu.	おねがいします。	Please (give me) . . .
Oyasuminasai.	おやすみなさい。	Good night.
Sayo(o)nara.	さよ（う）なら。	Goodbye.
Shibaraku desu ne.	しばらくですね。	I haven't seen you for a long time.
Shitsuree shimasu.	しつれいします。	Goodbye.
Sumimasen.	すみません。	Excuse me, thank you.

Questions

Doko desu ka.	どこですか。	Where is it?
Ikura desu ka.	いくらですか。	How much is it?
Nan desu ka.	なんですか。	What is it?
Nan-ji desu ka.	なんじですか。	What time is it?
. . . ga suki desu ka.	…がすきですか。	Do (you) like . . . ?

Classroom

booru-pen	ボールペン	ballpoint pen
chooku	チョーク	chalk
denki	でんき	light
doa	ドア	door
enpitsu	えんぴつ	pencil
gakusee	がくせい	student
hon	ほん	book
isu	いす	chair
jisho	じしょ	dictionary
kaban	かばん	bag
kami	かみ	paper
kokuban	こくばん	chalkboard
kurasu	クラス	class
kyookasho	きょうかしょ	textbook
kyooshitsu	きょうしつ	classroom
mado	まど	window
nooto	ノート	notebook
pen	ペン	pen
sensee	せんせい	teacher, professor
shaapupenshiru	シャープペンシル	mechanical pencil
teeburu	テーブル	table
tsukue	つくえ	desk

Numbers

ree, zero	れい、ゼロ	zero
ichi	いち	one
ni	に	two
san	さん	three
yon, shi	よん、し	four
go	ご	five
roku	ろく	six
shichi, nana	しち、なな	seven
hachi	はち	eight

ku, kyuu	く、きゅう	nine
juu	じゅう	ten
juu-ichi	じゅういち	eleven
juu-ni	じゅうに	twelve
juu-san	じゅうさん	thirteen
juu-yon, juu-shi	じゅうよん、じゅうし	fourteen
juu-go	じゅうご	fifteen
juu-roku	じゅうろく	sixteen
juu-shichi, juu-nana	じゅうしち、じゅうなな	seventeen
juu-hachi	じゅうはち	eighteen
juu-ku, juu-kyuu	じゅうく、じゅうきゅう	nineteen
ni-juu	にじゅう	twenty
san-juu	さんじゅう	thirty
yon-juu	よんじゅう	forty
go-juu	ごじゅう	fifty
roku-juu	ろくじゅう	sixty
nana-juu, shichi-juu	ななじゅう、しちじゅう	seventy
hachi-juu	はちじゅう	eighty
kyuu-juu	きゅうじゅう	ninety
hyaku	ひゃく	one hundred
ni-hyaku	にひゃく	two hundred
san-byaku	さんびゃく	three hundred
yon-hyaku	よんひゃく	four hundred
go-hyaku	ごひゃく	five hundred
rop-pyaku	ろっぴゃく	six hundred
nana-hyaku	ななひゃく	seven hundred
hap-pyaku	はっぴゃく	eight hundred
kyuu-hyaku	きゅうひゃく	nine hundred
sen	せん	one thousand
ni-sen	にせん	two thousand
san-zen	さんぜん	three thousand
yon-sen	よんせん	four thousand
go-sen	ごせん	five thousand
roku-sen	ろくせん	six thousand
nana-sen	ななせん	seven thousand
has-sen	はっせん	eight thousand
kyuu-sen	きゅうせん	nine thousand

Time Expressions

ichi-ji	いちじ	one o'clock
ni-ji	にじ	two o'clock
san-ji	さんじ	three o'clock
yo-ji	よじ	four o'clock
go-ji	ごじ	five o'clock

roku-ji	ろくじ	six o'clock
shichi-ji, nana-ji	しちじ、ななじ	seven o'clock
hachi-ji	はちじ	eight o'clock
ku-ji	くじ	nine o'clock
juu-ji	じゅうじ	ten o'clock
juu-ichi-ji	じゅういちじ	eleven o'clock
juu-ni-ji	じゅうにじ	twelve o'clock
go-hun	ごふん	five minutes
jup-pun, jip-pun	じゅっぷん、じっぷん	ten minutes
juu-go-hun	じゅうごふん	fifteen minutes
ni-jup-pun, ni-jip-pun	にじゅっぷん、にじっぷん	twenty minutes
ni-juu-go-hun	にじゅうごふん	twenty-five minutes
. . . han	…はん	. . . thirty (*when telling time*)
san-jup-pun, san-jip-pun	さんじゅっぷん、さんじっぷん	thirty minutes
san-juu-go-hun	さんじゅうごふん	thirty-five minutes
yon-jup-pun, yon-jip-pun	よんじゅっぷん、よんじっぷん	forty minutes
yon-juu-go-hun	よんじゅうごふん	forty-five minutes
go-jup-pun, go-jip-pun	ごじゅっぷん、ごじっぷん	fifty minutes
go-juu-go-hun	ごじゅうごふん	fifty-five minutes
asa	あさ	morning
gogo	ごご	P.M.
gozen	ごぜん	A.M.
hiru	ひる	noontime
maiasa	まいあさ	every morning
mainichi	まいにち	every day
yoru	よる	night
yuugata	ゆうがた	evening

Commands

Akete kudasai.	あけてください。	Please open (it).
Aruite kudasai.	あるいてください。	Please walk.
Dashite kudasai.	だしてください。	Please take (it) out.
Hashitte kudasai.	はしってください。	Please run.
Itte kudasai.	いってください。	Please say (it).
Kaite kudasai.	かいてください。	Please write (it).
Kakanai de kudasai.	かかないでください。	Please don't write.
Kiite (ite) kudasai.	きいて(いて)ください。	Please listen.
Kurikaeshite kudasai.	くりかえしてください。	Please repeat.
Minai de kudasai.	みないでください。	Please don't look.
Mite kudasai.	みてください。	Please look.
Pea o tsukutte kudasai.	ペアをつくってください。	Please make a pair.
Shite kudasai.	してください。	Please do (it).

Suwatte kudasai.	すわってください。	Please sit down.
Tatte kudasai.	たってください。	Please stand up.
Tojite kudasai.	とじてください。	Please close (it).

Other Useful Words

-ban	～ばん	Number _____(*counter for serial numbers*)
-en	～えん	¥_____(*counter for yen*)
-kai	～かい	_____-th floor (*counter for floors of a building*)
-san	～さん	Mr., Ms.
are	あれ	that (*thing over there*)
Chigaimasu.	ちがいます。	That's not right.
chikai	ちかい	close, near
chotto	ちょっと	a little
desu	です	to be
ee	ええ	yes
hai	はい	yes
Hai, soo desu.	はい、そうです。	Yes, that's right.
hayai	はやい	early
Hontoo desu ka.	ほんとうですか。	Really? (*lit.*, Is that true?)
iie	いいえ	no
ima	いま	now
jaa	じゃあ	well, then
ka	か	(*question marker*)
kirai	きらい	to dislike
kore	これ	this (*thing*)
no	の	(*possessive marker*)
Soo ja arimasen.	そうじゃありません。	That's not right.
suki	すき	to like
to	と	and
tooi	とおい	far
totemo	とても	very
watashi	わたし	I

Verbs

		(*I, you, he, she, we, they, etc.*)
benkyoo shimasu	べんきょうします	. . . study
hanashimasu	はなします	. . . speak
ikimasu	いきます	. . . go
kaerimasu	かえります	. . . return
kakimasu	かきます	. . . write
kikimasu	ききます	. . . listen
mimasu	みます	. . . look, watch

nemasu	ねます	. . . sleep
nomimasu	のみます	. . . drink
okimasu	おきます	. . . get up
renshuu shimasu	れんしゅうします	. . . practice
shimasu	します	. . . do
tabemasu	たべます	. . . eat
yomimasu	よみます	. . . read

Nouns

apaato	アパート	apartment
asagohan	あさごはん	breakfast
bangohan	ばんごはん	dinner, supper
benkyoo	べんきょう	study, studying
daigaku	だいがく	university
denwa	でんわ	telephone
eega	えいが	movie
gakkoo	がっこう	school
hirugohan	ひるごはん	lunch
hon	ほん	book
kagu	かぐ	furniture
kaimono	かいもの	shopping
kamera	カメラ	camera
kutsu	くつ	shoes
kutsushita	くつした	socks
meeshi	めいし	name card, business card
nyuusu	ニュース	news
ongaku	おんがく	music
shigoto	しごと	work
shinbun	しんぶん	newspaper
supootsu	スポーツ	sports
tokee	とけい	wristwatch
toshokan	としょかん	library
uchi	うち	house, home
zasshi	ざっし	magazine

Foods/Beverages

biiru	ビール	beer
hanbaagaa	ハンバーガー	hamburger
juusu	ジュース	juice
koocha	こうちゃ	tea
koohii	コーヒー	coffee
koora	コーラ	cola
kudamono	くだもの	fruit
menyuu	メニュー	menu
Nihon ryoori	にほんりょうり	Japanese dish
niku	にく	meat
nomimono	のみもの	beverage
o-cha	おちゃ	tea
o-sake	おさけ	alcoholic beverage
sakana	さかな	fish
sarada	サラダ	salad
suteeki	ステーキ	steak
suupu	スープ	soup
tabemono	たべもの	food
wain	ワイン	wine
yasai	やさい	vegetable

Countries/Languages

Amerika	アメリカ	America
Huransu	フランス	France
Huransugo	フランスご	French
Kanada	カナダ	Canada
Nihon	にほん	Japan
Nihongo	にほんご	Japanese
Oosutoraria	オーストラリア	Australia

Introduction to *Yookoso!*

Now that you have finished **Getting Started**, welcome (**Yookoso!**) to the heart of your textbook. Here you will begin studying grammar, **kanji** (*Chinese characters*), and other essentials to mastering Japanese. *Yookoso!* Volume I is divided into seven main chapters. Each chapter revolves around a single theme—classmates, daily life, food, shopping, and so on.

Each chapter starts with a section called **Vocabulary and Oral Activities**. This section contains several activities designed to help you build up vocabulary related to the chapter topic and to help you learn grammar structures in meaningful contexts.

The grammar section, **Grammar and Exercises**, contains brief dialogues that introduce each new grammar point as well as grammar explanations and exercises. When you see ㊙ **Study Grammar (number)** in **Vocabulary and Oral Activities**, you may read the corresponding grammar explanation and do the related grammar exercises before doing the oral activities; alternatively, you may elect to study the grammar *after* you've performed the activities with your instructor's guidance.

The following section, **Vocabulary**, lists the important vocabulary you have studied in the chapter's **Vocabulary and Oral Activities** and **Grammar and Exercises**. Also listed here are the **kanji** you are expected to learn in that chapter. You should review this section before proceeding to the **Reading and Writing** section.

Reading and Writing contains two reading practices and two writing practices. The reading materials relate to the chapter topics, and the writing focuses on the vocabulary and grammatical structures you have just studied. You will read many different types of writing in this section — travel guides, advertisements, essays, letters, and others.

In **Language Functions and Situations**, you will study important functional expressions used to ask for directions, ask someone to repeat, apologize, and so on. You'll practice how to communicate in such everyday situations as at a restaurant or a department store. Dialogues in this section offer models for interaction with native speakers in many real-life situations, and activities and role-play provide you with opportunities to practice handling those situations.

The last section of each chapter is **Listening Comprehension**. The conversations and narrations you will hear in this section will be on the now-familiar topics covered in the chapter.

Throughout the text you will see many printed items you would encounter in Japan — ads, tickets, magazine clippings, and so forth. (You have already seen some authentic materials in **Getting Started**.) You will also see many brief commentaries under several headings: 文化ノート (*culture notes*) offer useful cultural information;

言語ノート (*linguistic notes*) offer insights into interesting facts about the Japanese language; 文法ノート (*grammar notes*) provide brief explanations of useful grammar points; and コミュニケーション・ノート (*communication notes*) offer hints for communicating more effectively in Japanese.

Review Chapters appear after Chapter 4 and Chapter 7 in Volume I. There you will review important vocabulary and grammatical structures you have studied previously. Each **Review Chapter** consists of **Activities**, an **Interview**, **Situations**, **Cultural Reading**, and **This Is My Life!** The last two sections are designed to offer you more information about Japan, Japanese people, and Japanese lifestyles. In order to successfully communicate with Japanese people and to thrive in Japanese society, you need to understand the culture as well as the language. This text strives to introduce you to Japanese culture through culture notes, readings, authentic materials, and photographs.

1 第一章 クラスメート

Classmates

大学のキャンパス

OBJECTIVES

Topics

Nationalities and languages
Personal information
Around campus

Grammar

1. Identification: the copula です
2. Possessive particle の
3. Personal pronouns and demonstratives
4. Asking questions: interrogatives

Reading and Writing

My French classmate
We're looking for a pen pal!

Language Functions and Situations

Introducing friends
Introducing yourself

Vocabulary and Oral Activities

Nationalities and Languages

㊜ Study Grammar 1, 2, 3, and 4.

アクティビティー 1

ダイアログ：この人(ひと)はだれですか。(*Who is this person?*)

山口(やまぐち)さんとカワムラさんが写真(しゃしん)を見(み)ています。

山口：この人はだれですか。
カワムラ：その人はブラウンさんです。
山口：大学(だいがく)のクラスメートですか。
カワムラ：はい、そうです。

Kawamura is a Japanese family name. Because John Kawamura is an American citizen, however, his name is written in **katakana**.

Yamaguchi-san to Kawamura-san ga shashin o mite imasu.

YAMAGUCHI: Kono hito wa dare desu ka.
KAWAMURA: Sono hito wa Buraun-san desu.
YAMAGUCHI: Daigaku no kurasumeeto desu ka.
KAWAMURA: Hai, soo desu.

Now ask about the other people in the photograph, modeling your conversation after the dialogue. Replace the underlined words as necessary. An alternate ending to the dialogue follows.

いいえ、違(ちが)います。_____ です。(Iie, chigaimasu. _____ desu.)
(*No, that's not right. He/She is _____.*)

Mr. Yamaguchi and Mr. Kawamura are looking at a photo. YAMAGUCHI: Who is this person? KAWAMURA: That's Ms. Brown. YAMAGUCHI: Is she (your) classmate at the university? KAWAMURA: Yes, that's right.

Study Hint

This chapter continues to provide romanization, but try to refer to the Japanese writing as much as possible. From the next chapter on, you will be reading Japanese with no romanization as a crutch. Now is the time to start reading Japanese !

Vocabulary: People at School

クラスメート	**kurasumeeto**	classmate
友だち	**tomodachi**	friend
大学生	**daigakusee**	college student

Review: 学生（がくせい）、先生（せんせい）

NATIONALITIES AND LANGUAGES

Country	Nationality	Language
日本（にほん） Japan	日本人（にほんじん）	日本語（にほんご）
アメリカ U.S.	アメリカ人	英語（えいご）
イギリス England	イギリス人	英語
イタリア Italy	イタリア人	イタリア語（ご）
カナダ Canada	カナダ人	英語/フランス語
韓国（かんこく） South Korea	韓国人	韓国語
シンガポール Singapore	シンガポール人	英語/中国語
スペイン Spain	スペイン人	スペイン語
台湾（たいわん） Taiwan	台湾人	中国語
中国（ちゅうごく） China	中国人	中国語
ドイツ Germany	ドイツ人	ドイツ語
ブラジル Brazil	ブラジル人	ポルトガル語
フランス France	フランス人	フランス語
香港（ほんこん） Hong Kong	香港人	中国語
メキシコ Mexico	メキシコ人	スペイン語
ロシア Russia	ロシア人	ロシア語

言語ノート

Nationalities and Languages

With few exceptions, you can form the word for someone's nationality or language by attaching a suffix to the name of his country. Add the suffix 人 (じん : *people/person*) for the nationality and 語 (ご : *language*) for the language. To ask someone's nationality or what language(s) he speaks, use the following expressions. Remember that since the subject isn't explicitly stated here, context will determine whom you are talking about.

> お国(くに)はどちらですか。—アメリカです。
> *What country are (you) from? —(I) am from America.*
> 何語(なにご)を話しますか。—英語(えいご)を話します。
> *What language(s) do (you) speak? — I speak English.*

You can also ask someone's nationality by saying 何人(なにじん)ですか. However, this question sounds very rude when asked of someone directly.

アクティビティー 2

チンさんは中国人(ちゅうごくじん)です。(*Ms. Chin is Chinese. Who is this?*)

カワムラ：この人はチン・メイリンさんです。
山口：チンさんは中国人ですか。
カワムラ：はい、そうです。中国語(ご)を話(はな)します。

KAWAMURA: Kono hito wa Chin Meirin-san desu.
YAMAGUCHI: Chin-san wa Chuugoku-jin desu ka.
KAWAMURA: Hai, soo desu. Chuugoku-go o hanashimasu.

Practice the dialogue based on the following information

PERSON	COUNTRY
リンダ・ブラウン	アメリカ
ホセ・ロドリゲス	メキシコ
クロード・ミレー	フランス
ハンス・シュミット	ドイツ
アナ・ラポーソ	ブラジル
キム・チョンヒ	韓国(かんこく)

KAWAMURA: This is Ms. Mei-Lin Chin. YAMAGUCHI: Is Ms. Chin Chinese? KAWAMURA: Yes, that's right. She speaks Chinese.

アクティビティー 3

何人(なにじん)ですか。何語(なにご)を話(はな)しますか。(*What is his nationality? What language does he speak?*)

Answer these questions for each person listed below.

例 *means example(s)*

[例] ポール・マッカートニー→
ポール・マッカートニーはイギリス人です。英語(えいご)を話します。

1. フリオ・イグレシアス
2. マーガレット・サッチャー
3. 三船敏郎(みふねとしろう)
4. ソフィア・ローレン
5. プラシド・ドミンゴ
6. ジュリア・ロバーツ
7. ボリス・エリツィン
8. マイケル・J・フォックス
9. エビータ・ペロン
10. ブリジット・バルドー

Personal Information

Vocabulary: Personal Information

名前	**namae**	name
出身	**shusshin**	origin ; hometown
専攻	**senkoo**	major
学部	**gakubu**	(academic) department
学年	**gakunen**	year in school; school year
一年生	**ichinensee**	freshman
二年生	**ninensee**	sophomore
三年生	**sannensee**	junior
四年生	**yonensee**	senior
大学院生	**daigakuinsee**	graduate student

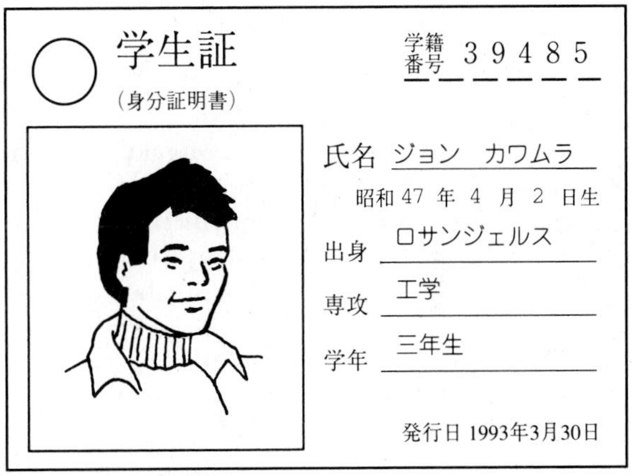

文化ノート

出身(しゅっしん) Origins

Japanese often ask the question ご出身はどちらですか。(*Where are you from?*) To this question, a variety of responses are possible. You can give your hometown, the place where you were born, as the answer. For example, ロサンゼルスの出身です。(*I am from Los Angeles.*) If you moved away from your birthplace as a child and you have a stronger attachment to a different place, you can give that place as the answer. To Japanese, 出身 means the place you identify with geographically, mentally, and emotionally, so it has more meanings than *birthplace*. For example, the word is also used to indicate what school you graduated from and what social group you are from. Someone who graduated from the University of Tokyo might say 東京大学(とうきょうだいがく)の出身です。(*I am a graduate of* [*lit., I am from*] *the University of Tokyo.*) Or you might hear 農家(のうか)の出身です。(*I am from a farmer's family.*)

One of the reasons Japanese people ask this question so often is that the notions of in-group and out-group are of central importance in Japanese society. Depending on whether or not someone is a member of your group, your language, behavior and attitude will differ. Asking this question is a way for Japanese to find out whether someone belongs to their in-group and to discover any common ground. To foreigners, Japanese will often substitute the question どちらのお国(くに)の方(かた)ですか。(*What country are you from?*) as a means to break the ice and identify any common experience.

Vocabulary Library

Academic Subjects and Majors

人類学	**jinruigaku**	anthropology
美術	**bijutsu**	art
生物学	**seebutsugaku**	biology
化学	**kagaku**	chemistry
コンピュータ・サイエンス	**konpyuuta·saiensu**	computer science
教育学	**kyooikugaku**	education
経済学	**keezaigaku**	economics
工学	**koogaku**	engineering
外国語	**gaikokugo**	foreign languages
歴史学	**rekishigaku**	history
法学	**hoogaku**	law
言語学	**gengogaku**	linguistics
文学	**bungaku**	literature
数学	**suugaku**	mathematics
音楽	**ongaku**	music
哲学	**tetsugaku**	philosophy
政治学	**seejigaku**	political science
物理学	**butsurigaku**	physics
社会学	**shakaigaku**	sociology

文化ノート

Japanese Universities and Colleges

In order to enter a Japanese university or college, you must take a nationally administered examination and/or an entrance exam specific to the school you wish to enter. These exams are usually held around January to March. (In Japan, the academic year starts in April.) The competition to enter prestigious national and private universities is severe, with medical schools and dental schools being the most difficult to get into. The extraordinary intense pressure has led some to call the phenomenon "examination hell." Many students who fail the entrance examination for the university of their choice decide to wait a year and retake the exam the following year, studying at a cram school or on their own in the meantime. These students are called 浪人 (ろうにん: *masterless samurai*). One of John Kawamura's classmates, Takashi Mimura, spent two years as a 浪人 until he was able to pass the exam to enter the prestigious University of Tokyo.

When students apply to universities, they specify which department they wish to enter (ie., choose a major in). However, they do not usually start studying specialized subjects in the department they're affiliated with until their junior year. During their freshman and sophomore years, students study a required core liberal arts curriculum consisting of 教養科目 (きょうようかもく: lit., *general education subjects*). As upperclassmen, they can study 専門科目 (せんもんかもく: *specialized subjects*).

I passed the entrance exam of the University of Tokyo!

言語ノート

Academic Subjects and Departments

Most academic subjects are expressed by adding 学 (がく : [*study*] *of*) to a relevant noun. For example, 経済学 (けいざいがく : *economics*) is a combination of 経済 (けいざい: *economy*) and 学. Academic department names are formed by adding 学部 (がくぶ: *academic department*) to the same relevant noun. Thus, 経済 plus 学部 becomes *Department of Economics*, or 経済学部(けいざいがくぶ). Similarly, 美術(びじゅつ: *fine arts*) plus 学部(*academic department*) becomes the *Department of Fine Arts*, or 美術学部(びじゅつがくぶ). Japanese undergraduates typically identify their department as a way of stating their major.

わたしは文学部の学生です。	*I am a student in the Department of Literature.*
カワムラさんは工学部の三年生です。	*Mr. Kawamura is a junior in the Engineering Department.*

アクティビティー　4

ダイアログ：専攻は何ですか。(*What is his/her major?*)

山口：ブラウンさんのご出身はどこですか。
ブラウン：ボストンの出身です。
山口：何年生ですか。
ブラウン：三年生です。
山口：専攻は何ですか。
ブラウン：歴史学です。

YAMAGUCHI: Buraun-san no go-shusshin wa doko desu ka.
BURAUN: Bosuton no shusshin desu.
YAMAGUCHI: Nannensee desu ka.
BURAUN: Sannensee desu.
YAMAGUCHI: Senkoo wa nan desu ka.
BURAUN: Rekishigaku desu.

Now talk about Linda Brown's classmates based on this table.

YAMAGUCHI: Where are you from, Ms. Brown? BROWN: I'm from Boston. YAMAGUCHI: What year student are you? BROWN: I'm a junior. YAMAGUCHI: What is your major? BROWN: It's history.

NAME 名前（なまえ）	HOMETOWN 出身（しゅっしん）	NATIONALITY 国籍（こくせき）	YEAR 学年（がくねん）	MAJOR 専攻（せんこう）
ジョン・カワムラ	ロサンゼルス	アメリカ	三年生（ねんせい）	工学（こうがく）
ヘザー・ギブソン	エドモントン	カナダ	二年生	経済学（けいざいがく）
チン・メイリン	ペキン	中国（ちゅうごく）	二年生	化学（かがく）
ヘンリー・カーチス	アトランタ	アメリカ	四年生	コンピュータ・サイエンス
林正男（はやしまさお）	阿蘇（あそ）	日本（にほん）	二年生	法学（ほうがく）
町田（まちだ）ひとみ	東京（とうきょう）	日本	三年生	フランス文学（ぶんがく）

アクティビティー 5

インタビュー：ご出身（しゅっしん）はどこですか。(*Where are you from?*)
Following the example, ask your classmates questions.

Student 1: ご出身はどこですか。
Student 2: シアトルです。
S1: 何年生（なんねんせい）ですか。
S2: 二年生（にねんせい）です。
S1: 専攻（せんこう）は何（なん）ですか。
S2: 生物学（せいぶつがく）です。

S1: Go-shusshin wa doko desu ka.
S2: Shiatoru desu.
S1: Nannensee desu ka.
S2: Ninensee desu.
S1: Senkoo wa nan desu ka.
S2: Seebutsugaku desu.

S1: Where are you from? S2: I'm from Seattle. S1: What year are you in? S2: I'm a sophomore. S2: What is your major? S2: It's biology.

コミュニケーション・ノート

Asking for Personal Information

Here are some common ways of eliciting personal information. Note the use of the honorific prefix **o-** or **go-** when referring to someone else's name, residence, etc.; remember to drop these prefixes when talking to an out-group member about your own name, residence, and so on, or that of a member of your in-group (for example, a sister or a co-worker).

お名前は(何ですか)。	O-namae wa(nan desu ka).	*(What is) your name?*
ご出身は(どちらですか)。	Go-shusshin wa (dochira desu ka).	*Where are you from?*
お国は(どちらですか)。	O-kuni wa (dochira desu ka).	*What country are you from?*
おすまいは(どちらですか)。	O-sumai wa (dochira desu ka).	*Where do you live?*
お年は(おいくつですか)。	O-toshi wa (o-ikutsu desu ka)	*How old are you?*
お電話番号は(何番ですか)。	O-denwa bangoo wa (nan-ban desu ka).	*What is your telephone number?*

In all of the above questions, you can omit the words in parentheses. Similarly, when answering these questions, you can say,

名前はジョン・カワムラです。	Namae wa Jon Kawamura desu.	*My name is John Kawamura.*

or simply

ジョン・カワムラです。	Jon Kawamura desu.	*(My name) is John Kawamura.*

Vocabulary : Age

The counter suffix **-sai** (*years old*) is used with the Sino-Japanese system of numerals to express a person's age. For ages 1 – 10 the Japanese system of numerals — 一つ、二つ、 etc. — may also be used. You will study more about these two number systems in **Chapter 2**. *Twenty* has its own special word, 二十 (はたち).

	SINO-JAPANESE SYSTEM	JAPANESE SYSTEM
1 year old	is-sai 一歳	hitotsu 一つ
2 years old	ni-sai 二歳	hutatsu 二つ
3 years old	san-sai 三歳	mittsu 三つ

	SINO-JAPANESE SYSTEM	JAPANESE SYSTEM
4 years old	yon-sai 四歳	yottsu 四つ
5 years old	go-sai 五歳	itsutsu 五つ
6 years old	roku-sai 六歳	muttsu 六つ
7 years old	nana-sai 七歳	nanatsu 七つ
8 years old	has-sai 八歳	yattsu 八つ
9 years old	kyuu-sai 九歳	kokonotsu 九つ
10 years old	jus-sai 十歳 jis-sai 十歳	too 十
11 years old	juu-is-sai 十一歳	
12 years old	juu-ni-sai 十二歳	
20 years old	ni-jus-sai 二十歳 ni-jis-sai 二十歳	hatachi 二十
25 years old	ni-juu-go-sai 二十五歳	
46 years old	yon-juu-roku-sai 四十六歳	
99 years old	kyuu-juu-kyuu-sai 九十九歳	
100 years old	hyaku-sai 百歳*	

To ask someone's age, use one of these expressions:

お年(おとし)は(おいくつですか)。
How old are (you)?
(山口(やまぐち)さんは)おいくつですか。
How old are (you, Mr. Yamaguchi)?
(カワムラさんは)何歳(なんさい)ですか。
How old are (you, Mr. Kawamura)?
— 22歳(さい)です。
— *(I am) 22 years old.*

The age of a baby under one year old is usually given with the counter ～ヶ月 (months), which is read かげつ. (This counter is also written ヵ月 or か月.)

— 7ヶ月(かげつ)です。
— *(He or she is) seven months old.*

---

* Japanese have the longest average lifespan of the people of any nation in the world: 75.9 for men and 81.7 for women (in 1989). In 1991 there were 749 men and 2,876 women over 100 years old in Japan. (Ministry of Health and Welfare)

Vocabulary: Months

一月	**ichi-gatsu**	January	七月	**shichi-gatsu**	July
二月	**ni-gatsu**	February	八月	**hachi-gatsu**	August
三月	**san-gatsu**	March	九月	**ku-gatsu**	September
四月	**shi-gatsu**	April	十月	**juu-gatsu**	October
五月	**go-gatsu**	May	十一月	**juu-ichi-gatsu**	November
六月	**roku-gatsu**	June	十二月	**juu-ni-gatsu**	December

Examples of how speakers talk about months follow.

今月は何月ですか。	Kongetsu wa nan-gatsu desu ka.	*What month is it this month?*
—十月です。	—Juu-gatsu desu.	*—It's October.*
カワムラさんは何月生まれですか。	Kawamura-san wa nan-gatsu umare desu ka.	*What month were you born in, Mr. Kawamura?*
—四月生まれです。	—Shi-gatsu umare desu.	*—I was born in April.*

アクティビティー 6

本当(ほんとう)ですか。違(ちが)いますか。(*True or False?*)

Look at the table. Are the statements below true or false?

NAME	AGE	MONTH OF BIRTH	HOMETOWN	RESIDENCE	TELEPHONE NUMBER
Masao Hayashi	19	May	Aso	Itabashi	03-3682-0961
Hitomi Machida	20	December	Tokyo	Mitaka	0422-45-4986
Kunio Sano	67	March	Yamagata	Nakano	03-3497-1276
Satomi Yamaguchi	22	May	Tokyo	Setagaya	03-5782-0876
Yuriko Yamaguchi	51	February	Hukushima	Setagaya	03-5782-0876

1. 林さんのご出身は阿蘇です。
2. 林さんのおすまいは板橋です。
3. 町田さんは二十歳です。
4. 町田さんは十一月生まれです。
5. 佐野さんは七十六歳です。
6. 佐野さんのご出身は中野です。
7. 佐野さんのお電話番号は03-3497-1276です。
8. 山口さとみさんは二十二歳です。
9. 山口さとみさんのご出身は福島です。
10. 山口さとみさんと山口ゆり子さんのおすまいは世田谷です。
11. 山口ゆり子さんは五十一歳です。

Remember that the particle と is used to connect two nouns.

文化ノート

Asking Personal Questions

If Japanese people sometimes seem overly curious about your age, it may be because age is one of the factors that go into determining the appropriate style and politeness level of speech. (Generally, a younger person speaks more politely to an older one.)

Similarly, don't be offended if Japanese ask lots of questions about your family. In Japan, despite weakening traditional values, the family is still the most important social unit and has much bearing on one's happiness and social standing. If your family is solid and supportive, Japanese will be happy for you. Those persistent questions arise from a desire to ascertain that you, too, have a good family you can rely on.

アクティビティー 7

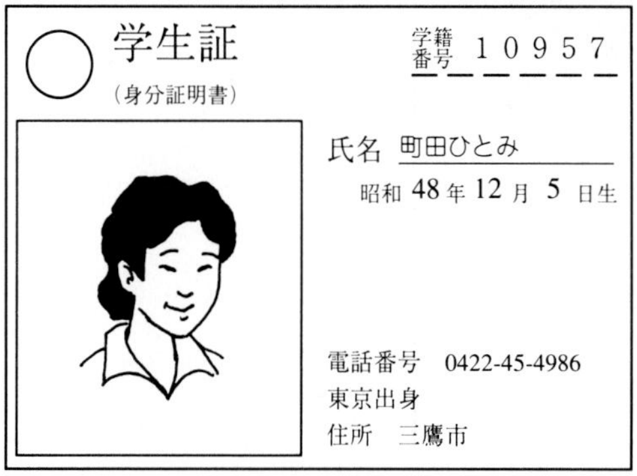

何月生まれですか。(*What month was he/she born in?*)

Based on the following ID, answer the questions.

1. 町田さんのご出身はどこですか。
2. 町田さんはおいくつですか。
3. 町田さんのおすまいは。
4. 町田さんは何月生まれですか。
5. 町田さんのお電話番号は。
6. 町田さんは何歳ですか。

アクティビティー 8

ダイアログ：もう一度(いちど)お願(ねが)いします。(*Once more, please.*)

大学(だいがく)の事務(じむ)室で

事務員(じむいん)：お名前(なまえ)は。
ブラウン：リンダ・ブラウンです。
事務員：お電話番号(でんわばんごう)は。
ブラウン：すみません。もう一度お願いします。
事務員：お電話番号は。
ブラウン：03-5871-8952です。
事務員：すみません。ゆっくりお願いします。
ブラウン：03-5871-8952です。

Daigaku no jimushitsu de

JIMUIN: O-namae wa。
BURAUN: Rinda Buraun desu.
JIMUIN: O-denwa bangoo wa。
BURAUN: Sumimasen. Moo ichido onegai-shimasu.
JIMUIN: O-denwa bangoo wa。
BURAUN: 03-5871-8952 desu.
JIMUIN: Sumimasen. Yukkuri onegai-shimasu.
BURAUN: 03-5871-8952 desu.

コミュニケーション・ノート

お願いします。

お願(ねが)いします (*lit., Please do me a favor*) is a polite, infinitely useful phrase that can mean *Please* (*do something for me*) or *Please give me* . . . For example, when making a purchase or when ordering in a restaurant, you might say これ、お願いします (*I would like this,* or *Please give me this*). In the same situations you could use お願いします to get the clerk's or waiter's attention (*Could you help me, please?*).

In fact, any time you would like someone to do something for you, you can simply use this expression instead of making a specific request. If you are on the receiving end of such a request, you will have to figure out from context what the speaker is asking you to do. For instance, in the preceding dialogue, もう一度(いちど)お願いします means *Please say it once more.*

At a university office CLERK: May I have your name? BROWN: Linda Brown. CLERK: May I have your phone number? BROWN: Excuse me, would you repeat that? (*lit.,* Excuse me. Once more, please.) CLERK: May I have your phone number? BROWN: 03-5871-8952. CLERK: Excuse me, would you say that slowly? BROWN: 03-5871-8952.

アクティビティー 9

お名前は。(*May I have your name?*)

Role play the situation in **Activity 8** using もう一度お願いします and ゆっくりお願いします as necessary. Student 1 (the office clerk) should write down the information provided by Student 2.

S1: お名前は。
S2: ______ です。
S1: ご出身は。
S2: ______ です。
S1: 何月生まれですか。
S2: ______ 生まれです。
S1: おすまいは。
S2: ______ です。
S1: お電話番号は。
S2: ______ です。

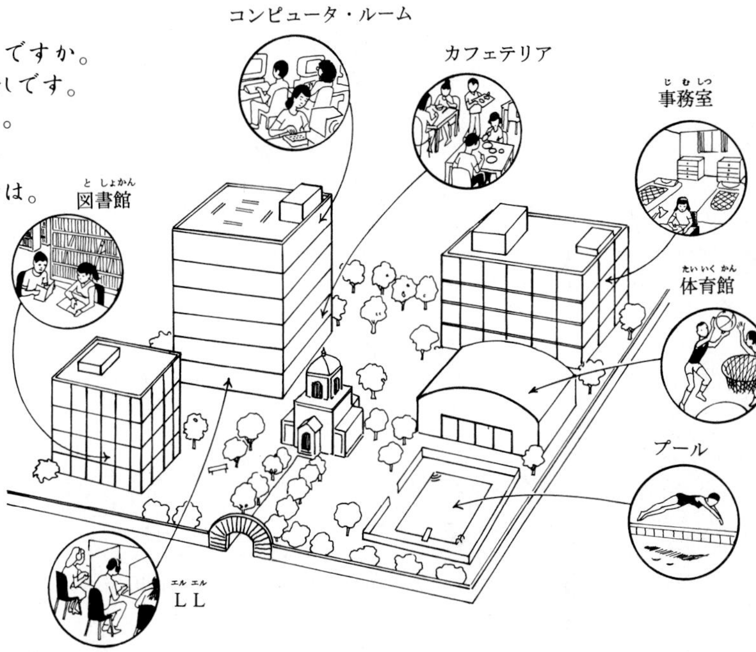

Around Campus

事務室	**jimushitsu**	administration office
ビル	**biru**	building
実験室	**jikkenshitsu**	laboratory

アクティビティー 10

ダイアログ：図書館はどこですか。(*Where is the library?*)

キャンパスで

ブラウン：すみません。図書館はどこですか。
学生：あそこです。
ブラウン：文学部はどこですか。
学生：あのビルの3階です。

On campus BROWN: Excuse me. Where is the library? STUDENT: It's over there. BROWN: Where is the Literature Department? STUDENT: It's on the third floor of that building.

Kyanpasu de

BURAUN: Sumimasen. Toshokan wa doka desu ka.
GAKUSEE: Asoko desu.
BURAUN: Bungakubu wa doko desu ka.
GAKUSEE: Ano biru no san-kai desu.

アクティビティー 11

大学(だいがく)のキャンパス (*University campus*)

Ask a classmate where other places on campus are.

S1: ＿＿＿はどこですか。

S2: このビルの＿＿＿です。

Bring a map of your campus to class and practice asking a classmate the location of several places.

Vocabulary : Days of the Week

日曜日	**nichiyoobi**	Sunday
月曜日	**getsuyoobi**	Monday
火曜日	**kayoobi**	Tuesday
水曜日	**suiyoobi**	Wednesday
木曜日	**mokuyoobi**	Thursday
金曜日	**kin'yoobi**	Friday
土曜日	**doyoobi**	Saturday
何曜日ですか。	**Nan'yoobi desu ka.**	What day of the week is it?

An apostrophe (') indicates that the preceding **n** is pronounced ん; it is not part of the following syllable.

アクティビティー 12

時間割(じかんわり) (*Class schedules*)

Answer the questions based on the schedules on page 71.

[例] 数学(すうがく)のクラスは何曜日(なんようび)ですか。→月(げつ)曜日です。

1. 日本文化(にほんぶんか) (*Japanese culture*)のクラスは何曜日ですか。
2. 歴史学(れきしがく)のクラスは何曜日ですか。
3. コンピュータのクラスは何曜日ですか。
4. 工学(こうがく)のクラスは何曜日ですか。

John's schedule

M	T	W	Th	F	S
math		German	physics		German
math	Japanese culture		engineering		
		computer science	engineering		
				Japanese	

Linda's schedule

M	T	W	Th	F	S
			history		
anthropology	Japanese culture	economics	history	political science	
literature		French		political science	
				Japanese	

5. 人類学（じんるいがく）のクラスは何曜日ですか。
6. フランス語（ご）のクラスは何曜日ですか。
7. 物理学（ぶつりがく）のクラスは何曜日ですか。

Now write down your class schedule and explain it to your classmates.

アクティビティー 13

ダイアログ：これはだれのボールペンですか。(*Whose ballpoint pen is this?*)

林（はやし）：これはだれのボールペンですか。
ギブソン：わたしのです。
林：あれもギブソンさんのボールペンですか。
ギブソン：いいえ、あれは町田（まちだ）さんのです。

HAYASHI: Kore wa dare no boorupen desu ka.
GIBUSON: Watashi no desu.
HAYASHI: Are mo Gibuson-san no boorupen desu ka.
GIBUSON: Iie, are wa Machida-san no desu.

HAYASHI: Whose ballpoint pen is this? GIBSON: It's mine. HAYASHI: Is that your ballpoint pen, too? GIBSON: No, it's Ms. Machida's.

アクティビティー 14

林(はやし)さんのです。(*It's Mr. Hayashi's.*)

S1: これはだれの本(ほん)ですか。
S2: 林さんのです。

Based on the following illustration, tell who each item belongs to.

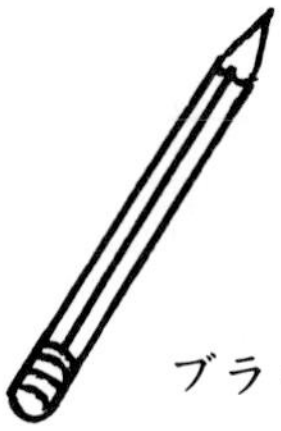

ブラウン

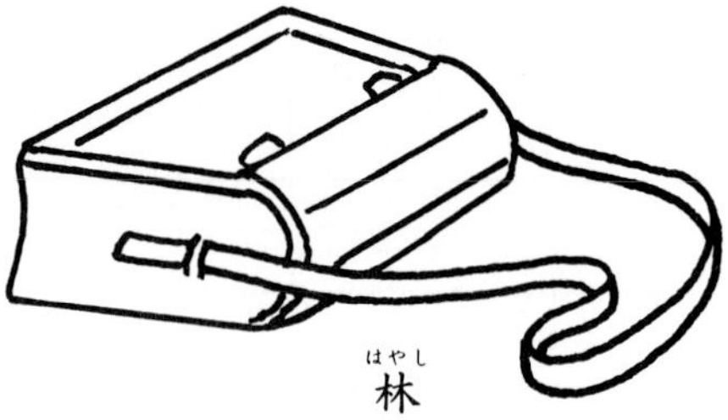

林(はやし)

三村(みむら)

チン

カーティス

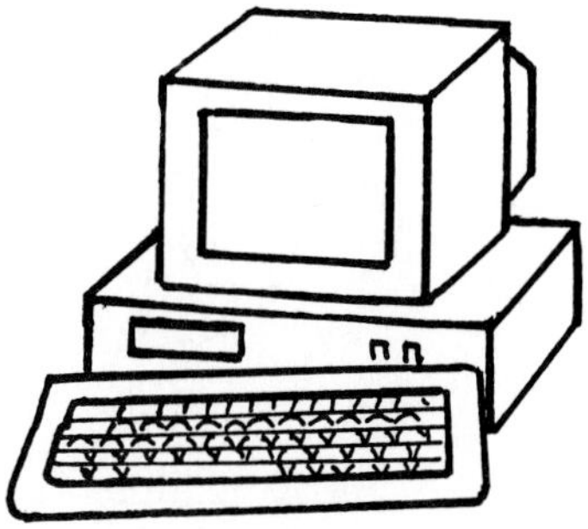

横井先生(よこいせんせい)

Grammar and Exercises

1. Identification: The Copula です

レストランで
　カワムラ：すみません。あれは何(なん)ですか。
ウエーター：あれは「すきやき」です。
　カワムラ：じゃ、あれをお願(ねが)いします。

受付(うけつ)けで
　ブラウン：すみません。高田(たかだ)さんをお願いします。
　　受付け：すみません。お名前(なまえ)は。
　ブラウン：わたしは東京大学(とうきょうだいがく)のブラウンです。
　　受付け：東京大学のブラウンさんですね。
　ブラウン：はい、そうです。

　ブラウン：あの人(ひと)は林(はやし)さんではありませんか。
　カワムラ：どの人ですか。
　ブラウン：ほら、あの人です。
　カワムラ：いいえ、林さんじゃありませんよ。

Reminder: 「 and 」 are quotation marks.

At a restaurant KAWAMURA: Excuse me. What is that? WAITER: That's sukiyaki. KAWAMURA: Then, please give me that.

At a reception desk BROWN: Excuse me. I would like (to see) Mr. Takada. RECEPTIONIST: Excuse me. May I have your name? BROWN: I am Brown of the University of Tokyo. RECEPTIONIST: Ms. Brown of the University of Tokyo, right? BROWN: Yes, that's right.

BROWN: Isn't that person Mr. Hayashi? KAWAMURA: Which person? BROWN: Over there. (*lit.*, Look.) (I mean) that person. KAWAMURA: No, that's not Mr. Hayashi.

1.1 To identify people and things in Japanese, you can use the following grammatical structure, where X and Y are nouns or pronouns.

X	は	Y	です	X is Y.
これ		ペン		*This is a pen.*
わたし		ブラウン		*I am Brown.*
すきやき	は	日本料理（にほんりょうり）	です	*Sukiyaki is a Japanese dish.*
町田（まちだ）さん		学生（がくせい）		*Ms. Machida is a student.*
カワムラさん		アメリカ人（じん）		*Mr. Kawamura is an American.*
受付（うけつ）け		あそこ		*The reception desk is over there.*

This structure means *X is equivalent to Y*, *X is a member of the group Y*, or *X is described (or modified) by Y.*

は is usually called a *topic particle*. It indicates that the preceding noun is the topic of the sentence. For instance, in this sentence the speaker would like to talk about Mr. Takada.

高田（たかだ）さんはエンジニアです。
Mr. Takada is an engineer.

Usage of the topic particle will be discussed in more detail later.

です is called the *copula*. It roughly corresponds to the verb *to be*. Like other Japanese verbs, です does not change form to agree with the subject of the sentence in number or person. In other words, (*I*) *am*, (*you*) *are*, (*he*) *is*, (*they*) *are*, and so on, are all expressed with the same form です. です also marks a certain level of politeness, which will be discussed later.

1.2 The negative form of です is ではありません (contracted to じゃありません in more informal speech).

X	は	Y	ではありません (じゃありません)	X isn't Y.
これ		ペン		*This is not a pen.*
わたし		ブラウン		*I am not Brown.*
すきやき	は	中国料理（ちゅうごくりょうり）	ではありません	*Sukiyaki is not a Chinese dish.*
町田（まちだ）さん		先生（せんせい）	(じゃありません)	*Ms. Machida is not a teacher.*
カワムラさん		フランス人		*Mr. Kawamura is not a French person.*
受付（うけつ）け		ここ		*The reception desk is not here.*

1.3 Yes/No questions are formed in Japanese simply by adding か (the *interrogative* or *question particle*) to the end of a sentence. You can think of か as a verbal question mark.

あの人は町田(まちだ)さんです。
That person is Ms. Machida.
あの人は町田さんですか。
Is that person Ms. Machida?

あの人は町田さんではありません。
That person is not Ms. Machida.
あの人は町田さんではありませんか。
Isn't that person Ms. Machida?
(rising intonation)

With falling intonation, this sentence can mean *Oh, I see. That person isn't Ms. Machida.*

Here are some typical ways to answer a yes/no question.

あの人は町田さんですか。
Is that Ms. Machida?

YES

はい、町田さんです。
Yes, it's Ms. Machida.
はい、そうです。
Yes, that's right.

NO

いいえ、町田さんではありません。
(いいえ、町田さんじゃありません。)
No, it's not Ms. Machida.
いいえ、そうではありません。
(いいえ、そうじゃありません。)
No, that's not right.
いいえ、ちがいます。
No, that's wrong (lit., different).

OTHER

わかりません。
I don't know.

コミュニケーション・ノート

Alternative Questions

To ask either/or questions, string the two alternate questions together: Aですか。Bですか (*Is it A? Is it B?* or in smoother English, *Is it A or B?*).

あれは日本料理(にほんりょうり)ですか。中国料理(ちゅうごくりょうり)ですか。
Is that Japanese food or Chinese food?
これは万年筆(まんねんひつ)ですか。ボールペンですか。
Is this a fountain pen or a ballpoint pen?

1.4 The particle も means *too*. Substitute も for は in the XはYです construction —XもYです— to say that *X is a member of Y, too* (or *X, too, is described by* [or *equivalent to*] *Y*).

わたしはアメリカ人(じん)です。
I am an American.
—本当(ほんとう)ですか。わたしもアメリカ人です。
—*Really? I am an American, too.*

2. Possessive Particle の

2.1 の is a particle used to connect and relate nouns (or pronouns). The result is a noun phrase. X の Y means *Y of X* in a broad sense, and thus carries the meanings *Y belongs to X, Y is a part of X, Y is possessed by X, Y has a characteristic of X*, and so on, depending on the context.

N1	の	N2	
わたし		本(ほん)	*my book*
大学(だいがく)		図書館(としょかん)	*the university library*
町田(まちだ)さん	の	万年筆(まんねんひつ)	*Ms. Machida's fountain pen*
アメリカ		州(しゅう)	*a state in America*
コットン		ジーンズ	*cotton jeans*

Throughout this book, N1 stands for *a noun* and N2 stands for *another noun*, or *Noun 1* and *Noun 2*.

The particle の can connect more than two nouns or pronouns.

わたしの友(とも)だちの大学(だいがく)
my friend's university
三村(みむら)さんのガールフレンドの家(いえ)
the house of Mr. Mimura's girlfriend

2.2 When the item possessed is clear from the context, it can be omitted as shown in the following examples.

これはだれのセーターですか。—ブラウンさんのです。
Whose sweater is this? —It's Ms. Brown's.
あれもブラウンさんのセーターですか。—いいえ、町田さんのです。
Is that also Ms. Brown's sweater? —No, it's Ms. Machida's.

3. Personal Pronouns and Demonstratives

山口(やまぐち)：かれはだれですか。
カワムラ：林(はやし)さんです。
山口：カワムラさんのクラスメートの林さんですか。
カワムラ：ええ、そうです。

ブラウン：この人(ひと)はだれですか。
町田(まちだ)：どの人ですか。
ブラウン：このセーターの人です。
町田：ああ、これはわたしの友(とも)だちのジョンソンさんです。

ブラウン：高田(たかだ)さんのオフィスはどこですか。
受付(うけつ)け：3 階(かい) です。
ブラウン：エレベーターはどこですか。
受付け：あちらです。

ブラウン：高田さん、こちらはカワムラさんです。
カワムラ：カワムラです。どうぞよろしく。

YAMAGUCHI: Who is he? KAWAMURA: That's Mr. Hayashi. YAMAGUCHI: You mean the Mr. Hayashi who's one of your classmates? KAWAMURA: Yes, that's right.

BROWN: Who is this person? MACHIDA: Which person? BROWN: This person wearing (*lit.*, of) a sweater. MACHIDA: Oh, that (*lit.*, this) is my friend Mr. Johnson.

BROWN: Where is Mr. Takada's office? RECEPTIONIST: It is on the third floor. BROWN: Where is the elevator? RECEPTIONIST: It's over there.

BROWN: Mr Takada, this is Mr. Kawamura. KAWAMURA: I am Kawamura. It's nice to meet you.

3.1 Personal pronouns are used to refer to a person without mentioning his or her name. Following are the most common personal pronouns in Japanese. Notice that this is one subject area where a singular/plural distinction is frequently made. Pronouns have varying levels of politeness and some are used only by or in reference to women or men, so you must be careful in selecting which pronoun to use.

SINGULAR		PLURAL	
私	I	私たち	we
僕	I (*male, informal*)	僕たち	we (*male, informal*)
あたし	I (*female, informal*)	あたしたち	we (*female, informal*)
あなた	you	あなたたち あなたがた	you you
彼	he	彼ら、彼たち	they (*male*)
彼女	she	彼女ら、彼女たち	they (*female*)
あの人	he/she	あの人たち	they
あの方	he/she (*polite*)	あの方たち	they (*polite*)

It is not necessary to use a pronoun if the context or other factors identify the person being discussed or addressed. In fact, Japanese tend to avoid the use of first person and second person pronouns whenever possible. It is considered rude to use あなた (a second person pronoun) in all but intimate situations. It is also considered impolite to use 彼 or 彼女 to refer to a social superior. Instead, use a person's family name plus a title such as 〜さん or 〜先生 when addressing or referring to other people. Both of the following statements are usually delivered without the pronouns (included here in parentheses),which are understood from context.

あの人 literally means *that person*.
方 is a polite substitute for 人 *person*.

(わたしは)カワムラです。どうぞよろしく。
I am Kawamura. It's nice to meet you.
(あなたは)ブラウンさんじゃありませんか。
Aren't you Ms. Brown?

3.2 Demonstrative pronouns are used to point out or to indicate a specific person, thing, place, or direction. This chart shows the primary demonstratives in Japanese.

	THING	PLACE	DIRECTION
こ-series	これ	ここ	こちら
そ-series	それ	そこ	そちら
あ-series	あれ	あそこ	あちら
ど-series	どれ	どこ	どちら

Each column follows the pattern of こ-そ-あ-ど (the first syllable of each word) from top to bottom. For this reason, Japanese demonstratives are often called こそあどことば or ***ko-so-a-do*** words.

The こ-series is used to point out whatever is close to the speaker.
The そ-series is used to point out whatever is close to the hearer.
The あ-series points out whatever is some distance from both the speaker and the hearer.
The ど-series are interrogatives used to ask which one, which place, or which direction.

これはブラウンさんの本(ほん)ですか。
Is this Ms. Brown's book?
それをお願(ねが)いします。
I would like that one.
図書館(としょかん)はあそこです。
The library is over there.
トイレはあちらですか。
Is the bathroom in that direction?
カワムラさんのコーヒーはどれですか。
Which one is Mr. Kawamura's coffee?

In most contexts, it is rude to use これ、それ、あれ、どれ to refer to people. Instead, こちら、そちら、あちら、どちら are used.

こちらは東京大学(とうきょうだいがく)の横井先生(よこいせんせい)です。
This is Professor Yokoi of the University of Tokyo.
ブラウンさんはどちらですか。
Which one of you is Ms. Brown?

Demonstrative adjectives, which modify nouns and come before them, also follow the **ko-so-a-do** pattern.

	DEMONSTRATIVE ADJECTIVES
こ-series	この
そ-series	その
あ-series	あの
ど-series	どの

この本(ほん)はブラウンさんの本です。
This book is Ms. Brown's book.
あの映画(えいが)は日本(にほん)の映画ですか。
Is that movie a Japanese movie?

どの means *which of three or more alternatives*. Similarly, どれ means *which one of three or more alternatives*.

> ブラウンさんの本はどの本ですか。
> *Which book is yours, Ms. Brown?* (out of three or more books)
> カワムラさんのかばんはどれですか。
> *Which bag is Mr. Kawamura's?* (out of three or more bags)

If the choice is between two alternatives, use どちら.

> 林(はやし)さんの本はどちらですか。
> *Which one is your book, Mr. Hayashi?* (There are two books.)

コミュニケーション・ノート

どちらへ Where to?

When you are on the way out of the door, friends, neighbors, or colleagues may ask you どちらへ (*Where to?*) or おでかけですか(*Are you going out?*). These are not nosy questions, but rather common formulaic greetings to those who are about to go somewhere. The feeling behind these expressions is that the speaker is happy because you are healthy enough to go out, or perhaps the speaker is concerned that you have to go out so often. Whichever the sentiment, the remark conveys a wish for a safe return.

In replying, you need not be specific about where you are going. The best answer to these questions is ええ、ちょっとそこまで (*Yes, just around the corner* [*lit., Yes, just to over there*]).

練習 1

Connect the appropriate words from column A and column B to make …は…です sentences.

A	B
マドンナ	飲(の)み物(もの)
わたし	日本人(にほんじん)
アコード	学生(がくせい)
川端康成(かわばたやすなり)	アメリカ人
コーラ	コンピュータ
マッキントッシュ	ホンダの車(くるま) (car)

練習 2

Formulate questions, following the example.

[例]　ラジカセ(combined radio and tape cassette player)→
　　これはラジカセですか。

1. ワープロ
2. スーツケース
3. 辞書（じしょ）
4. えんぴつ
5. ワイン

Now answer the questions you made, following the example.

[例]　これはラジカセですか。→
　　いいえ、ラジカセじゃありません。CDプレーヤーです。

1. コンピュータ
2. かばん
3. 教科書（きょうかしょ）
4. ペン
5. ジュース

Make dialogues following the example.

[例]　これはだれのラジカセですか。町田さん→
　　町田さんのラジカセです。

1. ブラウンさん
2. カーティスさん
3. 横井先生（よこいせんせい）
4. 林（はやし）さん
5. 佐野（さの）さん

練習 3

Complete the sentences to make dialogues.

[例]　カワムラさんですか。ブラウンさんですか。→ カワムラさんです。

1. ビールですか、_____。
   _____。
2. _____、ファクシミリですか。
   _____。
3. _____、テーブルですか。
   _____。
4. ギブソンさんはアメリカ人ですか、_____。
   _____。
5. _____、_____。(Make up your own dialogue.)
   _____。

練習　4

Make up appropriate follow-up sentences using も.

[例]　ブラウンさんはアメリカ人です。→ カワムラさんもアメリカ人です。

1. わたしの先生(せんせい)は45さいです。
2. わたしは学生(がくせい)です。
3. 「アミーゴ」はスペイン語(ご)です。
4. バナナはくだものです。
5. サッカーはスポーツです。
6. すきやきは日本(にほん)料理です。
7. パナソニックは日本のメーカーです。

練習　5

Complete these sentences with …です.

[例]　わたしは… →
　　わたしは東京大学(とうきょうだいがく)の学生(がくせい)です。 *or*
　　わたしは21さいです。 *or*
　　わたしは10月(がつ)生(う)まれです。

1. わたしの日本語(にほんご)の先生(せんせい)は…。
2. わたしのクラスメートの______さんは…。
3. わたしの先生のなまえは…。
4. マーガレット・サッチャーは…。
5. ジョン・カワムラさんは…。

4. Asking Questions: Interrogatives

ブラウン：あれは何(なん)ですか。
町田(まちだ)：あれは「のり」です。
山口(やまぐち)：あの人はだれですか。
カワムラ：クラスメートの林(はやし)さんです。
山口：ご出身(しゅっしん)はどこですか。
カワムラ：九州(きゅうしゅう)です。

BROWN: What is that?　MACHIDA: That's seaweed.

YAMAGUCHI: Who is he?　KAWAMURA: He is Mr. Hayashi, one of my classmates.　YAMAGUCHI: Where is he from?　KAWAMURA: He's from Kyushu.

山口：あの方はどなたですか。
カワムラ：あの方は横井先生です。
山口：何の先生ですか。
カワムラ：日本文化です。

山口：午後は何をしますか。
ブラウン：ショッピングに行きます。
山口：どこですか。
ブラウン：銀座です。

4.1 Questions starting with *who, why, where, when, what,* or *which* are sometimes called *wh-questions* in English. In Japanese, you can make questions corresponding to wh-questions quite easily.

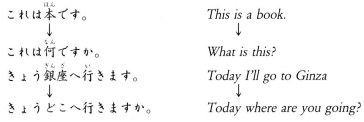

これは本です。	*This is a book.*
↓	↓
これは何ですか。	*What is this?*
きょう銀座へ行きます。	*Today I'll go to Ginza*
↓	↓
きょうどこへ行きますか。	*Today where are you going?*

Likewise, to answer a wh-question, simply replace the question word with the answer and drop the question particle か.

あの人はだれですか。	*Who is that person?*
↓	↓
(あの人は)ブラウンさんです。	*(That person) is Ms Brown.*

4.2 Three basic interrogatives are introduced in this chapter.

1. 何 (なに、なん) = *what*

When this interrogative is followed by a word starting with [d],[t],[k], or [n], it is pronounced なん. Otherwise, it is なに.

これは何ですか。
What is this?
これは何の本ですか。
What (kind of book) is this?

YAMAGUCHI: Who is that person? KAWAMURA: That's Professor Yokoi. YAMAGUCHI: What is she a professor of? KAWAMURA: Japanese culture.

YAMAGUCHI: What are you going to do this afternoon? BROWN: I'm going shopping. YAMAGUCHI: Where are you going? BROWN: Ginza.

何を食べますか。
What are you going to eat?

When this interrogative is attached to other words, it is pronounced なに when it means *what* and なん when it means *how many* or *how much.*

あなたのセーターは何色ですか。
What color is your sweater?
あなたのお父さんは何歳ですか。
How old is your father?

2. だれ、どなた = *who*

どなた is politer than だれ.

あの人はだれですか。
Who is that person?
あの方はどなたですか。
Who is that person? [much politer]

3. どこ = *where*

どこで昼ごはんを食べますか。
Where are you going to eat lunch?

Other interrogatives:

These interrogatives will be introduced gradually in this textbook. They are listed here only for quick reference. They are not active vocabulary at this stage.

いつ= *when*

いつデパートへ行きますか。
When are you going to the department store?

どちら、どっち = *which of two; where*
どっち is informal.
横井先生の研究室はどちらですか。
Where is Professor Yokoi's office?
ブラウンさんの本はどっちですか。
Which one (of the two) is Ms. Brown's book?

どれ = *which of three or more*

どれがギブソンさんの本ですか。
Which one is Ms. Gibson's book?

いくつ = *how many, how old*

いくつりんごを食べますか。
How many apples are you going to eat?
あなたのお父さんはおいくつですか。
How old is your father?

いくら = *how much (price)*

この雑誌はいくらですか

How much is this magazine?

The above interrogatives function like nouns. Connect them to other nouns with の. Remember the pattern X の Y (私の本).

これは何の教科書ですか。

What (kind of) textbook is this?

これはだれの本ですか。

Whose book is this?

どちらの本が好きですか。

Which book (of the two) do you like?

どんな = *what kind of*

どんな映画が好きですか。

What kind of movies do you like?

どう = *how, how about*

これはどうですか。

How about this one?

日本語のクラスはどうですか。

How is your Japanese class?

どうして、なぜ = *why*

どうして町田さんと話しましたか。

Why did you talk to Ms. Machida?

なぜ日本語を勉強しますか。

Why are you studying Japanese?

文法ノート

Particles は and が

Here are some general guidelines on when to use は and when to use が in the sentence construction X [は／が] Yです. You will study the difference between these particles in detail later, but for now remember the following.

1. Use が after a question word (who, where, etc.) and in the answer to a question using such a question word.

   どれがカワムラさんの本ですか。

   Which one is Mr. Kawamura's book?

これがカワムラさんの本です。
This is Mr. Kawamura's book.
どの人がブラウンさんですか。
Which person is Ms. Brown?
あの人がブラウンさんです。
That person is Ms. Brown.

2. Use は in statements or questions that seek to identify or describe X.

これは本です。
This is a book.
あれは本ですか。
Is that a book?
あの人はブラウンさんです。
That person is Ms. Brown.
あの人はだれですか。
Who is that person?

3. Use は in negative statements.

あれは本ではありません。
That is not a book.
あの人はカワムラさんではありません。
That person is not Mr. Kawamura.

練習 1

Fill in the blanks.

[例] これは(　)のペンですか。—それは町田さんのペンです。(だれ)

1. これは(　)の教科書ですか。—それは日本語の教科書です。
2. あの人は(　)ですか。—わたしの日本語の先生です。
3. ブラウンさんは(　)のご出身ですか。—ボストンの出身です。
4. きょうは(　)曜日ですか。—金曜日です。
5. 図書館は(　)ですか。—あそこです。
6. カワムラさんの本は(　)ですか。—これです。

練習 2

Fill in the blanks with これ、この、こちら、or ここ.

1. (　)はどこですか。—東京大学の図書館です。
2. (　)はどなたですか。—横井先生です。

3. (　　)はいくらですか。—300円(えん)です。
4. (　　)は日本語(にほんご)の本(ほん)ですか。—はい、そうです。

練習　3

These are answers to questions. What do you think the questions were? Write down possible questions.

[例]　450円(えん)です。→ この雑誌(ざっし)はいくらですか。

1. 横井先生(よこいせんせい)です。
2. カナダです。
3. あそこです。
4. カフェテリアです。
5. 明日(あす)いきます。
6. はい、そうです。
7. あちらです。
8. 95歳(さい)です。
9. わたしのコンピュータです。
10. 午前(ごぜん)10時(じ)です。

Vocabulary

Personal Information

がくねん	学年	academic year
だいがくせい	大学生	college student
いちねんせい	一年生	first-year student
にねんせい	二年生	sophomore
さんねんせい	三年生	junior
よねんせい	四年生	senior
だいがくいんせい	大学院生	graduate student
がくぶ	学部	academic department
こくせき	国籍	nationality
しゅっしん	出身	hometown, origin
せんこう	専攻	academic major
でんわばんごう	電話番号	telephone number
なまえ	名前	name

People

ともだち	友だち	friend

Loanwords: クラスメート
Review: 学生(がくせい)、先生(せんせい)

Places on Campus

けんきゅうしつ	研究室	professor's office
じむしつ	事務室	administration office
たいいくかん	体育館	gym
ビル		building
りょう	寮	dormitory

Loanwords: カフェテリア、キャンパス、プール

Review: 教室(きょうしつ)、大学(だいがく)、図書館(としょかん)

Nationalities/Languages

アメリカじん	アメリカ人	American (*person*)
イギリスじん	イギリス人	British (*person*)
イタリアじん／イタリアご	イタリア人／イタリア語	Italian (*person/language*)
えいご	英語	English (*language*)
かんこくじん／かんこくご	韓国人／韓国語	Korean (*person/language*)
カナダじん	カナダ人	Canadian (*person*)
スペインじん／スペインご	スペイン人／スペイン語	Spaniard/Spanish (*language*)
シンガポールじん	シンガポール人	Singaporean
たいわんじん	台湾人	Taiwanese (*person*)
ちゅうごくじん／ちゅうごくご	中国人／中国語	Chinese (*person/language*)
ドイツじん／ドイツご	ドイツ人／ドイツ語	German (*person/language*)
にほんじん／にほんご	日本人／日本語	Japanese (*person/language*)
ブラジルじん	ブラジル人	Brazilian (*person*)
フランスじん／フランスご	フランス人／フランス語	French (*person/language*)
ポルトガルじん／ポルトガルご	ポルトガル人／ポルトガル語	Portuguese (*person/language*)
ほんこんじん	香港人	Hong Kong native
メキシコじん	メキシコ人	Mexican (*person*)
ロシアじん／ロシアご	ロシア人／ロシア語	Russian (*person/language*)
くに	国	country

Review: 話(はな)す

Months

いちがつ	一月	January
にがつ	二月	February
さんがつ	三月	March
しがつ	四月	April
ごがつ	五月	May
ろくがつ	六月	June
しちがつ	七月	July
はちがつ	八月	August
くがつ	九月	September
じゅうがつ	十月	October
じゅういちがつ	十一月	November
じゅうにがつ	十二月	December
なんがつ	何月	what month

Days of the Week

にちようび	日曜日	Sunday	もくようび	木曜日	Thursday
げつようび	月曜日	Monday	きんようび	金曜日	Friday
かようび	火曜日	Tuesday	どようび	土曜日	Saturday
すいようび	水曜日	Wednesday	なんようび	何曜日	what day of the week

Question Words

だれ		who	なにじん	何人	what nationality
どこ		where	なんがつ	何月	what month
どちら		where (*polite*)	なんさい	何歳	how old
どなた		who (*polite*)	なんねんせい	何年生	what year (in school)
なに、なん	何	what	なんようび	何曜日	what day of the week
なにご	何語	what language			

Other Words

あそこ		that place over there	そちら		that place, there (*polite*)
あちら		that place over there (*polite*)	その		that. . .
あの		that. . . over there	それ		that thing
あれ		that thing over there	です		to be
か		(*question marker*)	ではありません		(*negative of* です)
が		(*subject marker*)	どこ		where
ここ		this place, here	どちら		where (*polite*); which (of two)
こちら		this place, here (*polite*)	どの		which. . . (of more than two)
この		this. . .	どれ		which thing (of more than two)
これ		this thing	は		(*topic marker*)
じゃありません		(*negative of* です)(*informal*)	も		too
そこ		that place, there	わたし	私	I, me

Study Hint

Learning New Vocabulary

Vocabulary is one of the most important tools for successful communication in a foreign language. What does it mean to know vocabulary? And what is the best way to learn vocabulary?

1. Memorization is only part of the learning process. Using new vocabulary to communicate requires practicing that vocabulary in context. What do you associate with this word? When might you want to use it? Create a context — a place, a situation, a person, or a group of people — for the

vocabulary that you want to learn, or use a context from the text. The more associations you make with the word, the easier it will be to remember. Practice useful words and phrases over and over, thinking about their meaning, until you can produce them automatically. You may find it useful to "talk to yourself," saying aloud the words you want to learn.

2. Carefully study the words in vocabulary lists and drawings. If a word is of English origin, be especially aware of its form and meaning. Sometimes the form and meaning are quite different from the original. For example, デパート came from the English phrase *department store* and has the same meaning as the English. コンセント means *plug outlet*, although it came from the English word *consent.*
3. After studying the list or illustration, cover the English and give the English equivalent of each Japanese word.
4. When you are able to translate the Japanese without hesitation and without error, reverse the procedure; cover the Japanese and give the Japanese equivalent of each English word. Write out the Japanese words in the appropriate script (but use **hiragana** if you haven't studied the appropriate **kanji** yet) once or several times and say them aloud.
5. Vocabulary lists and flash cards can be useful as a review or as a self-test.

Note that the best way to learn vocabulary is to use it constantly in actual contexts. Try to use new vocabulary as much as possible in conversation and in writing.

Kanji

Learn these **kanji.**

日	二	百	年	七	語
本	三	先	何	八	話
学	四	話	月	九	大
生	五	語	人	十	
名	六	先	一		

言語ノート

The Six Types of Kanji

Kanji (*Chinese characters*) originated in China. In China, **kanji** were categorized into one of six basic classifications depending primarily on how the character was formed. The pictograph, the most primitive type of **kanji**, was created as a representation of the physical appearance of an object. In modern Japanese there are relatively few of these characters.

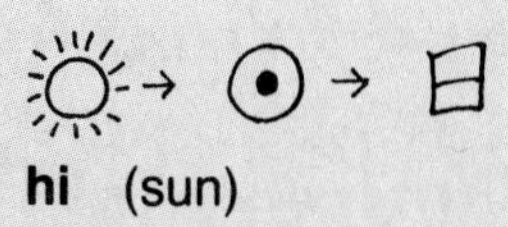

Kanji of the second type represent numbers, positional relations, or abstract concepts.

Kanji in the third group are a combination of two or more of the first two types of **kanji**.

The fourth and most important type of **kanji** consist of one part that represents meaning or a semantic class and another part that represents pronunciation. More than 80 percent of **kanji** used in modern Japanese fall into this category.

The fifth classification is **kanji** whose meanings have been altered by generalization or extension of the original meaning. For example, the character originally meaning *to play a musical instrument* has come to mean *to delight*, because playing music delights people.

Finally, there are **kanji** whose pronunciation led them to be used to express new concepts and words, regardless of their meaning. For example, the Chinese had no **kanji** for writing the Chinese word **hoku** (*north*), so they adopted the following character 北,because it was pronounced **hoku**, even though its meaning was totally unrelated.

ni (two)

木 + 木 → 林

hayashi (woods)

口 + 未 → 味

aji, mi (flavor)

楽

music → delight

北

north (originally meant people facing each other)

Reading and Writing

Reading 1 フランス人のクラスメート

Before You Read

The following passage describes a foreign student in Japan. Your task is to retrieve the following information.

1. the name of the student
2. the name of his university
3. where he is from
4. his nationality
5. his major
6. what year student he is
7. what classes he is taking

Here are some key words that will help you locate the information.

1. 名前(なまえ) *name*
2. 大学(だいがく) *university*
3. 出身(しゅっしん) *hometown, origin*
4. a word ending in ～人(じん)
5. 専攻(せんこう) *major*, a word ending in 学(がく)
6. a word ending in 年生(ねんせい)
7. words ending in 学(がく); if he is taking a language course, a word ending in 語(ご)

While reading you may want to refer to certain categories of the vocabulary list on page 60.

Now Read It!

Look for the preceding information while reading the passage as quickly as possible.

彼(かれ)の名前(なまえ)はピエール・ノワールです。学生(がくせい)です。彼はパリの出身(しゅっしん)です。フランス人です。今(いま)、東京大学(とうきょうだいがく)の三年生(さんねんせい)です。専攻(せんこう)は文学(ぶんがく)です。今、日本語(にほんご)、日本文学(にほんぶんがく)、社会学(しゃかいがく)、人類学(じんるいがく)のクラスをとっています。

今 *now*
～をとっています *is taking (courses)*

After You Finish Reading

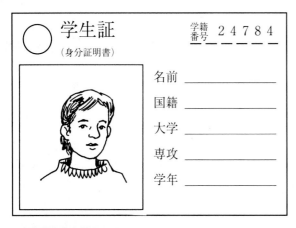

学生証 (身分証明書)	学籍番号 24784 _ _ _ _ _
名前	__________
国籍	__________
大学	__________
専攻	__________
学年	__________

Using the information you retrieved, complete the ID to the left. Don't use **kanji** you haven't learned to write yet. Just use **hiragana** for now.

Study Hint

Learning Kanji

The study of **kanji** should be approached systematically if you are to master their complexities. Each **kanji** may have several meanings. It most likely has several **on**-readings and **kun**-readings, and which reading applies depends on where it is used.

One way to study **kanji** would be to use flash cards to memorize the meanings and readings of characters by looking at them frequently. But knowing all the meanings and readings of a certain **kanji** would be useless without knowing in what context that character has a certain meaning and reading. For instance, 名 and 人 each have several meanings and readings and you could memorize all of them using flash cards. Then, while reading a Japanese passage, you see the **kanji** compound 名人 for the first time. How can you tell the meaning and reading of this compound? Your flash cards are of no help.

Probably the best way to study **kanji** is as the Japanese do: to study them in context. Read as many Japanese passages including **kanji** as possible. Study with which meaning and reading each **kanji** is used in the reading passages. For example, when you see the word 名人 in a sentence あの人(ひと)はつりの名人(めいじん)です, notice that when 名 is used with 人 it has the reading めい, and when 人 is preceded by 名 it has the reading じん. The compound, then, means *master, expert.* As you read more and more Japanese passages, you will find many different usages of these two **kanji** to add to your mental list of possible meanings, readings, and examples. By the way, 人 after あの has the reading ひと in this context. This shows that it is important for you to attend to contexts when learning **kanji**.

In other words, memorizing a list of meanings and readings of characters is not the best starting point for study. Rather, coming up with such a list as you work extensively with Japanese writing is part of the process of studying **kanji**. This method is time-consuming; even Japanese people study for a number of years to acquire a standard level of skill with **kanji**.

This textbook presents more **kanji** than other beginning textbooks. You need not study all **kanji** used in the passages, and don't worry if you forget some. Concentrate at first on recognizing various **kanji**. As you encounter the same **kanji** and **kanji** compounds several times in written passages, your ability to recognize them will grow.

To build your ability to write **kanji**, try to write using characters and compounds you can recognize. Writing **kanji** in context will develop your facility with them far more than simply writing the new **kanji** in each chapter forty or fifty times.

Writing 1

Write a short profile of yourself, following the format of **Reading 1**. Start with わたしの名前は….

After you finish writing, exchange profiles with a classmate. Is there any similarity in your profiles?

Reading 2　ペンパルをさがしています！

Before You Read

Next you will read a Penpal Wanted ad. First, make a list of points you would mention in describing yourself if you were to place such an ad in the paper. Among those points, how many can you express in Japanese?

Now Read It!

> **ペンパルをさがしています！**
>
> わたしたちはアメリカ人の大学生です。トリシア、デニース、ケートです。ウエスト・コースト大学の四年生です。２２歳です。日本語のクラスのクラスメートです。トリシアとデニースは経済学の専攻です。ケートはコンピューター・サイエンスの専攻です。日本人の大学生のペンパルをさがしています。かならず返事を書きます。日本語でけっこうです。
>
> Tricia Rosen
> P.O. Box 1481
> West Coast, CA 94156 U.S.A.

Don't worry about the new words and **kanji** you may run across. Just read quickly and find who is looking for a pen pal.

After You Finish Reading

Answer the following questions.

1. Who is looking for penpals?
2. Where and what are they studying?
3. What class are they taking together?
4. What kind of penpal are they looking for?

Guesswork

1. ペンパルをさがしています appears at the beginning and toward the end of the ad. What do you think さがしています means?
2. At the end of the ad, the word 日本語 appears in a short sentence. What do you think that sentence means?

Writing 2

1. First, write down in Japanese five to ten questions to ask your partner. The questions must ask for personal information.

2. Pair up and ask the questions you prepared.
3. Based on your partner's answers, write a brief profile of him or her in Japanese.

Language Functions and Situations

Introducing Friends

クラスで

ブラウン：横井先生(よこいせんせい)、ご紹介(しょうかい)します。こちらはローラ・ヒルさんです。
ヒルさんはわたしのアメリカの大学(だいがく)のクラスメートです。
横井先生：ヒルさん、はじめまして。どうぞよろしく。
ヒル：こちらこそ、どうぞよろしく。

Kurasu de

BURAUN: Yokoi-sensee, go-shookai shimasu. Kochira wa Roora Hiru-san desu.
Hiru-san wa watashi no Amerika no daigaku no kurasumeeto desu.
YOKOI SENSEE: Hiru-san, hajimemashite. Doozo yoroshiku.
HIRU: Kochira koso. Doozo yoroshiku.

コミュニケーション・ノート

こちらこそ

こちらこそ literally means *It's this side* or *It's my side*. For example, when you meet someone and he says はじめまして、どうぞよろしく, you can reply with こちらこそ, meaning *I am the one* (*who's glad to meet you*). When someone bumps into you and says どうもすみません (*I am sorry*), you can say こちらこそ (*I'm the one* [*who is to blame*]). *Or suppose you borrow a friend's car, notice a transmission problem, and repair it for him. When you return the car and thank him with* どうもありがとうございました, *he might say* いいえ、こちらこそ, *or I'm the one* (*who should say thank you*).

In class BROWN: Professor Yokoi. Let me introduce someone to you. This is Ms. Laura Hill. Ms. Hill is my classmate at my American university. PROFESSOR YOKOI: Ms. Hill, it's nice to meet you. HILL: Likewise, it's nice to meet you.

カフェテリアで

ブラウン：林さん、わたしの友だちをご紹介します。
ローラ・ヒルさんです。
アメリカの大学のクラスメートです。
林：ヒルさん、はじめまして。林です。
ブラウンさんからよく聞いています。
ヒル：はじめまして。ヒルです。

Kafeteria de

BURAUN: Hayashi-san, watashi no tomodachi o go-shookai shimasu. Roora Hiru-san desu. Amerika no daigaku no kurasumeeto desu.
HAYASHI: Hiru-san, hajimemashite. Hayashi desu.Buraun-san kara yoku kiiteimasu.
HIRU: Hajimemashite. Hiru desu.

コミュニケーション・ノート

Introductions

Here are some common expressions used in introductions.

ご紹介します。
Let me introduce(someone to you).
こちらはギブソンさんです。
This is Ms. Gibson.
はじめまして。
How do you do?(lit., This is the first time.)
どうぞよろしく。
It's nice to meet you.(lit., Please be kind to me.)

Role Play

Practice the following situations with your classmates.

1. Your friend is visiting your university. Introduce her to one of your professors. The professor will ask several questions of the visiting friend.
2. You have brought your friend to a student lounge. Introduce her to one of your classmates. Those who have been introduced will ask several questions of each other.

At a cafeteria BROWN: Mr. Hayashi, let me introduce my friend to you. This is Laura Hill. She is my classmate at my American university. HAYASHI: Ms. Hill, nice to meet you. I am Hayashi. I've heard a lot about you from Ms. Brown. HILL: Nice to meet you. I am Hill.

Introducing Yourself

カワムラ：自己紹介させていただきます。東京大学のジョン・カワムラです。ロサンゼルスの出身です。専攻は工学です。三年生です。どうぞよろしく。

KAWAMURA: Jikoshookai sasete itadakimasu. Tookyoo Daigaku no Jon Kawamura desu. Rosanzerusu no shusshin desu. Senkoo wa koogaku desu. Sannensee desu. Doozo yoroshiku.

Now introduce yourself to the class.

コミュニケーション・ノート

Self-Introductions

Self-introductions are a common occurrence at meetings and gatherings in Japan. A typical self-introduction starts this way.

自己紹介させていただきます。
Let me introduce myself.

If you want to be more humble, you can add 失礼ですが (*Excuse me but . . .*) before this expression. Then mention your name, affiliation, and so on. If you know someone who has a relationship with the person or group you are introducing yourself to, it's a good idea to mention that also.

横井先生の学生です。
I am a student of Professor Yokoi.
ブラウンさんのクラスメートです。
I am a classmate of Ms. Brown.

Conclude your self-introduction with どうぞよろしく and a polite bow.

KAWAMURA: Allow me to introduce myself. I am John Kawamura of the University of Tokyo. I am from Los Angeles. My major is engineering. I am a junior. It's nice to meet you.

Listening Comprehension

Sally MacDonald talks about five classmates in her Japanese culture class. While listening to her descriptions, complete the following table.

NAME	HOMETOWN	NATIONALITY	MAJOR	YEAR	AGE

2

第二章　わたしの町（まち）

My Town

東京の町

OBJECTIVES

Topics

Commuting
Cities and neighborhoods
Buildings and places around town
Counting

Grammar

5. Adjectives and adverbs
6. Expressing existence: the verbs あります and います
7. Indicating location
8. Positional words
9. Numerals and counters
10. Expressing likes and dislikes: 好（す）き and きらい

Reading and Writing

Linda Brown's neighborhood
Mr. Hayashi's hometown

Language Functions and Situations

Making communication work
Showing location on a map

Vocabulary and Oral Activities

Commuting

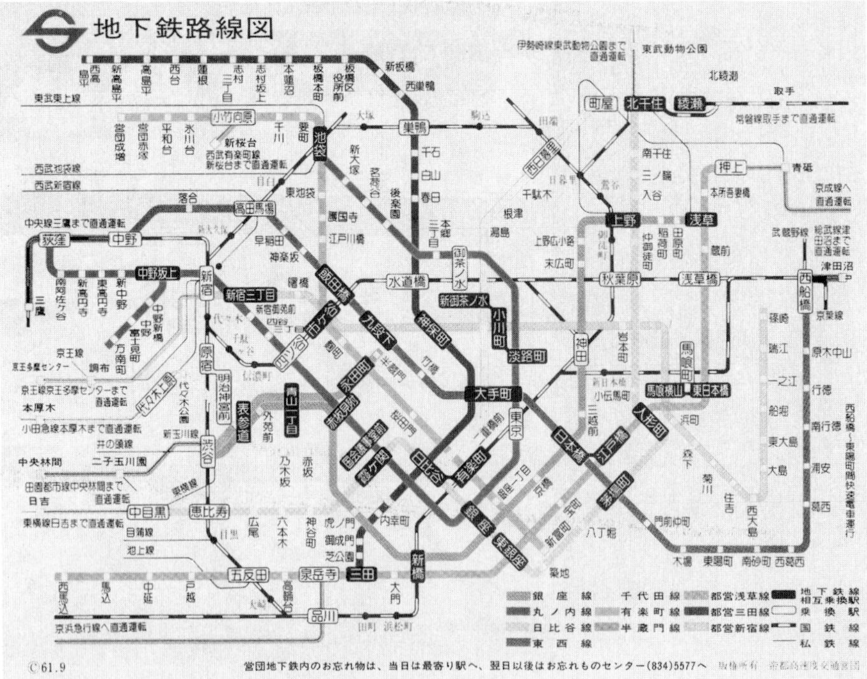

Vocabulary: Commuting

徒歩(で)	on foot	便利(な)	convenient
…に近いです	is close to . . .	不便(な)	inconvenient
…から遠いです	is far from . . .		

便利(不便) cannot be used to mean *suited (not suited) for one's schedule*. Japanese say 3時はつごうがいいです (*Three o'clock is convenient for me*) and 4時はつごうがわるいです (*Four o'clock is inconvenient for me.*)

(勉) Study Grammar 5.

アクティビティー 1

X で *via, by means of X;* Y から *from Y;* とても *very;* 上の *area of Tokyo.*

ダイアログ：地下鉄で10分ぐらいです。(*It's about 10 minutes by subway.*)

ブラウンさんと三村さんが話しています。

ブラウン：三村さんのアパートはどこですか。

三村：上野です。

ブラウン：大学に近いですね。

三村：ええ、地下鉄で10分ぐらいです。とても便利ですよ。

Vocabulary: Counting Minutes and Hours

To count minutes use the counter suffix, ～分(ふん; after some sounds, ぷん) with the Sino-Japanese series of numerals. The counter suffix for counting hours is 時間(じかん).

一分	いっぷん	one minute
二分	にふん	two minutes
三分	さんぷん	three minutes
四分	よんぷん	four minutes
五分	ごふん	five minutes
六分	ろっぷん	six minutes
七分	ななふん、しちふん	seven minutes
八分	はっぷん	eight minutes
九分	きゅうふん	nine minutes
十分	じゅっぷん、じっぷん	ten minutes
一時間	いちじかん	one hour
二時間	にじかん	two hours
一時間半	いちじかんはん	one and a half hours
三時間二十五分	さんじかんにじゅうごふん	three hours twenty-five minutes

Alternatively, the counter suffix ～分間(～ふんかん、～ぷんかん) may also be used when expressing duration of minutes: 五分話しました or 五分間話しました (*I talked for 5 minutes.*) But only ～分 can name a particular minute: 一時五分に行きました (*I went at 1:05*).

Ms. Brown and Mr. Mimura are talking BROWN: Where is your apartment, Mr. Mimura? MIMURA: It's in Ueno. BROWN: It's close to the university, isn't it? MIMURA: Yes. It's about ten minutes by subway. It's very convenient.

アクティビティー 2

どこですか。(*Where is it?*)

Practice the dialogue in アクティビティー **1,** substituting information from the chart below.

Useful word: ちょっと *a bit*

NAME/TYPE OF RESIDENCE	PLACE	PROXIMITY TO SCHOOL	TRANSPORTATION METHOD/TIME REQUIRED	CONVENIENCE
カワムラさんのうち	世田谷(せたがや)	ちょっと遠(とお)い	電車(でんしゃ) 50分(ぷん)	ちょっと不便(ふべん)
林(はやし)さんのアパート	板橋(いたばし)	近(ちか)い	バス 30分(ぷん)	便利(べんり)
横井先生(よこいせんせい)のうち	千葉(ちば)	遠い	車(くるま) 一時間半(いちじかんはん)	不便
チンさんのアパート	目白(めじろ)	とても近い	電車 15分(ふん)	とても便利
大野(おおの)先生のうち	横浜(よこはま)	とても遠い	電車 二時間(じかん)	とても不便

アクティビティー 3

インタビュー：大学(だいがく)に近(ちか)いですか。(*Is it close to university?*)

Pair up and ask the following questions.

S1: _____さんのうちはどこですか。
S2: _____です。
S1: 大学に近いですか。
S2: はい、近いです。_____で_____分です。
(いいえ、遠(とお)いです。_____で_____分です。)
S1: 便利(べんり)ですね。(不便(ふべん)ですね。)

文化ノート

Long Commutes

According to one recent survey, the average commuting time of workers living in the greater Tokyo area is one hour thirty-five minutes—each way! What's more, 20 percent of the surveyed workers spend over two hours getting to (or from) work. Because affordable housing is scarce in central Tokyo where many of the jobs are, the majority of workers have to live in outlying suburbs and cities some distance from the city center. Because the train and subway systems are so well-developed in Tokyo—they are extensive networks of punctual, frequent trains—about 50 percent of commuters use trains and/or subways, while only 25 percent use cars.

東京駅：電車で二時間です。—遠いですね。

Cities and Neighborhoods

Vocabulary: Cities and Towns

近所	きんじょ	neighborhood	人口	じんこう	population
区	く	ward of a city	所	ところ	place
郊外	こうがい	suburbs	町	まち	town
市	し	city	村	むら	village

…町 (*lit., town;* pronounced まち or ちょう) is usually subdivided into numbered districts called …丁目 (ちょうめ).

アクティビティー　4

ダイアログ：どんなところですか。(*What kind of place is it?*)

カワムラ：林(はやし)さんのご出身(しゅっしん)はどこですか。
　　林：九州(きゅうしゅう)の阿蘇(あそ)です。
カワムラ：どんなところですか。
　　林：小(ちい)さい町(まち)です。
カワムラ：きれいな町(まち)ですか。
　　林：ええ。

Now practice the dialogue replacing the underlined parts with the following words.

1. 大(おお)きい、古(ふる)い
2. きれいな、静(しず)かな
3. 古(ふる)い、小(ちい)さい

Useful Vocabulary: Basic Adjectives

大きい／大きな	おおきい／おおきな	big, large
小さい／小さな	ちいさい／ちいさな	small
多い	おおい	many
少ない	すくない	few
新しい	あたらしい	new
古い	ふるい	old
いい		good
悪い	わるい	bad
静か(な)	しずか(な)	quiet, peaceful
うるさい		noisy, disturbing
きれい(な)		attractive, clean
きたない		dirty
広い	ひろい	spacious, wide
狭い	せまい	small (*in area*), narrow
低い	ひくい	low
高い	たかい	high; expensive
安い	やすい	inexpensive
面白い	おもしろい	interesting
有名(な)	ゆうめい(な)	famous
にぎやか(な)		lively

In this textbook, adjectives are listed in their dictionary form. Na-adjectives are differentiated by adding (な) to the listed dictionary form.

KAWAMURA: Where are you from, Mr. Hayashi? HAYASHI: I am from Aso, Kyushu. KAWAMURA: What kind of place is it? HAYASHI: It's a small town. KAWAMURA: Is it an attractive town? HAYASHI: Yes.

アクティビティー 5

古山(ふるやま)さんのうちはどこですか。(*Where is Mr. Huruyama's house?*)

Talk about the commute experience and neighborhood of each student listed below.

[例] S1: 古山さんのうちはどこですか。
S2: 横浜(よこはま)の郊外(こうがい)です。
S1: 大学(だいがく)に近(ちか)いですか。
S2: いいえ、電車(でんしゃ)で1時間(じかん)20分(ぷん)です。
S1: どんなところですか。
S2: 静(しず)かなところです。

NAME	RESIDENCE	COMMUTES . . .	NEIGHBORHOOD
Mikawa	house in Koohu	2 hours by train	inconvenient
Hanada	apartment in Choohu	55 minutes by car	beautiful
Kanai	house in Shibuya	30 minutes by subway	convenient
Nomura	apartment in Ueno	5 minutes by bus	lively

Buildings and Places Around Town

(勉) Study Grammar 6.

道	みち	street, road
通り	とおり	avenue, street
建物	たてもの	building
家	いえ	house
うち		house, home; family
公園	こうえん	park
学校	がっこう	school
病院	びょういん	hospital
映画館	えいがかん	movie theater
銀行	ぎんこう	bank
郵便局	ゆうびんきょく	post office
交番	こうばん	police box
喫茶店	きっさてん	coffee (*lit.*, tea) shop

Both 家(いえ) and うち mean *house*, but the nuances are different. 家 usually refers to a private house in contrast to a company building, government office, or store. On the other hand, うち refers to the place where one leads one's life or where a family resides—in other words, a *home*. うち is sometimes used to mean the people who live in one house, or a *family*.

S1: Where is Mr. Furuyama's house? S2: It's in the suburbs of Yokohama. S1: Is it close to the university? S2: No, it's one hour twenty minutes away by train. S1: What kind of place is it? S2: It's a quiet place.

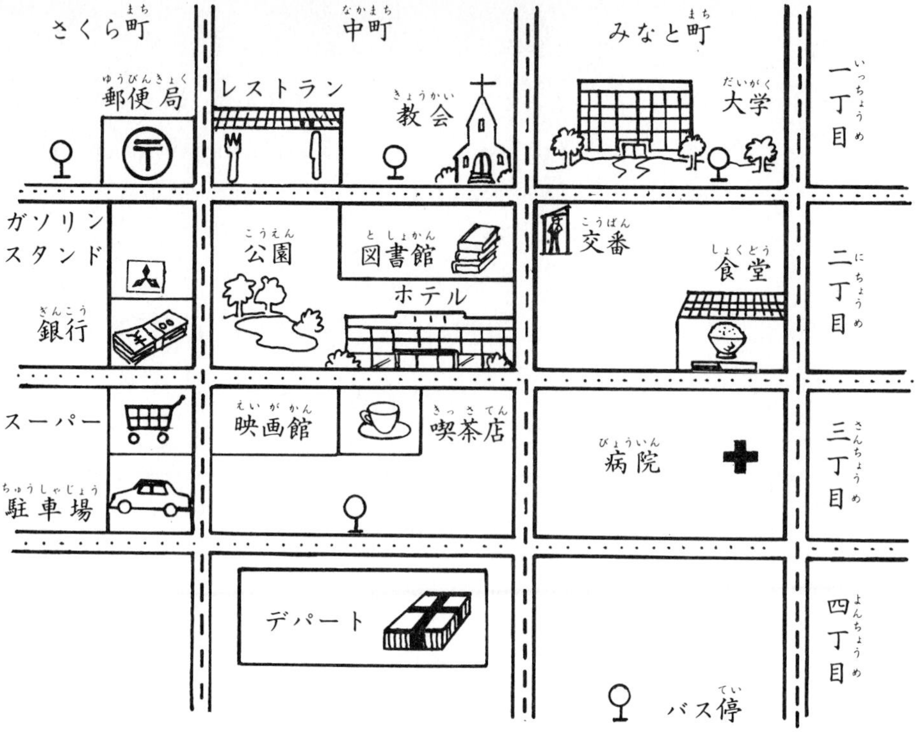

ホテル		hotel
(お)寺	(お)てら	Buddhist temple
神社	じんじゃ	Shinto shrine
教会	きょうかい	church
レストラン		restaurant
食堂	しょくどう	dining hall, informal restaurant
スーパー		supermarket
デパート		department store
ガソリン・スタンド		gas station
駐車場	ちゅうしゃじょう	parking lot
バス停	バスてい	bus stop

Review: 大学(だいがく)、図書館(としょかん)、ビル

文化ノート

交番(こうばん) *Police Boxes*

In Japan, you will see a *police box* or 交番 in almost every block of a city. The "box" may be a tiny freestanding structure or an office open to the street in a larger building. The policemen (おまわりさん) stationed at each police box patrol the neighborhood (often on bicycles) to help prevent crime, but probably their most frequently performed service is to give directions to people who are lost or don't know how to get to their destination. The boxes are usually open twenty-four hours a day, so citizens always know they can go there for help. It is said that the presence of these police boxes contributes, to a great extent, to the low crime rate in Japan.

プリンスホテルはどこですか。

アクティビティー 6

どこにありますか。(*Where is it?*)

Work in pairs. Look at the preceding map and tell where each place is.

[例]　銀行(ぎんこう)はどこにありますか。
　　　さくら町(ちょう)2丁目(ちょうめ)にあります。

文化ノート

Japanese Addresses

In Japan, most streets don't have names and individual houses don't have numbers. Rather, the address is given by naming the block or sub-block area where the house is located. Several houses may thereby share the same address. This is one reason why Japanese police spend so much time giving directions and why maps are often printed on business cards, party invitations, and so on. Being able to draw clear maps and read maps are skills useful to getting around in Japan. Note that Japanese addresses are given in the reverse order of American addresses; first comes the country, then prefecture (similar to a province or state), city, town (町 [まち]) numbered district (…丁目 [ちょうめ]), numbered block (…番地 [ばんち]), number (…号 [ごう]), etc. and finally the person's name.

アクティビティー 7

どこにいますか。(*Where is he/she?*)

The following company message board shows where each employee has gone. Practice asking where each person is with your classmates.

[例] 山田さんは今どこにいますか。—高田さんのオフィスにいます。

Name	Went to	Will be back
Yamada	Mr. Takada's office	3 p.m.
Tanaka	restaurant	2 p.m.
Yoshida	New York	tomorrow
Saitoo	library	4:30 p.m.
Sawai	Hiroshima	next Monday

勉 Study Grammar 7 and 8.

アクティビティー 8

ダイアログ：スーパーはどこにありますか。(*Where is the supermarket?*)

道で

A: すみません。このへんにスーパーはありますか。

B: ええ、駅の前にありますよ。

A: どんな建物ですか。

白い white

B: 白い、大きな建物ですよ。

A: どうもありがとうございました。

B: どういたしまして。

As you have seen, すみません is a useful expression that can be used in a variety of contexts. You have used it to convey an apology (*I'm sorry*) or your gratitude, especially when someone has gone out of their way for you (*thank you*). In this dialogue, すみません is used to get someone's attention in order to ask for help (*excuse me*).

On the street A: Excuse me. Is there a supermarket around here? B: Yes, there's one in front of the station. A: What kind of building is it? B: It's a large, white building. A: Thank you very much. B: You're welcome.

Vocabulary: Positional Words

上	うえ	on, above; up
下	した	under, below; down
左	ひだり	left
右	みぎ	right
中	なか	in, inside
外	そと	outside, out
前	まえ	front
後ろ	うしろ	back, behind
間	あいだ	between
向かい	むかい	facing, across from
隣	となり	next to, nextdoor
そば		nearby
回り	まわり	around
横	よこ	side

A と B の間 *between A and B*

アクティビティー 9

銀行のとなりにあります。(*It is next to the bank.*)

Practice the dialogue in アクティビティー **8**, substituting the following words and expressions for the underlined portions.

1. レストラン
   銀行のとなり
   グリーンのビル
2. 郵便局
   映画館と病院の間
   赤い (*red*)、小さな建物
3. 病院
   公園のそば
   白い、きれいな建物
4. 食堂
   図書館の前
   古い建物
5. ホテル
   映画館の右
   グレーのビル

文法ノート

Sentence-Final よ

The sentence-final particle よ is used by a speaker to indicate strong conviction about a statement or to indicate that he is giving new information to the listener; that is, information that the speaker thinks he or she, but not the listener, knows.

—カフェテリアはどこですか。
—*Where is the cafeteria?*
—あそこですよ。
—*It's over there.*
—わかりますか。
—*Do you understand?*
—ええ、もちろんわかりますよ。
—*Yes, of course, I understand.*

Note that, in general, sentence-final よ is not appropriate when speaking to a superior, because it can sound too direct or abrupt.

Vocabulary Library

More Positional Words

真ん中	まんなか	middle
はじ		edge
北	きた	north
南	みなみ	south
東	ひがし	east
西	にし	west
こちら側	こちらがわ	this side
向こう側	むこうがわ	the other side

アクティビティー 10

ボールは箱(はこ)の上(うえ)にあります。(*The ball is on the box.*)

What relation does the ball(s) have to the box in the following illustrations?

Useful words: 箱 *box*

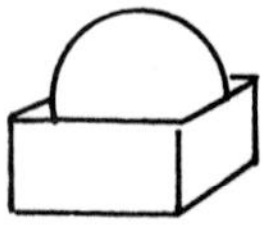
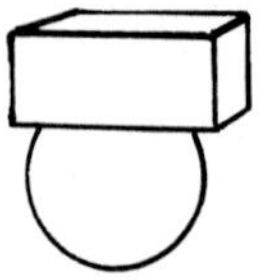
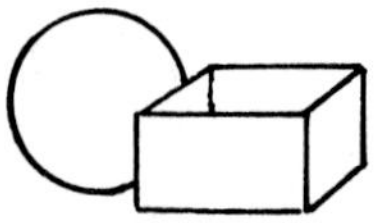

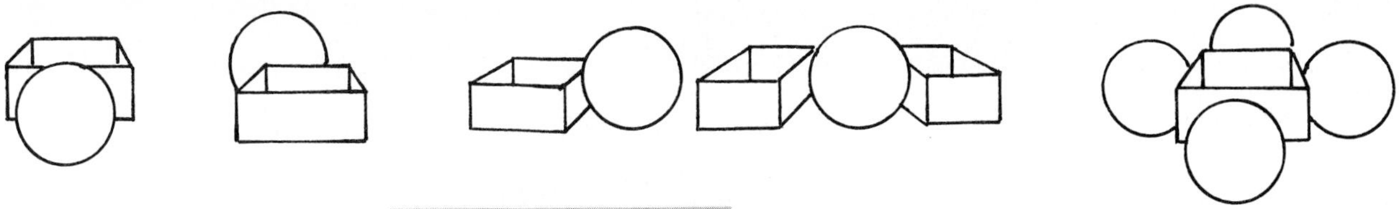

アクティビティー 11

どこにありますか。(*Where is it?*)

Look at this picture and answer the following questions.

1. スーパーはどこにありますか。
2. 郵便局(ゆうびんきょく)はどこにありますか。
3. レストラン「フラミンゴ」はどこにありますか。
4. 学校(がっこう)はどこにありますか。
5. 駐車場(ちゅうしゃじょう)はどこにありますか。
6. デパートはどこにありますか。
7. 地下鉄(ちかてつ)の駅(えき)はどこにありますか。
8. 公園(こうえん)の中(なか)に何(なに)がありますか。
9. 喫茶店(きっさてん)のとなりに何がありますか。

Make your own questions to ask your classmates.

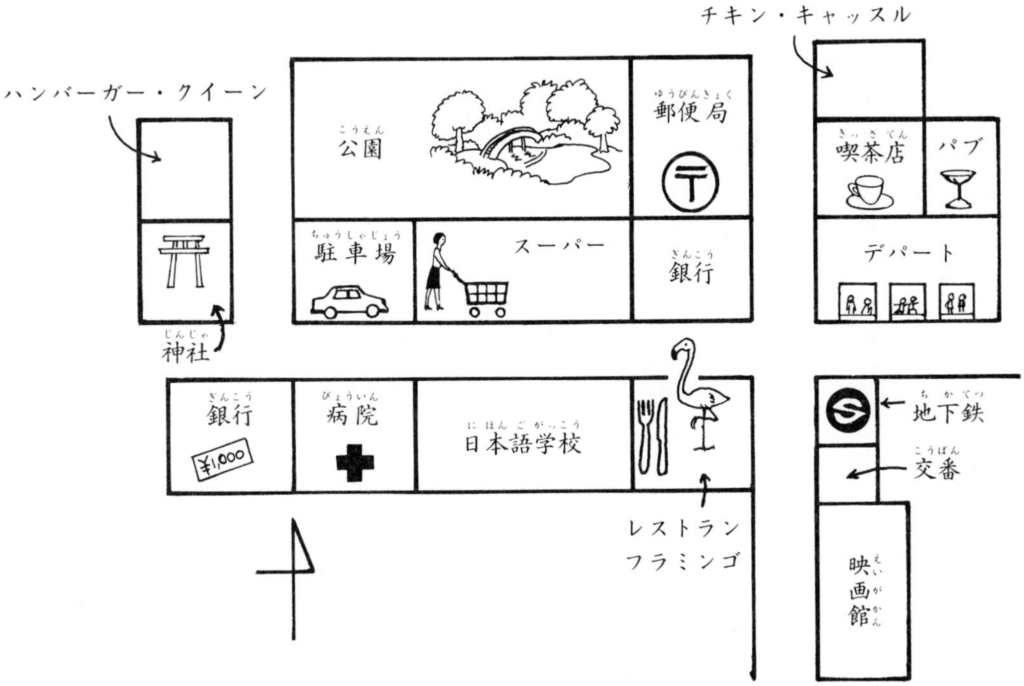

アクティビティー　12

ダイアログ：いいレストランはありますか (*Is there a good restaurant?*)

カワムラさんと町田(まちだ)さんが話(はな)しています。

カワムラ：この近所(きんじょ)にいいレストランはありますか。

　町田：ええ、ありますよ。となりのビルの4階(かい)にあります。

カワムラ：名前(なまえ)は。

　町田：「ナポレオン」です。

アクティビティー　13

いいホテルはありますか。(*Is there a good hotel?*)

Ask your classmates whether each of the following things exists near their house or apartment. If yes, ask specifically where it is (e.g., *Is it next to a shopping mall?*). In addition, ask what it's called.

1. bank
2. good restaurant
3. convenience store (コンビニエンス・ストア)
4. pretty park
5. movie theater
6. good hotel
7. hospital
8. large supermarket
9. tall building
10. famous school

アクティビティー　14

どこにいますか。(*Where is he?*)

Based on the illustration on page 113, answer the following questions.

1. チンさんはどこにいますか。
2. 町田(まちだ)さんはどこにいますか。
3. カーティスさんはどこにいますか。
4. 林(はやし)さんはどこにいますか。
5. ギブソンさんはどこにいますか。
6. カワムラさんの右(みぎ)にだれがいますか。
7. 横井先生(よこいせんせい)の前にだれがいますか。
8. 横井先生(よこいせんせい)の後(うし)ろにだれがいますか。

Mr. Kawamura and Ms. Machida are talking　KAWAMURA: Is there a good restaurant in this neighborhood?　MACHIDA: Yes, there is. There is one on the fourth floor of the building next-door. KAWAMURA: What's it called?　MACHIDA: "Napoleon."

Counting

㊙ Study Grammar 9.

アクティビティー 15

銀行は何軒ありますか。(*How many banks are there?*)

カワムラ：銀行はこの近所に何軒ありますか。
山口：三軒あります。

中野中央商店街

銀行
三井銀行
トマト銀行
東京銀行

レストラン
日本レストラン・竹田
ポパイ・サンドイッチ
松すし
マクドナルド
スキヤキ・ハウス

スーパー
ラッキー マート

デパート
丸井デパート

映画館
シネマ中野
中野日活

喫茶店
コーヒ・パレス
モーツァルト
ブルー・ムーン
オアシス
やすらぎ

ガソリン・スタンド
モービル
日本石油

図書館
中野中央図書館

Ask a classmate how many gas stations, movie theaters, and other establishments there are in the neighborhood.

KAWAMURA: How many banks are there in this neighborhood? YAMAGUCHI: There are three.

アクティビティー　16

ダイアログ：学生(がくせい)は何人(なんにん)いますか。(*How many students are there?*)

町田(まちだ)さんとブラウンさんが話(はな)しています。

町田：ブラウンさんの日本語(にほんご)のクラスに学生(がくせい)は何人(なんにん)いますか。
ブラウン：ええと、全部(ぜんぶ)で15人ぐらいいます。
町田：全部アメリカ人(じん)ですか。
ブラウン：いいえ、中国人(ちゅうごくじん)が五人(ごにん)とカナダ人が二人(ふたり)います。

Vocabulary: Counting People

一人	ひとり	one person	八人	はちにん	eight people
二人	ふたり	two people	九人	きゅうにん、くにん	nine people
三人	さんにん	three people	十人	じゅうにん	ten people
四人	よにん	four people	十一人	じゅういちにん	eleven people
五人	ごにん	five people	百人	ひゃくにん	one hundred people
六人	ろくにん	six people	何人	なんにん	how many people
七人	しちにん ななにん	seven people			

アクティビティー　17

何人(なんにん)いますか。(*How many people are there?*)

Answer these questions about your class.

1. このクラスに学生(がくせい)は何人いますか。
2. 先生(せんせい)は何人いますか。
3. 男(おとこ) (*male*) の学生は何人いますか。
4. 女(おんな) (*female*) の学生は何人いますか。
5. 日本人(にほんじん)は何人いますか。
6. アメリカ人は何人いますか。

Ms. Machida and Ms. Brown are talking MACHIDA: How many students are in your Japanese class, Ms. Brown? BROWN: Uh . . . there are a total of fifteen students. MACHIDA: Are they all Americans? BROWN: No, there are five Chinese and two Canadians.

㊝ Study Grammar 10.

アクティビティー 18

大きい町が好きですか。小さい町が好きですか。(*Do you like big towns or little towns?*)

Answer the following questions.

1. 日本料理が好きですか。
2. 勉強が好きですか。
3. どんなスポーツが好きですか。
4. どんな音楽が好きですか。
5. 静かなところが好きですか。にぎやかなところが好きですか。
6. 大きい町が好きですか。小さい町が好きですか。
7. どんな料理が好きですか。
8. どんな食べ物 (*food*) がきらいですか。

アクティビティー 19

この町が好きな人は何人いますか。(*How many people like this town?*)

Choose one question from the following list and ask it of ten classmates. Then report to the class how many people answered yes.

[例] 肉が好きですか。
— はい、好きです。
— いいえ、きらいです。
肉が好きな人は八人いました。
肉がきらいな人は二人いました。

1. 魚が好きですか。
2. サラダが好きですか。
3. 日本料理が好きですか。
4. パーティーが好きですか。
5. この大学が好きですか。
6. この町が好きですか。
7. スポーツが好きですか。
8. お酒 (*sake*) が好きですか。
9. バナナが好きですか。
10. 日本語のクラスが好きですか。

Grammar and Exercises

5. Adjectives and Adverbs

カワムラ：この赤いセーターはだれのですか。
町田：あっ、わたしのです。
カワムラ：いいセーターですね。
町田：いいえ、安いセーターですよ。

山口：日本語の先生はきびしいですか。
カワムラ：いいえ、とてもやさしいですよ。
山口：それはいいですね。わたしのフランス語の先生はとてもきびしいです。

カワムラ：あの人はだれですか。
チン：町田さんのボーイフレンドです。
カワムラ：ハンサムな人ですね。
チン：ええ。

林：ブラウンさんの大学は大きいですか。
ブラウン：いいえ、あまり大きくありません。
林：有名ですか。
ブラウン：いいえ、あまり有名じゃありません。

5.1 Adjectives are words that modify nouns. In the phrase *a red sweater, red* is an *adjective*. In Japanese as well, the adjective precedes the noun in such a phrase: 赤いセーター (*red sweater*). This usage is called *prenominal use,* meaning *before the noun*.

KAWAMURA: Whose red sweater is this? MACHIDA: Oh, that's mine. KAWAMURA: It's a nice sweater. MACHIDA: No, it's (just) a cheap thing (*lit.*, sweater).

YAMAGUCHI: Is your Japanese professor strict? KAWAMURA: No, she's very nice. YAMAGUCHI: You're lucky. (*lit.*,That's good). My French professor is very strict.

KAWAMURA: Who is that (person)? CHIN: That's Ms. Machida's boyfriend. KAWAMURA: He's nice-looking. (*lit.*, He is a nice-looking person.) CHIN: Yes.

HAYASHI: Is your university large, Ms. Brown? BROWN: No, it's not very large. HAYASHI: Is it famous? BROWN: No, it's not very famous.

Adjectives do not always precede nouns, however, as in *That sweater is red*. Likewise, in the equivalent Japanese sentence—あのセーターは赤いです—the adjective 赤(あか)いappears in the latter part of the sentence, which is called the predicate. (The predicate contains the verb and everything that comes after the subject.) We will call this use of an adjective the *predicate use*.

There are two types of adjectives in Japanese. We will call one type *i-adjectives* because their dictionary form (the form listed in dictionaries) always ends in the syllable い. (赤い is an i-adjective.) Another type of adjective is the *na-adjective*, named for the な that follows them in the prenominal use. These are some examples of these two types of adjectives in their dictionary form.

I-ADJECTIVES		NA-ADJECTIVES	
赤(あか)い	red	元気(げんき)	healthy
あまい	sweet	静(しず)か	quiet
やさしい	gentle	きれい	pretty
暑(あつ)い	hot	ハンサム	handsome
きびしい	strict	有名(ゆうめい)	famous

Note that there are several na-adjectives (like きれい) whose dictionary form ends in い. You'll just have to memorize those.

I-adjectives are of Japanese origin, while most na-adjectives are of foreign origin (from Chinese or Western languages).

5.2 The prenominal and predicate uses of i-adjectives and na-adjectives are summarized in the following chart.

I-ADJECTIVE	
prenominal use	おもしろい本(ほん) (*interesting book*)
predicate use (affirmative)	あの本はおもしろいです。 *That book is interesting.*
predicate use (negative)	あの本はおもしろくありません or あの本はおもしろくないです。 *That book is not interesting.*

NA-ADJECTIVE	
prenominal use	静(しず)かな町(まち) (*quiet town*)
predicate use (affirmative)	あの町は静かです。 *That town is quiet.*
predicate use (negative)	あの町は静かではありません or あの町は静かじゃないです。 *That town is not quiet.*

The affirmative of either type of adjective in the predicate use is formed by adding です to the dictionary form. To form the negative predicate use, you must distinguish between i-adjectives and na-adjectives. In the case of na-adjectives, simply change です to its negative form ではありません (or the colloquial contraction じゃありません). For i-adjectives, however, you must change the ending of the adjective. This process is called *conjugation*. Notice that the dictionary form of all i-adjectives ends in い. This い is actually an ending attached to the root of the adjective. To make a negative, simply replace this final い with く and add ありません or ないです. These two negative forms are identical in meaning and politeness level. Be aware that people often insert the particle は (**wa**) before ありません — for example, 赤くはありません. You will study this later.

Some adjectives have alternate conjugations in the prenominal use.

1. 大きい (*large*) and 小さい (*small*) may take な prenominally even though they are i-adjectives. In this usage the final い is dropped.

大きい人	大きな人	*large person*
小さい人	小さな人	*small person*

2. Some adjectives take the 〜くの form in front of a noun. Change the final い to く and add の.

近い	*near*	近くの大学	*nearby university*
遠い	*far*	遠くの大学	*faraway university*

5.3 *Adverbs* modify adjectives, verbs, and other adverbs and are usually positioned before the word they modify.

とてもきれいな女の人
a ***very*** *pretty woman*
わたしは肉をたくさん食べました。
I ate a ***lot of*** *meat.*
その大学はあまり有名ではありません。
That university is not ***very*** *famous.*

Both とても and あまり mean *very, so, or extremely*. But あまり is used only in negative sentences. In conversation あんまり, a variant of あまり, is often used instead.

練習 1

Practice the following as shown in the example.

[例] この大学は古いですか。(新しい)
→いいえ、この大学は古くありません。
新しいです。

Useful vocabulary

おもしろい	*interesting*	つまらない	*boring*
きびしい	*strict*	やさしい	*lenient, easy*
高(たか)い	*high, expensive*	安(やす)い	*cheap*
重(おも)い	*heavy*	軽(かる)い	*lightweight*
長(なが)い	*long*	短(みじか)い	*short*
厚(あつ)い	*thick*	うすい	*thin*
むずかしい	*difficult*	おいしい	*delicious*

1. そのビルは高いですか。(ひくい)
2. この本(ほん)はおもしろいですか。(つまらない)
3. この肉(にく)はおいしいですか。(まずい)
4. あの先生(せんせい)はきびしいですか。(やさしい)
5. このスーツは高いですか。(安い)
6. このテレビは重いですか。(軽い)
7. 日本語(にほんご)はむずかしいですか。(やさしい)
8. 山口(やまぐち)さんのスピーチは長いですか。(短い)
9. その本は厚いですか。(うすい)
10. あなたのうちは広いですか。(せまい)

練習 2

Practice, following the example.

[例] 古(ふる)い、ビル → あの古いビルは何(なん)ですか。

ハンサム、人(ひと) → あのハンサムな人はだれですか。

Useful vocabulary

きかい	*machine*	まじめ(な)	*serious*
もの	*thing, item*	まるい	*round*
親切(しんせつ)(な)	*kind*	器用(きよう)(な)	*skillful*
へん(な)	*strange*		

1. おもしろい、人
2. きれい、女(おんな)の人
3. 大(おお)きい、きかい
4. きたない、もの
5. 静(しず)か、人
6. 親切、男の人
7. やさしい、男(おとこ)の人
8. へん、もの
9. まじめ、男の人
10. 便利、きかい
11. まるい、もの
12. 器用、女の人

練習 3

Change affirmative sentences to negative, and negative sentences to affirmative.

[例] このアパートはとても便利です。→
このアパートはあまり便利ではありません。
その人はあまりきびしくありません。→
その人はとてもきびしいです。

Useful vocabulary

若い	*young*	車	*car*
安全(な)	*safe*	話	*tale, story*
元気(な)	*healthy*	おかしい	*funny, strange*

1. この近所はとても静かです。
2. あの男の人はあまり若くありません。
3. その大学はとても古いです。
4. この車はあまり安全じゃありません。
5. この町はとてもにぎやかです。
6. この話はとてもおかしいです。
7. カーティスさんはとても元気です。
8. あの人はあまりエレガントではありません。
9. このバナナはあまりおいしくありません。
10. このドレスはあまり安くありません。

練習 4

Rewrite these sentences following the examples.

[例] あれはつまらない本です。→ あの本はつまらないです。

Useful vocabulary

はで(な)	*gaudy, bright-colored*
にぎやか(な)	*lively*

1. これは安い時計です。
2. あれはとても静かな村です。
3. この町はとても小さいです。
4. これは古いカーテンです。
5. このネクタイははでです。
6. あの町はにぎやかです。
7. あれはとても有名なビルです。

練習 5

Choose one adjective that best fits the given noun and make a sentence. Translate the sentence into English.

[例] 日本語(にほんご)のクラス やさしい、おもしろい、むずかしい、つまらない
→日本語のクラスはつまらないです。(*Japanese class is boring.*)

1. わたし
   静(しず)か、にぎやか、元気(げんき)、まじめ、ハンサム、きれい
2. わたしの日本語の先生(せんせい)
   きれい、うつくしい、ハンサム、やさしい、エレガント、若(わか)い
3. ジュリア・ロバーツ
   エレガント、キュート、きれい、スマート、有名(ゆうめい)
4. アーノルド・シュワルツネーガー
   タフ、やさしい、若い、静か、いそがしい、ハンサム
5. エディー・マーフィー
   元気、やさしい、いそがしい、おもしろい、ハンサム
6. わたしの大学(だいがく)
   有名(ゆうめい)、大(おお)きい、むずかしい、やさしい、いい
7. わたしのうち
   大きい、小さい、きれい、ひろい、せまい、きたない
8. わたしのとなりの人(ひと) (*the person next to me*)
   うるさい、きれい、ハンサム、やさしい、へん、まじめ
9. この練習(れんしゅう) (*exercise*)
   むずかしい、やさしい、つまらない、長(なが)い

Study Hint

Learning Grammar

Learning a language is similar to learning any other skill; knowing about it is only part of what is involved. Consider how you would acquire another skill—swimming, for example. If you were to read all the available books on swimming, you would probably become an expert in talking about swimming and you would know what you should do in a pool. Until you actually got into a pool and practiced swimming, however, you would probably not swim very well. In much the same way, if you memorize all the grammar rules but spend little time practicing them, you will not be able to communicate very well in Japanese.

The best way to learn grammar is to use grammatical structures in actual contexts. Activities in the **Vocabulary and Oral Activities** sections of this textbook are designed so that you can practice grammatical structures as well as vocabulary in a variety of communicative contexts. The grammar point you are practicing is indicated by ㊝ **Study Grammar** in the textbook. If you prefer knowing grammar rules before trying them out, you can read the **Grammar and Exercises** section first. Or, you can read about the grammar after you have performed the oral activities with your instructor, thereby confirming the grammatical rules you have formulated through the activities.

As you study each grammar point in **Grammar and Exercises,** you will learn how the structure works; then you need to put your knowledge into practice. First, read the grammar discussion, and study and analyze the examples. Then begin to practice. Do the exercises and check your answers. When you are certain that your answers are correct, practice doing each exercise several times until the answers sound and "feel" right to you. As you do each item, think about what you are conveying and the context in which you could use each sentence, as well as about spelling and pronunciation.

Always remember that language learning is cumulative. This means that you are not finished with a grammar point when you go on to the next chapter. Even though you are now studying the material in Chapter 2, you must still remember how to inflect adjectives and how to use adverbs, because Chapter 2 builds on what you learned in Chapter 1—as all subsequent chapters will build on the material leading up to them. A few minutes spent each day reviewing "old" topics will increase your confidence—and success—in communicating in Japanese.

6. Expressing Existence: The Verbs あります and います

レストランで

カワムラ：すみません。ドイツのビールはありますか。

ウエイター：すみません。ありません。でも、オランダのビールはあります。

At a restaurant KAWAMURA: Excuse me, do you have German beer? WAITER: I'm sorry, we don't. But we have Dutch beer. KAWAMURA: I see. Then, I would like Dutch beer.

BROWN: Excuse me. Is there a phone (I could use)? HAYASHI: Yes, there's one there.

GIBSON: Is Mr. Hayashi here? KAWAMURA: No. BROWN: Oh, he's in the cafeteria. GIBSON: Really? He's always in the cafeteria.

カワムラ：そうですか。じゃ、オランダのビールをお願(ねが)いします。

ブラウン：すみません。電話(でんわ)はありますか。
　　林：ええ、そこにあります。

ギブソン：林(はやし)さんはいますか。
カワムラ：いいえ。
ブラウン：あっ、林さんはカフェテリアにいますよ。
ギブソン：本当(ほんとう)ですか。林さんはいつもカフェテリアにいますね。

6.1 To express existence in Japanese, you can use the verbs あります (dictionary form ある) and います (dictionary form いる). あります is used to denote the existence of inanimate objects and abstract concepts (e.g., notebooks, coffee, dead bodies, flowers, air, love, and ideas), while います is used to express the existence of living things (e.g., people, animals, and insects, but not plant life).

ある and いる are the plain forms of あります and います, respectively. (See 文法ノート.)

文法ノート

Polite Form Versus Plain Form

In Japanese, verbs, adjectives, and the copula all take different forms , depending on stylistic differences of speech. There are basically two different speech styles: polite and plain. The polite form is used when you speak with people outside your group or when you speak with people inside your group impersonally or nonintimately. The plain form is used when you speak intimately with someone in your group or to those considered much lower on the social scale, such as young children or pets. The plain form is also exclusively used in certain positions in sentences (that is, most positions except the end of the sentence and the end of an independent clause). In this case, the use of the plain form is motivated grammatically, rather than socially. The beginning of this textbook focuses on teaching you polite forms, which are more commonly used when you first meet Japanese people and are less likely to insult the listener than the informal plain form.

6.2 This is the simplest way to say *X exists* or *there is/are X*.

EXISTENT	PARTICLE	VERB [Affirmative]
N (inanimate)	が	ある (あります)
N (animate)	が	いる (います)

N stands for *noun*.

There is _____ ; *There are* _____.

6.3 The nonexistence of something is expressed by the negative forms of the same verbs.

EXISTENT	PARTICLE	VERB [Negative]
N (inanimate)	が	ない (ありません)
N (animate)	が	いない (いません)

ない and いない are the plain forms of ありません and いません, respectively.

There isn't _____ ; There aren't _____.

6.4 The location or position where something or someone exists usually occurs at the beginning of the above sentence structures and is marked with the particle に.

LOCATION	PARTICLE に	EXISTENT	PARTICLE が	VERB
N1	に	N2 (inanimate)	が	ある (あります)
N1	に	N2 (animate)	が	いる (います)

There is / are _____ at / in _____.

ここに本(ほん)があります。
There are books here.
ここに辞書(じしょ)はありません。
There are no dictionaries here.
そこにペンはありますか。
Is there a pen over there?
公園(こうえん)に何(なに)がありますか。
What is there in the park?
うちに犬(いぬ)がいます。
There is a dog at my house.
教室(きょうしつ)に三村(みむら)さんはいません。
Mr. Mimura is not in the classroom.
そこにカワムラさんはいますか。
Is Mr. Kawamura there?
今(いま)、教室(きょうしつ)にだれがいますか。
Who is in the classroom now?

Note that the particle は is used in negative and yes/no questions instead of が.

6.5 When you would like to say how many or how much of something exists, a phrase denoting quantity comes just before the verb of existence.

LOCATION	PARTICLE に	EXISTENT	PARTICLE が	QUANTITY	VERB
N1	に	N2 (inanimate)	が		ある (あります)
N1	に	N2 (animate)	が		いる (います)

N1 and *N2* stand for two different nouns.

There is one _____ at/in _____.
There are (number) _____s at / in _____.

ここにチョコレートがひとつあります。
Here is one piece of chocolate.
あそこに学生(がくせい)が三人(さんにん)います。
There are three students.
ここにアメリカ人(じん)は何人(なんにん)いますか。
How many Americans are here?

練習 1

Make sentences using あります or います based on the information provided.

1. (in this class) (chalkboard)
2. (in my room) (computer)
3. (in the cafeteria) (classmates)
4. (in Nakano) (Ms. Brown's apartment)
5. (in this class) (students)
6. (at home) (my bicycle)
7. (at the library) (books)

練習 2

Make five existential sentences based on inanimate and living things around you.

7. Indicating Location

ブラウン：すみません。カフェテリアはどこにありますか。
学生(がくせい)：あのビルの一階(いっかい)にあります。
ブラウン：どうもありがとうございます。
学生：どういたしまして。

BROWN: Excuse me. Where is the cafeteria? STUDENT: There is one on the first floor of that building.
BROWN: Thank you very much. STUDENT: You're welcome.

カワムラ：町田(まちだ)さんはどこにいますか。
チン：今(いま)、横井先生(よこいせんせい)の研究室(けんきゅうしつ)にいます。
カワムラ：横井先生の研究室はどこですか。
チン：このビルの三階(さんかい)です。

7.1 The simplest way to indicate the location of something or someone is to use the sentence structure N1 は N2 です, where N1 is a noun indicating a specific thing or person and N2 is a noun representing a place.

銀行(ぎんこう)はどこですか。—銀行はあそこです。
Where is the bank? —The bank is over there.
ブラウンさんはどこですか。—ブラウンさんは図書館(としょかん)です。
Where is Ms. Brown? —Ms. Brown is at the library.

7.2 In addition, you can use the following structures.

EXISTENT	PARTICLE は	LOCATION	PARTICLE に	QUANTITY	VERB
N1 (inanimate)	は	N2	に		ある (あります)
N1 (animate)	は	N2	に		いる (います)

(number) _____ is / are at / in _____.

銀行(ぎんこう)はどこにありますか。—銀行はあそこにあります。
Where is the bank? —It (the bank) is over there.
カワムラさんはカフェテリアにいますか。
Is Mr.Kawamura in a cafeteria?
学生(がくせい)はここに三人(さんにん)います。
There are three students here.

Note the differences between these structures and those expressing existence that are presented in **Grammer 6.5.** These structures require は instead of が and the location + に comes immediately before the verb. The structure presented in **Grammar 6.5** is used to state ***whether or not*** *people or things exist at a certain place*, whereas the structure presented here is used to state ***where*** *people or things exist.*

KAWAMURA: Where is Ms. Machida? CHIN: Right now she is in Professor Yokoi's office. KAWAMURA: Where is Professor Yokoi's office? CHIN: It's on the third floor of this building.

8. Positional Words

カワムラ：机(つくえ)の下(した)にかばんがありますよ。
ブラウン：だれのカバンですか。
カワムラ：さあ…かばんの中(なか)にペンとノートと財布(さいふ)がありますよ。
ブラウン：財布の中には何(なに)がありますか。
カワムラ：お金(かね)とクレジット・カードがあります。
ブラウン：銀座(ぎんざ)レストランはどこにありますか。
女(おんな)の人：銀座ホテルの2階(かい)にあります。銀座ホテルはあの高(たか)いビルの前にあります。
カワムラ：ブラウンさんはどこにいますか。
町田(まちだ)：あの部屋(へや)の中(なか)にいます。
カワムラ：あの赤(あか)いドアの部屋ですか。
町田：ええ、そうです。

8.1 Such phrases as *in front of* and *to the left of* are expressed in Japanese with the following structure.

N	POSSESSIVE PARTICLE の	POSITIONAL WORD	
机(つくえ)	の	上(うえ)	*on (top of) the desk*
ブラウンさん	の	右(みぎ)	*to the right of Ms. Brown*
東京大学(とうきょうだいがく)	の	そば	*near the University of Tokyo (lit., in the vicinity of the University of Tokyo)*

These locational phrases can modify nouns, in which case they precede the noun and are linked to it with the possessive particle の (*of*).

For a list of other important positional words, see p.140 of this chapter.

KAWAMURA: There is a bag under the desk (you know). BROWN: Whose bag is it? KAWAMURA: I wonder . . . There are pens, notebooks, and a wallet inside it. BROWN: What's inside the purse? KAWAMURA: There are money and credit cards.

BROWN: Where is the Ginza Restaurant? WOMAN: It's on the second floor of Ginza Hotel. Ginza Hotel is in front of that tall building.

KAWAMURA: Where is Ms. Brown? MACHIDA: She's in that room. KAWAMURA: You mean that room with the red door? MACHIDA: Yes, that's right.

机の上の本
the book on the desk (lit., the desk's top's book)

ギブソンさんの右の人
the person on Ms. Gibson's right (lit., Ms. Gibson's right side's person)

8.2 When these locational phrases are used as the location with existential verbs, they are followed by the particle に, as discussed in **Grammar 6.4** and **7.2**.

机の上に何がありますか。—机の上に本があります。
What is on the desk? —There is a book on the desk.

ブラウンさんの右にだれがいますか。—ブラウンさんの右にカワムラさんがいます。
Who is to the right of Ms. Brown? —Mr. Kawamura is on the right side of Ms. Brown.

銀行はどこにありますか。—銀行はホテルのとなりにあります。
Where is the bank? —The bank is next to the hotel.

練習 1

Make dialogues following the example.

[例] A: (レストラン) B: (映画館のとなり) →
A: レストランはどこにありますか。
B: 映画館のとなりにあります。

1. A: (カーティスさん) B: (図書館の前)
2. A: (交番) B: (銀行とスーパーの間)
3. A: (駐車場) B: (公園の後ろ)
4. A: (林さん) B: (ギブソンさんの右)
5. A: (喫茶店) B: (ホテルの中)

練習 2

Answer the following questions, using this illustration.

1. 机の上に何がありますか。
2. 箱の中に何がありますか。
3. 本の上に何がありますか。
4. かばんはどこにありますか。
5. カレンダーはどこにありますか。

6. ブラウンさんのうしろに何がありますか。
7. カワムラさんはどこにいますか。
8. ギブソンさんはどこにいますか。

練習　3

Answer the following questions, using this illustration.

Useful vocabulary

ベンチ	*bench*
車(くるま)	*car*
鳥(とり)	*bird*
犬(いぬ)	*dog*
木(き)	*tree*

1. ギブソンさんはどこにいますか。
2. ギブソンさんの右(みぎ)にだれがいますか。
3. ベンチの下(した)に何(なに)がいますか。
4. ベンチの横(よこ)にだれがいますか。
5. 町田さんはどこにいますか。
6. 木の上に何がいますか。
7. 車の中(なか)にだれがいますか。
8. 車の後(うし)ろにだれがいますか。

9. Numerals and Counters

ブラウン：日本(にほん)の人口(じんこう)は何人(なんにん)ですか。
町田(まちだ)：一億二千二百万人(いちおくにせんにひゃくまんにん)ぐらいです。
アメリカの人口は。
ブラウン：日本の人口の二倍(にばい)ぐらいです。

カワムラ：すみません。佐藤(さとう)さんのうちはどこでしょうか。
おまわりさん：このへんに佐藤さんは三軒(さんけん)あります。
どの佐藤さんですか。
カワムラ：佐藤良男(よしお)さんです。
おまわりさん：佐藤良男さんも二人(ふたり)います。

ブラウン：この家(いえ)には部屋(へや)がいくつありますか。
不動産屋(ふどうさんや)：五(いつ)つあります。
ブラウン：トイレはいくつありますか。
不動産屋：二つあります。一階(いっかい)に一(ひと)つ、二階に一つです。

9.1 There are two numerical systems in Japanese: the Japanese system and the Sino-Japanese system. In the Japanese system, which covers only from one to ten, つ is the general counter. After 11, there is only one system: the Sino-Japanese system.

Refer to Appendix 3.

Numbers 1 through 10

	JAPANESE SYSTEM	SINO-JAPANESE SYSTEM		JAPANESE SYSTEM	SINO-JAPANESE SYSTEM
1	ひとつ (一つ)	いち (一)	6	むっつ (六つ)	ろく (六)
2	ふたつ (二つ)	に (二)	7	ななつ (七つ)	しち／なな (七)
3	みっつ (三つ)	さん (三)	8	やっつ (八つ)	はち (八)
4	よっつ (四つ)	し／よん (四)	9	ここのつ (九つ)	きゅう／く (九)
5	いつつ (五つ)	ご (五)	10	とお (十)	じゅう (十)

BROWN: What is the population of Japan? (*lit.*, As for the population of Japan, how many people is it?) MACHIDA: About 122 million (people). How about the population of the U.S.? BROWN: It's about twice as large as Japan's.

KAWAMURA: Excuse me. Where is Mr. Satoo's residence? POLICEMAN: There are three Satoos in this neighborhood. Which Mr. Satoo do you mean? KAWAMURA: Mr. Yoshio Satoo. POLICEMAN: There are two Yoshio Satoos.

BROWN: How many rooms does this house have? REAL ESTATE AGENT: It has five. BROWN: How many bathrooms does it have? REAL ESTATE AGENT: It has two. There is one on the first floor, and another on the second floor.

9.2 Large numbers are expressed in units of 10,000 (万), 100,000,000 (億; *100 million*), and 1,000,000,000,000 (兆; *1 trillion*). If you divide large numbers with a comma every four digits starting at the right, it is easy to read them in Japanese. Think of the first comma from the right representing 万, the next 億, and the next 兆.

0 (zero) is read as ゼロ or 零 (れい)。

1234,5678,9876,5432

1 2 3 4 , 5 6 7 8 , 9 8 7 6 , 5 4 3 2
一千二百三十四兆五千六百七十八億九千八百七十六万五千四百三十二

When writing numerals in Japanese, however, place the commas every three digits starting from the right, as in English.

Large Numbers

10	じゅう (十)
100	ひゃく (百)
1,000	(いっ) せん ([一] 千)
10,000	いちまん (一万)
100,000	じゅうまん (十万)
1,000,000	ひゃくまん (百万)
10,000,000	(いっ) せんまん ([一] 千万)
100,000,000	いちおく (一億)
1,000,000,000	じゅうおく (十億)
10,000,000,000	ひゃくおく (百億)
100,000,000,000	(いっ) せんおく ([一] 千億)
1,000,000,000,000	いっちょう (一兆)

Notice these phonological (sound) changes when 1, 3, 6, 8, and 10 appear before 百、千、 or 兆.

1	一千 (いっせん)、一兆 (いっちょう)
3	三百 (さんびゃく)、三千 (さんぜん)
6	六百 (ろっぴゃく)
8	八百 (はっぴゃく)
10	十兆 (じゅっちょう *or* じっちょう)

9.3 When you count objects, you have to attach counter suffixes (a suffix is an element attached to the end of another element) to numbers. Which counter you use depends on the classification of what you count. Although there are many counters in Japanese (there is a dictionary just of counters), the number of commonly used counters is limited.

Some Important Counters

Bold characters indicate counters already introduced. You should know these.

a.	～人(にん)	people
b.	～ヶ月(かげつ)	number of months
c.	～台(だい)	heavy machinery, vehicles, office equipment, etc.
d.	～番(ばん)	number of order (No. 1, No. 2, etc.)
e.	～度(ど)	· · · times (occurrences, repetitions); degrees (temperature)
f.	～時間(じかん)	number of hours
g.	～枚(まい)	thin, flat items (paper, bedsheets, floppy disks, toast, etc.)
h.	～着(ちゃく)	clothes
i.	～課(か)	lessons
j.	～歳(さい)	age
k.	～冊(さつ)	books, notebooks, bound volumes
l.	～頭(とう)	large animals (elephant, whale, horse, etc.)
m.	～分(ふん)	minutes
n.	～杯(はい)	cupfuls or glassfuls
o.	～本(ほん)	long, thin items (pencil, banana, leg, tree, road, tapes, etc.)
p.	～階(かい)	floors of a building
q.	～足(そく)	shoes, socks, footwear
r.	～匹(ひき)	small animals (dog, cat, etc.)
s.	～羽(わ)	birds
t.	～軒(けん)	houses, buildings
u.	～倍(ばい)	· · · times (magnification)
v.	～回(かい)	· · · times (occurrences)
w.	～個(こ)	general counter

山口(やまぐち)さんのうちには車(くるま)が二台(にだい)あります。

There are two cars at Mr. Yamaguchi's house.

カウンターの上(うえ)にブラウスが三枚(さんまい)あります。

There are three blouses on the counter.

テーブルの上にバナナが五本(ごほん)あります。

There are five bananas on the table.

Blouses and sweaters are counted with ～枚. Pants are counted with ～本.

Depending on the numbers that come before the counters, some counters show phonological changes. Notice the exception for counting people (人). *One* and *two* use the Japanese system, while the rest use the Sino-Japanese system.

Refer to Appendix 4.

	～人(にん)	～台(だい)	～個(こ)	～分(ふん)	～軒(けん)
1	ひとり	いちだい	いっこ	いっぷん	いっけん
2	ふたり	にだい	にこ	にふん	にけん
3	さんにん	さんだい	さんこ	さんぷん	さんけん さんげん
4	よにん	よんだい	よんこ	よんぷん	よんけん

5	ごにん	ごだい	ごこ	ごふん	ごけん
6	ろくにん	ろくだい	ろっこ	ろっぷん	ろっけん
7	ななにん しちにん	ななだい しちだい	ななこ しちこ	ななふん しちふん	ななけん しちけん
8	はちにん	はちだい	はっこ はちこ	はっぷん はちふん	はっけん はちけん
9	きゅうにん くにん	きゅうだい	きゅうこ	きゅうふん	きゅうけん
10	じゅうにん	じゅうだい	じゅっこ じっこ	じゅっぷん じっぷん	じゅっけん じっけん

9.4 When you would like to ask *how many*, attach 何 (なん) before these counters. The interrogative corresponding to the general counter ～つ is いくつ.

このクラスに学生(がくせい)は何人(なんにん)いますか。
How many students are there in this class?
ここに本(ほん)が何冊(なんさつ)ありますか。
How many books are here?
まどはいくつありますか。
How many windows are there?

After 何, some counters undergo a sound change.

何杯 (なんばい)
何本 (なんぼん)
何匹 (なんびき)

練習 1

What counter do you think is used to count the following? Refer to the preceding list of counters.

1. socks
2. fingers
3. computers
4. horses
5. jackets
6. envelopes
7. movie theaters
8. streets
9. parks
10. goldfish

練習 2

These are answers. What are the questions in Japanese?

1. There are five pencils on the desk.
2. There are three cars at home.
3. There are two windows in the classroom.
4. There are three dogs in this room.
5. There is one person to the left of Mr. Yamada.
6. There are ten books in my bag.

7. There are six tea shops in this town.
8. There are eight books over there.
9. There are three bananas on the table.
10. There are three parks in this neighborhood.

練習 3

Read these numbers.

1. 3,052,196
2. 54,096,710
3. 100,094,312,093
4. 30,400,000,018
5. 6,701,100,990,778,156
6. 1,000,019,000

練習 4

Answer these questions using the following table.

Useful vocabulary: 面積(めんせき) *land area*, ～平方(へいほう)キロメートル ··· *square kilometers* (*km*^{2})

国(くに)	面積(平方キロメートル)	人口(じんこう)
日本(にほん or にっぽん)	373,000	117,057,000 (1980)
韓国(かんこく)	98,000	37,605,000 (1979)
アメリカ	9,363,000	220,580,000 (1979)
カナダ	9,976,000	23,690,000 (1978)
中国(ちゅうごく)	9,597,000	1,008,175,000 (1982)
台湾(たいわん)	36,000	18,270,000 (1981)
メキシコ	1,973,000	69,381,000 (1979)
ホンコン	1,031	5,100,000 (1980)
インド	3,288,000	650,980,000 (1979)

1. 日本の人口は何人(なんにん)ですか。
2. 日本の面積は何(なん)平方キロメートルですか。
3. 韓国の面積は何平方キロメートルですか。
4. アメリカの人口は何人ですか。
5. カナダの面積は何平方キロメートルですか。

6. 中国の人口は何人ですか。
7. 台湾の人口は何人ですか。
8. メキシコの面積は何平方キロメートルですか。
9. ホンコンの人口は何人ですか。
10. インドの人口は何人ですか。

10. Expressing Likes and Dislikes: 好き and きらい

カワムラ：林(はやし)さんの好(す)きな食(た)べ物(もの)は何(なん)ですか。
林：ハンバーガーです。
カワムラ：きらいな食べ物は何ですか。
林：ブロッコリーです。

林：ブラウンさんはお酒(さけ)が好きですか。
ブラウン：あまり好きではありません。
林さんは。
林：大好(だいす)きです。

町田(まちだ)：ブラウンさんはどんな学科(がっか)が好きですか。
ブラウン：歴史学(れきしがく)が好きです。
町田：きらいな学科はありますか。
ブラウン：ええ、数学(すうがく)が大(だい)きらいです。

Such meanings as *I like* and *I dislike* are expressed by na-adjectives 好き and きらい, respectively. You can use these adjectives both prenominally and predicatively.

わたしの好(す)きな町(まち)
a town I like, a favorite town of mine
わたしのきらいなところ
a place I dislike
山口(やまぐち)さんはあの喫茶店(きっさてん)が好きです。
Mr. Yamaguchi likes that coffee shop.
チンさんは大(おお)きい町(まち)がきらいです。
Ms. Chin doesn't like large cities.

Note that the object of liking and disliking (*tea shops* and *cities* in the above examples) is marked with the particle が.

KAWAMURA: What is your favorite food, Mr. Hayashi? HAYASHI: Hamburgers. KAWAMURA: What food don't you like? HAYASHI: It's broccoli.

HAYASHI: Do you like sake, (Ms. Brown)? BROWN: I don't like it very much. How about you, (Mr. Hayashi)? HAYASHI: I love it.

MACHIDA: What academic subject do you like, Ms. Brown? BROWN: I like history. MACHIDA: Is there any subject that you don't like? BROWN: Yes, I hate math.

コミュニケーション・ノート

Different Degrees of Liking and Disliking

野菜が好きですか。	*Do you like vegetables?*
—はい、大好きです。	*—Yes, I like them very much.*
—はい、好きです。	*—Yes, I like them.*
—まあまあです。	*—They're okay. (lit., So-so.)*
—あまり好きではありません。	*—I don't like them very much.*
—いいえ、きらいです。	*—No, I dislike them.*
—いいえ、大きらいです。	*—No, I hate them.*

練習 1

What's your Japanese-language and culture interest quotient? Ask a classmate the following questions. What's the score?

(5 points)	(4)	(3)	(2)	(1)
大好き	好き	まあまあ	きらい	大きらい

1. てんぷらが好きですか。
2. すしが好きですか。
3. ひらがなが好きですか。
4. カタカナが好きですか。
5. 漢字が好きですか。
6. 日本語のクラスが好きですか。
7. 日本語の先生が好きですか。(Be careful!)
8. 黒沢の映画が好きですか。
9. 歌舞伎が好きですか。
10. すもうが好きですか。

点 is a counter for points.

Total points: ______ 点

練習 2

Answer these questions.

1. 大きい町が好きですか。小さい町が好きですか。
2. 静かなところが好きですか。にぎやかなところが好きですか。
3. 新しい町が好きですか。古い町が好きですか。
4. どんな映画が好きですか。
   Useful words: アクション映画、SF映画、コメディー、ロマンス
5. どんな音楽が好きですか。
   Useful words: クラシック、ロック、ラップ、カントリーウエスタン、ゴスペル

6. どんな食べ物が好きですか。
7. どんな食べ物がきらいですか。
8. どんなスポーツが好きですか。
9. どんな学科 (*academic subject*) が好きですか。

Vocabulary

Transportation

ジェイアール	JR	JR (Japan Railways)
くるま	車	car
じてんしゃ	自転車	bicycle
ちかてつ	地下鉄	subway
でんしゃ	電車	electric train
とほ	徒歩	by walking, on foot

Loanwords: タクシー、バス

Places

いえ	家	house
うち		house; (my) home
えいがかん	映画館	movie theater
えき	駅	station
おてら	お寺	(Buddhist) temple
ガソリンスタンド		gas station
きっさてん	喫茶店	coffee (*lit., tea*) shop
きょうかい	教会	church
ぎんこう	銀行	bank
きんじょ	近所	neighborhood
こうえん	公園	park
こうがい	郊外	suburbs
こうばん	交番	police box
し	市	city
しょくどう	食堂	dining hall, informal restaurant
じんじゃ	神社	(Shinto) shrine
スーパー		supermarket
たてもの	建物	building
ちゅうしゃじょう	駐車場	parking lot
デパート		department store
とおり	通り	avenue, street
ところ	所	place
としょかん	図書館	library
バスてい	バス停	bus stop
びょういん	病院	hospital
まち	町	town
みち	道	street
むら	村	village
ゆうびんきょく	郵便局	post office

Loanwords: ホテル、レストラン
Review: 学校、大学、ビル

Nouns

じんこう	人口	population
たべもの	食べ物	food

Adjectives

あかい	赤い	red
あたらしい	新しい	new
あつい	暑い	hot
あまい		sweet
いい		good
うるさい		noisy, annoying
おおい	多い	many, much
おおきい／おおきな	大きい／大きな	large, big
きたない	汚い	dirty
きびしい		strict
きれい		attractive, pretty; clean
げんき(な)	元気(な)	healthy; energetic
しずか(な)	静か(な)	quiet, peaceful
しろい	白い	white
すくない	少ない	few
せまい	狭い	small in area; narrow
だいきらい(な)	大嫌い(な)	hated
だいすき(な)	大好き(な)	favorite, very well liked
たかい	高い	high; expensive
ちいさい／ちいさな	小さい／小さな	small
ちかい	近い	near, close
とおい	遠い	far
にぎやか(な)		lively
ひくい	低い	low
ひろい	広い	spacious; wide
ふべん(な)	不便(な)	inconvenient
ふるい	古い	old
べんり(な)	便利(な)	convenient
むずかしい		difficult
やさしい		easy; lenient; nice
やすい	安い	inexpensive, cheap
ゆうめい(な)	有名(な)	famous
わるい	悪い	bad

Loanword: ハンサム(な)

Review: 好(す)き(な)、嫌(きら)い(な)

Adverbs

あ(ん)まり	(+ *negative*) not so much
たくさん	a lot
まあまあ	so so

Review: とても

Verbs

ある	there is/are (*inanimate things*)
いる	there is/are (*people, animals*)

Counting Time

いっぷん	一分	one minute
にふん	二分	two minutes
さんぷん	三分	three minutes
よんふん	四分	four minutes
ごふん	五分	five minutes
ろっぷん	六分	six minutes
ななふん、しちふん	七分	seven minutes
はっぷん	八分	eight minutes
きゅうふん	九分	nine minutes
じゅっぷん、じっぷん	十分	ten minutes
いちじかん	一時間	one hour
いちじかんはん	一時間半	one and a half hours
にじかん	二時間	two hours

Counting People

ひとり	一人	one person
ふたり	二人	two people
さんにん	三人	three people
よにん	四人	four people
ごにん	五人	five people
ろくにん	六人	six people
しちにん	七人	seven people
はちにん	八人	eight people
きゅうにん、くにん	九人	nine people
じゅうにん	十人	ten people
じゅういちにん	十一人	eleven people
ひゃくにん	百人	hundred people

Large Numbers

じゅう	十	ten
ひゃく	百	hundred
せん	千	thousand
いちまん	一万	ten thousand
じゅうまん	十万	hundred thousand
ひゃくまん	百万	million
いっせんまん	一千万	ten million
いちおく	一億	hundred million
じゅうおく	十億	billion
ひゃくおく	百億	ten billion
いっせんおく	一千億	hundred billion
いっちょう	一兆	trillion

Counters

かい	～階	*(counter for floors of a building)*
けん	～軒	*(counter for houses)*
さい	～歳	*(counter for age)*
じかん	～時間	*(counter for hours)*
にん	～人	*(counter for people)*
ほん	～本	*(counter for long [often cylindrical] items)*

Review: 分(ふん)

Positional Words

あいだ	間	between
うえ	上	on, over; up
うしろ	後ろ	behind, back
した	下	below, under; down
そと	外	outside
そば		near
となり	隣	next to
なか	中	inside
ひだり	左	left
まえ	前	front
まわり	回り	around
みぎ	右	right
むかい	向かい	across from, facing
よこ	横	side

Kanji

Learn these **kanji**.

間	右	方
半	中	近
上	外	遠
下	前	有
分	後	
小	時	
好	山	
町	口	
田	千	
左	万	

Reading and Writing

Reading 1 ブラウンさんのアパートの近所

Before You Read

Linda Brown lives in an apartment in Nakano. The following passage describes her apartment and neighborhood. Before reading it, look at the map. Can you remember what the place labels mean? If not, go back to the **Vocabulary** section and find them.

Do you remember these words indicating positions?

回り	となり	上
右	前	間
左	向こう側	後ろ

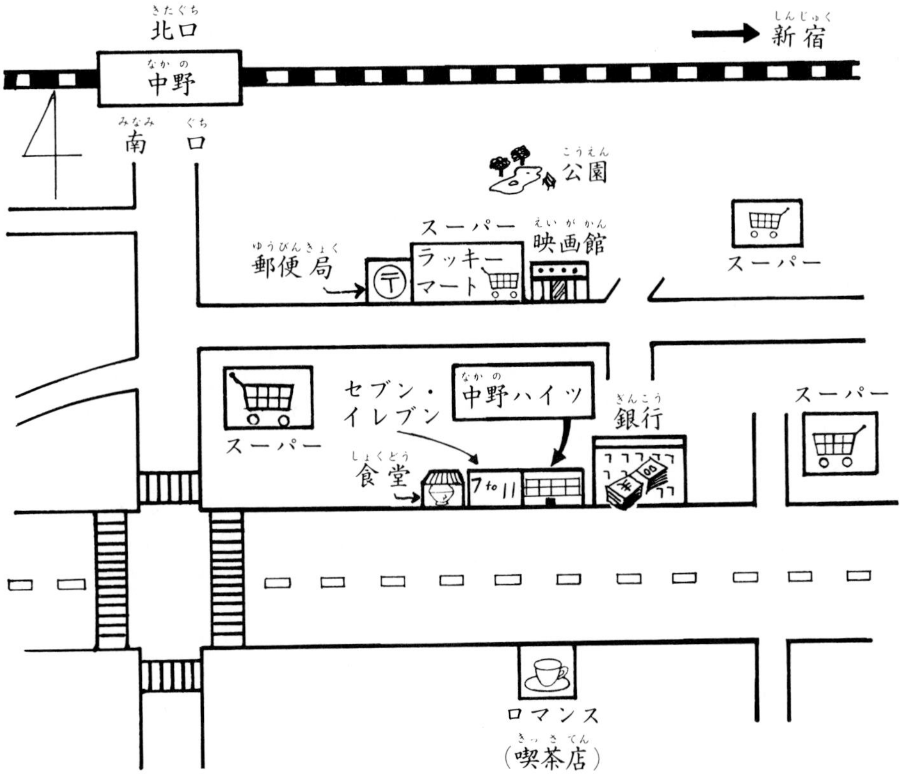

Now Read It!

ブラウンさんのアパートは東京の中野にあります。中野は電車で新宿から10分ぐらいです。ブラウンさんのアパートは駅から徒歩で5分です。東京大学まで地下鉄で30分です。とても便利です。

ブラウンさんのアパートの名前は「中野ハイツ」です。3階建てです。ブラウンさんのアパートは2階にあります。

アパートの回りにはいろいろなものがあります。アパートの右には銀行があります。アパートの左にはセブンイレブンがあります。セブンイレブンのとなりに食堂があります。とても小さな食堂です。でも、とてもおいしいです。ですから、いつもお客さんがたくさんいます。ブラウンさんはその食堂のカレーライスが大好きです。

アパートの前には広い道があります。道の向こう側に喫茶店があります。名前は「ロマンス」です。「ロマンス」にはウエートレスが3人います。ウエートレスの山本さゆりさんはブラウンさんのいい友だちです。「ロマンス」の上にパブがあります。

ブラウンさんのアパートの近所にはスーパーが4軒あります。ブラウンさんは「ラッキーマート」が好きです。このスーパーは郵便局と映画館の間にあります。小さなスーパーです。とても安いです。

スーパーの後ろに小さな公園があります。

ブラウンさんは中野が大好きです。

中野 *Nakano (a place in Tokyo)*
から *from*
まで *(up) to*
中野ハイツ *Nakano Heights (name of an apartment building)*
3階建て *three-story (building)*

いろいろ(な) *various* / もの *things*
でも *however, but*

おいしい *delicious* / ですから *therefore*
いつも *always* / お客さん *customer*

広い *wide*

パブ *pub*

安い *inexpensive, cheap*

After You Finish Reading

Answer these questions in English.

1. How long does it take to go from Shinjuku to Nakano by electric train?
2. How many minutes does it take to walk from Nakano Station to Linda's apartment?
3. How many floors does Linda's apartment building have?
4. What is to the left of Linda's apartment?
5. What is to the left of that?
6. Why does the small restaurant have many customers?
7. What does Linda like to eat there?
8. What is across the street from the apartment?
9. Where is the pub?
10. How many supermarkets are there in Linda's neighborhood?
11. Where is Lucky Mart?
12. What is behind Lucky Mart?

Fill in the blanks.

1. ブラウンさんのアパートから東京大学まで地下鉄で(　　)ぐらいです。
2. ブラウンさんのアパートは「中野ハイツ」の(　　)にあります。
3. アパートの(　　)にはいろいろなものがあります。
4. アパートの(　　)には銀行があります。
5. セブンイレブンのとなりの小さな食堂はとても(　　)です。
6. アパートの(　　)に広い道があります。
7. 「ロマンス」にはウエートレスが(　　)います。
8. 「ロマンス」の(　　)にパブがあります。
9. 「ラッキーマート」は郵便局と映画館の(　　)にあります。
10. 公園は「ラッキーマート」の(　　)にあります。

Writing 1

Imagine you live in the apartment marked with ● on the map below. Write a paragraph describing your neighborhood. Start with わたしのアパートのとなりにスーパーがあります.

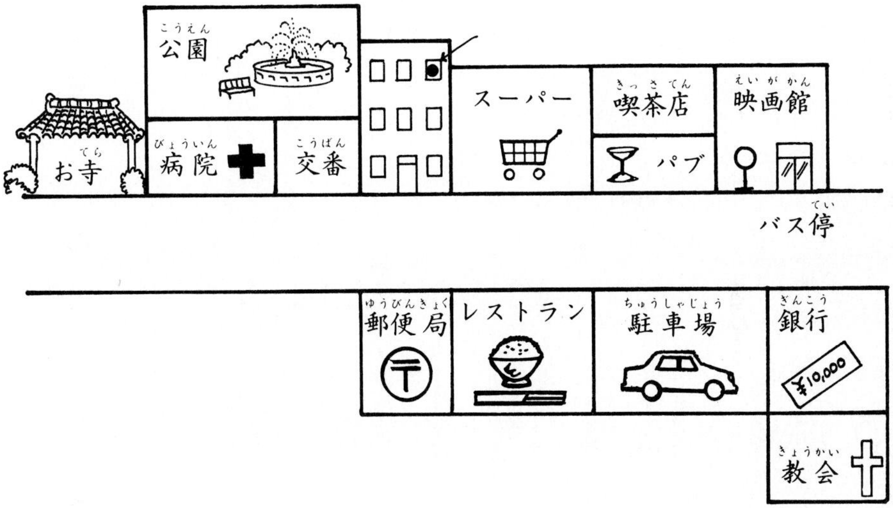

Reading 2　林さんのふるさと

| ふるさと hometown

Before You Read

Pair up with a classmate. Discuss which of the following you can find in large cities, in very small towns, or in both.

1. 電車の駅
2. 地下鉄の駅
3. 大学
4. バス停
5. 病院
6. 映画館
7. ホテル
8. 銀行
9. 喫茶店
10. デパート
11. スーパー
12. レストラン
13. 交番

What is the counter for each of the following?

1. 人
2. ベンチ
3. 家
4. 犬
5. 道

Now Read It!

This passage is a description of Mr. Hayashi's hometown village. What things listed in the first prereading activity can be found in his hometown? (Some may not be mentioned.)

九州の小さい村：山の向こうに大きい町があります。

カワムラさんのクラスメートの林さんは九州の小さい村の出身です。人口は八百人ぐらいです。家が百五十軒あります。とても小さい村です。病院はありません。ホテルもありません。デパートもありません。レストランもありません。

村は九州の真ん中にあります。村のまわりに高い山がたくさんあります。山の向こうに大きい町があります。村と町の間には道が一本あります。町からバスで一時間です。電車はありません。

村にバス停が一つあります。バス停は小さいスーパーの前にあります。このスーパーの前には犬が一匹いつもいます。スーパーの木下さんの犬です。

バス停の横に古いベンチが一つあります。ベンチの回りにいつも村の人がいます。スーパーのとなりに交番があります。交番の向かいに林さんの家があります。

九州 *Kyushu (large island in southern Japan)*

高い *high* / 山 *mountain*

向こう *over*

木下 *(family name)*

After You Finish Reading

1. What things listed in the first prereading activity exist in Mr. Hayashi's village?
2. Tell whether each of the following is true or false.
   a. Mr. Hayashi's village has a population of about 600.
   b. His village has 150 houses.
   c. His village is in the middle of Kyushu.
   d. His village is surrounded by mountains.
   e. There are two roads connecting his village and the next town.
   f. It takes two hours to travel by bus from his village to the next town.
   g. There is a bus stop in front of a small supermarket.
   h. A dog can always be found in front of a certain bench.
   i. The bench is new.
   j. There is a police box next to the supermarket.
   k. Mr. Hayashi's house is across the street from the police box.
3. Ask a classmate five questions in Japanese about the passage.

Writing 2

Write a short paragraph describing your neighborhood. Try to use あります and positional words.

Language Functions and Situations

Making Communication Work

Here are some useful techniques for making sure you're communicating effectively.

1. Ask someone to repeat something.

   A: スーパーは銀行(ぎんこう)の前(まえ)にあります。
   B: すみません。もう一度(いちど)ゆっくりお願(ねが)いします。
   A: スーパーは銀行の前にあります。

2. Check that you have understood.

   A: スーパーは銀行の前にあります。
   B: 銀行の前ですね。
   A: はい、そうです。

   A: 学生(がくせい)は26人(にん)います。
   B: 25人(にん)ですか。
   A: いいえ、26人です。

3. Say you have understood.

   A: ギブソンさんは図書館(としょかん)にいます。
   B: はい、わかりました。

4. Say you didn't understand.

   A: スーパーはあの映画館(えいがかん)のとなりにあります。
   B: すみません。わかりません。
   A: じゃ、つれていってあげましょう。(*Then, I'll take you there.*)

5. Show you are listening.

   A: あそこに銀行(ぎんこう)がありますね。
   B: ええ。
   A: そのとなりにレストランがありますね。
   B: はい、はい。
   A: 喫茶店(きっさてん)はあのレストランの上(うえ)にあります。

コミュニケーション・ノート

あいづち (*Yes, I'm following you . . .*)

One of the first things you notice when talking with Japanese people is that they frequently nod or interject はい, ええ, ああ, そうですか, うんうん, and so on after each phrase you utter. This is not a sign of impatience, boredom, or rudeness. Rather, they are engaging in the participatory style of communication that characterizes spoken Japanese. With these short interjections called あいづち, the listener is letting you know that he or she is still following you: "Yes, I'm following you, so please continue." (Even though はい [*yes*] is one of these **aizuchi,** here it doesn't necessarily mean *yes, I agree.*)

If the listener does *not* show any reaction a Japanese speaker may feel so uneasy that he will stop and ask わかりますか (*Do you understand?*) or start over at the beginning of the conversation, perhaps speaking more deliberately, on the assumption that the listener didn't understand. This happens frequently in telephone conversations; if the listener misses too many あいづち, the speaker will start over with もしもし (*Hello?*). Mastering the correct use of あいづち will go a long way toward enhancing your fluency.

Showing Location on a Map

道で

A: すみません。赤坂ホテルはどこですか。

B: 赤坂ホテルですか。ここに地図がありますから、見てください。

A: どうもすみません。

B: 今ここにいます。赤坂ホテルはここです。
となりに映画館と銀行があります。大きな白いビルです。

A: ここから何分ぐらいですか。

B: そうですね。10分ぐらいですね。

A: どうもありがとうございました。

B: どういたしまして。

On the street A: Excuse me. Where is Akasaka Hotel? B: Akasaka Hotel? Here is a map, so please take a look. A: Thank you for taking the trouble. B: (pointing to a spot on the map) We are here (now). (pointing to a different spot) Akasaka Hotel is here. Next to it are a movie theater and a bank. It is a large, white building. A: Approximately how many minutes is it from here? B: Let me see . . . it's about ten minutes. A: Thank you very much. B: You're welcome.

Role Play

Use the map below to practice showing location or giving directions to a classmate. Assume that you are standing in front of the station. Try to use some of the phrases you learned in **Making Communication Work**. Use your imagination to describe the building and how long it takes to get there.

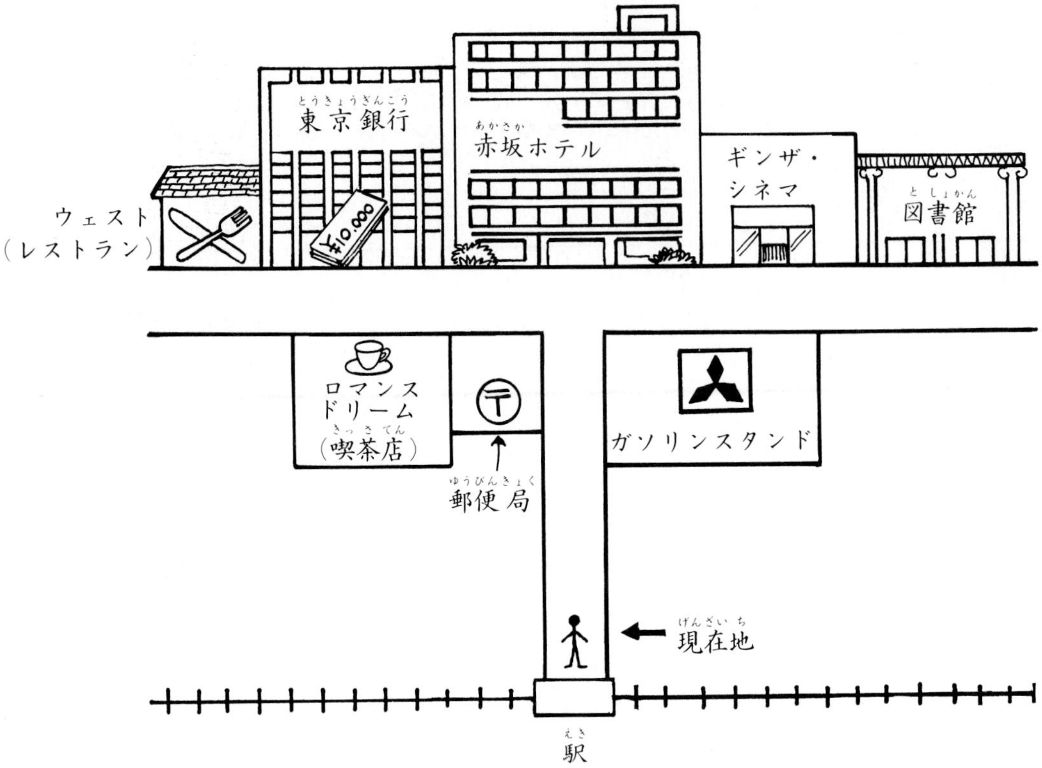

Listening Comprehension

While listening to your instructor, draw the mentioned items at the appropriate places in the picture.

3 Everyday Life

第三章

日常生活 (にちじょうせいかつ)

今日の晩ごはんはすきやきです。

OBJECTIVES

Topics

Schedules
Daily activities
Weekends and holidays

Grammar

11. Basic structure of Japanese verbs
12. The nonpast, polite form of verbs
13. The past, polite form of verbs
14. Particles showing grammatical relationships
15. Making suggestions: ～ましょう
16. Conjoining nouns: と and や

Reading and Writing

Daily activities
Linda Brown's weekend

Language Functions and Situations

Making a phone call
Extending an invitation

Vocabulary and Oral Activities

Schedules

Vocabulary : Days and Times of Day

今日	きょう	today
明日	あした	tomorrow
昨日	きのう	yesterday
あさって		the day after tomorrow
おととい		the day before yesterday
今朝	けさ	this morning
今日の午後	きょうのごご	this afternoon
今晩	こんばん	tonight

Review: 午前(ごぜん)、午後(ごご)、朝(あさ)、昼(ひる)、夕方(ゆうがた)、夜(よる)

アクティビティー 1

ダイアログ：いつも忙(いそが)しいですね。(*You are always busy.*)

ブラウン：三村(みむら)さん、明日(あした)の午後(ごご)はひまですか。
三村：残念(ざんねん)ですが、アルバイトがあります。
ブラウン：じゃあ、あさっての午後はどうですか。
三村：ううん。あさってはクラブのミーティングがあります。
ブラウン：三村さんはいつも忙しいですね。

Now practice the dialogue substituting your own schedule below.

BROWN: Mr. Mimura, are you free tomorrow afternoon? MIMURA: I'm sorry, but I have a part-time job. BROWN:Then, how about the morning of the day after tomorrow? MIMURA: Well, I have a club meeting the day after tomorrow. BROWN: You are always busy, aren't you?

コミュニケーション・ノート

Asking If Someone Has Free Time

These are common ways to ask if someone has free time and some ways to respond to the questions.

明日(あした)、ひまですか。
Are you free tomorrow?
ええ、ひまですが…
Yes, I'm free, but . . . (what do you have in mind?)
ちょっと用事(ようじ)があります。
I have some things to attend to.

明日、時間(じかん)がありますか。
Do you have any (free) time tomorrow?
はい、ありますよ。
Yes, I do.

ちょっと忙(いそが)しいです。
I'm (a bit) busy.
明日、忙しいですか。
Are you busy tomorrow?
ええ、ちょっと…
Yes, (sorry, but I'm) a bit (busy).
いいえ、ひまですよ。
No, I have no plans. (lit., I'm free.)

文化ノート

Part-Time Jobs for College Students

In Japanese, part-time jobs are commonly called アルバイト, or バイト for short, from the German word *arbeit* meaning *work*. Part- time workers are called アルバイター, or recently パートタイマー (from English *part-time*). Many Japanese college students have part-time jobs, most commonly as tutors (家庭教師[かていきょうし]) for elementary and secondary school children. Others work as waiters, waitresses, delivery workers, or shop clerks. Some students work part-time to earn tuition and living expenses; others earn pocket money for leisure activities. (The majority of college students in Japan are supported by their parents.) The student affairs office of any university has a bulletin board posting job opportunities, but the most popular sources of information are the daily and weekly magazines devoted to part-time job listings, such as とらばーゆ and 求人(きゅうじん)パートバイト情報(じょうほう).

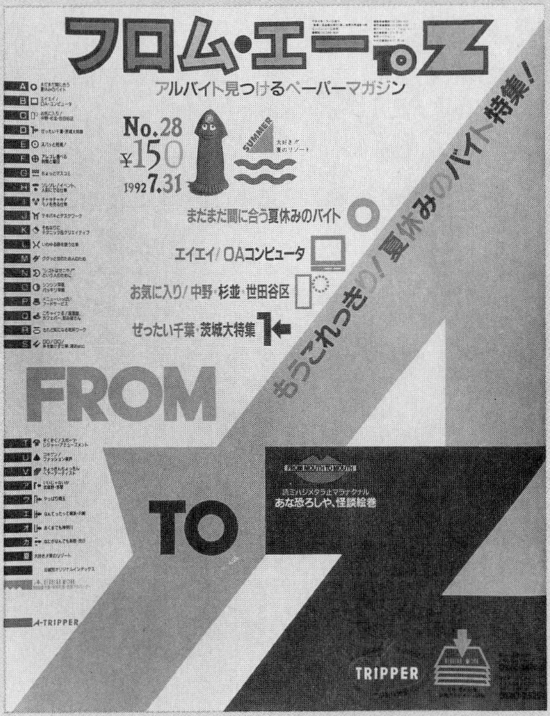

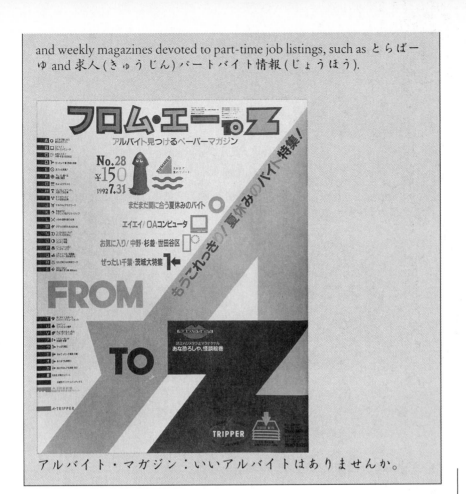

アルバイト・マガジン：いいアルバイトはありませんか。

Note that from the second through the tenth, Japanese numbers are used and that the first, fourteenth, twentieth, and twenty-fourth are irregular.

Vocabulary : Days of the Month

一日	ついたち	the first
二日	ふつか	the second
三日	みっか	the third
四日	よっか	the fourth
五日	いつか	the fifth
六日	むいか	the sixth
七日	なのか	the seventh
八日	ようか	the eighth
九日	ここのか	the ninth
十日	とおか	the tenth
十一日	じゅういちにち	the eleventh
十二日	じゅうににち	the twelfth
十三日	じゅうさんにち	the thirteenth
十四日	じゅうよっか	the fourteenth
十五日	じゅうごにち	the fifteenth
十六日	じゅうろくにち	the sixteenth
十七日	じゅうしちにち	the seventeenth
十八日	じゅうはちにち	the eighteenth
十九日	じゅうくにち	the nineteenth
二十日	はつか	the twentieth
二十四日	にじゅうよっか	the twenty-fourth

アクティビティー　2

ダイアログ：何日ですか。(*What is the date?*)

林：ギブソンさん、来週の金曜日はひまですか。
ギブソン：来週の金曜日…何日ですか。
林：ええと、14日です。
ギブソン：残念ですが、試験があります。

Practice this dialogue based on the following schedule.

January

S	M	T	W	Th	F	S
						1
ski club 2	3	4	today 5	part-time job 6	7	8
9	10	11	12	part-time job 13	exam 14	party 15
ski club 16	17	exam 18	19	part-time job 20	21	22
23	24	25	exam 26	part-time job 27	28	29
30	31					

Vocabulary : Weeks, Months, and Years.

今週	こんしゅう	this week
来週	らいしゅう	next week
先週	せんしゅう	last week
今月	こんげつ	this month
来月	らいげつ	next month
先月	せんげつ	last month
今年	ことし	this year
来年	らいねん	next year
去年	きょねん	last year
昨年	さくねん	last year

何日	なんにち	what day
何月	なんがつ	what month
何年	なんねん	what year
何曜日	なんようび	what day of the week
何年何月何日ですか。		What is the date (*lit., year, month, and day*)?

去年 sounds more informal than 昨年.

HAYASHI: Ms. Gibson, are you free next Friday? GIBSON: Next Friday . . . What is the date? HAYASHI: Uh . . . it is the fourteenth. GIBSON: I'm sorry, but I have an exam.

年号(ねんごう)

Japanese use both the Western system of identifying the year according to the Christian era as well as the Japanese system, which is based on the reigns of emperors. When following the Western system, Japanese write the year 1993 as numerals (1993年) or in **kanji** (千九百九十三年) and read it as the number 1,993. Although the Western calendar of months and days is standard in Japan, the Japanese system of identifying the year (borrowed from China and begun in 701 A.D.) remains prevalent even today. Since 1868, that system entails counting the years anew, from one, with the beginning of the reign of each new emperor. Emperor Heisei (平成天皇(へいせいてんのう)) ascended the throne in early 1989 of the Western calendar, so that year is called 平成一年(へいせいいちねん) or 平成元年(へいせいがんねん)(**Heisei** Year 1). 平成 is the 年号(ねんごう: era name). When the current emperor's son takes over the throne, a new 年号 will be created for him, and the count will start over again at one. Here are the 年号 of the recent past.

明治(1868–1912)	**Meiji** era, years 1–45
大正 (1912–26)	**Taisho** era, years 1–15
昭和(1926–89)	**Showa** era, years 1 –64

The names of eras are also used to classify generations of people who share common experience. Many forms and documents require you to fill in the year in the Japanese system, so it is important for you to know the year of your birth according to that system.

昭和49年生まれです。
*I was born in **Showa** (year) 49.*
昭和49年5月8日生まれです。
*I was born on May 8, **Showa**(year) 49.*
1974年5月8日生まれです。
I was born on May 8, 1974.
今日は1993年12月3日です。
Today is December 3rd, 1993.
今日は平成4年12月3日です。
*Today is December 3rd, **Heisei** (year) 4.*

Note that in Japanese dates are expressed in the order year-month-day whether the Western or Japanese system is used.

Review the words for months and days of the week.

アクティビティー 3

来週の水曜日は何日ですか。(*What day is next Wednesday?*)

Ask your partner the following questions.

1. 来週の水曜日は何日ですか。
2. 来週の月曜日は何日ですか。
3. 来月の三日は何曜日ですか。
4. 来月は何月ですか。
5. 来月の十四日は何曜日ですか。
6. 来週の金曜日は何月何日ですか。
7. 誕生日(*birthday*)は何月何日ですか。
8. 何年生まれですか。(*What year were you born in?*)

アクティビティー 4

誕生日は何月何日ですか。(*What day is your birthday?*)

Walk around the classroom and ask your classmates when their birthdays are. Then, ask them to sign on the appropriate blank line. Can you collect twelve signatures, one for each month?

ここにサインしてください。
Please sign here.

[例] S1：誕生日は何月何日ですか。
S2：四月一日です。
S1：ここにサインしてください。

四月一日 *Mary Smith*

	BIRTHDAY	SIGNATURE
一月	__________	__________
二月	__________	__________
三月	__________	__________
四月	__________	__________
五月	__________	__________
六月	__________	__________
七月	__________	__________
八月	__________	__________

	BIRTHDAY	SIGNATURE
九月		
十月		
十一月		
十二月		

Daily Activities

Vocabulary: Everyday Activities 1

夕ごはんを食べる	ゆうごはんをたべる	to eat dinner, supper
出かける	でかける	to step out, to leave for
買い物に出かける	かいものにでかける	to go out shopping

Review: 朝(あさ)ごはん(昼(ひる)ごはん、晩(ばん)ごはん)を食(た)べる、テレビを見(み)る、コーヒーを飲(の)む、仕事(しごと)をする

晩ごはん, which you studied in **Getting Started,** and 夕ごはん are identical in meaning.

1. 起(お)きる

2. 寝(ね)る

3. 新聞(しんぶん)を読(よ)む

4. 昼(ひる)ごはんを食(た)べる

5. お茶(ちゃ)を飲(の)む

6. 勉強(べんきょう)する

㊙ Study Grammar 11 and 12.

アクティビティー 5

ダイアログ：毎日何時に起きますか。(*What time do you get up every day?*)

カワムラさんと町田さんが、話しています。

カワムラ：町田さんは、毎日何時に起きますか。
町田：五時です。
カワムラ：わあ、はやいですね。
町田：ええ、五時半から六時までジョギングをします。

コミュニケーション・ノート

Expressions of Surprise

Here are some common ways to express surprise.

わあ。	*Wow!*
本当(ですか)。	*Really? (lit., Is that true?)*
うそ。	*You're kidding. (lit., That's a lie.) (frequently used by young women; very colloquial)*
まさか。	*Impossible!, That can't be!, No way!*
何ですって。	*What! (lit., What did you say?)*
信じられない。	*Incredible! (lit., I can't believe it.)*

アクティビティー 6

カワムラさんのスケジュール (*Mr. Kawamura's schedule*)

Use the table to answer the questions that follow it.

JOHN KAWAMURA'S DAILY SCHEDULE

6:00	get up
6:30	breakfast
8:30	Japanese class
12:00	lunch

Mr. Kawamura and Ms. Machida are talking KAWAMURA: What time do you get up every day, (Ms. Machida)? MACHIDA: I get up at five. KAWAMURA: Wow, that's early! MACHIDA: Yes, I go jogging from five-thirty to six.

1:30	study at the library
3:00	coffee break
4:00	return home
until 6:00	read (books)
6:15	dinner
7:00	watch TV
9:00	study Japanese
11:45	go to bed

1. カワムラさんは午前何時に起きますか。
2. 6時半に何をしますか。
3. 何時に昼ごはんを食べますか。
4. 午後1時半に何をしますか。
5. 何時にコーヒーを飲みますか。
6. 何時に家へ帰りますか。
7. 何時に夕ごはんを食べますか。
8. 午後7時から9時まで何をしますか。
9. 午後9時から何を勉強しますか。
10. カワムラさんは何時に寝ますか。
11. カワムラさんは何時間 (*how many hours*) ぐらい寝ますか。

アクティビティー 7

ダイアログ：そのあとは。(*What about after that?*)

林さんとギブソンさんが話しています。

林：ギブソンさん、今日の午後は忙しいですか。

ギブソン：ええ、とても。1時に日本語のクラスがあります。それから、図書館で勉強します。

林：じゃあ、そのあとは。

ギブソン：そのあと、友だちに会います。

林：そうですか。

The verb 会う *to meet with, see* (a person) takes the particle に or と to indicate the person met.

Describe Mr. Kawamura's schedule from **Activity 6** using the conjunctions presented in the **Communication Note**.

Mr. Hayashi and Ms. Gibson are talking HAYASHI: Ms. Gibson, are you busy this afternoon? GIBSON: Yes, very. I have a Japanese class at one o'clock. And then I'm going to study at the library. HAYASHI: Well, how about after that? GIBSON: After that, I'm meeting a friend. HAYASHI: I see.

コミュニケーション・ノート

Connecting Sequential Actions

Here are some conjunctions commonly used to connect sentences expressing sequential actions or events.

それから
and then . . . (lit., from that)
そして
and (then) . . . (lit., so doing)
そのあと
after that . . .

七時(じ)に朝(あさ)ごはんを食(た)べます。それから、新聞(しんぶん)を読(よ)みます。
I eat breakfast at 7:00. And then I read the newspaper.

図書館(としょかん)に行(い)きました。そして、本を読(よ)みました。
I went to the library. And (then) I read some books.

レストランで夕（ゆう）ごはんを食べます。そのあと、映画(えいが)を見（み）ます。それから、ディスコへ行きます。
I'll eat dinner at a restaurant. After that, I'll see a movie. And then, I'll go to a disco.

㊝ Study Grammar 13 and 14.

アクティビティー 8

あなたのスケジュールは。 (*What about your schedule?*)

Working in a pair, ask your partner questions about his or her daily schedule. Use the answers you get to write a schedule.

[例] S1：何時(なんじ)に起(お)きますか。
S2：_____時に起きます。
S1：それから、何をしますか。
S2：_____。

Vocabulary: Everyday Activities 2

シャワーを浴びる	シャワーをあびる	to take a shower
うちを出る	うちをでる	to leave home
(お)風呂に入る	(お)ふろにはいる	to take (*lit., enter*) a bath
歯を磨く	はをみがく	to brush one's teeth
顔を洗う	かおをあらう	to wash one's face
服を着る	ふくをきる	to put on clothes

…に乗る	…にのる	to ride or get on . . . (*a vehicle—train, bus, car, etc.*)
働く	はたらく	to work
休む	やすむ	to take a rest, to take time off

Review: 電話(を)する、買い物(を)する

寝坊する

料理する

音楽を聞く

運動する

アクティビティー 9

ダイアログ：寝坊しました。(*I overslept.*)

ブラウンさんと林さんが話しています。

ブラウン：今日は日本文化のクラスへ行きましたか。
林：ええ。ブラウンさん、クラスにいませんでしたね。
ブラウン：ええ、今朝、寝坊しました。
林：そうですか。

Ms. Brown and Mr. Hayashi are talking BROWN: Did you go to Japanese culture class today? HAYASHI: Yes. You weren't in class, were you? BROWN: No. I overslept this morning. HAYASHI: I see.

アクティビティー 10

林(はやし)さんのスケジュール (*Mr. Hayashi's schedule*)

Here is what Mr. Hayashi did yesterday. Describe his day in Japanese, or ask your classmates about his schedule.

Useful vocabulary: 法学(ほうがく) (*study of*) *law*

6:00	got up	1:00	studied at the library
6:15	took a shower	3:00	exercised
6:30	drank coffee	5:00	returned home
6:35	read a newspaper	6:00	cooked dinner
6:45	ate breakfast	7:30	ate dinner
7:15	watched TV	8:30	called a friend
8:00	left home	9:00	listened to the stereo
9:00	went to his Japanese culture class	9:30	studied law
10:30	went to his law class	10:30	took a bath
12:00	ate lunch with classmates	11:00	went to bed

アクティビティー 11

昨日(きのう)しましたか。(*Did you do that yesterday?*)

Ask a classmate if he or she did the following yesterday. If the answer is yes, ask related questions such as *What time did you do that?*

1. oversleep
2. take a shower
3. drink tea
4. exercise
5. read a newspaper
6. call a friend
7. listen to music
8. take a bath
9. go to a library
10. watch TV

アクティビティー 12

ダイアログ：一日(いちにち)に三回磨(さんかいみが)きます。(*I brush my teeth three times a day.*)

林(はやし)さんとブラウンさんが話しています。

林：ブラウンさんは歯(は)がきれいですね。
ブラウン：一日に三回磨きます。林さんは。

Mr. Hayashi and Ms. Brown are talking HAYASHI: Ms. Brown, you have such nice teeth (*lit., your teeth are pretty, aren't they*). BROWN: I brush them three times a day. How about you? HAYASHI: I don't brush them much. BROWN: Do you mean (*lit., is it*) once a day? HAYASHI: No, once a week. BROWN: You're kidding!

林：あまり磨きません。
ブラウン：一日に一回ですか。
林：いいえ、一週間（いっしゅうかん）に一回です。
ブラウン：うそ！

Vocabulary: Expressions of Frequency

〜回	〜かい	. . . times (*counter for occurrences*)
AにB回		B times per A
一日に何回	いちにちになんかい	how many times a day
一週間に二回	いっしゅうかんににかい	two times a week
一ヶ月に四回	いっかげつによんかい	four times a month
毎日	まいにち	every day
毎週	まいしゅう	every week
毎月	まいつき	every month
毎朝	まいあさ	every morning
毎晩	まいばん	every night
いつも		all the time
よく		often, a lot
時々	ときどき	sometimes
たまに		once in a while
あまり		(*with negative*) not very much, not very often
ほとんど		(*with negative*) hardly, almost never
全然	ぜんぜん	(*with negative*) not at all

…週間 and …ヶ月 are counters for the duration of weeks and months, respectively.

The kanji 々 is used to repeat the preceding kanji.

文法ノート

Adverbs Used in Negative Sentences

Some adverbs are used primarily in negative sentences. Two examples are あまり (*not very much, not very often*) and 全然（ぜんぜん）(*not at all*).

わたしはあまり映画（えいが）へ行きません。
I don't go to the movies very often.
わたしの父（ちち）はぜんぜんテレビを見ません。
My father doesn't watch TV at all.

ほとんど can be used in affirmative or negative sentences, but its meaning changes in these different contexts. In the affirmative it means *almost*, while in the negative it means *almost never* or *hardly ever*.

山田(やまだ)さんはほとんど毎日(まいにち)シャワーを浴(あ)びます。
Mr. Yamada takes a shower almost every day.
山田さんはほとんどお風呂(ふろ)に入(はい)りません。
Mr. Yamada hardly ever takes a bath.

Vocabulary Library

Everyday Activities 3

髪をとかす	かみをとかす	to comb one's hair
ひげをそる		to shave one's facial hair (*lit., beard*)
服を脱ぐ	ふくをぬぐ	to take off clothes
服を着替える	ふくをきがえる	to change clothes
運転する	うんてんする	to drive (*vehicles*)
散歩する	さんぽする	to take a walk, stroll
洗濯(を)する	せんたく(を)する	to do laundry
掃除(を)する	そうじ(を)する	to clean (*house, a room, etc.*)
眠る	ねむる	to sleep

アクティビティー 13

よくしますか。(*Do you do that often?*)

Tell how often you do the following, selecting from the following degrees of frequency (ordered from most frequent to least frequent).

1 = 毎日(まいにち)	3 = よく	5 = あまりしない
2 = ほとんど毎日	4 = 時々(ときどき)	6 = 全然(ぜんぜん)しない

a. ______ 歯(は)を磨(みが)く
b. ______ シャワーを浴(あ)びる
c. ______ お風呂(ふろ)に入(はい)る
d. ______ 朝(あさ)ごはんを食(た)べる
e. ______ コーヒーを飲(の)む
f. ______ 部屋(へや)(*room*)を掃除(そうじ)する
g. ______ 料理(りょうり)をする
h. ______ 買(か)い物(もの)をする
i. ______ 新聞(しんぶん)を読(よ)む
j. ______ 映画(えいが)を見(み)る
k. ______ ラジオを聞(き)く
l. ______ テレビを見(み)る
m. ______ お酒(さけ)を飲(の)む
n. ______ 運動(うんどう)する
o. ______ デートをする
p. ______ 勉強(べんきょう)する
q. ______ 電話(でんわ)する

Weekends and Holidays

Vocabulary: Holidays and Vacations

平日	へいじつ	weekday
週末	しゅうまつ	weekend
休みの日	やすみのひ	day off, holiday
休む	やすむ	to take time off, take a rest
祝日	しゅくじつ	national holiday
夏休み	なつやすみ	summer vacation
冬休み	ふゆやすみ	winter vacation
休暇	きゅうか	vacation
休暇を取る	きゅうかをとる	to take a vacation

アクティビティー 14

週末はひまです。(*I am free on weekends.*)

How do you spend your weekends? Did you do any of these activities last weekend?

1. 部屋を掃除する

2. 遅くまでテレビを見る

3. デートをする

4. 働く

5. 10時まで寝る
6. 勉強する
7. 映画を見る(*see a movie*)
8. 図書館に行く(*go to the library*)
9. 散歩する(*go on a walk*)
10. スポーツをする
11. 洗濯する(*do laundry*)
12. 何もしない(*not do anything*)

アクティビティー　15

平日と週末 (*Weekdays and weekends*)

Here are the weekday and weekend schedules of Mr. Takada, Linda Brown's next-door neighbor. Answer the following questions.

Useful vocabulary: ブランチ *brunch;* 会社 *company*

月曜日～金曜日＝平日

6:00	get up
6:05	take a shower
6:15	eat breakfast
6:45	leave home
7:00	get on a bus
8:00	start work
9:00	attend a meeting
10:30	drink coffee
12:00	eat lunch
1:00	drink coffee
2:00	meet with clients
4:45	leave the company
6:00	arrive home
6:30	cook dinner
7:30	eat dinner
8:00	watch TV
10:00	take a bath
11:00	go to bed

土曜日～日曜日＝週末

9:00	get up
9:30	drink coffee
9:45	read the newspaper
10:15	watch TV
11:00	eat brunch
12:00	clean the apartment
1:00	go shopping
2:30	do laundry
5:00	go to a restaurant
7:00	listen to the stereo
8:00	read a book
9:30	eat a snack
11:00	watch TV
12:30	go to bed

1. 高田さんは、平日、何時に起きますか。週末、何時に起きますか。
2. 高田さんは、週末、会社へ行きますか。
3. 高田さんは、平日、何時と何時にコーヒーを飲みますか。
   高田さんは、週末、何時にコーヒーを飲みますか。
4. 高田さんは、平日、洗濯をしますか。
5. 高田さんは、週末、朝ごはんを食べますか。
6. 高田さんは、平日も週末もテレビを見ますか。
7. 高田さんは、平日も週末も夕ごはんを作りますか。(作る *make, cook*)

Make your own questions to ask your classmates.

文法ノート

Connecting Disjunctive Sentences

Disjunctive conjunctions are words used to link two sentences that express contrasting ideas. A disjunctive conjunction frequently used in conversation is でも (*but, even so*). This conjunction begins the second sentence of the contrasting pair.

平日(へいじつ)、午前(ごぜん)6時(じ)に起(お)きます。でも、週末(しゅうまつ)、午前(ごぜん)10時に起きます。
I get up at 6:00 A.M. on weekdays. But I get up at 10:00 A.M. on weekends.

In written discourse, the conjunction しかし (*however*) is often used.

平日は会社(かいしゃ)へ行(い)く。しかし、週末は行かない。
I go to the office (lit., company) on weekdays. However, I don't go there on weekends.

A disjunctive conjunction is a word joining two contrasting independent clauses (that is, complete sentences) into a single compound sentence. One used very frequently in conversation is が (*but*). Unlike the English position of *but* at the beginning of the second clause, が attaches to the end of the first clause; the pause in speech and the comma in writing fall *after* が.

平日は午前6時に起きますが、週末は午前10時に起きます。
I get up at 6:00 A.M. on weekdays, but I get up at 10:00 A.M. on weekends.

Japanese often end sentences with this が and a trailing intonation, expecting the listener to know what the rest of the compound sentence would be from context.

すみませんが…
I'm sorry, but . . . (we don't have any; I can't do it this time; etc.)
Excuse me, but . . . (could you help me?; I have a question; etc.)

アクティビティー 16

平日(へいじつ)と週末(しゅうまつ) (*Weekdays and weekends*)

Add a contrasting clause to complete the following sentences comparing weekday and weekend schedules.

1. 平日の朝(あさ)はシャワーを浴(あ)びます。でも、＿＿
2. 週末はテニスをしますが、＿＿
3. 先週(せんしゅう)の平日は毎日勉強(まいにちべんきょう)しました。でも、＿＿

4. 平日は毎日図書館へ行きます。でも、＿＿
5. 平日はカフェテリアで昼ごはんを食べますが、＿＿
6. 平日は夜新聞を読みます。でも、＿＿
7. 平日は早く(*early*)寝ますが、＿＿

Useful Vocabulary: 遅く *late* (adverb)

Now recast the sentences to describe the differences between your weekday and weekend activities.

文化ノート

国民の祝日 ***National Holidays***

The following are national holidays in Japan.

1月1日	元日	*New Year's Day*
1月15日	成人の日	*Coming-of-Age Day*
2月11日	建国記念の日	*National Foundation Day*
3月21日 (variable)	春分の日	*Vernal Equinox Day*
4月29日	緑の日	*Greenery Day*
5月3日	憲法記念日	*Constitution Day*
5月5日	子供の日	*Children's Day*
9月15日	敬老の日	*Respect-for-the-Aged Day*
9月23日 (variable)	秋分の日	*Autumnal Equinox Day*
10月10日	体育の日	*Health-Sports Day*
11月3日	文化の日	*Culture Day*
11月23日	勤労感謝の日	*Labor Thanksgiving Day*
12月23日	天皇誕生日	*Emperor's Birthday*

成人の日：わたしたちは二十歳です。

成人の日—on this holiday, the Japanese celebrate those who turned 20 years old in the preceding year. You are considered an adult in Japan when you reach 20 years of age. (That is also the age of legal majority, when you can begin voting and drinking alcohol.)

憲法記念日 is the day commemorating the promulgation of the Constitution that was drafted after World War II.

文化の日 is the day celebrating. the development of culture and the proclamation of the new Constitution. On this day, those who have contributed to the enhancement of culture, technology, and community are awarded medals.

勉 Study Grammar 15.

アクティビティー 17

ダイアログ：何を見(み)ましょうか。(*What shall we see?*)

林(はやし)さんとギブソンさんが話しています。

林：ギブソンさん、今週(こんしゅう)の土曜日(どようび)、一緒(いっしょ)に映画(えいが)を見ませんか。
ギブソン：ええ。何を見ましょうか。
林：カラテ・キッドはどうですか。
ギブソン：いいですね。

Practice the preceding dialogue, substituting the following activities for the first and second underlined phrases. (Use the appropriate form.) Make up your own substitution for the third underlined phrase.

Useful Words: デパート *department store*; プール *swimming pool*

1. 買(か)い物(もの)に行(い)く、どこへ行く
2. ジョギングをする、どこでする
3. 夕(ゆう)ごはんを食(た)べる、どこで食べる
4. ドライブする (*to go on a drive*)、どこへ行く
5. 泳(およ)ぐ (*to swim*)、どこで泳ぐ

コミュニケーション・ノート

Making a Suggestion

In the preceding dialogue, the phrase …はどうですか is used to make a suggestion.

東急(とうきゅう)デパートはどうですか。
How about Tookyuu Department Store? (e.g. as a possible place to do shopping)
大学のプールはどうですか。
How about the college swimming pool? (e.g. as a possible place to swim)

The phrase …はいかがですか is a more formal equivalent of …はどうですか. A shop clerk at a department store might say the following while showing a pen to a customer.

このペンはいかがですか。
How about this pen? (as the one to buy)

Mr. Hayashi and Ms. Gibson are talking HAYASHI: Ms. Gibson, would you like to (*lit., won't you*) see a movie together this Saturday? GIBSON: Yes, what shall we see? HAYASHI: How about Karate Kid? GIBSON: That sounds good. (*lit., That's good.*)

アクティビティー 18

休(やす)みましょうか。(*Shall we take a rest?*)
Following the example, complete these conversations using 〜ましょう.

[例] 疲(つか)れましたね。(*I'm tired, aren't you?*) →
ええ、休みましょうか。(*Yes, shall we take a rest?*)

Useful Vocabulary: 食(た)べる、飲(の)む、家(いえ)に帰(かえ)る、図書館(としょかん)で勉強(べんきょう)する、先生(せんせい)に聞(き)く

1. おなかがすきましたね。(*I am hungry, aren't you?*)
2. のどがかわきましたね。(*I am thirsty, aren't you?*)
3. もう6時(じ)ですね。
4. ここはうるさいですね。(*It is noisy here, isn't it?*)
5. この問題(もんだい)、むずかしいですね。(*This question is difficult, isn't it?*)

アクティビティー 19

ダイアログ：ぼくが電話(でんわ)しましょう。(*I will make the phone call.*)

カワムラさんと林(はやし)さんが話しています。

カワムラ：今、何時(なんじ)ですか。
林：ええと、2時半(じはん)です。ブラウンさん、おそいですね。
カワムラ：ええ。ブラウンさんに電話しませんか。
林：ええ、ぼくが電話しましょう。
カワムラ：お願(ねが)いします。

Mr. Kawamura and Mr. Hayashi are talking KAWAMURA: What time is it now? HAYASHI: Uh, it's two thirty. Ms. Brown is late, isn't she? KAWAMURA: Yes, shouldn't we call her (*lit.*, Ms. Brown)? HAYASHI: Yes. I will make the call. KAWAMURA: Thank you. (*lit.*, Please do it for me.)

Grammar and Exercises

11. The Basic Structure of Japanese Verbs

11.1 In Chapter 2, you learned how to conjugate (change the form of) adjectives to form the negative (e.g., 大きい→大きくない). Japanese verbs also change form, or conjugate, to express a variety of meanings.

You have already studied several Japanese verbs, including 洗(あら)います [I] *wash,* 聞(き)きます [I] *listen,* 話(はな)します [I] *speak,* 立(た)ちます [I] *stand up,* 読(よ)みます [I] *read,* あります [*there*] *exists,* 泳(およ)ぎます [I] *swim,* 食(た)べます [I] *eat,* 寝(ね)ます [I] *go to bed* and 見(み)ます [I] *see, watch.* The verbs all end in ます because these are the ます forms of these verbs. In order to look up any of these verbs in a Japanese dictionary, you need to know the verb's dictionary form, which is listed in the following chart. Each dictionary form consists of two parts, a root and an ending.

DICTIONARY FORM	MEANING	ROOT	ENDING
Class 1 verbs			
洗う	to wash	洗	う
聞く	to listen	聞	く
話す	to speak	話	す
立つ	to stand up	立	つ
読む	to read	読	む
ある	to exist	あ	る
泳ぐ	to swim	泳	ぐ
Class 2 verbs			
食べる	to eat	食べ	る
寝る	to go to sleep	寝	る
見る	to see	見	る
着る	to wear	着	る

Notice the different endings between the two groupings of verbs. The ending of the first group is variable, while that of the second group is always る. In this textbook, the first group of verbs are called *Class 1* verbs, while the second group of verbs are called *Class 2* verbs. The simple (but not foolproof) rule for distinguishing between these two classes is this: if the dictionary form of a verb ends in a syllable from the i-column (い、き、し、ち、 etc.) or the e-column (え、け、せ、て、 etc.) of the **hiragana** syllabary ＋る, it is a Class 2 verb. Otherwise it is a Class 1 verb.

CLASS 2 VERBS

	-a	-i	-u	-e	-o	
食(た)				べ		＋る
				寝(ね)		＋る
		見(み)				＋る
		着(き)				＋る

The dictionary form of all Class 1 verbs ends in one of the syllables in the u-column of the **hiragana** syllabary. (Note that ある ends in る, but its root does not end in a syllable from the i-column or the e-column, so it is not a Class 2 verb.)

CLASS 1 VERBS

	-a	-i	-u	-e	-o	
洗(あら)			う			(あ row)
書(か)			く			(か row)
話(はな)			す			(さ row)
立(た)			つ			(た row)
読(よ)			む			(み row)
あ			る			(ら row)
泳(およ)			ぐ			(が row)

Class 1 and Class 2 verbs conjugate in different but regular ways.

In addition, there are two irregular verbs in Japanese: 来(く)る (*to come*) and する (*to do*). In this textbook these irregular verbs are called *Class 3* verbs. You will have to memorize the conjugation of these verbs individually. All compound verbs with する belong to Class 3: 勉強する(べんきょう) (*to study*), 運動(うんどう)する (*to exercise*), 電話(でんわ)する (*to call*), and so on.

Here are how some common verbs are classified.

You will learn more about these compound verbs with する (called nominal verbs) later on.

CLASS 1 VERBS		CLASS 2 VERBS		CLASS 3 VERBS	
洗う	to wash	食べる	to eat	する	to do
行く	to go	起きる	to get up	来る	to come
聞く	to listen	出(で)かける	to go out		
話す	to speak	出(で)る	to leave		
飲む	to drink	変(か)える	to change		
働(はたら)く	to work	見る	to see, watch		
休(やす)む	to take a rest	着る	to wear, put on		
乗(の)る	to ride				

11.2 The three primary meanings expressed in every Japanese verb form are tense, politeness, and affirmation/negation.

There are two basic tenses in Japanese: *past* and *nonpast*. The past tense is used to express past actions and events (*I played baseball, he remained in the hospital,* etc.). The nonpast tense is used to express present, habitual and future actions and events (*I get up at 6:00 every morning, I will go to school later, I'm going to study tomorrow*, etc).

Japanese verbs do not conjugate in terms of the person and number of the subject.

Japanese verbs also take different forms depending on the degree of politeness the speaker or writer wishes to show the listener or reader. The *plain form* is used, for example, when speakers address very familiar people on the same social level, such as close friends. It is also used in diaries and in newspaper articles. And as you will see later, verbs in certain positions in a sentence must be in the plain form. On the other hand, the *polite form* is used, for instance, to address people with whom one is not well acquainted or to speak not too intimately or personally with in-group people (such as one's superior). In addition, it is used to address most out-group people, such as a member of a client company. This form is also used in personal letters, TV news, and most public speeches. You have seen more use of polite forms than of plain forms in this textbook, because it is the appropriate speech register among adult speakers who are getting to know each other.

In Japanese, verbs take different endings depending on whether they are *affirmative* or *negative*.

In addition, different grammatical elements are added to the end of verb forms to express such meanings as ability and probability. The resultant forms consisting of verbs and grammatical elements also conjugate in terms of the three primary meanings.

11.3 The dictionary form of Japanese verbs is actually the *nonpast, plain, affirmative form*; for example, 書(か)く (*to write*) and 食(た)べる (*to eat*). When you look up a verb in the dictionary, this is the form you will find. The plain form can be considered a basis for conjugating the polite form.

The nonpast, plain, negative form is made as follows.

CLASS 1 VERBS

ROOT + the a-column **hiragana** corresponding to the dictionary form ending + ない

DICTIONARY FORM ROOT + ENDING	NONPAST, PLAIN, NEGATIVE FORM
書(か) + く	書(か) + か + ない
話(はな) + す	話(はな) + さ + ない
立(た) + つ	立(た) + た + ない
読(よ) + む	読(よ) + ま + ない
泳(およ) + ぐ	泳(およ) + が + ない

u-column	→	a-column
く	→	か
す	→	さ
つ	→	た
む	→	ま
ぐ	→	が

When the dictionary form ending of a Class 1 verb is う— for example, 洗う (*to wash*), 買う (*to buy*) —わ is inserted between the root and ない to form the nonpast, plain, negative.

DICTIONARY FORM ROOT + ENDING	NONPAST, PLAIN, NEGATIVE FORM
洗(あら) + う 買(か) + う	洗(あら) + わ + ない 買(か) + わ + ない

Although such verbs as 切る (*to cut*), 知る (*to know*), 帰る (*to go back*), 走る (*to run*), and 入る (*to enter*) look like Class 2 verbs and satisfy the (not foolproof) rule for identifying Class 2 verbs, they belong to Class 1 and conjugate as such. Thus, their nonpast, plain, negative form is made following the same rule presented above.

DICTIONARY FORM ROOT + ENDING	NONPAST, PLAIN, NEGATIVE FORM
切(き) + る 知(し) + る 帰(かえ) + る 走(はし) + る 入(はい) + る	切(き) + ら + ない 知(し) + ら + ない 帰(かえ) + ら + ない 走(はし) + ら + ない 入(はい) + ら + ない

Note that the nonpast, plain, negative form of ある (*to exist*) (see **Grammar 6,** Chapter 2) is simply ない. ない is an i-adjective representing negativity.

CLASS 2 VERBS

Root + ない

DICTIONARY FORM ROOT + ENDING	NONPAST, PLAIN, NEGATIVE FORM
食(た)べ + る 見(み) + る 着(き) + る	食(た)べ + ない 見(た) + ない 着(き) + ない

CLASS 3 VERBS

DICTIONARY FORM	NONPAST, PLAIN, NEGATIVE FORM
する 来(く)る	し + ない 来(こ) + ない

練習 1

Are these verbs Class 1, Class 2, or Class 3? Each is cited in its dictionary form.

ある *to exist*
いる *to exist*
できる *to be able to do*
歩(ある)く *to walk*
走(はし)る *to run*
踊(おど)る *to dance*
歌(うた)う *to sing*
泳(およ)ぐ *to swim*
待(ま)つ *to wait*
泣(な)く *to cry*
教(おし)える *to teach*
見(み)せる *to show*
使(つか)う *to use*
作(つく)る *to make*
笑(わら)う *to laugh*
休(やす)む *to take a rest*
料理(りょうり)する *to cook*
飛(と)ぶ *to fly*
考(かんが)える *to think*
会(あ)う *to meet*
住(す)む *to live*
わかる *to understand*
やめる *to quit*

練習 2

Write the nonpast, plain, negative form of these verbs. Use **hiragana** for **kanji** you have not yet studied.

起(お)きる *to get up*
食(た)べる *to eat*
みがく *to brush (teeth)*
洗(あら)う *to wash*
出(で)かける *to go out*
行(い)く *to go*
飲(の)む *to drink*
勉強(べんきょう)する *to study*
見(み)る *to see*
寝(ね)る *to go to bed*
着(き)る *to put on (clothes)*
浴(あ)びる *to take (a shower)*
入(はい)る *to enter*
言(い)う *to say*
歌(うた)う *to sing*
いる *to exist*
使(つか)う *to use*
話(はな)す *to speak*
乗(の)る *to ride*
働(はたら)く *to work*
休(やす)む *to rest*
眠(ねむ)る *to sleep*
会(あ)う *to meet*
洗濯(せんたく)する *to do laundry*
死(し)ぬ *to die*
とかす *to comb*

12. The Nonpast, Polite Form of Verbs

ブラウン：三村(みむら)さんは毎日何時(まいにちなんじ)に起(お)きますか。
三村：六時半(ろくじはん)に起(お)きます。
ブラウン：毎日朝(あさ)ごはんを食(た)べますか。
三村：いいえ、朝ごはんは食べません。
ブラウン：なぜですか。
三村：朝は時間(じかん)がありませんから…

チン：明日(あした)のパーティーに行(い)きますか。
町田：いいえ、行きません。
チン：なぜですか。
町田：夜(よる)、友だちが来(き)ますから…

ブラウン：あさっては何をしますか。
町田：あさっては何曜日(なんようび)ですか。
ブラウン：土曜日(どようび)です。
町田：土曜日ですか…何もしません。土曜日は家(いえ)で寝(ね)ます。

カワムラ：町田(まちだ)さんは大学へ何で来(き)ますか。
町田：バスで来ます。
カワムラ：何分(なんぷん)かかりますか。
町田：二十五分(ふん)ですね。

The nonpast, polite, affirmative and negative form of Class 1 and Class 2 verbs are made as follows.

CLASS 1 VERBS

Affirmative Root + i-column **hiragana** corresponding to the dictionary form ending + ます
Negative Root + i-column **hiragana** corresponding to the dictionary form ending + ません

BROWN: What time do you get up every day? MIMURA: I get up at six-thirty. BROWN: Do you eat breakfast every day? MIMURA: No, I don't eat breakfast. BROWN: Why not? MIMURA: Because I don't have time in the morning.

CHIN: Are you going to tomorrow's party? MACHIDA: No, I'm not going. CHIN Why not? MACHIDA: Because I have friends coming over (*lit., Because friends are coming*) *in the evening*.

BROWN: What are you doing the day after tomorrow? MACHIDA: What day of the week is it? BROWN: It's Saturday. MACHIDA: It's Saturday, is it . . . I'm not doing anything. I just sleep in on Saturdays. (*lit., I sleep at home on Saturdays.*)

KAWAMURA: How do you get (*lit., come*) to the university? MACHIDA: By bus. KAWAMURA: How many minutes does it take? MACHIDA: It takes (*lit., is*) twenty-five minutes.

DICTIONARY FORM ROOT+ENDING	AFFIRMATIVE FORM	NEGATIVE FORM
洗 + う	洗 + い + ます	洗 + い + ません
書 + く	書 + き + ます	書 + き + ません
話 + す	話 + し + ます	話 + し + ません
立 + つ	立 + ち + ます	立 + ち + ません
読 + む	読 + み + ます	読 + み + ません
あ + る	あ + り + ます	あ + り + ません
泳 + ぐ	泳 + ぎ + ます	泳 + ぎ + ません

u-column	→	i-column
く	→	き
す	→	し
つ	→	ち
む	→	み
る	→	り
ぐ	→	ぎ

CLASS 2 VERBS

Affirmative Root + ます
Negative Root + ません

DICTIONARY FORM ROOT + ENDING	AFFIRMATIVE FORM	NEGATIVE FORM
食 + べる	食べ + ます	食べ + ません
見 + る	見 + ます	見 + ません
着 + る	着 + ます	着 + ません

CLASS 3 VERBS

DICTIONARY FORM	AFFIRMATIVE FORM	NEGATIVE FORM
する	し + ます	し + ません
来る	来 + ます	来 + ません

The part preceding ます or ません in these conjunctions is called the *conjunctive form,* and it plays a key role in conjugating other forms of verbs. To summarize,

CLASS	CONJUNCTIVE FORM
Class 1	Root + the i-column *hiragana* corresponding to the dictionary form ending
Class 2	= Root
Class 3	(irregular) する→し 来る→来(き)

In other words, the nonpast, polite, affirmative and negative forms of verbs are formed by adding ます and ません to the conjunctive form.

言語ノート

送り仮名(おくりがな)

Most verb forms, whether they are dictionary form or conjugated form, are transcribed with a combination of **kanji** and **hiragana**. For example,

書く、書かない、書きます、書きません
見る、見ない、見ます、見ません
来る、来ない、来ます、来ません

The **kanji** part, in most cases, corresponds to the root or a part of the root, while the **hiragana** part corresponds to the conjugated ending. The **hiragana** part is called 送り仮名 (*the **kana** [syllabary] that follows*). Some adjectives are also written with a combination of **kanji** and 送り仮名 as well: 大きい、大きくない、静かだ、静かでした.

練習　1

Write the nonpast, formal, affirmative and negative forms of these verbs.

1.	起(お)きる	*to get up*	12.	会(あ)う	*to meet*
2.	洗(あら)う	*to wash*	13.	見(み)る	*to see*
3.	みがく	*to brush (teeth)*	14.	泳(およ)ぐ	*to swim*
4.	走(はし)る	*to run*	15.	する	*to do*
5.	食(た)べる	*to eat*	16.	帰(かえ)る	*to return*
6.	飲(の)む	*to drink*	17.	休(やす)む	*to rest*
7.	出(で)かける	*to go out*	18.	入(はい)る	*to enter*
8.	待(ま)つ	*to wait*	19.	読(よ)む	*to read*
9.	行(い)く	*to go*	20.	寝(ね)る	*to sleep*
10.	乗(の)る	*to ride*	21.	来(く)る	*to come*
11.	着(つ)く	*to arrive*	22.	話す	*to speak*

練習 2

Transform plain verbs into polite verbs, and vice versa.

[例] チンさんは毎日六時に起きる。→
チンさんは毎日六時に起きます。

1. ビールを飲みます。
2. 明日、ロサンゼルスへ行く。
3. 今日の午後、山田さんに会います。
4. ブラウンさんは来週、アメリカから帰る。
5. 毎日、運動します。
6. あなたは何を食べるか。
7. パーティーへ来るか。
8. わたしはテレビを見ない。
9. 町田さんを待ちますか。
10. シュミットさんは日本語を話さない。

練習 3

Make sentences using the words provided. (Change the verbs to their polite forms.)

[例] (六時)(毎日)(起きる)→わたしは毎日六時に起きます。

1. (七時)(いつも)(朝ごはんを食べる)
2. (七時半)(毎朝)(大学へ行く)
3. (八時)(毎日)(クラスが始まる)
4. (十二時)(毎日)(昼ごはんを食べる)
5. (三時)(いつも)(クラスが終わる)
6. (四時)(毎日)(図書館へ行く)
7. (五時)(いつも)(大学から帰る)
8. (六時)(毎日)(夕ごはんを食べる)
9. (七時)(いつも)(テレビを見る)
10. (九時)(毎日)(日本語を勉強する)
11. (十一時)(毎晩)(寝る)

練習　4

Make dialogues following the example.

[例]　(明日)(大学へ行く)　(いいえ)→
—明日大学へ行きますか。
—いいえ、行きません。

1. (毎朝)(運動する)　(いいえ)
2. (いつも)(コーヒーを飲む)　(はい)
3. (よく)(町田さんに会う)　(はい)
4. (毎日)(テレビを見る)　(いいえ)
5. (毎晩)(レストランで食べる)　(いいえ)

練習　5

Complete the following sentences. Your sentences must include the polite form of a verb.

[例]　毎朝六時に…→ 毎朝六時にシャワーを浴びます。

1. 日曜日の朝…
2. 毎日午前八時に…
3. わたしは毎日…
4. 日本語のクラスは…
5. わたしとガールフレンドはいつも…
6. わたしは来週の月曜日…
7. 土曜日の午後…
8. わたしは来年…

練習　6

Rewrite the following paragraph, substituting polite verb forms.

Useful vocabulary: 始まる *to start;* 終わる *to finish*

わたしは毎日午前五時に起きる。それから、家の回りを散歩する。午前六時にコーヒーを飲む。朝ごはんは食べない。午前七時に家を出る。午前七時のバスに乗る。午前八時に大学のクラスが始まる。十二時にカフェテリアで昼ごはんを食べる。午後一時にクラスへ行く。クラスは午後三時に終わる。わたしの友だちは図書館へ行く。でも、わたしは行かない。午後四時に家に帰る。それから、六時まで勉強する。六時に夕ごはんを食べる。そのあと、テレビを見る。午後十時にいつも寝る。

13. The Past, Polite Form of Verbs

林：昨日は何時に家に帰りましたか。
ブラウン：午後六時ごろです。
林：夕ごはんに何を食べましたか。
ブラウン：ステーキを食べました。

ブラウン：去年の夏はどこへ行きましたか。
カワムラ：シアトルへ行きました。
ブラウン：何をしましたか。
カワムラ：つりをしました。

ブラウン：今何時ですか。
チン：十時十五分です。
ブラウン：もうカワムラさんに電話をしましたか。
チン：いいえ、まだです。十時半にかけます。

The past, polite forms of verbs are formed as follows.

Affirmative the conjunctive form + ました
Negative the conjunctive form + ませんでした

DICTIONARY FORM	CONJUNCTIVE FORM	PAST, POLITE, AFFIRMATIVE FORM	PAST, POLITE, NEGATIVE FORM
Class 1 verbs			
洗う	洗い	洗いました	洗いませんでした
書く	書き	書きました	書きませんでした
話す	話し	話しました	話しませんでした
立つ	立ち	立ちました	立ちませんでした
読む	読み	読みました	読みませんでした
ある	あり	ありました	ありませんでした
泳ぐ	泳ぎ	泳ぎました	泳ぎませんでした

HAYASHI: What time did you return home yesterday? BROWN: About 6:00 P.M. HAYASHI: What did you eat for dinner? BROWN: I ate steak.

BROWN: Where did you go last summer? KAWAMURA: I went to Seattle. BROWN: What did you do? KAWAMURA: I went fishing.

BROWN: What time is it now? CHIN: It's 10:15. BROWN: Did you already call Mr. Kawamura? CHIN: No, not yet. I'll call him at 10:30.

DICTIONARY FORM	CONJUNCTIVE FORM	PAST, POLITE, AFFIRMATIVE FORM	PAST, POLITE, NEGATIVE FORM
Class 2 verbs 食べる 見る 着る	 食べ 見 着	 食べました 見ました 着ました	 食べませんでした 見ませんでした 着ませんでした
Class 3 verbs する 来る	 し 来	 しました 来ました	 しませんでした 来ませんでした

練習　1

Write the affirmative and negative past, polite forms of the verbs listed in **Grammar 12,** 練習 1.

練習　2

Give affirmative and negative answers to the following questions.

[例]　昨日、ビールを飲みましたか。→
　　はい、飲みました。
　　いいえ、飲みませんでした。

1. 先週、映画を見ましたか。
2. 昨日、日本語を勉強しましたか。
3. おととい、本を読みましたか。
4. 昨日はうちにいましたか。
5. 今日、朝ごはんを食べましたか。
6. 昨日、日本語のクラスがありましたか。
7. 去年、高田さんはアメリカへ行きましたか。
8. 昨日、たくさんテレビを見ましたか。
9. おととい、スポーツをしましたか。
10. 昨日、お風呂に入りましたか。

練習 3

Make dialogues following the example. Use the past, polite form of verbs.

[例]　(起きる) → — (*partner's name*)は昨日何時に起きましたか。
— 六時に起きました。

Useful vocabulary: お茶 *tea*; 手紙 *letter*

1. (朝ごはんを食べる)
2. (学校へ行く)
3. (お茶を飲む)
4. (図書館で勉強する)
5. (散歩をする)
6. (電話をかける)
7. (音楽を聞く)
8. (友だちと話す)
9. (手紙を書く)
10. (寝る)

練習 4

Make a dialogue based on the example below.

[例]　get up, 5:30 → — 昨日何時に起きましたか。
— 5時半に起きました。

1. get up, 5:30
2. go jogging, 6:00
3. eat breakfast, 6:30
4. leave home, 7:00
5. board a train, 7:15
6. go to class, 8:00
7. eat lunch, 12:20
8. drink coffee, 1:00
9. go to the library, 1:20
10. exercise, 3:40
11. go home, 5:30
12. watch TV, 6:00
13. eat dinner, 7:15
14. study Japanese, 8:45
15. listen to music, 10:40
16. go to bed, 11:30

練習 5

Complete these sentences. Use the past, polite form of verbs.

1. わたしは去年…
2. 田中さんは昨日の夜…
3. わたしと山口さんは先週、…
4. 昨日は…
5. 今日の朝、…
6. 先週の土曜日、…
7. いつもうちで…
8. 昨日、六時から十時まで…
9. うちの前に…
10. 大学からうちまで…

練習　6

Answer the following questions.

1. あなたは今日(きょう)、何時(なんじ)に起(お)きましたか。
2. あなたは先週(せんしゅう)、映画(えいが)を見(み)ましたか。
3. 今日はもう昼(ひる)ごはんを食(た)べましたか。
4. 昨日(きのう)何回(なんかい)、歯(は)をみがきましたか。
5. どこで生まれましたか。(*Where were you born?*)
6. いつこの学校(がっこう)に来ましたか。
7. 今日(きょう)、顔(かお)を洗(あら)いましたか。
8. 昨日、夕ごはんに何を食べましたか。
9. 昨日、何時間(なんじかん)日本語を勉強(べんきょう)しましたか。
10. 昨日、何時間寝(ね)ましたか。

14. Particles Showing Grammatical Relationships

In Japanese, the grammatical roles of some words in a sentence—subject, direct object, and so on—are identified by particles, also known as postpositions. These short words indicate the grammatical function of the word or phrase preceding them. Particles are a key element of Japanese grammar. The following explanation provides an overview of various particles. It is not a complete explanation by any means, but it should give you a good idea of why you have been using certain particles in particular situations, and prepare you for new usages you will encounter from now on.

14.1 が and は have similar but distinct uses. が is a *subject particle*. It marks a word or phrase that is the subject of a sentence. は (pronounced **wa**) is called the *topic particle* because it is often used to mark a word or phrase that is the topic of a sentence, that is, what the sentence is about.

Because topics and subjects are sometimes hard to distinguish from one another, in many cases either は or が would be grammatically acceptable. This does not mean, however, that they are interchangeable. For example

1. わたしはアメリカ人です。　*I am American.*
2. わたしがアメリカ人です。　*I am American.*

This section explains the usage of different particles for reference purposes only. Not all particles are considered active vocabulary at this stage.

Both sentences are grammatically correct. However, if someone asks だれがアメリカ人ですか(*Who is American?*) sentence 2 is the only appropriate answer. On the other hand, if you were standing up in front of others introducing yourself, sentence 1 is the only appropriate answer. The choice between は and が depends on context and is very complex. You will learn their use and differences gradually as you progress through this textbook. For now, it may help to think of は as being used to introduce a general topic (as in 1.) or to refer to a topic already in discussion, whereas が shifts emphasis to the subject it follows (***I** am American*).

14.2 The particle を has several uses.

1. を marks (follows) a direct object. (A direct object is something or someone directly affected by the action of a verb.) The direct objects are underlined in the following examples.

   わたしは朝ごはんを食べます。
   I will eat breakfast.

   チンさんは大学で日本語を勉強しました。
   Ms. Chin studied Japanese at a university.

   昨日スーパーでコーラを買いました。
   I bought cola at a supermarket yesterday.

   林さんはシャワーを浴びました。
   Mr. Hayashi took a shower.

   何を着ますか。
   What are you going to wear?

   Caution: Just because a word is a direct object in an English sentence doesn't mean its counterpart in the Japanese equivalent is also a direct object. Many Japanese verbs require に (*to*) where you might expect を. Here are some to watch out for.

   バスに乗りました。
   I rode a bus. (*lit., I got onto a bus.*)

   ブラウンさんは高田さんに会いました。
   Ms. Brown met Mr. Takada.

   日本が好きです。
   I like Japan.

   パーティーに出ました。
   I attended the party.

2. を is also used to indicate a place or object from which something or someone leaves. In this usage, it carries the sense of *from* or *out of.*

   午前八時に家を出ます。
   I leave home at 8:00 A.M.

   ブラウンさんは車をおりました。
   Ms. Brown got out of the car.

3. を is further used to indicate a place which something moves over, along, or through.

橋を渡りました。
I crossed the bridge.
道を歩きます。
I walk through the street.
スーパーマンはビルの上を飛びました。
Superman flew over the buildings.

14.3 に is one of the most versatile particles. Here are some of its many uses.

1. Point in time (*at, on, in*)

   カワムラさんは七時に朝ごはんを食べます。
   Mr. Kawamura eats breakfast at seven o'clock.
   月曜日にロサンゼルスへ行きました。
   I went to Los Angeles on Monday.
   1975年に生まれました。
   I was born in 1975.

   Some expressions of time (e.g., *today, next week, last year*) as well as frequency and duration of time do not take this particle.

   ギブソンさんは今日、東京へ来ます。
   Ms. Gibson will come to Tokyo today.
   来週忙しいです。
   I will be busy next week.
   昨日の午後、図書館へ行きました。
   I went to the library yesterday afternoon.
   毎日、ジョギングします。
   I jog every day.

2. Location of existence

   そこに銀行があります。
   There is a bank there (lit., in that place).
   高田さんはどこにいますか。
   Where is Mr. Takada?

3. Purpose (*for, in order to*) when the verb is 行く or 来る.

   昨日デパートへ買物に行きました。
   Yesterday I went shopping at the department store. (lit., Yesterday I went to the department store for shopping.)
   高田さんがあいさつに来ました。
   Mr. Takada came to greet me.

4. Direction of an action

山口さんは毎日お風呂に入ります。
Mr. Yamaguchi takes a bath every day. (*lit., Mr. Yamaguchi enters a bath every day.*)
わたしはそれにさわりました。
I touched that (indicating the hand's movement toward that).
林さんは八時の電車に乗りました。
Mr. Hayashi got on the eight o'clock train.

14.4 The particle へ also marks the direction toward which an action moves. While に marks movement toward a specific place, へ indicates motion in a general direction. However, the difference is unimportant in many cases, and the two particles are often interchangeable.

明日京都へ行きます。
I will go to Kyoto tomorrow.
チンさんはここへ来ますか。
Is Ms. Chin coming here?
いつ家へ帰りますか。
When will you return home?

14.5 で has three major uses. で marks the location where an action takes place.

カーティスさんはいつもここで昼ごはんを食べます。
Mr. Curtis always eats lunch here.
図書館で勉強します。
I will study at the library.

It also marks the instrument used to carry out an action.

ナイフでりんごを切りました。
I cut the apple with a knife.
電車で学校へ来ます。
I come to school by train.

The particle で also marks the reason or cause of an action. This usage corresponds to the English *because of* or *for.*

昨日、病気で学校を休みました。
Yesterday I was absent from school because of illness.
今、ビジネスでロサンゼルスにいます。
I am in Los Angeles now for business.

14.6 The particle から (*from*) is used to express the starting point in space or time of an action, and the particle まで ([*up*] *to, until*) is used to represent its ending point.

東京から京都まで新幹線で行きます。
I will go from Tokyo to Kyoto via Shinkansen (the bullet train).

わたしは一時から三時まで図書館にいます。
I will be at a library from 1:00 to 3:00.

ここからあそこまで二時間かかります。
It takes two hours (to go) from here to there.

かかる *to take (time, money)*

14.7 In Chapter 1, you learned that the particle も means *too* or *as much as*. When placed after a number it often means *as much as* or *as many as*. When placed after a regular noun or pronoun, it usually means *too*.

わたしもアイスクリームが好きです。
I also like ice cream (in addition to someone else).

わたしはアイスクリームも好きです。
I also like ice cream (in addition to something else).

三十人もパーティーに来ました。
As many as thirty people came to the party.

わたしの姉はフランス語も話します。
My elder sister speaks French, too (in addition to some other language).

去年、ローマへも行きました。
Last year, I went to Rome too (in addition to some other place).

アメリカからも学生が来ました。
Students came from the United States, too.

A も B も means *both A and B* (in affirmative sentences) and *neither A nor B* (in negative sentences).

わたしもブラウンさんも行きました。
Both Ms. Brown and I went there.

カーティスさんはすしもてんぷらも好きです。
Mr. Curtis likes both sushi and tempura.

林さんもギブソンさんもいませんでした。
Neither Mr. Hayashi nor Ms. Gibson were there.

山口さんはロックもラップも大きらいです。
Mr. Yamaguchi hates both rock music and rap.

When this particle is used in the subject or direct object position, it replaces は、が, or を. But it follows other particles, resulting in such combinations as にも、からも、までも、でも、 and へも. While the English *too* can appear in various positions in a sentence, も must follow the word or phrase that is being mentioned in addition to something else.

ブラウンさんは学生です。
Ms. Brown is a student.

わたしも学生です。
I am a student too.

すしを食べました。
I ate sushi.
てんぷらも食べました。
I ate tempura too.
その本は図書館にあります。
That book is at the library.

その本はわたしのうちにもあります。
That book is at my home too.

デパートへ行きます。
I will go to a department store.
スーパーへも行きます。
I will go to a supermarket too.

Here is a summary of these combinations and replacements of particles.

が	→	も
は	→	も
を	→	も
に	→	にも
へ	→	へも
で	→	でも

14.8 The particle と means *together with.*

ブラウンさんと映画へ行きました。
I went to the movies with Ms. Brown.
三村さんと会いましたか。
Did you meet with Mr. Mimura?

As you have already studied, this particle is also used to connect two or more nouns or pronouns in the sense of *and.*

アイスクリームとチョコレートが好きです。
I like ice cream and chocolate.

Remember: You cannot use と to connect adjectives, adverbs, verbs or sentences.

14.9 Japanese is sometimes called a "word order–free" language because its word order is not so strictly fixed as in English. A verb or a predicate comes in the sentence-final position, but other elements can be ordered more freely. This is possible because particles indicate the grammatical function of a word or a phrase. Therefore, even if you move a word or a phrase around, as long as it is followed by a particle you can tell its grammatical function. In English, however, the grammatical function of a word or phrase is often determined by word order.

Nevertheless, a natural word order does exist in Japanese, as shown here.

N は／が (time) (place) (indirect object) (direct object) **V**

わたしは明日ロサンゼルスから東京へ発ちます。

I will leave Los Angeles for Tokyo tomorrow.

わたしの妹は明日、デパートでくつを買います。

My sister will buy shoes at a department store tomorrow.

練習 1

Fill in the blanks.

[例] 七時(に)起きます。

1. 机(　　)上(　　)本があります。
2. テレビ(　　)見ます。
3. 毎晩、八時(　　)家(　　)帰ります。
4. 時々、ラジオ(　　)音楽 (*music*) (　　)聞きます。
5. よくレストラン(　　)行きます。
6. 来週東京(　　)行きます。東京(　　)ブラウンさん(　　)会います。東京(　　)来月帰ります。
7. 今日の朝、公園(　　)散歩しました (*took a walk*)。
8. そのアメリカ人はフォーク(　　)てんぷらを食べました。
9. わたしは大学(　　)うち(　　)電車で行きます。
10. 昨日カーティスさんはだれ(　　)話しましたか。
11. デパートへ買い物(　　)行きました。
12. どんな本(　　)好きですか。

練習 2

Fill in the blanks.

今日の朝、わたしは六時半(　　)起きました。そして、顔(　　)洗いました。七時(　　)七時半(　　)公園(　　)散歩しました。八時(　　)大学(　　)行きました。九時(　　)十二時(　　)クラス(　　)ありました。昼ごはんはカフェテリア(　　)ハンバーガー(　　)食べました。ミルク(　　)飲みました。三時(　　)町田さん(　　)としょかん

(　　)行きました。五時(　　)家(　　)帰りました。六時(　　)夕ごはん(　　)食べました。それから、ラジオ(　　)音楽(　　)聞きました。十時(　　)、友だち(　　)電話しました。十一時(　　)シャワー(　　)浴びました。十一時半(　　)寝ました。

練習　3

Make a dialogue using the words given in parentheses.

[例]　A: 町田さんは先週デパートへ行きましたか。
　　　B: (はい)→はい、行きました。

A: (いつ)
B: (先週の土曜日)
A: (だれと)
B: (山口さん)
A: (何)(買う)
B: (ブラウス)(買う)
A: 町田さんはよくレストランへ行きますか。
B: (あまり)
A: いつも家で夕ごはんを食べますか。
B: (いつも)
A: (昨日)(何)(食べる)
B: (ステーキ)(食べる)
A: (どんな)(食べ物)(好きです)
B: (ほとんど)(みんな *everything*)

15. Making Suggestions: ～ましょう

カワムラ：林さん、おそいですね。
ブラウン：ええ、どうしましょうか。
カワムラ：もう少し待ちましょう。
ブラウン：でも、もう9時ですよ。出かけましょうか。
カワムラ：ええ、そうですね。じゃ、そうしましょう。

KAWAMURA: Mr. Hayashi is late, isn't he? BROWN: Yes. What shall we do? KAWAMURA: Let's wait for him a little more. BROWN: But it's already nine o'clock. Shall we leave (now)? KAWAMURA: Yes, I guess you're right. Then, let's do that.

林(はやし)：チンさんがいませんね。
カワムラ：ええ。
林：チンさん、病気(びょうき)ですか。
カワムラ：さあ。
林：ぼくが家(いえ)に電話(でんわ)しましょうか。

15.1 The ましょう form, or the polite, volitional form of a verb, is made by adding ましょう to the conjunctive form.

DICTIONARY FORM	CONJUNCTIVE FORM	ましょう FORM
Class 1 verbs		
洗(あら)う	洗(あら)い	洗(あら)いましょう
書(か)く	書(か)き	書(か)きましょう
話(はな)す	話(はな)し	話(はな)しましょう
立(た)つ	立(た)ち	立(た)ちましょう
読(よ)む	読(よ)み	読(よ)みましょう
ある	あり	ありましょう
泳(およ)ぐ	泳(およ)ぎ	泳(およ)ぎましょう
Class 2 verbs		
食(た)べる	食(た)べ	食(た)べましょう
見(み)る	見(み)	見(み)ましょう
着(き)る	着(き)	着(き)ましょう
Class 3 verbs		
する	し	しましょう
来(く)る	来(き)	来(き)ましょう

15.2 The ましょう form is used to suggest, propose, or invite (*Let's . . .* or *Shall we . . . ?*).

一緒(いっしょ)に勉強(べんきょう)しましょうか。
Shall we study together?
昼(ひる)ごはんを食(た)べましょう。
Let's eat lunch.
電車(でんしゃ)で行(い)きましょうか。タクシーで行きましょうか。
Shall we go by train or taxi?

HAYASHI: Ms. Chin isn't here, is she? KAWAMURA: That's right. (*lit., Yes.*) HAYASHI: Is she sick? KAWAMURA: I don't know. HAYASHI: Shall I call her at home?

Because the ましょう form expresses the speaker's volition, without consideration to the hearer's preferences, it tends to sound somewhat pushy and forceful. It is politer to use the nonpast, plain, negative form of a verb ＋か when inviting someone to do something together or when making a suggestion.

一緒に夕ごはんを食べませんか。
Shall we eat dinner together?
Would you like to eat dinner together? (lit., Won't you eat dinner together [with me]?)

来週、デパートへ行きませんか。
Shall we go to a department store next week?
Would you like to go to a department store next week? (lit., Won't you go to a department store next week?)

When you already know that the hearer is willing to do something together, the use of the ましょう form does not sound pushy. For example,

レストランへ行きませんか。
Shall we go to a restaurant?
ええ、いいですね。
Yes, that sounds nice.
どこへ行きましょうか。
Where shall we go?

or

のどがかわきましたね。
I am thirsty, aren't you?
ええ、とても。
Yes, very much.
ジュースを飲みましょうか。
Shall we drink juice?

15.3 The ましょう form is also used when offering to do something for someone or when expressing one's own volition.

わたしがブラウンさんに話しましょう。
I will talk to Ms. Brown.
わたしがワインを買いましょうか。
Shall I buy wine?

When the first person subject is expressed explicitly as in the preceding examples, it implies that "I but not anyone else" will do something. When the first person subject is not expressed, it simply expresses the speaker's volition without such an implication.

さあ、勉強しましょう。
Well, I guess I will start studying.
Well, I'm going to study now.

コミュニケーション・ノート

Accepting and Declining Offers

To accept an offer, say

はい、お願いします。
Yes, please.
どうもありがとうございます。
Thank you very much.
どうもすみません。
Thank you for your trouble.(lit., I'm sorry for your trouble.)

To turn down an offer, say

いいえ、けっこうです。
No, thank you.
(lit., No, I'm fine.)

練　習　　1

Rewrite each sentence using the ましょう form.

[例]　コーラを飲む → コーラを飲みましょう。

1. 映画を見る
2. コンサートへ行く
3. ケーキを食べる
4. ジョギングする
5. 本を読む
6. 買物に出かける
7. プールで泳ぐ
8. 日本語で話す

練　習　　2

Complete the following dialogues using the ましょう form.

[例]　(ブラウンさんに電話する) (*accept*) →
— わたしがブラウンさんに電話しましょうか。
— ええ、おねがいします。
(掃除する) (*decline*) →
— わたしが掃除しましょうか。
— いいえ、けっこうです。

1. (山口さんに聞く) (*accept*)
2. (洗濯をする) (*decline*)
3. (横田先生の研究室に行く) (*accept*)
4. (その本を読む) (*accept*)
5. (料理する) (*decline*)

練習 3

For each of these sentences, compose a follow-up suggestion using the ましょう form.

[例] とても暑(あつ)いですね。→ とても暑いですね。ジュースを飲(の)みましょうか。

Useful Vocabulary

帰(かえ)る	*to go back*	プレゼント	*present, gift*
夕(ゆう)ごはん	*dinner*	買(か)う	*to buy*
出(で)かける	*to leave*	Aに聞(き)く	*to ask A*
電話(でんわ)する	*to make a phone call*	一緒(いっしょ)に	*together*

1. もう5時(じ)ですね。
2. 高田(たかだ)さん、おそいですね。
3. この質問(しつもん)はむずかしいですね。
4. 明日(あす)はカーティスさんの誕生日(たんじょうび)ですよ。
5. あっ、あそこに林(はやし)さんがいますよ。

16. Conjoining Nouns: と and や

カワムラ：横井(よこい)先生の研究室(けんきゅうしつ)にだれがいますか。
町田(まちだ)：横井先生とブラウンさんがいます。
カワムラ：チンさんは。
町田：研究室の外(そと)にいます。

ブラウン：机(つくえ)の上(うえ)に何がありますか。
カワムラ：ペンとノートと本があります。

ブラウン：事務室(じむしつ)にだれがいますか。
町田(まちだ)：カワムラさんや林(はやし)さんがいます。
ブラウン：カーティスさんは。
町田：ええ、カーティスさんもいます。

KAWAMURA: Who is in Professor Yokoi's office? MACHIDA: Professor Yokoi and Ms. Brown. KAWAMURA: How about Ms. Chin? MACHIDA: She is outside the office.

BROWN: What is on the desk? KAWAMURA: A pen, a notebook, a book.

BROWN: Who is in the administrative office? MACHIDA: Mr. Kawamura, Mr. Hayashi, and others. BROWN: How about Mr. Curtis? MACHIDA: Yes, he's there, too.

ブラウン：昨日(きのう)のパーティーにはだれが来(き)ましたか。
カワムラ：林(はやし)さんやカーティスさんや町田(まちた)さんが来(き)ました。

You can join nouns together with と or や. と (*and*) is used to enumerate *all* objects that exist in a certain place or *all* objects that belong to a certain category, while や (*and things like that*) is used to list only representative objects. Thus, と is exhaustive, and や is not. You may conjoin as many nouns as you like with these particles. Remember: you cannot use these particles to connect adjectives, verbs, or sentences.

練習

Answer each question two ways, first using と and then や.

1. 昨日(きのう)、だれが来(き)ましたか。(*Hayashi, Chin, and Gibson*)
2. 夕(ゆう)ごはんに何を食べましたか。(*steak, salad, and fruit*)
3. そこにだれがいますか。(*Brown, Kawamura, Curtis, and Chin*)
4. どんなコンピュータがありますか。(*IBM, Apple, NEC, and Toshiba*)
5. どんなスポーツが好(す)きですか。(*basketball, football, and tennis*)

Vocabulary

Time Expressions

あさって		the day after tomorrow	ことし	今年	this year
あした	明日	tomorrow	こんげつ	今月	this month
おととい		the day before yesterday	こんしゅう	今週	this week
きのう	昨日	yesterday	こんばん	今晩	tonight
きょう	今日	today	せんげつ	先月	last month
きょねん	去年	last year	せんしゅう	先週	last week
けさ	今朝	this morning	なんじかん	何時間	how many hours

BROWN: Who came to the party yesterday? KAWAMURA: Mr. Hayashi, Mr. Curtis, Ms. Machida, and others.

なんにち	何日	what day
なんねん	何年	what year
らいげつ	来月	next month
らいしゅう	来週	next week
らいねん	来年	next year

Review: 朝(あさ)、午前(ごぜん)、午後(ごご)、時間(じかん)、何月、何曜日(なんようび)、昼(ひる)、夕方(ゆうがた)、夜(よる)

Everyday Activities

いえをでる	家を出る	to leave home
うんどうする	運動する	to exercise
おふろにはいる	お風呂に入る	to take a bath
かおをあらう	顔を洗う	to wash one's face
シャワーをあびる	シャワーを浴びる	to take a shower
つかれる	疲れる	to become tired
でかける	出かける	to go out
でんわ(を)する	電話(を)する	to make a telephone call
ねぼうする	寝坊する	to oversleep
のる	乗る	to ride (a vehicle)
はたらく	働く	to work
はをみがく	歯を磨く	to brush one's teeth
ふくをきる	服を着る	to put on clothes
やすむ	休む	to take a rest, take time off
ゆうごはんをたべる	夕ごはんを食べる	to have dinner, supper
りょうり(を)する	料理(を)する	to cook

Review: 朝(あさ)ごはん、行(い)く、起(お)きる、買(か)い物(もの)(を)する、帰(かえ)る、聞(き)く、仕事(しごと)をする、食(た)べる、寝(ね)る、飲(の)む、話す、晩(ばん)ごはん、昼(ひる)ごはん、勉強(べんきょう)する、見(み)る、読(よ)む

Days of the Month

ついたち	一日	the first
ふつか	二日	the second
みっか	三日	the third
よっか	四日	the fourth
いつか	五日	the fifth
むいか	六日	the sixth
なのか	七日	the seventh
ようか	八日	the eighth
ここのか	九日	the ninth
とおか	十日	the tenth
じゅういちにち	十一日	the eleventh
じゅうににち	十二日	the twelfth
じゅうさんにち	十三日	the thirteenth
じゅうよっか	十四日	the fourteenth
じゅうごにち	十五日	the fifteenth
じゅうろくにち	十六日	the sixteenth
じゅうしちにち	十七日	the seventeenth
じゅうはちにち	十八日	the eighteenth
じゅうくにち	十九日	the nineteenth
はつか	二十日	the twentieth
にじゅうよっか	二十四日	the twenty-fourth

Frequency

あまり		(*with negative*) not very much
いつも		always
～かい	～回	. . . times (*counter for occurrences*)
ぜんぜん	全然	(*with negative*) not at all
たまに		once in a while
ときどき	時々	sometimes
ほとんど		almost
ほとんど～		(*with negative*) almost never, hardly
まいあさ	毎朝	every morning
まいしゅう	毎週	every week
まいつき	毎月	every month
まいにち	毎日	every day
まいばん	毎晩	every night
よく		often

Conjunctions

そして	and then
そのあと	after that
それから	and then

Particles

が	(*subject particle*)
から	from
で	at, by means of
と	with
に	(*indirect object particle*)
は	(*topic particle*)
へ	(*direction particle*)
まで	up to, until
も	too
を	(*direct object particle*)

Nouns

へいじつ	平日	weekday
しゅうまつ	週末	weekend
やすみのひ	休みの日	day off, holiday
なつやすみ	夏休み	summer vacation
ふゆやすみ	冬休み	winter vacation

Adjectives

いそがしい	忙しい	busy
ひま(な)	暇(な)	free (*not busy*)

Verb Endings

～ましょう	let's . . .
～ます	(*nonpast, polite, affirmative*)
～ません	(*nonpast, polite, negative*)
～ました	(*past, polite, affirmative*)
～ませんでした	(*past, polite, negative*)

Kanji

Learn these **kanji**.

朝	出	回
明	飲	見
午	入	起
昼	休	読
来	夕	火
行	今	水
聞	週	木
食	曜	金
会	毎	土

Reading and Writing

Reading 1 ブラウンさんの日常生活（にちじょうせいかつ）

Before You Read

The following passage describes Linda Brown's daily life. Before reading it, work with a partner to arrange the following activities in the order you think average students perform them.

______ 夕（ゆう）ごはんを食（た）べる
______ 大学へ行（い）く
______ 起（お）きる
______ 朝（あさ）ごはんを食べる
______ 家（いえ）に帰（かえ）る
______ クラスに出（で）る
______ 昼（ひる）ごはんを食べる
______ 寝（ね）る

Work in pairs. Which of the following activities do both you and your partner do every morning? Which do neither of you do?

______ 歯（は）をみがく
______ ラジオを聞（き）く
______ シャワーを浴（あ）びる
______ 朝（あさ）ごはんを食（た）べる
______ コーヒーを飲（の）む
______ テレビを見（み）る
______ 顔（かお）を洗（あら）う
______ パジャマを脱（ぬ）ぐ
______ 髪（かみ）をとかす
______ 服（ふく）を着（き）る
______ 電車（でんしゃ）に乗（の）る
______ 新聞（しんぶん）を読（よ）む
______ ジョギングをする

わたしは毎朝六時に起きます。まず、顔を洗います。そして、歯をみがきます。それから、ジョギングをします。七時ごろ朝ごはんを食べます。七時半にうちを出ます。わたしのアパートは中野駅のそばにあります。アパートから駅まで五分歩きます。そして、地下鉄で大学へ行きます。アパートから大学まで三十分ぐらいかかります。

クラスは八時に始まります。わたしの専攻は日本文化です。毎日、日本文化、日本語のクラスに出ます。　午前のクラスは十二時に終わります。いつも大学のカフェテリアで昼ごはんを食べます。　午後のクラスは一時から始まります。そして、四時に終わります。クラスの後、時々、図書館へ行きます。月曜日と水曜日と金曜日は友だちとエアロビクスのレッスンに行きます。

いつもアパートに五時か六時に帰ります。夕ごはんは七時半ごろ食べます。時々、アパートのそばの食堂へ行きます。

夜は日本語の勉強します。本もよく読みます。ミステリーが好きです。テレビはあまり見ません。カセットやCDで音楽をよく聞きます。毎日、十二時ごろ寝ます。

まず *first of all*

歩く *to walk*

かかる *to take*

始まる *to start*

終わる *to finish*

…の後 *after …*

五時か六時 *five o'clock or six o'clock*

文法ノート

Approximate Numbers

These words, when appended to quantities or points in time, make the numerical entities approximate.

1. ごろ (*around*) is used to express an approximate point in time, such as a day, month or hour.

   毎日5時ごろ起きます。
   I get up around 5:00 every day.

2. ぐらい or くらい (*about*) is used to express an approximate quantity. くらい and ぐらい are interchangeable.

   日本語のクラスには三十人ぐらいの学生がいます。
   There are about thirty students in the Japanese language class.
   東京から京都まで三時間ぐらいかかります。
   It takes about three hours from Tokyo to Kyoto.

その本は二千円(にせんえん)くらいです。
That book costs (lit., is) about 2,000 yen.

3. ほど (*about*) is also used to express approximate quantity. ほど is used in the sense of *as much as* with all but small numbers.

   レタスを二(ふた)つほどください。
   Can I have about two heads of lettuce?

   ここから十五分(じゅうごふん)ほどかかります。
   It takes (as much as) about fifteen minutes from here.

After You Finish Reading

1. Fill in the following schedule based on information provided in the passage.

LINDA BROWN'S DAILY SCHEDULE	
午前6:00	
7:00	
8:00	
9:00	
10:00	
11:00	
12:00	
午後1:00	
2:00	
3:00	
4:00	
5:00	
6:00	
7:00	
8:00	
9:00	
10:00	
11:00	
12:00	

2. Now look at the second paragraph carefully. Circle all the particles in the paragraph and explain how each is used.

Writing 1

Write a short paragraph about your daily life. Use this beginning.

わたしは毎朝_____時に起きます。それから…

Reading 2 ブラウンさんの週末

Before You Read

The following passage describes what Linda Brown did last weekend. Which of the following do you usually do on weekdays and which do you usually do on weekends?

_____ 寝坊する
_____ 勉強する
_____ 買い物をする
_____ 掃除をする
_____ 洗濯をする
_____ 図書館へ行く
_____ 映画を見る
_____ 友だちと電話で話す
_____ 大学へ行く
_____ レコードを聞く
_____ レストランへ行く

Match items in the left column to related items in the right column.

1. 誕生日 a. 日曜日
2. コインランドリー b. ギフト
3. パーティー c. デパート
4. 週末 d. ワイン
5. 買い物 e. 洗濯

Now Read It!

土曜日と日曜日は大学が休みです。土曜日は午前9時ごろ起きます。土曜日の朝はいつもアパートの前の喫茶店に行きます。この喫茶店のコーヒーはとてもおいしいです。お昼まで喫茶店でコーヒーを飲みます。土曜日の午後はアパートの掃除をします。夜はクラスメートと外に出かけます。先週の土曜日はカワムラさんと映画を見ました。今週の土曜日は町田さんとショッピングに行きます。土曜日はいつも午後11時か12時ごろアパートに帰ります。

おいしい *delicious*
お昼 *noontime*

日曜日はいつも、お昼ごろ起きます。午後は近くのコイン・ランドリーで洗濯をします。夜、ちょっと勉強します。来週の日曜日はカワムラさんの誕生日です。カワムラさんは二十一歳になります。町田さんの家でパーティーがあります。来週の日曜日は朝早く起きます。町田さんの家で、パーティーの準備を手伝います。町田さんと一緒にケーキやごちそうを作ります。

昨日、カワムラさんのバースデー・プレゼントを買いました。カワムラさんはコンピュータが好きです。それで、コンピュータのソフトウェアを買いました。

コイン・ランドリー *laundromat*

…になる *to become*

早く *early*

準備 *preparation*
手伝う *to help, assist*
一緒に *together*
ごちそう *delicious food*
作る *to make, cook*
それで *therefore*

After You Finish Reading

1. Tell whether each of the following is true or false.
    1. Linda drinks coffee at a coffee shop until noon on Saturdays.
    2. Linda went out with Hitomi Machida last Saturday.
    3. Linda goes to bed at 11:00 P.M. or 12:00 midnight on Saturdays.
    4. Linda cleans her apartment and does her laundry on Sundays.
    5. Next Sunday is John Kawamura's twenty-first birthday.
    6. Hitomi Machida will come to Linda's apartment next Sunday to help Linda prepare for the party.
    7. Linda will buy computer software for John Kawamura.
2. Arrange the following activities in the order Linda Brown does them on Saturday. Don't forget to use conjunctions.

    _____ アパートに帰る
    _____ 喫茶店へ行く
    _____ 掃除をする
    _____ コーヒーを飲む
    _____ 午前9時ごろ起きる
    _____ 友だちと出かける

Writing 2

Drawing from the journal notations on the following page, write a short paragraph about what John Kawamura did last weekend.

DIARY	
Sat	Sun
10:00 got up read paper	9:30 got up
11:00 watched TV	10:00 took shower
12:00 ate lunch	11:00 listened to music
1:00 did laundry	12:00 called Linda Brown
2:00 cleaned house	2:00 went shopping with Linda
4:00 went to movie	5:00 went to McDonald's
7:00 ate at a tempura restaurant	7:00 came home
10:00 went to pub	8:00 studied Japanese
12:00 returned home and went to bed	10:30 went to bed

Language Functions and Situations

Making a Phone Call

山口：もしもし、山口です。
ブラウン：もしもし、ブラウンです。カワムラさんをお願いします。
山口：ちょっとお待ちください。

YAMAGUCHI: Hello. This is Yamaguchi speaking. BROWN: Hello. This is Brown. May I speak to Mr. Kawamura? (*lit., Please give me Mr. Kawamura.*) YAMAGUCHI: Wait a moment, please. KAWAMURA: Hello. This is Kawamura speaking. BROWN: This is Brown.

カワムラ：もしもし、カワムラです。
ブラウン：ブラウンです。

田中(たなか)：もしもし。
ブラウン：もしもし、山口(やまぐち)さんですか。
田中：いいえ、違(ちが)います。
ブラウン：3567-3981ですか。
田中：いいえ、3567-3891です。
ブラウン：あっ、どうもすみません。間違(まちが)えました。
田中：いいえ。

山口(やまぐち)：もしもし、山口です。
ブラウン：もしもし、ブラウンです。カワムラさんをお願(ねが)いします。
山口：カワムラさんは大学へ行(い)きましたよ。
ブラウン：そうですか。では、また電話(でんわ)します。じゃ、失礼(しつれい)します。
山口：失礼します。

山口(やまぐち)：もしもし、山口です。
ブラウン：もしもし、カワムラさんはいますか。
山口：今(いま)、いませんよ。
ブラウン：そうですか。ブラウンですが、電話(でんわ)をお願(ねが)いします。
山口：電話番号(ばんごう)をお願いします。
ブラウン：3965-9133です。

コミュニケーション・ノート

Talking on the Telephone

もしもし。
Hello.
林(はやし)です。
This is Hayashi speaking.
This is the Hayashi residence.
(lit., This is Hayashi.)
チンさんをお願(ねが)いします。
May I speak to Ms. Chin? (lit., Please give me Ms. Chin.)

TANAKA: Hello. BROWN: Hello. Is this Mr. Yamaguchi? TANAKA: No, it isn't. (*lit., No, it's different.*) BROWN: Is this 3567-3981? TANAKA: No, this is 3567-3891. BROWN: Oh, I'm very sorry. I must have made an error. (*lit., I made a mistake.*) TANAKA: That's OK. (*lit., Not at all.*)

YAMAGUCHI: Hello. This is the Yamaguchi residence. BROWN: Hello. This is Brown. May I speak to Mr. Kawamura? YAMAGUCHI: Mr. Kawamura went to the university. BROWN: I see. Then, I will call him back. Goodbye. YAMAGUCHI: Goodbye.

YAMAGUCHI: Hello. This is the Yamaguchi residence. BROWN: Hello. Is Mr. Kawamura there? YAMAGUCHI: Mr. Kawamura is not here now. BROWN: I see. This is Brown. Can you ask him to call me? YAMAGUCHI: May I have (*lit., Please give me*) your phone number? BROWN: 3965-9113.

間違(まちが)い電話(でんわ)です。
You've dialed the wrong number. (lit., This is the wrong number.)
間違えました。
I made a mistake.
また電話します。
I will call back.
伝言(でんごん)をお願いします。
May I leave a message?

Role Play

Working with a partner, practice the following situations.

1. Call the Yamamoto residence and ask for Ms. Moore, who is boarding there.
2. You have received a call, but it is the wrong number.
3. Call the Muranaka residence. You learn that Mr. Muranaka is not there and say that you will call back later.
4. Call the Sano residence. Ms. Sano is not there. Say that you would like to leave a message.

Extending an Invitation

大学で

林(はやし)：ギブソンさん、今日(きょう)の午後(ごご)、ひまですか。
ギブソン：ええ。
林：一緒(いっしょ)に夕(ゆう)ごはんを食(た)べませんか。
ギブソン：ええ、もちろん。どこがいいですか。
林：「さくらレストラン」はどうですか。
ギブソン：ええ、それはいいですね。

大学で

チン：今日(きょう)は何時(なんじ)にクラスが終(お)わりますか。
カーティス：3時です。
チン：映画(えいが)に行(い)きませんか。

At the university HAYASHI: Ms. Gibson, are you free this afternoon? GIBSON: Yes. HAYASHI: Shall we have dinner together? GIBSON: Yes, certainly (*lit., of course*). Where shall we go? (*lit., Where is good*?) HAYASHI: How about the Sakura Restaurant? GIBSON: Yes, that sounds good.

At the university CHIN: What time is your class over today? CURTIS: At three o'clock. CHIN: Shall we go to the movies? CURTIS: Yes, that would be good. CHIN: Which movie shall we see? (*lit., Which movie is good?*) CURTIS: How about *Ninja*? CHIN: Yes, that would be good. CURTIS: Where shall we meet? CHIN: How about in front of the library? CURTIS: (Yes,) That would be fine.

カーティス：ええ、いいですね。
チン：どの映画がいいですか。
カーティス：「ニンジャ」はどうですか。
チン：ええ、いいですね。
カーティス：どこで会(あ)いましょうか。
チン：図書館(としょかん)の前(まえ)はどうですか。
カーティス：ええ、いいですよ。

三村(みむら)：ギブソンさん、明日(あした)コンサートに行(い)きませんか。
ギブソン：すみません。明日はちょっと仕事(しごと)があります。
三村：そうですか。残念(ざんねん)ですね。

コミュニケーション・ノート

Let's Do Something Together

The ましょう form or the nonpast, negative form of a verb is commonly used to suggest doing something together. (See **Grammar 15** in this chapter for more about the ましょう form.)

一緒(いっしょ)に夕(ゆう)ごはんを食(た)べましょう。
Let's have dinner together.
一緒に夕ごはんを食べませんか。
Would you like to have dinner together?
(*lit., Won't you have dinner together* [*with me*]*?*)

To agree, say

ええ、いいですね。
Yes, that sounds good.

To decline, say

すみません。またこの次(つぎ)。
I'm sorry, but (let's do it) next time.
いいですね。でも、また今度(こんど)。
That would be nice, but (let's make it) next time.
どうもありがとうございます。でも、今はちょっと…。
Thank you very much. But I am afraid now is a bit . . . (inconvenient).

To offer or suggest something to someone else, use X はどうですか。(*How about X?*)

この本はどうですか。
How about this book (to read, to buy, to borrow, etc.)?

MIMURA: Ms. Gibson, would you like to go to a concert tomorrow? GIBSON: I'm sorry. I have (*lit., a little*) work tomorrow. MIMURA: I see. That's too bad.

A politer equivalent is X はいかがですか。This expression is commonly used to offer something to a guest.

コーヒーはいかがですか。
How about (having) a cup of coffee?

Role Play

林さんへ

来週の土曜日、わたしのアパートに来ませんか。
アメリカのビデオを見ます。
カーティスさんも来ます。

ブラウン
2月24日

Practice the following situations with your classmates.

1. Ask one of your classmates when his or her classes are over today, and issue an invitation to do the following.
   a. jog with you after class
   b. drink beer with you after class
   c. eat pizza with you after class
   d. go shopping with you after class
2. Invite a classmate to have lunch with you next Monday. Suggest eating at your favorite restaurant near the university. If your classmate is busy next Monday, ask when he or she is free. Remember that it is rude to say no directly in Japanese; if you are busy next Monday use one of the responses you learned in the Communication Note on page 303a. For example,
3. Call one of your classmates and invite him or her to your home this Saturday. Give simple directions and use descriptions of your house and neighborhood.

Listening Comprehension

1. Mr. Kunio Hasegawa, one of the richest Japanese who ever lived, was murdered in the British-style garden of his large mansion in Kamakura last night. You are a police chief in Kamakura. One of your detectives, Nobuo Maruyama, interviewed six suspects about their activities last night. Listen to his report and fill in the following table. The six suspects are Mr. Hasegawa's wife, Tamako; his daughter, Sawako; his son, Muneo; his mistress, Junko Suzuki; his chauffeur, Kazuo Morimoto; and his brother-in-law, Haruki Kameda.

NAME	7–8 P.M.	8–9 P.M.	9–10 P.M.	10–11 P.M.	11 P.M.–MIDNIGHT

2. Listen to the results of a survey on the lifestyle of Japanese people. Complete the following table by filling in the appropriate numbers.

Japanese who get up before 6:30 A.M.	%
Japanese who eat breakfast	%
Japanese who start work before 8:30 A.M.	%
Japanese who eat lunch between noon and 1:00 P.M.	%
Japanese workers who return home before 7:00 P.M.	%
Japanese workers who go drinking after work	%
Japanese who watch TV every night	%
Japanese who go to bed before 11:00 P.M.	%

Review Chapter 1

Tokyo, the capital of Japan, is home to over 10 percent of the nation's population.

Culture Reading: Geography

Japan consists of four large islands (島).

北海道　本州　四国　九州

Honshu, the main island, is divided into five different regions (地方).

東北地方　関東地方　中部地方　近畿地方　中国地方

Administratively, Japan is divided into one 都, one 道, two 府, and forty-three 県 (*prefectures*).

東京都
北海道
大阪府、京都府
千葉県、埼玉県、…

Read the following passage and identify five regions on the island of Honshu.

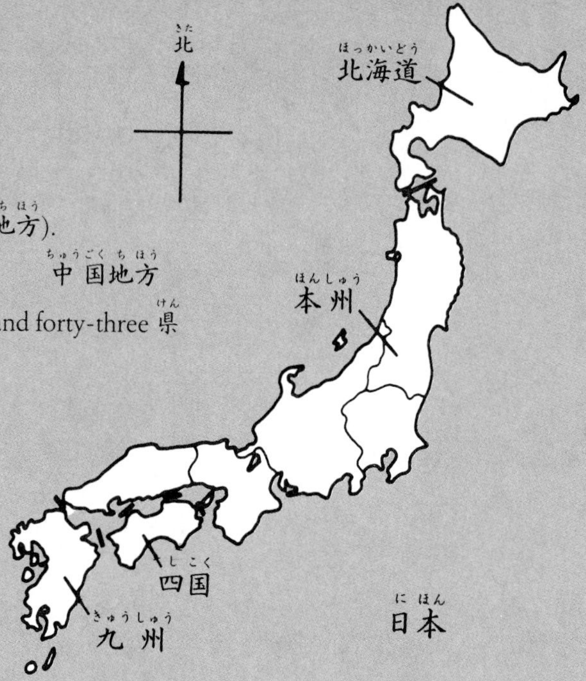

日本は四つの大きい島からなります。北海道、本州、四国、九州です。本州は一番大きい島です。北海道は本州の北にあります。九州は一番南にあります。
本州には五つの地方があります。東北地方、関東地方、中部地方、近畿地方、中国地方です。東北地方は一番北にあります。関東地方は東北地方の南にあります。中部地方は関東地方と近畿地方の間にあります。中国地方は近畿地方の西にあります。中国地方の南に四国があります。東京都は関東地方にあります。関東地方には東京都と六つの県があります。大阪府と京都府は近畿地方にあります。近畿地方にはこの二つの府と五つの県があります。中国には県が五つ、四国には四つ、九州には七つあります。九州の南に沖縄県があります。

からなる *to consist of. . .*
一番 *most*
北 *north*
南 *south*
西 *west*

Oral Activities

アクティビティー 1

どこでしますか。(*Where do you do that?*)

Where do you usually do each of the following activities? Answer in complete sentences, drawing on the options listed below.

Options: ランゲージ・ラボ、映画館、図書館、カフェテリア、教室

1. 本を読む
2. 映画を見る
3. 勉強する
4. 日本語のテープを聞く
5. 昼ごはんを食べる

アクティビティー 2

Katakana practice

Circle all the **katakana** words in this page from a Japanese magazine. Can you guess what each word means?

アクティビティー 3

Vocabulary review

Which of the words listed in parentheses is most closely connected to the first word given?

[例] 朝ごはん (ステーキ、ピザ、シリアル、ビール、本) →
シリアルです。朝ごはんにいつも食べます。

1. 朝六時 (寝る、勉強する、起きる、電話する、話す)
2. クラス (起きる、寝る、勉強する、食べる、飲む)
3. 図書館 (昼ごはん、寝る、ビールを飲む、本を読む)
4. 見る (ステレオ、夕ごはん、テレビ、新聞、トイレ)
5. 読む (新聞、朝ごはん、寝る、シャワー、お風呂)
6. 運動 (朝ごはん、エアロビクス、図書館、本、勉強、寝る)
7. 顔 (みがく、飲む、出かける、洗う、浴びる)
8. お風呂 (みがく、浴びる、入る、起きる、寝る)
9. 週末 (木曜日、金曜日、土曜日、月曜日、火曜日)
10. 着る (ラジオ、ステレオ、ベッド、服、図書館)

アクティビティー 4

Combining sentences

Connect the following pairs of sentences with そして or でも, whichever is appropriate.

1. 朝8時に起きました。顔を洗いました。
2. 図書館へ行きます。本を読みます。
3. 三村さんは学生です。あまり勉強しません。
4. チンさんは中国人です。いつも日本語を話します。
5. いつも6時に起きます。週末は10時に起きます。

アクティビティー 5

月間スケジュール (*Monthly schedule*)

Using the following calendar page, discuss Heather Gibson's activities. Assume that today is March 15th.

[例] 昨日、パーティーに行きました。

S	M	T	W	Th	F	S
			March			
	shopping 1	cleaning judo 2	see prof. 3	4	part-time job 5	free 6
free 7	study 8	library judo 9	study 10	exam 11	part-time job 12	see Hayashi 13
party 14	today 15	study judo 16	exam 17	movie 18	part-time job 19	shopping 20
see Hayashi 21	22	library judo 23	study 24	exam 25	part-time job 26	party 27
laundry cleaning 28	see Brown 29	concert judo 30	movie 31			

アクティビティー 6

学生証(しょう) (*Student ID*)

What do you think the following words mean? Look for hints on Henry Curtis' student ID.

学生証
(身分証明書)

学籍番号 1 0 9 5 7

氏名 ヘンリー・カーティス

年齢 22
生年月日 1971.7.14
国籍 アメリカ
出身地 アトランタ市
住所 横浜市西区中央 2-18
学部 工学
専攻 コンピューター・サイエンス

1. 年齢(ねんれい)
2. 生年月日
3. 出身地(しゅっしんち)
4. 専攻(せんこう)
5. 住所(じゅうしょ)
6. 国籍(こくせき)
7. 学部(がくぶ)

アクティビティー 7

この近所においしいレストランはありませんか。(*Isn't there a good restaurant in this neighborhood?*)

Practice this dialogue.

A: この近所においしいフランス・レストランはありませんか。
B: ええ、ありますよ。
A: 名前は。
B: 「マルセイユ」です。
A: どこですか。
B: 住友銀行のとなりです。
A: じゃ、大学に近いですね。
B: ええ、車で10分くらいです。一緒に行きませんか。
A: ええ、いいですね。いつがいいですか。
B: 金曜日の6時ごろはどうですか。
A: ええ、いいですよ。どこで会いましょうか。
B: 大学の前はどうですか。
A: ええ、けっこうですよ。
B: じゃ、金曜日に。
A: ええ、じゃ、また。

Work in pairs. Practice the preceding dialogue, substituting as appropriate. Use some of the following words in the opening question.

Adjectives: おいしい、安い、便利、いい、きれい、有名、静か
Places: 食堂、喫茶店、公園、ディスコ、パブ、博物館 (*museum*)、美術館 (*art museum*)

アクティビティー 8

ここにサインしてください。(*Please sign here.*)

Fill in the blanks to make questions. Then ask your classmates these questions. If you find someone who answers yes, ask for his or her signature. Don't ask one person more than two questions in a row.

[例] 今日の朝_____か。→

S1: 今日の朝、オレンジ・ジュースを飲みましたか。
S2: はい、飲みました。
S1: ここにサインしてください。

サイン

1. ＿＿＿がとても好きですか。 ＿＿＿
2. 昨日(きのう)＿＿＿か。 ＿＿＿
3. 明日(あした)＿＿＿か。 ＿＿＿
4. ＿＿＿がきらいですか。 ＿＿＿
5. あなたの＿＿＿ですか。 ＿＿＿
6. 日本語の＿＿＿か。 ＿＿＿
7. あなたは＿＿＿ですか。 ＿＿＿

Interview

You have studied a variety of ways to elicit information from others. Here is a chance to practice what you've learned. First, with a partner write questions that ask about the listed information. Then, split up and ask the questions of one classmate you have not talked with often. Feel free to ask other questions, too.

1. name
2. age
3. where he or she lives now
4. where he or she is from
5. what year student he or she is
6. academic major
7. nationality
8. what he or she likes
9. what he or she doesn't like
10. whether he or she studies on weekends

Situations

Listen to you teacher as he or she role plays the following situations. You will then role play the same situations with a classmate.

1. This is the first day of class. Introduce yourself to a student sitting next to you. Ask questions to try to find out about him or her.
2. You get tired easily lately. You are talking with a doctor now. He or she asks questions about your daily schedule: what time you get up, do exercise, etc.
3. Your friend is thinking about moving from his or her current apartment because of a noisy neighbor. Your friend asks about your neighborhood: What's in your neighborhood? Is it convenient? and so on.
4. While you are walking on campus, someone asks you where the cafeteria is. You point it out.
5. One of your classmates has a birthday next week. You would like to celebrate with a party at your home. Invite your classmates.

This Is My Life! : 永田マリ(学生)

こんにちは。永田マリです。今年、21歳になります。東京女子大学の三年生です。専攻はフランス文学です。私の大学は西荻窪にあります。私の家は三鷹にあります。電車で大学に行きます。家から大学まで20分ぐらいかかります。

私は毎朝六時に起きます。そして、七時に家を出ます。クラスは八時に始まります。毎日フランス語やフランス文学のクラスに行きます。クラスは一時に終わります。昼ごはんは大学のカフェテリアで食べます。カフェテリアはとても安いです。昼ごはんのあと、新宿のマクドナルドへアルバイトに行きます。午後3時から7時までの仕事です。午後7時45分に家に帰ります。家で夕ごはんを食べます。

私の家族は母と妹です。母は45歳、妹は17歳です。妹は高校生です。妹は毎日バレーボールと勉強で忙しいです。

土曜日と日曜日はクラスがありません。母も仕事がありません。週末の朝は十時まで寝ます。午後、母と買い物に行きます。渋谷や銀座のデパートによく行きます。私はショッピングが大好きです。二週間に一回くらいアルバイトのお金で新しい服を買います。

東京女子大学 *Tokyo Women's College*
西荻窪 *area in outskirts of Tokyo*

家族 *family* 母 *mother*
妹 *younger sister*
高校生 *high school student*

渋谷 *town in Tokyo*
銀座 *town in Tokyo*

お金 money 服 *clothes*

ビッグマック二つ、マックナゲッツ一つ、コーラ三つ、フレンチフライ一つですね。

Answer these questions.

1. 永田マリさんは今年何歳ですか。
2. 大学の何年生ですか。
3. 専攻は何ですか。
4. 学校に何で行きますか。
5. クラスは何時に始まりますか。
6. どんなクラスに行きますか。
7. 昼ごはんはどこで食べますか。
8. アルバイトは何時から何時までですか。
9. 家に何時に帰りますか。
10. 週末は何時に起きますか。
11. どこへ買い物に行きますか。

4

第四章

天気(てんき)・気候(きこう)

Weather and Climate

今日は雨です。

OBJECTIVES

Topics

Weather reports
Enjoying the four seasons
Forecasting

Grammar

17. Conjugating adjectives
18. Comparatives and superlatives
19. The past, plain forms of verbs
20. Explaining a reason: …のだ
21. The te-form of adjectives and the copula
22. The te-form of verbs
23. Expressing probability and conjecture

Reading and Writing

A letter to Linda Brown
Reading a travel guide: The climate of Iroha

Language Functions and Situations

Asking questions about the Japanese language
Asking for assistance with **kanji**

Vocabulary and Oral Activities

Weather Reports

今日のお天気

雨です

晴です

曇です

雪です

風が強いです

暑いです

寒いです

Vocabulary: Weather and Climate

(お)天気	(お)てんき	weather
気候	きこう	climate
天気予報	てんきよほう	weather forecast
天気図	てんきず	weather map
いい天気	いいてんき	good weather
悪い天気	わるいてんき	bad weather
晴れる	はれる	to clear up
くもる		to become cloudy, to be cloudy
雨が降る	あめがふる	to rain (*lit., Rain falls*)
雪が降る	ゆきがふる	to snow (*lit., Snow falls*)
気温	きおん	(air) temperature
…度	…ど	. . . degrees (*counter*)
暖かい	あたたかい	warm
涼しい	すずしい	cool
むし暑い	むしあつい	sultry, hot and humid
風が吹く	かぜがふく	The wind blows.
風が弱い	かぜがよわい	There is a slight breeze. (*lit., The wind is weak.*)
台風	たいふう	typhoon

Review: 高(たか)い、低(ひく)い

寒(さむ)い and 冷(つめ)たい both translate as *cold* in English. 寒い is used to refer to seasons, climates, atomosphere, while 冷たい refers to the cold object that a person can touch or sense directly. Therefore, 寒い気候 *cold climate*, but 冷たい飲み物 *a cold drink*, 冷たい風 *a cold wind*, and 冷たい人 *a cold (-hearted) person*. The parallel terms for *hot* are both pronounced あつい. The difference is apparent only when writing: 暑い refers to seasons, climates, etc. while 熱い refers to other things, such as 熱いコーヒー *hot coffee*.

コミュニケーション・ノート

Talking About the Weather

Discussing the weather is a ritual of daily conversation in many cultures, and Japan is no exception. In Japanese, a reference to the weather—いいお天気(てんき)ですね (*It's fine weather, isn't it?*)—can serve as a greeting, a substitute for *Hello, how are you?* This is partly because in former times Japan's economy was based on agriculture, especially rice cultivation; many people were concerned about the weather because it affected their livelihoods. In Japan today the weather is a neutral, impersonal topic for everyday conversations with new or old acquaintances. As you will see in **Reading 1** of this chapter, a reference to the weather or season is also a standard opening line for a personal letter.

アクティビティー 1

ダイアログ：今日はどんなお天気ですか。(*What is the weather like today?*)

電話で

ブラウン：長野は今日、どんなお天気ですか。
友だち：晴れですよ。
ブラウン：気温は何度ぐらいですか。
友だち：10度ぐらいです。とても涼しいです。
ブラウン：風はありますか。
友だち：いいえ、ありません。

Practice this dialogue, drawing on information in the following table.

(Temperatures are in degrees centigrade. See the **Culture Note** following the table).

PLACE	WEATHER	TEMPERATURE	WIND
Nara	Rainy	18 degrees, warm	Weak wind
Kumamoto	Cloudy	25 degrees, warm	Weak wind
Yamagata	Snow	0 degrees, cold	Strong wind
Kanazawa	Cloudy	5 degrees, cool	No wind
Naha	Fine	30 degrees, hot	Weak wind

文化ノート

℃

When Japanese say 20度 (ど) (*20 degrees*), they mean *20 degrees centigrade*. In Japan only the centigrade, or Celsius, system is used to measure temperature. To specify which system you are using, you can say 摂氏 (せっし) 20度 (*20℃*) or 華氏 (かし) 68度 (*68°F*), but don't expect Japanese to know the Fahrenheit (華氏) system. If you are good at calculating in your head, the formula for converting ℃ to °F is (℃ × 9/5) + 32 . Otherwise, you might want to start learning the system by remembering a few benchmark equivalents: the Celsius freezing point is 0

On the phone BROWN: What is the weather like in Nagano today? FRIEND: It's sunny and clear. BROWN: (About) what is the temperature? FRIEND: It's about 10 degrees. It's quite cool. BROWN: Is there a breeze (*lit., wind*)? FRIEND: No, there isn't.

degrees, the boiling point is 100 degrees, and so on (see the scale below for more guideposts). One way or another, you will have to get used to the metric system in order to function freely in Japan.

Centigrade	−20	−10	0	10	20	30	40
Fahrenheit	−4	14	32	50	68	86	104

アクティビティー　2

雨(あめ)がよく降(ふ)りますか。(*Does it rain often?*)

For words expressing frequency, review Chapter 3, p.163

Ask your partner what the weather is like in January where he or she grew up. Complete the table following the example of Tokyo.

	東京(とうきょう)	YOUR HOMETOWN	YOUR PARTNER'S HOMETOWN
晴(は)れる	よく晴れます。		
くもる	時々(ときどき)くもります。		
雨(あめ)	時々(ときどき)降ります。		
雪(ゆき)	ほとんど降(ふ)りません。		
気温(きおん)	5度(ど)ぐらいです。		
風(かぜ)	時々強(つよ)い風が吹(ふ)きます。		

勉 Study Grammar 17.

アクティビティー　3

ダイアログ：暑(あつ)かったです。(*It was hot.*)

林(はやし)：ギブソンさん、沖縄(おきなわ)*はどうでしたか。
ギブソン：海(うみ)がとてもきれいでした。
林：暑かったですか。
ギブソン：ええ、とても暑かったですよ。

HAYASHI: Ms. Gibson, how was Okinawa?　GIBSON: The ocean was very pretty.　HAYASHI: Was it hot?　GIBSON: Yes, it was very hot.

*Okinawa, a prefecture located south of Kyushu, consists of the Okinawa Islands and Sakishima Islands.

アクティビティー 4

昨日はどんなお天気でしたか。(*What was the weather like yesterday?*)

Use this summary of yesterday's weather in five Japanese cities to answer the questions that follow.

PLACE	WEATHER	TEMPERATURE	WIND
Sapporo	Snow	−5 degrees, cold	Strong wind
Sendai	Gloudy	7 degrees, cool	No wind
Maebashi	Rain	9 degrees, cool	Strong wind
Hiroshima	Fine	15 degrees, warm	No wind
Kagoshima	Fine	27 degrees, hot	Weak wind

1. 昨日、札幌はどんなお天気でしたか。寒かったですか。暑かったですか。風はありましたか。
2. 仙台はどんなお天気でしたか。気温は何度でしたか。風はありましたか。
3. 前橋はどんなお天気でしたか。涼しかったですか。暖かかったですか。風は強かったですか。弱かったですか。
4. 広島のお天気はよかったですか。涼しかったですか。暖かかったですか。
5. 鹿児島のお天気はよかったですか、悪かったですか。寒かったですか。暑かったですか。気温は何度でしたか。

Now talk about yesterday's weather in your town with your classmates.

(勉) Study Grammar 18.

アクティビティー 5

ダイアログ：どちらのほうが寒いですか。(*Which is colder?*)

ブラウン：仙台と山形とどちらのほうが寒いですか。
三村：山形のほうが寒いです。

ブラウン：じゃ、どちらのほうが雪がたくさん降りますか。
三村：やはり、山形のほうですね。1メートル†ぐらい降ります。

BROWN: Which is colder, Sendai or Yamagata? MIMURA: Yamagata is colder. BROWN: Then, which has more snow? MIMURA: As you might expect, Yamagata. It snows about one meter.

†One meter is about 3.3 feet. Some people say メーター instead of メートル.

アクティビティー 6

どちらのほうが暖かいですか。(*Which place is warmer?*)

Look at the following table of Japanese cities (arranged in order of northernmost to southernmost) while your instructor describes the weather for tomorrow.

TOMORROW'S WEATHER

City	Weather	Temperature	Wind	Notes
Sapporo	Snow (30 cm)	−15℃	North, 20 km/h	Heavy snowfall
Aomori	Fine	−12℃	West, 5 km/h	Foggy
Akita	Snow (15 cm)	−20℃	No wind	Snow till Friday
Sendai	Cloudy	−9℃	North, 3 km/h	Heavy snow Thursday
Niigata	Snow (10 cm)	−11℃	North, 30 km/h	Snowstorm
Takasaki	Rain (2 mm)	−2℃	North, 25 km/h	Cold in the morning
Tokyo	Cloudy	5℃	No wind	Rain in the afternoon
Shizuoka	Cloudy	14℃	South, 5 km/h	Rain at night
Nagoya	Rain (5 mm)	18℃	No wind	Cloudy in the afternoon
Kyoto	Cloudy	13℃	No wind	Foggy
Osaka	Fine	9℃	East, 5 km/h	Fine till Saturday
Hiroshima	Rain (15 mm)	17℃	South, 5 km/h	Cloudy in the afternoon
Nagasaki	Rain (30 mm)	20℃	West, 35 km/h	Storm
Kagoshima	Rain (40 mm)	21℃	West, 50 km/h	Typhoon No. 2
Naha	Fine	30℃	No wind	Sultry

km = kilometer (5⁄8 of a mile)
. . . km/h is read 時速(じそく)…キロ(メートル)

Typhoons are identified by number, starting with 1 each year. The counter …号(ごう [*number*]) is used with typhoons.

Now look at the preceding table and describe the weather in several cities to a classmate.

[例] A: 東京は、どんなお天気ですか。

B: くもりです。午後は雨です。気温は5度ぐらいです。風はありません。

Answer the following questions.

1. 札幌(さっぽろ)と青森(あおもり)とどちらのほうが寒(さむ)いですか。
2. 札幌と秋田(あきた)とどちらのほうが雪(ゆき)がたくさん降(ふ)りますか。
3. 青森(あおもり)と仙台(せんだい)と新潟(にいがた)の中でどこが一番(いちばん)寒いですか。
4. 静岡(しずおか)と京都(きょうと)とどちらのほうが暖(あたた)かいですか。
5. 大阪(おおさか)と那覇(なは)とどちらのほうが暑(あつ)いですか。
6. 広島(ひろしま)と長崎(ながさき)と鹿児島(かごしま)の中でどこが一番雨が降りますか。
7. 新潟(にいがた)と高崎(たかさき)とどちらのほうが風が強(つよ)いですか。
8. どこが一番風が強いですか。
9. どこが一番寒いですか。
10. どこが一番暑いですか。

Vocabulary Library

Precipitation and Other Weather Terms

空	そら	sky
霧	きり	fog
洪水	こうずい	flood
日照り	ひでり	drought
湿度	しつど	humidity
気圧	きあつ	air pressure

Rain

小雨	こさめ	light rain
にわか雨	にわかあめ	shower
夕立	ゆうだち	evening shower
大雨	おおあめ	heavy rain
どしゃぶり		downpour (*of rain*)
梅雨	つゆ	rainy season (*in June and July*)
雷	かみなり	thunder
稲光	いなびかり	lightning

Other Precipitation

降水量	こうすいりょう	precipitation
嵐	あらし	storm
吹雪	ふぶき	snowstorm
大雪	おおゆき	heavy snow
みぞれ		sleet
あられ		hail
霜	しも	frost
露	つゆ	dew

Types of Rain

Rain has exerted a strong influence on Japanese life and culture since ancient times. For centuries the majority of Japanese people made their living in agriculture, for which rainfall is crucial. The amount and type of rain could spell success or failure for a farmer's crop. Over the years, the Japanese coined many words to distinguish different types of rain. Among them are さみだれ (*early summer rain*), しぐれ (*drizzle*), にわかあめ (*shower*), はるさめ (*spring rain*), あきさめ (*autumn rain*), and むらさめ (*passing rain*). There are also numerous ways to describe the manner of the rain's fall with onomatopoeia. (The Japanese language includes so many onomatopoeia that entire dictionaries are devoted to them.)

雨(あめ)がザーザー降(ふ)ります。
It rains cats and dogs. (*lit., It rains "zaa zaa."*)
雨がシトシト降ります。
It drizzles. (*lit., It rains "shito shito."*)
雨がポツポツ降ります。
It rains in big scattered drops. (*lit., It rains "potsu potsu."*)

Although a greater volume of rain falls in the autumn, Japan has a rainy season—called 梅雨 (つゆ)—that consists of more or less constant drizzle for a month or so starting in mid-June. While the rainy season is uncomfortably cold and damp or hot and humid, it is, as the Japanese frequently remind themselves, good for the farmers.

今日は雨がシトシト降ります。

アクティビティー 7

何月が一番寒いですか。(*Which month is coldest?*)

Using this table* of actual average temperatures and rainfall in Tokyo, answer the questions that follow.

東京

Month	1	2	3	4	5	6	7	8	9	10	11	12
Temp. (℃)	5	6	8	14	18	22	25	27	23	17	12	7
Precip. (mm)	54	63	102	128	148	181	125	137	193	181	93	56

1. 東京は7月と8月とどちらが暑いですか。
2. 何月が一番寒いですか。
3. 4月と5月とどちらのほうがたくさん雨が降りますか。
4. 1月と2月と3月のなかで何月が一番雨が多いですか。
5. 何月が一番雨が多いですか。

Now, look at these statistics about the climate in five international cities and answer the questions. (Temperature is in degrees centigrade, and precipitation is in millimeters.)

Month	1	2	3	4	5	6	7	8	9	10	11	12
LONDON												
Temperature	4	4	7	9	12	16	18	17	15	11	7	5
Precipitation	53	40	37	38	46	46	56	59	50	57	64	48
PARIS												
Temperature	3	4	7	10	14	17	19	18	16	11	7	4
Precipitation	54	43	32	38	52	50	55	62	51	49	50	49
SYDNEY												
Temperature	22	22	21	18	16	13	12	13	15	18	19	21
Precipitation	104	125	129	101	115	141	94	83	72	80	77	86
MOSCOW												
Temperature	−10	−9	−4	5	12	17	19	17	11	4	−2	−7
Precipitation	31	28	33	35	52	67	74	74	58	51	36	36
BUENOS AIRES												
Temperature	24	23	20	17	13	11	10	11	14	16	20	22
Precipitation	92	84	122	87	78	55	42	58	88	100	79	90

---

*Source: *Science Almanac 1991*. Figures are the average for the period 1951 to 1980.

1. ロンドンでは何月が一番気温が高いですか。何月が一番気温が低いですか。
2. ロンドンでは何月が一番降水量 (*precipitation*) が多いですか。何月が一番降水量が少ないですか。
3. シドニーとブエノスアイレスとどちらが1月の気温が高いですか。
4. シドニーとブエノスアイレスとどちらが7月の降水量が多いですか。
5. ロンドンとパリとモスクワの中でどこが8月の気温が一番高いですか。

Make up similar questions about the table to ask your classmates.

(勉) Study Grammar 19, 20.

アクティビティー 8

ダイアログ：アルバイトがあったんです。(*Because I had a part-time job.*)

林：昨日はクラスに来ませんでしたね。
三村：ええ、アルバイトがあったんです。
林：今日はクラスに出るんですか。
三村：ええ、雨が降ったから、テニスの練習がないんです。

アクティビティー 9

なぜですか。(*Why?*)

Make dialogues, following the example.

[例] パーティーに行かない →
S1: パーティーに行かなかったんですか。
S2: ええ、病気 (*sick*) だったんです。

Useful expressions (reasons)

雪が降る	暇(な)	天気がいい	週末	暑い	時間がある
雨が降る	寒い	きたない	誕生日	病気	仕事がある

1. スキーに行く
2. 家にいた
3. レストランで夕ごはんを食べる
4. 映画を見る
5. クラスに行かない
6. 掃除する
7. 10時に起きる
8. プールで泳ぐ
9. 12時まで勉強する

HAYASHI: You didn't come to class yesterday, did you? MIMURA: No (*lit., Yes*), because I had a part-time job. HAYASHI: Are you going to attend class today? MIMURA: Yes. Because it rained, I don't have (*lit., there isn't*) tennis practice.

コミュニケーション・ノート

Asking and Answering *Why?*

Two interrogative pronouns are used to ask why: なぜ and どうして. In very informal speech, either can be used alone to mean *Why?* Otherwise follow the examples of usage below.

なぜですか。
Why (is that)?
どうしてですか。
Why (is that)?
なぜピクニックに行きませんでしたか。
Why didn't you come to the picnic?
どうしてクラスを休(やす)みましたか。
Why did you miss class?

To answer why or to give a reason, use the conjunction から (*because*) or ので (*because; it being that . . .*).

雨(あめ)が降(ふ)ったから、行きませんでした。
Because it rained, I didn't go.
病気(びょうき)だったので、休(やす)みました。
Because I was sick, I took the day off.

Or you can simply say

雨が降ったからです。
(It's) Because it rained.
病気(びょうき)だったのです or 病気だったんです。
It's that I was sick.

アクティビティー 10

暑(あつ)いから、海(うみ)へ行(い)きましょう。(*Because it's hot, let's go to the ocean.*)

Complete the following sentences. How many different sentences can you make?

[例] 暑いから、…→
暑いから、海へ行きましょう。
暑いから、アイスクリームを食(た)べます。
暑いから、クーラーを買(か)います。

1. 昨日(きのう)はとても寒(さむ)かったので、
2. 台風(たいふう)が来(き)たので、
3. 今日(きょう)は暖(あたた)かいから、
4. 風(かぜ)がとても強(つよ)いので、
5. 天気(てんき)がいいから、
6. 雪(ゆき)がたくさん降(ふ)ったから、

Enjoying the Four Seasons

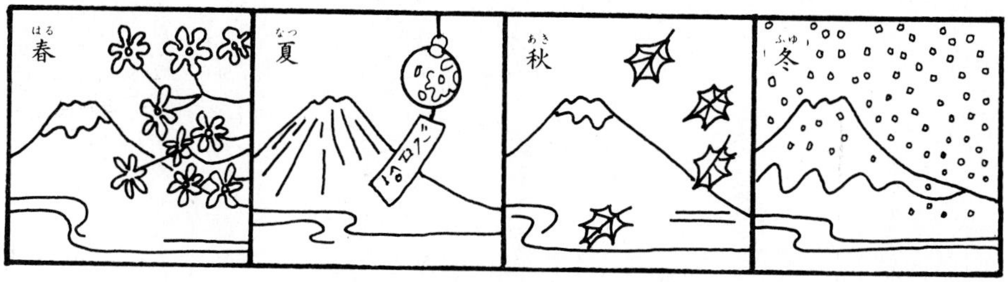

Vocabulary: Seasons and Seasonal Activities

季節	きせつ	season
四季	しき	four seasons
カレンダー		calendar
泳ぐ	およぐ	to swim
スキーをする		to ski
スケートをする		to skate
山登りをする	やまのぼりをする	to climb mountains
つりをする		to fish
キャンプ(に行く)	キャンプ(にいく)	(to go) camping
ハイキング(に行く)	ハイキング(にいく)	(to go) hiking
花見(に行く)	はなみ(にいく)	(to go) cherry blossom viewing

アクティビティー 11

どの季節が一番好きですか。(*Which season do you like best?*)

Answer the following questions.

1. 春は何月から何月までですか。
2. 夏は何月から何月までですか。
3. 秋は何月から何月までですか。
4. 冬は何月から何月までですか。
5. シドニーの8月はどんな季節ですか。
6. ニューヨークの8月はどんな季節ですか。
7. シドニーの1月はどんな季節ですか。
8. ニューヨークの1月はどんな季節ですか。
9. どの季節が一番暑いですか。
10. どの季節が一番寒いですか。
11. どの季節が一番雨が降りますか。
12. どの季節が一番好きですか。

クラスメートと花見に来ました。

アクティビティー 12

Do you remember? The interrogative どの asks which one of three or more alternatives. To ask which one of two, use どちら. Review **Grammar 4, Chapter 1**.

どの季節にしますか。(*In what season do you do that?*)

In what season(s) do you do these activities? Ask your partner, following the example.

[例]　スキーをする →
　S1: どの季節にスキーをしますか。
　S2: 冬です。

1. 海で泳ぐ
2. ピクニックに行く
3. スケートをする
4. 山登りをする
5. キャンプに行く
6. 釣りをする
7. ゴルフをする
8. 花見に行く

What activities do you do in each of the four seasons? Discuss in class. Are there any activities you can do only in a specific season?

アクティビティー 13

今年の夏は暖かいですけれども… (*This summer is warm but . . .*)

Complete the sentences, following the example.

[例]　今年の夏は暖かいですけれども、去年の夏は… →
　今年の夏は暖かいですけれども、去年の夏は涼しかったです。

1. 今年の夏は雨が多いですが、去年の夏は…
2. 夏は雨がたくさん降りますが、冬は…
3. 今年の冬は暖かいですけれども、去年の冬は…
4. おととしの冬は雪がたくさん降りましたが、去年の冬は…
5. 夏は台風がたくさん来ますが、冬は…
6. 今週は暑いですけれども、先週は…
7. 今年は雨が多いですけれども、去年は…
8. 今日は風が弱いですが、昨日は…
9. 今月は気温が高いですけれども、先月は…

文法ノート

Linking Disjunctive Clauses with けれども

You've already learned several ways to link disjunctive or contrasting ideas, including が (*but*), でも (*but*), and しかし (*however*). Another common connector is けれども. Unlike those you have studied so far, けれども can be used either as a conjunction (i.e., to join two independent clauses into one sentence) or as a transitional phrase at the beginning of the second of two contrasting sentences. It is roughly equivalent to *although* or *however.*

ここは冬は寒いですけれども、雪はあまり降りません。
Although winters are cold here, it doesn't snow much.
ここは冬は寒いです。けれども、雪はあまり降りません。
Winters are cold here. Nevertheless, it doesn't snow much.

Of the linking words considered here, が is most common and expresses the least contrast. でも is common in informal conversation, while しかし tends to sound bookish or formal. けれども may be shortened to けども in informal conversation, and も is often dropped (yielding けれど or けど) to express a lesser degree of contrast.

As shown in the preceding examples, the particle は often marks items being compared or contrasted, regardless of which conjunction or transition is used. Here are some more examples.

今日は忙しいですけれども、明日は暇です。
I am busy today, but I will be free tomorrow.
ブラウンさんは来ましたが、カワムラさんは来ませんでした。
Ms. Brown came, but Mr. Kawamura didn't.

㊗ Study Grammar 21 and 22.

アクティビティー 14

ダイアログ：冬はどんな気候ですか。(*What is the climate like in winter?*)

林：エドモントンの冬はどんな気候ですか。
ギブソン：雪がたくさん降って、とても寒いです。
林：夏はどうですか。
ギブソン：夏は涼しくて、おだやかな気候です。

Practice the dialogue, using the following pattern and information.

—(place) の (season) はどんな気候ですか。
— ______。

1. —New York, winter
   —rainy and cold
2. —Seattle, fall
   —fine and warm
3. —Sapporo, spring
   —cloudy and cool
4. —Tokyo, summer
   —fine and sultry

アクティビティー 15

夏、何をしましたか。(*What did he do in the summer?*)

Using the information provided, tell what each person did.

[例] —カワムラさんは夏、何をしましたか。
—アメリカに帰って、友だちに会いました。

1. winter, go to the mountains, ski
2. spring, go to a park, view cherry blossoms
3. fall, go to Nagano, hike
4. summer, go to the ocean, swim

HAYASHI: What is the climate like in Edmonton in winter? GIBSON: It snows a lot, and it's very cold. HAYASHI: What about summer? GIBSON: Summers are cool, and the weather is mild.

Forecasting

(勉) Study Grammar 23.

アクティビティー 16

ダイアログ：雨が降るかもしれません。(*It might rain.*)

ブラウン：いやなお天気ですね。

林：ええ、空が暗いですね。

ブラウン：午後は雨が降るでしょうか。

林：ええ、嵐が来るかもしれません。

アクティビティー 17

明日はどんなお天気でしょうか。(*What will the weather be like tomorrow?*)

While looking at the table, listen to your instructor forecast tomorrow's weather.

[例]　函館は雪が降るでしょう。

Useful words: 東 *east;* 西 *west;* 南 *south;* 北 *north*

CITY	WEATHER	TEMPERATURE	WIND
Hakodate	Snow	−3, cold	North, strong
Yamagata	Cloudy, P.M. snow	−5, cold	North, strong
Hukushima	Fine, occasionally cloudy	−1, cold	West, weak
Chiba	Fine	16, warm	South
Kamakura	Rain, occasionally cloudy	12, cool	No wind
Gihu	Rain	8, cool	East, weak
Kobe	Cloudy, occasionally fine	17, warm	South, weak
Okayama	Fine	20, warm	No wind
Kochi	Rain	27, hot	No wind
Hukuoka	Cloudy, P.M. rain	24	East, weak
Miyazaki	Fine	28, hot	No wind
Yakushima	Fine	30, hot	South, weak

Ms. Brown and Mr. Hayashi are talking BROWN: The weather is unpleasant, isn't it? HAYASHI: Yes. The sky is dark (isn't it?) BROWN: I wonder if it will rain this afternoon. HAYASHI: Yes. It just might storm. (*lit., A storm might come.*)

アクティビティー 18

明日は雨が降るでしょう。(*It will rain tomorrow.*)

You are a TV meteorologist. Using the following data, give a weather forecast. Don't forget to use でしょう or かもしれません.

Kushiro	cloudy, occasional snow, very cold −15 degrees, very strong north wind
Okayama	sunny, very good weather 20 degrees, warm, no wind
Nara	cloudy in the morning, rain in the afternoon a little cold, 5 degrees, weak west wind
Miyazaki	cloudy, occasional rain in the morning foggy in the morning, warm, 22 degrees, no wind.

アクティビティー 19

明日のお天気は？(*What about tomorrow's weather?*)

Working with a partner, draw a map of your town or region. One of you will play a TV meteorologist predicting tomorrow's weather. As you make your predictions, draw appropriate weather symbols and temperatures on the map. The second person will play a TV anchor asking the meteorologist questions about the weather. Be creative.

Grammar and Exercises

17. Conjugating Adjectives

ブラウン：昨日寒かったですね。
林：ええ、本当に。
ブラウン：わたしのアパートには、ストーブがまだありませんから、こまりました。
林：それはたいへんでしたね。

BROWN: It was cold yesterday, wasn't it? HAYASHI: Yes, really. BROWN: I had a hard time, because there isn't a heater in my apartment yet. HAYASHI: That must have been awful! (*lit., That was awful, wasn't it?*)

町田：プールはどうでしたか。
チン：人がとても多かったです。
町田：水はきれいでしたか。
チン：いいえ、あまりきれいではありませんでした。
町田：それはよくありませんでしたね。

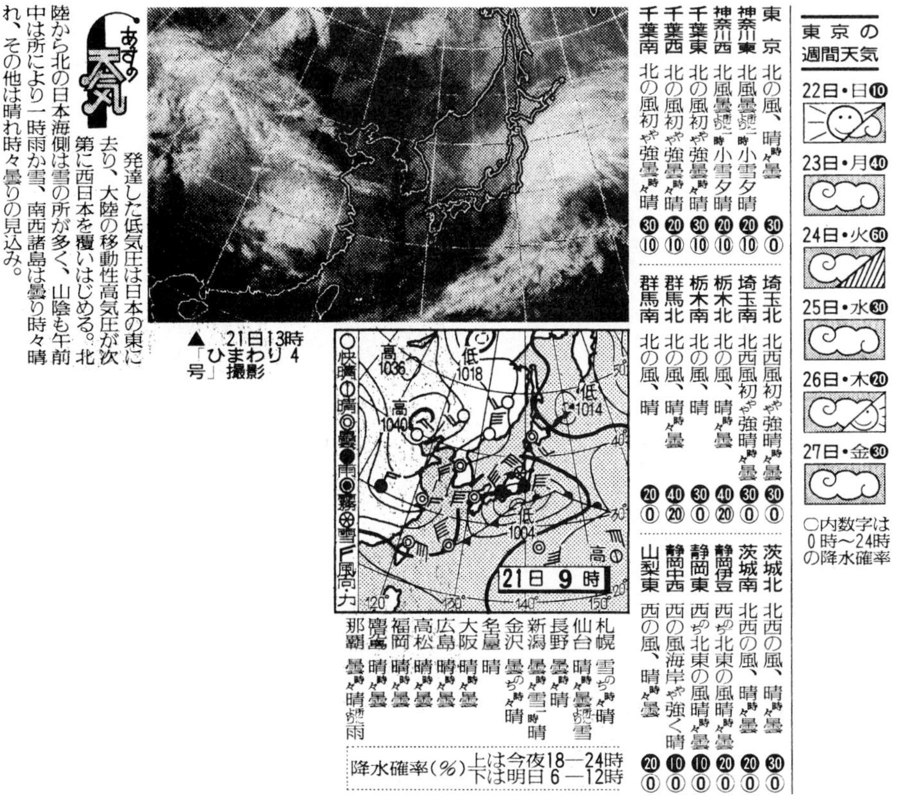

あすの天気

発達した低気圧は日本の東に去り、大陸の移動性高気圧が次第に西日本を覆いはじめる。北陸から北の日本海側は雪の所が多く、山陰も午前中は所により一時雨か雪、南西諸島は曇り時々晴れ、その他は晴れ時々曇りの見込み。

▲21日13時「ひまわり4号」撮影

地域	予報	今夜	明日
東京	北の風、晴時々曇	30	0
神奈川東	北風曇所により一時小雪夕晴	20	10
神奈川西	北風曇所により一時小雪夕晴	20	10
千葉東	北の風初やや強曇時々晴	30	10
千葉西	北の風初やや強曇時々晴	20	10
千葉南	北の風初やや強曇時々晴	30	10
埼玉北	北西風初やや強晴時々曇	30	0
埼玉南	北西風初やや強晴時々曇	30	0
栃木北	北の風、晴時々曇	40	20
栃木南	北の風、晴	30	0
群馬北	北の風、晴時々曇	40	20
群馬南	北の風、晴	20	0
茨城北	北西の風、晴時々曇	30	0
茨城南	北西の風、晴時々曇	20	0
静岡伊豆	西のち北東の風晴時々曇	20	0
静岡東	西のち北東の風晴時々曇	10	0
静岡中西	西の風海岸やや強く晴	10	0
山梨東	西の風、晴時々曇	20	0

札幌	雪のち時々晴
仙台	晴時々曇所により雪
長野	曇時々晴
新潟	曇時々雪一時晴
金沢	曇のち時々晴
名古屋	晴
大阪	晴時々曇
広島	晴時々曇
高松	晴時々曇
福岡	晴時々曇
鹿児島	晴時々曇
那覇	曇時々晴所により雨

降水確率（%）上は今夜18—24時 下は明日6—12時

東京の週間天気

日	降水確率
22日・日	10
23日・月	40
24日・火	60
25日・水	30
26日・木	20
27日・金	30

○内数字は0時～24時の降水確率

17.1 You have already studied the two types of Japanese adjectives, i-adjectives and na-adjectives. Both types of adjectives, like verbs, conjugate in terms of tense, politeness, and affirmation/negation and have at least eight basic conjugated forms when used as predicates (that is, when not in prenominal position).

MACHIDA: How was the swimming pool? CHIN: There were many people. MACHIDA: Was the water clean? CHIN: No, it wasn't very clean. MACHIDA: That's not good. (*lit., That wasn't good.*)

17.2 The nonpast forms of i- and na-adjectives are formed as follows.

I-ADJECTIVES: 寒(さむ)い (*cold*)

Nonpast	Plain	Polite
Affirmative	Root + い (i.e., dictionary form) = 寒(さむ)い	Dictionary form + です = 寒(さむ)いです
Negative	Root + く + ない = 寒(さむ)くない	Root + く + ない + です = 寒(さむ)くないです or Root + く + ありません = 寒(さむ)くありません

ないです expresses a stranger level of regation than ありません.

NA-ADJECTIVES: 静(しず)か (*quiet*)

だ is the plain, nonpast, affirmative form of the copula です.

Past	Plain	Polite
Affirmative	Dictionary form + だ 静(しず)かだ	Dictionary form + です = 静(しず)かです
Negative	Dictionary form + ではない or じゃない = 静(しず)かではない or 静(しず)かじゃない	Dictionary form + ではありません or じゃありません = 静(しず)かではありません or 静(しず)かじゃありません

じゃ is a contraction of では and is somewhat less formal and more colloquial than では.

Notice that na-adjectives themselves do not conjugate. Rather, the conjugated forms of the copula です (see **Grammar 1,** Chapter 1) are appended to the dictionary form of a na-adjective.

17.3 The past forms of i-adjectives are formed as follows.

I-ADJECTIVES: 寒い (*cold*)

Past	Plain	Polite
Affirmative	Root + かった = 寒(さむ)かった	Plain, past + です = 寒(さむ)かったです

Past	Plain	Polite
Negative	Root + く + なかった = 寒(さむ)くなかった	Root + く + なかったです = 寒(さむ)くなかったです or Root + く + ありませんでした = 寒(さむ)くありませんでした

大野先生(おおのせんせい)はとてもきびしかったです。
Professor Oono was very strict.
その問題(もんだい)はあまりむずかしくありませんでした。
That problem wasn't very difficult.
あのバースデー・ケーキは大きかった。
That birthday cake was big.
その映画(えいが)はぜんぜんおもしろくなかった。
That movie wasn't at all interesting.

The past forms of na-adjectives are formed by adding the conjugated forms of the copula です to their dictionary form.

NA-ADJECTIVES: 静か (*quiet*)

Past	Plain	Polite
Affirmative	静(しず)かだった	静(しず)かでした
Negative	静(しず)かではなかった or 静(しず)かじゃなかった	静(しず)かではありませんでした or 静(しず)かじゃありませんでした

その女(おんな)の人は静(しず)かでした。
That woman was quiet.
チンさんはあまり元気(げんき)ではありませんでした。
Ms. Chin wasn't feeling very well (lit., wasn't very healthy).
空(そら)がとてもきれいだった。
The sky was quite lovely.
あの人はあまり親切(しんせつ)じゃなかった。
That person was not very kind.

17.4 よい (or いい) meaning *good* shows some irregularity, although it is an i-adjective.

Nonpast	Plain	Polite
Affirmative	よい or いい	いいです
Negative	よくない	よくありません or よくないです

Past	Plain	Polite
Affirmative	よかった	よかったです
Negative	よくなかった	よくありませんでした or よくなかったです

いい and いいです are colloquial forms of よい and よいです. These colloquial forms are more commonly used than よい (です) in informal conversations.

あの辞書(じしょ)はよくなかった。
That dictionary wasn't good.

練習 1

Disagree with these statements, following the example.

[例] ボストンは寒(さむ)かったですか。(暑(あつ)い) →
いいえ、寒くなかったです (寒くありませんでした)。暑かったです。

1. お天気(てんき)は悪(わる)かったですか。(いい)
2. 東京(とうきょう)は涼(すず)しかったですか。(暖かい)
3. その本はおもしろかったですか。(つまらない)
4. そこはきれいでしたか。(きたない)
5. その人は静(しず)かでしたか。(うるさい)
6. 東京の冬(ふゆ)は長(なが)かったですか。(短(みじか)い)
7. その人は忙(いそが)しかったですか。(ひま)
8. その先生はきびしかったですか。(やさしい)
9. その山(やま) (*mountain*) は高(たか)かったですか。(低(ひく)い)
10. その学生はまじめ (*serious*) でしたか。(ふまじめ *lazy, not serious*)

練習 2

Change these sentences to the past tense, preserving the politeness level, as shown in the example.

[例]　あの映画はおもしろくない。→ あの映画はおもしろくなかった。

1. アラスカはいつも寒いです。
2. 日本の夏はむし暑い。
3. 4月は毎日暖かい。
4. 今年の夏は涼しい。
5. あの部屋はとても暑い。
6. 12月は気温が高くない。
7. ブラウンさんは元気じゃありません。
8. あの本はよくない。
9. 天気がいつも悪い。
10. カワムラさんはハンサムだ。
11. ギブソンさんはエレガントです。
12. この大学は有名ではない。

練習 3

Complete the following sentences by filling in each blank with the past form of an adjective.

[例]　あの人は昨日は（　　）が、今日は病気です。→
　　あの人は昨日は元気でしたが、今日は病気です。

1. わたしは昨日は（　　）が、今日はひまです。
2. 昨日は（　　）が、今日は暑いです。
3. 東京は昨日は気温が（　　）が、今日は低い。
4. そのショッピングセンターは昨日は人が（　　）が、今日は少ない。
5. あの学生は昨日は（　　）が、今日はうるさい。
6. 昨日は風が（　　）が、今日は弱いです。
7. 昨日は天気が（　　）が、今日は悪い。
8. 「ジョーズⅠ」は（　　）が、「ジョーズⅣ」はつまらないです。

練習 4

Substituting 昨日 for 今日, change each predicate in the following passage to the corresponding past form.

今日は一月二十三日です。朝からとても寒いです。でも、お天気はとてもいいです。空がとてもきれいです。風がありますが、あまり強くありません。今日は土曜日ですから、クラスがありません。宿題(*homework*) もありません。だから (*because of that*)、わたしはひまです。今日は部屋 (*room*) を掃除します。わたしの部屋はとてもきたないです。それから、洗濯もします。わたしのルームメートは病気です。部屋にいます。

18. Comparatives and Superlatives

林：ロサンゼルスはマイアミより暑いですか。
カワムラ：いいえ、マイアミのほうが暑いです。
林：では、ロサンゼルスとマイアミとどちらのほうがたくさん雨が降りますか。
カワムラ：マイアミのほうがたくさん降ります。

チン：札幌と仙台と東京の中でどこが一番寒いですか。
町田：札幌です。
チン：その三つの中でどこが一番北にありますか。
町田：札幌が一番北にあります。
チン：なるほど。

町田：食べ物の中で何が一番好きですか。
カワムラ：チョコレートです。
町田：では、何が一番きらいですか。
カワムラ：レバーです。

HAYASHI: Is it hotter in Los Angeles than in Miami? KAWAMURA: No, it's hotter in Miami. HAYASHI: Well, which has more rain—Los Angeles or Miami? KAWAMURA: It rains more in Miami.

CHIN: Which is coldest—Sapporo, Sendai, or Tokyo? MACHIDA: Sapporo. CHIN: Among them, which is furthest north? MACHIDA: Sapporo is furthest north. CHIN: I see.

MACHIDA: What food do you like most? KAWAMURA: Chocolate. MACHIDA: Well then, what food do you like least (*lit., dislike most*)? KAWAMURA: Liver.

18.1 A sentence that compares *two* quantities or qualities, such as *John is taller than Mary* or *John ate more than Mary,* is called a *comparative sentence.* A Japanese comparative sentence takes one of two forms, as follows. Y より means *more than Y* or *compared to Y.*

Note that unlike English, adjectives in Japanese do not have comparative or superlative forms.

X	は	Y	より	adjective

X is more . . . than Y. (*lit., More than Y, X is. . . .*)

東京(とうきょう)は大阪(おおさか)より大きい。

Tokyo is larger than Osaka. (*lit., More than Osaka, Tokyo is large.*)

あの町はこの町よりきれいでした。

That town was prettier than this town.

林(はやし)さんは三村(みむら)さんよりまじめですか。

Is Mr. Hayashi more serious than Mr. Mimura? (*lit., More than Mr. Mimura, is Mr. Hayashi serious?*)

X	は	Y	より	adverb + verb

X does . . . more (. . .) than Y. (*lit., More than Y, X does. . . .*)

今年(ことし)の冬(ふゆ)は去年(きょねん)の冬より雨(あめ)がたくさん降(ふ)りました。

It rained more this winter than last winter.

ブラウンさんはギブソンさんより早(はや)く起(お)きました。

Ms. Brown got up earlier than Ms. Gibson.

18.2 To ask a comparative question, use the following construction, which means *Of X and Y, which* (*alternative*) *is/does* (*more*). . . .

X	と	Y	と	どちら(のほう)が	adjective or adverb + verb	か

Which (alternative) is more . . . — X or Y?
Which (alternative) does . . . more (. . .) — X or Y?

The answer to this question takes the following form, meaning *The* (*alternative of*) *X is* (*more*). . . .

X	(のほう)が	adjective or adverb + verb

X is more. . . .
X does (something) more. . . .

横井先生と大野先生とどちら(のほう)がきびしいですか。
Who is stricter—Professor Yokoi or Professor Oono? (lit., Of Professor Yokoi and Professor Oono, which [alternative] is strict?)

大野先生のほうがきびしいです。
Professor Oono is stricter. (lit., The alternative of Professor Oono is strict.)

ブラウンさんとギブソンさんとどちら(のほう)が早く起きますか。
Who gets up earlier—Ms. Brown or Ms. Gibson? (lit., Of Ms. Brown and Ms. Gibson, which [alternative] gets up early?)

ブラウンさんのほうが早く起きます。
Ms. Brown gets up earlier. (lit., The alternative of Ms. Brown gets up early.)

Notice that when はやい is used in its temporal meaning of *early*, the character 早い is used. When はやい means fast or quick, use the character 速い.

文法ノート

Adverbs Used with Comparatives

The following adverbs expressing degree are often used in comparative sentences.

ずっと	*by far*
もっと	*more*
少し or ちょっと	*a little*

この大学はあの大学よりずっと大きい。
This university is far bigger than that university.

アンカレッジはバンクーバーよりもっと寒いです。
Anchorage is colder (lit., more cold) than Vancouver.

山口さんは高田さんより少し(ちょっと)若い。
Mr. Yamaguchi is a bit younger than Mr. Takada.

The counter …倍 (*times,* as in magnification) or a specific number (plus the appropriate counter, if necessary) specifies the extent of the difference in comparisons. These expressions come before adjectives or adverbs.

この電車はあの電車より3倍速い。
This train is three times faster than that train.

カプチーノはカフェオレより200円高いです。
Cappuccino costs 200 yen more than cafe au lait.

今日は昨日より3度暖かい。
It is 3 degrees warmer today than yesterday.
今日は昨日より一時間早く起きた。
Today I got up one hour earlier than yesterday.

18.3 A **superlative sentence** is one that compares the quality or quantity of *three or more* entities and specifies which entity has most of that quality or quantity. For instance, *Who is the most popular actress in the United States — Julia Roberts, Vanna White, or Pia Zadora?*

A Japanese superlative sentence takes one of the following forms. (一番 [*lit., number one*] means *most*.)

XとYとZ	の中で or のうちで	Xが (or other particle)	一番	adjective or adverb	+ verb

X is the most . . . among X, Y, and Z.
X does . . . the most (. . .) among X, Y, and Z.

ロンドンとパリとモスクワの中で、モスクワが一番寒い。
Among London, Paris, and Moscow, Moscow is the coldest.
東京と横浜と大阪の中で、東京が一番大きい。
Among Tokyo, Yokohama, and Osaka, Tokyo is the largest.
あの四人のうちで、ギブソンさんが一番速く走ります。
Among those four people, Ms. Gibson runs fastest.
ビール、ジュース、コーラの中でコーラを一番よく飲みます。
Among beer, juice, and cola, I drink cola most often.

18.4 An *equative sentence* is one that equates two entities. For example, *He is as tall as I am*. Equative sentences in Japanese are expressed as follows.

X	は	Y	と	同じぐらい	adjective or adverb	+ verb

As you remember, 同じ means *same* and ぐらい means *about*. The phrase 同じぐらい means *to (about) the same extent* or *to (about) the same degree*. This sentence means *X is about the same as Y with regard to. . . .*

広島の三月は鹿児島の三月と同じぐらい暖かいです。
March in Hiroshima is about as warm as March in Kagoshima.
町田さんは林さんと同じぐらいよくここに来ます。
Ms. Machida comes here about as often as Mr. Hayashi.

A negative equative sentence such as A *is not as . . . as B* is expressed with this structure. (ほど means *as much as.*)

X	は	Y	ほど	negative form of adjective or adverb + negative form of verb

X is/does not . . . as much as Y.
春の夜は秋の夜ほど寒くない。
Spring evenings aren't as cold as fall evenings.
あの人はチンさんほど速く話しません。
That person doesn't talk as fast as Ms. Chin.

練習 1

Make dialogues, following the example.

[例] (この大学)(あの大学)(大きい) →
—この大学とあの大学とどちらが大きいですか。
—この大学のほうが大きいです or この大学です。

1. (この町)(フローレンス)(きれい)
2. (ペプシ)(コーク)(おいしい [*tasty*])
3. (日本の車)(アメリカの車)(安い)
4. (フロリダ)(ネバダ)(雨がたくさん降る)
5. (ニューヨーク)(ボストン)(寒い)
6. (カール・ルイス)(ベン・ジョンソン)(速く [*fast*] 走る)
7. (去年の夏)(今年の夏)(暑い)
8. (トロント)(エドモントン)(雪が多い)
9. (昨日)(今日)(涼しい)
10. (南日本)(北日本)(台風がたくさん来る)

練習 2

Fill in the blanks to complete the sentences.

[例] このセーターはあのセーターより (高いです)。

1. 東京はニューヨークより (　　)。
2. アメリカは日本より人口が (　　)。
3. アメリカ人は日本人より (　　)。
4. 日本はメキシコより (　　)。
5. わたしはカワムラさんより (　　)。
6. わたしの日本語の先生は横井先生より (　　)。
7. 日本語はラテン語より (　　)。
8. この本はあの本より (　　)。

練習 3

Change the following into negative sentences.

[例] この大学はあの大学より大きいです。→
この大学はあの大学ほど大きくありません。

1. 林さんはカワムラさんよりたくさん食べます。
2. 東京は京都より古いです。
3. 昨日は今日よりむし暑かった。
4. 林さんは三村さんよりお酒が好きだ。
5. チンさんはシュミットさんより日本語をじょうずに (*skillfully, well*) 話す。
6. 札幌は秋田より雪が多く (*a lot*) 降ります。
7. 町田さんは本田さんよりキュートです。
8. この映画はあの映画よりおもしろかった。

練習 4

Use the interrogative だれ (*who*) when asking about people, どれ (*which one*) when asking about things, concepts, and events, and どこ (*where*) when asking about places.

Make dialogues using the words provided, as shown in the example.

[例] (ヘミングウェー)(ホーソン)(クラベル)(有名) →
—ヘミングウェーとホーソンとクラベルの中でだれが一番有名ですか。
—ヘミングウェーが一番有名です。

1. (日本語)(ロシア語)(アラビア語)(むずかしい)
2. (プレリュード)(ミヤタ)(アクラ・レジェンド)(高い)
3. (シカゴ)(ロサンジェルス)(ダラス)(風が強い)

4. （ミシガン）（フロリダ）（アイダホ）（暖かい）
5. （バス）（車）（電車）（便利）
6. （スーパー）（デパート）（セブン・イレブン）（安い）
7. （ビール）（お茶）（コーヒー）（よく飲む）

練習　5

Answer the following questions in Japanese.

1. アメリカで一番大きい都市 (*city*) はどこですか。
2. アメリカで一番古い都市 はどこですか。
3. 世界 (*world*) で一番高い建物は何ですか。
4. アメリカで一番きれいな都市はどこですか。
5. アメリカで一番有名な日本人はだれですか。
6. 日本の食べ物の中で何が一番好きですか。
7. 一年中 で何月が一番暑いですか。
8. 一年中で何月が一番寒いですか。
9. 一年中で何月が一番 忙しい (*busy*) ですか。
10. スポーツの中で何が一番おもしろいですか。
11. 日本語の中でどのことば (*word*) が一番好きですか。

19. The Past, Plain Forms of Verbs

さとみ：昨日、映画に行ったの。
大助：うん。
さとみ：何を見たの。
大助：「ニンジャ」。おもしろかったよ。
ゆり子：さとみ、昼ごはんを食べたの。
さとみ：ええ、カワムラさんと「ユアーズ」で食べたわ。
ゆり子：「ユアーズ」…どこにあるの。
さとみ：先月、駅の前にできたのよ。
知らないの？

SATOMI: Did you go to the movies yesterday? DAISUKE: Yeah. SATOMI: What did you see? DAISUKE: *Ninja*. It was good. (*lit., It was interesting.*)

YURIKO: Satomi, did you eat lunch? SATOMI: Yes, I ate with Mr. Kawamura at Yours. YURIKO: Yours? Where is it? SATOMI: It opened in front of the station last month. Don't you know (about it)?

19.1 You have studied the past, polite forms of the three classes of verbs. The formation of the past, plain forms of Class 2 verbs is very simple.

Affirmative: Root + た	Negative: Root + なかった

For the definition of *past, plain*, and the three classes of verbs, review **Grammar 11** in Chapter 3. For the sake of explanation, we will start with Class 2 verbs here.

DICTIONARY FORM	ROOT	PAST, PLAIN, AFFIRMATIVE	PAST, PLAIN, NEGATIVE
食(た)べる *to eat*	食(た)べ	食(た)べた	食(た)べなかった
見(み)る *to see*	見(み)	見(み)た	見(み)なかった
着(き)る *to wear*	着(き)	着(き)た	着(き)なかった
変(か)える *to change*	変(か)え	変(か)えた	変(か)えなかった

19.2 The past, plain forms of Class 3 verbs (the irregular verbs する and くる) are as follows.

DICTIONARY FORM	PAST, PLAIN, AFFIRMATIVE	PAST, PLAIN, NEGATIVE
する *to do*	した	しなかった
来(く)る *to come*	来(き)た	来(こ)なかった

Note that plain forms of verbs and adjectives are used in these conversations between family members (between brother and sister in the first dialogue and between mother and daughter in the second). As discussed in **Grammar 11,** Chapter 3, plain forms are common in conversations among members of the same in-group.

19.3 The past, plain, negative form of Class 1 verbs is formed according to the following rule. Root + the a-column hiragana corresponding to the dictionary form ending + なかった.

DICTIONARY FORM ROOT + ENDING	PAST, PLAIN, NEGATIVE FORM
書(か) + く	書(か) + か + なかった
話(はな) + す	話(はな) + さ + なかった
立(た) + つ	立(た) + た + なかった
死(し) + ぬ	死(し) + な + なかった
読(よ) + む	読(よ) + ま + なかった
乗(の) + る	乗(の) + ら + なかった
泳(およ) + ぐ	泳(およ) + が + なかった

u-column	→	a-column
く	→	か
す	→	さ
つ	→	た
ぬ	→	な
む	→	ま
る	→	ら
ぐ	→	が

When the dictionary form ending of a Class 1 verb is う, わ, rather than あ, is inserted between the root and なかった.

DICTIONARY FORM ROOT + ENDING	PAST, PLAIN, NEGATIVE FORM
洗(あら) + う	洗(あら) + わ + なかった
言(い) + う	言(い) + わ + なかった

The past, plain, negative form of ある *to exist* is simply なかった.

Remember that this rule applies to the formation of the nonpast, plain, negative form of these verbs: 洗わない、言わない.

The past, plain, affirmative form of Class 1 verbs depends on the dictionary form ending.

1. When the dictionary ending is く

   Rule: Change it to いた.
   書(か)く → 書(か)いた (*wrote*)

   There is only one exception to this rule: 行く (*to go*).
   行(い)く → 行(い)った (*went*)

2. When the dictionary ending is ぐ

   Rule: Change it to いだ.
   泳(およ)ぐ → 泳(およ)いだ (*swam*)

3. When the dictionary ending is う、つ、or る

   Rule: Change it to った.
   買(か)う → 買(か)った (*bought*)
   立(た)つ → 立(た)った (*stood*)
   乗(の)る → 乗(の)った (*rode*)

4. When the dictionary ending is ぬ、む、or ぶ

   Rule: Change it to んだ.
   死(し)ぬ → 死(し)んだ (*died*)
   読(よ)む → 読(よ)んだ (*read [past]*)
   呼(よ)ぶ → 呼(よ)んだ (*called*)

5. When the word ending is す

   Rule: Change it to した.
   話(はな)す → 話(はな)した (*spoke*)

As mentioned in **Grammar 11**, Chapter 3, ない in 書(か)かない、食(た)べない、しない、etc. (the nonpast, plain, negative form) is an adjective expressing negativity. It is an i-adjective and conjugates as such. In this chapter, you have already studied how to form the past, plain forms of i-adjectives. In the past, plain, negative forms 書かなかった、食べなかった、しなかった、etc., なかった is the past, plain form of ない.

Note that the past, plain, affirmative forms of 読む and 呼ぶ happen to have the same sound sequence: よんだ. Their accent patterns, however, are different.

The conjugations of the past, plain, affirmative form of Class 1 verbs are summarized in the following table.

DICTIONARY ENDING	PAST, PLAIN, AFFIRMATIVE ENDING	EXAMPLES
く	→いた	書(か)く→書(か)いた exception 行(い)く→行(い)った
ぐ	→いだ	泳(およ)ぐ→泳(およ)いだ
う、つ、る	→った	買(か)う→買(か)った 立(た)つ→立(た)った 乗(の)る→乗(の)った
ぬ、む、ぶ	→んだ	死(し)ぬ→死(し)んだ 読(よ)む→読(よ)んだ 呼(よ)ぶ→呼(よ)んだ
す	→した	話(はな)す→話(はな)した

Here are some sample sentences using the past, plain form of verbs.

昨日(きのう)の夜(よる)、雨(あめ)がたくさん降(ふ)った。
It rained a lot last night.
強(つよ)い風(かぜ)が一日中(いちにちじゅう)吹(ふ)いた。
A strong wind blew all day.
山田(やまだ)さんはアメリカへ行(い)ったが、わたしは行かなかった。
Mr. Yamada went to America, but I didn't.
昨日(きのう)は八時から十時までテレビを見(み)た。その後、ラジオを聞いた。
I watched TV from 8:00 to 10:00 yesterday. After that, I listened to the radio.
かれは夕(ゆう)ごはんをぜんぜん食(た)べなかった。
He didn't eat any dinner at all.

The past, plain, affirmative form of a verb is used to express a past action or event in an informal context. It is also used as a component of several other grammatical structures you will study later on. These other significant grammatical structures require the ability to conjugate this verb form, so it is important that you master this form now.

In most cases, the past, plain, affirmative form of a verb ends in **-ta,** so we will refer to this form as the ta-form.

The past, plain, affirmative form of an adjective is also called the ta-form of an adjective.

練習　1

Put these sentences into the past tense, maintaining the plain form of the verb.

[例]　チンさんは中国語で話す。→ チンさんは中国語で話した。

1. ブラウンさんは五時半に起きる。
2. 顔を洗う。
3. 歯を一日に三回みがく。
4. 毎日10キロ走る。
5. サラダをたくさん食べる。
6. オレンジ・ジュースを飲む。
7. 高田さんは7時に出かける。
8. デパートの前でギブソンさんを待つ。
9. 毎日クラスへ行く。
10. 家から大学までバスに乗る。
11. 8時に大学に着く (*to arrive*)。
12. 図書館でチンさんに会う。
13. テレビでニュースを見る。
14. 午後プールで泳ぐ。
15. フランス語を勉強する。
16. 10時ごろ家に帰る。
17. 土曜日は家で休む。
18. お風呂に入る。
19. 電車の中で新聞を読む。
20. 12時に寝る。
21. いつもパーティーに来る。

練習　2

Rewrite the following sentences changing the verb form from polite to plain.

[例]　昨日東京へ来ました。→ 昨日東京へ来た。

1. 先週は雨がたくさん降りました。
2. デパートでプレゼントを買いました。
3. パーティーでは山田さんに会いませんでした。
4. 高田さんは昨日、ワシントンから帰りました。

5. わたしはぜんぜん勉強(べんきょう)しませんでした。
6. 昨日、ブラウンさんと話しませんでした。
7. かれのおじいさん (*grandfather*) は去年(きょねん)死(し)にました。(死ぬ: *to die*)
8. 今朝(けさ)、歯(は)をみがきませんでした。
9. 昨日(きのう)はお酒(さけ)を飲みましたか。
10. 昨日顔(かお)を洗(あら)いませんでした。
11. もうテレビのニュースは見(み)ましたか。
12. ここに何時(なんじ)に着(つ)きましたか。
13. 昨日(きのう)の夜(よる)はあまり寝(ね)ませんでした。
14. ディズニーランドでコーヒーカップに乗(の)りました。
15. 林(はやし)さんはもう出(で)かけましたか。
16. 高田さんはスーパーへ行(い)きました。
17. 一週間(いっしゅうかん)お風呂に入(はい)りませんでした。
18. シャワーは浴(あ)びましたか。

20. Explaining a Reason: …のだ

佐野(さの)：何をしているんですか。
ブラウン：日本語を勉強(べんきょう)しているんです。
佐野：そうですか。むずかしいんですか。
ブラウン：ええ、とても。

ブラウン：林(はやし)さんは何を笑(わら)っているのですか。
町田：さあ、わかりません。
ブラウン：林さん、何がおかしいんですか。
林：今(いま)、漫画(まんが)を読(よ)んでいるんです。ハハハ…

カーティス：ストーブはどこですか。
チン：寒(さむ)いんですか。
カーティス：風邪(かぜ)をひいたんです。
チン：いつからですか。
カーティス：昨日(きのう)からです。

SANO: What are you doing? BROWN: I am studying Japanese. SANO: I see. Is it difficult? BROWN: Yes, very.

BROWN: What is Mr. Hayashi laughing at? MACHIDA: I don't know. BROWN: Mr. Hayashi, what is funny? HAYASHI: I'm reading a comic book (now). Ha, ha, ha . . . .

CURTIS: Where is the heater? CHIN: Are you cold? CURTIS: (It's that) I caught a cold. CHIN: Since when? CURTIS: Since yesterday.

林：北海道は寒かったんじゃありませんか。
ギブソン：はい、とても寒かったです。
林：雪はたくさんありましたか。
ギブソン：いいえ、ぜんぜんなかったんです。
林：ぜんぜんなかったんですか。
ギブソン：はい、ぜんぜん。

Sentences ending in のだ (polite form のです) explain the reason for some event or information known to both speaker and hearer. In colloquial speech んだ (polite form んです) commonly replaces のだ (のです).

Consider these two sentences, for example.

寒いですか。
寒いんですか。

In the first sentence, the speaker has no idea whether or not the person addressed feels cold. Therefore, it is simply a straightforward question: *Are you cold?* In the second, the speaker assumes that the person addressed feels cold because, say, he is shivering or wearing a thick sweater. The second sentence, then, asks for an explanation: *Is it that you're cold?*

Similarly, if you see a friend getting ready to do something, it would be odd to say

何をしますか。
What are you going to do?

because you have actually seen his or her preparations and know that he or she is about to do something. This information is shared between the two of you, so it's more appropriate to say

何をするんですか。
What are you going to do? (*lit., What is it that you are going to do?*)

Verbs, adjectives, and nouns may precede のです (んです). In the case of verbs, the plain form is used.

チンさんにもう言ったんですか。
Did you already tell Ms. Chin? (*lit., Is it that you already told Ms. Chin?*)
林さんに電話しないのですか。
Aren't you going to call Mr. Hayashi?

The plain form of i-adjectives may also precede のです.

なぜ顔が赤いんですか。
Why is your face red?

HAYASHI: Wasn't it cold in Hokkaido? GIBSON: Yes, it was very cold. HAYASHI: Was there a lot of snow? GIBSON: No, there wasn't any at all. HAYASHI: There wasn't any at all? GIBSON: That's right, (*lit., Yes*) none at all.

夏でしたが、あまり暑くなかったんです。
It was summer, but it wasn't very hot.

When the nonpast, affirmative form of na-adjectives or nouns is used, な precedes のです (んです).

あの人が山口さんなんですか。
Is that person Mr. Yamaguchi?
三村さんはどうして有名なんですか。
Why is Mr. Mimura famous?
林さんは学生ではないんですか。
Isn't Mr. Hayashi a student?
チンさんは元気だったんですか。
Was Ms. Chin well?

コミュニケーション・ノート

Answering Negative Questions

In English, you answer in the same way whether you are asked a question affirmatively or negatively. Thus, whether you are asked, "Will you attend today's class?" or "Won't you attend today's class?" you would say "Yes, I will attend" or "No, I won't attend."

In Japanese, the way you answer a negative question depends on the addressee's presupposition or previous knowledge. In the dialogue on p. 252, Hayashi asks 北海道(ほっかいどう)は寒(さむ)かったんじゃありませんか (*Wasn't it cold in Hokkaido?*), assuming that it must have been cold in Hokkaido around that time. In this case, you would answer

はい、寒かったです。
Yes, it was cold.
いいえ、寒くありませんでした。
No, it wasn't cold.

On the other hand, when he asks the question ぜんぜんなかったんですか (*Wasn't there snow at all?*), Hayashi already knows that there was no snow at all. In this case, you would answer

はい、ぜんぜんありませんでした。
Lit., Yes, there wasn't any at all.
いいえ、たくさんありました。
Lit., No, there was a lot.

Let's consider another example. Someone asks you クラスへ行かないんですか (*Aren't you going to class?*) If you think the questioner assumes you won't go to class, you would respond

はい、行きません。
Lit., Yes, I won't go.
いいえ、行きます。
Lit., No, I will go.

If you think the questioner assumes you *will* go to class, you would respond

はい、行きます。
Yes, I will go.
いいえ、行きません。
No, I won't go.

You have to decide how to answer based on your guess about the questioner's knowledge, his or her facial expression, and other contextual factors. In addition, the intonation pattern of the question differ depending on the assumption. For example,

クラスへ行かないんですか。↑ (rising intonation) assumes that you will go
クラスへ行かないんですか。↓ (falling intonation) assumes that you won't go

練習

Complete these dialogues using the cue in parentheses and んです.

[例] デパートへ行くんですか。(ブラウスを買います。) →
はい、ブラウスを買うんです。

1. 林さん、たくさん飲みますね。(お酒が好きです。)
2. 映画に行かないんですか。(明日、試験 (exam) です。)
3. スキーへ行くんですか。(雪がたくさん降りました。)
4. ヒーターを買ったんですか。(とても寒いです。)
5. この問題はわかりませんか。(先週、休みました。)
6. 昨日学校へ来ませんでしたね。(アルバイトがありました。)
7. 明日家にいないんですか。(スケートに行きます。)
8. アパートは便利なんですか。(駅にとても近いです。)
9. 学校へ行かないんですか。(今、休みです。)

21. The Te-Form of Adjectives and the Copula

カワムラ：町田さんの家のそばにスーパーはありますか。
町田：ええ。
カワムラ：どんなスーパーですか。
町田：大きくて、安いです。
カワムラ：いい肉はありますか。
町田：ええ、新しくて、おいしい肉がたくさんあります。
カワムラ：町田さんはいつもそのスーパーで買い物するんですか。
町田：ええ、近くて、便利ですから。

チン：山田さんのガールフレンドはどんな人ですか。
林：とてもきれいで、やさしい人ですよ。
チン：本当ですか。山田さんはけちで、いじわるでしょう。
なぜ、そんないいガールフレンドがいるんですか。
林：さあ、わかりませんね。

21.1 An important conjugated form of adjectives and verbs is what we shall call the *te-form*. In **Grammar 21** and **22,** you will study the te-form of adjectives, the copula, and verbs.

21.2 The te-form of adjectives may be used to link together adjectives or whole clauses in a sentence, as *and* is used in English. The te-form can be used only when adjectives are in nonfinal position in a sentence.

Form the te-form of i-adjectives by adding くて to the root.

DICTIONARY FORM	ROOT	TE-FORM
赤い *red*	赤	赤くて
おいしい *tasty*	おいし	おいしくて
寒い *cold*	寒	寒くて
いい (よい) *good*	よ	よくて (irregular)

KAWAMURA: Is there a supermarket near your house Mr. Machida? MACHIDA: Yes. KAWAMURA: What kind of supermarket is it? MACHIDA: It is big and inexpensive. KAWAMURA: Do they have good meat? MACHIDA: Yes, they have lots of fresh, tasty meat. KAWAMURA: Do you always shop there? MACHIDA: Yes, because it is nearby and convenient.

CHIN: What kind of person is Mr. Yamada's girlfriend? HAYASHI: Yes, she's a very pretty, sweet person. CHIN: Really? Mr. Yamada is miserly and mean. Why does he have such a nice girlfriend? HAYASHI: Hmm, I don't know.

21.3 The te-form of na-adjectives is formed by adding で to the dictionary form.

DICTIONARY FORM	TE-FORM
きれい *pretty*	きれいで
静か *quiet*	静かで
便利 *convenient*	便利で
ハンサム *handsome*	ハンサムで

21.4 Study these sample sentences.

彼女は若くて、きれいだ。
She is young and pretty.

あの子はおしゃべりで、うるさい。
That kid is talkative and noisy.

静かで、便利なところが好きです。
I like quiet, convenient places.

In the following four examples, the clause ending in the te-form of adjectives indicates a reason or cause for the following clause.

これは大きくて、重い教科書ですね。
This is a large, heavy textbook (don't you agree?)

この辞書は大きくて、不便です。
This dictionary is large and (therefore it's) inconvenient.

父はお酒が大好きで、いつもたくさん飲みます。
My father loves sake and always drinks a lot.

日本語のクラスが好きで、日本語をたくさん勉強する。
I like my Japanese class, and (that's why) I study Japanese a lot.

When you conjoin two or more adjectives this way, they must be all favorable or all unfavorable in meaning. For instance, the following sentence sounds unnatural.

あのスーパーはきれいで、高いです。
That supermarket is clean and expensive.

In such a case, you must use a conjunction for joining contrasting or contradictory statements.

あのスーパーはきれいですが、高いです。
あのスーパーはきれいだけれども、高いです。
That supermarket is clean, but it's expensive.

You can use either the plain or polite form in front of けれども.

21.5 The te-form of the copula です (plain form だ) is で. It is used to conjoin nouns.

町田さんは日本人で、東京の出身です。
Ms. Machida is a Japanese national, and is from Tokyo.
カワムラさんは東京大学の学生で、専攻は工学です。
Mr. Kawamura is a student at the University of Tokyo, and his major is engineering.

A clause ending in a noun ＋ でcan explain a reason or cause for what follows.

病気で、クラスを休みました。
I was sick and (so I) missed class.

練習 1

Make sentences by combining the words and phrases provided.

[例] (あのレストラン)(高い)(まずい [*not tasty*]) →
あのレストランは高くて、まずいです。もう行きません！

1. (あの人のスピーチ)(長い)(つまらない)
2. (日本語の先生)(やさしい)(しんせつ)
3. (このケーキ)(あまい)(おいしい)
4. (このラップトップ・コンピュータ)(重い)(不便)
5. (カナダの冬)(寒い)(長い)
6. (わたしの大学)(大きい)(有名)
7. (山口さん)(エレガント)(きれい)
8. (カワムラさん)(ハンサム)(やさしい)
9. (高田さん)(26歳)(サラリーマン)
10. (チンさん)(中国人)(ペキンの出身)

練習 2

Answer the following questions using two adjectives.

[例] あの町は静かですか。→
ええ、静かで、いいところです。(*or* いいえ、車が多くて、うるさい [*noisy*] です。)

Useful vocabulary

うるさい	*noisy*	遠い	*far*
たいへん	*terrible, awful*	つまらない	*boring*
静か	*quiet*		

1. あなたの近所は便利ですか。
2. 12月は雪が多いですか。
3. 日本の夏は暑いですか。
4. 駅は近いですか。
5. ボーイフレンドはハンサムですか。
6. 大野先生のクラスは好きですか。

練習 3

Make sentences about each topic, combining as many appropriate adjectives as possible from those listed.

[例] 日本語のクラス
(やさしい、おもしろい、むずかしい、つまらない) →
日本語のクラスはやさしくて、おもしろいです。(*or* 日本語のクラスはやさしいですが、つまらないです。)

1. わたし
(静か、にぎやか、元気、いんき [*gloomy*]、ようき [*cheerful*])
2. ジュリア・ロバーツ
(エレガント、若い [*young*]、きれい、スマート [*slim*]、元気、やさしい、ようき、いんき)
3. アーノルド・シュワルツネーガー
(タフ、やさしい、元気、若い、いんき、静か、強い)
4. エディー・マーフィー
(元気、いんき、きびしい、若い、やさしい、忙しい、おもしろい)
5. わたしの学校
(大きい、むずかしい、やさしい、いい、静か、有名)
6. わたしの家
(大きい、小さい、きれい、広い [*spacious*]、せまい [*small in area*]、きたない)
7. わたしのとなりの人 (*the person next to me*)
(うるさい、きれい、ハンサム、いんき、ようき、若い、やさしい、へん [*strange*]、まじめ)
8. この練習 (*exercise*)
(むずかしい、やさしい、つまらない、長い、短かい [*short*]、おもしろい)

22. The Te-Form of Verbs

ブラウン：新しいビデオがあるんですよ。うちに来て、見ませんか。
ギブソン：ええ、ぜひ。
ブラウン：じゃ、明日5時ごろにうちに来てください。
ギブソン：はい、じゃあ、明日。
高田：明日は何をするんですか。
ギブソン：部屋を掃除して、洗濯をします。高田さんは。
高田：会社へ行って、仕事をします。
ギブソン：明日は日曜日ですよ！

22.1 If you have mastered formation of the past, plain, affirmative form of verbs (that is, the ta-form), you can master the te-form very easily. Observe the following.

	TA-FORM	TE-FORM
Class 1		
書く	書いた	書いて
行く	行った	行って
泳ぐ	泳いだ	泳いで
買う	買った	買って
立つ	立った	立って
知る	知った	知って
読む	読んだ	読んで
死ぬ	死んだ	死んで
呼ぶ	呼んだ	呼んで
話す	話した	話して

BROWN: I have a new video. Won't you come over (*lit., to my home*) and watch it? GIBSON: Yes, by all means. BROWN: Then please come over (*lit., to my home*) around five tomorrow. GIBSON: Yes. See you tomorrow.

TAKADA: What are you going to do tomorrow? GIBSON: I'll clean my room and do some laundry. How about you? TAKADA: I'll go to my company and work. GIBSON: Tomorrow is Sunday, you know!

	TA-FORM	TE-FORM
Class 2		
食べる	食べた	食べて
見る	見た	見て
Class 3		
する	した	して
来る	来た	来て

As you can see, the te-form of verbs is formed by changing the た to て or だ to で.

22.2 The te-form of verbs is usually combined with other components to form grammatical constructions. For instance, the te-form of a verb + ください (*please give me*) is used to ask someone to do something for you. It literally means *Please give me your doing of (something)*, in other words, *Please do. . . .*

This is a fairly direct way to make a request and should therefore be used with caution, especially when speaking with superiors or strangers.

五時にここに来てください。
Please come here at five.
ギブソンさんと会ってください。
Please meet with Ms. Gibson.
ここに名前を書いてください。
Please write your name here.
日本語で話してください。
Please speak in Japanese.

どうぞ (*Please, go ahead*) is often added to the beginning of these request sentences to make your request sound politer.

どうぞたくさん食べてください。
Please eat as much as you want. (*lit., Please eat a lot.*)

22.3 You can express a succession of actions or events simply by connecting clauses that end in the te-form of a verb. For example,

スーパーに行って、アイスクリームを買う。
I will go to the supermarket and buy ice cream.
わたしは六時に起きて、歯をみがいて、顔を洗いました。
I got up at 6:00, brushed my teeth, and washed my face.

There is no grammatical limit on the number of verb clauses you can string together with this construction. The actions or events must usually take place within a short period of time and be related to one another in some sense. In most cases, they also should be listed in the same order in which the events occurred.

The tense and the speaker's attitude are expressed in the sentence-final verb—in the examples above, 買(か)う and 洗(あら)いました. All the preceding te-forms of verbs assume the same tense and other attributes of the sentence-final verb. Therefore, since 洗いました is past tense, you know that the first two actions—getting up and brushing teeth—also took place in the past. Because of the politeness level of 洗いました, you can tell that the speaker is speaking politely. In the first example, by the plain form of the final verb you can tell that the speaker is conveying information informally.

To summarize, you cannot know the tense and the speaker's attitude or emotion until you hear the last verb.

文法ノート

Conjoining Sequential Actions

You already studied how to express sequential actions and events using the transitions そして、それから、 and そのあと (Chapter 3). In addition to these transitions and the te-form of verbs, you can also link sequential actions with a te-form of a verb + から. This pattern adds a temporal emphasis: A から, B (after A, B).

夕ごはんを食べて新聞を読んでから、日本語を勉強しました。
After eating dinner and reading the newspaper, I studied Japanese.

ブラウンさんに会ってから、話しましょう。
Let's talk about it after we meet Ms. Brown.

22.4 The te-form of verbs can be used to express a cause-and-effect relationship where the first clause explains a reason for the second. You will have to determine from context whether a causal connection is intended. For example,

寝坊して、学校におくれた。
I overslept and (so) I was late for school.

古いケーキを食べて、病気になりました。
I ate some old cake, and (because of that) I got sick.

練習 1

Change each verb to its te-form + ください.

[例] ギブソンさんと話す → ギブソンさんと話してください。

1. 早く起きる
2. 顔を洗う
3. 夕ごはんを食べる
4. お茶を飲む
5. 大学の前で待つ
6. スーパーへ行く

7. タクシーに乗る
8. ブラウンさんに会う
9. このかばんを見る
10. 今日の新聞を読む
11. 中に入る (*to enter*)
12. 4時にここに来る

練習 2

Using te-forms, combine the sentences provided into one past tense sentence.

[例] (朝起きる)(コーヒーを飲む) → 朝起きて、コーヒーを飲んだ。

1. (お風呂から出る)(ビールを飲む)
2. (バスに乗る)(デパートへ行く)(セーターを買う)
3. (シャワーを浴びる)(ひげをそる)
4. (ドレスを着る)(デートに出かける)
5. (夕ごはんを食べる)(日本語を勉強する)
6. (カワムラさんの家へ行く)(話す)
7. (家に帰る)(寝る)
8. (ワープロを使う [*to use a word processor*])(手紙 [*letter*] を書く)

練習 3

What would you say to these people? Answer by using the te-form + ください.

[例] To a student who is very lazy → 勉強してください。

1. To a guest you want to start eating dinner
2. To someone who is sleeping and is late for an appointment
3. To a student who is speaking English in a Japanese language class
4. To someone you want to come to your home tomorrow
5. To someone who was sprayed by a skunk
6. To someone who is considering buying books from you

練習 4

Complete the following sentences based on your own experience.

[例] 朝起きて、→ 朝起きて、トイレに行きます。

1. 日本語のクラスへ行って、
2. カフェテリアへ行って、
3. 昼ごはんを食べて、

4. バスに乗って、
5. スニーカーをはいて、
   Useful vocabulary: はく *to wear (shoes, socks, etc.)*
6. セーターを着て、
7. 本を読んで、
8. うちに帰って、

23. Expressing Probability and Conjecture

ブラウン：林さんは来るでしょうか。
町田：さあ、どうでしょうか。

ブラウン：来ないかもしれませんね。
町田：さあ、わかりませんね。

林：今シアトルはどんなお天気でしょうか。
カワムラ：そうですね。毎日、雨が降っているでしょう。
林：そうですか。では、傘がいりますね。
カワムラ：多分寒いでしょうから、コートもいるかもしれません。

ブラウン：昨日のパーティーはどうでしたか。おもしろかったでしょう。*
町田：ええ、とてもおもしろかったです。
ブラウン：ギブソンさんはパーティーにいましたか。
町田：ええと、いたかもしれません。いや、いなかったかもしれません。

カーティス：ハワイは暑かったでしょう。
三村：ええ、ほんとうに。気温が40度くらいあったかもしれません。
カーティス：それは暑いですね。たいへんだったでしょう。
三村：ええ、でも、きれいで、とてもいいところですね。

BROWN: Do you suppose Mr. Hayashi will come? MACHIDA: Hmm, I wonder. BROWN: He may not come, isn't that right? MACHIDA: Hmm, I don't know.

HAYASHI: What do you suppose the weather is like in Seattle now? KAWAMURA: Let me see. It's probably raining every day. HAYASHI: I see. Then I'll need an umbrella, won't I. KAWAMURA: It's probably cold, so you may need a coat, too.

BROWN: How was the party yesterday? It must have been fun, huh? MACHIDA: Yes, it was great fun. BROWN: Was Ms. Gibson there? MACHIDA: Uhh, she may have been. No, maybe she wasn't.

CURTIS: Hawaii was hot, I'll bet. (*lit., It was hot in Hawaii, wasn't it?*) MIMURA: Yes, very. The temperature may have been 40 degrees. CURTIS: That's hot! It must have been awful. MIMURA: Yes . . . but it's a beautiful, very good place.

*In the third dialogue, おもしろかったでしょう。ends in a rising intonation.

23.1 There are a variety of ways to express conjecture or uncertainty in Japanese. Two of the most commonly used expressions are でしょう (plain form だろう) meaning *probably* and かもしれません (plain form かもしれない) meaning *may* or *maybe*. The major difference between these two expressions is that かもしれません expresses a greater degree of uncertainty.

When making a conjecture relating to yourself, かもしれない—not だろう—is used.

ジョンソンさんは日本語がわかるでしょう。
Ms. Johnson probably understands Japanese.
ジョンソンさんは日本語がわかるかもしれません。
Ms. Johnson might understand Japanese.

Nouns, adjectives and verbs precede these expressions. When the speaker is guessing what will happen in the present or future, the following forms are used.

noun i-adjective (nonpast, plain) na-adjective (dictionary form) verb (nonpast, plain form)	+	でしょう (だろう) *or* かもしれません (かもしれない)

When the preceding nouns, adjectives, and verbs are negative, they take the following forms.

noun + で(は)ない i-adjective (nonpast, plain, negative) na-adjective (dictionary form + で(は)ない) verb (nonpast, plain, negative form)	+	でしょう (だろう) *or* かもしれません (かもしれない)

明日(あした)は雨(あめ)でしょう。
It probably will rain tomorrow.
あの人は学生ではないでしょう。
That person probably is not a student.
明日は暑(あつ)いでしょう。
It probably will be hot tomorrow.
明日は寒(さむ)くないでしょう。
It probably won't be cold tomorrow.
あの人はまじめかもしれません。
That person might be serious.
あの人は暇(ひま)ではないかもしれません。
He might not be free.

明日は雪(ゆき)が降(ふ)るかもしれません。
It might snow tomorrow.
明日はここに来(こ)ないかもしれません。
I might not come here tomorrow.

To express a conjecture or to guess about what happened in the past, use these forms.

noun だった i-adjective (past, plain) na-adjective (past, plain) verb (past, plain)	+	でしょう (だろう) *or* かもしれません (かもしれない)

When the elements that precede a conjecture about the past are negative, the following forms are used.

noun ではなかった (じゃなかった) i-adjective (past, plain, negative) na-adjective (past, plain, negative) verb (past, plain, negative)	+	でしょう (だろう) *or* かもしれません (かもしれない)

昨日(きのう)東京(とうきょう)は雨(あめ)だったでしょう。
It probably rained in Tokyo yesterday.
あの人は先生ではなかったでしょう。
That person probably wasn't a teacher.
昨日東京は寒(さむ)かったでしょう。
It probably was cold in Tokyo yesterday.
昨日大阪(おおさか)は暑(あつ)くなかったでしょう。
It probably wasn't hot in Osaka yesterday.
あの学生はまじめだったかもしれません。
That student might have been serious.
Maybe that student was serious.
あの町はきれいではなかったかもしれません。
That town might not have been clean.
Maybe that town wasn't clean.
ブラウンさんはあそこに行(い)ったかもしれません。
Ms. Brown might have gone there.
Maybe Ms. Brown went there.

高田さんはあそこに行かなかったかもしれません。
Mr. Takada might not have gone there.
Maybe Mr. Takada didn't go there.

23.2 でしょう is often accompanied by adverbs expressing degrees of certainty, such as the following (listed in order of increasing certainty).

多分	*probably*
おそらく	*possibly, in all likelihood*
きっと	*certainly, surely*

Because of the strong probability expressed by きっと, it cannot be used with かもしれません.

かれは多分来るでしょう。
He will probably come.
かれはおそらく山下さんに電話をかけるでしょう。
Most likely he will call Mr. Yamashita.
あの学生はきっと日本語を勉強しているでしょう。
That student surely must be studying Japanese.

でしょう is often used to ask an indirect question, in which case the question particle か is pronounced with a falling intonation. As you might have guessed, this is a somewhat more formal way to ask a question.

かれはもう起きましたか。
Did he get up already?
かれはもう起きたでしょうか。
Do you suppose he already got up?
I wonder if he already got up.

でしょう pronounced with a rising intonation asks for the hearer's confirmation —*isn't it? aren't you? don't you agree?*

あなたも来るでしょう。↑
You're coming too, aren't you?
その映画はおもしろかったでしょう。↑
That movie was interesting, don't you think?

練習　1

Respond to the following questions using でしょう or かもしれません.

1. あの人はどこの国の人ですか。
2. あの人は何歳ですか。

3. 明日はどんなお天気でしょうか。
4. あの人は昨日どこへ行きましたか。
5. あのセーターは安いですか。高いですか。
6. 今、東京は暑いですか。
7. あの人はどんな人ですか。
8. 十二月はニューヨークとワシントンとどちらが寒いですか。
9. ここから一番近い駅まで何分かかりますか。
10. あの人は昨日何をしましたか。

練習　2

What can you guess about each of these pictures? State your conjectures.

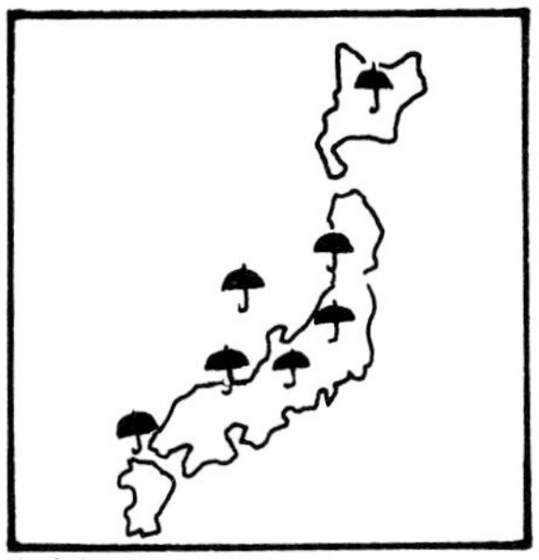

1. 明日はどんなお天気ですか。

2. 林さんは大丈夫ですか。

3. あのレストランはおいしいですか。

4. ジョンソンさんは日本語がわかりますか。

5. 台風は来ますか。

Vocabulary

Weather

あたたかい	暖かい	warm	たいよう	太陽	sun
あめ	雨	rain	てんき	天気	weather
かぜ	風	wind	てんきず	天気図	weather map
きあつ	気圧	air pressure	てんきよほう	天気予報	weather forecast
きおん	気温	temperature	…ど	…度	. . . degrees (*counter*)
きこう	気候	climate	はれ	晴れ	clear weather, sunny and clear
くも	雲	cloud	ふく	吹く	to blow (*used with wind*)
くもり	曇	cloudy	ふる	降る	to fall (*used with rain, snow, etc.*)
さむい	寒い	cold	むしあつい	むし暑い	sultry, hot and humid
すずしい	涼しい	cool	ゆき	雪	snow
たいふう	台風	typhoon			

Review: 暑(あつ)い

Seasons

あき	秋	fall, autumn	なつ	夏	summer
きせつ	季節	season	はる	春	spring
しき	四季	four seasons	ふゆ	冬	winter

Loanword: カレンダー

Adjectives

あかるい	明るい	bright (*vs. dark*)
おだやか (な)		calm (*ocean, personality*), gentle (*breeze*)
おもい	重い	heavy
おもしろい	面白い	interesting, fun
くらい	暗い	dark
スマート (な)		slender (*person*)
たいへん (な)	大変 (な)	terrible, awful
つまらない		boring
つよい	強い	strong

ながい	長い	long
にぎやか (な)		lively
はやい	早い; 速い	early; quick, fast
ふまじめ (な)	不まじめ (な)	not serious, lazy (*person*)
へん (な)	変 (な)	strange
まじめ (な)		serious (*person*)
みじかい	短い	short
むずかしい		difficult
ゆうめい (な)	有名 (な)	famous
よわい	弱い	weak
わかい	若い	young

Loanwords: エレガント (な)、キュート (な)、タフ (な)、ハンサム (な)

Review: 新(あたら)しい、いい、忙(いそが)しい、うるさい、(…が) 多(おお)い、きたない、きびしい、きれい (な)、元気(げんき) (な)、静(しず)か (な)、親切(しんせつ) (な)、(…が) 少ない、せまい、高(たか)い、低(ひく)い、暇(ひま) (な)、広い、不便(ふべん) (な)、古い、便利(べんり) (な)、やさしい、安(やす)い、悪(わる)い

Nouns

うみ	海	ocean, sea
かさ	傘	umbrella
きた	北	north
つり	釣り	fishing
てがみ	手紙	letter
にし	西	west
はなみ	花見	(cherry) blossom viewing
ひがし	東	east
びょうき	病気	sick
みなみ	南	south
やま	山	mountain
やまのぼり	山登り	mountain climbing
ワープロ		word processor

Loanwords: キャンプ、コート、スキー、スケート、ハイキング

Verbs

およぐ	泳ぐ	to swim
しぬ	死ぬ	to die
つかう	使う	to use

Other Words

おなじ	同じ	same
ぐらい、くらい		about, approximately
はやく	早く; 速く	early; quickly (*adverb*)

Review: たくさん、よく

Grammar

…でしょう	probably (*conjecture, polite*)	…が、	but (*conjunction*)
…だろう	probably (*conjecture, plain*)	…から、	because (*conjunction*)
…かもしれません	may, might (*conjecture, polite*)	～てください	please do . . .
…かもしれない	may, might (*conjecture, plain*)		

Kanji

Learn these characters.

天	東
気	西
雨	南
雪	北
度	高
風	多
台	少
春	強
夏	弱
秋	昨
冬	暑
空	寒

Reading and Writing

Reading 1 ブラウンさんへの手紙

Before You Read

You are writing a letter in English to a friend, telling her about your ski vacation. How do you start your letter? What are the standard elements of an English personal letter (e.g., date, your name, etc.)? Where do you place them in a letter?

Japanese letters usually start with 拝啓 (はいけい), which roughly corresponds to *Dear Sir* or *Dear Madam*. This introductory greeting is generally followed by a reference to the weather or season. In what season do you think the following phrases would be used in a Japanese letter?

1. 毎日暑(まいにちあつ)いです。
2. 最近雪(さいきんゆき)が多(おお)くて、たいへんです。
3. そちらは梅雨(つゆ)の季節(きせつ)でしょうか。ここは毎日雨(あめ)が降(ふ)ります。
4. さくらがとてもきれいです。
5. 北風(きたかぜ)が吹いて、寒いです。
6. 台風(たいふう)の季節(きせつ)に入りました。
7. 南風(みなみかぜ)が吹いて、とても暖(あたた)かいです。

Now Read It!

Yooichi Takada wrote this letter to Linda Brown from Hokkaido, where he has been vacationing.

拝啓
ブラウンさん、お元気ですか。私は元気です。こちらは寒くて、たいへんですが、東京はどうですか。
さて、私は先週の土曜日に北海道に着きました。日曜日に雪がたくさん降りました。私の家の近くに山があります。月曜日に友だちとその山へ行って、スキーをしました。月曜日はいいお天気で、朝から夕方までスキーをしました。
火曜日は私の誕生日でした。家のそばの喫茶店でバースデー・パーティーがありました。友だちがたくさん来ました。
あさって、東京に帰ります。おみやげを買って、帰りますので、楽しみにしてください。
今日はこれで失礼します。寒いですから、お体に気をつけてください。

敬具

二月十五日

高田洋一

リンダ・ブラウン様

After You Finish Reading

1. Find the following information in the letter.

   Date
   Sender's name
   Addressee's name
   Reference to weather or season
   Inquiry about addressee's health
   Reference to sender's health
   Closing remarks
   Closing (e.g., Sincerely)

2. Discuss in class the differences between English letters and Japanese letters.
3. How many details did you understand? Answer the following to test yourself.
   a. What is the weather like in Hokkaido?
   b. When did Mr. Takada go to Hokkaido?
   c. When did it snow?
   d. When did Mr. Takada go skiing?
   e. What was the weather like the day he went skiing?
   f. When was Mr. Takada's birthday?
   g. What did he do on his birthday?
   h. When is Mr. Takada returning to Tokyo?
   i. When did Mr. Takada write this letter?

文化ノート

How to Write a Letter in Japanese

Here is the standard format of a Japanese personal letter.

1. opening word or phrase, such as 拝啓 (はいけい)
2. preliminary remarks: reference to the weather or season, inquiry about the addressee's health (often followed by reference to the writer's health), etc.
3. main body
4. concluding remarks: best wishes for the addressee's health, regards to the addressee's family, etc.
5. closing word or phrase such as 敬具 (けいぐ)
6. date
7. sender's full name
8. addressee's full name (the title 様 (さま), not さん, is usually used in personal letters)
9. postcript: anything sender forgot to include in the main body.

When writing a letter, you generally use politer language than when talking directly to the addressee.

拝啓 ｝頭語

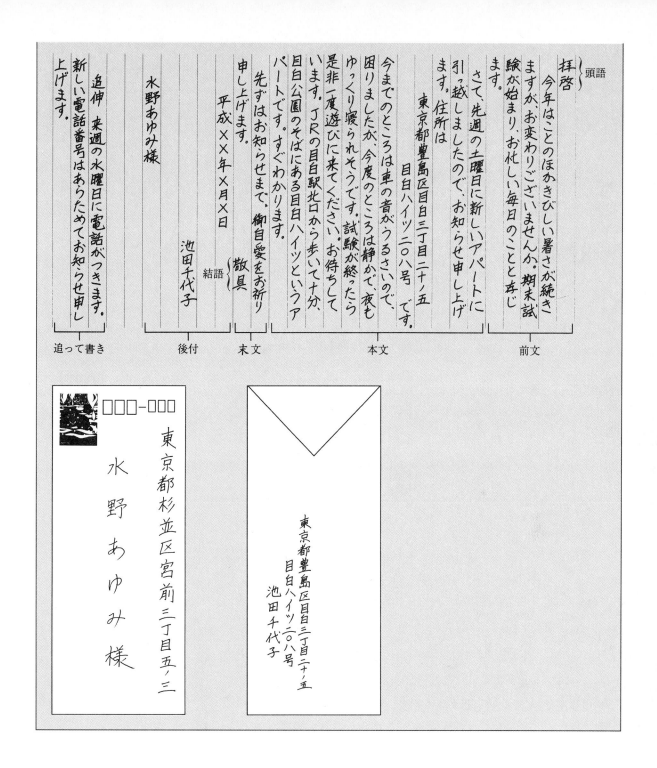

今年はことのほかきびしい暑さが続きますが、お変わりございませんか。期末試験が始まり、お忙しい毎日のことと存じます。

（前文）

さて、先週の土曜日に新しいアパートに引っ越しましたので、お知らせ申し上げます。住所は

東京都豊島区目白三丁目二十ノ五
目白ハイツ二〇八号　です。

今までのところは車の音がうるさいので、困りましたが、今度のところは静かで、夜もゆっくり寝られそうです。試験が終ったら是非一度遊びに来てください。お待ちしています。JRの目白駅北口から歩いて十分、目白公園のそばにある目白ハイツというアパートです。すぐわかります。

（本文）

先ずはお知らせまで、御自愛をお祈り申し上げます。

（末文）

敬具 ｝結語

平成××年×月×日

池田千代子

水野あゆみ様

（後付）

追伸　来週の水曜日に電話がつきます。新しい電話番号はあらためてお知らせ申し上げます。

（追って書き）

□□□-□□□

東京都杉並区宮前三丁目五ノ三

水野あゆみ様

東京都豊島区目白三丁目二十ノ五
目白ハイツ二〇八号
池田千代子

Writing 1

Write a short letter to a friend in Japanese. Include the following in your letter.

1. reference to the season or weather
2. inquiry about your friend's health
3. description of your Japanese language study
4. invitation to visit your house next month

Reading 2 トラベル・ガイド：いろは町の気候

Before You Read

You are planning to make a short trip during a school break. You have decided to visit Iroha, a small town near Kyoto. You would like to know the climate there and what clothes you should take, so you consult a travel guidebook. It includes many words you haven't learned, but you can read enough to get the information you need. Before reading the following page from the guidebook, list words relating to each of these topics.

季節(きせつ)	雨(あめ)	雪(ゆき)
気温(きおん)	風(かぜ)	

Describe in Japanese the kind of weather you associate with these items.

1. オーバー
2. レインコート
3. ショートパンツ
4. セーター
5. 傘(かさ) (*umbrella*)
6. T-シャツ
7. ノースリーブス

Now Read It!

いろは町の気候(きこう)

春(はる)は昼間(ひるま)は暖(あたた)かいが、朝夕(あさゆう)はまだ寒(さむ)い。セーターがいる。雨はほとんど降(ふ)らない。四月は桜(さくら)がきれいだ。山も美(うつく)しくて、多(おお)くの人がハイキングを楽(たの)しむ。

昼間 *daytime*
まだ *still*
…がいる *one needs . . .*
桜 *cherry blossoms*
山 *mountain*

　六月から七月の梅雨の季節は、雨が多い。ちょっと寒い日が多い。傘やレインコートがいる。この季節は、お寺の庭がとても美しい。
いろは町の夏はむし暑い。夏の平均気温は28度、平均湿度は90%だ。カジュアルな服がいい。夕方雨がよく降る。傘がいる。
　秋は毎日いい天気が続く。山がとても美しい。秋は一年中で一番美しい季節だ。昼間は15度ぐらいだ。朝夕は涼しいので、セーターやコートがいる。
　十一月から、寒い北風が吹いて、気温も下がる。いろは町の冬はきびしい。京都より気温が2～3度低い。十二月から二月まで雪が降る。お寺の庭にも雪が降って、本当に美しい。お寺や神社には暖房がないので、お寺や神社の中でもオーバーがいる。

美しい *beautiful*
楽しむ *to enjoy*
庭 *garden*
平均 *average*
湿度 *humidity*
カジュアル *casual, informal*

下がる *to go down*

暖房 *heater*

After You Finish Reading

Tell what the weather is like in each season in Iroha.

季節	気候
春	
夏	
秋	
冬	

In what season should these people visit Iroha?

1. ギブソン　雪が好きです。
2. 町田　ハイキングが好きです。
3. 横井先生　雨の季節のお寺はきれいで、いいですね。
4. 林　暑い季節が好きです。

京都の夏祭 (summer festival)：祇園祭

Writing 2

Write a short description in Japanese of the weather and the four seasons at some place in your home country.

Language Functions and Situations

Asking Questions About the Japanese Language

Japanese native speakers are a good source of information about the language. Here are some simple ways to ask someone for help when studying Japanese.

1. asking about pronunciation

すみません。これはどう発音(はつおん)しますか。—「とうざいなんぼく」です。

Excuse me. How do you pronounce this? —**Too-zai-nan-boku.** (*East-west-south-north.*)

東西南北

Alternative expression: これを発音してくださいますか。 *Would you pronounce this for me?*

2. asking how to read **kanji**

すみません。この漢字(かんじ)はどう読(よ)みますか。—「あさゆう」です。

Excuse me. How do you read these **kanji**? —**Asayuu.** (*Morning and evening.*)

朝夕

Alternative expression: この漢字を読んでくださいますか。 *Would you read this (these) kanji for me?*

3. asking about writing

すみません。「あつい」は漢字でどう書(か)きますか。—こう書きます。

*Excuse me. How do you write **hot** in* **kanji**? —*You write it like this.* (said while writing)

暑い

Alternative expression:「あつい」という漢字を書いてくださいますか。*Would you write the kanji for* **"atsui"** *for me?*

4. asking about meaning

すみません。「湿度(しつど)」はどういう意味(いみ)ですか。—空気(くうき)の中の水(みず)のことです。英語(えいご)で *humidity* といいます。

Excuse me. What does **shitsudo** *mean?* —*It means **the moisture in the air.** In English, you say **humidity.***

Alternative expression:「湿度」の意味を教えてくださいますか。*Would you please tell me the meaning of* **"shitsudo"**?

Asking for Assistance with **Kanji**

ギブソン：林(はやし)さん、ちょっとすみません。日本語を教(おし)えてください。
林：ええ、いいですよ。何ですか。
ギブソン：「ゆき」は漢字(かんじ)でどう書(か)きますか。
林：雨(あめ)の下にカタカナの「ヨ」です。
ギブソン：ちょっと書いてください。
林：こう書きます。
ギブソン：ありがとうございます。

GIBSON: Mr. Hayashi, excuse me. Can you teach me some Japanese? HAYASHI: Yes, sure. What can I do for you? (*lit., What is it?*) GIBSON: How do you write *snow* in **kanji**? HAYASHI: Write a **katakana yo** under the character for *rain*. (*lit., It is a **katakana yo** under **rain**.*) GIBSON: Please write it for me. HAYASHI: You write it like this. GIBSON: Thank you.

ブラウン：横井先生、質問があるんですが、…
横井：ええ、何ですか。
ブラウン：この漢字は何と読みますか。
横井：「しつど」と読みます。*humidity* のことです。
ブラウン：「温度」とは違いますか。
横井：ええ、違います。
ブラウン：「温度」を書いていただけますか。
横井：こう書きます。
ブラウン：ありがとうございます。

コミュニケーション・ノート

Making Polite Requests

The most common way to make a request is to use the te-form of a verb + ください (*please give me the doing of . . .*).

名前を書いてください。
Please write down your name.

As discussed above, どうぞ makes your request more polite.

どうぞ教えてください。
Please tell me. or *Please teach me.*

Politer forms of request include the following, in increasing order of politeness.

te-form of verb +
- くださいますか
- くださいませんか
- いただけますか
- いただけませんか

明日電話してくださいますか。
Would you call me tomorrow?
ブラウンさんと話していただけませんか。
Would you please talk with Ms. Brown?

BROWN: Professor Yokoi, I have a question but . . . (could you help me?) YOKOI: Yes, what is it? BROWN: How do you read this **kanji**? YOKOI: You read it **shitsudo**. It means *humidity*. BROWN: Is it different from **ondo**? YOKOI: Yes, it's different. BROWN: Would you please write **ondo** for me? YOKOI: You write it like this. BROWN: Thank you very much.

アクティビティー

Find a native speaker of Japanese on your campus and ask for the following information.

1. pronunciation and meaning of these characters

   a. 南西　　b. 空気　　c. 日中

2. how to write these phrases in **kanji**

   a. こうてい *high and low*
   b. こうてん *good weather*
   c. だんじょ *man and woman*

Don't forget to use polite requests when you ask these questions.

Listening Comprehension

While listening to tomorrow's weather forecast for a number of Japanese cities, fill in the table in English.

PLACE	WEATHER	TEMPERATURE	WIND	OTHERS
Sapporo				
Sendai				
Hukushima				
Utsunomiya				
Tokyo				
Nagoya				
Wakayama				
Hiroshima				
Hukuoka				
Miyazaki				

5

第五章

趣味・余暇（しゅみ・よか）

Hobbies and Leisure Activities

趣味は何ですか。

OBJECTIVES

Topics

Hobbies and Pastimes
Sports
Family

Grammar

24. Interrogative ＋か／も／でも
25. Describing abilities
26. Nominalizers: こと and の
27. More uses of the particle も
28. Potential form of verbs
29. The te-form of verbs ＋います
30. Relative clauses
31. Describing a change in state : なる

Reading and Writing

Sunrise Culture Center announcement
Survey on Japanese leisure time

Language Functions and Situations

Responding to compliments
Introducing a family member

Vocabulary and Oral Activities

Hobbies and Pastimes

Vocabulary: Hobbies and Leisure Activities

余暇	よか	free time, leisure
趣味	しゅみ	hobby
娯楽	ごらく	pastime, entertainment
遊ぶ	あそぶ	to play
楽しむ	たのしむ	to enjoy
特技	とくぎ	special talent, skill
切手集め	きってあつめ	stamp collecting
写真	しゃしん	photography, photograph
料理	りょうり	cooking
園芸	えんげい	gardening
手芸	しゅげい	handicrafts
読書	どくしょ	reading books
絵画	かいが	painting
音楽鑑賞	おんがくかんしょう	music appreciation, listening to music
歌	うた	song
楽器	がっき	musical instrument
コンサート		concert
旅行	りょこう	travel
カルチャーセンター		culture education center, adult school
クラブ		club
レジャー		leisure

Review: 映画(えいが)、音楽(おんがく)、スポーツ、釣り(つ)(に行く)、暇(ひま)(な)

㊙ Study Grammar 24.

アクティビティー　1

ダイアログ：趣味(しゅみ)は何ですか。(*What is your hobby?*)

町田さんと林(はやし)さんが話しています。

When asking a social superior about his or her hobbies, use the polite alternate 御趣味(ごしゅみ). See Grammar Note on p.196.

林：町田さんは何か趣味がありますか。
町田：そうですね、音楽鑑賞(おんがくかんしょう)ですね。
林：スポーツは何かしますか。
町田：テニスやバレーボールをします。
　　　林さんの趣味は何ですか。
林：いやあ、何もないんですよ。

アクティビティー　2

この週末(しゅうまつ)何をしますか。(*What are they going to do this weekend?*)

Using the following table, discuss what hobby each person has and what he or she is going to do this weekend.

[例]　S1: 町田さんは何か趣味(しゅみ)がありますか。
　　　S2: クラシック音楽(おんがく)です。
　　　S1: 週末は何かしますか。
　　　S2: 日曜日、コンサートへ行きます。

名前	趣味(しゅみ)	土曜日	日曜日
ジョン・カワムラ (21歳(さい)、大学生)	映画(えいが)	映画を見る	ジョギングをする
町田ひとみ (20歳、大学生)	クラシック音楽	ステレオを聞く	コンサートへ行く
林正男(はやしまさお) (19歳、大学生)	ない	一日中寝(ね)る	テレビを見る
チン・メイリン (19歳、大学生)	読書(どくしょ)	本を読む	本を読む

Ms. Machida and Mr. Hayashi are talking HAYASHI: Do you (*lit., Ms. Machida*) have any hobbies? MACHIDA: Let me see. My hobby is listening to music. HAYASHI: Do you play any sports? MACHIDA: I play tennis,volleyball, and the like.What is your hobby, Mr. Hayashi? HAYASHI: Well, I don't have any.

名前	趣味	土曜日	日曜日
山本さゆり (18歳、ウエイトレス)	買い物	デパートへ行く	ブティックへ行く
高田洋一 (26歳、会社員)	ない	仕事をする	仕事をする
山口健次 (54歳、会社員)	つり	仕事をする	釣りに行く
ヘザー・ギブソン (20歳、大学生)	スポーツ	エアロビクスをする	スキーに行く

| 会社員 *company employee*

Vocabulary Library

More Hobbies

Art

絵をかく	えをかく	to draw a picture
油絵	あぶらえ	oil painting
水彩画	すいさいが	watercolor
墨絵	すみえ	**sumi** ink painting
生花	いけばな	flower arranging
書道	しょどう	brush calligraphy

Music and Performing Arts

バイオリン		violin
こと		**koto** (*Japanese zither*)
三味線	しゃみせん	**samisen** (*Japanese banjo-like instrument*)
日本舞踊	にほんぶよう	Japanese traditional dancing
弾く	ひく	to play (*string instruments*)
吹く	ふく	to play (*wind instruments*)
歌(を歌う)	うた(をうたう)	(to sing) a song
カラオケ		**karaoke** (*singing to recorded accompaniment*)
クラシック音楽	クラシックおんがく	classical music
演劇	えんげき	(*theatrical*) play

Loanwords: オペラ、ギター、ジャズ、ダンス、ピアノ、ミュージカル、ラップ、ロック

Games

テレビゲーム		video game
トランプ(をする)		(to play) cards
碁	ご	go (*a board game*)
将棋	しょうぎ	shogi (*a board game*)
マージャン		mah-jongg
カルタ		Japanese playing cards
パチンコ		**pachinko** (*Japanese pinball*)

Loanwords: コンピュータゲーム、チェス

Photography

写真(を撮る)	しゃしん(をとる)	(to take) a photo
白黒写真	しろくろしゃしん	black-and-white photo (graphy)
カラー写真	カラーしゃしん	color photo (graphy)

Loanwords: アルバム、カメラ、ビデオカメラ、フィルム

Other Hobbies

切手(を集める)	きって(をあつめる)	(to collect) stamps
骨董品	こっとうひん	antiques
刺繍	ししゅう	embroidery
編物	あみもの	knitting, crochet
手品	てじな	juggling
茶道	さどう	tea ceremony
盆栽	ぼんさい	bonsai
ペット(を飼う)	ペット(をかう)	(to keep, raise) a pet
犬	いぬ	dog
猫	ねこ	cat
鳥	とり	bird
金魚	きんぎょ	goldfish

Loanwords: コンピュータ、ハンティング、ヨガ

文化ノート

碁、将棋、マージャン、パチンコ

Four popular games, among the many played in Japan, are go, shogi, mah-jongg, and pachinko. The first two, go and shogi, are portable board games, but pachinko must be played in a pachinko parlor equipped with pachinko machines. Mah-jongg may be played either at home or at a mah-jongg parlor where refreshments are served and high-tech devices "shuffle" and deal the game pieces for you.

チーン、ジャラジャラ！パチンコ屋の中はいつもにぎやかです。

Go is a two-player game of sophisticated strategy. Each player in turn places a black or white stone on one of the 361 intersections of the 19 × 19 grid board with the aim of surrounding and otherwise capturing territories and the opponent's stones.

Shogi is a two-player board game similar to chess. Each player manipulates twenty pieces headed by a king. Go and shogi, both originally imported from China, are very popular in Japan. Indeed over 500 Japanese make their living as professional go and shogi players, and the results of their competitions are reported regularly in the newspapers.

Mah-jongg is a game played by four people using 136 tiles (game pieces resembling dominoes). Each player tries to complete combinations of tiles by collecting and discarding them in turn. This game is extremely popular among college students, especially male students who may stay up all night playing. Partly because of the loud noise created when "shuffling" the tiles, students often play at mah-jongg parlors in commercial districts near their universities.

Pachinko is a Japanese version of pinball that began its rise to phenomenal popularity in the late 1940s. With a flipper or knob the player sends small steel balls into the vertically oriented pinball machine, aiming at specific holes. Depending on which hole a ball enters, varying quantities of steel balls are discharged at the bottom of the machine as the player's winnings. These balls can be reinserted into the machine for extended play or exchanged for such merchandise as cigarettes and candy. Minors are not allowed to play pachinko.

Despite the rise of video games and computer technology, these four games continue to attract large followings. The computer version of go may be a better option than not playing at all, but the distinctive sound of a go stone striking the wooden playing board and the pleasures of interacting with a live opponent have yet to be replicated.

文法ノート

Nominal Verbs

Countless new verbs can be formed by appending the verb する (*to do*) to certain foreign loanwords and compound nouns (those composed of two or more characters) of Chinese origin. These are called *nominal verbs*. Add する to 旅行(りょこう) (*travel*) and you get 旅行する (*to travel*). Here are some more nominal verbs you already know.

勉強(べんきょう)する、運動(うんどう)する、料理(りょうり)する
ドライブする、ジョギングする、スポーツする

You cannot make verbs this way out of all loanwords and Chinese-origin compound nouns. For instance, you cannot say 銀行(ぎんこう)する (*to bank*); a completely different verb is required. Nor can you say 会議(かいぎ)する; you have to say 会議(かいぎ)をする (*to have a meeting*). Most (but not all) nouns that can be turned into nominal verbs can also be used as the direct object of する.

勉強をする、運動をする、料理をする
ドライブをする、ジョギングをする、スポーツをする

アクティビティー 3

ヨガのクラスは何曜日の何時ですか。(*What time on what day of the week is yoga class?*)

東京カルチャーセンター

クラス・スケジュール

クラス	先生	曜日	時間	場所
ヨガ	プラート	月	3〜4	東ビル3階
写真	吉田	水	10〜12	西ビル1階
生花	沢井	火	1〜3	東ビル2階
エアロビクス	水沢	金	2〜3:30	南ビル4階
絵画	岩村	水	9〜12	北ビル4階
フルート	神田	木	2〜4	北ビル5階
茶道	木下	月・水	11〜1	南ビル3階
ボーリング	花田	金	10〜12	東京ボーリング
手芸	北野	火・木	2〜4	西ビル1階
ピンポン	村上	月	12〜2	ジム
フランス語	ラルー	土	9〜12	西ビル2階

Ask your classmates questions about classes at the Tokyo Culture Center. Refer to the schedule below.

[例] S1: すみません。ヨガのクラスは何曜日の何時ですか。
S2: 月曜日の3時から4時までです。
S1: 先生はどなたですか。
S2: プラート先生です。
S1: クラスはどこですか。
S2: 東ビルの3階です。
S1: どうもありがとうございます。
S2: どういたしまして。

アクティビティー 4

余暇をどのように過ごしますか。(*How do you spend your free time?*)

Here is how Japanese answer this question. The activities are listed in decreasing order of popularity. Answer the questions that follow the table.

順位	女性	%	男性	%
1	ショッピングをする	46.0	テレビを見る	49.0
2	旅行をする	45.9	寝る	34.8
3	手芸・編物をする	45.9	音楽を聞く	34.7
4	テレビを見る	41.1	旅行をする	32.7
5	読書をする	33.4	スポーツをする	30.3
6	友だちと話す	33.2	読書をする	27.8
7	音楽を聞く	30.8	釣りをする	24.8
8	映画を見る	30.2	映画を見る	24.3
9	レストランへ行く	23.4	マージャンをする	23.5
10	スポーツをする	20.6	パチンコをする	21.7

順位 *rank* 女性 *women* 男性 *men* ～番目 is a counter for ordinal numbers (first, second, third, etc.)

に of 女性に means *among* in this context.

1. 女性に一番人気がある(*popular*)ことは何ですか。
2. 男性に一番人気があることは何ですか。
3. 女性と男性とどちらがスポーツをするのが好きですか。
4. 女性が7番目に好きなことは何ですか。

Decimal point is 点 in Japanese. Thus, 45.9 % is read 四十五点九パーセント. 49.0 % is read 四十九点ゼロ(or 零)パーセント.

5. 男性が７番目に好きなことは何ですか。
6. 男性がして、女性がしないことは何ですか。
7. 女性がして、男性がしないことは何ですか。
8. アメリカ人があまりしないことは何ですか。

Make your own questions ask your classmates.

Vocabulary: Sports

スポーツ		sports
運動	うんどう	exercise
試合	しあい	game
ジョギング		jogging
マラソン		marathon; long-distance running
野球	やきゅう	baseball
バスケットボール		basketball
バレーボール		volleyball
テニス		tennis
ゴルフ		golf
フットボール		football
サッカー		soccer
水泳	すいえい	swimming
ダイビング		diving
プール		(*swimming*) pool
ヨット		yacht
キャンピング		camping
エアロビクス		aerobics
サイクリング		bicycling

Review: 泳(およ)ぐ、ハイキング、山登(のぼ)り

㊙ Study Grammar 25.

アクティビティー 5

ダイアログ：野球(やきゅう)が上手(じょうず)ですね。(*You are good at baseball.*)

カワムラ：三村(みむら)さんは野球が上手ですね。
三村：いいえ、野球は好きですが、下手(へた)です。
カワムラ：そんなことありませんよ。
三村：いいえ、ぜんぜんダメですよ。

KAWAMURA: You (*lit., Mr. Mimura*) sure are good at baseball. MIMURA: No, I like baseball, but I'm no good at it. KAWAMURA: That's not true. (*lit., No, there isn't such a case.*) MIMURA: Yes it is. (*lit., No, I am no good at all.*)

後楽園ドーム：野球は日本で一番人気 **(popularity)** があります。

コミュニケーション・ノート

When You Are Praised

It is usually difficult for Japanese to say no, but there are a few situations where Japanese say no immediately. One of those situations is receiving praise. When praised, whether for one's skills, a possession, a family member, or another in-group person, a Japanese first denies the praise or mentions something negative. *No, I'm still learning, No, it's a cheap item, No, my son is not talented.* It is considered rude and unsophisticated to accept praise right away or to boast about one's own skills or talent (or that of an in-group member), even if that skill is self-evident. Predictably, the person making the compliment offers further praise, which is again denied. After two or three exchanges of this kind, the person being praised finally accepts the praise somewhat reluctantly. See **Language Functions and Situations** in this chapter for more examples of how to respond to compliments.

Selecting from the sports listed, answer the questions.

Sports: バスケットボール、バレーボール、空手、テニス、ピンポン、ゴルフ、スキー、野球、ソフトボール、サッカー

1. どのスポーツが好きですか。
   (Choose as many as you like and rank them in order of preference.)
2. どのスポーツができますか。
   (Rank the sports you can play in order of your skill level.)

Now compare your answers with your classmates'.

1. みんな、どのスポーツが好きですか。
2. みんなが上手なスポーツは何ですか。

Vocabulary: Skills

上手(な)	じょうず(な)	good, skillful at
下手(な)	へた(な)	bad, unskillful at
だめ(な)		no good
得意(な)	とくい(な)	good at and fond of something
苦手(な)	にがて(な)	bad at and dislike something
できる		to be able to do
できない		cannot do

アクティビティー 6

一人でしますか。(*Do you do it alone?*)

Tell what sports satisfy each of the following conditions.

…人で *as . . . person/people*

…以上 means . . . *or more*. Thus, 三人以上 means *three people or more*. …以下 means *less than*. . . . 三人以下 means *fewer than three people* (that is, zero, one, or two people).

1. 一人でします。
2. 二人でします。
3. 三人以上でします。
4. ボールを使います。
5. 外 (*outdoors*) でします。
6. 海でします。
7. オリンピックの種目 (*event*) です。
8. 冬のスポーツです。
9. 危険な (*dangerous*) スポーツです。

Vocabulary Library

More Sports Terms

投げる	なげる	to throw
受ける	うける	to catch(a ball)
打つ	うつ	to hit
ピンポン、卓球	たっきゅう	table tennis, Ping-Pong
プロ		professional
アマ		amateur
体操	たいそう	gymnastics
乗馬	じょうば	horseback riding
射撃	しゃげき	shooting
空手	からて	karate
柔道	じゅうどう	judo
剣道	けんどう	**kendo**(*Japanese fencing*)
相撲	すもう	sumo wrestling
陸上競技	りくじょうきょうぎ	track and field
選手	せんしゅ	athlete

Loanwords: ウエイト・リフティング、ジム、バドミントン、ボート、ボーリング、ボクシング、ラケット、ラグビー、ランニング、ロッククライミング、レスリング

文化ノート

日本のスポーツ

Sumo, a form of wrestling, is considered the Japanese national sport. It started some 2,000 years ago as a religious ritual and is still surrounded in ceremony today. Two sumo wrestlers compete in a dirt ring 4.55 meters in diameter. The object is to force one's opponent out of the ring or to force any part of his body but the soles of his feet to touch the ground. Professional sumo tournaments, each lasting fifteen days, are held six times a year and are televised nationwide. Top-ranked sumo wrestlers attain hero status, including a few foreigners over the years who have excelled as professional sumo wrestlers.

Most Japanese study at least one martial art, most commonly judo or kendo, during their secondary schooling. Judo has a long history, but the current form of judo was established by Jigoro Kano about 110 years ago. In judo, a player assumes a natural loose stance and tries to defeat his opponent by using his opponent's power and movement to get him off balance. Judo is now played worldwide and is an Olympic event.

すもうは日本の国技 **(national sport)** です。小錦 (右) はハワイの出身です。

Karate originated in China and was further developed in Okinawa. It has become popular in many countries. This martial art relies on kicks, thrusts, and strikes to best one's opponent.

Kendo, swordfighting with bamboo staffs, developed from the swordmanship of samurai. Of the various martial arts, judo and kendo place particular emphasis on moral and spiritual training as well as physical training.

Although in recent years soccer and football have garnered growing interest in Japan, the most popular team sport by far is baseball. Japanese professional baseball consists of twelve teams divided into two leagues, the Pacific League and the Central League. Since the teams are owned by corporations, they sport such names as the Nippon Ham Fighters, Chunichi Dragons, Yakult Swallows, and Yomiuri Giants. Baseball is popular as an amateur sport, too, and the annual nationwide competition among high school baseball teams commands the nation's attention for several days when the playoffs are televised.

Japanese participate in and avidly follow many other Western sports as well, including golf, tennis, marathon running, rugby, and skiing.

勉 Study Grammar 26 and 27.

アクティビティー 7

ダイアログ：見るのは好きです。(*I like watching it.*)

カワムラ：林(はやし)さんはフットボールが好きですか。
林：見るのは好きですが、するのはちょっと…
カワムラさんは。
カワムラ：わたしは見るのも、するのも大好きです。
林：上手(じょうず)ですか。
カワムラ：まあまあです。

アクティビティー 8

私(わたし)の好きなスポーツ (*Sports I like*)

Describe your favorite sport to a classmate in Japanese.

[例] わたしはテニスをするのが好きです。いつも近くのテニスコートで友だちとテニスをします。テニスは小さいボールとラケットを使(つか)います。
わたしは野球(やきゅう)を見るのが好きです。週末(しゅうまつ)はテレビで野球を見ます。好きなチームはメッツです。

勉 Study Grammar 28.

アクティビティー 9

ダイアログ：泳(およ)げますか。(*Can you swim?*)

カワムラ：チンさんの特技(とくぎ)は何ですか。
チン：水泳(すいえい)です。
カワムラ：どれぐらい泳げますか。
チン：そうですね。10キロぐらい泳げます。
カワムラ：本当(ほんとう)ですか。それはすごいですね。

Answer these questions.

See the Grammar Note on p.294 for an explanation of this use of particle か.

1. 将棋(しょうぎ)か碁(ご)ができますか。
2. マージャンをすることができますか。
3. 上手(じょうず)に写真(しゃしん)が撮(と)れますか。
4. 手芸(しゅげい)ができますか。
5. 絵(え)が上手に描(か)けますか。
6. 編物(あみもの)ができますか。

KAWAMURA: Do you (*lit., Mr. Hayashi*) like football? HAYASHI: I like watching it, but I don't like playing it. (*lit., I like watching it, but playing it is a bit. . . .*) How about you? KAWAMURA: I like both watching and playing it very much. HAYASHI: Are you good at it? KAWAMURA: I'm so-so.

KAWAMURA: What is your special talent? CHIN: It's swimming. KAWAMURA: How far can you swim? CHIN: Let me see. I can swim about ten kilometers. KAWAMURA: Really? That's terrific!

7. 何か楽器(がっき)がひけますか。
8. 日本料理(りょうり)が作(つく)れますか。
9. 日本語が上手に話せますか。
10. 漢字(かんじ)が上手に書けますか。

アクティビティー　10

インタビュー：できますか？ (*Can you do it?*)

Ask one of the following questions of ten students in your class. Then report to the class how many students responded yes and how many said no.

1. 日本語の歌(うた)が歌(うた)えますか。
2. 100メートル泳(およ)げますか。
3. スケートができますか。
4. 刺繍(ししゅう)(*embroidery*)ができますか。
5. スペイン語が話せますか。
6. 自転車(じてんしゃ)(*bicycle*)に乗れますか。
7. テニスができますか。
8. 柔道(じゅうどう)か空手(からて)ができますか。

文法ノート

か *or*

The particle か, used between two nouns, means *or*.

将棋(しょうぎ)か碁(ご)ができますか。
Can you play ***shogi*** *or go?*
ジュースかコーラを飲みませんか。
Would you like some (lit., won't you drink) juice or cola?
ブラウンさんかカワムラさんが行きます。
Ms. Brown or Mr. Kawamura will go.

You may add another か after the second noun with no change in meaning.

ブラウンさんかカワムラさんかが行きます。
柔道(じゅうどう)か空手(からて)ができますか。
Can you do judo or karate?
はい、柔道ができます。
Yes, I can do judo.
はい、両方(りょうほう)できます。
Yes, I can do both.
はい、どちらもできます。
Yes, I can do both.
いいえ、どちらもできません。
No, I can't do either.

Both 両方(りょうほう) and どちらも mean *both (or either) of two.*

Vocabulary: Family

家族	かぞく	family
両親	りょうしん	parents
父	ちち	father
母	はは	mother
子供	こども	child, children
息子	むすこ	son
娘	むすめ	daughter
兄弟	きょうだい	siblings
兄	あに	older brother
姉	あね	older sister
弟	おとうと	younger brother
妹	いもうと	younger sister
祖父	そふ	grandfather
祖母	そぼ	grandmother
孫	まご	grandchild, grandchildren
夫婦	ふうふ	husband and wife
夫	おっと	husband
主人*	しゅじん	husband
妻	つま	wife
家内*	かない	wife
おじ		uncle
おば		aunt
親戚	しんせき	relative

Important note: These words are used to refer only to your own family members and relatives. You will study another set of family terms for referring to other people's family members and relatives later in this chapter.

アクティビティー 11

Note the use of the polite 方 and どなた to refer to an older person in contrast to the neutral 子 and だれ for a child.

ダイアログ：父(ちち)です。(*This is my father.*)

町田さんとブラウンさんが写真(しゃしん)を見ています。

ブラウン：これは私(わたし)の家族(かぞく)の写真(しゃしん)です。

町田：ブラウンさんの右の男(おとこ)の方(かた)はどなたですか。

ブラウン：父です。

---

* Although in common use, these words are spurned by some Japanese for their sexist implications. 主人 literally means *master* and 家内, *one inside the home*.

Ms. Machida and Ms. Brown are looking at a photo BROWN: This is a photograph of my family. MACHIDA: Who is the man on your (*lit., Ms. Brown's*) right? BROWN: My father. MACHIDA: Who is this girl? BROWN: My younger sister.

町田：この女(おんな)の子(こ)はだれですか。
ブラウン：妹(いもうと)です。

Practice the dialogue, substituting the following for the underlined parts.

1. ブラウンさんの左(ひだり)の女(おんな)の方 — 母(はは)
   水玉(みずたま) (*polka-dot*) のブラウスの女の方 — 姉(あね)
2. ブラウンさんの後ろの男の方 — 兄(あに)
   ストライプ (*stripes*) のシャツの男の子 — 弟(おとうと)
3. 白(しろ)いブラウスの女の方 — 祖母(そぼ)
   サングラスの男の方 — 祖父(そふ)

Vocabulary: People

男	おとこ	male	子*	こ	child
女	おんな	female	男の子	おとこのこ	boy
人	ひと	person	女の子	おんなのこ	girl
方	かた	person (*polite*)			

Note: While grammatically correct, referring to people as その男 or その女 is rude. You should say その男の人、あの女の人 or, more politely, その男の方、あの女の方.

文法ノート

Words Expressing Respect and Politeness

Japanese has a wide range of expressions and structures to convey different levels of speakers' or writers' feeling of respect and politeness. (These expressions and structures are generally called honorifics (敬語[けいご]), which will be introduced gradually, beginning here. Let's take, for example, words meaning *person, people*. In a neutral situation, 人 (ひと) is used. To show respect, 方 (かた) is used.

The prefixes お or 御 (ご) are often added to a word to express respect or politeness. For instance, お年寄 (としより) is the honorific counterpart of 年寄 (*old person*). 御趣味 (ごしゅみ) is the honorific counterpart

*子(こ) and 子供(こども) both mean *child* or *children*. 子 must be used with modifiers — e.g., その子、うちの子、男の子 — but 子供 can be used alone as well as with modifiers.

of 趣味 (*hobbies*), and it is used to refer to the hobbies of socially superior people. These prefixes do not make honorifics of all words, however. When they are used, the choice of お or 御 depends on each word.

アクティビティー　12

わたしは林正男(はやしまさお)です。(*I am Masao Hayashi.*)

Masao Hayashi is describing his family. Are his statements accurate? Correct any that are wrong.

1. 林俊男(としお)はわたしの父(ちち)です。
2. 林やすとはわたしの弟(おとうと)です。
3. 林すみ子はわたしの姉(あね)です。
4. 林くみ子(こ)はわたしの母(はは)です。
5. 林太郎はわたしの祖母(そぼ)です。
6. 林よし子はわたしのおばです。
7. 林はなはわたしのおじです。

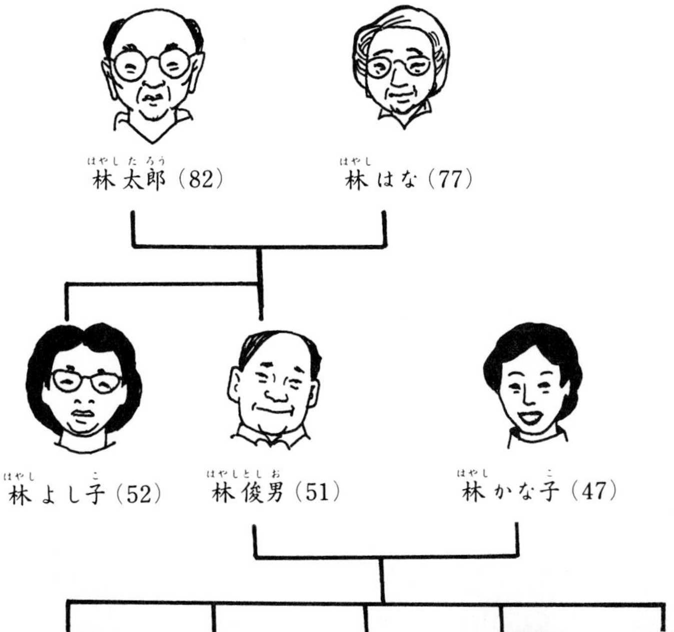

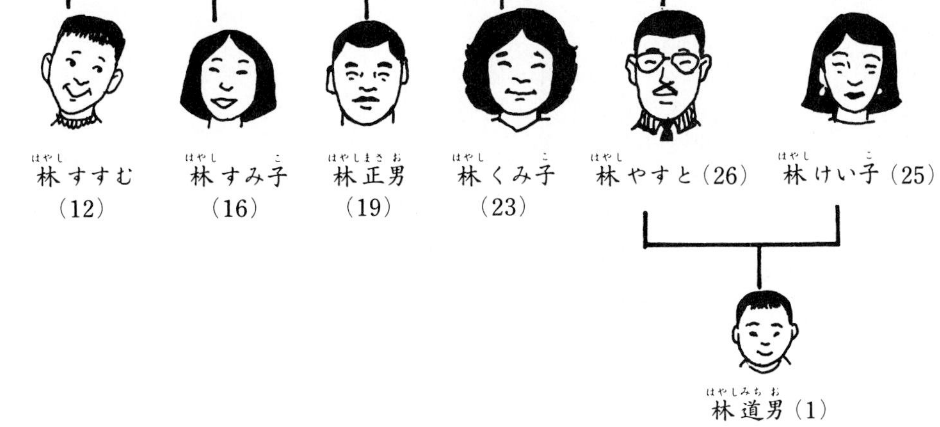

Now look at Masao Hayashi's family from another perspective, and at your own family.

8. Assume you are a member of the Hayashi family (other than Masao). Describe your family.
9. From that person's standpoint, make five statements (accurate or not). Ask a classmate if each is right or wrong.
10. Draw your own family tree. Explain it to a classmate.

文化ノート

The Japanese Family

Unlike the prewar years, when families were large and several generations lived under one roof, the average Japanese household today consists of a single nuclear family — two parents with one or two children. There is strong social pressure to marry by age thirty if not earlier. In 1985, the average age of marriage for Japanese men was 28.2 years old, while that of Japanese women was 25.5 years old. The typical couple has their first child within one to three years of marriage, whereupon the wife is expected to quit her job to take care of the child (unless she already quit her job to get married).

Women are also in charge of running the home — managing the family budget, the children's education, and the family's social schedule — while husbands are occupied with their company jobs, long commutes, and after-hours business socializing. As more and more women enter the workforce, these gender-based social roles have begun to change, especially among the younger generation. But married women, even those who have part-time or full-time jobs, still bear the greatest responsibility for managing the household, even after the children have left the nest.

As women have gained economic independence through increased job opportunities, the divorce rate has risen. The number of single-parent families is also increasing. Family life in Japan usually revolves around the children, and their education is the central focus of their parents. Even if the father is transferred to a branch office in a different city or country, the rest of the family may stay behind, for years, so the children can complete their education without disruption. While some Japanese lament the dissolution of the extended and even nuclear family in Japan, blaming it on Western influence, others welcome the options offered by more than one socially acceptable life pattern. Despite the changes, the family (not the individual) is still seen as the vital social unit in modern Japan.

家族(かぞく)みんなでお茶(ちゃ)の時間(じかん)です。

Vocabulary: Other People's Families

御家族	ごかぞく	family
御両親	ごりょうしん	parents
お父さん	おとうさん	father
お母さん	おかあさん	mother
お子さん	おこさん	child, children
息子さん	むすこさん	son
娘さん	むすめさん	daughter
お嬢さん	おじょうさん	daughter
御兄弟	ごきょうだい	siblings
お兄さん	おにいさん	older brother
お姉さん	おねえさん	older sister
弟さん	おとうとさん	younger brother
妹さん	いもうとさん	younger sister
おじいさん		grandfather
おばあさん		grandmother
お孫さん	おまごさん	grandchild, grandchildren
御夫婦	ごふうふ	husband and wife
御主人	ごしゅじん	husband
奥さん	おくさん	wife
おじさん		uncle
おばさん		aunt
御親戚	ごしんせき	relative

Important note: These terms are used when referring to someone else's family members or relatives. These words are respectful in contrast to the humble terms for your own family; be careful not to confuse the two sets of terms.

言語ノート

My Father, Your Father

In Japanese, there are at least two words for identifying each family member or relative, one word for identifying your own family member or relative and another for identifying someone else's. For example, 父(ちち) refers to the speaker's own father, and お父(とう)さん refers to someone else's father. (You will study some exceptions later.) The former is humble, while the latter is respectful. (Did you recognize the honorific prefix お and honorific suffix さん?) You would never call someone else's father 父(ちち), so it is redundant to say わたしの父 (*my father*). Similarly, when asking someone about his or her father, just use お父さん; in that context it would mean *your father*. These two sets of terms for family members reflect the careful distinction between in-group and out-group in Japanese language and society.

アクティビティー 13

ギブソンさんのお父さんは51歳です。(*Ms. Gibson's father is 51 years old.*)

Now Masao Hayashi is describing Heather Gibson's family. Are the following statements true or false?

1. ギブソンさんのお父さんは49歳です。
2. ギブソンさんのお母さんの名前はマリアンです。
3. ギブソンさんのお兄さんは28歳です。
4. ギブソンさんのお姉さんはコンピュータ・プログラマーです。
5. ギブソンさんのおじいさんは70歳です。
6. ギブソンさんのおばあさんの名前はジュリーです。
7. ギブソンさんの妹さんは20歳です。

Now try some other family descriptions.

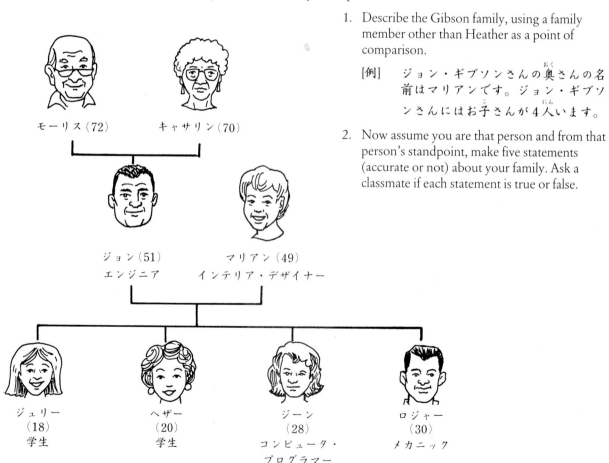

1. Describe the Gibson family, using a family member other than Heather as a point of comparison.

   [例]　ジョン・ギブソンさんの奥さんの名前はマリアンです。ジョン・ギブソンさんにはお子さんが4人います。

2. Now assume you are that person and from that person's standpoint, make five statements (accurate or not) about your family. Ask a classmate if each statement is true or false.

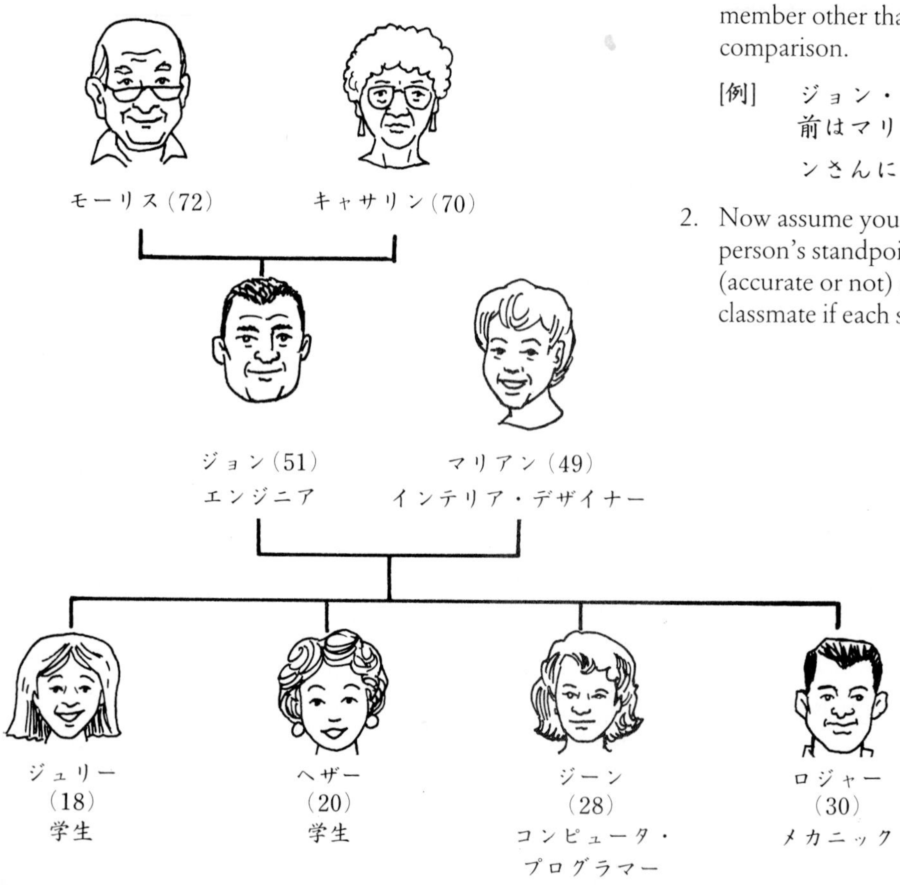

Vocabulary Library

More Family Terms

義理の(母)	ぎりの(はは)	(mother)-in-law
養子	ようし	adopted child
独身	どくしん	single (*not married*) person

Humble Form		Respectful Form		
長男	ちょうなん	御長男	ごちょうなん	oldest son
長女	ちょうじょ	御長女	ごちょうじょ	oldest daughter
甥	おい		おいごさん	nephew
姪	めい		めいごさん	niece
いとこ			おいとこさん	cousin

アクティビティー　14

お姉(ねえ)さんの趣味(しゅみ)は何ですか。(*What are your older sister's hobbies?*)

This chart summarizes your family's hobbies and interests. Work with a partner, and answer your classmate's questions about each family member.

[例]　—お姉さんの趣味は何ですか。
　　　—姉(あね)の趣味は音楽(おんがく)です。ピアノが得意(とくい)です。

家族(かぞく)	趣味(しゅみ)	注(ちゅう) (*Note*)
父(ちち)	仕事(しごと)	土曜日，日曜日も働(はたら)く
母(はは)	生花(いけばな)	園芸(えんげい)が好き
兄(あに)	音楽(おんがく)を聞く	クラシック音楽が大好(す)き
姉(あね)	音楽	ピアノが得意(とくい)
わたし	読書(どくしょ)	いつもフランス語の本を読む
弟(おとうと)	テレビを見る	12時までテレビを見る
妹(いもうと)	スポーツ	空手(からて)が好き

*Replace the parenthetical family term with its respectful alternate to refer respectfully to someone else's in-law. Thus, 義理のお母さん *(your/his) mother-in-law.*

Study Grammar 29.

アクティビティー 15

ダイアログ：何をしていますか。(*What is he doing?*)

電話で

　　山口：もしもし、山口です。
ブラウン：もしもし、ブラウンです。カワムラさんはいますか。
　　山口：ええ、今、<u>テレビを見ています</u>。
ブラウン：ちょっとお願いします。

Practice the dialogue, substituting the following activities for the underlined phrase.

1. 料理をする
2. ステレオで音楽を聞く
3. コンピュータ・ゲームをする
4. 写真を撮る
5. 犬と遊ぶ

アクティビティー 16

本を読んでいます。(*He is reading a book.*)

Describe the following illustrations.

[例]　カーティスさんは本を読んでいます。

Study Grammar 30.

アクティビティー 17

テレビゲームをしている男の人はだれですか。(*Who is the man who is playing video games?*)

On the phone YAMAGUCHI: Hello. This is Yamaguchi speaking. BROWN: Hello. This is Brown. Is Mr. Kawamura there? YAMAGUCHI: Yes, <u>he is watching TV</u> now. BROWN: May I talk to him?

Using the preceding illustrations, answer these questions.

1. ブラウンさんと話している女(おんな)の人はだれですか。
2. テレビゲームをしている男の人はだれですか。
3. 手紙(てがみ)を書(か)いている男の人はだれですか。
4. エアロビクスをしている女の人はだれですか。
5. カーティスさんが読んでいる本は何ですか。
6. Ｔシャツを着(き)ている男の人はだれですか。
7. 三村(みむら)さんが飲んでいるもの(*thing*)は何ですか。

アクティビティー 18

フランス語が話せる人はだれですか。(*Who is the person who can speak French?*)

Walk around the classroom interviewing your classmates to find out who satisfies which of the following conditions. Report your results to the class.

1. 空手(からて)のできる人
2. カメラを持(も)っている人
3. ピアノが弾(ひ)ける人
4. 歌(うた)が上手(じょうず)に歌(うた)える人
5. 昨日(きのう)ジョギングをした人
6. 先週、映画(えいが)を見た人
7. ひまがない人
8. 泳(およ)げない人

アクティビティー 19

たくさんお金のかかる趣味(しゅみ) (*Hobbies requiring a lot of money*)

List hobbies, games, and sports that satisfy each of the following conditions. Later, compare your list with your classmates' lists.

1. たくさんお金のかかる趣味
2. あまりお金のかからない趣味
3. ４人でするゲーム
4. カードを使(つか)うゲーム
5. とても疲(つか)れる趣味、スポーツ(*hobbies and sports that tire you*)
6. 家(いえ)の中でできる趣味
7. アメリカ人がよくするスポーツ
8. 冬(ふゆ)、よくするスポーツ

アクティビティー 20

趣味は何ですか。(*What are their hobbies?*)

Various people made these statements. Identify their hobbies.

1. 毎日プールへ行って、泳いでいます。
2. 昨日、図書館で12時まで本を読みました。
3. 去年、ボストンとニューヨークで走りました。
4. 「マダム・バタフライ」が好きです。
5. 昨日、ジャイアンツの試合を見ました。
6. カメラをいつも持っています。
7. シチューを作るのが上手です。
8. 去年、中国とメキシコとフランスとエジプトへ行きました。

(勉) Study Grammar 31.

アクティビティー 21

ダイアログ：上手になりましたね。(*You have become good at it.*)

カワムラ：さとみさん、フランス語を練習しているんですか。
山口：ええ。毎日練習していますが、なかなか上手になりません。
カワムラさんは日本語が上手になりましたね。
カワムラ：いいえ、まだまだですよ。
山口：そんなことありませんよ。本当に上手ですよ。

アクティビティー 22

好きになりました。(*I've come to like it.*)

Following the example, explain how each person has changed.

[例]　ゴルフがきらいでした。でも、今は好きです。→
ゴルフが好きになりました。

1. ピアノが下手でした。でも、今は上手です。
2. ブロッコリがきらいでした。でも、今は好きです。

KAWAMURA: Satomi, are you practicing French?　YAMAGUCHI: Yes. Although I practice every day, I don't seem to be getting better (*lit., I cannot become good at it easily*). You have become good at Japanese, haven't you?　KAWAMURA: No. I'm still poor at it.　YAMAGUCHI: That's not true. You really are good, you know.

3. 読書(どくしょ)が好きでした。でも、今はきらいです。
4. 中国(ちゅうごく)語が苦手でした。でも、今は得意(とくい)です。
5. スピーチが苦手でした。でも、今は得意です。
6. ドイツ語が上手でした。でも、今は下手(へた)です。
7. 料理(りょうり)が得意でした。でも、今は苦手(にがて)です。

Grammar and Exercises

24. Interrogative ＋ か／も／でも

24.1 By appending the particles か、も、 or でも to an interrogative (question word), you can express a whole range of new meanings.

1. An interrogative followed by か yields a word meaning *some*. . . .
2. An interrogative followed by も means *every* . . . in affirmative sentences; it means *no* . . . in negative sentences.
3. An interrogative followed by でも means *any*.

These meanings are summarized in the following table. Note the two exceptions where other terms are used instead of the interrogative ＋ も.

INTERROGATIVE	＋ か	＋ も **In Affirmative Sentences**	＋ も **In Negative Sentences**	＋ でも
何(なに)	何(なに)か *something*	みんな、みな 全(すべ)て、全部(ぜんぶ) *everything*	何(なに)も *nothing*	何(なん)でも *anything, whatever*
だれ (どなた)	だれか (どなたか) *someone*	みんな、みな (みなさん) *everyone*	だれも (どなたも) *no one*	だれでも (どなたでも) *anyone, whoever*
いつ	いつか *sometime*	いつも *always, all the time*	いつも *never*	いつでも *anytime, whenever*
どこ	どこか *somewhere*	どこも *everywhere*	どこも *nowhere*	どこでも *anywhere, wherever*

INTERROGATIVE	+ か	+ も	+ も	+ でも
		In Affirmative Sentences	**In Negative Sentences**	
どれ	どれか *one of them*	どれも *every one, everything, all of them*	どれも *none of them*	どれでも *any of them, whichever one*
どちら	どちらか *either of two*	どちらも *both of them*	どちらも *neither of them*	どちらでも *either of them, whichever of the two*

何か食べますか。—ええ、何でもけっこうです。
Will you eat something?—Yes, anything is fine.
昨日(きのう)は何か食べましたか。—いいえ、何も食べませんでした。
Did you eat something yesterday?—No, I ate nothing (or No, I didn't eat anything.)
だれか来ますか。—いいえ、だれも来ません。
Is someone coming?—No, no one is coming.
いつかそこへ行きましょうか。—ええ、いつでもいいですよ。
Shall we go there someday?—Yes, any time is OK.
三村(みむら)さんはいつもいませんね。—アルバイトで忙(いそが)しいんですよ。
Mr. Mimura is never present.—He's busy with his part-time jobs, you know.
この三つの中からどれか選(えら)んでください。—じゃ、これをください。
Please choose one of these three.—Well then, please give me this one.
どれがいいでしょうか。—どれでも同(おな)じです。
Which one is good?—All of them are the same.
どちらか選(えら)んでください。—わたしはどちらでもいいですよ。
Please choose one of these (two).—Either is fine with me.

Reminder: どれ is used when talking about three or more things. どちら is used when discussing two things.

24.2 When the particles に、へ、から and まで are part of a sentence containing the interrogative + か／も／でも construction, they fall between the interrogative and も or でも.

みんなに会(あ)いますか。—いいえ、だれにも会いませんよ。
Will you see everyone?—No, I won't see anyone.
どこかへ行きましたか。—いいえ、どこへも行(い)きませんでした。
Did you go somewhere?—No, I didn't go anywhere.

The particle を is dropped whenever these interrogative-particle combinations are used.

何を見ますか。—何でも見ますよ。
What will you see?—I will see everything.

24.3 Here are some useful expressions formed by combining interrogatives with か.

なぜか *somehow (for some reason)*

なぜか村山(むらやま)さんが好きではありません。
Somehow I don't like Ms. Murayama.

どうか *somehow* (often used in requests)

どうか教(おし)えてください。
Please (find a way to) instruct me.

いくつか *some (number of), several*

日本語のことばをいくつか習(なら)いました。
I learned some Japanese words.

練習 1

Fill in each blank with the appropriate interrogative + particle(s) and complete the dialogues.

1. A: (　　　)飲みますか。
   B: ええ、コーラはありますか。
2. A: (　　　)へ行きましょうか。
   B: そうですね。デパートはどうですか。
3. A: そこに(　　　)いますか。
   B: ええ、林(はやし)さんがいます。
4. A: この映画(えいが)の中で(　　　)を見ましたか。
   B: いいえ、どれも見ていません。
5. A: この三冊(さつ)の本の中のどれがいいですか。
   B: (　　　)いいですよ。

冊 is a counter for books.

6. A: 今年の夏(なつ)はどこへ旅行(りょこう)しましょうか。
   B: わたしは(　　　)いいですよ。
7. A: この問題(もんだい)はやさしいですね。
   B: ええ、(　　　)簡単(かんたん)に(*easily*)できますね。
8. A: 土曜日がいいですか。日曜日がいいですか。
   B: (　　　)いいですよ。
9. A: あそこにだれがいましたか。
   B: (　　　)いませんでした。
10. A: (　　　)へ行きましょうか。
    B: いいえ、家(いえ)にいましょう。今日は(　　　)こんでいます(こんでいる *to be crowded*)。

練習 2

Answer these questions. Use interrogatives +か、も、 or でも only if appropriate.

1. 先週の日曜日、どこかへ行きましたか。
2. 何を食べますか。
3. いつか映画(えいが)を見ませんか。
4. このコンピュータはどれも同(おな)じですか。
5. コーラとジュースとビールのどれがいいですか。
6. 今日の午後、何もしないんですか。
7. あの先生はいつもやさしいですか。
8. だれもこの練習(れんしゅう)ができないんですか。

25. Describing Abilities

カワムラ：町田さんはピンポンが上手(じょうず)ですね。
町田：いいえ、あまり上手じゃありませんが、大好きです。
カワムラ：一度一緒(いちどいっしょ)にしませんか。
町田：ええ、いいですね。

林(はやし)：ブラウンさんの趣味(しゅみ)は何ですか。
ブラウン：そうですね。料理(りょうり)が好きです。
林：わたしは料理がまったく苦手(にがて)なんです。
ブラウン：わたしもそんなに上手じゃないんです。
林：得意(とくい)な料理は。
ブラウン：そうですね。オムレツですね。

林(はやし)：町田さんは何か外国語(がいこくご)ができますか。
町田：ええ、フランス語がちょっとできます。
林：それはすごいですね。
町田：林さんは。
林：わたしは外国語がぜんぜんダメです。

Note the similarity between these expressions and those for stating likes and dislikes (**Grammar 10,** Chapter 2).

KAWAMURA: You are good at playing table tennis! MACHIDA: No, I'm not that good at it, but I love it. KAWAMURA: How about playing together sometime (*lit., once*)? MACHIDA: Yes, that would be good.

HAYASHI: What is your hobby, Ms. Brown? BROWN: Let me see. I like cooking. HAYASHI: I'm a complete failure at cooking. (*lit., I am totally bad at cooking and don't like it.*) BROWN: I am not all that good at it, either. HAYASHI: What is your best dish? (*lit., As for cooking you're good at?*) BROWN: Let me see . . . omelets.

HAYASHI: Can you speak any foreign languages? MACHIDA: Yes, I can speak French a little bit. HAYASHI: That's great. MACHIDA: How about you? HAYASHI: I am totally bad at foreign languages.

25.1 Here is how to express skills and abilities in Japanese.

A	+	は	+	B	+	が	上手(じょうず) です (だ)	*A is good at B*
(person)				(noun)			下手(へた) です (だ)	*A is poor at B*
							得意(とくい) です (だ)	*A is good at and likes B*
							苦手(にがて) です (だ)	*A is poor at and dislikes B*
							できます(できる)	*A can do B*

ブラウンさんはダンスが上手(じょうず)ですね。
Ms. Brown, you are good at dancing, aren't you?
歌(うた)が下手(へた)で、いつもこまる。
I am poor at singing and that always gives me trouble.
ギブソンさんはスケートが得意(とくい)だ。
Ms. Gibson is quite a skater (lit., is good at and likes skating).
わたしはフランス語が苦手(にがて)だ。
I am poor at French (lit., and dislike it).
チンさんは水泳(すいえい)ができますか。
Ms. Chin, can you swim (lit., can you do swimming)?

25.2 上手(じょうず) and 下手(へた) are na-adjectives. 得意(とくい) and 苦手(にがて) are na-adjectives that may also be used as nouns. When used as a noun 得意 means *special skill* or *specialty* and 苦手 means *weakness* or *weak point*.

得意(とくい)な外国語(がいこくご)はスペイン語です。
My best foreign language is Spanish. (lit., The foreign language I'm good at and like is Spanish.)
歌(うた)が上手(じょうず)な人はだれですか。
Who is (a person who is) good at singing?
料理(りょうり)が下手(へた)な人はたくさんいます。
There are many people who are bad cooks (lit., poor at cooking).
得意(とくい)な楽器(がっき)はトランペットです。
The musical instrument I'm most skilled at (and like) is trumpet.
私(わたし)の得意(とくい)はオムレツです。(得意 used as noun)
My special dish is omlettes.
苦手(にがて)なクラスは数学(すうがく)です。
The class I am poor at (and don't like) is math.
料理(りょうり)が私(わたし)の苦手(にがて)です。(苦手 used as noun)
Cooking is my weak point.

25.3 できます (dictionary form できる) is a Class 2 verb meaning *can do, is possible* and conjugates as such.

兄は楽器ができません。
My older brother cannot play (lit., do) musical instruments.
雨が降って、ハイキングができなかった。
It rained, and (so) we couldn't go hiking.

25.4 In these expressions notice that the direct object (B in the **Grammar 25.1** chart) is marked with the particle が, not を. This is an exception to the rule that direct object nouns and pronouns are marked with the particle を. You already studied two similar exceptions: the na-adjectives 好き and 嫌い. In addition to the na-adjectives and verb (できます) in the chart, this rule also applies to the verb わかります (*to understand*; dictionary form わかる).

兄はドイツ語がわかります。
My older brother understands German.
このことば (word) の意味 (meaning) がわかりますか。
Do you understand the meaning of this word?
その答え (answer) がわからなかった。
I didn't understand that answer.

練習　　1

Following the example, make complete sentences.

[例]　(父)(ダンス)(得意) → 父はダンスが得意です。

1. (山口さんの奥さん)(ボーリング)(上手)
2. (林さん)(バスケットボール)(下手)
3. (シュミットさん)(日本語)(上手ではない)
4. (佐野さん)(あみもの)(得意)
5. (カワムラさん)(フランス語)(苦手)
6. (父)(インドネシア語)(できる)
7. (兄)(スポーツ)(苦手)
8. (ギブソンさん)(スキー)(得意)
9. (私)(料理)(できない)
10. (妻)(イタリア語)(わかる)

練習 2

Make dialogues, following the example.

[例] (バレー／できる)(できない)→
—あなたはバレーができますか。
—いいえ、できません。

1. (スポーツ／得意(とくい))(苦手(にがて))
2. (ロシア語／上手(じょうず))(下手(へた))
3. (バイオリン／上手)(まあまあ)
4. (ピンポン／できる)(できる)
5. (タガログ語／わかる)(わからない)

練習 3

Answer these questions truthfully.

1. 車(くるま)の運転(うんてん)(*driving*)が上手(じょうず)ですか。
2. どんな料理(りょうり)が一番得意(とくい)ですか。
3. 日本語が上手(じょうず)ですか。
4. ご家族(かぞく)は日本語ができますか。
5. どんなスポーツが上手ですか。
6. どんな楽器(がっき)が上手ですか。
7. 食べ物(もの)の中で何が一番きらいですか。
8. 苦手(にがて)なもの (*thing*) は何ですか。
9. どんな外国語ができますか。
10. ショッピングが上手ですか。

26. Nominalizers: こと and の

ブラウン：野球(やきゅう)は好きですか。
林(はやし)：ええ、見るのは好きです。
ブラウン：野球はしないんですか。
林：ええ、するのはあまり好きじゃありません。

BROWN: Do you like baseball? HAYASHI: Yes, I like watching it. BROWN: You mean you don't play it? HAYASHI: That's right. (*lit., Yes.*) I don't like playing it very much.

高田：日本語は得意ですか。
カワムラ：話すのは下手ですが、好きです。
高田：書くのはどうですか。
カワムラ：むずかしいです。でも、漢字を書くのはおもしろいです。

A：高田さんはいますか。
B：ええ。でも、高田さんと今話すことは無理です。
A：無理なことはわかりますが、どうか…
B：ダメです。高田さんは今忙しいんです。

カワムラ：チンさんが昨日ペキンへ帰ったことを聞きましたか。
町田：いいえ。なぜですか。
カワムラ：お母さんが病気なんです。
町田：お父さんが病気だったことは聞いていましたが、お母さんもですか。

Nominalizers are grammatical elements that change verbs, adjectives, etc., into nouns or noun phrases. In English, for instance, by adding *-ing* to the end of a verb, you form the gerund or noun form. (For example: *see* → *seeing* in *Seeing is believing*.) Thus, *-ing* can be considered a nominalizer in English.

26.1 Generally speaking, only nouns, pronouns, noun phrases, and noun-like elements can be in the subject and object positions of a sentence. When you would like to use verbs and adjectives in those positions, you must change them into noun phrases. In Japanese, こと and の are used to nominalize verbs and adjectives (change them into noun phrases). These two elements are called *nominalizers*. Add one of them to the *plain* form of a verb or adjective to form a noun phrase.

plain form of verb, i-adjective, or na-adjective + こと or の

TAKADA: Are you good at Japanese? KAWAMURA: I am poor at speaking it, but I like it. TAKADA: How about writing it? KAWAMURA: It's difficult, but it's fun to write Chinese characters.

A: Is Mr. Takada in? B: Yes, but it's impossible for you to talk to him now. A: I know it's impossible, but please . . . (let me see him). B: No way. Mr. Takada is busy now.

KAWAMURA: Did you hear that Ms. Chin returned to Beijing yesterday? MACHIDA: No. Why? KAWAMURA: Because her mother is ill. MACHIDA: I had heard that her father was ill, but her mother, too?

Here are some examples of each.

1. plain form of verb + nominalizer

読むこと	読むの
読まないこと	読まないの
読んだこと	読んだの
読まなかったこと	読まなかったの

2. plain form of i-adjective + nominalizer

大きいこと	大きいの
大きくないこと	大きくないの
大きかったこと	大きかったの
大きくなかったこと	大きくなかったの

3. plain form of na-adjective + nominalizer

きれいなこと	きれいなの
きれいではないこと	きれいではないの
(きれいじゃないこと)	(きれいじゃないの)
きれいだったこと	きれいだったの
きれいではなかったこと	きれいではなかったの
(きれいじゃなかったこと)	(きれいじゃなかったの)

You can use these noun phrases in the subject or object position of a sentence.

日本語を読むのはやさしいです。
Reading Japanese is easy.
SF を読むことが好きです。
I like reading science fiction.

SF (エスエフ) *science fiction*

父(ちち)がわたしの手紙(てがみ)を読んだことは知(し)りませんでした。
I didn't know that my father had read my letter.
その町がきれいなことは有名(ゆうめい)です。
その町がきれいなのは有名です。
It's well known that that town is pretty. (*lit., The fact that that town is pretty is famous.*)

26.2 Although both こと and の can be used to nominalize verbs, adjectives, and sentences, there is some difference in nuance between the two. の is used in sentences that express something subjective (i.e., something directly related to the speaker or something perceived or experienced by the speaker). こと is used when talking more generally or objectively. For example,

日本語を話すのはやさしいです。
日本語を話すことはやさしいです。
Speaking Japanese is easy.

The implication of the first sentence is that the speaker is basing the observation on personal experience. The second sentence does not imply a personal opinion, but rather simply makes a generally known observation that Japanese is easy to speak (compared, say, to writing it). For this reason, こと sometimes sounds a bit formal or bookish. Note the difference in meaning between these two sentences.

> ブラウンさんが日本語で話すのを聞いた。
> *I heard Ms. Brown speak in Japanese.*
> ブラウンさんがいつも日本語で話すことを聞いて、感心(かんしん)した。
> *I heard that Ms. Brown always speaks in Japanese and I was impressed.*

In many contexts, you can use either こと or の with little difference in meaning other than the implication just explained. In some contexts, however, only こと or の can be used. For instance

> わたしは父がお酒(さけ)を飲むのを見ていた。
> *I was watching my father drink sake.*

In this sentence, の must be used, because the statement involves the speaker's direct perception.

> 見ることは信(しん)じることだ。
> *Seeing is believing.*

This sentence expresses a general fact, so only こと can be used.

練習 1

Complete each sentence, choosing an appropriate phrase from the right-hand column. (More than one alternative is possible.)

1.	日本語を話すのは	a.	おもしろい
2.	料理(りょうり)をすることは	b.	やさしい
3.	テニスをすることは	c.	むずかしい
4.	音楽(おんがく)を聞くことは	d.	おかしい (*strange*)
5.	山田(やまだ)さんが来たのは	e.	体(からだ)にいい (*good for one's health*)

練習 2

Following the example, complete each sentence.

[例] (ブラウンさん)(料理(りょうり)を作(つく)ります)(好き)
→ブラウンさんは料理を作るのが好きです。

1. (カワムラさん)(バスケットボールをします)(好き)
2. (林(はやし)さん)(運動(うんどう)をします)(きらい)
3. (ギブソンさん)(日本語を話します)(上手(じょうず))
4. (チンさん)(歌(うた)を歌(うた)います)(きらい)

5. (町田さん)(ピアノをひきます)(得意)
6. (三村さん)(英語を書きます)(苦手)

練習 3

Complete the following sentences using こと or の.

1. わたしは…が好きです。
2. …はむずかしいです。
3. …はやさしいです。
4. …はおもしろいです。
5. わたしは…が得意です。
6. わたしは…が苦手です。
7. わたしの日本語の先生は…が上手です。
8. わたしは…が下手です。
9. …はつまらないです。
10. わたしは…がきらいです。

27. More Uses of the Particle も

林：カワムラさんはテニスかゴルフをしますか。
カワムラ：ええ、テニスもゴルフもしますよ。林さんは。
林：わたしはテニスもゴルフもしません。スポーツが苦手ですから…
カワムラ：本当ですか。

ブラウン：山本さん、週末はどうでしたか。
山本：土曜日も日曜日も仕事がありました。
ブラウン：それはたいへんでしたね。こんどの休みはいつですか。
山本：今週も来週も休みはありません。
ブラウン：本当ですか。2週間も休みがないんですか。

カワムラ：山口さんの趣味は何ですか。
山口：写真を撮ることです。
カワムラ：カメラは何台ありますか。
山口：今は5台です。
カワムラ：へえ、5台もあるんですか。

台 is a *counter for cameras*

HAYASHI: Do you (*lit., Mr. Kawamura*) play tennis or golf? KAWAMURA: Yes, I play both tennis and golf. How about you (*lit., Mr. Hayashi*)? HAYASHI: I don't play either tennis or golf. I'm not good at sports so. . . . KAWAMURA: Really?

BROWN: Ms. Yamamoto, how was your weekend? YAMAMOTO: I had to work on both Saturday and Sunday. BROWN: That must have been awful. When is your next day off? YAMAMOTO: I don't have a day off this week or next week. BROWN: Really? You don't have a day off for two whole weeks?

KAWAMURA: What is your (*lit., Mr. Yamaguchi's*) hobby? YAMAGUCHI: My hobby is taking photos. KAWAMURA: How many cameras do you have? YAMAGUCHI: Now I have five. KAWAMURA: Wow, you have *five*?

27.1 A も B も means *both A and B* or *A as well as B* in affirmative sentences, and (*n*)*either A* (*n*)*or B* in negative sentences.

> カワムラさんもブラウンさんもアメリカ人です。
> *Both Mr. Kawamura and Ms. Brown are American.*
> もう山口さんのご主人(しゅじん)にも奥(おく)さんにも会(あ)いました。
> *I have already met the Yamaguchis, both husband and wife.*
> クラシック音楽(おんがく)もロックもあまり好きじゃありません。
> *I don't like either classical music or rock music very much.*
> *I like neither classical music nor rock music very much.*
> ここは春(はる)も夏(なつ)も秋(あき)も雨(あめ)がたくさん降(ふ)る。
> *Here it rains a lot in spring, summer, and fall as well.*

27.2 Numeral + counter + も means *as much as* or *as many as* the stated quantity; in other words, the number is higher than the speaker expected or more than usual. When this form is used in negative sentences, the implication is the opposite: the number is smaller than expected, *not even the stated quantity*.

> うちから駅(えき)まで2時間もかかりました。
> *It took as much as two hours to get from home to the station.*
> 先週のパーティーには300人も来た。
> *As many as 300 people came to last week's party.*
> 今日のクラスは学生が5人もいない。
> *There aren't even five students in today's class.*
> わたしは学校(がっこう)を1日も休(やす)みませんでした。
> *I didn't miss even one day of school.*

文法ノート

Particles That Connect Nouns

Several particles can be used to connect nouns. You have already studied some of these particles.

1. と *and*

   バレーボールとバスケットボールが好きです。
   I like volleyball and basketball.

2. か *or*

   バレーボールかバスケットボールをしますか。
   Do you play volleyball or basketball?

3. や *X, Y and the like, among others, X and Y*

   バレーボールやバスケットボールをしました。
   We played volleyball, basketball, and the like.

4. …も…も *both X and Y, neither X nor Y*

   バレーボールもバスケットボールもします。
   I play both volleyball and basketball.
   バレーボールもバスケットボールもしません。
   I don't play either volleyball or basketball.

5. とか *for example, X and Y; X, Y, and others* (very similar to や)

   バレーボールとかバスケットボールをしました。
   We played volleyball and basketball, for example.

練習 1

Following the example, complete these sentences using …も…も.

[例] カワムラさんはビールが好きです。
カワムラさんはワインが好きです。→
カワムラさんはビールもワインも好きです。

1. チンさんはパーティーに来ました。
   林(はやし)さんはパーティーに来ました。
2. 机(つくえ)の上にペンがあります。
   机の上にえんぴつがあります。
3. 林さんはブロッコリがきらいです。
   林さんはアスパラガスがきらいです。

4. 17日、雨(あめ)が降りました。
   18日、雨(あめ)が降りました。
5. 三村(みむら)さんはテニスが上手(じょうず)です。
   三村さんはピンポンが上手です。

練習　2

Following the example, make a dialogue for each exercise item.

[例]　日本語を勉強(べんきょう)する／5年→
—日本語を何年勉強したんですか。
—5年です。
—5年も勉強したんですか。

Review counters in Chapter 2.
冊 is a *counter for books*
杯 is a *counter for glassfuls*

1. 寝(ね)る／12時間
2. 旅行(りょこう)する／3週間
3. ハンバーガーを食べる／6つ
4. 本を読む／3冊(さつ)
5. ワインを飲む／グラスで7杯(はい)
6. ボーイフレンドがいる／3人

28. Potential Form of Verbs

ブラウン：林(はやし)さん、明日(あす)、学校へ早(はや)く来ることができますか。
林：何時ですか。
ブラウン：6時です。
林：すみませんが、そんなに*早く起きることはできません。

カワムラ：町田さんはフランス語ができますか。
町田：話せませんが、ちょっと読めます。
カワムラ：書(か)けますか。
町田：ええ、やさしい文(ぶん)は書けます。

カワムラ：これはおさしみですか。
山口：ええ、そうです。
カワムラ：食べられますか。
山口：昨日のですから、もう食べられません。

BROWN: Mr. Hayashi, can you come to school early tomorrow? HAYASHI: At what time? BROWN: Six o'clock. HAYASHI: I am sorry, but I cannot get up that early.

KAWAMURA: Do you know French? (*lit., Can you, Ms. Machida, do French?*) MACHIDA: I can't speak it, but I can read a little. KAWAMURA: Can you write it? MACHIDA: Yes, I can write easy sentences.

KAWAMURA: Is this raw fish? YAMAGUCHI: Yes, that's right. KAWAMURA: Is it edible? (*lit., Can we eat it?*) YAMAGUCHI: It's yesterday's, so it's no longer edible.

*そんな, one of the **ko-so-a-do** words, means *that kind of*. そんなに means *like that, that much*.

ブラウン：町田さんは、一人で着物(きもの)を着(き)られますか。
町田：いいえ、着物を着るのはたいへんです。一人ではちょっと…
ブラウン：じゃあ、どうするんですか。
町田：近くの美容院(びよういん)に行きます。

Grammatical constructions expressing abilities, such as *I can swim* and *he is able to come tomorrow* are called *potential expressions* or *potentials*.

28.1 In Japanese, there are two different ways to express abilities or potential. Both correspond to the English auxiliary verb *can*.

28.2 The first potential structure is a combination of the dictionary form (non-past, plain, affirmative form) of a verb and ことができる.

dictionary form of verb ＋ ことができる

Note that in this sentence structure you cannot use の in place of こと.

できる is a Class 2 verb, used here to mean *can* or *is able to do*. The entire structure literally means *the doing of* [*verb*] *is possible*.

日本語を話すことができます。
I can speak Japanese.
山口さんは2キロ泳(およ)ぐことができる。
Mr. Yamaguchi can swim two kilometers.
明日、6時に来ることができますか。
Can you come at 6:00 tomorrow?
母(はは)はラテン語を読むことができた。
My mother could read Latin.
昨日(きのう)、ブラウンさんに会(あ)うことができましたか。
Were you able to see Ms. Brown yesterday?
この電話(でんわ)は使(つか)うことができません。
You cannot use this telephone.
弟(おとうと)はハイキングに行くことができなかった。
My younger brother couldn't go hiking.

BROWN: Ms. Machida, can you put on a kimono by yourself? MACHIDA: No. It's difficult to put on a kimono. To do that myself is . . . (impossible). BROWN: Then, what do you do? MACHIDA: I go to a nearby beauty salon.

As you can see from these examples, tense, negativity, and formality are expressed in the conjugation of できる; the dictionary form of the preceding verb remains unchanged.

28.3 You can also express abilities and possibilities by conjugating a verb. The conjugated verb forms expressing abilities and possibilities are called the potential forms of a verb and are formed in the following way.

	CLASS 1	CLASS 2	CLASS 3
Rules	root + e-column **hiragana** corresponding to the dictionary ending + る	root + られる	irregular
Examples	書(か)く→書(か)ける 読(よ)む→読(よ)める 会(あ)う→会(あ)える 話(はな)す→話(はな)せる 待(ま)つ→待(ま)てる	食(た)べる→食(た)べられる 見(み)る →見(み)られる 着(き)る →着(き)られる	来(く)る→来(こ)られる する→できる

u-column	→	e-column
く	→	け
む	→	め
う	→	え
す	→	せ
つ	→	て

These potential forms all end in -る (the ending of the dictionary form of Class 2 verbs), and indeed, they conjugate like Class 2 verbs, whether they are derived from Class 1, 2, or 3 verbs. For example,

CLASS 1	CLASS 2	CLASS 3	CLASS 3
書ける	食べられる	できる	来られる
書けない	食べられない	できない	来られない
書けた	食べられた	できた	来られた
書けなかった	食べられなかった	できなかった	来られなかった
書けます	食べられます	できます	来られます
書けません	食べられません	できません	来られません
書けました	食べられました	できました	来られました
書けませんでした	食べられませんでした	できませんでした	来られませんでした

漢字(かんじ)が上手(じょうず)に書けます。
*I can write **kanji** well.*

父(ちち)はすしが食べられない。
My father cannot eat sushi.

わたしの子(こ)どもはまだ話せません。
My child still cannot speak.

ピンポンができますか。
Can you play table tennis?
山口さんは昨日(きのう)来(こ)られなかった。
Mr. Yamaguchi couldn't come yesterday.

In these potential sentences, direct objects are marked with が. In sentences that use the potential form of verbs, the direct object can be marked with either が or を. Therefore

わたしは漢字(かんじ)が上手(じょうず)に書けます。
わたしは漢字を上手に書けます。

are both grammatically correct. Although the meaning is equivalent whether you use が or を, Japanese speakers tend to prefer が in most contexts.

Although some grammarians consider the root + られる to be the only correct potential form of Class 2 verbs, many Japanese speakers use a shortened form: the root + れる. In fact, nowadays the shortened form is more widely used than the longer form, especially among the younger generation, in informal conversation and writing. For now, learn to produce the traditionally "correct" form and to understand the shortened form.

	-られる FORM (LONG FORM)	-れる FORM (SHORT FORM)
食(た)べる	食(た)べられる	食(た)べれる
見(み)る	見(み)られる	見(み)れる
着(き)る	着(き)られる	着(き)れる

For speakers who use these shortened forms, there is no difference other than accent pattern between the potential forms of 切る (*to cut*; Class 1 verb) and 着(き)る (*to wear*; Class 2 verb).

練習 1

Following the example, complete each sentence using ことができます。

[例] (土曜日に来られます) → 土曜日に来ることができます。

1. 午後図書館(としょかん)へ行けます
2. 今日の午後、林(はやし)さんに会(あ)えます
3. 10キロ走(はし)れます
4. 駅(えき)まで歩(ある)けます
5. ここで泳げますか
6. 今、ブラウンさんと話せます
7. 母(はは)に電話(でんわ)できます

練習 2

Make dialogues using the potential form of each verb.

[例] (play the guitar) →
—チンさんはギターがひけますか。
—はい、ひけます。(いいえ、ひけません。)

1. (play tennis)
2. (sing Japanese songs)
3. (run fast)
   Useful word: 走(はし)る *to run*
4. (draw pictures well)
5. (go to a concert with me)
6. (ski)
7. (watch TV with me this afternoon)
8. (read books together with me)
9. (swim in the ocean)
10. (come to my home)

練習 3

Answer the following questions.

1. あなたはピアノがひけますか。
2. あなたは上手(じょうず)に写真(しゃしん)が撮(と)れますか。
3. あなたは自転車(じてんしゃ) (*bicycle*) に乗(の)れますか。
4. あなたはバレーボールができますか。
5. あなたはフランス語で歌(うた)えますか。
6. あなたは1キロ泳(およ)げますか。
7. あなたは10キロ走(はし)れますか。
8. あなたの家族(かぞく)は日本語が話せますか。
9. 明日、映画(えいが)へ行けますか。
10. 土曜日、大学へ来られますか。

練習 4

Change the verbs in parentheses to their potential forms.

Useful vocabulary: ショパン *Chopin,* とくに *especially*

今日はわたしの家族(かぞく)の趣味(しゅみ)、特技(とくぎ)の話をします。わたしの趣味はピアノをひくことです。ショパンのノクターンが上手(じょうず)に(ひく)。わたしの父(ちち)の趣味は外国語(がいこくご)を勉強(べんきょう)することです。父はフランス語、スペイン語、英語(えいご)が上手に(話す)。また、ラテン語、ギリシャ語が(読む)。母(はは)の特技(とくぎ)は写真(しゃしん)を撮ることです。たくさんのカメラを持(も)っています。一台(だい)のカメラは夜も写真が(

持っています *owns*
一台のカメラ *one camera*

とる)。兄の趣味は水泳です。兄は10キロ(泳ぐ)。妹の趣味は絵をかくことです。とくに、ポートレートが上手に(かく)。弟の趣味は食べることです。一度にすしを100個(食べる)。

29. The Te-Form of Verbs + います

村井：あそこで男の人と女の人が話していますね。
山口：ええ。
村井：あっ、キスをしていますよ。いいですね。
山口：あれは、娘さんではありませんか。

A：すみません。高田さんはいますか。
B：ええ、でも、電話をしています。
A：そうですか。じゃ、ここで待ちます。
B：ブラウンさんも高田さんを待っていますよ。

A：あの人はいつもすてきな服を着ていますね。
B：今日はデザイナーズ・ブランドを着ていますよ。
A：ええ。いいドレスですね。
B：あのドレスは駅の前のブティックで売っていますよ。

カワムラ：大助さん、おそいですね。
山口：1時から公園で運動をしているんですよ。
カワムラ：大助さんが、運動をしているんですか。
山口：ええ、1ヶ月前から始めたんです。
毎日、1時間ぐらい運動しているんですよ。

MURAI: A man and a woman are talking over there. YAMAGUCHI: Yes. MURAI: Oh, they are kissing each other! That's nice. YAMAGUCHI: Isn't that your daughter?

A: Excuse me. Is Mr. Takada in? B: Yes, but he is on the phone. A: I see. Then, I will wait here. B: Ms. Brown is also waiting for him, you know.

A: She always wears nice clothes. B: She's wearing a designer brand today. A: Yes. It's a fine dress. B: They sell that dress at the boutique in front of the station, you know.

KAWAMURA: Daisuke is late, isn't he? YAMAGUCHI: He has been exercising at the park since one o'clock. KAWAMURA: Daisuke is exercising? YAMAGUCHI: Yes, he started a month ago. He is exercising about an hour every day.

29.1 The te-form of a verb + the auxiliary verb います (いる) can be used to express these two meanings.

1. a continuing action at a certain point in time (like the English progressive tense: *I am reading, He was jogging, They will be eating*, etc.)
2. a state or condition that was created by a previous action or event and that is still maintained at a certain point in time.

Whether this construction has the first or second meaning depends on the nature of the verb being used.

Auxiliary verbs are used with main verbs to express a variety of meanings, such as tense. The following verbs cannot be used with the auxiliary verb います：ある to exist, いる to exist, いる to need, できる can. While the "can do" meaning of できる does not allow ～ている , the combination できている does occur with the meaning of "is finished."

29.2 If the verb indicates an action that can continue once started, such as 食べる or 話す, it has the first meaning. Thus, 食べている = *I am eating*. Other verbs of this kind are 飲む、歩く、走る、歌う、泳ぐ、書く、見る、使う、作る、休む、勉強する、会う.

山口さんはうちでビールを飲んでいた。
Mr. Yamaguchi was drinking beer at home.
学生が先生と話している。
A student is speaking with the teacher.
母は今、テニスをしています。
My mother is playing tennis now.

29.3 When the verb indicates an action that is non-continuous, such as 知る (*to come to know*) or 晴れる (*to clear up*), it has the second meaning. Thus, 知っている = I know (that is, *I came to know and I am still in that state*). Other verbs of this type include 死ぬ、忘れる、立つ、座る、起きる、言う、乗る、着く、寝る.

あの人を知っていますか。
Do you know that person?
クラスは始まっています。
The class has already started. or *The class is in progress.* (*That is, the class started and is still in that state.*)
母は起きていた。
My mother was up. (*That is, she got up and was still up.*)
今日、空は晴れています。
The sky's clear today. (*That is, the sky cleared up and it's still in that state.*)

The affirmative answer to this question is はい、知っています *Yes, I know him.* The negative answer is いいえ、知りません *No, I don't know him.*

When such movement verbs as 行く (*to go*), 来る (*to come*), 帰る (*to return*), 入る (*to enter*), and 出る (*to go out*) appear in this construction, the meaning expressed is (2).

ギブソンさんが来ています。
Ms. Gibson is here (*she came and is still here now*).
父はトイレに入っている。
My father is in the bathroom (*he entered the bathroom and is still there*).

～ています is often shortened to ～てます in conversations. (That is, い is dropped.)

29.4 In some cases, either meaning (1) or (2) is possible, as shown in the following two examples. Verbs in this category include 着る、取る、and おぼえる.

カーティスさんはセーターを着ています。
Mr. Curtis is putting on a sweater. (1)
Mr. Curtis is wearing a sweater. (*That is, he put it on and it's still on.*) (2)
その学生は日本語のたんごをおぼえています。
Those students are memorizing Japanese words (*now*). (1)
Those students know Japanese words. (*That is, they memorized them and still remember them.*) (2)

> CAUTION: The いる of the te-いる construction and the いる you learned meaning *to exist* are identical in form, but grammatically they are completely different. In the te-form verb + いる construction, *only* いる is used whether or not the subject is animate.

29.5 Sometimes, this construction is used to express a habitual action, one that takes place repeatedly.

わたしは毎朝ジョギングをしています。
I jog every morning.
山口さんは田中さんと毎日デートをしています。
Ms. Yamaguchi has a date with Mr. Tanaka every day.

The difference between these sentences and regular nonpast sentences is that these emphasize the habitual nature of the actions more than do regular nonpast sentences. For example

カワムラさんは毎日ジョギングをします。
カワムラさんは毎日ジョギングをしています。
Mr. Kawamura jogs every day.

The first example simply states the fact that John Kawamura jogs every day. The second example, on the other hand, points out that he makes jogging part of his daily activities.

文法ノート

Did You Already Eat?

When you are asked whether you have finished doing something and you have not done so, you will answer using the te-いる form. For example,

昼ごはんをもう食べましたか。
Did you already eat lunch?

—いいえ、まだ食べていません。
—No, I haven't eaten yet.
—いいえ、まだです。
—No, not yet.

When you have already eaten, you answer using the regular past tense form.

—はい、もう食べました。
—Yes, I already ate.

文法ノート

Some Time Expressions

Here are several expressions for indicating how long or since when an action or event has been taking place.

1. Point in time + から = since. . .

   先週からカルチャーセンターへ行っています。
   Since last week, I have been going to (study at) a cultural center.
   去年からスペイン語を勉強(べんきょう)している。
   Since last year, I have been studying Spanish.

2. Time expression + 前から = since . . . ago

   五日前から電車(でんしゃ)で学校(がっこう)へ行っています。
   I have been commuting to school by train since five days ago.
   三年前から山口さんを知(し)っています。
   I have known Mr. Yamaguchi since three years ago.
   二時間前からここにいます。
   I have been here since two hours ago.

You can reword the last sentence as follows.

二時間ここにいます。
I have been here for two hours.

You will study these and other time expressions in detail later.

練習 1

Using the following illustrations, make dialogues.

[例]　—ギブソンさんは今何をしていますか。
　　　—新聞(しんぶん)を読んでいます。

練習 2

Rewrite these sentences following the example.

Reminder: The particle に following a time expression means *at* (*a certain point in time*). In the same position, the particle から means *from* or *since* (*a certain point in time*).

[例]　山口さんは11時に寝(ね)ました。→ 山口さんは11時から寝ています。

1. わたしはブラウンさんを２年前に知(し)りました。
2. カワムラさんは30分前にお風呂(ふろ)に入りました。
3. 山口さんの奥(おく)さんは３時にデパートに行きました。
4. カーティスさんは去年(きょねん)、日本に来ました。
5. さとみさんは先週、キャンプに出かけました。

練習　3

Answer the following questions.

1. 今クラスをいくつ取っていますか。どんなクラスを取っていますか。
(取る *to take*)
2. いつから日本語を勉強していますか。
3. 毎日日本語を勉強していますか。
4. 漢字をいくつ知っていますか。
5. 日本語の辞書を持っていますか。
6. あなたはだれか日本人を知っていますか。
7. 今雨が降っていますか。
8. あなたは今ボールペンを使っていますか。
えんぴつを使っていますか。
9. あなたは今何を着ていますか。
10. あなたは今、立っていますか。すわっていますか。
11. あなたはどこに住んでいますか。(住む *to live*)

30. Relative Clauses

横井：明日のハイキングに行く人はいますか。
ブラウン：はい、カワムラさんと私です。
横井：ハイキングに行く人のミーティングが1時にあります。
来てください。
ブラウン：わかりました。

カワムラ：山口さんの趣味は何ですか。
山口：テニスです。
カワムラ：よくしますか。
山口：いいえ、まわりにテニスができる人があまりいないんです。

ブラウン：村山さんの趣味は何ですか。
村山：外国語を勉強することです。

YOKOI: Is anyone here going on tomorrow's hike? BROWN: Yes. Mr. Kawamura and I will go. YOKOI: There's a meeting at one o'clock for those who are going hiking. Please come. BROWN: OK. (*lit., I understand.*)

KAWAMURA: What is your hobby? YAMAGUCHI: It's tennis. KAWAMURA: Do you play often? YAMAGUCHI: No. There aren't many people I know (*lit., around*) who can play.

BROWN: What is your hobby, Ms. Murayama? MURAYAMA: Learning foreign languages. BROWN: How many languages have you studied? MURAYAMA: About thirty. BROWN: Of the foreign languages you have studied so far, which is the most difficult?

ブラウン：いくつぐらい勉強しましたか。
村山：30ぐらいです。
ブラウン：今まで勉強した外国語で一番(ばん)むずかしいことばは何ですか。

ブラウン：チンさんは大学で、スポーツをしましたか。
チン：勉強(べんきょう)で忙(いそが)しくて、スポーツする時間がありませんでした。

30.1 You have already learned that adjectives modifying nouns precede the noun.

おもしろいクラス	*interesting class; fun class*
きれいな部屋(へや)	*clean room*

In the examples above, a word modifies another word. When a whole clause modifies a noun, the clause usually takes the form of a relative clause. In English, the relative clause follows the noun it modifies.

the person who came here yesterday
the person whom I saw yesterday
the hamburger that I ate three days ago
a house where I lived for ten years

In English a relative clause (sometimes also called sentential modifiers) is introduced with a relative pronoun or adverb such as *who, whom, which, and where.*

30.2 Japanese relative clauses, like their English counterparts, modify nouns. However, there are some striking differences between the two languages.

1. Relative clauses in Japanese *precede* nouns that they modify.
2. There are no relative pronouns or adverbs required in Japanese. Relative clauses *directly* precede the nouns they modify.

わたしが昨日食べた *I ate yesterday*	ピザ *pizza → the pizza I ate yesterday*
あなたが会った *you met*	人 *person → the person you met*
山田(やまだ)さんと話している *is talking with Yamada*	男(おとこ)の人 *man → the man who is talking with Mr. Yamada*
わたしが勉強(べんきょう)した *I studied*	ところ *place → the place where I studied*

As you see from the examples, to form a relative clause in Japanese you simply position a clause before a noun.

BROWN: Did you participate in (*lit., do*) sports at college? CHIN: I was busy studying, so I didn't have time for sports.

30.3 Note that verb forms used in relative clauses must be plain forms.

> カワムラさんがいつも勉強(べんきょう)する時間
> *the time when Mr. Kawamura always studies*
> カワムラさんが見ないテレビの番組(ばんぐみ)
> *the TV programs Mr. Kawamura doesn't watch*
> 父(ちち)が買(か)ったステレオ
> *the stereo my father bought*
> その話を聞かなかった学生
> *the students who didn't listen to that story*
> とても面白かった映画
> *the movie that was very interesting*
> 山口さんが好きだった食べ物
> *the food that Mr. Yamaguchi liked*

Polite forms are not used in relative clauses. A noun modified by a relative clause (double-underlined) is a noun clause (single-underlined), and may be used in a sentence anywhere a noun can be used.

> 昨日食べたピザはおいしかったですか。
> *Was the pizza you ate yesterday delicious?*
> 父(ちち)が買(か)ったステレオを見ますか。
> *Do you want to (lit., will you) look at the stereo my father bought?*

30.4 The possessive marker の is often substituted for the subject particle が in relative clauses and other noun-modifying clauses.

> 父(ちち)の買(か)ったステレオ
> *the stereo that my father bought*
> 母(はは)の好きだった本
> *the book that my mother liked*

The topic particle は is not used within relative clauses.

練習 1

Complete these sentences using a phrase chosen from the list following the exercise items.

[例] (　　)はゴルフをする人です。→
(ゴルファー)はゴルフをする人です。(*A golfer is a person who golfs.*)

1. (　　)はギャンブルをする人です。
2. (　　)はレスリングをする人です。
3. (　　)は勉強(べんきょう)するところです。
4. (　　)は本がたくさんあるところです。

5. (　　　) は水泳をする人です。
6. (　　　) は写真をとる機械 (*machine*) です。
7. (　　　) はひまな時間です。
8. (　　　) は日本人が話す言葉(*language*)です。
9. (　　　) は映画を見るところです。
10. (　　　) は水泳をするところです。

学校、図書館、プール、カメラ、ギャンブラー、レスラー、日本語、余暇、スイマー、映画館

練習　2

Combine these sentences by using a relative clause. In this practice, use the second sentence as the main clause of the resultant sentence. In other words, make sentences in which the predicate of the second sentence comes at the end.

Note that while わたし is marked with が in the resultant sentence, わたし is the topic of the relative clause, not of the sentence. The topic of the sentence is 公園 and is marked with は. The が can be replaced by の as explained in **Grammar 30.4.**

[例]　わたしは昨日公園へ行きました。
その公園はきれいでした。→ わたしが昨日行った公園はきれいでした。
わたしは先週映画を見ました。
その映画はアメリカのです。→ わたしが先週見た映画はアメリカのです。

1. 父は昨日カメラを買いました。
そのカメラは高かったです。
2. わたしは毎日プールで泳ぎます。
そのプールはうちのそばにあります。
3. 昨日の夜レコードを聞きました。
そのレコードは町田さんのレコードです。
4. カルチャーセンターで先生がヨガを教えています。(教える to teach)
その先生はインドから来ました。
5. わたしはいつも近くのレストランへ行きます。
そのレストランは安くて、おいしいです。
6. ブラウンさんは中野に住んでいます。
中野は静かで、便利です。

練習　3

Using the illustration on Page 327 (**Grammar 29,** 練習 1), make sentences containing a relative clause.

[例]　新聞を読んでいる女の人はギブソンさんです。

練習 4

Complete the sentences using relative clauses.

[例] あの方は(　　)先生ですか。→ あの方は(日本語を教えている)先生ですか。

1. (　　)パーティーはどうでしたか。
2. あなたは(　　)本を読みましたか。
3. (　　)時間は3時間でした。
4. (　　)写真はあまりよくありません。
5. (　　)レストランは大学の北にあります。
6. これは(　　)レコードです。
7. これは(　　)学生の部屋です。
8. (　　)コンサートはつまらなかったです。
9. (　　)女の人は中国人です。
10. (　　)人をマラソン・ランナーといいます。

練習 5

Answer these questions.

できるhere means *to be constructed, to be completed.*

1. 日本語を上手に話せる外国人を知っていますか。
2. あなたの家のそばにボーリングができるところがありますか。
3. あなたの家のそばに24時間あいているスーパーはありますか。(あく: *to become open*)
4. あなたの学校に安く昼ごはんを食べられるところがたくさんありますか。
5. あなたの学校の中にはコンサートができるところがありますか。
6. あなたの町のそばにスキーができるところがありますか。
7. あなたはマージャンができる人を知っていますか。
8. あなたはいいステレオを持っている人を知っていますか。
9. あなたは趣味を楽しむ時間がありますか。(楽しむ: *to enjoy*)
10. あなたがいつも飲んでいる飲み物は何ですか。

31. Describing a Change in State: なる

カワムラ：林さんのアパートは便利ですか。
林：前は不便でした。でも、近くにスーパーができたので、便利になりました。
カワムラ：それはよかったですね。
林：それに、最近、地下鉄の駅ができたので、もっと便利になりました。

高田：山田さんの娘さんはおいくつですか。
山田：先月６歳になりました。
高田：もうそんなに大きくなったんですか。
山田：ええ、いつの間にか。

ブラウン：カーティスさんのお兄さんのお仕事は何ですか。
カーティス：画家です。
ブラウン：本当ですか。
カーティス：ええ、絵をかくのが大好きで、画家になったんです。

The verb なる (Class 1) means *to become, to turn into.*

noun ＋ に na-adjective ＋ に root of i-adjective ＋ く	＋ なります(なる)

来年、大学生になります。
I will be (lit., become) a college student next year.
夜になって、静かになりました。
After night fell, it became quiet. (lit., It became night and it became quiet.)
お酒を飲んだので、顔が赤くなった。
Because I drank sake, my face turned red.

KAWAMURA: Is your apartment convenient? HAYASHI: It was inconvenient before, but since a supermarket opened nearby it has become convenient. KAWAMURA: That was lucky (*lit., good*). HAYASHI: In addition, a subway station was built (nearby) recently, so it has become more convenient.

TAKADA: How old is your daughter, Mr.Yamada? YAMADA: She turned six last month. TAKADA: She's already gotten that old (*lit., big*) ? YAMADA: Yes, before you know it . . . (these things happen).

BROWN: What is your older brother's job? CURTIS: He is an artist. BROWN: Really? CURTIS: Yes, because he loved drawing pictures, he became an artist.

練習 1

Fill in the blanks with appropriate adjectives from the list that follows.

少ない、多い、長い、ひま(な)、上手(な)、赤い、安い、大きい、暖かい、便利(な)、好き(な)、きれい(な)、白い、

1. 息子は8歳になって、体 (*body*) も(　　　)なりました。
2. 床屋 (*barber shop*) へ行かなかったので、髪が(　　　)なった。
3. となりに銀行ができて、とても(　　　)なりました。
4. 夏になって、仕事は(　　　)なった。
5. ピアノを毎日練習しているので、(　　　)なった。
6. 秋になって、葉 (*leaves*) が(　　　)なりました。
7. セールなので、なんでも(　　　)なりました。
8. 春になって、(　　　)なった。
9. 6月に入って、雨の日が(　　　)なった。
10. 年をとって (*getting older*)、髪が(　　　)なった
11. 掃除をしたので、部屋が(　　　)なった。
12. 最近 (*recently*)、すしが(　　　)なりました。

練習 2

Following the example, complete the sentences.

[例]　(ピアノが上手だ)(ピアニスト)→
ピアノが上手なので、ピアニストになりました。

1. (エアロビクスが好きだ　(エアロビクスのインストラクター)
2. (英語が話せる)(英語の先生)
3. (車が好きだ)(カー・レーサー)
4. (プログラミングができる)(プログラマー)
5. (体が大きくて、強い)(ボディーガード)

Vocabulary

Hobbies and Pastimes

あそぶ	遊ぶ	to play
あつめる	集める	to collect
いけばな	生け花	flower arranging
え	絵	picture
えんげい	園芸	gardening
えんそうする	演奏する	to play (*a musical instrument*)
かいが	絵画	painting
かく		to draw (*a picture*)
がっき	楽器	musical instrument
カルチャーセンター		culture center
きって	切手	stamp
きってあつめ	切手集め	stamp collecting
ごらく	娯楽	entertainment, pastime
さどう	茶道	tea ceremony
しゃしん	写真	photography, photograph
しゅげい	手芸	handicrafts
しゅみ	趣味	hobby
たのしむ	楽しむ	to enjoy
とくぎ	特技	special talent
どくしょ	読書	reading (*books*)
とる	取る、撮る	to take (*a class*); to take (*a photo*)
よか	余暇	free time
りょうり	料理	cooking
りょこう	旅行	travel

Loanwords: クラブ、コンサート、ダンス、ドライブ、ヨガ、レジャー

Review: 映画(えいが)、音楽(おんがく)、スポーツ、釣(つ)り、暇(ひま)(な)、練習(れんしゅう)する

Sports

しあい	試合	game
すいえい	水泳	swimming
たっきゅう	卓球	table tennis, Ping-Pong
やきゅう	野球	baseball

Loanwords: エアロビクス、キャンピング、ゴルフ、サイクリング、サッカー、ジョギング、ダイビング、テニス、ハイキング、バスケットボール、バドミントン、バレーボール、ピンポン、プール、フットボール、ボート、ボーリング、マラソン、ヨット、ラグビー、ランニング
Review: 運動(うんどう)、泳(およ)ぐ、スキー、スケート、スポーツ、山登り

Family Terms

かぞく	家族	family
あに	兄	older brother
あね	姉	older sister
いもうと	妹	younger sister
いもうとさん	妹さん	younger sister (*respectful*)
おかあさん	お母さん	mother (*respectful*)
おくさん	奥さん	wife (*respectful*)
おこさん	お子さん	child (*respectful*)
おじ		uncle (*respectful*)
おじいさん		grandfather (*respectful*)
おじさん		uncle (*respectful*)
おじょうさん	お嬢さん	daughter (*respectful*)
おっと	夫	husband
おとうさん	お父さん	father (*respectful*)
おとうと	弟	younger brother
おとうとさん	弟さん	younger brother (*respectful*)
おにいさん	お兄さん	older brother (*respectful*)
おねえさん	お姉さん	older sister (*respectful*)
おば		aunt
おばあさん		grandmother (*respectful*)
おばさん		aunt (*respectful*)
おまごさん	お孫さん	grandchild (*respectful*)
かない	家内	wife
きょうだい	兄弟	siblings, brothers
ごかぞく	御家族	family (*respectful*)
ごきょうだい	御兄弟	siblings, brothers (*respectful*)
ごしゅじん	御主人	husband (*respectful*)
ごしんせき	御親戚	relative (*respectful*)
こども	子供	child
ごふうふ	御夫婦	married couple (*respectful*)
ごりょうしん	御両親	parents (*respectful*)
しゅじん	主人	husband
しんせき	親戚	relative
そふ	祖父	grandfather
そぼ	祖母	grandmother
ちち	父	father
つま	妻	wife

はは	母	mother
ふうふ	夫婦	married couple
まご	孫	grandmother
むすこ	息子	son
むすこさん	息子さん	son (*respectful*)
むすめ	娘	daughter
むすめさん	娘さん	daughter (*respectful*)
りょうしん	両親	parents

Nouns

おとこ	男	male, man
おとこのこ	男の子	boy
おとこのひと	男の人	man
おんな	女	female, woman
おんなのこ	女の子	girl
おんなのひと	女の人	woman
かた	方	person (*polite*)
こ	子	child
ひと	人	person
みな		all, everyone
みんな		all, everyone
もんだい	問題	question, issue, problem

Na-Adjectives

じょうず(な)	上手(な)	good at, skilled at
とくい(な)	得意(な)	good at and like; forte
にがて(な)	苦手(な)	bad at and dislike; weak point
へた(な)	下手(な)	poor at

Adverbs

いっしょに	一緒に	together
とくに	特に	especially
まったく	全く	totally

Verbs and Verb Forms

できる	to be able to do
なる	to become, to turn into
わかる	to understand, to be clear
～れる	(*shorten form of potential*)
～ている	(*progressive*)
～られる	(*potential*)

Words Formed From Interrogatives

いつか		sometime, someday
いくつか		some, several
いつでも		anytime
いつも		always
すべて	全て	all
ぜんぶ	全部	all

だれか	someone	どなたか	someone (*polite*)
だれでも	anyone	どなたでも	anyone (*polite*)
だれも	everyone; no one	どなたも	everyone (*polite*)
どうか	somehow	どれか	one of them
どこか	somewhere	どれでも	any of them
どこでも	anywhere	どれも	all of them; none of them
どこも	everywhere; nowhere	なぜか	somehow, for some reason
どちらか	either	なにか　何か	something
どちらでも	whichever	なにも　何も	everything; nothing
どちらも	both; neither	なんでも　何でも	anything

Kanji

Learn these characters.

手	族
家	勉
男	道
女	使
子	国
母	音
父	楽
兄	全
姉	部
弟	運
妹	動
作	

Reading and Writing

Reading 1　サンライズ・カルチャーセンターのお知らせ

Before You Read

Suppose you have decided to take a class at a local culture center. What information would you like to know about the class? Here are headings from the class schedule for a culture center in Tokyo. Does it include all the information you would need?

クラスの名前　　先生　　曜日　　時間　　クラス　　授業料

What do you think 授業料 means?

Association: What words from the list below are related to each of the following: 外国語、手紙 (*letter*)、料理、and ワイン? You may use the same word more than once.

書く、飲む、食べる、フランス語、紙 (*paper*)、ペン、エプロン、コルク、キッチン、話す、練習、作る、夕ごはん、スペイン語、ランゲージ・ラボ、読む、ことば (*word*)、朝ごはん、グラス、辞書、郵便局、シェフ

Now Read It!

サンライズ・カルチャーセンター

春学期のクラスのお知らせ

サンライズ・カルチャーセンターの春学期のクラスは4月1日から始まります。春学期のクラスをいくつか紹介しましょう。

学期 *semester, quarter*
お知らせ *notice, announcement*
始まる *to start*
いくつか *some, several*
紹介する *to introduce*

■英文レター入門

「英語は話せるが、書くのは苦手だ。」

「英語で手紙を書くのはむずかしい。」

「英語で手紙が書けない。」

英文の *in English (writing)*
…入門 *introduction to . . .*

このクラスでは、英語で手紙を書くことを練習します。先生は東京外国語大学の吉田京子先生です。クラスは毎週火曜日、木曜日午後6時から8時までです。授業料は3万5千円です。クラスは東ビル1304号室。

練習する *to practice*
…号室 *Room No.*

■ワイン・テイスティング

ワインが大好きな方！ワイン・テイスティングを楽しみましょう。このクラスでは、フランス、ドイツ、イタリア、スペイン、ポルトガル、アメリカのカリフォルニアの赤ワイン、白ワインを楽しみます。先生はオーシャン・ホテルの川口はじめさんです。クラスは毎週金曜日午後7時から9時までです。授業料は4万6千円です。クラスは南ビル2415号室。学生は20歳以上の方に限ります。

…以上 *more than -* (compare …以下 *less than*)
限る *to be limited to*

■中国語入門

中国語は世界で一番多くの人が話していることばです。あなたも中国語を勉強しませんか。春学期のおわりには、簡単な会話をすることができます。

世界 *world*
ことば *language*
おわり *end*
簡単(な) *simple*
会話 *conversation*

先生は日本で20年中国語を教(おし)えているリン・ホンミン先生です。クラスは毎週月曜日、水曜日、金曜日５時から７時までです。授業料は４万円です。クラスは月曜日と水曜日は北(きた)ビル320号室です。金曜日は南ビル140号室のランゲージ・ラボです。

■男性(だんせい)のためのクッキング・クラス

食べるのは好きだが、料理(りょうり)をするのは苦手(にがて)な男性はいませんか。このクラスでは男性でもできる簡単な料理を勉強します。先生はテレビでもラジオでも有名(ゆうめい)な土井森男先生(どいもりおせんせい)です。クラスは毎週土曜日午前９時半から12時までです。昼ごはんにはクラスで作(つく)ったものをみんなで食べます。授業料は2万8千5百円です。クラスは西(にし)ビル654号室です。エプロンを忘(わす)れないで下さい。

他(ほか)に、スペイン語、フランス語、モダン・ダンス、イラスト、生花(いけばな)、ヨガ、書道(しょどう)、ピアノ、フルート、ゴルフ、ピンポンなどのクラスがあります。

男性 *male*
…のため *for (the sake of) . . .*

作る *to make*

忘れないでください。*please don't forget* (from 忘れる *to forget*)

他に *in addition*
など *etc.*

After You Finish Reading

The preceding passage describes four classes offered by the Sunrise Culture Center during this coming spring semester. Using the information in the passage, fill in the following table in English.

COURSE TITLE	INSTRUCTOR	CLASS DATE	CLASS TIME	TUITION

Check your answers with a classmate by using the following dialogue.

S1: すみません。_____ のクラスは何曜日の何時からですか。
S2: _____ です。
S1: 先生はどなたですか。
S2: _____先生です。
S1: 授業料はいくらですか。
S2: _____円です。

Which class would you recommend to each of the following people?

1. わたしは来年ペキンとシャンハイへ行きます。
2. わたしは商社(しょうしゃ)(*trading company*)で働(はたら)いています。アメリカの会社(かいしゃ)(*company*)によく手紙を書きますが、英語はちょっと…

3. 去年(きょねん)20歳になって、はじめてお酒(さけ)を飲みました。お酒の中ではワインが一番好きです。

4. ぼくは、中野(なかの)のアパートに一人で住(す)んでいます。夕ごはんはいつもレストランか食堂(しょくどう)で食べますが、高(たか)くてこまります (*have difficulty*)。

Now study the reading more closely for the following exercises.

1. Find the nominalizers (の and こと) in the description of the English letter-writing class.
2. Find the relative clauses used in the descriptions of the Chinese language and cooking classes.

コミュニティプラザ・新百合　新規開講サークル

知性と教養とヘルシーな明日のための42講座。

〈8月10日㈮より受付スタート〉

	サークル名	開催週	時　間	受　講　料
月	指圧でリラックス	1・3	10:30～12:00	9,300円 (3ヵ月)
	辰巳流日本舞踊	2・4	10:15～12:00	9,300円 (3ヵ月)
	ヨーロピアンフォークアート	2・4	10:30～12:30	9,300円 (3ヵ月)
	フィットネスフラダンス	毎週	12:30～13:30	12,400円 (2ヵ月)
	作詞入門	1・3	13:00～14:30	12,400円 (3ヵ月)
	シャンソンを楽しく	2・4	15:30～17:00	12,400円 (3ヵ月)
	真向法	毎週	15:30～16:30	12,400円 (2ヵ月)
火	郷土の日本史探訪	2	10:30～12:30	12,400円 (6ヵ月)
	彫金	1・3	10:30～12:30	9,300円 (3ヵ月)
	デンマークラグメーキング	2・4	10:30～12:30	9,300円 (3ヵ月)
	手まり手芸	1・3	13:00～15:00	9,300円 (3ヵ月)
	"書"を学ぶ	1・3	13:00～15:00	9,300円 (3ヵ月)
	暮らしに生かすインテリア	2・4	13:00～14:30	12,400円 (3ヵ月)
	短歌に親しむ	2・4	15:30～17:30	9,300円 (3ヵ月)
水	パッチワークキルト(初級)	2・4	10:30～12:30	9,300円 (3ヵ月)
	ペン習字	毎週	10:30～12:30	12,400円 (2ヵ月)
	話し方と朗読	1・3	13:00～14:30	9,300円 (3ヵ月)
	スウェーデン刺繍	1・3	13:00～15:00	9,300円 (3ヵ月)
	日本画入門	2・4	13:00～15:00	9,300円 (3ヵ月)
	万葉集を読む	1・3	15:30～17:00	9,300円 (3ヵ月)
	エッセイの書き方（入門）	2・4	15:30～17:30	9,300円 (3ヵ月)
木	キーボードを楽しむ	1・3	10:30～12:00	9,300円 (3ヵ月)
	美容気功	毎週	11:00～12:00	12,400円 (2ヵ月)
	木版画を楽しむ	1・3	13:00～15:00	12,400円 (3ヵ月)
	俳画	2	13:00～15:00	9,300円 (6ヵ月)
	三味線の手ほどき	毎週	13:00～15:00	12,400円 (2ヵ月)
	エッグクラフト	2・4	13:00～15:00	9,300円 (3ヵ月)
	般若心経を読む	2・4	15:30～17:30	9,300円 (3ヵ月)
金	日本の庭園とその歴史	1・3	10:30～12:00	12,400円 (3ヵ月)
	レザー工芸	1・3	10:30～12:30	9,300円 (3ヵ月)
	童話を書く	2・4	10:30～12:00	9,300円 (3ヵ月)
	ブラッシュアップ英会話	毎週	10:30～12:00	12,400円 (2ヵ月)
	茶道の歴史と日本文化	2	13:00～15:00	12,400円 (6ヵ月)
	インテリジェンス・チェス	2・4	13:00～15:00	9,300円 (3ヵ月)
	英会話（初級）	毎週	13:00～15:00	12,400円 (2ヵ月)
	御家流　香道	4	15:00～16:00	13,500円(3ヵ月)(材料費込)
	フォトレッスン	1・3	15:30～17:30	9,300円 (3ヵ月)
	コミュニケーション手話	2・4	15:30～17:30	9,300円 (3ヵ月)
土	40's ピクス	毎週	11:00～12:15	12,400円 (2ヵ月)
	中国語入門	毎週	13:00～14:30	12,400円 (2ヵ月)
	リフレッシュ体操	毎週	13:30～15:00	12,400円 (2ヵ月)
	カードマジック	4	15:30～17:30	9,300円 (6ヵ月)

Class schedule from a culture center in Tokyo.

Writing 1

You have decided to enroll in one of the courses offered by the Sunrise Culture Center. Complete the following application form (申込書 (もうしこみしょ)) in Japanese. What special

サンライズ・カルチャーセンター
クラス受講申込書

名前

男・女

電話番号

クラスの名前

学期　春・夏・秋・冬

曜日・時間

場所

授業料

領収書

平成　年　月　日　＿＿＿＿＿＿＿＿＿＿様

¥

但し　クラスの授業料として

サンライズ・カルチャー・センター校長

山中一男　印

領収書 *receipt*
平成 *Heisei (era)*
但し *conditions*
校長 *school principal*
印 *seal*
…として *as...*
クラス受講申込書 *class attendance application form*

skill do you have that you could teach to other people? You have been hired by the Sunrise Culture Center to teach a class. Write your own course description in Japanese. What days of the week will you teach? At what time? How much will you charge for tuition?

Reading 2 学生とサラリーマンの余暇調査

Before You Read

If you had some free time, how would you most like to spend it? Rank the following activities in order of preference.

ゴロゴロする (*to loaf around*)
コンサートへ行く
テレビを見る
スポーツをする
友(とも)だちと話す
旅行(りょこう)をする

Compare your ranking with those of your classmates.

Which of the following do you think are meaningful activities? Rank them in order of most to least meaningful.

映画(えいが)を見る
旅行(りょこう)する
ステレオを聞く
読書(どくしょ)をする
友(とも)だちとレストランへ行く
スポーツをする

Compare your ranking with those of your classmates.

Now Read It!

学生とサラリーマンの余暇(よか)調査(ちょうさ)
日本の学生は余暇に何をしているのか。学生500人にこの質問(しつもん)をした。
テレビを見ている学生が一番(いちばん)多かった。2位(い)は「家(いえ)でゴロゴロする」、3位

調査 *survey*
質問 *question*
…位 *No.*… (*rank*)

は「スポーツをする」、4位は「喫茶店へ行く」、5位は「友だちとレストランへ行く」だった。テレビを見ている時間は女子学生よりも男子学生のほうが長い。

では、サラリーマンはどうだろうか。同じ質問をサラリーマン500人にした。旅行をするサラリーマンが一番多い。2位は「スポーツをする」、3位は「映画を見る」、4位は「読書をする」、5位は「コンサートへ行く」だった。この調査から、サラリーマンは映画、読書、コンサートなど、教養を深める活動をしていることがわかる。一方、学生は余暇をあまり有効に使っていないことがわかる。

女子 *female* 男子 *male*

サラリーマン *company worker*

教養 *knowledge*

深める *to deepen, increase*
活動 *activity*
一方 *on the other hand*
有効に *profitably*

After You Finish Reading

Using information from the passage, fill in the following table in English.

POPULAR LEISURE ACTIVITIES OF JAPANESE STUDENTS AND COMPANY WORKERS

Students	Ranking	Company Workers
	1	
	2	
	3	
	4	
	5	

Do you agree with the claim that company workers spend their free time more productively than students?

List all the relative clauses used in the above passage.

Writing 2

Conduct a survey in your class on what your classmates do during their free time. Using your survey results, write a short report in Japanese. Follow the format used in the reading.

Useful expression:
余暇に何をしていますか。*What do you usually do during your free time?*

言語ノート

Sound Words

Japanese has a vast number of words that represent sounds. One category of such words, called 擬声語 (ぎせいご: onomatopoeia in English), includes those that imitate natural sounds: for example, the sound of a cat's cry is *meow* in English, ニャー in Japanese. A second category, called 擬態語(ぎたいご), is composed of sound words that represent the manner of an action, a situation, or an image, as if the sound expressed those states. *Zigzag* is one of the few such words found in English. Japanese contains an enormous number of these 擬態語. Some examples are ゴロゴロ ([*the "sound" of someone*] *rattling around — i.e., being idle*), シーン ([*the "sound" of*] *dead silence*), and キラキラ ([*the "sound" of*] *shining*). Note that these sound words are written in **katakana**. Entire dictionaries are devoted to these sound words in Japanese. You will learn more of them as you proceed through this textbook.

Language Functions and Situations

Responding to Compliments

カワムラ：これは山口さんがかいた絵(え)ですか。
山口：ええ、そうです。

カワムラ：山口さんは絵が上手(じょうず)ですね。
山口：いいえ、まったくダメなんですよ。
カワムラ：いいえ、そんなことありませんよ。
山口：そうですか。

ギブソン：町田さん、きれいなブラウスですね。高(たか)かったでしょう。
町田：いいえ、安(やす)かったんですよ。

In written Japanese, emphasis may be added to a word by writing it in **katakana**, even if the word is not a foreign loanword or a sound word. だめ is written in **katakana** here for this reason.

KAWAMURA: Is this the picture you drew, Ms. Yamaguchi? YAMAGUCHI: Yes, that's right. KAWAMURA: You are skilled at drawing, aren't you? YAMAGUCHI: Oh, no. I am no good at all. KAWAMURA: No, that's not true. YAMAGUCHI: Do you think so?

GIBSON: Ms. Machida, that's a pretty blouse. It must have been expensive. MACHIDA: No, it was cheap. GIBSON: No, that can't be. It suits you well. MACHIDA: Do you think so?

ギブソン：いいえ、そんなことないでしょう。よく似合いますよ。
町田：そうですか。

ブラウン：佐野さん、かわいいお孫さんですね。
佐野：いいえ、わがままな子で、こまります。
ブラウン：いいえ、おとなしくて、いいお子さんですよ。
佐野：そうですか。

How would you respond to the following compliments?

1. スペイン語を話すのが上手ですね。
2. ファッションのセンスがいいですね。
3. わあ、新しい車ですか。カッコイイですね。(*It looks great.*)
4. ハンサムなボーイフレンドですね。
5. テニスが上手ですね。

Role Play

Work in pairs. One person praises the other for the following. The person complimented responds using the patterns in the dialogues.

1. being good at speaking Japanese
2. being good at cooking
3. his or her **kanji** writing is good
4. his or her hairstyle is nice
   Useful word: ヘアースタイル
5. his or her younger sister is pretty

Introducing a Family Member

山口：ああ、ブラウンさん、おひさしぶりですね。
ブラウン：ああ、山口さん。お元気ですか。
山口：ええ、まあ、何とか。あっ、ご紹介します。兄の大助です。
大助：山口大助です。妹がいつもお世話になっております。
どうぞよろしく。
ブラウン：妹さんにはいつもお世話になっております。どうぞよろしく。

BROWN: Ms. Sano, your grandchild is cute. SANO: No, she is a spoiled child, and I have a hard time. BROWN: No, she is a quiet, good child, you know. SANO: Do you think so?

YAMAGUCHI: Oh, Ms. Brown. I haven't seen you for a long time. BROWN: Oh, Ms. Yamaguchi. How are you? YAMAGUCHI: Oh, I'm getting along. (*lit., Yes, well, somehow* . . .) Let me introduce someone to you. This is my older brother, Daisuke. DAISUKE: I am Daisuke Yamaguchi. Thank you very much for taking care of my younger sister all the time. Nice meeting you. BROWN: I am always taken care of by your younger sister. Nice meeting you.

コミュニケーション・ノート

お世話(せわ)になっております。

When you are introduced by an acquaintance (Mr. X) to one of his family members or colleagues or someone else from his in-group, you may say to the person introduced, X さんにいつもお世話になっております (*I am always taken care of by Mr. X* or *I am always indebted to Mr. X*). This expression indicates that you and Mr. X are very close and have a good relationship. Also, the compliment makes Mr. X feel good in front of his in-group member. The other party may say, いいえ、X がいつもお世話になっております (*No, X is always taken care of by* ***you*** or *No, Mr. X is always indebted to* ***you***) or X からいつもうかがっております (*I always hear about you from X*). Either statement now makes you feel good. The latter statement indicates that you are such an important person in X's life that he always talks about you. Alternatively, the other party may say, X がいつもご迷惑(めいわく)をおかけしています (*X is always giving you trouble*). This means *Thank you very much for tolerating X's behavior and forgiving him for it.* These expressions are commonly used in such introductions, whether or not your acquaintance really is taking care of you, and whether or not he really gives you much trouble. Think of them as formalities. The point here is that the distinction between in-group and out-group plays a crucial role in the language behavior of Japanese people.

町田：お母さん、こちらは大学のカワムラさん。

母：まあ、ようこそ、カワムラさん。娘(むすめ)からいつもうかがっております。

カワムラ：ジョン・カワムラです。はじめまして。ひとみさんにはいつもお世話(せわ)になっております。

母：いいえ、娘がいつもご迷惑(めいわく)をおかけしております。

言語ノート

How to Address Family Members

Japanese family members may address one another by their first names, but they also use terms that define their relationships. Naturally enough, Japanese children address their father as お父(とう)さん (*father*) and their mother as お母(かあ)さん (*mother*). パパ *papa* and ママ *mama* are terms of

---

MACHIDA: Mother, this is Mr. Kawamura from school (*lit., the university*). MOTHER: Oh, welcome, Mr. Kawamura. I often hear about you from my daughter. KAWAMURA: I'm John Kawamura. How do you do? I am always taken good care of by Hitomi. MOTHER: Oh, no. My daughter is always troubling you.

address commonly used by young children. (Other variations also exist.) A husband addresses his wife by her first name (without さん) or おまえ *you* (vulgar) or calls her with おい *hey*. A wife calls her husband by his first name (*with* さん) or as あなた *you*. おまえ and あなた are the closest everyday Japanese comes to *dear* or *honey*. When a couple has a child, they may call each other by the same terms their child would use: お父さん／パパ and お母さん／ママ. Parents call their child by his or her first name (without any title) — for example, 太郎(たろう) (*a boy*) or 裕子(ひろこ) (*a girl*) — or they may append the diminutive title suffix 〜ちゃん to a young child's name — 太郎ちゃん、裕子ちゃん. Adding 〜ちゃん to a name is like making Tommy out of Thomas or Tom. To boys' names 〜君(くん) (a familiar title suffix appended to male names of equals or inferiors) may be added; thus, 太郎君. When a family has more than one child, the terms of address are determined by the youngest child. That child is called by his or her first name. An older brother or sister is called お兄(にい)ちゃん *older brother* or お姉(ねえ)ちゃん *older sister* (affectionate forms of お兄さん and お姉さん) by other family members. This helps the youngest member of the family understand his or her relationship to the other family members.

Role Play

Practice the following situations with your classmates.

1. You are at home, and a good friend stops by for a few minutes. Introduce him or her to your family. Tell something about him or her. The friend greets the family members and talks about what you are doing at school.
2. You are shopping with your father or mother at a department store. You happen to run into a classmate from school. Introduce your parents and your classmate.

Listening Comprehension

1. Your teacher will explain what hobby each of the following people has, and what he or she will do this weekend. Fill in the table in English.

NAME	HOBBIES	THIS WEEKEND
Sasaki		
Motoyoshi		
Kuramoto		
Tamamura		

2. Listen to the advertisement of some courses offered by a cultural center. Fill in the table in English.

COURSE TITLE	TEACHER	DAY/TIME	PLACE	NOTES (TUITION, ETC.)

6 Food

第六章 食べ物(たもの)

ファミリーレストランで昼ごはんです。

OBJECTIVES

Topics
Foods and beverages
Meals and restaurants
Cooking: flavors and seasonings

Grammar
32. Expressing experience ことがある
33. Expressing a desire: ほしい、ほしがる、～たい、and ～たがる
34. Expressing an opinion:…と思(おも)う
35. ～すぎる
36. Quoting speech: …と言(い)う
37. Expressing intention: つもり and the volitional form of verbs
38. The te-form of a verb ＋みる、しまう、いく、and くる
39. Expressing simultaneous actions: ～ながら

Reading and Writing
Murasaki: All-you-can-eat restaurant
Check your diet

Language Functions and Situations
Asking and expressing opinions
At a restaurant

Vocabulary and Oral Activities

Vocabulary: Foods and Beverages

食べる	たべる	to eat
食べ物	たべもの	food
飲む	のむ	to drink
飲み物	のみもの	drinks, beverages
食料品	しょくりょうひん	foodstuffs

Meat

肉	にく	meat
牛肉	ぎゅうにく	beef
豚肉	ぶたにく	pork
鳥肉	とりにく	chicken
ラム		lamb

Fish

魚	さかな	fish
貝	かい	shellfish
まぐろ		tuna
さけ		salmon
いか		cuttlefish
たこ		octopus

Vegetables

野菜	やさい	vegetable
レタス		lettuce
にんじん		carrot
豆	まめ	bean, pea
じゃがいも		potato
きゅうり		cucumber
玉ねぎ	たまねぎ	onion
トマト		tomato
ピーマン		green pepper

Fruit

果物	くだもの	fruit
バナナ		banana
みかん		mandarin orange
りんご		apple
なし		pear
ぶどう		grape
レモン		lemon
パイナップル		pineapple
メロン		melon
いちご		strawberry

Beverages

(お)茶	(お)ちゃ	tea (*in general*); Japanese tea
紅茶	こうちゃ	black tea
コーヒー		coffee
牛乳、ミルク	ぎゅうにゅう	milk
ジュース		juice
(お)酒	(お)さけ	sake; alcoholic beverage
ワイン		wine
ビール		beer
カクテル		cocktail
ウイスキー		whiskey
水	みず	water (*cold to tepid in temperature*)
(お)湯	(お)ゆ	hot water, boiling water

アクティビティー 1

何が一番好きですか。(*What do you like best?*)

Answer each question. Then rank the items in the order of your preference.

1. どの肉が一番好きですか。牛肉、豚肉、鳥肉
2. どの野菜が一番好きですか。レタス、にんじん、ピーマン
3. どの果物が一番好きですか。バナナ、りんご、ぶどう
4. どの飲み物が一番好きですか。お茶、コーヒー、コーラ
5. どのジュースが一番好きですか。りんご、みかん、ぶどう
6. どのアイスクリームが一番好きですか。バニラ、チョコレート、ストロベリー

お茶(おちゃ)

When you go to a restaurant in America, a waiter or waitress first brings a glass of water. In Japan, when you go to a Japanese restaurant, the first thing you are served is green tea. When you visit a residence or a company, a cup of green tea is served soon after your arrival. (Recently, young people seem to prefer black tea — 紅茶(こうちゃ) literally *crimson tea* or coffee rather than 緑茶(りょくちゃ) *green tea*). Many people enjoy 茶道(さどう) (*tea ceremony* [*lit., the way of tea*]), which through ritualized preparation and serving of tea to guests teaches the practitioner the art of hospitality. Young women often study it as part of their preparation for marriage. When you want to chat with someone or take him or her out, you might say お茶でも飲みませんか (*Shall we drink tea?*). People go to 喫茶店 (きっさてん: *coffee shops* [*lit., tea shops*]) and enjoy chatting with friends or talking about business matters over tea. In short, tea plays an important role in Japanese life. Most neighborhoods have a tea specialty store that sells many different kinds of tea. These are some of the common offerings.

煎茶(せんちゃ)	sencha (*good-quality green tea*)
番茶(ばんちゃ)	bancha (*an everyday, coarser green tea*)
麦茶(むぎちゃ)	*barley tea* (*served chilled in summer*)
げんまい茶	*brown-rice tea* (*contains popcorn-like bits of puffed rice*)
抹茶(まっちゃ)	*powdered tea* (*used in the tea ceremony; a popular ice cream flavor*)
ウーロン茶	*oolong tea* (*chilled in summer*)
昆布茶(こんぶちゃ)	*seaweed "tea"* (*actually, powdered seaweed*)
一番茶(いちばんちゃ)	*the first tea picked in a given year*

茶道(さどう)：抹茶(まっちゃ)の味(あじ)はいかがでしょうか。

アクティビティー 2

何ですか。(*What is it?*)

1. ぶどうから作るお酒です。
2. チキンバーガーに使う (*use*) 肉です。
3. オレンジ色の果物です。
4. アメリカでバーベキューによく使う肉です。日本ではすきやきに使います。
5. 日本や中国でよく飲む飲み物です。
6. 赤 (*red*) やみどり (*green*) の果物です。コンピュータの会社 (*company*) の名前です。
7. 黄色 (*yellow*) の果物です。
8. フレンチフライを作る野菜です。
9. ごはん (*cooked rice*) の上にこれをのせて (*put on*)、すしを作ります。
10. 果物から作る飲み物です。

Vocabulary: Meals and Restaurants

Meals

食事	しょくじ	meal つくる
ごはん		meal; cooked rice
朝ごはん	あさごはん	breakfast
昼ごはん	ひるごはん	lunch
夕ごはん	ゆうごはん	supper, dinner
おやつ、スナック		snack
夜食	やしょく	evening snack

Places to Eat

レストラン		restaurant
食堂	しょくどう	dining hall, cafeteria
喫茶店	きっさてん	coffee (*lit.*, *tea*) shop
台所	だいどころ	kitchen
キッチン		kitchen

Types of Food

ファーストフード		fast food
デザート		dessert
和食	わしょく	Japanese cuisine
洋食	ようしょく	Western cuisine
中華料理	ちゅうかりょうり	Chinese cuisine
…料理	…りょうり	. . . cuisine, . . . cooking

Review: 料理(を)する

言語ノート

米(こめ)、ライス、ごはん

Rice is a staple food in Japan. Many Japanese eat rice more than once a day, often three times a day, and don't feel as if they have eaten a meal unless they've had rice. Waiters at Western-style restaurants in Japan usually ask if you would like to have bread or rice along with your entree. Reflecting the importance of rice in Japanese life, the language has several words referring to rice. A *rice plant* is called 稲(いね). *Uncooked rice* is 米 or お米(こめ). *Cooked rice served in a bowl* is ごはん, while *cooked rice served on a plate* is ライス. ごはん also means *meals* in general. While bread has made inroads into the consumption of rice over the past decade, rice retains an important role in the diet and in the Japanese people's collective identity as a nation of rice eaters.

アクティビティー 3

朝ごはんに何を食べましたか。(*What did you eat for breakfast?*)

Discuss in class.

1. いつも昼ごはんを食べますか。昨日昼ごはんを食べましたか。何を食べましたか。
2. 昨日夕ごはんを食べましたか。何時に食べましたか。何を食べましたか。
3. 朝ごはんの時、何か飲みましたか。何を飲みましたか。
4. いつも朝ごはんを食べますか。今日朝ごはんを食べましたか。
5. どんな食べ物(もの)が一番好きですか。
6. どんな飲み物が一番好きですか。
7. レストランによく行きますか。どんなレストランに行きますか。
8. ファーストフード・レストランへよく行きますか。何を食べますか。
9. どんなデザートが好きですか。
10. 料理(りょうり)は得意(とくい)ですか。よく料理をしますか。

文化ノート

What Do Japanese Eat?

Thanks to increasing interaction with foreign countries, Japanese people eat a wider variety of foods than ever before. While some prefer the traditional breakfast—rice, miso soup, seaweed, raw egg (cracked in a bowl, mixed with soy sauce, and poured on the rice), and fish—others choose a Western breakfast of buttered toast, an egg (usually hardboiled or fried), coffee, and perhaps a small portion of green salad or small sausages.

For lunch, most Japanese workers and students eat at the company or university cafeteria or at small restaurants in the neighborhood. The most popular fare is simple dishes like noodles (cold or hot, in broth or for dipping, made of buckwheat or wheat), rice with something on top (a pork cutlet, say, or curry sauce), or the special set menu of the day (soup, rice, green salad, and a main dish such as tempura). Some people take their lunch to work in a reusable rectangular container wrapped in a square cloth. Shops also sell such boxed lunches, or 弁当 (べんとう), daily.

Suppers cooked at home range from fried chicken, spaghetti, or stew, to sushi, sukiyaki, and tempura. Chinese, Korean, and French are the most widespread foreign cuisines. As the number of working women has grown in Japan, take-out food (テークアウト) and dining out (外食 [がいしょく]) have become popular. Some Japanese take rice, instant noodles, or other Japanese food when they travel abroad for fear they won't be able to eat foreign cuisines. The overwhelming success of chains such as McDonald's, KFC (Kentucky Fried Chicken), and Baskin Robbins in Japan, however, bespeaks a changing palate that relishes new flavors.

Whatever and wherever the Japanese eat, before they begin they usually say いただきます (*lit., I receive this*) and after they finish they say ごちそうさまでした (*lit., It was a feast*). Both are expressions of gratitude directed toward the people and things that made the meal possible—that is, the farmers, the fishermen, the people who prepared the meal, the rain that enabled the crops to grow, and so on.

レストランの前で：
何を食べますか。

(勉) Study Grammar 32.

アクティビティー 4

ダイアログ：イタリアン・レストランへ行ったことがありますか。(*Have you ever been to an Italian restaurant?*)

ブラウンさんとチンさんが話しています。

ブラウン：イタリアン・レストランへ行ったことがありますか。
チン：ええ、ありますよ。
ブラウン：どのレストランですか。
チン：いつも「ナポリ」へ行きます。
ブラウン：ああ。あそこのラザーニャを食べたことがありますか。
チン：ええ。本当(ほんとう)においしいですね。

Now answer these questions.

1. イタリアン・レストランへ行ったことがありますか。何を食べましたか。
   Italian foods: ピザ、パスタ、スパゲッティ
2. スペイン料理(りょうり)の店(みせ)へ行ったことがありますか。何を食べましたか。
   Spanish foods: パエーヤ、ガスパーチョ、スパニッシュ・オムレツ
3. ベトナム料理の店へ行ったことがありますか。何を食べましたか。
4. インド料理の店へ行ったことがありますか。何を食べましたか。
   Indian foods: カレー、インドのパン、ライタ
5. メキシコ料理の店へ行ったことがありますか。何を食べましたか。
   Mexican foods: タコス、ブリート、エンチラダ、チミチャンガ
6. どんな料理(りょうり)を作(つく)ったことがありますか。おいしかったですか。
7. アフリカ料理を食べたことがありますか。
8. ロシア料理を作ったことがありますか。食べたことがありますか。
9. フランス料理を作ったことがありますか。

Vocabulary Library

More Food Words

缶詰	かんづめ	canned food
冷凍食品	れいとうしょくひん	frozen food
前菜	ぜんさい	appetizer
お菓子	おかし	sweets (cakes and confections)
卵	たまご	egg
パン		bread
ラーメン		**ramen** (*Chinese-style wheat noodles*)

Ms. Brown and Ms. Chin are talking BROWN: Have you ever been to an Italian restaurant? CHIN: Yes, I have. BROWN: Which restaurant? CHIN: I always go to Napoli. BROWN: Oh. Have you ever eaten their lasagna? CHIN: Yes. It's really delicious.

Japanese Food

うどん		**udon** (*thick, flat wheat noodles*)
そば		**soba** (*buckwheat noodles*)
てんぷら		tempura (*dipped in batter and fried vegetables and fish*)
すきやき		sukiyaki
漬物	つけもの	pickled vegetable
しいたけ		shiitake mushroom
海苔	のり	a kind of seaweed
みりん		sweet cooking sake
とうふ		tofu, bean curd

Meals

朝食	ちょうしょく	breakfast
昼食	ちゅうしょく	lunch
夕食	ゆうしょく	dinner, supper
軽食	けいしょく	light meal, snack

Loanwords: インスタント・フード、オレンジ、クッキングオイル、ケーキ、サンドイッチ、スパゲッティ、ソーセージ、チーズ、チョコレート、トースト、ハム、バター、マーガリン、ヨーグルト

アクティビティー 5

日本料理の通(つう)ですか。(*Are you a connoisseur of Japanese cuisine?*)

Answer these questions. Circle the letter of your response.

1. あなたは日本レストランへ行ったことがありますか。
   a. はい、あります。　b. いいえ、ありません。
2. あなたはてんぷらを食べたことがありますか。
   a. はい、あります。　b. いいえ、ありません。
3. あなたはすしを食べたことがありますか。
   a. はい、あります。　b. いいえ、ありません。
4. あなたははし (*chopsticks*) が上手に使(つか)えますか。
   a. はい、使えます。　b. いいえ、使えません。
5. あなたは日本語のメニューが読めますか。
   a. はい、読めます。　b. いいえ、読めません。
6. あなたは日本料理を作ったことがありますか。
   a. はい、あります。　b. いいえ、ありません。
7. あなたは日本料理を作るのが得意(とくい)ですか。
   a. はい、得意です。　b. いいえ、得意じゃありません。
8. あなたは日本料理が好きですか。
   a. はい、好きです。　b. いいえ、きらいです。

9. あなたは昨日日本料理を食べましたか。
　a. はい、食べました。　　b. いいえ、食べませんでした。
10. あなたは明日日本料理を食べますか。
　a. はい、食べます。　　b. いいえ、食べません。

Now rate yourself. How many times did you answer *a*?

7 or more:	You are a true connoisseur of Japanese cuisine.
4–6:	You can appreciate Japanese food but can't shake that craving for hamburgers.
2–3:	You need more practice with chopsticks!
0–1:	Are you in the right class?

(勉) Study Grammar 33.

アクティビティー　6

ダイアログ：どこへ行きたいですか。(*Where do you want to go?*)

町田さんとブラウンさんが話しています。

町田：土曜日、どこかへ行きませんか。
ブラウン：ええ。町田さんはどこへ行きたいですか。
町田：そうですね。いいレストランへ行きたいですね。
ブラウン：それはいいですね。何かおいしいものを食べたいですね。

Practice the dialogue, substituting the following for the underlined sentences.

1. イタリア・レストランへ行く
　スパゲッティをたべる
2. 映画館(えいがかん)へ行く
　おもしろい映画を見る
3. ショッピングセンターへ行く
　買(か)い物(もの)をする
4. ゲームセンターへ行く
　テレビゲームで遊(あそ)ぶ
5. 林(はやし)さんのアパートへ行く
　林さんと話す

アクティビティー　7

何が食べたいですか。(*What do you want to eat?*)

Answer these questions.

1. 今、午前6時半です。何が食べたいですか。
2. 今、午後6時です。とてもおなかがすいています (*You are very hungry*)。
　何が食べたいですか。

Ms. Machida and Ms. Brown are talking　MACHIDA: Shall we go somewhere on Saturday?　BROWN: Yes. Where do you want to go?　MACHIDA: Let me see. I would like to go to a good restaurant, wouldn't you?　BROWN: That's a good idea. (*lit., That's good.*) I would like to eat some good food. (*lit., I want to eat something delicious, don't you?*)

3. 今日はデートです。どんなレストランへ行きたいですか。
4. 今、午後10時です。日本語を勉強(べんきょう)しています。とてもおなかがすきました。何が食べたいですか。
5. 今、日本レストランにいます。何が食べたいですか。
6. 今日の夕ごはんは何が食べたいですか。
7. テニスをしました。のどがかわきました (*You are thirsty*)。何が飲みたいですか。

Now pair up. Find out what your partner wants to do on the following occasions. Take notes and save them for アクティビティー **8**.

8. 今、何が一番食べたいですか。
9. デートの時、どんなレストランへ一番行きたいですか。
10. 今、何が一番買(か)いたいですか。
11. この週末、何がしたいですか。
12. 今、だれに一番会いたいですか。
13. 今、どの映画(えいが)が見たいですか。
14. 次(つぎ)の (*next*) 夏休みにどこへ行きたいですか。
15. 次の冬休みにどこへ行きたいですか。

アクティビティー 8

ダイアログ：ロブスターを食べたがっています。(*She wants to eat lobster.*)

ブラウンさんと林(はやし)さんが話しています。

ブラウン：林さん、お出かけですか。
林：ええ、ギブソンさんとシーフード・レストランへ行くんです。
ブラウン：それはいいですね。
林：ええ、ギブソンさんがロブスターを食べたがっているんです。

Practice the dialogue, substituting the following expressions for the underlined phrases.

1. ショッピング・センターへ行く
   新(あたら)しいドレスを買(か)う
2. コンサートへ行く
   クラシック音楽(おんがく)を聞く
3. プールへ行く
   泳(およ)ぐ

Ms. Brown and Mr. Hayashi are talking BROWN: Mr. Hayashi, are you going out? HAYASHI: Yes, I'm going to a seafood restaurant with Ms. Gibson. BROWN: That should be nice. (*lit., That's good, isn't it?*) HAYASHI: Yes. We are going because Ms. Gibson wants to eat lobster. (*lit., It's that Ms. Gibson wants to eat lobster.*)

Now report the results of the interview you conducted in アクティビティー 7 to the class. Use ～たがっています.

[例]　ジョンソンさんは今すしを一番食べたがっています。
　　　キムさんはメキシコ料理の店へ一番行きたがっています。

Vocabulary: Flavors, Tastes, and Seasonings

Flavors and Taste

味	あじ	flavor, taste
味がいい	あじがいい	to taste good
味がない	あじがない	to have no taste
味見する	あじみする	to taste a sample
おいしい		tasty, delicious
まずい		not tasty, tastes bad
甘い	あまい	sweet
苦い	にがい	bitter
辛い	からい	spicy; hot (*spicy*); salty
塩辛い	しおからい	salty
酸っぱい	すっぱい	sour
渋い	しぶい	astringent

Seasonings

調味料	ちょうみりょう	seasoning
塩	しお	salt
砂糖	さとう	sugar
胡椒	こしょう	pepper
醤油	しょうゆ	soy sauce
味噌	みそ	miso (*fermented soybean paste*)
酢	す	vinegar
ソース		*a prepared sauce somewhat like steak sauce*

㊝ Study Grammar 34 and 35.

アクティビティー 9

どう思(おも)いますか。(*What do you think?*)

林(はやし)さんとギブソンさんが台所(だいどころ)で話しています。

ギブソン：これ、ちょっと味見(あじみ)してください。
林：ああ、いいにおいですね。
ギブソン：どう思いますか。
林：ウーン、ちょっと甘(あま)すぎると思います。

Practice the dialogue, substituting the underlined part with the following.

1. とてもおいしい
2. ちょっと酸(す)っぱい
3. おもしろい味だ
4. ちょっと辛(から)すぎる
5. ぜんぜん味がない

アクティビティー 10

値段 *price* / おすすめ品 *recommended dish* / 休み *day(s) closed*

どのレストランがいいと思いますか。(*Which restaurant do you think is good?*)

Answer the following questions according to the table. Use …と思(おも)います。

名前	タイプ	値段(ねだん)	味(あじ)	おすすめ品(ひん)	休み
ふじ	日本	¥	★★★	すきやき	月
アミーゴ	メキシコ	¥¥	★	タコス	日
マキシム	フランス	¥¥¥	★★★	エスカルゴ	火
モナリザ	イタリア	¥¥¥	★	ピザ	月
ホンコン	中国(ちゅうごく)	¥¥	★★	全部(ぜんぶ)	日
バーガー・クイーン	ファーストフード	¥	★	ハンバーガー	24時間オープン

[例] —「ふじ」はどんなレストランですか。
—安(やす)くて、おいしいレストランだと思います。

Mr. Hayashi and Ms. Gibson are talking in the kitchen. GIBSON: Please taste this for me. HAYASHI: Mm, it smells good. (*lit., Mm, it's a good smell, isn't it?*) GIBSON: What do you think? HAYASHI: Hmm . . . , I think it is a little too sweet.

1. 「ふじ」は何がおいしいですか。
2. 「アミーゴ」は何曜日が休みですか。
3. 「マキシム」は高いですか。安いですか。
4. 「モナリザ」はおいしいですか。まずいですか。
5. 「ホンコン」は何がおいしいですか。
6. 「バーガー・クイーン」は休みがありますか。
7. 今日はデートです。どのレストランがいいですか。
8. 今日はお金があまりありません。どのレストランがいいですか。
9. 中国料理(ちゅうごくりょうり)が大好きです。どのレストランがいいですか。
10. 安くて、おいしいレストランはありませんか。

コミュニケーション・ノート

Asking For and Expressing Opinions

To ask for someone's opinion, say

…(を)どう思(おも)いますか。
What do you think about . . . ?

To state your opinion, say

…と思います。
I think (that) . . . .

For example

あのレストランのステーキをどう思いますか。
What do you think of that restaurant's steaks?
とてもおいしいと思います。
I think they are quite delicious.

When you don't have an opinion, or wish to avoid expressing an opinion, you can say

さあ、わかりません。
Hmm, I don't know.

When soliciting agreement with your view, you can say

…と思いませんか。
Don't you think (that) . . . ?

For instance

あのレストランは、高すぎると思いませんか。
Don't you think that restaurant is too expensive?

In addition, you can use this phrase to try to change someone's opinion.

でも、サービスがいいと思いませんか。
But don't you think that their service is good?

アクティビティー 11

ダイアログ：「ふじ」というレストランへ行ったことがありますか。
(*Have you ever been to the restaurant Huji?*)

カーティス：「ふじ」というレストランへ行ったことがありますか。
チン：ええ。よく行きますよ。
カーティス：どんなレストランですか。
チン：安くて、おいしいレストランだと思います。

Practice the dialogue, substituting information from the table in アクティビティー 10 for the underlined phrases.

(勉) Study Grammar 36.

アクティビティー 12

ダイアログ：何と言ったんですか。(*What did he say?*)

カワムラ：町田さん、泣いているんですか。
町田：ええ、林さんがひどいことを言ったんですよ。
カワムラ：何と言ったんですか。
町田：私の作ったケーキがまずいと言ったんですよ。
カワムラ：それはひどいですね。

Practice the dialogue, substituting the following insensitive comments for the underlined phrase. Remember to change each to the appropriate quoted form.

1. 「町田さんは料理がへたですね。」
2. 「町田さんのヘアースタイルは面白いですね。」
3. 「町田さんの作ったクッキーは味がぜんぜん ([*not*] *at all*) ありませんね。」
4. 「町田さんのファッション・センスはあまりよくないですね。」
5. 「町田さんのボーイフレンドがきれいな女の人と歩いていましたよ。」

アクティビティー 13

有名人にインタビューしました。(*I interviewed famous people!*)

Following the example, tell who made each statement. Choose from the famous people listed here.

CURTIS: Have you ever been to the restaurant Huji? CHIN: Yes, I go there often. CURTIS: What kind of restaurant is it? CHIN: I think the food's good and it's inexpensive. (*lit., I think it is an inexpensive, delicious restaurant.*)

KAWAMURA: Ms. Machida, are you crying? MACHIDA: Yes, Mr. Hayashi said a terrible thing (to me). KAWAMURA: What did he say? MACHIDA: He said that the cake I made tastes bad. KAWAMURA: That's terrible, you're right.

フアン・バルデス、コロネル・サンダース、ジュリア・チャイルド、サラ・リー、ジェニー・クレイグ

[例]　「エアロビクスが好きです。」→
ジェーン・フォンダがエアロビクスが好きだと言いました。

1. 「料理の本(*cookbook*)をたくさん書きました。」
2. 「コロンビアでコーヒーを作っています。」
3. 「私の作ったケーキはおいしいですよ。」
4. 「みんながわたしのダイエットをしています。」
5. 「KFC(ケンタッキー・フライド・チキン)は、わたしが始めました(*began*)。」

What do you think the following people said?

ビル・クリントン、マイク・タイソン、マドンナ、ボー・ジャクソン

Vocabulary Library

More Cooking Terms

Food Preparation

料理の本	りょうりのほん	cookbook
材料	ざいりょう	ingredient(s)
生	なま	raw
切る	きる	to cut
煮る	にる	to boil (to cook in liquid)
焼く	やく	to broil, to grill, to bake
いためる		to stir-fry
あげる		to deep fry
蒸す	むす	to steam
ゆでる		to cook in boiling water

Utensils and Appliances

包丁	ほうちょう	cleaver, big cutting knife
鍋	なべ	pan, pot
かんきり		can opener
せんぬき		bottle opener
皿	さら	plate, dish
コップ		glass
茶碗	ちゃわん	rice bowl or teacup
(お)椀	(お)わん	soup bowl
箸	はし	chopsticks
冷蔵庫	れいぞうこ	refrigerator

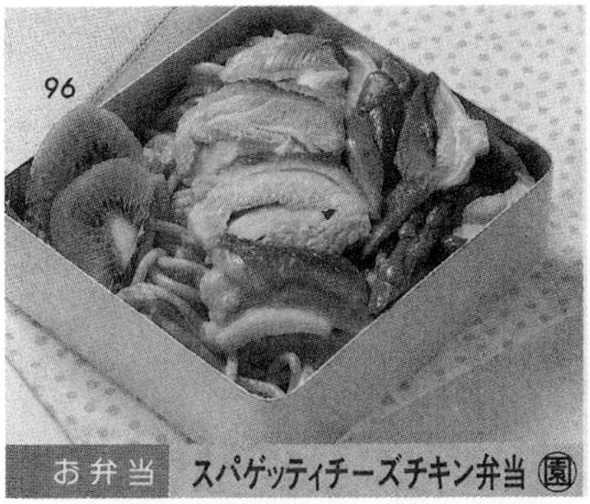

96
お弁当
スパゲッティチーズチキン弁当 園

酒蒸しにした鶏肉小¼枚は厚みに切り込みを入れてチーズをはさみ、両面を油焼きにする。ゆでたスパゲッティは炒めて塩、胡椒、ケチャップで調味する。スパゲッティの上にチキンをのせ、グリーンアスパラと生椎茸のソテー、キーウィを添える。

副　菜　**レバーのシナモン煮**

鶏レバー400gは塩水で血抜きして一口大に切り、葱の葉先などを加えて下ゆでする。鍋にレバー、葱のぶつ切り、生姜の薄切り各少少、小玉葱10個を入れ、醤油¼カップ、みりんまたは砂糖少々、シナモン大さじ½を加えて汁けがなくなるまで煮る。

おやつ　**フルーツタルト**

バター70g、粉砂糖50g、卵黄1個分、おろしレモン皮1個分、小麦粉120gで生地を作り、小さな型に敷いて焼き上げ、ケースに。卵黄2個分、大さじで砂糖2、小麦粉1、牛乳150ccでカスタードを作ってケースにつめ、フルーツとホイップクリームで飾る。

Loanwords: オーブン、クッキング・スクール、グラス、スプーン、ナイフ、ナプキン、フォーク、フライパン、レシピー、レンジ

アクティビティー　14

何がいりますか。(*What do you need?*)

Work in pairs. Ask your partner what ingredient you need to prepare the following dishes.

Useful expression: …がいります。 *You need . . . .*

[例]　S1: サンドイッチを作(つく)ります。何がいりますか。
　　　S2: パンとハムとレタスとチーズです。

1. すきやき
2. フルーツ・サラダ
3. 野菜(やさい)サラダ
4. すし
5. てんぷら

Now change partners. Report your first partner's answers as done in the example.

[例]　パンとハムとレタスとチーズがいると言いました。

(勉) Study Grammar 37.

アクティビティー　15

ダイアログ：パーティーをするつもりです。(*I'm planning to have a party.*)

カワムラ：土曜日はチンさんの誕生日(たんじょうび)ですね。
町田：ええ、それで、うちでパーティーをするつもりです。
カワムラ：それはいい考(かんが)えですね。
町田：バースデー・ケーキを作(つく)ろうと思(おも)っています。

Now practice the dialogue, substituting the following phrases for the underlined phrase.

1. バースデー・ケーキを買(か)う
2. チンさんのボーイフレンドも呼(よ)ぶ (*invite*)
3. みんなでゲームをする
4. たくさん写真(しゃしん)をとる

アクティビティー　16

こんな時、どうしますか。(*What are you going to do on this occasion?*)

For each phrase in Column A, choose an appropriate phrase from Column B and connect them in a logical sentence.

[例]　とても暑い　　アイスティーを飲む→
とても暑いので、アイスティーを飲もうと思います。

	A	B
1.	ピザが好きだ	卵(たまご)をたくさん買う
2.	料理(りょうり)が上手になりたい	夕ごはんはすきやきにする
3.	今日は牛肉(ぎゅうにく)が安(やす)かった	サラダを作る
4.	ギブソンさんは肉を食べない	イタリア・レストランで食べる
5.	オムレツを作(つく)りたい	クッキング・スクールへ行く

KAWAMURA: This Saturday is Ms. Chin's birthday, isn't it? MACHIDA: Yes, so I'm planning to have a party at my home. KAWAMURA: That's a good idea. MACHIDA: I'm thinking of making a birthday cake.

文法ノート

…にする

X にする means *to decide on X.*

飲み物は何にしますか。—寒いから、ココアにします。
What drink will you have? (lit., As for drink, what will you decide on?—It's cold, so I'll have cocoa. (lit., Because it's cold, I will decide on cocoa.)

この三つのうちでどれにしますか。—これにします。
Which one of these three will you choose (lit., decide on)?—I'll choose this one. (lit., I will decide on this one.)

勉 Study Grammar 38.

アクティビティー 17

ダイアログ：食べてみてください。(*Please eat it and see what you think.*)

カワムラ：さとみさんはクッキング・スクールに通っているんですか。
さとみ：ええ、今日も行ってきたんですよ。
カワムラ：今日は何を習ってきたんですか。
さとみ：オムレツです。今夜、作ってみますから、食べてみてください。

アクティビティー 18

どこで聞きましたか。だれが言いましたか。(*Where did you hear that? Who said that?*)

Where do you think the following statements were made? Choose from the places listed here.

台所、図書館、デパート、スーパー、レストラン

1. もう少し甘いほうがいいですかねえ。
2. このブラウスをためして (*try on*) みてください。
3. この本を読んでみよう。
4. このステーキをたのんで (*order*) みましょう。
5. この新しいステーキ・ソースを買ってみましょう。

Who do you think made the following statements? Choose from the people listed here.

KAWAMURA: Are you going (*lit., commuting*) to a cooking school? SATOMI: Yes, I went there today, too. KAWAMURA: What did you learn today? SATOMI: How to make omelets. (*lit., It's omelets.*) Tonight, I will try making one, so please (come and) eat it and see what you think.

日本のサラリーマン、日本語の学生、イメルダ・マルコス、コック(*cook*)、スチュワーデス

6. パリとロンドンとローマに行ってきました。
7. 料理をたくさん作ってきました。
8. 夜十時まで働いてきました。
9. 漢字をたくさん勉強してきました。
10. 靴(*shoes*)をたくさん買ってきました。

㊚ Study Grammar 39.

アクティビティー 19

ダイアログ：勉強しながら、食べます。(*I will eat while studying.*)

山口：カワムラさん、ごはんですよ。
カワムラ：今、勉強で忙しいんです。
山口：じゃ、あとにしますか。
カワムラ：いいえ、勉強しながら、食べます。

Practice the dialogue, substituting the following for the underlined portions.

1. 今、テレビを見ています
   テレビを見ながら、食べます
2. 今、ステレオを聞いています
   ステレオを聞きながら、食べます
3. 今、お酒を飲んでいます
   お酒を飲みながら、食べます

アクティビティー 20

いいと思いますか。悪いと思いますか。(*Do you think it's good or bad?*)

State your opinion about the following.

1. テレビを見ながら、
   ごはんを食べる。
2. 野菜を毎日食べる。
3. 朝ごはんを食べない。
4. コーヒーを一日に三杯飲む。
5. 電話で話しながら、食事をする。
6. 毎日、日本料理を食べる。
7. 毎日、お酒をたくさん飲む。
8. 毎日、ファーストフード・
   レストランへ行く。

YAMAGUCHI: Mr. Kawamura, dinner is ready (*lit., it's dinner*)! KAWAMURA: I'm busy studying now. (*lit., I'm busy with studying now.*) YAMAGUCHI: Then, will you eat (*lit., decide on*) later? KAWAMURA: No, I will eat while studying.

Grammar and Exercises

32. Expressing Experience: The Ta-Form of Verbs + ことがある

カワムラ：町田さんはロシア料理(りょうり)を食べたことがありますか。
町田：ええ、あります。
カワムラ：どんな味(あじ)でしたか。
町田：なかなかよかったですよ。

林(はやし)：ブラウンさんは東急(とうきゅう)デパートの食堂(しょくどう)へ行ったことがありますか。
ブラウン：いいえ、まだありません。
林：じゃ、今度一緒(こんどいっしょ)に行きませんか。
ブラウン：林さんもまだなんですか。
林：ええ。

カワムラ：レストラン「九州(きゅうしゅう)」を知(し)っていますか。
山口：ええ、新聞(しんぶん)で読んだことがあります。
カワムラ：行ったことはないんですか。
山口：はい、ないんです。

32.1 The following construction is used to express past experiences, with a meaning of *to have* (*done something*) *before, to have* (*done something*) *once* or literally, *to have the experience of having* (*done something*).

Ta-form of a verb + ことがある (ことがあります)

こと in this construction is a nominalizer (see, **Grammar 26** Chapter 5).

The ta-form of a verb is equivalent to the plain, past form of verbs.

KAWAMURA: Have you ever eaten Russian food? MACHIDA: Yes, I have. KAWAMURA: What did it taste like? (*lit., What kind of taste was it?*) MACHIDA: It was quite good, you know.

HAYASHI: Have you ever been (*lit., gone*) to the dining hall at Tokyu Department Store? BROWN: No, I haven't yet. HAYASHI: Then, shall we go there together sometime (*lit., next time*)? BROWN: You haven't gone yet, either? HAYASHI: No. (*lit., Yes* [*i.e., that's right*].)

KAWAMURA: Do you know of the restaurant Kyushu? YAMAGUCHI: Yes. I've read (about it) in the newspaper. KAWAMURA: Haven't you been (*lit., gone*) there? YAMAGUCHI: No (*lit., Yes*), I haven't.

タイ料理(りょうり)を食べたことがありますか。
Have you ever eaten Thai food?
はい、あります。
Yes, I have.
いいえ、ありません。
No, I haven't.
わたしはさくらレストランへ行ったことがある。
I have been to Restaurant Sakura.
父(ちち)も料理(りょうり)をしたことがあります。
My father has cooked, too. (lit., My father also has the experience of having cooked.)
レストランでウエーターをしたことがあります。
I have worked as a waiter in a restaurant before.

Notice the difference between this construction and the simple past tense.

三年前にダイエットしました。
三年前にダイエットしたことがあります。
I was on a diet three years ago.

The first sentence (simple past) describes the speaker's diet simply as a past event — I was on a diet three years ago. The second sentence (experience) describes the diet as an experience the speaker had at some time in his life — I have been on a diet before, it was three years ago.

32.2 You can express a lack of experience by using the negative forms of ある.

ポルトガルのワインは飲んだことがありません。
I have never had (lit., drunk) Portuguese wine.
こんなにおいしいすしは食べたことがない。
I have never eaten such delicious sushi.

Remember that ない, the plain, negative form of ある, is an adjective and conjugates as such.

32.3 Here are several adverbs that are commonly used with this construction.

…年前に *. . . years ago*

十年前にカナダへ行ったことがあります。
I went to Canada ten years ago. (I have been to Canada before—it was ten years ago.)
五年前にブラウンさんに会ったことがあります。
I've met Ms. Brown before—five years ago.

これまでに、今までに *up to now*

これまでに(今までに)外国語(がいこくご)を勉強(べんきょう)したことがありますか。
Have you ever studied a foreign language? (lit., Up to now, have you had the experience of studying a foreign language?)

一度 *once*, 一度も *never, not once*, 何度も *many times*

一度横井先生と話したことがある。
I have talked with Professor Yokoi once before.
こんなまずいものを食べたことは一度もありません。
I have never eaten such bad food in my life.
メキシコ料理を食べたことがありますか。
Have you ever eaten Mexican food?
はい、一度あります。
Yes, once.
いいえ、一度もありません。
No, not ever.

度 is a counter meaning *times* as well as *degrees* (*temperature*). 一度 literally means *one time*. 一度も is used in negative sentences.

まだ + negative *not yet*

インスタント・ラーメンはまだ食べたことがありません。
I haven't eaten instant noodles yet. (*That is, I have never eaten them.*)
この本を読んだことがありますか。—いいえ、まだです。(short for まだ読んだことはありません。)
Have you ever read this book? —No, not yet.

Note: You cannot use words indicating the recent past with this construction.

昨日テレビを見たことがある。(ungrammatical)
I have watched TV yesterday.

練習 1

Make a question using the ta-form of the verb + ことがある, and answer the question according to your own experience.

[例] お酒を飲む →
—お酒を飲んだことがありますか。
—はい、あります。(or いいえ、ありません。)

1. 料理をする
2. 日本へ行く
3. ゴルフをする
4. 日本の音楽を聞く
5. すきやきを食べる
6. お金 (*money*) をおとす (*lose*)
7. お金をひろう (*find*)

練習 2

Make dialogues as shown in the example, using the ta-form of the verb + ことがある. Choose a negative or positive answer depending on the second phrase provided.

[例]　(てんぷらを食べる)(一度も)→
—てんぷらを食べたことがありますか。
—いいえ、一度も食べたことがありません。

1. (あのレストランへ行く)(三度)
2. (あのコーラを飲む)(何度も)
3. (ロシア語を勉強(べんきょう)する)(一度)
4. (スピルバーグの映画(えいが)を見る)(五年前)
5. (日本の食べ物(もの)を買(か)う)(二回ぐらい)
6. (コンピュータを使(つか)う)(一度)
7. (町田(まちだ)さんに会う)(三年前に一度)
8. (あのプールで泳(およ)ぐ)(一度も)
9. (この町で雪が降(ふ)る)(一度も)
10. (ウェートレスをする)(五年前)

Review **Grammar 9** Chapter 2 for the use of 〜回.

練習　3

Ask a friend if he or she has had the following experiences.

1. been to Japan
2. studied French
3. eaten sushi
4. had a party at home
   Useful expression: パーティーをする *to have a party*
5. received a D at school
   Useful expression: Dを取(と)る *to receive a D*
6. cleaned his or her room
   Useful expression: 部屋(へや)を掃除(そうじ)する *to clean a room*

練習　4

Answer these questions.

1. 日本レストランへ行ったことがありますか。
2. どんなレストランへ行ったことがありますか。
3. 自分(じぶん)で (*by yourself*) 料理(りょうり)をしたことがありますか。
4. お酒をたくさん飲んだことがありますか。
5. レストランで働(はたら)いたことがありますか。

33. Expressing a Desire: ほしい、ほしがる、～たい、and ～たがる

町田：カワムラさんは今、何が一番ほしいですか。
カワムラ：そうですね。いい日本語の辞書がほしいですね。
町田：大学の前の本屋にいい辞書がありますよ。
カワムラ：本当ですか。すぐに買いたいですね。

林：明日はギブソンさんの誕生日ですね。
ブラウン：そうですね。バースデー・プレゼントは何にしましょうか。
林：ギブソンさんは何をほしがっていますか。
ブラウン：さあ、よくわかりません。
でも、いつもすしを食べたがっていますよ。
林：そうですか。じゃあ、一緒にすし屋へ行きましょうか。

ブラウン：カワムラさん、新しいカメラですか。
カワムラ：ええ、昨日買ったんです。
林：いいですね。ぼくもほしいなあ。
ブラウン：林さんは新しいものをすぐほしがるんですね。

The sentence-final particle な(あ) is used to express the speaker's emotion directly, to try to convince others, to confirm another's opinion, to express a wish, and so forth.

言語ノート

食(た)べ物屋(ものや) *Eateries*

You can make words representing specialized restaurants by adding 屋 to the names of foods. For instance

すし→すし屋	**sushi** *restaurant*
そば→そば屋	**soba** *restaurant*
ラーメン→ラーメン屋	**ramen** *restaurant*

MACHIDA: What do you want most now? KAWAMURA: Let me see. . . I want a good Japanese dictionary. MACHIDA: There are good dictionaries at the bookstore in front of the university, you know. KAWAMURA: Really? I would like to buy one right now.

HAYASHI: Tomorrow is Ms. Gibson's birthday, isn't it? BROWN: That's right. What shall we give her for a birthday gift? (*lit., As for a birthday gift, what shall we decide on?*) HAYASHI: What does she want? (*lit., What is Ms. Gibson wanting?*) BROWN: Hmm, I don't really know. But she wants (*lit., is always wanting*) to eat sushi. HAYASHI: Is that right? Well then, let's go to a sushi restaurant together.

BROWN: Mr. Kawamura, is that a new camera? KAWAMURA: Yes, I bought it yesterday. HAYASHI: It looks like a fine camera. I'd sure like one. (*lit., It's good, isn't it? I want one, too.*) BROWN: You (always) want to get new things, don't you?

てんぷら→てんぷら屋	**tempura** *restaurant*
うなぎ→うなぎ屋	*barbecued eel restaurant*
カレー→カレー屋	*curry restaurant*
中華料理→中華料理屋	*Chinese restaurant*

33.1 In Japanese, there is no single verb meaning *to want* as in *I want a new car.* Instead you must choose between two constructions, depending on who is doing the wanting.

(a)	Xは	+	Yが	+	ほしい
(b)	Xは	+	Yを	+	ほしがる

X want(s) Y

Construction (a) is used when expressing one's own desire or when directly asking another person about his or her desire. ほしい is an i-adjective and conjugates as such.

わたしは新しい車がほしいです。
I want a new car.
いいカメラがほしかった。
I wanted a good camera.
今、コーヒーはほしくありません。
I don't want coffee now.
このドレスはほしくない。
I don't want this dress.

As you've studied before, in negative sentences the particle が is often replaced with は.

Construction (b) is used when discussing a third person's desire. ほしがる is a Class 1 verb. The te-form of ほしがる＋いる (ほしがっている) is used when expressing a current desire, whereas the nonpast form (ほしがる) expresses a longer term desire.

林さんはもっと本をほしがっています。
Mr. Hayashi wants more books.
町田さんはもっとレモンをほしがっていますか。
Does Ms. Machida want more lemon?
弟はいつもわたしのペンをほしがります。
My younger brother always wants my pen.
妹はあまりお金をほしがらない。
My younger sister doesn't want money very much.

Notice that the object of desire is marked with が in sentences using the predicate ほしい and with を in those using ほしがる.

わたしは新しい車がほしい。
I want a new car.
妻は新しい車をほしがっている。
My wife wants a new car.

文法ノート

〜がる

In Japanese, different grammatical constructions are needed when describing your own emotional state as opposed to that of others. You know your own emotional state, but you can only guess about that of other people from their appearance, behavior, or statements. To describe someone else's emotional state, you can attach 〜がる to the root of an adjective to mean *has the appearance of* or *appears to (be)*. Thus, when *you* are lonely, you say

さびしいです。
I am lonely.

But when someone else is lonely, you say

さびしがっています。
He is lonely. (lit., He appears to be lonely.)

33.2 Similar to the ほしい／ほしがる pair is the pair of patterns used to express *to want to (do something)*, as in *I want to eat sushi.*

(a)	Xは	+	Yが／を	+	conjunctive form of verb + たい
(b)	Xは	+	Yを	+	conjunctive form of verb + たがる

As with ほしい and ほしがる, (a) is used when the speaker expresses a desire or asks about the hearer's desire. (b) is used to describe a third person's desire. The ending 〜たい is an i-adjective and conjugates as such, whereas 〜たがる is a Class 1 verb.

In sentences using 〜たい, the direct object of the verb can be marked with either が or を. However, in sentences using 〜たがる, the direct object is marked only with を.

ヨーグルトが食べたい。
ヨーグルトを食べたい。
I want to eat yogurt.
林(はやし)さんはヨーグルトを食べたがっている。
Mr. Hayashi wants to eat yogurt.

Here are some more examples.

ステーキが食べたい。
I want to eat steak.
レストランへ行きたいです。
I want to go to a restaurant.
わたしは今朝(けさ)ごはんは食べたくありません。
I don't want to eat breakfast now.
明日どこへ行きたいですか。
Where do you want to go tomorrow?
わたしはお酒(さけ)が飲みたかった。
I wanted to drink sake.

The ～たい form is often used to ask for permission. For instance

ちょっと早(はや)く帰(かえ)りたいんですが、…
I want to leave a little early, but . . . (is it OK?)
このコンピュータを使(つか)いたいのですが、…
I want to use this computer, but . . . (is it OK?)
中に入りたいんですが、よろしいですか。
I would like to go inside, but is that all right?
ここにもう少しいたいんですが、いいでしょうか。
I would like to stay here a little longer (lit., more), but would that be OK?

Like the contrast between ほしがる and ほしがっている discussed above, the te-form ofたがる +いる (たがっている) expresses a current desire, whereas the nonpast expresses a longer term desire.

タマーラさんは日本語を勉強(べんきょう)したがっています。
Mr. Tamara wants to study Japanese.
山口さんはアメリカに来たがっている。
Mr. Yamaguchi wants to come to the United States.
チンさんは家(いえ)に帰(かえ)りたがりません。
Ms. Chin doesn't want to go back home.

コミュニケーション・ノート

Asking What Someone Wants

In Japanese, it is considered rude to ask someone what he or she desires directly. This is especially true regarding the desires of socially superior people. For instance, it is very rude to ask someone

すきやきが食べたいですか。
Do you want to eat sukiyaki?

どこへ行きたいですか。
Where do you want to go?

どの映画(えいが)を見たいですか。
Which movie do you want to see?

Rather, Japanese speakers tend to ask

すきやきを食べませんか。
Won't you eat sukiyaki?
すきやきはいかがですか。
How about some sukiyaki?

どこかへ行きませんか。
Shall we go somewhere?

映画を見ませんか。
Shall we see movies?

練習 1

Change these sentences as shown in the examples.

[例] 昼ごはんを食べる → 昼ごはんが食べたいです。
ビールを飲まない → ビールは飲みたくないです。
ジュースが飲みたいです。

1. ちょっと休む
2. 朝早(はや)く起きない
3. フランス語の辞書(じしょ)を買(か)う
4. スーパーへ行かない
5. 働(はたら)かない
6. 町田さんに会う
7. 映画(えいが)を見る
8. 林(はやし)さんと話す
9. 日本語を練習(れんしゅう)する
10. 今日、宿題(しゅくだい)をしない

練習 2

Rewrite the sentences you made in 練習 1 starting each new sentence with ブラウンさんは.

[例] ブラウンさんは昼ごはんを食べたがっています。
ブラウンさんはビールを飲みたがっていません。

練習 3

Using the information in the pictures, answer these questions.

1. ブラウンさんは今年の夏、どこへ行きたがっていますか。
2. ブラウンさんは今夜、何を食べたがっていますか。
3. ブラウンさんはだれに会いたがっていますか。
4. ブラウンさんは明日、何をしたがっていますか。
5. ブラウンさんは何を飲みたがっていますか。
6. ブラウンさんは何をしたがっていますか。
7. ブラウンさんはどんなレコードを聞きたがっていますか。
8. ブラウンさんはどのビデオを見たがっていますか。

1.

2.

3.

4.

5.

6.

7.

8.

練習 4

Complete the following sentences.

[例]　とても寒(さむ)いので、(　　　)がほしいです。→ とても寒いので、(セーター)がほしいです。

1. 日本語の勉強(べんきょう)のために (*for studying Japanese*)、(　　　)がほしいです。
2. 今日はいいお天気だから、(　　　)たいです。
3. つかれた (*I'm tired*) から、(　　　)たいです。
4. おなかがすいた (*I'm hungry*) から、(　　　)たいです。
5. 町田さんは昼ごはんに(　　　)たがっています。
6. 音楽(おんがく)の好きな山本(やまもと)さんは(　　　)をほしがっています。

練習 5

Answer these questions.

1. 今、何が一番食べたいですか。
2. 今、何が一番買いたいですか。
3. 今週の土曜日、何をしたいですか。
4. 今、何がほしいですか。
5. 今、どこへ一番行きたいですか。
6. 今、だれに一番会いたいですか。
7. あなたが一番勉強(べんきょう)したい外国語(がいこくご)は何ですか。
8. あなたが一番したくないことは何ですか。

34. Expressing an Opinion …と思(おも)う

ギブソン：林(はやし)さん、このシチューの味(あじ)、どう思(おも)いますか。
林：ううん、とてもいい味だと思いますよ。
ギブソンさんが作(つく)ったんですか。
ギブソン：いいえ、インスタントです。
林：本当(ほんとう)ですか。ギブソンさんが作ったんだと思いました。

GIBSON: Mr. Hayashi, what do you think about the taste of this stew?　HAYASHI: Mm. I think that it tastes good. Did you make it?　GIBSON: No, it's instant.　HAYASHI: Really? I thought that you made it.

カーティス：チンさん、明日、ハイキングに行きますか。
チン：ええ、行けると思いますが、カーティスさんは？
カーティス：明日はアルバイトがあるんです。
それに、明日は雨が降(ふ)ると思いますよ。
チン：そう思いますか。

ブラウンさんと町田さんが写真(しゃしん)を見ています。
ブラウン：町田さん、この男(おとこ)の人、知(し)ってますか。
町田：ええ、どこかで見たことがありますね。
ブラウン：わたしもそう思(おも)ったんです。
町田：そうそう、思(おも)い出(だ)しました。
この人は先週のパーティーに来ていたと思いますよ。

文法ノート

そう

そう is one of the following list of **ko-so-a-do** words used to express manner. (See **Grammar 3** *Chapter 1*, for more on **ko-so-a-do** words.)

こう	*like this*
そう	*like that*
ああ	*like that*
どう	*how, in what manner*

そう is used in many common expressions.

はい、そうです。
Yes, that's right. (lit., Yes, it's like that.)
そうですね。
Well . . . (or, *Let me see. . . .*) or *That's right.* (*depending on intonation*)
はい、そうします。
Yes, I will do so.
そうしましょう。
Let's do that.
はい、そう思(おも)います。
Yes, I think so.

CURTIS: Ms. Chin, are you going hiking tomorrow? CHIN:Yes, I think I can go. How about you? CURTIS: I have a part-time job tomorrow. Also, I think it will rain (tomorrow). CHIN: Do you think so?

Ms. Brown and Ms. Machida are looking at a photograph BROWN: Ms. Machida, do you know this man? MACHIDA: Yes, I have seen him somewhere. BROWN: I thought so, too. MACHIDA: That's right! I just remembered. I think that he was at last week's party.

An opinion can be expressed with the following construction in Japanese, which means *to think (that)* . . . .思う is a Class 1 verb meaning *to think*.

Plain form of verb, adjective, or copula + と思う (思います)

ギブソンさんはタクシーで来ると思います。
I think that Ms. Gibson will come by cab.
山本さんは今日は働いていないと思う。
I think that Ms. Yamamoto is not working today.
明日は寒いと思いますか。
Do you think that it will be cold tomorrow?
あのステーキはとてもおいしかったと思いますよ。
I think that steak was very tasty.
ブラウンさんはカワムラさんがちょっと遅いと思った。
Ms. Brown thought that Mr. Kawamura was a little late.

What one believes or recalls is also expressed by this construction.

その日はレストランで食事をしたと思います。
I think I ate at a restaurant on that day.
あの人は高田さんのお父さんだと思う。
I think that person is Mr. Takada's father.
林さんはだれが好きだと思いますか。—ギブソンさんが好きだと思います。
Who do you think Mr. Hayashi likes? —I think that he likes Ms. Gibson.

練習 1

Following the example, rewrite each sentence using と思います。

[例] 今夜 (*tonight*)、山口さんはいません。→
今夜、山口さんはいないと思います。

1. 林さんと話しませんでした。
2. その日、そのレストランは休みでした。
3. その人に会ったことがありました。
4. 山口さんの家の台所はとてもきれいです。
5. ブラウンさんの作ったケーキはとてもおいしかったです。
6. あの男の人はコック (*cook*) です。
7. さとみさんは料理をしています。

練習　2

Look at the illustrations and answer the following questions.

1. カワムラさんはよく勉強(べんきょう)すると思(おも)いますか。
2. ブラウンさんは日本語が上手に話せると思いますか。
3. この近所(きんじょ)は静(しず)かだと思いますか。
4. ギブソンさんは料理(りょうり)が上手だと思いますか。
5. 林(はやし)さんはたくさん食べると思いますか。
6. 町田さんは何をほしがっていると思いますか。
7. チンさんはどこへ行ったと思いますか。

35. ～すぎる

町田：大野(おおの)先生のクラスはどうですか。
ブラウン：宿題(しゅくだい)が多くて、たいへんです。
町田：そうですか。大野先生はちょっときびしすぎますよね。
ブラウン：ええ、本当(ほんとう)に。

MACHIDA: How is Professor Ono's class? BROWN: There is lots of homework, so it's tough. MACHIDA: Is that right? Professor Ono is a little too strict, isn't he? BROWN: Yes, really.

カワムラ：林さん、大丈夫(だいじょうぶ)ですか。
林：ええ、ちょっと飲みすぎましたね。
カワムラ：一人で帰(かえ)れますか。
林：ええ、何とか。

To add the meaning *too much* or *excessively* to a verb or adjective, add the verb すぎる to the appropriate form, as shown. すぎる is a Class 2 verb meaning *to exceed*.

VERBS	**Conjunctive Form**	
	飲む → 飲み	
	食べる → 食べ	
	する → し	
	来る → 来(き)	
I-ADJECTIVES	**Root**	+ すぎる
	むずかしい → むずかし	
	大きい → 大き	
NA-ADJECTIVES	**Root (Dictionary Form)**	
	静(しず)か(な) → 静(しず)か	
	はで(な) → はで	

あの人はちょっと話しすぎますね。
That person talks a little too much.
アイスクリームを食べすぎて、おなかがいたい。
Because I ate too much ice cream, I have a stomach ache.
この部屋(へや)はちょっと暑すぎませんか。
Isn't this room a little too hot?
このケーキは甘(あま)すぎて、食べられない。
This cake is too sweet to eat. (lit., This cake is too sweet, so I can't eat it.)
あの冷蔵庫(れいぞうこ)はこの小さいキッチンに大きすぎる。
That refrigerator is too large for this small kitchen.
あの喫茶店(きっさてん)はにぎやかすぎて、話ができません。
That coffee shop is so noisy that you cannot talk.
この問題(もんだい)はわたしにはむずかしすぎる。
This question is too difficult for me.

KAWAMURA: Mr. Hayashi, are you all right? HAYASHI: Yes, I have drunk a little too much. KAWAMURA: Can you get home yourself? HAYASHI: Yes, I can manage. (*lit., Yes, somehow.*)

練習 1

Fill in the blanks with the appropriate forms of the words listed here.

長い、あつい、飲む、広い、からい、食べる、高い、にぎやか、静か

1 このコーヒーは(　　　)すぎて、飲めません。
2. 昨日はすきやきを(　　　)すぎました。
3. 父はちょっとお酒を(　　　)すぎます。
4. あのダイヤはちょっと(　　　)すぎて、買えません。
5. この家は部屋が8つもあって、(　　　)すぎます。
6. あのレストランのカレーは(　　　)すぎる。
7. あの映画は4時間で、ちょっと(　　　)すぎる。

練習 2

What do you say in these situations? Answer using ～すぎる。

[例]　when a cake is too sweet → このケーキは甘すぎます。

1. when an exam is very difficult
2. when there are many difficult **kanji** in a reading passage
3. when someone is working too much
4. when the room is too cold
5. when someone is playing music too loudly
6. when an exam is very easy
7. when a sweater is too big for you

36. Quoting Speech: …と言う

カワムラ：すみません。*Plug outlet* はどこですか。
町田：プラグアウトレット？ああ、日本語ではコンセントといいます。
カワムラ：日本語では *plug outlet* をコンセントというんですか。
町田：ええ、おかしいですか。

KAWAMURA: Excuse me. Where is the plug outlet? MACHIDA: Plug outlet? Oh, it's called **konsento** in Japanese. KAWAMURA: You call a plug outlet **konsento** (*consent*)? MACHIDA: Yes, is it funny?

ギブソン：あの角の新しいレストランへ行きましたか。
チン：「ハングリーベアー」というレストランですか。
ギブソン：ええ、そうです。
チン：昨日行きました。ブラウンさんも行ったと言っていましたよ。

けど is a colloquial form of けれども.

ブラウン：わたしのケーキがないんですけど…
林：カワムラさんが食べたと言っていましたよ。
ブラウン：えっ！わたしのケーキだと言ったんですよ。
林：おいしかったと言っていました。
ブラウン：ひどい人！

36.1 The verb 言う means *to say, to tell,* or *to be called.* This verb is used in the following construction to say what something or someone is called or named.

(Aは) + Xを + Yと + 言う (言います)

A calls X Y

日本人はこれを何と言いますか。
What do Japanese call this?
日本人はこれをたこと言います。
Japanese call this **tako** *(octopus).*

When the topic (Aは) is omitted (when A is unknown or understood from context), X is usually marked with the topic marker は instead of を.

これはいかと言います。
This is called **ika** *(cuttlefish).*

In colloquial speech, …と言う (言います) very often changes to …って言う (言います), as in これはいかって言います。

36.2 Use the same verb to make a noun phrase meaning *X called (or named) Y.*

Y + という + X

ジョン・カワムラという学生
a student named John Kawamura

GIBSON: Did you go to the new restaurant at that corner? CHIN: Do you mean the restaurant called Hungry Bear? GIBSON: Yes, that's right. CHIN: I went yesterday. Ms. Brown also said that she had been there.

BROWN: I cannot find my cake. (*lit., There is not my cake, but . . .*) HAYASHI: Mr. Kawamura said that he ate it. BROWN: What! I told him that it was my cake. HAYASHI: He said it was delicious. BROWN: What a terrible man!

東京(とうきょう)大学という大学
a university called the University of Tokyo

ジョン・カワムラという学生(がくせい)は東京大学という大学の学生です。
A student named John Kawamura is a student at the university called the University of Tokyo.

島根(しまね)という県(けん)はどこにありますか。
Where is the prefecture ***Shimane****?*

これは何という料理(りょうり)ですか。
What is this dish called? (lit., As for this, it is a dish called what)?

In colloquial speech, …っていう… is often used rather than …という…. For example, 東京大学っていう大学.

文法ノート

Quote Marker と

The particle と in という is called a *quote marker* and is used to mark the end of a quotation. In addition, it indicates the content of thinking (…と思う), writing (…と書(か)く), and hearing (…と聞く).

あの人は先生だろうと思った。
I thought that that person was probably a teacher.

今日は寒かったと日記(にっき)に書いた。
I wrote in my diary that it was cold today.

林(はやし)さんは九州(きゅうしゅう)に帰(かえ)ると聞きました。
I heard that Mr. Hayashi will return to Kyushu.

36.3 There are two ways to quote someone's words—*direct quotation* and *indirect quotation*. Direct quotation is the quoting of someone's words verbatim, exactly as they were spoken. In English, direct quotations are set off with quotation marks. For example

He said, "I am hungry."

Indirect quotation, on the other hand, may be a paraphrasing of someone else's words; the object is to convey the basic content of the utterance, not the specific words. For example

He said that he was hungry.

In Japanese, direct quotations usually take the following structure.

「　　」, と言(い)う (or some other communication verb)

「　　」, called かぎ括弧 (かぎかっこ), are equivalent to quotation marks. The information contained within the quotation marks is as it was spoken, so you can use either polite or plain forms of predicates.

「早く起きてください。」と山口さんは言いました。
Mr. Yamaguchi said, "Please get up early."
高田さんは、「明日来ますか。」とわたしに聞きました。
Mr. Takada asked me, "Are you coming tomorrow?"
林さんは、「おなかがすいたよ。」と言いました。
Mr. Hayashi said, "I am hungry."

Indirect quotations take the following structure.

Clause ending in a plain form of verb, adjective, or copula	+	と言う (言います) (or other verb of communication)

No quotation marks are used, and only the plain form of a verb, adjective, or the copula can be used in front of と in this case.

三村さんは明日来ると言いました。
Mr. Mimura said he will come tomorrow.
そこに行かなかったとカーティスさんは言った。
Mr. Curtis said that she didn't go there.
そのりんごは甘いとブラウンさんは言っています。
Ms. Brown says (lit., is saying) those apples are sweet.

When the subject of the clause preceding と言う is in the third person, and the tense of 言う is nonpast, it is better to use 言っている.

Some communication verbs often used in these constructions are 言う *to say, to tell*, 伝える *to convey*, 述べる *to state*, 聞く *to hear, to ask*, and 話す *to speak*.

かれのお父さんは有名だったと聞きました。
I heard that his father had been famous.

練習 1

Answer these questions.

1. 日本語で *breakfast* を何といいますか。
2. 日本語で *vegetable* を何といいますか。
3. この教科書は何といいますか。
4. あなたの学校は何といいますか。
5. 英語で「料理」を何といいますか。
6. 日本語で電話をかけます。何と言いますか。
7. これからごはんを食べます。何と言いますか。
8. ごはんが終わりました。何と言いますか。

練習 2

Fill in the blanks.

1. わたしはマッキントッシュという(　　)を使(つか)っています。
2. わたしは「ようこそ!」という(　　)を使っています。
3. わたしは(　　)という大学の学生です。
4. わたしは(　　)という町に住(す)んでいます (*reside in*)。
5. わたしは(　　)という食べ物(もの)が好きです。

練習 3

Following the example, make dialogues.

[例]　(これ)(飲み物(もの))(カルピス)→
—これは何という飲み物ですか。
—カルピスという飲み物です。

カルピス, or **Calpis** (sold in America as *Calpico*), is a sweet, fermented milk drink popular in the summertime.

1. (あれ)(映画館(えいがかん))(テアトロシアター)
2. (あれ)(果物(くだもの))(キィウィ)
3. (ここ)(町)(中野(なかの))
4. (これ)(車(くるま))(セリカ)
5. (あそこ)(レストラン)(セブンシーズ)
6. (これ)(教科書(きょうかしょ))(ようこそ)

練習 4

Make a dialogue, following the example.

[例]　ブラウンさんはカワムラさんのクラスメートです。→
—ブラウンさんという人を知(し)っていますか。
—ええ、カワムラさんのクラスメートです。

1. アコードは日本の車(くるま)です。
2. 東京(とうきょう)大学はブラウンさんの大学です。
3. ラッキーマートはブラウンさんの近所(きんじょ)のスーパーです。
4. おでんは日本の食べ物(もの)です。
5. しょうゆは日本の調味料(ちょうみりょう)です。

おでん is a Japanese stew of vegetables, fish rolls, tofu, and hard-boiled eggs.

練習 5

Rewrite these direct quotation sentences into their indirect quotation equivalents.

[例] かれは「そのメロンが好きです。」と言いました。→
かれはそのメロンが好きだと言いました。

1. 町田さんは「レストランへ行きました。」と言った。
2. チンさんはわたしに「中国語を教(おし)えています。」と言いました。
3. カワムラさんは「ハンバーガーが好きですか。」と聞きました。
4. テレビのレポーターは「ハワイはとても暑いですよ。」と言っています。
5. 林(はやし)さんは「英語(えいご)が話せません。」と言った。
6. 山口さんは「毎日料理(りょうり)しました。」と言いました。
7. 山本(やまもと)さんは「新聞(しんぶん)を読んでいません。」と言いました。
8. カーティスさんは「昼ごはんを食べましたか。」と聞いた。
9. ギブソンさんは「二十日(はつか)は土曜日です。」と言いました。
10. ブラウンさんは「雨の日が好きではありません。」といつも言っています。

練習 6

Complete the following sentences by inserting a statement likely to be uttered in the given context.

[例] (今は夏です。)
カワムラさんは「　　」と言いました。→
カワムラさんは「サーフィンをしましょう。」と言いました。

1. (ここはレストランです。)
山口さんは「　　」と言いました。
2. (ここは図書館(としょかん)です。)
カーティスさんは「　　」と言いました。
3. (ここはクラスです。)
チンさんは「　　」と言いました。
4. (今は朝の6時です。)
三村(みむら)さんは「　　」と言いました。
5. (今は夜の11時です。)
町田さんは「　　」と言いました。

37. Expressing Intention: つもり and the Volitional Form of Verbs

ブラウン：町田さん、昼ごはんはどうするつもりですか。
町田：ええと、カフェテリアで食べるつもりです。ブラウンさんは。
ブラウン：学校の外で食べようと思います。カフェテリアには
あきましたから…
町田：そうですね。私も学校の外で食べようかなあ…

ブラウン：高田さん、明日、うちで夕ごはんを食べませんか。
ビーフ・シチューを作(つく)るつもりなんです。
高田：本当ですか。うれしいなあ。ブラウンさんは料理(りょうり)が上手だから。
ブラウン：山本さんも呼(よ)ぼうと思うんです。
高田：それはもっとうれしいなあ。

37.1 One way to express one's intention is with this construction. (つもり is a noun meaning *plan, intention.*)

Dictionary form of verb + つもりだ (つもりです)

to intend to . . . or to plan to . . .

毎日野菜(やさい)を食べるつもりです。
I intend to eat vegetables every day.

チンさんの誕生日(たんじょうび)にすしを作(つく)るつもりです。
I plan to make sushi for Ms. Chin's birthday.

37.2 Another way to express one's intention is with the following construction. Here the intention is weaker and more tentative.

Plain, volitional form of verbs + と思(おも)う (と思います)

BROWN: Ms. Machida, what are you planning to do about lunch? MACHIDA: Uh . . . I'm planning to eat at the cafeteria. What about you? BROWN: I'm thinking of eating off campus (*lit., outside school*). I'm tired of the cafeteria. MACHIDA: You're right. Maybe I should eat off campus, too. . . .

BROWN: Mr. Takada, would you like to have dinner at my home tomorrow? I'm planning to make beef stew. TAKADA: Really? I'd be happy to! You're a good cook. (*lit., I'm so happy! Because you're good at cooking.*) BROWN: I'm thinking of inviting Ms. Yamamoto, too. TAKADA: That makes me (even) happier.

to think one will (do) . . . or to think of (doing) . . .

The plain, volitional form of verbs is formed in the following way.

CLASS 1 VERBS	CLASS 2 VERBS	CLASS 3 VERBS
Root + the o-column **hiragana** corresponding to the dictionary ending + う	Root + よう	Irregular
買う → 買おう 書く → 書こう 話す → 話そう 立つ → 立とう 死ぬ → 死のう 読む → 読もう 乗る → 乗ろう 泳ぐ → 泳ごう	食べる → 食べよう 見る → 見よう 着る → 着よう	する → しよう 来る → 来よう

u-column	→	o-column
う	→	お
く	→	こ
す	→	そ
つ	→	と
ぬ	→	の
む	→	も
る	→	ろ
ぐ	→	ご

The polite, volitional form of verbs is what you know as the ましょう form of verbs (see **Grammar 15,** Chapter 3).

The ましょう form of verbs, as you will remember, is used to ask someone to do something with you or to offer to do something for someone.

PLAIN VOLITIONAL FORM	(POLITE VOLITIONAL FORM) ましょう FORM
一緒に昼ごはんを食べよう。 *Let's eat lunch together.*	一緒に昼ごはんを食べましょう。
わたしがその肉を買おう。 *I will buy that meat.*	わたしがその肉を買いましょう。

牛肉が安いので、スキヤキを作ろうと思います。
Since beef is cheap, I think I'll make sukiyaki.
そのレストラン・ガイドを読もうと思う。
I think I'll read that restaurant guide.

When you have had an intention for some time, use the volitional form of a verb + と思っています (と思っている) rather than と思います (と思う).

今度のデートにはあのレストランへ行こうと思っています。
I have been thinking of going to that restaurant on our next date.

37.3 To say you don't intend to do something, use either of the following constructions. The second is the stronger of the two.

37.35 To express dowt such as, what should I do
volitional verb + かなあ. . . .

何を食べようかなあ... what should I eat

nai form of verb + つもりだ (つもりです)

to intend not to (do) . . .

Dictionary form of verb + つもりはない (つもりはありません)

The nai form of a verb is the plain, nonpast, negative form of a verb.

to have no intention of (doing) . . .

あの辞書を買わないつもりです。
I intend not to buy that dictionary.

あの辞書を買うつもりはありません。
I have no intention of buying that dictionary.

37.4 As discussed before, the nonpast form of verbs can also express intention or will.

明日、カワムラさんと一緒に宿題をします。
Tomorrow I will do homework together with Mr. Kawamura.
Tomorrow I am going to do homework together with Mr. Kawamura.

This sentence implies that it has been decided to do homework together with Mr. Kawamura, so I intend to do so or I will do so. On the other hand,

明日、カワムラさんと一緒に宿題をするつもりです。

simply means: *I intend to do homework together with Mr. Kawamura tomorrow.*

コミュニケーション・ノート

Talking about Plans

You can ask about someone's plans with the following expressions.

明日何かするつもりですか。
Are you planning to do something tomorrow?

明日何をする予定ですか。
What are you planning to do tomorrow? (lit., Tomorrow, your schedule is to do what?)

You can state your own plans using ～つもりです, as discussed above.

映画に行くつもりです。
I am planning to go to the movies.

When you don't have any plans, you can say

予定はありません。
I don't have any plans.

別に何もしません。
I won't do anything in particular.

When you don't know what you are going to do or you would like to avoid answering specifically, just say

わかりません。
I don't know.

練習 1

Rewrite the following using the volitional form of the verb + と思います。

1. 朝早く起きる
2. 毎朝ジョギングをする
3. 朝ごはんを毎日食べる
4. コーヒーを飲むのをやめる (*stop, quit*)
5. スーパーで夕ごはんの材料 (*ingredients*) を買う

練習 2

Answer these questions.

Note that it is rude to ask your superior's intention using …つもりですか。You should use …おつもりですか, as in 何をするおつもりですか。

1. 今日の夕ごはんは何を食べるつもりですか。
2. 明日何をするつもりですか。
3. 今週の週末は何をしようと思いますか。
4. 今年の夏はどこかへ行くつもりですか。
5. 今年の冬休みは何をしようと思いますか。

練習 3

Make sentences based on the following table.

[例] 学校へ行くつもりでしたが、病気で家にいました。(*I planned to go to school, but I stayed home because of illness.*)

ORIGINAL INTENTION	ACTUAL RESULTS
go to school	stayed home because of illness
make sukiyaki	couldn't make it because there was no meat
buy pork	couldn't buy any because I didn't have the money
call Ms. Brown	forgot
go hiking	couldn't go because of rain

Study Hint

How to Remember Verb Conjugations

The verb conjugation system of Japanese is simple compared with, say, Latin or Greek. Basically, only two Class 3 verbs, する and 来る, are irregular verbs whose conjugation you have to memorize. For Class 2 verbs, auxiliary verb endings and other expressions are attached to the root (i.e., the dictionary form minus る: 食べ for 食べる、見 for 見る). The conjugation of Class 1 verbs may seem somewhat complicated, but there is some regularity. Look at the following chart of Class 1 verb conjugations.

	書く	話す	立（た）つ	読む	乗（の）る	泳（およ）ぐ
PLAIN, NEGATIVE, NONPAST	書かない	話さない	立たない	読まない	乗らない	泳がない
POLITE, AFFIRMATIVE, NONPAST	書きます	話します	立ちます	読みます	乗ります	泳ぎます
DICTIONARY FORM	書く	話す	立つ	読む	乗る	泳ぐ
IMPERATIVE FORM	書け	話せ	立て	読め	乗れ	泳げ
VOLITIONAL FORM	書こう	話そう	立とう	読もう	乗ろう	泳ごう

Notice that the sequence of sounds following the root of each verb follows the same sequence of the Japanese syllabary: *a, i, u, e, o*. It's easy to learn these conjugated forms of Class 1 verbs by studying what vowel comes after the root for each form. (You will study the imperative form later.)

38. The Te-Form of Verbs + Verbs みる、しまう、いく、and くる

カワムラ：インドネシア・レストランへ行ったことがありますか。
ブラウン：いいえ、一度もありません。
カワムラ：じゃあ、行ってみましょうか。
ブラウン：ええ、いいですね。

KAWAMURA: Have you ever been to an Indonesian restaurant? BROWN: No, I haven't been even once. KAWAMURA: Well then, shall we go and see (what it's like)? BROWN: Yes, that would be good.

カワムラ：今日、あのレストランはあいているでしょうか。
山田：さあ、わかりませんね。
カワムラ：電話(でんわ)をして、聞いてみましょう。
山口：ぼくが電話をしてみます。

カーティス：夕ごはんは食べましたか。
林(はやし)：ええ、もう食べてしまいました。
カーティス：そうですか。それはざんねんですね。
ピザを買ってきたんですが、…
林：まだ、食べられますよ。お皿(さら)を持(も)ってきます。

ギブソン：コンサートは何時からですか。
林(はやし)：7時からです。
ギブソン：じゃあ、夕ごはんを食べていきましょう。
林：うん、そうしましょう。

38.1 The te-form of a verb is combined with other verbs to express several important meanings in Japanese. In this section, you will study four of these combinations. The te-form of a verb ＋ みる means *to do (something) in order to see what happens or what it's like*. Sometimes this translates as *to try* in the sense of *to sample (something)* or *to give (something) a try*.

Note: When used with the te-form of verbs, these four verbs are written in **hiragana**, not **kanji**.

一度すしを食べてみました。
I ate some sushi to see what it's like.
I tried sushi once.
そこへ行ってみましょう。
Let's go there and see what it's like.
そのお酒(さけ)を飲んでみたが、味(あじ)は悪(わる)かった。
I tried some of that liquor, and (lit., but) it tasted bad.

38.2 The te-form of a verb ＋ しまう means *to finish doing (something)*. In other words, it is used to express the completion of an action or an event. This construction focuses on the completed state of an action or an event.

Another way to say *to finish doing* is the conjunctive form of a verb ＋ 終(お)わる: 食べ終わる (*to finish eating*). By the way, the meaning *to start doing* is expressed by the conjunctive form of a verb ＋ 始(はじ)める: 飲み始める (*to start drinking*).

KAWAMURA: Is that restaurant open today do you think? YAMAGUCHI: Hmm, I don't know. KAWAMURA: Let's call and ask. YAMAGUCHI: I'll call and see.

CURTIS: Have you eaten dinner? HAYASHI: Yes, I already ate. CURTIS: Oh really? That's too bad. I went and bought a pizza but . . . (I guess you don't want any). HAYASHI: I still have room, you know. (*lit., I still can eat.*) I'll bring a plate.

GIBSON: What time does the concert start? (*lit., From what time is the concert?*) HAYASHI: It starts at seven o'clock. (*lit., It's from seven o'clock.*) GIBSON: Well then, let's eat dinner and then go. HAYASHI: Yeah, let's do that.

わたしはもう宿題をしてしまいました。
I already finished doing my homework.
そのアイスクリームはぜんぶ食べてしまった。
I ate all of that ice cream.

文法ノート

もう and まだ

When the adverb もう is used in affirmative sentences, it means *already, yet.*

もう5時になりましたか。
Is it five o'clock yet? (lit., Did it already become five o'clock?)
ええ、もう5時15分です。
Yes, it's already 5:15.

When used in negative sentences, もう means *anymore.*

もうあのレストランへは行きません。サービスが本当に悪いんですから。
I won't go to that restaurant anymore. Because the service is really bad.

The adverb まだ, on the other hand, means *still* in affirmative sentences.

まだ時間がありますか。
Is there still time?
林さんはまだ寝ていますよ。多分疲れているんでしょう。
Mr. Hayashi is still sleeping. Maybe he is tired.

まだ means (*not*) *yet* in negative sentences.

三村さんはまだ来ていません。寝坊したんでしょう。
Mr. Mimura has not come in yet. He probably overslept.
日本へはまだ行ったことがありません。
I haven't been to Japan yet.

The usages of もう and まだ are summarized in the following table.

	AFFIRMATIVE	NEGATIVE
もう	already, yet	(not) any more, any longer
まだ	still	not yet

しまう itself is a Class 1 verb and conjugates as such.

This construction sometimes implies that something happened that should not have happened or someone did something that should not have been done. In these cases, this construction implies the speaker's or the agent's regret.

わたしは妹(いもうと)のデザートを食べてしまった。
I ate my sister's dessert (*by mistake*).

10時まで寝(ね)てしまいました。
I slept until ten o'clock.

It depends on the context which of the two meanings しまう expresses.

38.3 The te-form of a verb + いく has the following meanings.

1. to do something and then leave that place

   山田さんは父(ちち)と話していきました。
   Ms. Yamada talked with my father and then left.
   夕ごはんを食べていきましょう。
   Let's eat dinner and then go.

2. to do something in a direction moving away from the speaker's or subject's current location (or away from the speaker's or subject's location before the action began)

   わたしは学校(がっこう)へ走(はし)っていきました。
   I ran to school (said when at home).

3. some currently ongoing action or state will keep changing into the future

   コンピュータはどんどん小さくなっていく。
   Computers will get smaller and smaller rapidly.
   この映画はこれからおもしろくなっていきますよ。
   This movie will get interesting from this point on.

38.4 The te-form of a verb + くる can mean the following.

1. to do something and then come toward the speaker

   山田さんは朝ごはんを食べてきました。
   Mr. Yamada ate breakfast and then came here.
   母(はは)は学校(がっこう)でわたしの先生と話してきました。
   My mother talked with my teacher at school and then came here.
   スーパーに行って、リンゴを買ってきてください。
   Please go to a supermarket and buy apples (*and then, come back here*).

2. to do something in a direction moving toward the speaker's current location

   わたしは学校(がっこう)へ歩(ある)いてきました。
   I walked to school (said when at school).

3. some action or event begins or is in progress

わたしは少し日本語がわかってきました。
I have started understanding Japanese a little. (or, *I have come to understand a little Japanese.*)

雨が降ってきた。
It has started raining.

Both te-form ＋ いく and te-form ＋ くる express ongoing actions or events, as illustrated in the third definition of each form. In deciding which to use, take into consideration these nuance differences: くる is more subjective and personal, whereas いく is more objective and impersonal. In other words, くる indicates more physical or psychological involvement on the part of the speaker.

言語ノート

行くと来る

行く and 来る do not necessarily correspond to English *to come* and *to go*. For example, when called in English, you might respond *I'm coming*. In Japanese, however, you would respond すぐ行きます (*I'll go right away*). 行く is used when the speaker, or someone or something else, moves away from the speaker's current position. On the other hand, 来る is used when the speaker, or someone or something else, moves to the speaker's current position.

練習 1

Make dialogues using the te-form of the verb in parentheses ＋ みる. Be creative!

[例] そのステーキはおいしいですか。(食べる)→
—そのステーキはおいしいですか。
—食べてみてください。*or* ちょっと食べてみます。

1. この問題 (*question*) がわかりますか。(聞く)
2. ペプシとコークとどちらがおいしいですか。(飲む)
3. 明日、山田さんが来ます。(会う)
4. これが料理の本です。(作る)
5. これはとてもおもしろい本ですよ。(読む)
6. あのレストランはおいしいですよ。(行く)

練習　2

Make a dialogue by using the te-form of the verb + しまう.

[例]　(あの本)(読む)
—あの本はどうしましたか。(*What happened to that book?*)
—もう読んでしまいました。

1. (カワムラさん)(帰(かえ)る)
2. (昨日買(か)ったアイスクリーム)(食べる)
3. (手紙(てがみ))(書く)
4. (ビデオ)(見る)
5. (ウイスキー)(飲む)
6. (宿題(しゅくだい) [*homework*])(する)
7. (ナイフとフォーク)(洗(あら)う)
8. (チンさんのバースデー・ケーキ)(買(か)う)

練習　3

Make dialogues using the te-form of the verb + いく.

[例]　コンサートまでまだ時間がありますよ。(ショーウインドーを見る)→
—コンサートまでまだ時間がありますよ。
—じゃあ、ショーウインドーをちょっと見ていきましょう。

1. 安(やす)いりんごがありますよ。(買(か)う)
2. 今日は寒いですよ。(セーターを着(き)る)
3. もう12時ですね。(昼ごはんを食べる)
4. もう1時ですよ。ミーティングは1時15分からですよ。(走(はし)る)
5. カーティスさんがいますよ。(話す)
6. つかれましたね。(*I'm tired, aren't you?*)　(休む)
7. 新(あたら)しいCDがありますよ。(聞く)
8. ビールがたくさんあります。どうぞ。(*Please . . . [have some].*)　(飲む)

練習　4

Make dialogues using the te-form of the verb + くる.

[例]　ペンはありますか。(買(か)う)→
—ペンはありますか。
—ええ、買(か)ってきました。

1. 一緒に夕ごはんを食べませんか。(食べる)
2. 山田さんと話しましたか。(話す)
3. 日本語は勉強しましたか。(教科書を読む)
4. 肉はありますか。(買う)
5. 早かったですね。(*You are early, aren't you?*) (走る)
6. 顔 (*face*) が赤いですね。(お酒を飲む)
7. 山下さんは家にいますか。(3時に帰る)
8. なぜわらっているんですか。(*Why are you laughing?*)
(おもしろい映画を見る)

39. Expressing Simultaneous Actions: 〜ながら

カワムラ：おなかがすきましたね。お昼ごはんにしましょうか。
町田：ええ、そうしましょう。ここにすわりましょう。
カワムラ：外のけしきを見ながら、食べられますね。
町田：そうですね。

To express two actions taking place simultaneously, use 〜ながら (*while*) in this construction.

Clause 1: conjunctive form of a verb	+	ながら,	Clause 2

The agent of the two actions must be identical. Thus, although you can use this construction to say *While studying, I ate,* you cannot use it to say *While my wife was talking on the phone, I was cooking dinner*. Notice that in English the clause beginning with while (the subordinate action) usually comes last.

コーヒーを飲みながら、ブラウンさんと話した。
I talked with Ms. Brown while drinking coffee.
レコードを聞きながら、朝ごはんを食べましょう。
Let's eat breakfast while listening to a record.

KAWAMURA: I'm hungry, aren't you? Shall we have lunch? (*lit., Shall we make it lunch?*) MACHIDA: Yes, let's do that. Let's sit here. KAWAMURA: We can eat while looking at the scenery outdoors, can't we? MACHIDA: Yes.

練習

Join the clauses into a complete sentence using ～ながら.

[例] (ポップコーンを食べた)(本を読む)→
ポップコーンを食べながら、本を読んだ。

1. (ワインを飲む)(ステーキを食べた)
2. (町を歩(ある)く)(写真(しゃしん)をたくさん取りました)
3. (テレビを見る)(勉強(べんきょう)しました)
4. (メモ [*notes*] を取(と)る)(三村(みむら)さんの話を聞く)
5. (昼はアルバイトをする)(夜は学校(がっこう)へ行っています)

Vocabulary

Meals

おやつ		snack
きっさてん	喫茶店	coffee (tea) shop
ごはん		meal; cooked rice
しょくじ	食事	meal
しょくどう	食堂	dining hall
だいどころ	台所	kitchen
たべもの or たべもの	食べ物	food
ちゅうかりょうり	中華料理	Chinese cuisine
のみもの	飲み物	beverage
やしょく	夜食	evening snack
ようしょく	洋食	Western cuisine
りょうり	料理	cooking, cuisine
わしょく	和食	Japanese cuisine

Loanwords: キッチン、コック、スナック、デザート、ファーストフード、レストラン

Review: 朝ごはん、食べる、飲む、昼ごはん、夕ごはん、料理する

Foods

いか		cuttlefish	なし		pear
かい	貝	shellfish	にく	肉	meat
ぎゅうにく	牛肉	beef	にんじん		carrot
きゅうり		cucumber	ピーマン		green pepper
くだもの	果物	fruit	ぶたにく	豚肉	pork
こめ	米	rice (*uncooked*)	ぶどう		grape
さけ		salmon	まぐろ		tuna
じゃがいも		potato	まめ	豆	bean, pea
しょくりょうひん	食料品	foodstuffs	みかん		mandarin orange
たこ		octopus	やさい	野菜	vegetable
たまねぎ	玉ねぎ	onion	りんご		apple
とりにく	鳥肉	chicken			

Loanwords: スープ、トマト、パイナップル、バナナ、メロン、ラム、レタス、レモン

Review: 魚

Beverages

(お)さけ	(お)酒	liquor; sake	(お)みず	(お)水	water
(お)ちゃ	(お)茶	tea	ぎゅうにゅう	牛乳	milk
(お)ゆ	(お)湯	hot water, boiling water	コーヒー		coffee

Loanwords: ウイスキー、カクテル、ジュース、ビール、ミルク、ワイン

Taste and Flavors

あじ	味	taste	ちょうみりょう	調味料	seasoning
あじがいい	味がいい	to taste good	にがい		bitter
あじみする	味見する	to taste a sample	まずい		not tasty
あまい	甘い	sweet	みそ	味噌	miso
おいしい		delicious, tasty			
からい	辛い	spicy; hot (*spicy*); salty			
クッキングオイル		cooking oil			
こしょう	胡椒	pepper			
さとう	砂糖	sugar			
しお	塩	salt			
しおからい	塩辛い	salty			
しぶい	渋い	astringent			
しょうゆ	醤油	soy sauce			
す	酢	vinegar			
すっぱい	酸っぱい	sour			
ソース		*a prepared sauce (somewhat like steak sauce)*			

Other Words

ああ		like that
いう	言う	to say
おもう	思う	to think
おわる	終わる	to finish
こう		like this
…ことがある		to have done . . . , to have experience doing . . .
～すぎる		to do . . . too much, to be excessively . . .
そう		like that
～たい		to want to (do)
～たがる		to want to (do)
つかう	使う	to use
…つもりだ		to intend to...
～ていく		to do and leave
～てくる		to do and come
～てしまう		to complete
～てみる		to try to
と		(*quote marker*)
…という	と言う	to say that . . . ; called/named . . .
どう		how
…とおもう	と思う	to think that . . .
～ながら		while
…にする		to decide on
はじめる	始める	to start
ほしい		to want
ほしがる		to want
まだ		not yet
もう		already, yet
～ようとおもう	ようと思う	to think of (doing) . . .
よてい	予定	plan

Kanji

Learn these **kanji**.

思	湯	洋	茶	理
終	野	夜	酒	米
始	魚	言	牛	品
物	味	貝	鳥	和
肉	悪			
事	料			

Reading and Writing

Reading 1 バイキング料理「むらさき」

Before You Read

Work in pairs. Discuss with your partner what information is included in restaurant guides. Then look at the following words, which are commonly used in Japanese restaurant guides. Can you guess what each means?

営業時間
駐車場
料理
値段
休み
電話番号

Here are a few exercises to prepare you for new words in the reading.

1. As you have already studied, 英語 means *English language* in Japanese. An English-Japanese dictionary is called 英和辞典, while a Japanese-English dictionary is called 和英辞典. Now, what do you think 和食 means?
2. 和室 means *Japanese-style room*, while 洋室 means *Western-style room*. 和風 means *Japanese style*, whereas 洋風 means *Western style*. Now, what do you think 洋食 means?
3. Odd man out. Which word doesn't belong in each group?
   和食：てんぷら、すし、すきやき、野菜、豆腐
   洋食：ステーキ、箸、オムレツ、スパゲッティー
   サラダ：野菜、フルーツ、ピザ、シェフ、ポテト
   サラダドレッシング：イタリアン、フレンチ、ジュース、ビネガー
   デザート：チーズケーキ、アイスクリーム、パスタ、プリン
   果物：りんご、ナイフ、みかん、バナナ、メロン
   飲み物：お茶、コーヒー、スプーン、コーラ、ジュース

Now Read It!

レストラン・ガイド
バイキング料理「むらさき」

バイキング料理を食べたことはありますか。バイキング料理のレストランはたくさんあります。しかし、高くて、まずいのがふつうです。東京・上野にある「むらさき」はバイキング料理のレストランですが、ここの料理は安くて、おいしいことで有名です。昼ごはん、夕ごはんは、いつも満員です。

メニューはサラダ、スープ、和食、洋食、デザート、フルーツ、パン、ごはん、飲み物など、全部で150種類以上あります。サラダは、野菜サラダ、フルーツサラダ、ツナサラダ、エッグサラダなど。ドレッシングはフレンチ、イタリアン、和風、など。スープは野菜、オニオン、コーン、クラムチャウダー、コンソメなど。和食はてんぷら、すきやき、さしみ、すしなど20種類。洋食はステーキ、とんかつ、ハンバーグなど25種類。デザートはチーズケーキ、キャロットケーキ、プリン、アップルパイ、チョコレートケーキ、アイスクリームなどがあります。果物の好きな人はみかん、りんご、バナナ、パイナップル、パパイアなども食べられます。

値段は大人が4500円で、子供は1500円です。お酒は飲み放題で2000円です。日本酒、ウイスキー、赤ワイン、白ワイン、カクテル、ビールなどがあります。

日曜日午前9時から午後2時まではシャンペンを無料でサービスしています。場所は、上野デパートのとなり、上野駅から歩いて、10分で、とても便利です。駐車場は上野デパートの地下にあります。営業時間は火曜日から土曜日は午前11時から午後10時まで。日曜日は午前9時から午後9時まで。月曜日はお休みです。予約は(03)3781-3945まで。

バイキング料理 *all-you-can-eat dining (lit., Viking food)*
ふつう *usual*
上野 *Ueno (district in Tokyo)*
満員 *full capacity*
など *et cetera*
種類 *kinds, varieties*
〜以上 *more than . . .*
とんかつ *pork cutlet*
値段 *price, charge*
大人 *adult*
飲み放題 *all you can drink*
日本酒 *sake (lit., Japanese liquor)*
無料 *free of charge*
サービスする *to offer for free*
場所 *place, location*
駐車場 *parking lot* / 地下 *underground*
営業時間 *business hours (hours open to business)*
予約 *reservation*

After You Finish Reading

1. Lately, the number of foreign customers has been increasing at Murasaki restaurant. The owner has decided to produce a simple brochure about his restaurant in English. Help him compose the brochure by filling in the missing information in English.

RESTAURANT MURASAKI

All You Can Eat!

Price: Adult ¥

(all you can drink, additional ¥)

Child ¥

MENU

Salad:

Soup:

Main dishes: Japanese varieties Western varieties

Dessert:

Fruit:

Alcoholic Beverages:

Business Hours: Tue – Sat from to
Sun from to
(free champagne from to)
Closed Monday

Location: next to

Parking:

---

2. You work for Murasaki. One of your jobs is to answer questions telephoned in by potential customers. How do you respond to these questions?
   a. 場所はどこですか。
   b. 営業時間は何時から何時までですか。
   c. バイキングの値段はいくらですか。
   d. 和食はどんなものがありますか。
   e. 洋食は何種類ありますか。
   f. サラダはどんなものがありますか。
   g. お酒は無料ですか。
   h. 日曜日はあいています (*open*) か。
   i. 駐車場はありますか。
   j. 休みは何曜日ですか。

Writing 1

Using the following brochure, write down a short description of this restaurant.

ホテル東京　レストラン・やまと
朝食(ちょうしょく)食べ放題（ビュッフェ・スタイル）
日曜日午前9時から午後3時まで

大人1500円（シャンペン無料）
子供800円

メニュー

フルーツ：　オレンジ、バナナ、パイナップル、メロン
サラダ：　シェフ・サラダ
スープ：　オニオン、コーン、野菜、チキン・ヌードル
：　パン、卵(たまご)料理、ベーコン、ソーセージ、フライド・ポテト
デザート：　チーズケーキ、アイスクリーム、プリン、パイ

Reading 2 あなたの食事(しょくじ)チェック

Before You Read

Work in pairs and discuss the following with your partner.

1. What time do people generally eat the following meals or snacks?
   a. 朝ごはん
   b. 昼ごはん
   c. おやつ
   d. 夕ごはん
   e. 夜食(やしょく)
2. What do you usually eat for each of the above meals? Are your meals well balanced?

Now Read It!

A Japanese women's weekly magazine runs a column called "Check Your Diet," in which a dietitian analyzes the diet of a chosen reader. Last month, Hitomi Machida was interviewed for this section.

あなたの食事チェック

町田ひとみ（20）学生

今週の「あなたの食事チェック」は東京大学でフランス文学を専攻している町田ひとみさんです。町田さんは東京の三鷹にご両親と住んでいます。趣味は料理で、一週間に3回ぐらい夕ごはんを作ります。

朝ごはん	6:45 a.m. 家で パン、牛乳、ジュース、バナナ
昼ごはん	12:00 大学のカフェテリアで ポークソテー、サラダ、ヨーグルト、 コンソメ・スープ、パン
おやつ	3:00 p.m. 喫茶店で コーヒー、チーズケーキ
夕ごはん	7:00 p.m. 家で ごはん、みそ汁、漬物、サラダ、 クリーム・シチュー、みかん
夜のおやつ	ポップコーン、コーヒー
カロリー	2865 Kcal

「町田さんの話」　最近、太ってきたので、食事の量を少なくしています。でも、2月24日は、とてもおなかがすいていたので、ちょっと食べ過ぎたと思います。前は、一日3回ごはんを食べていましたが、今は一回で、朝ごはんと昼ごはんはパンを食べています。和食より洋食のほうが好きなので、昼ごはんも夕ごはんも洋食が多いです。母も働いているので、インスタント食品、冷凍食品、テークアウト、外食も増えてきました。一日にコーヒーを4杯飲むので、少なくしたいと思っています。

「栄養士・金井さと子先生の話」　町田さんの食事はバランスがとてもいいと思います。昼ごはんも肉を食べていますが、サラダを食べているので、問題はありません。コーヒーの飲みすぎはよくありませんね。

After You Finish Reading

You interviewed Hitomi Machida for the magazine column. Answer Ms. Kanai's questions about Ms. Machida, following the example.

[例]　どこに住んでいますか。→
—どこに住んでいますか。
—三鷹に住んでいると言いました。

1. 趣味は何ですか。
2. 一週間に何回ぐらい夕ごはんを作りますか。
3. 2月24日の朝ごはんに何を食べましたか。
4. 昼ごはんはどこで食べましたか。
5. 2月24日は食べすぎたと思いますか。
6. ごはんは一日何回食べていますか。
7. 和食と洋食、どちらが好きですか。
8. インスタント食品をよく食べますか。
9. コーヒーを一日何杯（なんばい）(*glassfuls*) 飲みますか。

Work in pairs. Ask your partner what he or she ate yesterday. Do you think your partner's meals are well balanced?

Writing 2

Write a short paragraph about your eating habits, meals, and so on. Cover at least the following points.

1. what you usually eat
2. your favorite foods
3. foods you don't like
4. whether you drink coffee a lot
5. whether you eat instant foods or frozen foods a lot

Language Functions and Situations

Asking and Expressing Opinions

台所(だいどころ)で

カワムラ：この肉(にく)、どう思(おも)いますか。
町田：新(あたら)しくて、いい肉だと思います。いくらでしたか。
カワムラ：ええと、100 g 千円(せんえん)でした。
町田：ええ！ちょっと高すぎると思いませんか。
カワムラ：そうですか。

ギブソン：林(はやし)さんをどう思(おも)いますか。
町田：そうですね。とてもやさしい人だと思います。
ギブソン：ハンサムだと思いますか。
町田：さあ…

In the kitchen KAWAMURA: What do you think of this meat? MACHIDA: I think it tastes good and fresh. (*lit., I think it's fresh, good meat.*) How much was it? KAWAMURA: Uh, it was 1,000 yen per 100 grams. MACHIDA: What? Don't you think that's a bit too expensive? KAWAMURA: Do you think so? (*lit., Is that so?*)

GIBSON: What do you think of Mr. Hayashi? MACHIDA: Hmm. I think he's very sweet. GIBSON: Do you think he's handsome? MACHIDA: Hmm . . . .

Role Play

Work with a partner. One of you is a reporter and the other is a restaurant critic. The reporter asks for the critic's opinion of a certain local restaurant. The reporter must ask about price, what dishes are served, whether the service is good, whether alcoholic beverages are available, and so on. The reporter should take notes.

At a Restaurant

ウェイター：いらっしゃいませ。メニューをどうぞ。
カワムラ：どうも。
ウェイター：ご注文（ちゅうもん）は。
カワムラ：サラダとステーキをお願（ねが）いします。
ウェイター：はい。お飲み物（もの）は。
カワムラ：赤（あか）ワインをお願いします。
ウェイター：デザートは。
カワムラ：いいえ、けっこうです。
ウェイター：かしこまりました。

ウェイター：ステーキです。どうぞ。
カワムラ：お勘定（かんじょう）をお願いします。

コミュニケーション・ノート

Useful Expressions When Dining Out

Here are some expressions that are useful in restaurants.

6時に予約（よやく）があります。
I have a reservation for six o'clock.
四人ですが、テーブルはありますか。
I'd like a table for four. (lit., We're four, but do you have a table [to accommodate us] ?)
どんな飲み物（もの）がありますか。
What kinds of drinks do you have?
注文（ちゅうもん）したいんですが、…。
Can I order now? (lit., I want to order but. . . .)

WAITER: Welcome. Here is a menu. KAWAMURA: Thank you. WAITER: May I have your order? KAWAMURA: I would like a salad and steak. WAITER: Yes. How about a drink? KAWAMURA: I would like red wine. WAITER: How about dessert? KAWAMURA: No, thank you. WAITER: As you wish, (*lit., Certainly.*) . . . WAITER: Here is your steak . . . . KAWAMURA: I would like the bill, please.

今日は何がおいしいですか。
What is good today?
サラダはけっこうです。
No salad, thank you.
初(はじ)めに、スープをお願(ねが)いします。
I'd like to start with soup.
お水をお願(ねが)いします。
May I have some water?
すきやきにします。
I'll have sukiyaki.
デザートは後でお願いします。
I'd like dessert later.
メニューを見せてください。
Would you bring me a menu? (lit., Please show me a menu.)

Role Play

You are at a restaurant with several classmates. One of you is the waiter or waitress and the others are customers. Use the menu below to order your meal.

イタリア料理の店　ミラノ

メニュー

<u>サラダ</u>

アンティパスタ（コンビネーション、二人前）	1600
シーザーサラダ	760
シーフードサラダ（いか、たこ、えび、貝）	850
パイナップルとアーモンドのサラダ	670

<u>スープ</u>

ミネストローネスープ	350
ポタージュ	400

<u>パスタ</u>

シーフードスパゲッティ	780
ミートボールスパゲッティ	760
カルボナーダ	690
ラザーニャ	800
トルテリーニ（ペストソース付き）	730
ラビオリ	780

<u>ピザ</u>

ミラノオリジナルピザ	760
ペパローニピザ	710
ハワイアンピザ	820
シーフードピザ	840
ベジタリアンピザ	650

<u>ピラフ</u>

シーフードピラフ	680
ドリア（ライスグラタン）	660

<u>ディナーセット</u>

（ディナーセットにはサラダかスープ、ライスかパン、アイスクリーム、コーヒーが付きます。）

Aセット（イタリア風ステーキ）	4500
Bセット（えびのクリームソース煮）	3800
Cセット（ポテトグラタン）	3200

<u>デザート</u>

ティラミス	390
ナポリタンアイスクリーム	290
ビスコーティ（3種類のクッキー）	330
エクレア	390
ナポレオン	360
アマレートチーズケーキ	400

<u>飲み物</u>

（ブレンドコーヒーとアメリカンコーヒーは、おかわり自由です。）

ブレンドコーヒー	350
アメリカンコーヒー	370
紅茶（レモン・ミルク）	350
カプチーノ	450
エスプレーソ	450
カフェオーレ	400
ウインナーコーヒー	430
オレンジスカッシュ	450
レモンスカッシュ	470
ミルク（アイス・ホット）	350
ミネラルウオーター	500
ビール　中	680
大	900
ワイン（赤・ロゼ・白）	700
アマレート	600
キアンティ	700

Listening Comprehension

Ms. Yamamoto and Ms. Okada are talking about the eating habits of Japanese while looking at the results of a recent survey. While listening to their conversation, fill in the following table. Their conversation won't provide exhaustive information, so you won't be able to fill in all the blanks.

	RANK AND PERCENTAGE				
	1 (%)	2 (%)	3 (%)	4 (%)	5 (%)
What kind of cuisine do Japanese like most?					
What kind of food do Japanese cook most?					
What food do Japanese children like most?					
What foods don't Japanese children like?					
What beverages do Japanese children drink most?					

7

第七章

買(か)い物(もの)

Shopping

今日は新宿にショッピングに来ました。

OBJECTIVES

Topics

Shops and stores
Shopping
Buying clothes

Grammar

40. Saying when something happens: temporal clauses ending in 時
41. Indefinite pronoun の
42. The ～たら conditional
43. Using the particle に to express purpose
44. Reporting hearsay: …そうだ
45. Saying whether or not something is true: …かどうか
46. Giving reasons with …し、…し

Reading and Writing

Grand opening sale at Sun Road
My fashion

Language Functions and Situations

Shopping
Saying whether two things are the same or different

Vocabulary and Oral Activities

Vocabulary: Shops and Stores

ショッピング		shopping
売る	うる	to sell
買う	かう	to buy
商店街	しょうてんがい	shopping mall, shopping street
店	みせ	store, shop
市場	いちば	market, marketplace
肉屋	にくや	butcher shop
魚屋	さかなや	fish store
八百屋	やおや	vegetable store, green grocer's
果物屋	くだものや	fruit store
パン屋	パンや	bakery
ケーキ屋	ケーキや	pastry shop

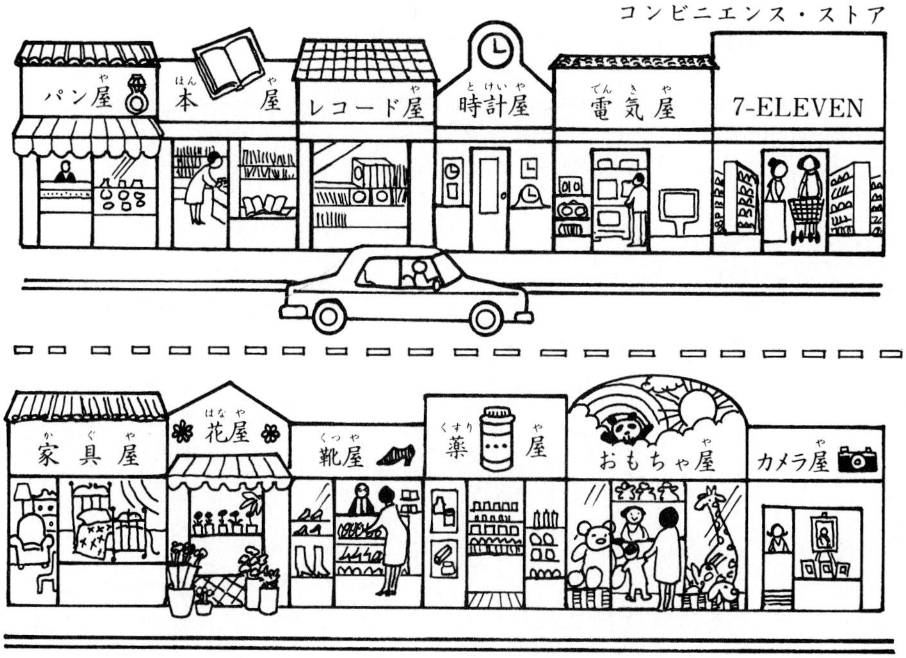

酒屋	さかや	liquor store
本屋	ほんや	bookstore
文房具屋	ぶんぼうぐや	stationery store
レコード屋	レコードや	record store, music store
時計屋	とけいや	watch shop
電気屋	でんきや	electric appliance store
家具屋	かぐや	furniture shop
花屋	はなや	flower shop, florist
靴屋	くつや	shoe store
薬屋、薬局	くすりや、やっきょく	drugstore, pharmacy
眼鏡屋	めがねや	eyeglasses store, optician's
クリーニング屋	クリーニングや	dry cleaner's
カメラ屋	カメラや	camera shop

Review: 買い物、スーパー、デパート

言語ノート

屋 (や) と店 (てん)

Shop names ending in 屋 (や) are also used to refer to the shop owners or salespeople working at the shops. For example, the owner of a 時計屋 (とけいや) (*watch store*) may be called 時計屋 or 時計屋さん. Use the politer さん to those in the watch vendor's in-group (including him). As in English, in Japanese you can say 肉屋 (にくや) に行った (*I went to the butcher shop*) or 肉屋さんに行った (*I went to the butcher's*) with no change in meaning. The 屋 of a store name can sometimes be replaced with 店 (*shop*). For example, レコード屋 and レコード店 (レコードてん) are both used to mean *record store*. Unlike 屋, however, shop names ending in 店 (てん) cannot be used to refer to a person at the shop.

アクティビティー 1

どこにいますか。(*Where are you?*)

Where are you when you say this? Match the statement with the appropriate store.

1. ______ このバッファリンはいくらですか。
2. ______ このスカート、ドライ・クリーニングお願いします。
3. ______ このスニーカーのサイズは何センチですか。
4. ______ 日本語の教科書はありますか。

a. 文房具屋
b. 果物屋
c. 本屋
d. ケーキ屋
e. レコード屋

For ～すぎる、refer to **Grammar 35,** Chapter 6.

5. ＿＿このサングラス、ちょっと大きすぎますね。
6. ＿＿明日は「母の日」ですから、カーネションを買いましょう。
7. ＿＿今日はバナナが安いですね。
8. ＿＿そのチーズケーキ二つとアップルパイ三つください。
9. ＿＿U2の新しいCDはありますか。
10. ＿＿鉛筆10本ください。

f. 花屋
g. 薬屋
h. 眼鏡屋
i. クリーニング屋
j. 靴屋

アクティビティー 2

Review the potential form of verbs (**Grammar 28,** Chapter 5) and the te-form ＋ います construction (**Grammar 29,** Chapter 5).

どこで買えますか。どこで売っていますか。(*Where can you buy them? Where do they sell them?*)

Tell where you can buy these things. Which item in each group is not available there?

1. りんご、みかん、バナナ、トースター、パイナップル
2. レタス、キャベツ、いす、じゃがいも、にんじん
3. 牛肉、マトン、鳥肉、豚肉、ケーキ
4. アスピリン、バンドエイド、ハンマー、ワセリン、ダイバー
5. ベーゲル、クロワッサン、フランスパン、ブーツ、サンドイッチ
6. ウイスキー、酒、米、ビール、ワイン
7. テレビ、ドレス、ラジオ、テープ・レコーダー、ステレオ
8. 辞書、雑誌、まんが (*comic books*)、本、時計

アクティビティー 3

(勉) Study Grammar 40.

ダイアログ：ケーキ屋さんに行った時、金井さんに会いました。(*When I went to the pastry shop, I saw Mr. Kanai.*)

カワムラ：昨日、ケーキ屋さんに行った時、金井さんに会いました。
山口：そうですか。
カワムラ：バースデー・ケーキを買っていましたよ。
山口：だれかの誕生日だったんでしょう。

Practice the dialogue, substituting the following words for the first and second underlined portions. Change the third underlined portion on your own.

1. カメラ屋　フィルム
2. おもちゃ屋　プラモデル (*plastic model*)

KAWAMURA: When I went to the pastry shop yesterday, I saw Mr. Kanai. YAMAGUCHI: Is that right? KAWAMURA: He was buying a birthday cake. YAMAGUCHI: It was probably someone's birthday.

3. 本屋　ガイドブック
4. レコード屋　クラシック音楽のレコード
5. 文房具屋　ノート

Vocabulary Library

More Stores

米屋	こめや	rice dealer
食料品店	しょくりょうひんてん	grocery store
金物屋	かなものや	hardware store
洋品店	ようひんてん	Western clothing store
婦人服店	ふじんふくてん	women's wear store
ふとん屋	ふとんや	futon store
呉服屋	ごふくや	kimono store
化粧品店	けしょうひんてん	cosmetics store
床屋	とこや	barbershop
美容院	びよういん	beauty parlor
お菓子屋	おかしや	confectionery shop sweet shop
おもちゃ屋	おもちゃや	toy store

Loanwords: コンビニエンス・ストア、ブティック

アクティビティー 4

こんな時、どこへ行きますか。(*Where do you go on this occasion?*)

On these occasions, what store do you go to?

[例] おなかがすきました。ポテトチップがほしいです。→
ポテトチップがほしい時は、スーパーに行きます。

1. 今夜はすきやきが食べたいんですが…
2. うちの時計(とけい)がこわれました (*is broken*)。
3. 頭(あたま)がいたいんですが… (*my head hurts . . .*)
4. 野菜ジュースを作りたいんですが…
5. 夏だから、髪(かみ) (*hair*) をみじかく切(き)りたい (*want to cut*) んですが…
6. 今夜はすしを作りましょう。
7. 明日、パーティーをします。
8. デザイナーズ・ブランドのドレスがほしいんですが…
9. ペンのインキがもうありません。
10. このスカート、きたないですね。

Useful vocabulary: 持(も)っていく *to take*

Vocabulary: Colors

色	いろ	color
白、白い	しろ、しろい	white
黒、黒い	くろ、くろい	black
赤、赤い	あか、あかい	red
青、青い	あお、あおい	blue
黄色、黄色い	きいろ、きいろい	yellow
緑	みどり	green
茶色、茶色い	ちゃいろ、ちゃいろい	brown (*lit., tea color*)
灰色	はいいろ	gray
水色	みずいろ	light blue (*lit., water color*)
派手(な)	はで(な)	bright, gaudy
地味(な)	じみ(な)	quiet (*in color*)
暗い	くらい	dark
明るい	あかるい	light, bright
薄い	うすい	light (*in color*), pale
濃い	こい	dark (*in color*), deep

Note: Where two words are given for a color, the first is a noun, and the second is an i-adjective.

アクティビティー 5

Association:

What color(s) do you associate with the following?

1. お金
2. アメリカ
3. 冬
4. 夏
5. 秋
6. 日本
7. りんご
8. レモン
9. 夢(*dream*)
10. 愛(*love*)
11. 情熱(*passion*)
12. 嫉妬(*envy*)
13. 結婚(*marriage*)

文化ノート

色(いろ): *Colors*

Learning a foreign language means learning to see the world in a new way. The color spectrum provides a good example of this. In Japanese the color 青(あお) encompasses both blue and green. This color is used in such set phrases as 青空(あおぞら: *blue sky*) and 青信号(あおしんごう: *green light, in a traffic signal*). Nowadays, distinction is often made between green and blue with 緑(みどり) or グリーン used to indicate green and 青 meaning blue. 緑 is the same word used to name the national holiday 緑の日 (みどりのひ: *Greenery Day*) and symbolizes greenery, nature, and the environment. Other color symbolism includes the combination of red and white to represent festivity or congratulations. Black and white combined are used in decorations for funerals.

In another shift of the color spectrum, blue movies are known as ピンク映画 (ピンクえいが) in Japan. A number of colors derive their names from the environment. 茶色 (ちゃいろ: *brown*) literally means tea color, 灰色 (はいいろ: *gray*) literally translates as ash color, 桃色 (ももいろ: *pink*) is peach color, and so on. Notice that in traditional kimono as well as Western fashions, bright colors are considered suitable for wear by children and young women, but in general the older one gets, the more subdued are the colors one is expected to wear, with the elderly wearing muted tones of brown, gray, and navy.

hat color do you like?)

子きですか。
「か。
色ですか。
んな色ですか。
ですか。
ですか。
「か。
ですか。
)(*thing*)はありますか。
)はありますか。

Vocabulary Library

More Colors

藍色	あいいろ	indigo blue	金色	きんいろ	gold
クリーム色	クリームいろ	cream-colored	銀色	ぎんいろ	silver
オレンジ色	オレンジいろ	orange	透明(な)	とうめい(な)	transparent
紫	むらさき	purple			

Loanwords: ブルー、ダークブルー、ライトブルー、グリーン、ピンク、グレー

(勉) Study Grammar 41.

アクティビティー 7

ダイアログ：この赤(あか)いのはどうですか。(*How about this red one?*)

ブラウン：この白(しろ)いブラウスはいくらですか。
店員(てんいん)：9500円でございます。
ブラウン：もっと<u>安(やす)い</u>のはありますか。
店員：では、<u>この赤い</u>のはどうでしょうか。7600円でございます。

てございます is a very polite form of です. Note that the shop clerk is using a very polite level of speech with the customer.

Practice the dialogue, substituting the following for the underlined portions.

1. はでな　　　　このピンク
2. 小さい　　　　あの青(あお)い
3. フォーマルな　あのケースの中にある
4. カジュアルな　その白いブラウスの右にある

Vocabulary: Shopping

バーゲンセール		bargain sale	領収書	りょうしゅうしょ	receipt (*usually handwritten*)
(お)客(さん)	(お)きゃく(さん)	customer	レシート		receipt (*usually printed by cash registers*)
主人	しゅじん	store owner	レジ		cash register, cashier
店員	てんいん	store clerk			
値段	ねだん	price			
おつり		change			
お金	おかね	money			
払う	はらう	to pay			

Review: 安い、高い

BROWN: How much is this white blouse? CLERK: It's 9,500 yen. BROWN: Do you have a <u>cheaper</u> one? CLERK: Well, how about <u>this red</u> one? It's 7,600 yen.

アクティビティー 8

いくらですか。(*How much is it?*)

Look at the illustration and answer the following questions.

1. 大きいアルバムはいくらですか。小さいのはいくらですか。
2. 日本製の万年筆 (*fountain pen*) はいくらですか。ドイツ製のはいくらですか。
3. 日本製の万年筆の下にあるかばんはいくらですか。カウンターのうしろにあるのはいくらですか。
4. ショーケースの上にあるボールペンはいくらですか。ブラウンさんが持っているのはいくらですか。
5. ショーケースの中にあるワープロはいくらですか。カワムラさんが見ているのはいくらですか。

(country name) 製 (の) means *made in . . .* For example, フランス製 means *made in France.*

Handling Japanese Money

The denominations of coins currently circulated in Japan are 1 yen, 5 yen, 10 yen, 50 yen, 100 yen, and 500 yen. 5-yen and 50-yen coins have a hole in the middle. The denominations of Japanese bills are 1,000 yen, 5,000 yen, and 10,000 yen. The portraits on these bills are of Soseki Natsume, a writer in the Meiji era (1868–1912), for the 1,000-yen bill, Inazo Nitobe, a diplomat in the Meiji era, for the 5,000-yen bill, and Yukichi Hukuzawa, an educator in the same era, for the 10,000-yen bill.

Traditionally, Japanese people have considered it improper to talk about or show money in public, so when they give or return money, it is likely to be in an envelope. If they don't have an envelope, they might say はだかで申し訳(もうしわけ)ありません (*Sorry about the naked money*). When Japanese count out change, they use subtraction rather than addition. Thus, when you pay 5,000 yen for a 4,300-yen item, the shop clerk gives you 700 yen after subtracting 4,300 yen from 5,000 yen. The shop clerk says something like

> 4,300円です。5,000円頂戴(ちょうだい)いたします。700円のおつりでございます。
>
> *That's 4,300 yen.* (Then, on receiving the customer's money) *I have received 5,000 yen . . . . Here is your change, 700 yen.*

In most stores and shops the clerks use a tray to return change to you.

日本のお金

Vocabulary Library

More on Shopping

商品	しょうひん	goods, merchandise

Customer Service

セール		sale
売り出し	うりだし	bargain sale
見本	みほん	sample items
包み紙	つつみがみ	wrapping paper
包む	つつむ	to wrap
サービス		something given for free (*lit., service*)
広告	こうこく	advertisement
注文(する)	ちゅうもん(する)	order (*n.*); (to order)
配達(する)	はいたつ(する)	delivery; (to deliver)
返品(する)	へんぴん(する)	returned merchandise; (to return merchandise)

Loanwords: カタログ、ショーウインドー、メールオーダー

Paying

価格	かかく	price
値切る	ねぎる	to haggle over price
請求書	せいきゅうしょ	bill
現金	げんきん	cash
分割払い	ぶんかつばらい	installment purchase
割引(する)	わりびき(する)	discount (*n.*); (to discount)

Loanwords: クレジットカード

アクティビティー 9

ショッピングが好きですか。(*Do you like shopping?*)

Discuss in class.

1. ショッピングが好きですか。
2. バーゲンセールによく行きますか。
3. バーゲンセールでは何%の割引(わりびき) (*discount*) がありますか。
4. 現金(げんきん) (*cash*) で買い物をしますか。クレジットカードで買い物をしますか。
5. クレジットカードを何枚持(も)っています (*have*) か。どんなカードを持っていますか。
6. 買ったものを返品(へんぴん)した (*returned*) ことがありますか。
7. どんなものを分割払(ぶんかつばら)い (*on installment*) で買いますか。
8. どんなものをメールオーダーで買いますか。

勉 Study Grammar 42.

アクティビティー 10

ダイアログ：安かったら買うんですが。(*If it were cheaper, I would buy it.*)

ブティックで

町田：あのセーターいいですね。
ブラウン：ええ、きれいな色ですね。買わないんですか。
町田：ええ、もう少し安かったら、買うんですが…
ブラウン：そうですね。2万円はちょっと高すぎますね。

Practice the dialogue, substituting the following words in Machida's role. Make up appropriate substitutions for the underlined portions of Brown's role.

1. 冷蔵庫、もう少し小さい
2. スカート、サイズが大きい
3. ステレオ、CDプレーヤーがついている (*a CD player is attached*)
4. コンピュータ、もう少しメモリーが大きい
5. ワープロ、日本語が使える
6. バッグ、違う色
7. スポーツ・カー、お金がある

アクティビティー 11

えり好みするお客さん (*Picky shoppers*)

Look at the following illustrations. Under what circumstances would you buy each item?

[例]　1万円だったら、買います。

1

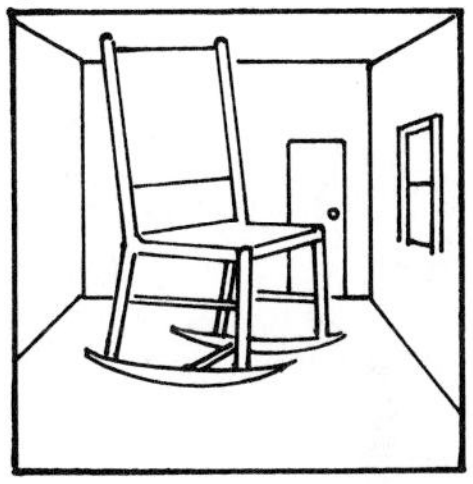

2

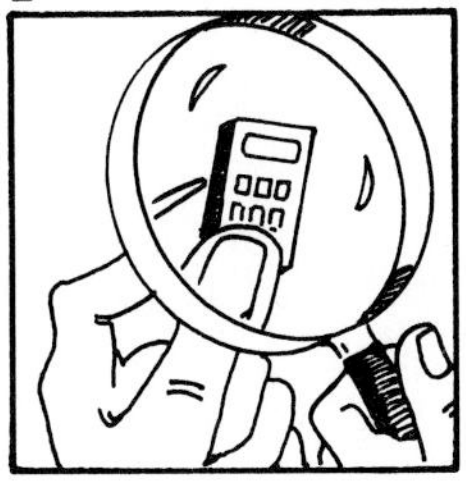

3

4

5

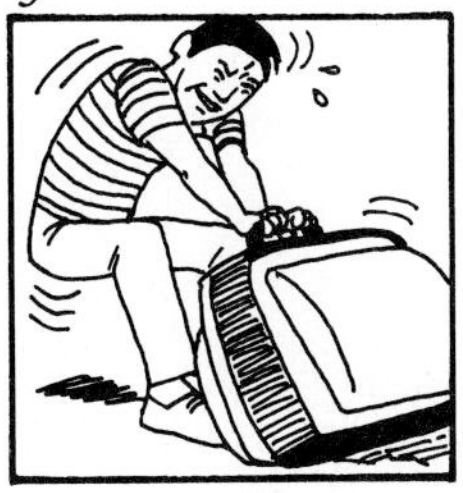

6

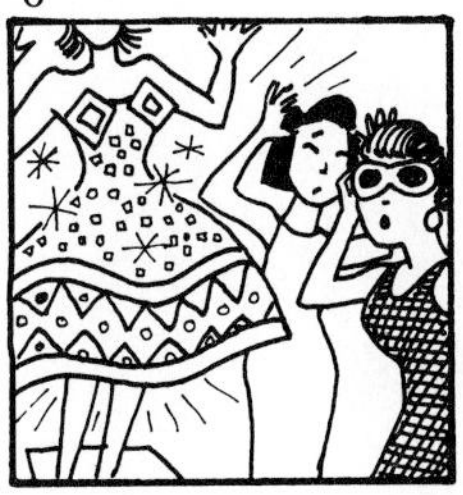

At a boutique MACHIDA: That sweater is nice, isn't it? BROWN: Yes, it's a pretty color, isn't it? Aren't you going to buy it? MACHIDA: No. If it were a little cheaper, I would buy it . . . . BROWN: That's true. Twenty thousand yen is a bit expensive.

Vocabulary: Clothes

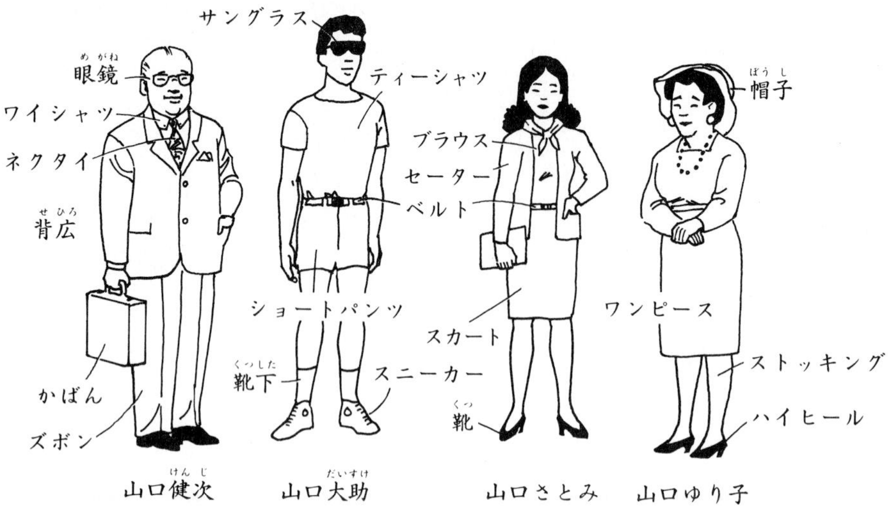

着る	きる	to wear; to put on
はく		to wear; to put on (*your legs or feet; pants, shoes, etc.*)
かぶる		to wear; to put on (*your head; hats, helmets, etc.*)
つける		to wear; to put on (*things that need attaching; earrings, bras, etc.*)
脱ぐ	ぬぐ	to take off
洋服	ようふく	Western-style clothes
和服	わふく	Japanese-style clothes
着物	きもの	kimono
背広	せびろ	suit
ワイシャツ		(men's) dress shirt (*lit., white shirt*)
ネクタイ		necktie
ドレス		dress
ワンピース		dress (*lit., one piece*)
セーター		sweater
ブラウス		blouse
マフラー		muffler
ハンカチ		handkerchief
眼鏡	めがね	glasses
サングラス	サングラス	sunglasses
ズボン		trousers
スカート		skirt
コート		coat
下着	したぎ	underwear

シャツ		shirt
パンツ		briefs (*lit., pants*)
パンティー		panties
ブラジャー		bra (*lit., brassiere*)
パジャマ		pajamas
ネグリジェ		negligee
水着	みずぎ	bathing suit
靴	くつ	shoe
ブーツ		boot
靴下	くつした	sock
ストッキング		stockings (*especially women's*)
帽子	ぼうし	hat, cap
ベルト		belt
スポーツウェア		sportswear
ティーシャツ		T-shirt
ジーンズ、ジーパン		jeans
ショートパンツ		shorts

アクティビティー 12

どんなお天気ですか。 (*What is the weather like?*)

Review vocabulary relating to weather and climate (p. 219).

What is the weather like in each city, if the following are descriptions of appropriate dress?

1. 東京(とうきょう)：道子(みちこ)さんはレインコートを着(き)ています。傘(かさ)もさしています。(*She is using an umbrella, too.*) いいお天気ですか。お天気が悪(わる)いですか。
2. 札幌(さっぽろ)：吉田(よしだ)さんはあついコートを着ています。スノーブーツもはいています。帽子もかぶっています。夏ですか。冬ですか。何が降(ふ)っていますか。
3. 熊本(くまもと)：金井(かない)さんはショートパンツをはいています。半袖(はんそで) (*short sleeves*) のシャツを着ています。サンダルをはいています。夏ですか。冬ですか。暑いですか。寒いですか。
4. 岡山(おかやま)：友子(ともこ)さんはブラウスを着ています。ジャケットもコートも着ていません。どんな季節(きせつ)ですか。寒いですか。
5. 金沢(かなざわ)：山下(やました)さんはセーターを着ています。そして、その上に、ジャケットを着ています。暑いですか。寒いですか。

Vocabulary Library

More on Clothes

Clothing

衣服	いふく	clothes
長袖(の)	ながそで(の)	long sleeves (*n.*); (long-sleeved)
半袖(の)	はんそで(の)	short sleeves (*n.*); (short-sleeved)
上着	うわぎ	jacket, suitcoat
制服	せいふく	uniform
手袋	てぶくろ	gloves
着替える	きがえる	to change clothes

Loanwords: サンダル、スリッパ、ポケット

Accessories

指輪	ゆびわ	ring

Loanwords: イヤリング、ネックレス、ピアス (*pierced earring*)、ブレスレット、ブローチ (*brooch*)

Fashion

Loanwords: ファッション、ファッション・ショー、モデル、デザイン、デザイナー

Sewing

縫う	ぬう	to sew
繕う	つくろう	to mend
編む	あむ	to knit
ミシンをかける		to use a sewing machine
はさみ		scissors
糸	いと	thread
針	はり	needle
アイロンをかける		to iron
ファスナー		zipper
ボタン		button

シャツにアイロンをかける
to iron a shirt

Fabric and Fiber

絹	きぬ	silk	縞	しま	stripe
綿	めん	cotton	模様	もよう	pattern
毛皮	けがわ	fur	厚い	あつい	thick
無地	むじ	plain (*no pattern*), solid color	薄い	うすい	thin

Loanwords: ウール、ストライプ、チェック、ナイロン、プリント、ポリエステル

アクティビティー 13

何を着ますか。(*What are you going to wear?*)

Tell what you will wear on the following days.

1. 今は五月です。春です。いいお天気です。暖かいです。
2. 今は十二月です。今日はスキーへ行きます。
3. 今は八月です。夏です。とてもむし暑いです。わたしは日本の会社 (*company*) のサラリーマンです。
4. 今は八月です。今日もむし暑いです。今日は休みです。海へ行きます。
5. 今は六月です。梅雨の季節です。毎日雨が降ります。デパートへ買い物に行きます。
6. 今は十月です。秋です。昼は暖かいですが、夜はちょっと寒いです。
7. 今は三月です。まだ、寒いです。雨も時々降ります。

言語ノート

着る、はく、かぶる、つける

Japanese use different verbs meaning *to put on or wear*, depending on what part of the body the clothing is worn on or how the item is attached. Study the chart that follows. 着(き)る is a general term that includes items worn on the torso or upper torso, such as dresses or shirts. はく covers items worn on the legs or feet, such as slacks or socks. Headgear requires the verb かぶる. Items for the hand, such as gloves or rings, call for はめる.

ITEMS	TO PUT ON OR WEAR	TO TAKE OFF
背広 ワンピース セーター 上着 シャツ コート 着物	**(on torso)** 着る	脱ぐ
ズボン スカート ジーンズ 靴 靴下	**(on legs or feet)** はく	

ITEMS	TO PUT ON OR WEAR	TO TAKE OFF
帽子(ぼうし) ヘルメット	**(on head)** かぶる	脱(ぬ)ぐ、取(と)る
ネクタイ	しめる	取(と)る、はずす
ベルト ブラジャー 時計(とけい) イヤリング	**(accessories; things that need "attaching")** する つける	
指輪(ゆびわ)	**(on hands or fingers)** はめる	
眼鏡(めがね)	かける (*lit., to hang on*)	

アクティビティー 14

ダイアログ: はいてみますか。(*Will you try them on?*)

ブラウン：どの靴(くつ)がいいでしょうか。
店員(てんいん)：これはいかがでしょうか。
ブラウン：そうですね。
店員：ちょっとはいてみますか。
ブラウン：ええ。

Practice the dialogue, substituting the following items. Change the underlined verb (*put on*) as appropriate.

1. ワンピース
2. スカート
3. 指輪(ゆびわ) (*ring*)
4. 眼鏡(めがね)
5. セーター
6. ブーツ
7. 帽子(ぼうし)

BROWN: Which shoes do you recommend (*lit., are good*)? CLERK: How about these? BROWN: Hmm . . . CLERK: Will you try them on? BROWN: Yes.

アクティビティー 15

ファッション・ショー！ (*Fashion show!*)

Work in pairs. You will describe what your partner is wearing today. But first, ask several questions about your partner's clothing.

[例] 町田さんは今日(きょう)はピンクと白のブラウスを着(き)ています。このブラウスは去年(きょねん)の誕生日(たんじょうび)のプレゼントでした。町田さんが今日はいているスカートは今年の三月に伊勢丹(いせたん)デパートで買いました。町田さんがはいている赤(あか)のハイヒールはイタリア製(せい)です。町田さんがしているイヤリングとネックレスはパールです。

(勉) Study Grammar 44.

アクティビティー 16

ダイアログ：ワープロを見に行くんです。(*I will go look at word processors.*)

アパートの前で

高田：ブラウンさんもお出かけですか。

ブラウン：ええ、本屋(ほんや)へ雑誌(ざっし)を買(か)いに行ってきます。高田さんは。

高田：ぼくは電気屋(でんきや)にワープロを見にいくんです。

ブラウン：同(おな)じ方向(ほうこう)ですね。一緒(いっしょ)に行きましょうか。

高田：ええ、そうしましょう。

Practice the dialogue substituting the following stores or places for 本屋 and 電気屋. Change the rest of the underlined phrases appropriately.

1. パン屋　　家具屋(かぐや)
2. 肉屋(にくや)　　レストラン
3. 図書館(としょかん)　　銀行(ぎんこう)

Useful expressions: 本を借(か)りる／返(かえ)す *to borrow/return a book,* お金をおろす *to withdraw money,* 貯金(ちょきん)をする *to deposit money*

4. 郵便局(ゆうびんきょく)　　映画館(えいがかん)

Useful expression: 手紙(てがみ)を出す *to mail a letter*

5. スーパー　　コンビニエンス・ストア

In front of the apartment TAKADA: Are you also going out? BROWN: Yes, I am going to the bookstore to buy a magazine. What about you? TAKADA: I am going to an electric appliance shop to look at word processors. BROWN: We're going in the same direction, aren't we? (*lit., It's the same direction, isn't it?*) Shall we go together? TAKADA: Yes, let's do that.

(勉) Study Grammar 44 and 45.

アクティビティー 17

ダイアログ：とても安(やす)かったそうです。(*I heard that it was very inexpensive.*)

町田：ギブソンさんのあのセーター、とてもいいデザインですね。
ブラウン：ええ、昨日、近所(きんじょ)のブティックで買(か)ったそうです。
町田：高かったでしょうね。
ブラウン：いいえ、バーゲンセールで、とても安かったそうです。
町田：本当(ほんとう)ですか。わたしもほしいわ。
ブラウン：じゃ、まだバーゲンセールをしているかどうか聞(き)いてみましょう。

言語ノート

Sentence-Final Particles

You have already studied that some important meanings such as interrogatives and speaker's emotions and attitudes are expressed by sentence-final particles. In the preceding dialogue, わ in わたしもほしいわ is the particle used by female speakers to express their admiration, desire, or surprise; to try to convince the hearer of their claim or judgment; or to confirm their judgment. In this context, male speakers would say ぼくもほしいな(あ). な(あ) is a sentence-final particle expressing exclamation, desire, or wish and can be used by both male and female speakers. These sentence-final particles are more often used in colloquial speech than in formal speech.

As students in Professor Yokoi's class get acquainted with each other and come to feel closer to each other, their speech style will change to more informal, colloquial speech and diversified sentence-final particles will be used. You will learn them gradually in Volume Two.

アクティビティー 18

家計簿(かけいぼ) (*Household accounts log*)

Work in a group of three. Here is Mrs. Yamaguchi's log where she keeps track of household expenses. First, Student 1 asks Student 2 the following questions, as in the first part of the example. Then, Student 3 asks Student 1 the same questions, as in the second part of the example.

MACHIDA: That sweater of Ms. Gibson's has a very good design, doesn't it? BROWN: Yes, I heard that she bought it at a boutique in her neighborhood yesterday. MACHIDA: It must have been expensive. (*lit., It probably was expensive, huh?*) BROWN: No, I heard that, due to a sale, it was very inexpensive. MACHIDA: Really? I want (to get) one, too. BROWN: Then, let's ask (Ms. Gibson) whether or not the sale is still going on (and see what she says).

8月 August	15日（土） 日（ ） 旧暦6月21日 自由日付欄		16日（日） 日（ ） 旧暦6月22日		17日（月） 日（ ） 旧暦6月23日	
	品　目	金額 (千 百 十)	品　目	金額 (千 百 十)	品　目	金額 (千 百 十)
収　入						
レシート添付欄						
肉・魚 乳製品類	牛肉 100g 560円× 400g	2240				
野菜類	レタス1つ150円 ×2つ トマト100g60円 ×400g	300 240				
調味料 その他の食品	りんご100g230円 ×300g	690				
副食計		3470				
主　食						
外　食						
嗜好品	ビール1本560円 ×6本	3360				
食費合計		6830				
住居・備品						
光熱・水道						
衣　服						
医療・衛生	バンドエイド	480				
教　育						
教養・娯楽	本2冊	1950				
交　際						
交通・通信	切手	560				
花	ダリア	420				
貯蓄・保険						
支出合計						
現在高						
クレジット使用控え						
★印の料理は、巻頭に写真と作り方つき	スパゲッティ　★夏野菜のスープ煮　卵サラダ（レタス・胡瓜）		冷凍いかとセロリの中国風うま煮　辛子あえ（げそ・胡瓜）　高野豆腐の煮物		かき玉汁　鶏ささ身とえびのくず打ち　なすとピーマンの醤油炒め	
日記欄	明日から18日までサミットストアでセール。 明日，バナナ，スイートコーン，パン 牛乳を買う。		カワムラさん，夜出かける。 さとみ，20日まで長野でキャンプ。		南さんと銀座でショッピング。	

[例]

S1: りんごは100gいくらでしたか。

S2: 100g 230円（えん）でした。

S3: りんごは100gいくらでしたか。

S1: 100g 230円だったそうです。

1. 肉屋（にくや）で何を買（か）いましたか。
2. 花屋（はなや）で何を買いましたか。
3. 八百屋（やおや）で何を買いましたか。
4. 酒屋（さかや）でビールを何本買いましたか。一本いくらでしたか。
5. バンドエイドはいくらでしたか。
6. 明日何を買うつもりですか。
7. サミットストアのセールはいつからいつまでですか。

文化ノート

Metric System

Japanese use the metric system of measurement. Instead of pounds and ounces, grams (g) and kilograms (kg) are used to quantify weight. Liquids (milk, gasoline, rainwater, etc.) are measured in cubic centimeters (cc) and liters (l). When measuring linear distance, Japanese use centimeters (cm), meters (m), and kilometers (km). Here is a conversion table for figuring metric measurements from those used in the United States.

インチ (*inch*) × 2.54 = センチ (メートル) (*cm*)
フィート (*feet*) × 0.31 = メートル (*m*)
マイル (*mile*) × 1.61 = キロ (メートル) (*km*)
オンス (*oz*) × 28 = グラム (*g*)
ポンド (*lb*) × 0.45 = キロ (グラム) (*kg*)

Now answer these questions.

あなたは何キログラムありますか。

あなたの家から大学(だいがく)まで何キロメートルありますか。

あなたの身長(しんちょう) (*height*) は何センチメートルですか。

アクティビティー 19

インタビュー

Work in pairs. Follow these instructions, and report the results to class later.

1. 買(か)い物(もの)が好きかどうか聞(き)いてください。
2. 昨日、買い物に行ったかどうか聞いてください。
3. クレジットカードをよく使(つか)うかどうか聞いてください。
4. 今、クレジットカードを持(も)っている (*is carrying*) かどうか聞いてください。
5. 今、現金(げんきん)を持っているかどうか聞いてください。
6. 今日か明日、買い物に行くつもりかどうか聞いてください。
7. バーゲンセールの時によく買い物をするかどうか聞いてください。
8. 洋服(ようふく)にたくさんお金をかける (*to spend*) かどうか聞いてください。
9. 1万ドル以上(いじょう)のものを買ったことがあるかどうか聞いてください。

〜以上 *equal to or more than . . .*

(勉) Study Grammar 46.

アクティビティー 20

ダイアログ：軽(かる)いし、はきやすいし…(*They are light and easy to wear. . . .*)

店員：この靴(くつ)はいかがでしょうか。
三村：ううん、なかなかいいですね。
店員：ええ、軽いし、はきやすいし、申(もう)し分(ぶん)ありません。
三村：じゃあ、これをください。

Practice the dialogue, substituting the following.

1. ジャケット　デザインもいいし、着(き)やすいし
2. カメラ　オートマチックだし、小さいし
3. エアコン (air conditioner)　音(おと) (*sound*) が静(しず)かだし、リモコン (*remote control*) だし
4. ワープロ　ポータブルだし、使(つか)いやすい(*easy to use*) し
5. 帽子(ぼうし)　色(いろ)もきれいだし、デザインもいいし

文法ノート

～やすい、～にくい

やすい and にくい are i-adjectives meaning *easy* and *hard* respectively. They are used in the following construction.

Conjunctive form of verb + やすい (*easy to . . .*) or にくい (*difficult, hard to . . .*)

このぺんは書きやすいです。
This pen is easy to write with.
山下さんは話しにくい。
Mr. Yamashita is hard to talk to.
このサンドイッチは食べにくいです。
This sandwich is hard to eat.
これは使(つか)いやすいアイロンですね。
This is an easy-to-use iron.
あれは持(も)ちにくいバッグですね。
This is a hard-to-carry bag.

CLERK: How about these shoes? MIMURA: Hmm. They are quite nice. CLERK: Yes. They are lightweight and easy to wear. . . . They are perfect. (*lit., There is nothing to say against them.*) MIMURA: Then, I will take them.

このシャツは着やすい。
This shirt is easy to wear (i.e., comfortable).
この靴ははきにくい。
These shoes are hard to put on.

Grammar and Exercises

40. Saying When Something Happens: Temporal Clauses Ending in 時

山口：ちょっと買い物に行ってきます。
カワムラ：あっ、ぼくもすぐ出かけるつもりです。
山口：じゃあ、出かける時、鍵をかけていってください。
カワムラ：わかりました。

ブラウン：きれいなブラウスですね。
町田：このあいだ、デパートでセールがあった時、買ったんです。
ブラウン：町田さんはよく買い物に行くんですか。
町田：ええ、今度行く時、ブラウンさんもさそいましょう。

カーティス：林さん暇な時は、何をしますか。
林：天気がいい時は、散歩します。天気が悪い時は、うちで本を読みます。

YAMAGUCHI: I'm going out shopping. KAWAMURA: Oh, I'm planning to go out in a moment, too. YAMAGUCHI: Then, please lock the door when you leave. KAWAMURA: OK. (*lit., I understood.*)

BROWN: That's a pretty blouse. MACHIDA: I bought it the other day when there was a sale at the department store. BROWN: Do you go shopping often? MACHIDA: Yes, I'll invite you along next time I go.

CURTIS: What do you do when you have free time? HAYASHI: When the weather is good, I take a walk. When the weather is bad, I read books at home.

文法ノート

だけ

だけ is a particle meaning *only*, *just*, *alone*. As seen in the following examples, it modifies the preceding noun (or pronoun).

薬局ではアスピリンだけ(を)買った。
I bought only aspirin at the drugstore.
ブラウンさんだけ(が)来ました。
Only Ms. Brown came.

Only the particles は、が、and を can follow だけ in standard speech. Note that these sentences including だけ can be rewritten by using しか + negative.

薬局ではアスピリンしか買わなかった。
ブラウンさんしか来ませんでした。

だけ also can modify a clause or a sentence. For example

聞いただけです。
I just asked. (*i.e., All I did was ask.*)
チーズケーキを買っただけです。
I just bought cheesecake. (*i.e. All I did was buy cheesecake.*)

41.2 Note that the indefinite pronoun の is different from the possessive particle の (**Grammar 2**, Chapter 1) and the nominalizer の (**Grammar 26**, Chapter 5).

POSSESSIVE PARTICLE

ブラウンさんのネックレスはきれいですね。
Your (lit., Ms. Brown's) necklace is pretty, isn't it?
ブラウンさんのはきれいですね。
Yours (lit., Ms. Brown's) is pretty, isn't it? (omission of ネックレス)

INDEFINITE PRONOUN

黒い靴がほしいです。
I want black shoes.
黒いのがほしいです。
I want black ones. (の *refers to shoes.*)

NOMINALIZER

ギブソンさんが帽子を買ったのを知っていますか。
Do you know that Ms. Gibson bought a hat?

INDEFINITE PRONOUNS

ギブソンさんが買ったのは何ですか。
What is it (lit., the one) that Ms. Gibson bought?

練習 1

Following the example, make dialogues.

[例]　ケーキ、甘い、甘くない→
　A: すみません。ケーキをください。
　B: 甘いのがいいですか。甘くないのがいいですか。
　A: 甘いのをおねがいします。

1. スカート、長い、短い
2. テープレコーダー、大きい、小さい
3. アイロン、重い (*heavy*)、軽い (*lightweight*)
4. ネクタイ、派手、地味
5. リボン、黒い、赤い

練習 2

Rewrite the second sentence of each question using the indefinite pronoun の.

[例]　小さい車がいいです。→小さいのがいいです。

1. その赤いセーターはいいですね。でも、この黒いセーターはわたしには似合いません (*doesn't suit*) ね。
2. この紙はちょっとうすい (*thin*) ですね。あつい (*thick*) 紙はありますか。
3. このアパートは不便です。もっと便利なアパートを探しましょう。(探す *to look for*)
4. こんなブランドは聞いたことがありません。有名なブランドはありますか。
5. このカレーはからすぎます。からくないカレーがあちらにありますから、それを食べましょう。

練習 3

Following the example, change these sentences using the indefinite pronoun の.

[例]　昨日、わたしがスーパーへ行きました。→
　昨日、わたしが行ったのはスーパーです。
　山口さんは、わたしの右にいます。→わたしの右にいるのは山口さんです。

1. 先週ブラウスを買いました。
2. あの店でおいしいケーキを売っています。

3. わたしがブラウンさんに電話しました。
4. 昨日、林さんはステーキを食べました。
5. この本はたいへん有名です。
6. 東京の電車はとても便利です。

42. Making If-Then Statements: The たら Conditional

カワムラ：ブラウンさんはまだ来ませんか。
林：ええ、まだです。おそいですね。
カワムラ：タクシーだったら、10分もかからないんですがね…
林：おかしいですね。
カワムラ：とにかく、来たら、すぐ教えてください。

カワムラ：あの車、いいですね。
チン：ええ、お金があったら、買うんですが…
カワムラ：もう少し安かったら、ぼくも買いたいんですがね…
チン：カワムラさん、そんなにお金があるんですか。

カワムラ：三村さんのアパートは駅に近くて便利ですね。
三村：ええ。でも、もう少し新しかったら、いいんですが…
カワムラ：そんなに古くないでしょう。
三村：それに、となりの人が静かだったら、もっといいんですが…

42.1 *If it rains, I will stay at home* is called a conditional sentence. In such a sentence, the clause introduced by *if* expresses the condition under which the second clause will occur. The first *if* clause is usually called the conditional clause, and the other is called the resultant clause. There are several types of conditionals in Japanese; you will study them gradually. The one presented here, the たら conditional, is used to express a simple relationship between a conditional clause and the resultant clause.

KAWAMURA: Hasn't Ms. Brown arrived yet? HAYASHI: No, not yet. She's late, isn't she? KAWAMURA: If she used a taxi, it wouldn't take even ten minutes. . . . HAYASHI: Something's not right. (*lit., It's strange, isn't it.*) KAWAMURA: Anyway, when she comes, please let me know immediately.

KAWAMURA: That's a great car, isn't it! CHIN: Yes, if I had the money, I'd buy it but. . . . KAWAMURA: If it were a little cheaper, I would like to buy it, too. CHIN: Mr. Kawamura, do you have that much money?

KAWAMURA: Your apartment is conveniently close to the station, isn't it? MIMURA: Yes. But I wish it were a little newer. (*lit., But if it were a little newer, it would be good, but. . . .*) KAWAMURA: It's not that old, is it? MIMURA: Besides, I wish the neighbors were quiet. (*lit., If the people next door were quiet, it would be nicer.*)

CONDITIONAL CLAUSE			
	Affirmative	**Negative**	
Verb I-adjective Na-adjective Copula	the past, plain form + ら	the past, plain, negative form + ら	+ RESULTANT CLAUSE

The conditional clause is often preceded by もしも or, more commonly, もし (*if, supposing*), both of which emphasize the suppositional nature of the clause.

雨が降ったら、ハイキングには行きません。
If it rains, I won't go hiking.
もしそこにブラウンさんがいなかったら、お金を払えませんでした。
If Ms. Brown had not been there, I would not have been able to pay (lit., the money).
もし暑かったら、窓を開けてください。
If you are hot, please open the window.
そんなに寒くなかったら、外で食べましょう。
If it is not that cold, let's eat outside.
もっと元気だったら、みんなと山へ行くんですが…
If I were healthier, I would go to the mountains with everyone.
大切でなかったら、読みません。
If it is not important, I don't read it.
わたしが林さんだったら、ギブソンさんにプロポーズします。
If I were Mr. Hayashi, I would propose to Ms. Gibson.
もしそれが絹ではなかったら、店に返します。
If it is not silk, I will return it to the store.

42.2 This conditional is typically used when the resultant clause expresses a request, suggestion, permission, volition, or prohibition.

買い物から帰ったら、勉強しましょう。
Let's study after we return from shopping.
新しい靴を買ったら、見せてください。
If you buy a new pair of shoes, please show them to me.

42.3 This conditional may be used to express a hypothetical situation.

お金があったら、いいコンピューターを買いたい。
If I had money, I would like to buy a good computer.

林(はやし)さんがもっとハンサムだったら、デートするんですが…
If Mr. Hayashi were more handsome, I would date him.

42.4 This conditional may be used to indicate actual (i.e., not hypothetical) sequences of actions or events. The resultant clause is commonly in the past tense. When used in this sense, 〜たら is similar to *when.*

林さんのアパートへ行ったら、ギブソンさんがいた。
When I went to Mr. Hayashi's apartment, Ms. Gibson was there.

42.5 The expression 〜たらいい can be used to express a wish, regret, suggestion, etc.

明日晴(は)れたらいいですね。
I hope the weather will be good tomorrow. (lit., It would be nice if it's clear tomorrow, wouldn't it?)
あなたもパーティーに来られたらよかったですね。
I wish you could have come to the party. (lit., It would have been nice if you too had been able to come to the party.)
土曜日、いいお天気だったら、ピクニックに行きませんか。
If the weather is good on Saturday, would you like to go on a picnic?

練習 1

Fill in the blanks with the たら form.

[例] (　　)、買(か)いましょう。(安(やす)い)→安かったら、買いましょう。

1. パーティーに(　　)、ブラウンさんに会った。(行く)
2. カーティスさんに(　　)、わかりますよ。(聞く)
3. (　　)、家にいます。(寒い)
4. あなたがステレオを(　　)、わたしも買(か)います。(買う)
5. ライトを(　　)、暗(くら)くなった。(消(け)す[*to turn off*])
6. その部屋(へや)が(　　)、そこで話しましょう。(静(しず)か)
7. 今、そこに家を(　　)、とても高いですよ。(たてる[*to build*])
8. チンさんが(　　)、教(おし)えてください。(来る)
9. その本が(　　)、かして(*lend*)ください。(おもしろい)

練習 2

Following the example, make hypothetical conditional sentences. Make up an appropriate final clause.

[例]　わたしは病気(びょうき)です。→もし病気(びょうき)でなかったら、学校へ行くでしょう。

1. 明日、試験(しけん)があります。
2. わたしは日本語が上手ではありません。
3. わたしはお金があまりありません。
4. わたしはステレオを持っていません。
5. 雨が降(ふ)っています。

練習　3

Make conditional sentences, following the example.

[例]　おなかがすく→おなかがすいたら、何か食べます。

1. マドンナが来る。
2. 6時になる。
3. 1万ドルある。
4. マイケル・ジャクソンから電話(でんわ)が来る。
5. そのコートが安(やす)い。
6. フランス語が上手だ。
7. 春が来る。
8. 車(くるま)がある。
9. 日本へ行く。

43. Going Somewhere with a Purpose: Using the Particle に to Express Purpose

カワムラ：林(はやし)さんはどこに行ったんですか。
ブラウン：花(はな)を買(か)いに行きました。
カワムラ：そうですか。チンさんは?
ブラウン：服(ふく)を着替(きが)えに、アパートに帰(かえ)りました。

山口：シンさんは何をしに来たのですか。
カワムラ：本を借(か)りに来たんです。
山口：そうですか。あの人も学生ですか。
カワムラ：ええ、日本文化(ぶんか)を勉強(べんきょう)しに来ているんです。

KAWAMURA: Where did Mr. Hayashi go?　BROWN: He went to buy flowers.　KAWAMURA: I see. What about Ms. Chin?　BROWN: She returned to her apartment to change clothes.

YAMAGUCHI: Why did Mr. Shin come here? (*lit., What did Mr. Shin come to do?*)　KAWAMURA: He came to borrow some books.　YAMAGUCHI: I see. Is he a student, too?　KAWAMURA: Yes, he came here to study Japanese culture.

In the following construction, the particle に expresses purpose. Here に corresponds to *to* or *in order to* in English.

Conjunctive form of a verb + the particle に + {
(motion verb)
行く *to go*
来る *to come*
帰(かえ)る *to return home*
もどる *to return*
出かける *to go out*
出る *to leave*
}

to go (come, etc.) in order to (do) . . .

テニスをしに行きませんか。
Shall we go play tennis? (lit., Won't you go to play tennis?)

ブラウンさんが本を返(かえ)しに来ました。
Ms. Brown came to return some books.

父は友人(ゆうじん)に会いに出かけました。
Father went out to see his friend.

高田さんは昼ごはんを食べに出ました。
Mr. Takada left to eat lunch.

練習 1

Following the example, combine two sentences into one.

[例] 山本(やまもと)さんは出かけました。カワムラさんに会います。→
山本さんはカワムラさんに会いに出かけました。

1. 三村(みむら)さんは行きました。電話(でんわ)をかけます。
2. ブラウンさんは出かける。スキーをします。
3. チンさんは来ました。カーティスさんと話します。
4. 山口さんとカワムラさんは行きました。映画(えいが)を見ます。
5. 山口さんは帰(かえ)りました。昼ごはんを食べます。
6. 町田さんはもどりました。服(ふく)を着(き)替(が)えます。

練習　2

Look at the picture and make a dialogue starting with 何をしに行きましたか.

[例]　—何をしに行きましたか。
　　　—コーヒーを飲みに行きました。

1

2

3

4

5

44. Reporting Hearsay: . . . そうだ

林(はやし)：ブラウンさんのアパートはとてもいいそうですね。
ブラウン：ええ、新(あたら)しいし、いいアパートですよ。
林：駅(えき)に近くて、便利(べんり)だそうですね。
ブラウン：ええ、駅から歩いて、5分です。

HAYASHI: I hear that your apartment is very nice.　BROWN: Yes, it's new and (thus) it's a good apartment.
HAYASHI: I hear that it is conveniently close to the station.　BROWN: Yes, it's five minutes from the station on foot.

ブラウン：伊勢丹デパートでセールがあるそうですよ。
ギブソン：本当ですか。
ブラウン：ええ、セーターやコートが40%引きだそうです。
ギブソン：わあ、今日の午後行ってみませんか。

チン：ねえ、ねえ、聞いて下さい。
三村：何ですか。
チン：ギブソンさんが林さんにプロポーズしたそうです。
三村：冗談でしょう。信じられない。

44.1 Here is one way to report hearsay, that is, information you have heard secondhand.

I-adjectives	Plain forms	
Na-adjectives	Dictionary form ＋だ／だった	＋そうだ(そうです)
Verbs	Plain forms	
Copula	Plain forms	

I hear(d) that, they say that, it is said that. . .
あの魚屋はとても安いそうです。
I hear that that fish store is very inexpensive.
東京の地下鉄は便利だそうだ。
It is said that subways in Tokyo are convenient.
林さんは病気だったそうです。
I heard that Mr. Hayashi was sick.
カワムラさんはクリーニング屋に行くそうです。
I heard that Mr. Kawamura is going to the dry cleaner's.
林さんはレコード屋でチンさんに会ったそうです。
I heard that Mr. Hayashi met Ms. Chin in a record store.
あの人はパン屋さんだそうです。
They say that that person is a baker.
あの人は肉屋さんだったそうです。
They say that person was a butcher.

BROWN: I hear there's a sale at Isetan Department Store. GIBSON: Really? BROWN: Yes, I heard that sweaters, coats, and some other items are 40 percent off. GIBSON: Wow. Shall we go there this afternoon (and see what we find)?

CHIN: Say, listen to this. MIMURA: What (is it)? CHIN: I heard that Ms. Gibson proposed to Mr. Hayashi. MIMURA: You must be kidding. (*lit., It must be a joke.*) I cannot believe it.

44.2 To clarify the source, preface your statement with (*source*) によると or (*person's name*) の話では both of which mean *According to. . . .*

新聞によると、今野菜がとても高いそうです。
According to the newspaper, vegetables are very expensive now.

チンさんによると、その人は眼鏡をかけているそうです。
According to Ms. Chin, that person wears glasses.

ギブソンさんの話では、エドモントンにとても大きい商店街があるそうです。
According to Ms. Gibson, there is a very large shopping mall in Edmonton.

コミュニケーション・ノート

Other Ways to Report Hearsay

Here are three other ways to report hearsay.

1. と言っていました。 [*someone*] *was saying that . . .*
2. と聞きました。 *I heard that . . .*
3. …(ん)ですって(female speakers only), …(ん)だって(informal), …って (informal) [*Someone*] *said that . . .* (って, here, is a variant of quote marker と.)

ブラウンさんが、デパートでバーゲンセールがあると言っていました。
Ms. Brown was saying that there is a sale at the department store.

林さんから、明日試験がないと聞きました。
I heard from Mr. Hayashi that there won't be an exam tomorrow.

カワムラさんが新しいステレオを買ったんですって。
I heard that Mr. Kawamura bought a new stereo. (female speaker)

練習 1

Following the example, make sentences.

[例] ブラウン：あの店はサービスがいいですよ。→
ブラウンさんの話では、あの店はサービスがいいそうです。

1. 林：ギブソンさんはカナダの出身です。
2. チン：このケーキはあそこのお菓子屋で買いました。
3. カワムラ：そのビールは酒屋で売っています。
4. カーティス：あのワープロは高かったですよ。

5. 山口：主人は若い時、ハンサムでした。
6. 山本：高田さんのネクタイはちょっとはででした。
7. 高田：フィルムはデパートでも買えますよ。

練習　2

Following the example, make sentences.

[例]　カワムラ：林さんはどこの出身ですか。
　　　林：九州です。　→
　林さんは九州の出身だそうです。

1. ブラウン：高田さんの車は新しいんですか。
　高田：いいえ、古いです。
2. 町田：チンさんのアパートは便利ですか。
　チン：あまり便利じゃありません。
3. カワムラ：北海道はどうでしたか。
　山口：雪が降って、とても寒かったです。
4. 山本：ブラウンさん、しばらくですね。
　ブラウン：ええ、京都へ行っていたんです。
5. 町田：夏休みはどうしますか。
　ブラウン：近所の洋品店でアルバイトをします。

45. Saying Whether or Not Something Is True: …かどうか

チン：本を探しているんですが…
本屋さん：あるかどうか、見てみましょう。
チン：すみません。

ブラウン：そば、おそいですね。
町田：ええ、もう出たかどうか、電話してみます。
ブラウン：お願いします。

CHIN: I am looking for a book but . . . (can you help me?)　BOOKSTORE OWNER: Let me check if we have it. (*lit., I'll look and see whether or not we have it.*)　CHIN: Thank you.

BROWN: The **soba** noodles have not arrived yet. (*lit., The **soba** is late, isn't it?*)　MACHIDA: Yes. I'll call and see whether or not they already left.　BROWN: Thank you. (*lit., I make a request of you.*)

けど is a colloquial form of けれども.

ブラウン：これ、町田さんが作ったんですか。
町田：ブラウンさんが好きかどうかわからなかったけど、作ってみたんです。
ブラウン：わたし、天ぷらが大好きなんですよ。
町田：おいしいかどうかわかりませんが、食べてみてください。
ブラウン：ウーン、おいしい。

X かどうか means *whether or not X*. X may be a noun, adjective, or predicate.

NOUN		
	Noun or noun ＋だった	＋かどうか
I-adjective	Plain form	＋かどうか
Na-adjective	Root or root ＋だった	＋かどうか
Verb	Plain form	＋かどうか

このペンが林さんのかどうかわかりません。
I don't know whether or not this pen is Mr. Hayashi's.
その人が日本人だったかどうかおぼえていません。
I don't remember whether or not that person is (lit., was) Japanese.
そのレストランがいいかどうかだれかに聞いてみましょう。
Let's ask someone whether or not that restaurant is good.
このセーターが高かったかどうかおぼえていない。
I cannot remember whether or not this sweater was expensive.
ブラウンさんのアパートが便利かどうか聞いてみました。
I asked Ms. Brown whether or not her apartment was convenient.
その車を買うかどうかまだわからない。
I still don't know whether or not I will buy that car.
カワムラさんが買い物から帰ってきたかどうか見てきます。
I will go see whether or not Mr. Kawamura has come back from shopping.

練習

Answer these questions, following the example.

[例]　そのセーターはデパートで買えますか。(母に聞く)→
買えるかどうかわからないから、母に聞いてみます。

BROWN: Did you make this?　MACHIDA: I didn't know whether or not you would like it, but (yes) I made it.　BROWN: I love tempura.　MACHIDA: I don't know whether or not it tastes good, but please try it (*lit., eat it and see*).　BROWN: Mm, this is delicious.

1. カワムラさんはパーティーに来ましたか。(ブラウンさんに聞く)
2. 明日雨が降りますか。(テレビの天気予報を見る)
3. カナダはロシアより大きいですか。(図書館で調べる [*check at the library*])
4. ギブソンさんはカナダ人ですか。(ギブソンさんに聞く)
5. カワムラさんは部屋 (*room*) で勉強していますか。(見る)
6. カーティスさんはコンサートに行きますか。(電話で聞く)
7. この肉は新しいですか。(肉屋さんに聞く)

46. Giving Reasons with …し、…し

町田：ギブソンさんはこのスーパーでいつも買い物するんですか。
ギブソン：ええ、アパートに近いし、大きいし、店員さんも親切です。
町田：そうですか。新しいし、きれいだし、いいスーパーですね。

林：今、何時ですか。
ギブソン：ええと、もう3時ですよ。
林：買い物もしたし、映画も見たし、もう帰りましょうか。
ギブソン：ええ。

三村：カワムラさん、お酒を飲んでいきませんか。
カワムラ：もうおそいし、…
三村：一杯だけ、どうですか。
カワムラ：明日、試験もあるし、…

46.1 し, coming after adjectives, verbs, and the copula, is used to enumerate mutually compatible facts or conditions in an emphatic way. Often the enumerated factors lead up to a conclusion or result which may be stated or understood from context.

あのレストランは安いし、おいしい。
That restaurant is cheap and what's more, the food is delicious. (lit., That restaurant is cheap ***and*** *delicious.)*

MACHIDA: Do you always shop at this supermarket? GIBSON: Yes, it's close to my apartment, it's large, and the clerks are nice. MACHIDA: I see. It's new and clean—it's a good supermarket, isn't it?

HAYASHI: What time is it now? GIBSON: Um, it's already three o'clock. HAYASHI: We went shopping *and* saw a movie, so shall we go home now (*lit., already*)? GIBSON: Yes.

MIMURA: Mr. Kawamura, do you want a drink before going back home? KAWAMURA: It's already late, so . . . . MIMURA: How about just one drink (*lit., one glassful*)? KAWAMURA: I have an exam tomorrow, so . . . .

The wording of the preceding example is more emphatic than あのレストランは安くて、おいしい。Some more examples follow.

カーティスさんはハンサムだし、やさしいし、とてもいい人です。
Mr. Curtis is handsome and sweet—he is a very nice person.

明日は会議(かいぎ)もあるし、忙(いそが)しいです。
I have a meeting tomorrow, among other things (lit., too), so I will be busy.

お昼ごはんも食べたし、出かけようか。
We've eaten lunch (and gotten ready in other ways)—(so) shall we leave?

寒かったし、雨が降(ふ)っていたから、外に出たくなかった。
It was cold and it was raining (among other similar reasons), so I didn't want to go out.

The following forms of predicate precede し.

I-adjective	Plain form	+ し
Na-adjectives	Dictionary form + だ / だった	+ し
Verbs	Plain form	+ し
Copula	Plain form	+ し

46.2 This construction can be used to avoid saying no by ending the sentence after し so the listener has to fill in the unstated negative conclusion.

もう少しいかがですか。—ええ、でも、もうたくさん食べたし、…
How about a little bit more? — Well (lit., yes), but I already ate a lot . . . (so no, thank you).

コミュニケーション・ノート

Saying No Politely

Japanese tend to avoid saying no directly. It is one way to avoid confrontation and preserve harmony, at least on the surface. For this purpose, Japanese employ a variety of ways to say no indirectly, that is, politely. Here are several of these tactics.

1. First agree and then give a reason that you must say no. (*Yes, but. . . .*)

   もう少しいかがですか。ええ、でも、もうおなかがいっぱいですから。
   How about a little more? — Yes, but since I'm already full . . . (no, thank you).

   Sometimes, this is shortened to simply

   ええ、でも、…
   . . . Yes, however. . . .

2. Give an ambiguous answer, one that can be taken as positive or negative.

   明日、デパートへ行きませんか。—多分。
   Would you like to go to the department store tomorrow?
   —Maybe.

3. Say you will consult with someone before answering.

   これ買いませんか。—妻に聞いてみます。
   Won't you buy this?—I will ask my wife (and see what she says).

4. Try to delay your answer.

   来週、一緒に東京へ行きませんか。—明日、お答えします。
   Would you like to go to Tokyo with me next week?—I'll give you my answer tomorrow.

5. Simply apologize.

   これ買いませんか。—すみません。ちょっと…
   Won't you buy this?—I'm sorry. It's just. . . .

練習 1

Following the example, complete the sentences.

[例] (広いです)(明るいです)(いい部屋ですね)→
広いし、明るいし、いい部屋ですね。

1. (きれいな色です)(よく似合います)(いいセーターですね。)
2. (おいしいです)(安いです)(いいレストランですね。)
3. (やさしいです)(親切です)(いい人ですね。)
4. (速いです)(便利です)(東京のタクシーはいいですね。)
5. (わたしの家に近いです)(静かです)(この公園によく来ます。)

練習 2

Complete the sentences, following the example.

[例] あのレストランは安いし、…→
あのレストランは安いし、サービスもいいし、申し分ありません。

1. わたしのアパートはせまい (*small*) し、
2. 町田さんは頭がいいし (*smart*) 、

3. この町は車が多いし、
4. このハンドバッグは軽(かる)いし、
5. この計算機(けいさんき) (*calculator*) は小さいし、
6. カーティスさんはハンサムだし、
7. 今日はたくさん食べたし、

Vocabulary

Stores

いちば	市場	market
かぐや	家具屋	furniture store
カメラや	カメラ屋	camera shop
くすりや	薬屋	drugstore, pharmacy
くだものや	果物屋	fruit store
くつや	靴屋	shoe store
クリーニングや	クリーニング屋	dry cleaner's
ケーキや	ケーキ屋	pastry store
さかなや	魚屋	fish store, fishmonger's
さかや	酒屋	liquor store
しょうてんがい	商店街	shopping mall, shopping street
でんきや	電気屋	electric appliance store
とけいや	時計屋	watch shop
にくや	肉屋	butcher shop
はなや	花屋	flower shop, florist's
パンや	パン屋	bakery
ぶんぼうぐや	文房具屋	stationery store
ほんや	本屋	bookstore
みせ	店	shop, store
めがねや	眼鏡屋	eyeglasses store, optician's
やおや	八百屋	vegetable store, green grocer's
やっきょく	薬局	drugstore, pharmacy
レコードや	レコード屋	record store, music store

Loanword: ブティック

Shopping

うりだし	売り出し	sale	てんいん	店員	shop clerk
うる	売る	to sell	ねだん	値段	price
(お)かね	(お)金	money	はらう	払う	to pay
(お)つり		change	～びき	～引き	reduced —%
きゃく	客	customer	りょうしゅうしょ	領収書	receipt
しゅじん	主人	shop owner	レジ		cash register, cashier

Loanwords: クレジットカード、ショーウインドー、ショッピング、セール、バーゲンセール、レシート
Review: 買い物、買う

Color

あおい	青い	blue, green	くろい	黒い	black
あか	赤	red	こい	濃い	dark (*in color*)
いろ	色	color	じみ(な)	地味(な)	quiet (*in color*), plain
うすい	薄い	light (*in color*), pale	しろ	白	white
あお	青	blue	ちゃいろ	茶色	brown
きいろ	黄色	yellow	はいいろ	灰色	gray
きいろい	黄色い	yellow	はで(な)	派手(な)	bright, gaudy
くろ	黒	black	みどり	緑	green

Loanwords: グリーン、グレー、ダークブルー、ピンク、ブルー、ライトブルー
Review: 赤い、明るい、暗い、白い

Clothes

かぶる		to wear; to put on (*the head*)
きもの	着物	kimono
きる	着る	to wear; to put on (*the torso*)
くつ	靴	shoe
くつした	靴下	sock
したぎ	下着	underwear
ショートパンツ		shorts
ズボン		trousers
セーター		sweater
せびろ	背広	business suit
つける	付ける	to wear; to put on (*something that "attaches"*)
ぬぐ	脱ぐ	to take off
はく		to wear; to put on (*the feet or legs*)
ハンカチ		handkerchief
パンツ		briefs
ふく	服	clothes

ブラジャー		bra (*lit., brassiere*)
ぼうし	帽子	cap, hat
みずぎ	水着	bathing suit, swimwear
めがね	眼鏡	eyeglasses
ようふく	洋服	Western-style clothes
ワイシャツ		(men's) dress shirt (*lit., white shirt*)
わふく	和服	Japanese-style clothes
ワンピース		dress (*lit., one piece*)

Loanwords: コート、サングラス、ジーンズ、シャツ、スカート、ストッキング、スポーツウェア、ティーシャツ、ドレス、ネクタイ、ネグリジェ、パジャマ、パンティー、ブーツ、ブラウス、ブリーフ、ベルト、マフラー

Nouns

あたま	頭	head	きって	切手	stamp
かさ	傘	umbrella	ちょきん(する)	貯金	deposit (*of money*); (to deposit)
かみ	髪	hair	てがみ	手紙	letter

Loanwords: アスピリン、アルバム、サイズ

Verbs

(おかねを)おろす	お金をおろす	to withdraw (money)
かえす	返す	to return
かりる	借りる	to borrow
こわれる		to become broken
だす	出す	to send out, to mail
ねぎる	値切る	to bargain
でございます		(*very polite form of* です)

Adjectives

いたい　painful

Loanwords: カジュアル(な)、フォーマル(な)

Other Words

…かどうか	whether	…とき	…時	when . . .
…し、	and (*emphatic*)	～にくい		difficult to . . .
…そうだ	they say	の		one, ones (*pronoun*)
だけ	only	～やすい		easy to . . .
～たら	if			

Kanji

Learn these **kanji**.

同	白	売	赤	員
長	屋	着	服	暗
場	黒	切	返	円
市	色	店	花	
主	買	引	黄	
電	青			

Reading and Writing

Reading 1「サン・ロード」グランド・オープニング・セール

Before You Read

Look at today's (or a recent) newspaper and check out the sale ads. What are the most typical discounts offered?

Match the stores in the first column with the merchandise sold there.

1. ______ 靴(くつ)屋	a. 辞書(じしょ)
2. ______ 宝石(ほうせき)屋 (*jewelry store*)	b. フィルム
3. ______ 花(はな)屋	c. 野菜(やさい)
4. ______ 呉服(ごふく)屋 (*kimono store*)	d. クロワッサン
5. ______ パン屋	e. ソファー
6. ______ 肉(にく)屋	f. ダイヤモンド
7. ______ 魚(さかな)屋	g. チューリップ
8. ______ 八百屋(やおや)	h. テレビ
9. ______ 本(ほん)屋	i. 着物(きもの)
10. ______ カメラ屋	j. スニーカー
11. ______ 家具(かぐ)屋	k. まぐろ
12. ______ 電気(でんき)屋	l. ハム

Guess the meaning of the given term.

1. If 全部(ぜんぶ) means *all*, and 商品(しょうひん) means *merchandise*, what do you think 全品(ぜんぴん) means?
2. If 半分(はんぶん) means *half* and 金額(きんがく) means *amount of money*, what do you think 半額(はんがく) means?
3. 部分(ぶぶん) means *part*. What do you think 一部(いちぶ) means?
4. 五割(ごわり) means *50 percent*. What do you think 二割(にわり) means?

Now Read It!

Linda Brown received an announcement about the grand opening sale at a shopping mall that will open soon near her apartment. Read the announcement. What stores and shops are in the mall? Look at Linda's shopping list following the announcement. What items on her list are on sale? Concentrate on retrieving this information; you need not understand every word in the passage.

ごあいさつ

今月１４日、中野駅南口駅ビルに新しく「サン・ロード」がグランド・オープニングします。１４日は午前１０時から、「サン・ロード」前でオープニング・セレモニーを行ないます。

グランド・オープニングを記念して、１４日から２１日まで「サン・ロード」全店が、大売り出しを行ないます。皆様のお出を、お待ちしています。

「サン・ロード」のお店と大売り出しの一部をご紹介します。

靴のアイザワ	アディダス、ナイキ２５％引
井上宝石店	ダイヤモンド・リング３０％引
上田呉服店	着物３～４割引
エノモト・ベーカリー	全品半額
薬の小川	化粧品２０％引
香川肉店	スキヤキ用牛肉２割引
八百松	全野菜２０％引
魚定	おさしみ２０～４０％引
高松クリーニング	背広・ドレスクリーニング２５％引
山本金物店	全品半額
ケーキのコトブキ	チーズ・ケーキ１００円
	アップル・パイ１２０円
佐藤ブックス	辞書２０％引
ビューティー・コンドー	パーマ４５００円
	カット１６００円
サン・ロード・フラワー	ブーケ１５％引
山口カメラ	３５mmカラー・フィルム２４枚撮り
	３００円、ＤＰＥ３０％引
カメイ電気	カラー・テレビ、ステレオ１０％引
本田家具	ソファー、ベッド３５％引
ブティック・サン	高級ドレス半額
キッチン・ウエスト	ハンバーガー２１０円

「サン・ロード」の営業時間は

月～金	10:00 A.M. – 8:00 P.M.
土	10:00 A.M. – 10:00 P.M.
日	12:00 P.M. – 8:00 P.M.

This is Linda Brown's shopping list. Check the items or services that are on sale during the grand opening sale at Sun Road shopping mall.

買い物リスト
・ドレス
・机
・ラジカセ
・フランスパン
・日本語の辞書
・イヤリング
・ブーツ
・マスカラ
・レタス
・にんじん
・フィルム
・スカートのクリーニング

After You Finish Reading

Answer these questions.

1. On what side of Nakano Station is Sun Road?
2. When will Sun Road mall open?
3. How long is the opening sale?
4. What time does Sun Road mall open on Saturdays and Sundays?
5. The **kanji** 引 is used repeatedly in the above advertisement. What do you think it means in this context?

Writing Practice 1

Write an advertisement based on the following information.

Shopping Center Mercado (メルカード)
Opening: July 14
Opening sale: From July 14 through July 20

Shoe store Okada: all shoes 30% off
Furniture store Murai: sofas 50,000 yen – 100,000 yen
Stationery store Yamamoto: all notebooks and pens 50% off
Electric appliance store Electric Land: television sets, stereos 15% off
Hunai Bakery: all bread half price

Business hours: M–Sat 10 A.M.–6 P.M.
Sun 12 noon–9 P.M.

Reading 2 マイ・ファッション

Before You Read

1. _____ ストッキング
2. _____ 背広
3. _____ ワンピース
4. _____ ブーツ
5. _____ スカート
6. _____ ジーンズ
7. _____ ネックレス
8. _____ ハイヒール

a. 着る
b. はく
c. つける

Answer these questions.

1. とてもフォーマルなパーティーに行く時は、何を着ていきますか。
2. 学校に行く時は、何を着ていきますか。
3. ビジネスの旅行をする時、ビジネスマンやビジネスウーマンは何を着ていきますか。
4. テニスをする時、何を着ますか。
5. 山にハイキングに行く時、何を着ていきますか。
6. 海で泳ぐ時、何を着ますか。
7. 寝る時、何を着ますか。

What kind of clothes do you associate with the following words?

1. インフォーマル
2. シンプル
3. ニュートラ (*New Traditionals*)
4. カジュアル

言語ノート

Shortened *Katakana* Words

When a Western word enters the Japanese language, it may become quite long because each **katakana** character is a syllable, most of which combine a consonant and a vowel. For example, the one-syllable English word *dress* becomes ドレス, a three-syllable word, in Japanese. Many long **katakana** words are shortened or abbreviated in Japanese by cutting off the latter part of the word or, in the case of a two-word loanword, the latter part of both words. The resulting term's meaning may not be readily apparent to a speaker of the source language, but with practice you will get better at guessing what such shortened **katakana** words mean. Here are some examples. デパート (*department store*); テレビ (*television*); マスコミ (*mass communication*); ハンスト (*hunger strike*); ワープロ (*word processor*); パソコン (*personal computer*); ラジカセ (*radio cassette player*), コンビニ (*convenience store*), and パンスト (*panty hose* [*stockings*]).

Now Read It!

Linda Brown and John Kawamura were featured in the *My Fashion* section of a monthly magazine widely read among college students.

マイ・ファッション

今月は東京大学のアメリカ人留学生のリンダ・ブラウンさんとジョン・カワムラさんです。二人は去年の九月に日本文化を勉強しに来日しました。最初は日本語の勉強で大変でしたが、今は日本語もだんだんわかってきて、勉強にレジャーに忙しい毎日を送っています。

リンダ・ブラウン

わたしが今着ているブルーグリーンのワンピースは、ロサンゼルスでおととし買いました。500ドルくらいでした。サマンサー・リーのデザインです。彼女のデザインはシンプルで大好きです。日本では彼女の服が買えないのが、残念です。日本でも買えたら本当にいいですね。今度アメリカに帰ったら、ワンピースかジャケットを買うつもりです。フォーマルなパーティーにも着ていけます。その時には、同じ色のハイヒール、黒のストッキング、ゴールド・ネックレスと組み合わせます。黒い靴もいいですね。

時々学校へ着ていきます。その時には、上に白いジャケットを着ます。絹100%で、とても着やすいので、わたしの大好きな服です。

ジョン・カワムラ

ぼくはかたくるしい服装は大嫌いです。背広は着たことがありません。いつもジーンズをはいています。靴もスニーカーしかはきません。今ぼくがはいているのはウオッシュアウトしたブルージーンズです。新宿のジーンズ専門店で今年買いました。12,000円くらいでした。ジーンズはたくさん持っています。ストレートが多いですね。黒や白のジーンズも持っています。

留学生 *foreign student*

来日しました *came to Japan*

最初 *first*

送っています *are spending*

残念(な) *regrettable, too bad*

組み合わせる *to combine*

絹 *silk*

かたくるしい *overly restrained, formal*

服装 *clothes*

新宿 *Shinjuku (area of Tokyo)*

専門店 *specialty shop*

持っています *owns, has*

このワインレッドのトレーナーは東京(とうきょう)大学のです。安(やす)いし、着やすいし、トレーナーはたくさん持っています。赤(あか)いのや青(あお)いのやたくさんあります。一枚(まい)2,000円ぐらいでした。夏はTシャツを着ます。寒い時には、この上にセーターを着たり、ジャンパーを着たりします。

このスニーカーはアメリカで買いました。とても歩(ある)きやすいので大好きです。

フォーマルなパーティーには、ブルーのブレザーを着て、ネクタイをしていきます。もちろん、下はジーンズとスニーカーです。ジーンズとスニーカーがだめだったら、パーティーには出ません。ジーンズとスニーカーがウエストコースト出身(しゅっしん)のぼくのファッションのトレードマークです。

トレーナー *sweatshirts*

ジャンパー *windbreaker*

After You Finish Reading

1. Unfortunately, Linda's and John's pictures were black-and-white. What color clothes are they wearing in the photos according to the article?
2. Answer these questions.
   a. Where did Linda buy her favorite dress? How much was it?
   b. Who designed the dress?
   c. Can you buy that designer's garments in Japan?
   d. What is Linda planning to buy when she returns to the United States?
   e. What kind of shoes does Linda wear with her favorite dress when she goes to a formal party?
   f. What kind of shoes does Linda wear with it when she goes to school?
   g. Why does Linda like this dress?
   h. What kind of clothes does John Kawamura dislike?
   i. Has he ever worn a suit?
   j. What kind of jeans does he have?

   Useful expression: 持(も)っている *to own, have*

   k. What color sweatshirts (トレーナー) does he have?
   l. What does he wear in summer? What does he wear when it is cold?
   m. What does he wear when he goes to a formal party?

Writing Practice 2

Write a description of the clothes you are wearing or of a favorite outfit. Model your description after **Reading 2**.

Language Functions and Situations

Shopping

店員：いらっしゃいませ。

カワムラ：チーズ・ケーキはありますか。

店員：はい、一つ250円です。

カワムラ：じゃあ、三つください。チーズ・ケーキのとなりのケーキは何ですか。

店員：レモン・ケーキです。

カワムラ：いくらですか。

店員：一つ230円です。

カワムラ：それも三つください。

店員：ほかには。

カワムラ：それでけっこうです。

店員：いらっしゃいませ。

林：シェーバーがほしいんですが、いいのはありますか。

店員：これはいかがでしょうか。

林：いくらですか。

店員：14,500円です。

林：ちょっと、大きすぎて、使いにくいんじゃないですか。
それに、ちょっと高いですね。
もう少し安くて、小さいのはありませんか。

店員：それでは、これはいかがでしょうか。9,800円です。
とても使いやすいです。

林：いいデザインですね。じゃ、これをください。

店員：ありがとうございます。

CLERK: Welcome. KAWAMURA: Do you carry cheesecake? CLERK: Yes, it's 250 yen a piece. KAWAMURA: Then please give me three pieces. What is the cake next to the cheesecake? CLERK: That's lemon cake. KAWAMURA: How much is it? CLERK: It's 230 yen a piece. KAWAMURA: Please give me three of them, too. CLERK: Anything else? KAWAMURA: This will be fine.

CLERK: Welcome. HAYASHI: I'm looking for an electric shaver. (*lit., I want to buy an electric shaver, but. . . .*) Do you have a good one? CLERK: How about this one? HAYASHI: How much is it? CLERK: It's 14,500 yen. HAYASHI: It's a bit too large and hard to use, isn't it? Besides, it's a bit expensive. Don't you have a small one that's a bit cheaper? CLERK: Then how about this one? It's 9,800 yen. It is very easy to use. HAYASHI: It's a nice design, isn't it? I will take this one. CLERK: Thank you very much.

店員：いらっしゃいませ。
ブラウン：ブラウスを探しているんですが、…
店員：ブラウスはこちらですが、どんなものがよろしいでしょうか。
ブラウン：ピンクのブラウスはありますか。
店員：サイズは。
ブラウン：11です。
店員：では、これはいかがでしょうか。
ブラウン：ううん、ちょっと派手すぎますね。もっと地味なのはありますか。
店員：では、こんなのはいかがですか。
ブラウン：きれいな色ですね。絹ですか。
店員：はい、絹100%です。
ブラウン：試してみてもいいですか。
店員：ええ、試着室はあちらです。
ブラウン：なかなかいいですね。
店員：たいへんよくお似合いです。とても着やすいでしょう。
ブラウン：ここがちょっときついんですが。
店員：いいえ、よくフィットしています。
ブラウン：そうですか。これ、いくらですか。
店員：33,000円です。
ブラウン：ちょっと高いですね。
店員：フランス製ですので、…
ブラウン：ううん、でもデザインもいいから、…じゃ、これをいただきます。
店員：ありがとうございます。

コミュニケーション・ノート

Useful Expressions for Shopping

1. saying what you are looking for
   文房具売場はどこですか。
   Where is the stationery section?
   ワイシャツがほしいんですが、…
   I would like a dress shirt (lit., I want a dress shirt but . . . [do you have any?])

CLERK: Welcome. BROWN: I am looking for a blouse. CLERK: Blouses are over here. What kind would you like? (*lit., what kind is good?*) BROWN: Do you have a pink blouse? CLERK: What size? BROWN: Eleven. CLERK: Then how about this one? BROWN: Hmm. It's too bright. Do you have a more subdued one? CLERK: Well, how about this one? BROWN: It's a pretty color, isn't it? Is this silk? CLERK: Yes, it's 100 percent silk. BROWN: May I try it on? CLERK: Yes. The fitting room is over there. . . . BROWN: It's quite nice. CLERK: It looks very good on you. It's very comfortable (*lit., easy to wear*), don't you think? BROWN: It is too tight here. CLERK: No, it fits very well. BROWN: Do you think so? How much is this? CLERK: It's 33,000 yen. BROWN: It's a bit expensive. CLERK: It is made in France, so . . . . BROWN: Hmm. But the design is good, too, so . . . I will get it (*lit., I will receive this one*). CLERK: Thank you very much.

ドライバーはありますか。
Do you have any screwdrivers?
スーツを見せてください。
Please show me some suits.

2. asking prices

これ、いくらですか。
How much is this?
これはおいくらですか。
How much is this? (politer)
全部(ぜんぶ)でいくらですか。
How much is it in total?
一ついくらですか。
How much is one of them?

3. asking to be shown something else

ほかのを見せてください。
Please show me a different one.
もっと軽(かる)いのはありませんか。
Don't you have a lighter (i.e. more lightweight) one?
もう少し大きいのがいいんですが、…
I prefer a somewhat larger one (lit., a somewhat larger one would be good, but . . . [do you have one?])

4. asking whether you can try something on

着(き)てみてもいいですか。
May I try it on?
試(ため)してみてもいいですか。
May I try it out?
試食(ししょく)できますか。
Can I taste a sample?

5. saying you have decided to buy something

これをいただきます。
I will take this. (lit., I'll receive this.)
これをください。
Please give me this.
これにします。
I have decided on this one.
これでけっこうです。
This will be fine.

6. saying you have decided not to make a purchase

今日はやめておきます。
I'll refrain from buying today.

クレジットカードでお願いします。

また、この次にします。
I will buy (lit., do) it next time.
今日はけっこうです。
I won't buy it today (lit., Today, I'm fine.)

7. paying

はい、3,000円です。
Here's 3,000 yen.
クレジットカードでお願いします。
I would like to pay with a credit card.

8. expressions used by shop clerks

いらっしゃいませ。
Welcome (to our store).
何をお探しでしょうか。
What are you looking for?
何をさしあげましょうか。
What can (lit., shall) I show you?
こちらはいかがですか。
How about this one?
かしこまりました。
Certainly. (i.e., I understand. I will do that.) (Responding to customer's request.)
セーターはこちらにございます。
Sweaters are over here.
申し訳ありませんが、品切れです。
I am sorry, but it's out of stock.
領収書をどうぞ。
Here is your receipt.
どうもありがとうございました。またお越し下さい。
Thank you very much. Please come again.

Role Play

Using the following shopping lists and receipts, practice buying a variety of things. Pair up with a classmate; one of you is the store clerk, the other the shopper. Make sure you buy an item that's just the right size, color, etc.

Useful vocabulary

きつい	*tight*
ゆるい	*loose*

毎度ありがとうございます。

サン・ストア

中野南口店

(電) 03(3374)8891

93.09.03 (金) 10:28

ギュウニュウ	¥90
ヨーグルト	¥100
ドールオレンジジュース	¥98
フランスパン	¥210
マーガリン	¥345
マーマレード	¥288
小計 6個	¥1,131
消費税	¥33
合計	¥1,164
現金	¥1,200
お釣り	¥36

レジ2・ノグチサトシ

買い物リスト

りんご	300g
バナナ	400g
レタス	2つ
じゃがいも	1Kg
たまねぎ	5つ
トマト	3つ
にんじん	4本

領収書 **Isemaru**

新宿店 03(3352)1111

93/09/10 10 0047 08895 99999

0310 011	セーター	1	12,000
0345 011	ソックス	5	2,500
0551 034	ベルト	1	4,600
小計			19,100
消費税			573
計			19,573
預り			20,000
釣銭			327

ショッピング・リスト

ビデオテープ(VHS)	5本
カセットテープ(120分)	10本
M.C.ハマーのCD	
「ホームアローン」のビデオ	

Saying Whether Two Things Are the Same or Different

Compare these two pictures. How are they identical? How are they different?

コミュニケーション・ノート

Same or Different?

1. saying two items are the same

   AはBと同じです。
   A is the same as B.
   AはBとCが同じです。
   A is the same as B with regard to C.
   このセーターはあのセーターとサイズが同じです。
   This sweater is the same as that sweater with regard to the size.

2. saying two items are different

   AはBと違います。
   A is different from B.
   AはBとCが違います。
   A is different in C from B.
   わたしのブーツと町田さんのブーツは色が違います。
   My boots are different in color from Ms. Machida's.

3. asking whether two items are the same or different

   AとBは同じですか、違いますか。
   Are A and B the same or different?
   このネクタイとあのネクタイは同じですか、違いますか。
   Are this necktie and that necktie the same or different?

Listening Comprehension

1. Five people are talking about what they bought over the weekend. While listening to your instructor, fill in the blanks.

NAME	STORES	ITEMS/PRICE

2. While listening to your instructor, fill in the blanks. He or she will describe what the following four people were wearing last night.

NAME	CLOTHES
Nakamura	
Hara	
Saeki	
Nonoyama	

3. There was a robbery at a convenience store last night. The above four people are questioned by the police because they were seen walking near the store around the time of the robbery. The store owner will describe to the police what the robber was wearing. Who do you think the robber is?

Review Chapter 2

札幌の雪祭：北海道の冬はとても寒いです。

Culture Reading: Japan's Climate

Despite the apparently small size of Japan, the Japanese islands stretch over 2,000 kilometers (1,300 miles) from north to south, so the climate of Hokkaido, the northernmost island, differs considerably from Okinawa, the southernmost island. For example, the date on which one popular strain of cherry blossoms reaches full bloom varies by as much as six weeks across Japan. See the map in this section, which is much like those displayed as part of Japanese TV weather reports during cherry-blossom viewing season. In addition, the eastern side of Japan faces the Pacific Ocean, exposing these areas to typhoons, while the western side faces the Asian continent, a relatively short distance across the Japan Sea, which exposes the western areas to frigid continental air in winter. Also of note are the high mountains running north to south down the middle of Honshu, which split this island into different climatic zones in the east and the west.

Read the following.

日本の気候

日本は北から南に長く(なが)のびているので、一番北の北海道(ほっかいどう)と一番南の沖縄(おきなわ)は気候(きこう)が違(ちが)います。
北海道の冬はきびしくて、寒いですが、夏は涼(すず)しいです。沖縄は夏はとても暑くて、冬もあまり寒くありません。

のびる *to extend*
違う *to be different*

沖縄の海岸 (beach): 一緒に泳ぎませんか。

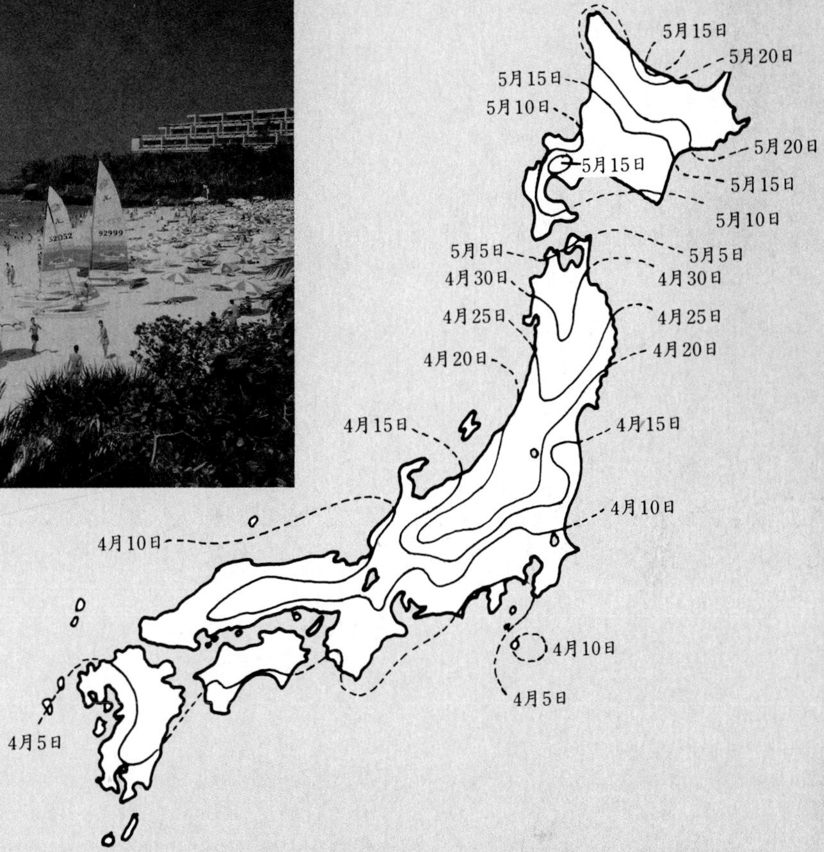

東京は3月でもちょっと寒いです。4月には、暖かくなって、さくらが咲きます。たくさんの人が花見に行きます。5月はいい天気の日が多いです。

6月は梅雨の季節で、雨の日が多いです。梅雨は7月10日ごろ、終わります。

7月の後半から暑さがきびしくなります。東京の夏はとてもむし暑くて、最高気温は30度を超えます。

8月後半から秋には台風がたくさん来ます。台風は時々、大きな被害をあたえます。

10月から11月は天気のいい日が続きます。山々の木々が赤や黄色になって、とてもきれいです。気温もだんだん低くなります。

11月後半から北西の風が吹いて、寒くなります。11月には北海道で雪が降ります。冬は、日本海側は天気の悪い日が多いですが、太平洋側はいい天気が続きます。

さくら *cherry tree*
咲く *to bloom*
終わる *to finish*
後半 *latter half*
超える *to exceed*
被害をあたえる *cause damage*
続く *to continue*
山々 *mountains*
木々 *trees*
だんだん *gradually*
日本海側 *the Japan Sea side (of Japan)*
太平洋側 *the Pacific Ocean side (of Japan)*

Oral Activities

アクティビティー 1

Odd man out

In each of the following groups of words, one word does not belong in the same category as the others. Identify it and tell why it doesn't belong.

[例] ロンドン、東京、ニューヨーク、モスクワ、パリ→
ニューヨークです。アメリカにあります。外国の都市 (*city*) ではありません。*or*「東京」です。カタカナではありません。

1. 妻、母、父、兄、町、妹
2. 暑い、いい、寒い、涼しい、暖かい
3. 晴れ、くもり、雨、高い、雪
4. 北、南、風、東、西
5. 月曜日、水曜日、木曜日、火曜日、日曜日
6. トランペット、ギター、ピアノ、スケート、フルート
7. 碁、将棋、トランプ、チェス、生け花
8. バスケットボール、バレーボール、マラソン、サッカー、ゴルフ
9. すもう、テニス、スキー、ラグビー、レスリング、ボクシング
10. お父さん、祖父、お兄さん、弟さん、妹さん
11. 水泳、山登り、ボート、ヨット、ダイビング
12. ステーキ、サラダ、ビーフシチュー、フライドチキン、ポークソテー
13. 高い、甘い、辛い、塩辛い、にがい
14. ワイン、ビール、ウイスキー、カクテル、お茶
15. 八百屋、果物屋、ケーキ屋、そば屋、ブティック
16. 赤い、緑、ピンク、白い、黒い、明るい

アクティビティー 2

Katakana review

Match each **katakana** word with its meaning.

1. _____ ジョギング		a. calendar
2. _____ エアロビクス		b. handicrafts
3. _____ ウインドサーフィン		c. aerogram

4.	______ ジュース	d.	ticket
5.	______ エアログラム	e.	chicken burger
6.	______ ウィンタースポーツ	f.	jogging
7.	______ ロッククライミング	g.	weightlifting
8.	______ フットボール	h.	aerobics
9.	______ ロックンロール	i.	juice
10.	______ チケット	j.	rock 'n' roll
11.	______ ケチャップ	k.	ketchup
12.	______ バレリーナ	l.	football
13.	______ ハンドクラフト	m.	ballerina
14.	______ チキン・バーガー	n.	French dressing
15.	______ バケーション	o.	windsurfing
16.	______ カレンダー	p.	rock climbing
17.	______ ウェートリフティング	q.	vacation
18.	______ フレンチ・ドレッシング	r.	winter sports

アクティビティー 3

Trip to Niigata

You would like to go from Tokyo to Niigata by car. Your car is very old. It doesn't have windshield wipers. It doesn't have a good radiator. Simply speaking, your car doesn't run well in bad weather. Also, it cannot climb steep hills. After listening to a weather report and highway information read by your instructor, decide what route you have to take to make it all the way to Niigata from Tokyo.

Useful expression: 工事中(こうじちゅう) *under construction*

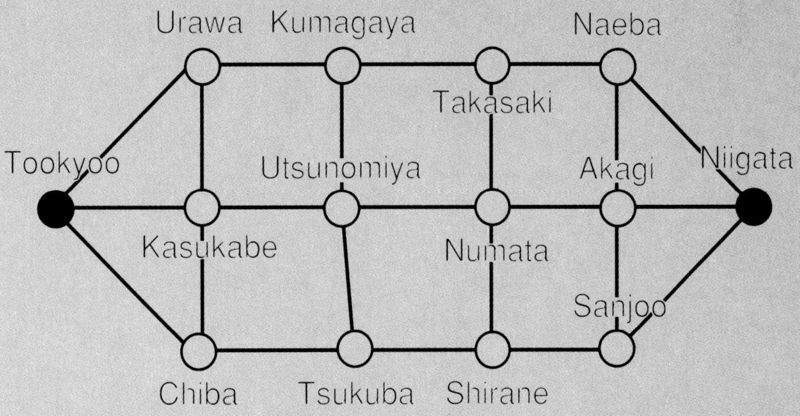

アクティビティー 4

Who's who?

Work in pairs. Student 1 covers the answer key in the footnote and asks who is who. Student 2 answers by describing what each person is wearing, based on the answer key. Follow the example.

[例] S1: 山田(やまだ)さんはどの人ですか。
S2: ドレスを着ている人です。
S1: 山田さんはXですか。
S2: はい、そうです。／ いいえ、違います。

1. 木村(きむら)さん
2. 本間(ほんま)さん
3. 鈴木(すずき)さん
4. 佐藤(さとう)さん
5. 丸山(まるやま)さん
6. 今野(こんの)さん
7. 星(ほし)さん
8. 野村(のむら)さん

アクティビティー 5

At a ticket agency

Following the dialogue, practice buying tickets for events listed in the following schedule.

S1: すみません。オペラの切符(きっぷ) (*ticket*) を2枚(まい)ください。
S2: 何日ですか。
S1: 15日です。
S2: 何時ですか。
S1: 7時です。
S2: S席(せき) (*seat*) とA席がございますが。
S1: S席をお願いします。
S2: 2枚で14,000円です。

ございます is a politer word for あります.

料金 *price*

	イベント	日時(にちじ)	席／料金(りょうきん)
スポーツ	サッカー	10, 11日 3:00, 8:00	S ¥1,000 A ¥750
	レスリング	11, 12日 12:00, 6:00	S ¥13,000 A ¥10,000 B ¥7,000

Activity 4 answers: 1 = b 2 = h 3 = a 4 = f 5 = c 6 = e 7 = g 8 = d

	イベント	日時	席／料金
音楽	バイオリンコンサート	4, 5日 12:00, 6:30	S ¥20,000 A ¥15,000
	オペラ	11, 12日 2:30, 7:00	S ¥7,000 A ¥5,000 B ¥3,500 C ¥2,000
	ミュージカル	1〜9日	S ¥5,500 A ¥4,500 B ¥3,500
コンテスト等	サーカス	20, 21日 12:00, 3:00, 7:00	S ¥3,000 A ¥1,800
	東京ペットショー	28, 29日 10:00 A.M., 2:00 P.M.	S ¥4,000 A ¥2,000
	ミスター日本コンテスト	24日 9:00 A.M., 6:00 P.M.	A ¥6,300 B ¥4,800

アクティビティー 6

Which do you prefer?

You are thinking of going on vacation this winter. You are wondering whether you should go to Nagano or Okinawa. Look at the following brochures of two hotels, one from each place, and discuss the following questions in class.

SNOW PRINCE HOTEL

長野

夏は涼しく (七月、八月 16〜21 度)、冬はスキーに最適。(ホテルの後ろにスキー場)

客室 245 室
東京から電車で 2 時間半
喫茶店、グリル、日本レストラン
ゲームセンター、ビリヤード
ディスコ、温泉浴場
ルームサービスあり、
各室カラーテレビ、電話付き
シングル： 12000円
ダブル： 15000円
ツイン： 16000円
ご予約は 0266 (54) 8709 まで

一年中暖かく (19〜29度)、スイミング、スキューバダイビング、釣りが楽しめる。

ホテルの前にはきれいなビーチが広がっています。

客室 132室、東京から飛行機で 2時間半、大阪から 2時間

喫茶店・シアターレストラン・ナイトクラブ
フランスレストラン・ヘルスクラブ・会議室
コンベンションホール・ガーデンプール・パブ
ルームサービスあり、各室カラーテレビ、冷蔵庫、電話付

シングル：15000円　ダブル：17000円
ツイン：19000円　スイート：28000円〜

ご予約は 0998 (21) 6198 まで

Okinawa Summer Resort Hotel

1. 長野(ながの)と沖縄(おきなわ)とどちらが暖(あたた)かいですか。
2. どちらでスキーができますか。
3. どちらでスキューバダイビングができますか。
4. 電車(でんしゃ)で行けるところはどちらですか。
5. 長野スノープリンスホテルと沖縄サマーリゾートホテルとどちらのほうが高いですか。
6. ヘルスクラブがあるホテルはどちらですか。
7. 日本料理(りょうり)が食べられるホテルはどちらですか。
8. ゲームもビリヤードもできるホテルはどちらですか。
9. フランスレストランがあるホテルはどちらですか。
10. どちらのホテルもルームサービスがありますか。
11. 長野スノープリンスホテルの後ろには何がありますか。
12. 沖縄サマーリゾートホテルの前には何がありますか。
13. どちらのホテルのほうが部屋(へや) (*rooms*) がたくさんありますか。
14. あなたはどちらへ行きたいですか。

アクティビティー　7

Ms. Machida's family

Here is a scene at Hitomi Machida's home. Answer these questions.

1. 町田さんのお父さんは何をしていますか。
2. 町田さんのおばあさんはどんな人ですか。
3. 本を読んでいる人はだれですか。
4. 町田さんのお父さんの趣味(しゅみ)は何だと思(おも)いますか。
5. 町田さんの家族はどんな家族ですか。

Make your own questions about Ms. Machida's family to ask your classmates. Now describe your ideal family. What would your spouse be like? How many children do you want to have? How many sons? How many daughters?

アクティビティー 8

My family and food

When it comes to eating habits, even members of the same family may have quite different preferences. First, answer these questions about the eating habits of one member of your family (not yourself). Then compare your answers with your classmates. See if you can find any customs your families have in common.

1. 一日に何回食事(しょくじ)をしますか。何時に食べますか。
2. 食事は家族一緒(いっしょ)にしますか。
3. だれが食事を作りますか。
4. 食事をしながら、話をしますか。誰(だれ)が一番話しますか。誰(だれ)が一番静(しず)かですか。
5. 食事をしながら、テレビを見ますか。食事をしながら、音楽を聞きますか。
6. 食事をしながら、何を飲みますか。

7. 食卓 (*dinner table*) のマナーはいいですか。悪いですか。
   普通 (*average*) ですか。
8. 一週間に何回外食します (*dine out*) か。
9. どんな食べ物が好きですか。きらいですか。

アクティビティー 9

どう思いますか。(*What do you think?*)

Describe the following picture. Use the following questions as a guide and invent necessary details. As you describe the scene, express your own opinions and conjectures.

1. 何時ですか。
2. ここはどこですか。
3. 男の人はだれですか。
4. 女の人はだれですか。
5. 男の人は何と言っていますか。
6. 女の人は何と言っていますか。
7. 二人はどこへ行くつもりですか。

Interview

In Chapters 4, 5, 6 and 7 of *Yookoso!* you gained practice asking questions and greatly increased the number of topics you can discuss in Japanese. This interview activity will help you review the major topics you have worked with so far.

First, read over the following topics and think about what your answers will be when someone asks you questions about them in Japanese. You may want to jot down things to say or additional points to raise about the same questions. Then find someone in class with whom you have spoken only infrequently and interview him or her about these topics. Finally, organize the information you have learned about your classmate into a brief presentation.

1. Is your diet healthy?
   Ask your partner what he or she ate and drank yesterday.

	朝ごはん	昼ごはん	夕ごはん	おやつ
食べた物(もの)				
飲んだ物				

Then ask your partner the following questions in Japanese.

Useful vocabulary: 健康的(けんこうてき) (な) *healthy*, コレステロール *cholesterol*

a. Is your diet healthy?
b. Is your diet expensive?
c. Do your meals include a lot of cholesterol?

2. Talk about a family member.
   Select one family member of your partner to talk about.

   SOCIAL LIFE

   a. 結婚(けっこん)していますか。独身(どくしん)ですか。(*Is he/she married? or single?*)
   b. 結婚している人：結婚して、何年になりますか。(*How many years has he/she been married?*)
   奥(おく)さん (御主人(ごしゅじん)) はどんな方ですか。
   独身の人：恋人(こいびと) (*boyfriend/girlfriend*) はいますか。
   結婚したことがありますか。
   はやく結婚したがっていますか。
   c. どこに住(す)んでいますか。(*Where does he/she live?*)
   d. どんな仕事(しごと)をしていますか。

e. どんな学校を卒業していますか。(卒業する *to graduate [from]*)
Possibilities: 小学校 *elementary school*, 中学校 *middle school*, 高校 *high school*, 大学、大学院 *graduate school*

f. 趣味は何ですか。

g. どんなスポーツが好きですか。するのが好きですか。見るのが好きですか。

h. ショッピングが好きですか。

CULINARY INTERESTS

i. どんな食べ物が好きですか。

j. 料理が上手ですか。

k. 日本料理を食べたことがありますか。

OTHER QUESTIONS

l. 誕生日はいつですか。何歳ですか。

m. どの季節が好きですか。

n. 去年の夏、どこかへ行きましたか。

o. 来年の夏、どこへ行きたがっていますか。

3. What sport or hobby do you recommend?
Your partner is a sports and hobby expert. Ask what hobby or sport he or she recommends for the following people. The expert must give one or two reasons why each particular hobby or sport is recommended.

a. 体が大きい人 (*a large person [lit., a person whose body is large]*)

b. 花が好きな人

c. 音楽が好きな人

d. 頭のいい人 (*an intelligent person [lit., a person whose head is good]*)

e. 海のそばに住んでいる (*lives*) 人

f. お金がたくさんある人

g. 時間があまりない人

Situations

Listen to your instructor as he or she role plays the following situations. You may not understand all you hear. Make some educated guesses about what your instructor says as he or she enacts the roles. While listening, think about whether you would say or do the same thing.

After your instructor finishes role playing, act out the situations with your instructor or one of your classmates. Try to use most of the vocabulary you know that fits each situation.

1. You are a travel agent in Japan. A customer comes to you in January asking for information about the weather in Hawaii, New York, and Buenos Aires. The customer intends to take a vacation starting next week and asks which of these cities would be the best destination. What do you suggest?
2. You would like to enroll in a hobby class at a nearby cultural center. You talk with the receptionist there and decide which course you should take.
3. You go to a Japanese/French/Mexican/American restaurant. Ask a waiter for a table near a window, away from the kitchen, and then order a meal. After you finish eating, the waiter brings your check. The total amount is more than you have in your wallet. What do you do?
4. Today is your payday. You take your boyfriend or girlfriend to an expensive restaurant. You order soup. Before you eat any, you find a fly (はえ) in the soup. What do you do? You would like to talk with your date, but the singer at the restaurant is singing very loudly while playing the piano. What's more, his singing is atrocious. What do you do?
5. You are a private investigator and are asked by the family of a prospective bride to gather information about the family of her prospective groom, Mr. Yoshida. Interview a neighbor about the Yoshida family.
6. You bought a sweater at a department store last week. When you bought it, you liked the color and the size seemed just right for you. When you returned home, however, for some reason you didn't like the color and the size was large for you. Return the sweater to the department store.

This Is My Life!: 金井貞夫(かないさだお)(サラリーマン)

4年前に大学を卒業(そつぎょう)して、今は東京駅(とうきょうえき)のそばにあるコンピュータの会社(かいしゃ)につとめています。コンピュータのセールスの仕事(しごと)をしています。大学では経済学(けいざいがく)を専攻(せんこう)していました。

仕事はきついです。今日は日曜日ですから、朝10時に起きました。でも、いつもは6時に起きます。うちから会社までは電車(でんしゃ)で1時間半かかりますから、うちを7時15分に出ます。時々、夜11時や12時まで会社で仕事をします。(残業(ざんぎょう)といいます。)残業した日は、うちに1時か2時に帰(かえ)ってきます。次(つぎ)の日の朝は、起きるのが大変(たいへん)です。

今日はお昼までゆっくり新聞(しんぶん)を読んで、午後からガールフレンドのりえさんと新宿(しんじゅく)に買(か)い物(もの)に行こうと思(おも)っています。夕ごはんも一緒(いっしょ)に食べようと思います。彼女も同(おな)じ会社につとめています。会社で知(し)り合(あ)いました。会社の仕事(しごと)が忙(いそが)しくて、彼女とデートする時間はあまりありません。今日は久(ひさ)しぶりのデートです。来年、結婚しようと話しています。

卒業して *graduated*
つとめています *work for*
経済学 *economics*
きつい *tough, hard*
残業 *overtime work*
…といいます *we call it . . .*
次の *the following*
大変 *difficult, terrible*
ゆっくり *leisurely*
知り合いました *got acquainted with*
結婚する *to get married*

金井さん、今日も残業ですか。

彼女は美人じゃありませんけれども、とてもやさしい女の人です。私の趣味は切手集めです。世界中の珍しい切手を集めています。ドライブも好きです。トヨタのセリカを持っていますが、仕事が忙しくて、ドライブする時間はあまりありません。今年の夏は彼女と九州にドライブするつもりです。

家族は両親と妹です。父は出版社につとめています。碁が大好きで、今日も近所の友だちの家で朝から碁をしています。母は主婦ですが、時々、近所のスーパーでパートタイムの仕事をしています。母の趣味は生け花です。妹は私より二つ年下です。短大を卒業して、デパートにつとめています。妹は旅行が大好きで、今、友だちとハワイに行っています。私はまだハワイに行ったことがありません。ハネムーンにはハワイに行きたいと思っています。でも、りえさんはヨーロッパに行きたがっています。結婚まで一年ありますから、二人でもっと話し合ってみるつもりです。

美人 *beautiful woman*
世界中 *all over the world*
珍しい *rare, unusual*
持っています *have, own*
出版社 *publishing company*
碁 *go (the game)*
主婦 *housewife*
年下 *younger*
短大 *junior college*
もっと *more*
話し合って *talk to each other*

Answer these questions in English.

1. What company does Mr. Kanai work for?
2. What type of work does he do?
3. What time does he get up on weekdays?

4. How long does it take to go by train from his home to his company?
5. What is he going to do this afternoon?
6. What company does Mr. Kanai's girlfriend work for?
7. When are Mr. Kanai and his girlfriend planning to get married?
8. What is Mr. Kanai's hobby?
9. Where is he planning to go this summer?
10. What does his younger sister like?
11. What is Mr. Kanai planning to talk about more with his girlfriend before their wedding?

Appendices

APPENDIX 1: Verb Conjugation

	CLASS 1						
Dictionary form	あ 会う	か 書く	はな 話す	た 立つ	し 死ぬ*	よ 読む	の 乗る
Root	会 (わ)	書	話	立	死	読	乗
Plain, Nonpast, Negative	会わない	書かない	話さない	立たない	死なない	読まない	乗らない
Polite, Nonpast, Affirmative	会います	書きます	話します	立ちます	死にます	読みます	乗ります
ましょう **Form (Polite Volitional)**	会いましょう	書きましょう	話しましょう	立ちましょう	死にましょう	読みましょう	乗りましょう
たい **Form**	会いたい	書きたい	話したい	立ちたい	死にたい	読みたい	乗りたい
Polite Command	会いなさい	書きなさい	話しなさい	立ちなさい	死になさい	読みなさい	乗りなさい

Note: Don't forget! Horizontal bold lines in this chart set off verb forms whose endings contain the same sound from the **hiragana** syllabary. For more on remembering verb conjugations by relating them to **a-i-u-e-o** order, see the Study Hint on p. 395.

	CLASS 1		CLASS 2		CLASS 3	
Dictionary form	泳ぐ	呼ぶ	How to create forms	食べる	する	来る
Root	泳	呼	Drop る ending	食べ	Irregular	Irregular
Plain, Nonpast, Negative	泳がない	呼ばない	Root + ない	食べない	しない	来ない
Polite, Nonpast, Affirmative	泳ぎます	呼びます	Root + ます	食べます	します	来ます
ましょう **Form (Polite Volitional)**	泳ぎましょう	呼びましょう	Root + ましょう	食べましょう	しましょう	来ましょう
たい **Form**	泳ぎたい	呼びたい	Root + たい	食べたい	したい	来たい
Polite Command	泳ぎなさい	呼びなさい	Root + なさい	食べなさい	しなさい	来なさい

	CLASS 1						
Dictionary Form	会う	書く	話す	立つ	死ぬ	読む	乗る
Potential	会える	書ける	話せる	立てる	死ねる	読める	乗れる
Imperative	会え	書け	話せ	立て	死ね	読め	乗れ
ば Conditional	会えば	書けば	話せば	立てば	死ねば	読めば	乗れば
Volitional	会おう	書こう	話そう	立とう	死のう	読もう	乗ろう
Ta-Form	会った	書いた	話した	立った	死んだ	読んだ	乗った
Te-Form	会って	書いて	話して	立って	死んで	読んで	乗って
Other Verbs	洗う 使う 歌う 買う 手伝う 笑う 言う 習う	聞く 行く† 磨く 働く はく 歩く	探す 直す	持つ 勝つ 待つ		飲む 休む 住む 楽しむ	帰る 入る 知る 降る 走る 泊まる 止まる 取る 切る 終わる 始まる

*死ぬ is the only verb whose dictionary form ends in ぬ.
† The ta-form and te-form of 行く are 行った and 行って, respectively.

	CLASS 1		CLASS 2		CLASS 3	
Dictionary Form	泳ぐ	呼ぶ		食べる	する	来る
Potential	泳げる	呼べる	Root ＋ られる	食べられる	できる	来られる
Imperative	泳げ	呼べ	Root ＋ ろ	食べろ	しろ	来い
ば Conditional	泳げば	呼べば	Root ＋ れば	食べれば	すれば	来れば
Volitional	泳ごう	呼ぼう	Root ＋ よう	食べよう	しよう	来よう
Ta-Form	泳いだ	呼んだ	Root ＋ た	食べた	した	来た
Te-Form	泳いで	呼んで	Root ＋ て	食べて	して	来て
Other Verbs	脱ぐ 急ぐ	飛ぶ 遊ぶ		見る 起きる 寝る 出かける 出る 着る 教える All potential verb forms	Nominal verbs (勉強する、洗濯する)	連れてくる 持ってくる

APPENDIX 2: Adjective and Copula Conjugation

Adjectives

	DICTIONARY FORM	PRENOMINAL	PREDICATE			
			Plain			
			Non-past		**Past**	
			Affirmative	**Negative**	**Affirmative**	**Negative**
I-Adjectives	赤(あか)い	赤い	赤い	赤くない	赤かった	赤くなかった
	いい	いい	いい	よくない	よかった	よくなかった
Na-Adjectives	静(しず)か	静かな	静かだ	静かではない／静かじゃない	静かだった	静かではなかった／静かじゃなかった

Copula

DICTIONARY FORM	PRENOMINAL	PREDICATE			
		Plain			
		Non-past		**Past**	
		Affirmative	**Negative**	**Affirmative**	**Negative**
だ	の／である	だ／である	ではない／じゃない	だった	ではなかった／じゃなかった

	PREDICATE						ADVERBIAL
	Polite				Te-Form	Conditional	
	Non-past		Past				
	Affirmative	Negative	Affirmative	Negative			
I-Adjectives	赤いです	赤くありません/赤くないです	赤かったです	赤くありませんでした/赤くなかったです	赤くて	赤ければ	赤く
	いいです	よくありません/よくないです	よかったです	よくありませんでした/よくなかったです	よくて	よければ	よく
Na-Adjectives	静かです	静かではありません/静かじゃありません	静かでした	静かではありませんでした/静かじゃありませんでした	静かで	静かならば/静かであれば	静かに

PREDICATE						ADVERBIAL
Polite				Te-Form	Conditional	
Non-past		Past				
Affirmative	Negative	Affirmative	Negative			
です	ではありません/じゃありません	でした	ではありませんでした/じゃありませんでした	で	なら(ば)/であれば	N/A

APPENDIX 3: Numbers

NATIVE JAPANESE SYSTEM	SINO-JAPANESE SYSTEM				
1 ひと 一つ	1 いち 一	11 じゅういち 十一			
2 ふた 二つ	2 に 二	12 じゅうに 十二		200 にひゃく 二百	2,000 にせん 二千
3 みっ 三つ	3 さん 三	13 じゅうさん 十三	30 さんじゅう 三十	300 さんびゃく 三百	3,000 さんぜん 三千
4 よっ 四つ	4 し、よん 四	14 じゅうし、じゅうよん 十四	40 よんじゅう 四十	400 よんひゃく 四百	4,000 よんせん 四千
5 いつ 五つ	5 ご 五	15 じゅうご 十五	50 ごじゅう 五十	500 ごひゃく 五百	5,000 ごせん 五千
6 むっ 六つ	6 ろく 六	16 じゅうろく 十六	60 ろくじゅう 六十	600 ろっぴゃく 六百	6,000 ろくせん 六千
7 なな 七つ	7 しち、なな 七	17 じゅうしち、じゅうなな 十七	70 ななじゅう、しちじゅう 七十	700 ななひゃく 七百	7,000 ななせん 七千
8 やっ 八つ	8 はち 八	18 じゅうはち 十八	80 はちじゅう 八十	800 はっぴゃく 八百	8,000 はっせん 八千
9 ここの 九つ	9 く、きゅう 九	19 じゅうく、じゅうきゅう 十九	90 きゅうじゅう 九十	900 きゅうひゃく 九百	9,000 きゅうせん 九千
10 とお 十	10 じゅう 十	20 にじゅう 二十	100 ひゃく 百	1,000 (いっ)せん (一)千	10,000 いちまん 一万

Large Numbers

100,000	十万(じゅうまん)	1,000,000,000 *(one billion)*	十億(じゅうおく)
1,000,000 *(one million)*	百万(ひゃくまん)	10,000,000,000	百億(ひゃくおく)
10,000,000	(一)千万((いっ)せんまん)	100,000,000,000	(一)千億((いっ)せんおく)
100,000,000	一億(いちおく)	1,000,000,000,000 *(one trillion)*	一兆(いっちょう)

Notes

1. Zero is 零(れい) or ゼロ.
2. 0.314 is read 零点三一四(れいてんさんいちよん). 2.236 is read 二点二三六(にてんにさんろく).(点(てん) = point)
3. The native Japanese system exists for 1 through 10 only. After 11, only the Sino-Japanese system can be used.
4. Some people read 1,000, 10,000,000, and 100,000,000,000 as 一千(いっせん)、一千万(いっせんまん)、and 一千億(いっせんおく), respectively.

APPENDIX 4: Counters

The following chart lists common counters (suffixes appended to numbers for counting or naming things), most of which are introduced in this book. Notice the phonological changes that occur when some numbers and counters are joined. The first column (～番) represents the simplest case: the Sino-Japanese number is followed by the counter with no phonological changes. In other columns, phonological changes occur in some cases. Such variations are marked with an asterisk (*). Where two pronunciations are provided, either may be used, although a particular pronunciation may predominate in a given situation. (For example, *seven o'clock* is usually pronounced しちじ, except over train station public address systems where ななじ is often used to prevent confusion with *one o'clock* いちじ.) Counters that name something are so indicated; all others are used to count. Each chart groups together counters that vary in similar ways. For more on counters, see **Grammar 9, Chapter 2**.

COUNTERS:	～番 (ばん)	～時 (じ)	～月 (がつ)	～回 (かい)
WHAT IS BEING COUNTED OR NAMED:	**Serial Numbers (*Number . . .*)**	**Hours of the Day (Name) (*...o'clock*)**	**Months (Name)**	**Occurrences (*...times*)**
1	一番 (いちばん)	一時 (いちじ)	一月 (いちがつ)	一回 (いっかい)*
2	二番 (にばん)	二時 (にじ)	二月 (にがつ)	二回 (にかい)
3	三番 (さんばん)	三時 (さんじ)	三月 (さんがつ)	三回 (さんかい)
4	四番 (よんばん)	四時 (よじ)*	四月 (しがつ)*	四回 (よんかい)
5	五番 (ごばん)	五時 (ごじ)	五月 (ごがつ)	五回 (ごかい)
6	六番 (ろくばん)	六時 (ろくじ)	六月 (ろくがつ)	六回 (ろっかい)*
7	七番 (ななばん、しちばん)	七時 (しちじ、ななじ)	七月 (しちがつ)*	七回 (ななかい、しちかい)
8	八番 (はちばん)	八時 (はちじ)	八月 (はちがつ)	八回 (はっかい)*
9	九番 (きゅうばん)	九時 (くじ)*	九月 (くがつ)*	九回 (きゅうかい)

10	十番 (じゅうばん)	十時 (じゅうじ)	十月 (じゅうがつ)	十回 (じっかい、じゅっかい*)
OTHER COUNTERS WITH SAME PATTERN OF VARIATION	…枚 (まい) thin, flat objects, …度 (ど) ...degrees (temperature), ...times (occurrences), …倍 (ばい) ...*times* (magnifications)	…時間 (じかん) hours, …年 (ねん) years (number and name)		…個 (こ) pieces, …ヶ月 (かげつ) month, …課 (か) lessons

COUNTERS:	…階 (かい)	…本 (ほん、ぽん、ぼん)	…分 (ふん)	…冊 (さつ)
WHAT IS BEING COUNTED OR NAMED:	**Floors (of a building) (Number and Name)**	**Long, Cylindrical Objects**	**Minutes (Number and Name)**	**Books, Bound Volumes**
1	一階* (いっかい)	一本* (いっぽん)	一分* (いっぷん)	一冊* (いっさつ)
2	二階 (にかい)	二本 (にほん)	二分 (にふん)	二冊 (にさつ)
3	三階 (さんがい、さんかい*)	三本* (さんぼん)	三分* (さんぷん)	三冊 (さんさつ)
4	四階 (よんかい)	四本 (よんほん)	四分 (よんふん)	四冊 (よんさつ)
5	五階 (ごかい)	五本 (ごほん)	五分 (ごふん)	五冊 (ごさつ)
6	六階* (ろっかい)	六本* (ろっぽん)	六分* (ろっぷん)	六冊 (ろくさつ)
7	七階 (ななかい、しちかい)	七本 (ななほん、しちほん)	七分 (ななふん、しちふん)	七冊 (ななさつ、しちさつ)
8	八階* (はっかい)	八本* (はっぽん)	八分* (はっぷん)	八冊* (はっさつ)
9	九階 (きゅうかい)	九本 (きゅうほん)	九分 (きゅうふん)	九冊 (きゅうさつ)
10	十階 (じっかい、じゅっかい*)	十本 (じっぽん、じゅっぽん*)	十分 (じっぷん、じゅっぷん*)	十冊 (じっさつ、じゅっさつ*)
OTHER COUNTERS WITH SAME PATTERN OF VARIATION		…杯 (はい) glass (ful)s, cup (ful)s, …匹 small animals	…泊 (はく) overnight stays	…章 (しょう) chapters

COUNTERS:	～足（そく）	～ページ	～頭（とう）	～人（にん）
WHAT IS BEING COUNTED OR NAMED	**Pair of Footwear (Shoes, Socks, etc.)**	**Pages (Number and Name)**	**Large Animals**	**People**
1	一足（いっそく）*	一（いっ）ページ*	一頭（いっとう）*	一人（ひとり）*
2	二足（にそく）	二（に）ページ	二頭（にとう）	二人（ふたり）*
3	三足（さんぞく）	三（さん）ページ	三頭（さんとう）	三人（さんにん）
4	四足（よんそく）	四（よん）ページ	四頭（よんとう）	四人（よにん）*
5	五足（ごそく）	五（ご）ページ	五頭（ごとう）	五人（ごにん）
6	六足（ろくそく）	六（ろっ）ページ*	六頭（ろくとう）	六人（ろくにん）
7	七足（ななそく、しちそく）	七（なな、しち）ページ	七頭（ななとう、しちとう）	七人（しちにん、ななにん）
8	八足（はっそく）*	八（はっ）ページ*	八頭（はっとう）	八人（はちにん）
9	九足（きゅうそく）	九（きゅう）ページ	九頭（きゅうとう）*	九人（きゅうにん、くにん）
10	十足（じっそく、じゅっそく*）	十（じっ、じゅっ）ページ*	十頭（じっとう、じゅっとう*）	十人（じゅうにん）
OTHERS COUNTERS WITH SAME PATTERN OF VARIATION		…ポンド pounds	…通（つう） letters (i.e., pieces of correspondence), …トン tons, ～点（てん） points (e.g., in games, grades), …滴（てき） drops of liquid	

COUNTERS:	…日	…日 (にち)	…晩 (ばん)	…歳 (さい)
WHAT IS BEING COUNTED OR NAMED:	**Days of the month (Name)**	**Days (Number)**	**Nights**	**Age (. . . *years old*)**
1	一日 (ついたち)*	一日 (いちにち)	一晩 (ひとばん)	一歳 (いっさい)、一つ (ひと)*
2	二日 (ふつか)*	二日 (ふつか)*	二晩 (ふたばん)*	二歳 (にさい)、二つ (ふた)*
3	三日 (みっか)*	三日 (みっか)*	三晩 (みばん)*	三歳 (さんさい)、三つ (みっ)*
4	四日 (よっか)*	四日 (よっか)*	四晩 (よばん)*	四歳 (よんさい)、四つ (よっ)*
5	五日 (いつか)*	五日 (ごにち、いつか*)	五晩 (ごばん)	五歳 (ごさい)、五つ (いつ)*
6	六日 (むいか)*	六日 (ろくにち、むいか*)	六晩 (ろくばん)	六歳 (ろくさい)、六つ (むっ)*
7	七日 (なのか)*	七日 (しちにち、なのか*)	七晩 (ななばん)	七歳 (ななさい)、七つ (なな)*
8	八日 (ようか)*	八日 (はちにち、ようか*)	八晩 (はちばん)	八歳 (はっさい)、八つ (やっ)*
9	九日 (ここのか)*	九日 (くにち、ここのか*)	九晩 (きゅうばん)	九歳 (きゅうさい)、九つ (ここの)*
10	十日 (とおか)*	十日 (とおか)	十晩 (じゅうばん)	十歳 (じっさい、じゅっさい)、十 (とお)*
OTHER IRREGULAR PRONUNCIATIONS OF NUMBERS AND COUNTERS	十四日 (じゅうよっか)* 二十日 (はつか)* 二十四日 (にじゅうよっか)*	十四日 (じゅうよっか)* 二十日 (はつか)* 二十四日 (にじゅうよっか)*		二十歳 (はたち)*

SUFFIXES FOR ORDINAL NUMBERS:	～目（め） (Used with Japanese numbers) (*the first*, *the second*, etc.)	～番目（ばんめ） (Used with Sino-Japanese Numbers)
1	一つ目（ひとつめ）	一番目（いちばんめ）
2	二つ目（ふたつめ）	二番目（にばんめ）
3	三つ目（みっつめ）	三番目（さんばんめ）
4	四つ目（よっつめ）	四番目（よんばんめ）
5	五つ目（いつつめ）	五番目（ごばんめ）
6	六つ目（むっつめ）	六番目（ろくばんめ）
7	七つ目（ななつめ）	七番目（ななばんめ、しちばんめ）
8	八つ目（やっつめ）	八番目（はちばんめ）
9	九つ目（ここのつめ）	九番目（きゅうばんめ、くばんめ）
10	—	十番目（じゅうばんめ）

How to form ordinal numbers

Note: Another way to make ordinal numbers is to add the prefix 第（だい）··· (Number . . .) to the Sino-Japanese numbers (第一（だいいち）、第二（だいに）、第三（だいさん）、第四（だいよん）、第五（だいご）、第六（だいろく）、第七（だいなな）、第八（だいはち）、第九（だいきゅう）、第十（だいじゅう） and so on). This prefix may be used in combination with some counter suffixes to name ordered things. Examples are, 第三章（だいさんしょう） (*Chapter Three*) and 第五課（だいごか） (*Lesson Five*). The suffix ～目（め） is commonly used in combination with counters to indicate *the...th*. For example, 九回目（きゅうかいめ） (*the ninth time*), 三日目（みっかめ） (*the third day*) 五足目（ごそくめ）, (*the fifth pair of footwear*), 二人目（ふたりめ） (*the second person*) and so on. When indicating items having no assigned counter or when you are unsure of the counter, you can usually use the general terms above for *the first* (*one*), *the second* (*one*), and so on.

APPENDIX 5: Time, Days, Months and Years

TELLING TIME

	A.M.	P.M.
	午前 (ごぜん)	午後 (ごご)

1 : 00 一時 (いちじ)	2 : 00 二時 (にじ)	3 : 00 三時 (さんじ)	4 : 00 四時 (よじ)	5 : 00 五時 (ごじ)	6 : 00 六時 (ろくじ)
7 : 00 七時 (しちじ、ななじ)	8 : 00 八時 (はちじ)	9 : 00 九時 (くじ)	10 : 00 十時 (じゅうじ)	11 : 00 十一時 (じゅういちじ)	12 : 00 十二時 (じゅうにじ)

一分 (いっぷん)	二分 (にふん)	三分 (さんぷん)	四分 (よんぷん)	五分 (ごふん)	六分 (ろっぷん)	七分 (ななふん、しちふん)	八分 (はっぷん)	九分 (きゅうふん)	十分 (じっぷん、じゅっぷん)

(and so on through 59 minutes)

[例] 午前五時二十六分 (ごぜんごじにじゅうろっぷん) 5 : 26A.M.　午後八時四十七分 (ごごはちじよんじゅうななふん) 8 : 47P.M.

DAYS OF THE WEEK

週末 (しゅうまつ) *weekend*	平日 (へいじつ) *weekday*					週末 (しゅうまつ) *weekend*
日曜日 (にちようび) *Sunday*	月曜日 (げつようび) *Monday*	火曜日 (かようび) *Tuesday*	水曜日 (すいようび) *Wednesday*	木曜日 (もくようび) *Thursday*	金曜日 (きんようび) *Friday*	土曜日 (どようび) *Saturday*

DAYS OF THE MONTH

1 一日 (ついたち)	2 二日 (ふつか)	3 三日 (みっか)	4 四日 (よっか)	5 五日 (いつか)	6 六日 (むいか)	7 七日 (なのか)
8 八日 (ようか)	9 九日 (ここのか)	10 十日 (とうか)	11 十一日 (じゅういちにち)	12 十二日 (じゅうににち)	13 十三日 (じゅうさんにち)	14 十四日 (じゅうよっか)
15 十五日 (じゅうごにち)	16 十六日 (じゅうろくにち)	17 十七日 (じゅうしちにち)	18 十八日 (じゅうはちにち)	19 十九日 (じゅうくにち)	20 二十日 (はつか)	21 二十一日 (にじゅういちにち)
22 二十二日 (にじゅうににち)	23 二十三日 (にじゅうさんにち)	24 二十四日 (にじゅうよっか)	25 二十五日 (にじゅうごにち)	26 二十六日 (にじゅうろくにち)	27 二十七日 (にじゅうしちにち)	28 二十八日 (にじゅうはちにち)
29 二十九日 (にじゅうくにち)	30 三十日 (さんじゅうにち)	31 三十一日 (さんじゅういちにち)				

MONTHS

いちがつ 一月 *January*	にがつ 二月 *February*	さんがつ 三月 *March*	しがつ 四月 *April*	ごがつ 五月 *May*	ろくがつ 六月 *June*
しちがつ 七月 *July*	はちがつ 八月 *August*	くがつ 九月 *September*	じゅうがつ 十月 *October*	じゅういちがつ 十一月 *November*	じゅうにがつ 十二月 *December*

Years

Western year:	1988年 (ねん)	1989年	1990年	1991年	1992年	1993年	1994年	1995年
Era:	しょうわ 昭和*	へいせい 平成						
Japanese year:	六十三年	一年 or がんねん 元年	二年	三年	四年	五年	六年	七年

*The **Showa** era began in 1926 and ended when the **Heisei** era began on January 8, 1989. Technically, the first days of 1989 fall in the **Showa** era, so events that occurred within those days (such as someone's birth) are often dated **Showa 64**.

RELATIVE TIME EXPRESSIONS

Days	おととい *the day before yesterday*	きのう 昨日 *yesterday*	きょう 今日 *today*	あした 明日 *tomorrow*	あさって *the day after tomorrow*
Weeks	せんせんしゅう 先々週 *the week before last*	せんしゅう 先週 *last week*	こんしゅう 今週 *this week*	らいしゅう 来週 *next week*	さらいしゅう 再来週 *the week after next*
Months	せんせんげつ 先々月 *the month before last*	せんげつ 先月 *last month*	こんげつ 今月 *this month*	らいげつ 来月 *next month*	さらいげつ 再来月 *the month after next*
Years	いっさくねん 一昨年 *the year before last*	きょねん さくねん 去年 or 昨年 *last year*	ことし 今年 *this year*	らいねん 来年 *next year*	さらいねん 再来年 *the year after next*

TIME DURATIONS

	なんぷんかん 何分(間) ***minutes***	なんじかん 何時間 ***hours***	なんにちかん 何日(間) ***days***	なんしゅうかん 何週間 ***weeks***	なんかげつ 何ケ月 ***months***	なんねんかん 何年(間) ***years***
1	いっぷんかん 一分(間)	いちじかん 一時間	いちにちかん 一日(間)	いっしゅうかん 一週間	いっかげつ 一ケ月	いちねんかん 一年(間)
2	にふんかん 二分(間)	にじかん 二時間	ふつかかん 二日(間)	にしゅうかん 二週間	にかげつ 二ケ月	にねんかん 二年(間)
3	さんぷんかん 三分(間)	さんじかん 三時間	みっかかん 三日(間)	さんしゅうかん 三週間	さんかげつ 三ケ月	さんねんかん 三年(間)
4	よんふんかん 四分(間)	よじかん 四時間	よっかかん 四日(間)	よんしゅうかん 四週間	よんかげつ 四ケ月	よねんかん 四年(間)
5	ごふんかん 五分(間)	ごじかん 五時間	いつかかん 五日(間)	ごしゅうかん 五週間	ごかげつ 五ケ月	ごねんかん 五年(間)
6	ろっぷんかん 六分(間)	ろくじかん 六時間	むいかかん 六日(間)	ろくしゅうかん 六週間	ろっかげつ 六ケ月	ろくねんかん 六年(間)
7	しちじかん ななふんかん 七分(間)	ななじかん 七時間	なのかかん 七日(間)	ななしゅうかん 七週間	しちかげつ ななかげつ 七ケ月	しちねんかん ななねんかん 七年(間)
8	はっぷんかん 八分(間)	はちじかん 八時間	ようかかん 八日(間)	はっしゅうかん 八週間	はっかげつ 八ケ月	はちねんかん 八年(間)
9	きゅうふんかん 九分(間)	くじかん 九時間	ここのかかん 九日(間)	きゅうしゅうかん 九週間	きゅうかげつ 九ケ月	きゅうねんかん 九年(間)
10	じゅっぷんかん じっぷんかん 十分(間)	じゅうじかん 十時間	とおかかん 十日(間)	じゅっしゅうかん じっしゅうかん 十週間	じゅっかげつ じっかげつ 十ケ月	じゅうねんかん 十年(間)
14	じゅうよんふんかん 十四分(間)	じゅうよじかん 十四時間	じゅうよっかかん 十四日(間)	じゅうよんしゅうかん 十四週間	じゅうよんかげつ 十四ケ月	じゅうよねんかん 十四年(間)
20	にじゅっぷんかん にじっぷんかん 二十分(間)	にじゅうじかん 二十時間	はつかかん 二十日(間)	にじゅっしゅうかん にじっしゅうかん 二十週間	にじっかげつ 二十ケ月	にじゅうねんかん 二十年(間)
24	にじゅうよんふんかん 二十四分(間)	にじゅうよじかん 二十四時間	にじゅうよっかかん 二十四日(間)	にじゅうよんしゅうかん 二十四週間	にじゅうよんかげつ 二十四ケ月	にじゅうよねんかん 二十四年(間)

APPENDIX 6: **Ko-so-a-do** Words

	こ-SERIES (*this*)	そ-SERIES (*that*)	あ-SERIES (*that over there*)	ど-SERIES (*which, what, etc.*)
Demonstrative pronoun (*this one, that one, that one over there, which one, etc.*)	これ	それ	あれ	どれ
Demonstrative Adjective (*this, that, that over there, which, etc.*)	この	その	あの	どの
Location (*here, there, over there, where*)	ここ	そこ	あそこ	どこ
Direction* (polite) (*this way, that way, yonder, which way*)	こちら	そちら	あちら	どちら
Direction* (informal) (*this way, that way, yonder, which way*)	こっち	そっち	あっち	どっち
Kind or type (*this kind of, that kind of, that kind of [far away], what kind of*)	こんな	そんな	あんな	どんな
Extent (*to this extent, to that extent, to that [far] extent, to what extent*)	こんなに	そんなに	あんなに	どんなに
Manner (*[in a manner] like this / that / that over there, in what manner*)	こう	そう	ああ	どう

* These **ko-so-a-do** words can also be used to refer to people, things, and locations. Here are some examples.

> こちらは横井先生(よこいせんせい)です。
> *This is Professor Yokoi.*
> あっちのセーターは9千円(せんえん)ですよ。
> *That sweater over there is 9,000 yen.*
> カーティスさんはそちらにいますか。
> *Is Mr. Curtis there (lit., at that place)?*

APPENDIX 7: Japanese Accent

Basic Rules

1. In standard Japanese speech, a syllable is pronounced with high pitch or low pitch. Pitch is relative; high or low pitch means higher or lower pitch than that of other syllables in a given word or utterance.
2. In standard Japanese, the pitch of the first syllable of a word is always different from that of the second syllable. Thus, if the first syllable has high pitch, the second one has low pitch, and vice versa.
3. Within a single word, once the pitch falls, it doesn't rise again.

Symbols

In many accent dictionaries published in Japan, accent is indicated with two symbols: — and ─┐ . A horizontal bar over a syllable means that this syllable is pronounced with high pitch. A syllable with no bar over it is pronounced with low pitch. A downturn at the end of a bar ─┐ indicates a fall in pitch — that is, the syllable after the downturn is pronounced with low pitch. Here are some examples.

o ma wa ri sa n   inu   ushi

In the word **omawarisan** (*police officer*), the first syllable is pronounced with low pitch, the second and third syllables are pronounced with high pitch, and the last three syllables are pronounced with low pitch. The two words **inu** (*dog*) and **ushi** (*cow*) have the same accent pattern low-high when pronounced independently. However, the difference in notations indicates that the pitch of, for example, particles (**wa**, **ga**, **o**, etc.) following these words will differ. Note that the particles do not have fixed pitch; rather, their pitch (high or low) is determined by the preceding word.

inu ga   ushi ga

Accent Patterns of Words

The following chart shows the possible accent patterns of one-through four-syllable words in standard Japanese speech (using the notation system of this textbook). Also shown is the accent of one-syllable particles when they follow words with these accent patterns. ○ represents a syllable in a given word, and ● denotes a particle.

ONE SYLLABLE	TWO SYLLABLES	THREE SYLLABLES	FOUR SYLLABLES
き (木; *tree*)	ねこ (猫; *cat*)	いのち (命; *life*)	こんばん (今晩; *tonight*)
	いぬ (犬; *dog*)	こころ (心; *heart*)	やまやま (山々; *mountains*)
		おんな (女; *female*)	かがりび (かがり火; *bonfire*)
き (気; *spirit*)	うし (牛; *cow*)	さくら (桜; *cherry tree*)	ともだち (友だち; *friend*)

APPENDIX 8: Answers to Exercises

GETTING STARTED

Part One

Activity 1 1. Konnichi wa. 2. Okagesama de, genki desu. (Ee, genki desu.) 3. Ja, mata. 4. Konban wa. 5. Doo itashimashite. 6. Hajimemashite. 7. Ee. Ogenki desu ka. (Ohisashiburi desu ne.) 8. Ohayoo gozaimasu. 9. Ee, soo desu ne. 10. Oyasuminasai.

Activity 2 1. Ohayoo gozaimasu. 2. Shibaraku desu ne. Ogenki desu ka. 3. Konban wa. Hidoi ame desu ne. 4. Konban wa.

Part Two

Activity 3 Ni-ji desu. Ku-ji desu. Ichi-ji desu. Juu-ni-ji desu. Juu-ji han desu. Yo-ji desu. Shichi-ji desu. Roku-ji han desu.

Linguistic Notes: Katakana Kuizu apartment, alarm clock, [electric] shaver, toothbrush, toast, butter, coffee, automatic [transmission] car, car stereo, sun roof, air conditioner, cassette tapes, popular music, building, underground parking, office, elevator, lunch time, restaurant, curry and rice, coffee shop, tea with lemon, date, fiancée, computer programmer, engagement ring, dinner, French restaurant, drive, neon, date, whiskey, shower, bed.

Part Three

Activity 2 1. san-juu-yon (san-juu-shi) 2. roku-juu-roku 3. hachi-juu-nana (hachi-juu-shichi) 4. hyaku-hachi 5. hyaku-kyuu-juu-roku 6. yon-hyaku-go-juu-kyuu (yon-hyaku-go-juu-ku) 7. go-hykau-go-juu-go 8. hap-pyaku-san 9. sen-ichi 10. sen-go-hykau-roku-juu-ni 11. ni-sen-nana-juu-san 12. go-sen-go-hyaku-go-juu-go 13. has-sen-kyuu-hyaku-roku 14. kyuu-sen-nana-hyaku-juu-san

Activity 5 1. Gozen shichi-ji desu. 2. Gozen hachi-ji desu. 3. Juu-ni-ji desu. 4. Gogo san-ji desu. 5. Gogo shichi-ji desu. 6. Gogo ku-ji desu. 7. Ju-ni-ji desu.

CHAPTER 1

3. Personal Pronouns and Demonstratives

練習1 マドンナはアメリカ人です。/わたしは学生です。/
アコードはホンダの車です。/かわばたやすなりは日本人です。/コーラは飲み物です。/マッキントッシュはコンピュータです。

練習2 1. これはワープロですか。 2. これはスーツケースですか。 3. これは辞書ですか。 4. これはえんぴつですか。 5. これはワインですか。
1. いいえ、ワープロじゃありません。コンピュータです。 2. いいえ、スーツケースじゃありません。かばんです。 3. いいえ、辞書じゃありません。教科書です。 4. いいえ、えんぴつじゃありません。ペンです。 5. いいえ、ワインじゃありません。ジュースです。
1. これはだれのワープロですか。ブラウンさんのワープロです。 2. これはだれのスーツケースですか。カーティスさんのスーツケースです。 3. これはだれのじしょですか。横井先生の辞書です。 4. これはだれのえんぴつですか。林さんのえんぴつです。 5. これはだれのワインですか。佐野さんのワインです。

練習3 (sample answers) 1. ビールですか、ワインですか。ビールです。 2. コンピュータですか、ファクシミリですか。コンピュータです。 3. つくえですか、テーブルですか。つくえです。 4. ギブソンさんはアメリカ人ですか、日本人ですか。アメリカ人です。 5. カワムラさんは一年生ですか、二年生ですか。二年生です。

練習4 (sample answers) 1. かのじょも45さいです。 2. はやしさんも学生です。 3.「アディオス」もスペイン語です。 4. りんごもくだものです。 5. バスケットボールもスポーツです。 6. てんぷらも日本料理です。 7. ソニーも日本のメーカーです。

練習5 1. わたしの日本語の先生は45さいです。 2. わたしのクラスメートのはやしさんは8月生まれです。 3. わたしの先生のなまえはよこいです。 4. マーガレット・サッチャーはイギリス人です。 5. ジョン・カワムラさんは学生です。

4. Asking Questions: Interrogatives

練習1　1. 何　2. だれ　3. どこ　4. 何　5. どこ　6. どれ
練習2　1. ここ　2. こちら　3. これ　4. これ
練習3 (sample answers)　1. あの人はどなたですか。 2. どこのごしゅっしんですか。/ごしゅっしんはどこですか。 3. としょかんはどこですか。 4. あそこは何ですか。 5. いつデパートへいきますか。 6. これは本ですか。 7. 先生のけんきゅうしつはどちらですか。 8. はやしさんは何歳ですか。/お年はおいくつですか。 9. これはだれのコンピュータですか。 10. 今何時ですか。

CHAPTER 2

5. Adjectives and Adverbs

練習1　1. いいえ、そのビルは高くないです。ひくいです。 2. いいえ、この本はおもしろくないです。つまらないです。 3. いいえ、この肉はおいしくないです。まずいです。 4. いいえ、あの先生はきびしくないです。やさしいです。 5. いいえ、このスーツは高くないです。安いです。 6. いいえ、このテレビは重くないです。軽いです。 7. いいえ、日本語はむずかしくないです。やさしいです。 8. いいえ、山口さんのスピーチは長くないです。短いです。 9. いいえ、その本は厚くないです。うすいです。 10. いいえ、わたしのうちは広くないです。せまいです。
練習2　1. あのおもしろい人はだれですか。 2. あのきれいな女の人はだれですか。 3. あの大きいきかいは何ですか。 4. あのきたないものは何ですか。 5. あの静かな人はだれですか。 6. あの親切な男の人はだれですか。 7. あのやさしい男の人はだれですか。 8. あのへんなものは何ですか。 9. あのまじめな男の人はだれですか。 10. あの便利なきかいは何ですか。 11. あのまるいものは何ですか。 12. あの器用な女の人はだれですか。
練習3　1. この近所はあまり静かではありません。 2. あの男の人はとても若いです。 3. その大学はあまり古くありません。 4. この車はとても安全です。 5. この町はあまりにぎやかではありません。 6. この話はあまりおかしくありません。 7. カーティスさんはあまり元気ではありません。 8. あの人はとてもエレガントです。 9. このバナナはとてもおいしいです。 10. このドレスはとても安いです。
練習4　1. この時計は安いです。 2. あの村はとても静かです。 3. これはとても小さい町です。 4. このカーテンは古いです。 5. これははでなネクタイです。 6. あれはにぎやかな町です。 7. あのビルはとても有名です。
練習5 (sample answers)　1. わたしはきれいです。(*I am pretty.*)　2. わたしの日本語の先生はハンサムです。(*My Japanese teacher is handsome.*)　3. ジュリア・ロバーツは有名です。(*Julia Roberts is famous.*)　4. アーノルド・シュワルツネーガーはタフです。(*Arnold Schwarzenegger is tough.*)　5. エディ・マーフィーはおもしろいです。(*Eddie Murphy is funny.*)　6. わたしの大学は大きいです。(*My university is big.*)　7. わたしのうちは小さいです。(*My house is small.*)　8. わたしのとなりの人はまじめです。(*The person next to me is serious.*)　9. この練習はやさしいです。(*This exercise is easy.*)

6. Expressing Existence: The Verbs あります and います

練習1　1. このクラスに黒板があります。 2. わたしのへやにコンピュータがあります。 3. カフェテリアにクラスメートがいます。 4. なかのにブラウンさんのアパートがあります。 5. このクラスに学生がいます。 6. うちにわたしのじてんしゃがあります。 7. としょかんに本があります。
練習2 (sample sentences)　クラスに学生がいます。クラスにまどがあります。へやにつくえがあります。アパートにテレビがあります。としょかんに本があります。...

8. Positional Words

練習1　1. A: カーティスさんはどこにいますか。 B: 図書館の前にいます。 2. A: 交番はどこにありますか。 B: 銀行とスーパーの間にあります。 3. A: 駐車場はどこにありますか。 B: 公園の後ろにあります。 4. A: 林さんはどこにいますか。 B: ギブソンさんの右にいます。 5. A: 喫茶店はどこにありますか。 B: ホテルの中にあります。
練習2　1. はこと本と紙があります。 2. ペンがあります。 3. かみがあります。 4. いすの上にあります。 5. こくばんの右にあります。 6. まどがあります。 7.こくばんの前にいます。 8. チンさんとカーティスさんの間にいます。
練習3　1. カワムラさんとチンさんの間にいます。 2. チンさんがいます。 3. いぬがいます。 4. カーティスさんがいます。 5. 木の下にいます。 6. とりがいます。 7. みむらさんがいます。 8. はやしさんがいます。

9. Numerals and Counters

練習1 1. 足 (そく) 2. 本 (ほん) 3. 台 (だい) 4. 頭 (とう) 5. 着 (ちゃく) 6. 枚 (まい) 7. 軒 (けん) 8. 本 (ほん) 9. つ 10. 匹 (ひき)

練習2 1. つくえの上にえんぴつが何本ありますか。 2. うちに車が何だいありますか。 3. きょうしつにみむらさんがいますか。 4. このへやにいぬは何びきいますか。 5. 山田さんの左に人が何人いますか。 6. かばんの中に本が何さつありますか。 7. この町にきっさてんが何けんありますか。 8. あそこに本が何さつありますか。 9. テーブルの上にバナナが何本ありますか。 10. このきんじょにこうえんがいくつありますか。

練習3 1. 三百五万二千百九十六 2. 五千四百九万六千七百十 3. 千億九千四百三十一万二千九十三 4. 三百四億十八 5.六千七百一兆千九億九千七十七万八千百五十六 6. 十億一万九千

練習4 1. 一億千七百五万七千人です。 2. 三十七万三千平方キロメートルです。 3. 九万八千平方キロメートルです。 4. 二億二千五十八万人です。 5. 九百九十七万六千平方キロメートルです。 6. 十億八百十七万五千人です。 7. 千八百二十七万人です。 8. 百九十七万三千平方キロメートルです。 9. 五百十万人です。 10. 六億五千九十八万人です。

10. Expressing Likes and Dislikes: 好き and きらい

練習2 (sample answers) 1. 大きい町が好きです。 2. にぎやかなところが好きです。 3. 古い町が好きです。 4. コメディーが好きです。 5. ゴスペルが好きです。 6. 日本りょうりが好きです。 7. ブロッコリがきらいです。 8. フットボールが好きです。 9. 日本語が好きです。

CHAPTER 3

11. The Basic Structure of Japanese Verbs

練習1 Class 1 ある、歩く、走る、踊る、歌う、泳ぐ、待つ、泣く、使う、作る、笑う、休む、飛ぶ、会う、住む、わかる

Class 2 いる、できる、教える、見せる、考える、やめる

Class 3 料理する

練習 2 起きない、食べない、みがかない、洗わない、出かけない、行かない、飲まない、勉強しない、見ない、寝ない、着ない、浴びない、入らない、言わない、歌わない、いない、使わない、話さない、乗らない、働かない、休まない、眠らない、会わない、洗濯しない、死なない、とかさない

12. The Nonpast, Polite Form of Verbs

練習1 1. 起きます、起きません 2. 洗います、洗いません 3. みがきます、みがきません 4. 走ります、走りません 5. 食べます、食べません 6. 飲みます、飲みません 7. 出かけます、出かけません 8. 待ちます、待ちません 9. 行きます、行きません 10. 乗ります、乗りません 11. 着きます、着きません 12. 会います、会いません 13. 見ます、見ません 14. 泳ぎます、泳ぎません 15. します、しません 16. 帰ります、帰りません 17. 休みます、休みません 18. 入ります、入りません 19. 読みます、読みません 20. 寝ます、寝ません 21. 来ます、来ません 22. 話します、話しません

練習2 1. ビールを飲む。 2. 明日、ロサンジェルスへ行きます。 3. 今日の午後、山田さんに会う。 4. ブラウンさんは来週、アメリカから帰ります。 5. 毎日、運動する。 6. あなたは何を食べますか。 7. パーティーへ来ますか。 8. わたしはテレビを見ません。 9. 町田さんを待つか。 10. シュミットさんは日本語を話しません。

練習3 1. いつも七時に朝ごはんを食べます。 2. 毎朝七時半に大学へ行きます。 3. 毎日八時にクラスが始まります。 4. 毎日十二時に昼ごはんを食べます。 5. いつも三時にクラスが終わります。 6. 毎日四時に図書館へ行きます。 7. いつも五時に大学から帰ります。 8. 毎日六時に夕ごはんを食べます。 9. いつも七時にテレビを見ます。 10. 毎日九時に日本語を勉強します。 11. 毎晩十一時に寝ます。

練習4 —毎朝運動しますか。—いいえ、しません。 2. —いつもコーヒーを飲みますか。—はい、飲みます。 3. —よく町田さんに会いますか。—はい、会います。 4. —毎日テレビを見ますか。—いいえ、見ません。 5. —毎晩レストランで食べますか。—いいえ、食べません。

練習5 (sample answers) 1. 日曜日の朝うんどうします。 2. 毎日午前八時にテレビを見ます。 3. わたしは毎日シャワーをあびます。 4. 日本語のクラスは午後二時にはじまります。 5. わたしとガールフレンドはいつもカフェテリアであいます。 6. わたしは来週の月曜日ニューヨークへ行きます。 7. 土曜日の午後せんたくします。 8. わたしは来年スペイン語をべんきょうします。

練習6　わたしは毎日午前五時に起きます。それから、家の回りを散歩します。午前六時にコーヒーを飲みます。朝ごはんは食べません。午前七時に家を出ます。午前七時のバスに乗ります。午前八時に大学のクラスが始まります。十二時にカフェテリアで昼ごはんを食べます。午後一時にクラスへ行きます。クラスは午後三時に終わります。わたしの友だちは図書館へ行きます。でも、わたしは行きません。午後四時に家に帰ります。それから、六時まで勉強します。六時に夕ごはんを食べます。そのあと、テレビを見ます。午後十時にいつも寝ます。

13. The Past, Polite Form of Verbs

練習1　1. 起きました、起きませんでした　2. 洗いました、洗いませんでした　3. みがきました、みがきませんでした　4. 走りました、走りませんでした　5. 食べました、食べませんでした　6. 飲みました、飲みませんでした　7. 出かけました、出かけませんでした　8. 待ちました、待ちませんでした　9. 行きました、行きませんでした　10. 乗りました、乗りませんでした　11. 着きました、着きませんでした　12. 会いました、会いませんでした　13. 見ました、見ませんでした　14. 泳ぎました、泳ぎませんでした　15. しました、しませんでした　16. 帰りました、帰りませんでした　17. 休みました、休みませんでした　18. 入りました、入りませんでした　19. 読みました、読みませんでした　20. 寝ました、寝ませんでした　21. 来ました、来ませんでした　22. 話しました、話しませんでした

練習2　1. はい、見ました。いいえ、見ませんでした。 2. はい、勉強しました。いいえ、勉強しませんでした。 3. はい、読みました。いいえ、読みませんでした。 4. はい、いました。いいえ、いませんでした。 5. はい、食べました。いいえ、食べませんでした。 6. はい、ありました。いいえ、ありませんでした。 7. はい、行きました。いいえ、行きませんでした。 8. はい、見ました。いいえ、見ませんでした。 9. はい、しました。いいえ、しませんでした。 10. はい、入りました。いいえ、入りませんでした。

練習3 (sample answers)　1. 田中さんは昨日何時に朝ごはんを食べましたか。八時に食べました。2. 田中さんは昨日何時に学校へ行きましたか。九時に行きました。 3. 田中さんは昨日何時にお茶を飲みましたか。三時に飲みました。 4. 田中さんは昨日何時に図書館で勉強しましたか。四時に勉強しました。 5. 田中さんは昨日何時に散歩をしましたか。五時にしました。 6. 田中さんは昨日何時に電話をかけましたか。六時にかけました。 7. 田中さんは昨日何時に音楽を聞きましたか。七時に聞きました。 8. 田中さんは昨日何時に友だちと話しましたか。八時に話しました。 9. 田中さんは昨日何時に手紙を書きましたか。九時に書きました。 10. 田中さんは昨日何時に寝ましたか。十一時に寝ました。

練習4　1. —昨日何時に起きましたか。—5時半に起きました。 2. —昨日何時にジョギングしましたか。—6時にジョギングしました。 3. —昨日何時に朝ごはんを食べましたか。—6時半に食べました。 4. —昨日何時にいえを出ましたか。—7時に出ました。 5. —昨日何時に電車に乗りましたか。—7時15分に乗りました。 6. —昨日何時にクラスへ行きましたか。—8時に行きました。 7. —昨日何時に昼ごはんを食べましたか。—12時20分に食べました。 8. —昨日何時にコーヒーを飲みましたか。—1時に飲みました。 9. —昨日何時に図書館へ行きましたか。—1時20分に行きました。 10. —昨日何時に運動をしましたか。—3時40分にしました。 11. —昨日何時に家に帰りましたか。—5時半に帰りました。 12. —昨日何時にテレビを見ましたか。—6時に見ました。 13.—昨日何時に夕ごはんを食べましたか。—7時15分に食べました。 14. —昨日何時に日本語を勉強しましたか。—8時45分に勉強しました。 15. —昨日何時に音楽を聞きましたか。—10時40分に聞きました。 16. —昨日何時に寝ましたか。—11時30分に寝ました。

練習5 (sample answers)　1. わたしは去年日本へ行きました。 2. 田中さんは昨日の夜九時にねました。 3. わたしと山口さんは先週、すしを食べました。 4. 昨日はねませんでした。 5. 今日の朝、さんぽをしました。 6. 先週の土曜日、パーティーがありました。 7. いつもうちでテレビを見ました。 8. 昨日、六時から十時までとしょかんでべんきょうしました。 9.　うちの前にいぬがいました。 10. 大学からうちまではしりました。

練習6 (sample answers)　1. 九時に起きました。 2. いいえ、見ませんでした。 3. はい、食べました。 4. 三回みがきました。 5.　シカゴで生まれました。 6. 昨年来ました。 7. はい、洗いました。 8. ステーキを食べました。 9. 三時間勉強しました。 10. 七時間寝ました。

14. Particles Showing Grammatical Relations

練習1　1. の、に　2. を　3. に、へ　4. で、を　5. に (へ)　6. に (へ)、で、に (と)、から　7. を　8. で　9. から、まで　10. と　11. に　12. が

練習2　に、を、から、まで、を、に、に (へ)、から、まで、が、で、を、を、に、と、に (へ)、に、へ (に)、に、を、で、を、に、に、に、を、に

練習3 A: いつデパートへ行きましたか。 B: 先週の土曜日に行きました。 A: だれと行きましたか。 B: 山口さんと行きました。 A: 何を買いましたか。 B: ブラウスを買いました。. . . B: いいえ、あまり行きません。. . . B: はい、いつも家で夕ごはんを食べます。 A: 昨日何を食べましたか。 B: ステーキを食べました。 A: どんな食べ物が好きですか。 B: ほとんどみんな好きです。

15. Making Suggestions: ～ましょう

練習1 1. 映画を見ましょう。 2. コンサートへ行きましょう。 3. ケーキを食べましょう。 4. ジョギングしましょう。 5. 本を読みましょう。 6. 買い物に出かけましょう。 7. プールで泳ぎましょう。 8. 日本語で話しましょう。

練習2 1. —わたしが山口さんに聞きましょうか。—ええ、おねがいします。 2. —わたしが洗濯しましょうか。—いいえ、けっこうです。 3. —わたしが横井先生の研究室に行きましょうか。—ええ、おねがいします。 4. —わたしがその本を読みましょうか。—ええ、おねがいします。 5. —わたしが料理しましょうか。—いいえ、けっこうです。

練習3 (sample answers) 1. もう5時ですね。帰りましょうか。 2. 高田さん、おそいですね。電話しましょうか。 3. この質問はむずかしいですね。先生に聞きましょうか。 4. 明日はカーティスさんの誕生日ですよ。プレゼントを買いましょうか。 5. あっ、あそこに林さんがいますよ。一緒にかえりましょうか。

16. Conjoining Nouns: と and や

練習 1. はやしさんとチンさんとギブソンさんが来ました。はやしさんやチンさんが来ました。 2. ステーキとサラダとくだものを食べました。ステーキやサラダを食べました。 3. ブラウンさんとカワムラさんとカーティスさんとチンさんがいます。ブラウンさんやカワムラさんがいます。 4. アイ・ビー・エムとアップルとエヌ・イー・シーととうしばがあります。アイ・ビー・エムやアップルがあります。 5. バスケットボールとフットボールとテニスが好きです。バスケットボールやフットボールが好きです。

CHAPTER 4

17. Conjugating Adjectives

練習1 1. いいえ、悪くなかったです (悪くありませんでした)。よかったです。 2. いいえ、涼しくなかったです (涼しくありませんでした)。暖かかったです。 3. いいえ、おもしろくなかったです (おもしろくありませんでした)。つまらなかったです。 4. いいえ、きれいではなかったです (きれいではありませんでした)。きたなかったです。 5. いいえ、静かではなかったです (静かではありませんでした)。うるさかったです。 6. いいえ、長くなかったです (長くありませんでした)。短かったです。 7. いいえ、忙しくなかったです (忙しくありませんでした)。ひまでした。 8. いいえ、きびしくなかったです (きびしくありませんでした)。やさしかったです。 9. いいえ、高くなかったです (高くありませんでした)。低かったです。 10. いいえ、まじめではなかったです (まじめではありませんでした)。ふまじめでした。

練習2 1. アラスカはいつも寒かったです。 2. 日本の夏はむし暑かった。 3. 4月は毎日暖かかった。 4. 今年の夏は涼しかった。 5. あの部屋はとても暑かった。 6. 12月は気温が高くなかった。 7. ブラウンさんは元気じゃありませんでした。 8. あの本はよくなかった。 9. 天気がいつも悪かった。 10. カワムラさんはハンサムだった。 11. ギブソンさんはエレガントでした。 12. この大学は有名ではなかった。

練習3 1. いそがしかったです 2. 寒かったです 3. 高かった 4. 多かった 5. 静かだった 6. 強かったです 7. よかった 8. おもしろかったです

練習4 昨日は一月二十三日でした。朝からとても寒かったです。でも、お天気はとてもよかったです。空がとてもきれいでした。風がありましたが、あまり強くありませんでした。昨日は土曜日でしたから、クラスがありませんでした。宿題もありませんでした。だから、わたしはひまでした。昨日は部屋を掃除しました。わたしの部屋はとてもきたなかったです。それから、洗濯もしました。わたしのルームメートは病気でした。部屋にいました。

18. Comparatives and Superlatives

練習1 1. —この町とフローレンスとどちらがきれいですか。—この町のほうがきれいです。 2. —ペプシとコークとどちらがおいしいですか。—コークのほうがおいしいです。 3. —日本の車とアメリカの車とどちらが安いですか。—日本の車のほうが安いです。 4. —フロリダとネバダとどちらが雨がたくさん降りますか。—フロリダのほうが雨がたくさん降ります。 5. —ニューヨークとボストンとどちらが寒いですか。—ボストンのほうが寒いです。 6. —カール・ルイスとベン・ジョンソンとどちらが速く走りますか。—ベン・ジョンソンのほうが速く走ります。 7. —去年の夏と今年の夏とどちらが暑いですか。—今年の夏のほうが暑いです。 8. —トロントとエドモントンとどちらが雪が多いですか。—エドモントンのほうが雪が多いです。 9. —昨日と今日とどちらが涼しいですか。—今日のほうが涼しいです。 10. —南日本の北日本とどちらが台風がたくさん来ますか。—南日本のほうが台風がたくさん来ます。
練習2 (sample answers) 1. 暑いです 2. 多いです 3. たくさんはたらきます 4. 小さいです 5. わかいです 6. きびしいです 7. かんたんです 8. おもしろいです
練習3 1. 林さんはカワムラさんほどたくさん食べません。 2. 東京は京都ほど古くないです。 3. 昨日は今日ほどむし暑くなかった。 4. 林さんは三村さんほどお酒が好きではない。 5. チンさんはシュミットさんほど日本語をじょうずに話さない。 6. 札幌は秋田ほど雪が多く降りません。 7. 町田さんは本田さんほどキュートではありません。 8. この映画はあの映画ほどおもしろくなかった。
練習4 1. —日本語とロシア語とアラビア語の中でどれが一番むずかしいですか。—アラビア語が一番むずかしいです。 2. —プレリュードとミヤタとアクラ・レジェンドの中でどれが一番に高いですか。—アクラ・レジェンドが一番高いです。 3. —シカゴとロサンジェルスとダラスの中でどこが一番風が強いですか。—シカゴが一番風が強いです。 4. —ミシガンとフロリダとアイダホの中でどこが一番暖かいですか。—フロリダが一番暖かいです。 5. —バスと車と電車の中でどれが一番便利ですか。—車が一番便利です。 6. —スーパーとデパートとセブン・イレブンの中でどこが一番安いですか。—スーパーが一番安いです。 7. —ビールとお茶とコーヒーの中でどれを一番よく飲みますか。—お茶を一番よく飲みます。
練習5 (sample answers) 1. ニューヨークです。 2. ボストンです。 3. シアーズ・タワーです。 4. シアトルです。 5. オノ・ヨーコです。 6. すしが一番好きです。 7. 8月が一番暑いです。 8. 1月が一番寒いです。 9. 6月が一番忙しいです。 10. フットボールが一番おもしろいです。 11. 「さよなら」が一番好きです。

19. The Past, Plain Forms of Verbs

練習1 1. ブラウンさんは五時半に起きた。 2. 顔を洗った。 3. 歯を一日に三回みがいた。 4. 毎日10キロ走った。 5. サラダをたくさん食べた。 6. オレンジ・ジュースを飲んだ。 7. 高田さんは7時に出かけた。 8. デパートの前でギブソンさんを待った。 9. 毎日クラスへ行った。 10. 家から大学までバスに乗った。 11. 8時に大学に着いた。 12. 図書館でチンさんに会った。 13. テレビでニュースを見た。 14. 午後プールで泳いだ。 15. フランス語を勉強した。 16. 10時ごろ家に帰った。 17. 土曜日は家で休んだ。 18. お風呂に入った。 19. 電車の中で新聞を読んだ 20. 12時に寝た。 21. いつもパーティーに来た。
練習2 1. 先週は雨がたくさん降った。 2. デパートでプレゼントを買った。 3. パーティーでは山田さんに会わなかった。 4. 高田さんは昨日、ワシントンから帰った。 5. わたしはぜんぜん勉強しなかった。 6. 昨日、ブラウンさんと話さなかった。 7. かれのおじいさんは去年死んだ。 8. 今朝、歯をみがかなかった。 9. 昨日はお酒を飲んだか。 10. 昨日顔を洗わなかった。 11. もうテレビのニュースは見たか。 12. ここに何時に着いたか。 13. 昨日の夜はあまり寝なかった。 14. ディズニーランドでコーヒーカップに乗った。 15. 林さんはもう出かけたか。 16. 高田さんはスーパーへ行った。 17. 一週間お風呂に入らなかった。 18. シャワーは浴びたか。

20. Explaining a Reason: …のだ

練習 1. はい、お酒が好きなんです。 2. はい、明日、試験なんです。 3. はい、雪がたくさん降ったんです。 4. はい、とても寒いんです。 5. はい、先週、休んだんです。 6. はい、アルバイトがあったんです。 7. はい、スケートに行くんです。 8. はい、駅にとても近いんです。 9. はい、今、休みなんです。

21. The Te-Form of Adjectives and the Copula

練習1 1. あの人のスピーチは長くて、つまらないです。 2. 日本語の先生はやさしくて、しんせつです。 3. このケーキはあまくて、おいしいです。 4. このラップトップ・コンピュータは重くて、不便です。 5. カナダの冬は寒くて、長いです。 6. わたしの大学は大きくて、有名です。 7. 山口さんはエレガントで、きれいです。 8. カワムラさんはハンサムで、やさしいです。 9. 高田さんは26歳で、サラリーマンです。 10. チンさんは中国人で、ペキンの出身です。
練習2 (sample answers) 1. ええ、便利で、いいところです。 2. ええ、雪が多くて、寒いです。 3. ええ、暑くて、たいへんです。 4. いいえ、とおくて、ふべんです。 5. ええ、ハンサムで、しんせつです。 6. いいえ、つまらなくて、好きではありません。

練習3 (sample answers) 1. わたしはにぎやかで、元気です。 2. ジュリア・ロバーツは若くて、きれいです。 3. アーノルド・シュワルツネーガーはタフで、強いです。 4. エディー・マーフィーは元気で、おもしろいです。 5. わたしの学校はむずかしくて、有名です。 6. わたしの家はせまいですが、きれいです。 7. わたしのとなりの人はハンサムですが、へんです。 8. この練習はむずかしいですが、おもしろいです。

22. The Te-Form of Verbs

練習1 1. 早く起きてください。 2. 顔を洗ってください。 3. 夕ごはんを食べてください。 4. お茶を飲んでください。 5. 大学の前で待ってください。 6. スーパーへ行ってください。 7. タクシーに乗ってください。 8. ブラウンさんに会ってください。 9. このかばんを見てください。 10. 今日の新聞を読んでください。 11. 中に入ってください。 12. 4時にここに来てください。

練習2 1. お風呂から出て、ビールを飲んだ。 2. バスに乗って、デパートへ行って、セーターを買った。 3. シャワーを浴びて、ひげをそった。 4. ドレスを着て、デパートに出かけた。 5. 夕ごはんを食べて、日本語をべんきょうした。 6. カワムラさんの家へ行って、話した。 7. 家に帰って、寝た。 8. ワープロを使って、手紙を書いた。

練習3 1. 食べてください。 2. 起きてください。 3. 日本語を話してください。 4. 明日、うちに来てください。 5. シャワーを浴びてください。 6. 本を買ってください。

練習4 (sample answers) 1. 日本語のクラスへ行って、日本語を話します。 2. カフェテリアへ行って、コーヒーを飲みます。 3. 昼ごはんを食べて、はをみがきます。 4. バスに乗って、デパートへ行きます。 5. スニーカーをはいて、運動します。 6. セーターを着て、大学へ行きます。 7. 本を読んで、勉強します。 8. うちに帰って、テレビを見ます。

23. Expressing Probability and Conjecture

練習1 (sample answers) アメリカ人でしょう。 2. 30歳くらいでしょう。 3. 雪がふるかもしれません。 4. デパートへ行ったかもしれません。 5. 多分高いでしょう。 5. きっと暑いでしょう。 7. 多分まじめな人でしょう。 8. ニューヨークのほうが寒いかもしれません。 9. 10分くらいかかるでしょう。 10. 日本語を勉強したかもしれません。

練習2 1. 雨が降るでしょう。 2. 病気かもしれません。 3. 多分おいしいでしょう。 4. わからないかもしれません。 5. 今日の午後、台風が来るでしょう。

CHAPTER 5

24. Interrogative ＋か／も／でも

練習1 1. 何か 2. どこか 3. だれか (どなたか) 4. どれか 5. どれも 6. どこでも 7. だれでも (どれも) 8. どちらでも 9. だれも 10. どこか どこも

練習2 (sample answers) 1. いいえ、どこへも行きませんでした。 12. 何でも食べます。 3. はい、いつでもいいです。 4. はい、どれも同じです。 5. どれでもいいです。 6. はい、何もしません。 7. はい、いつもやさしいです。 8. いいえ、だれかできるでしょう。

25. Describing Abilities

練習1 1. 山口さんの奥さんはボーリングが上手です。 2. 林さんはバスケットボールのが下手です。 3. シュミットさんは日本語が上手ではありません。 4. 佐野さんはあみものが得意です。 5. カワムラさんはフランス語が苦手です。 6. 父はインドネシア語ができます。 7. 兄はスポーツが苦手です。 8. ギブソンさんはスキーが得意です。 9. わたしは料理ができません。 10. 妻はイタリア語がわかります。

練習2 1. —スポーツが得意ですか —いいえ、苦手です。 2. —ロシア語が上手ですか —いいえ、下手です。 3. —バイオリンが上手ですか。—まあまあです。 4. —ピンポンができますか。—はい、できます。 5. —タガログ語がわかりますか。—いいえ、わかりません。

練習3 (sample answers) 1. いいえ、下手です。 2. カレーライスが一番得意です。 3. はい、上手です。 4. いいえ、できません。 5. テニスが上手です。 6. ピアノが上手です。 7. てんぷらが一番きらいです。 8. そうじが苦手です。 9. フランス語ができます。 10. はい、上手です。

26. Nominalizers: こと and の

練習1 (sample answers) 日本語を話すのはやさしい。 2. 料理をすることはむずかしい。 3. テニスをすることは体にいい。 4. 音楽を聞くことはおもしろい。 5. 山田さんが来たのはおかしい。

練習2 1. カワムラさんはバスケットボールをするのが好きです。 2. 林さんはうんどうをするのがきらいです。 3. ギブソンさんは日本語を話すのが上手です。 4. チンさんは歌を歌うのがきらいです。 5. 町田さんはピアノをひくのがとくいです。 6. 三村さんは英語を書くのが苦手です。
練習3 (sample answers) 1. わたしはテニスをするのが好きです。 2. ドイツ語を話すことはむずかしいです。 3. すきやきをつくるのはやさしいです。 4. SFを読むのはおもしろいです。 5. わたしは日本語を話すのがとくいです。 6. わたしはダンスするのがにがてです。 7. わたしの日本語の先生は歌を歌うのが上手です。 8. わたしは料理をするのが下手です。 9. あの人の話を聞くのはつまらないです。 10. わたしは勉強するのがきらいです。

27. More Uses of the Particle も

練習1 1. チンさんも林さんもパーティーに来ました。 2. 机の上にペンもえんぴつもあります。 3. 林さんはブロッコリもアスパラガスもきらいです。 4. 17日も18日も雨が降りました。 5. 三村さんはテニスもピンポンも上手です。
練習2 1. —何時間寝たんですか。—12時間です。—12時間も寝たんですか。 2. —何週間旅行したんですか。—3週間です。—3週間も旅行したんですか。 3. —ハンバーガーをいくつ食べたんですか。—6つです。—6つも食べたんですか。 4. —本を何冊読んだんですか。—3冊です。—3冊も読んだんですか。 5. —ワインを何杯飲んだんですか。—グラスで7杯です。—7杯も飲んだんですか。 6. —ボーイフレンドが何人いますか。—3人です。—3人もいるんですか。

28. Potential Form of Verbs

練習1 1. 午後図書館へ行くことができます。 2. 今日の午後、林さんに会うことができます。 3. 10キロ走ることができます。 4. 駅まで歩くことができます。 5. ここで泳ぐことができます。 6. 今、ブラウンさんと話すことができます。 7. 母に電話することができます。
練習2 1. —テニスができますか。—はい、できます。(いいえ、できません。) 2. —日本のうたをうたえますか。—はい、うたえます。(いいえ、うたえません。) 3. —はやく走れますか。—はい、走れます。(いいえ、走れません。) 4. —じょうずにえがかけますか。—はい、かけます。(いいえ、かけません。) 5. —わたしとコンサートへ行けますか。—はい、行けます。(いいえ、行けません。) 6. —スキーができますか。—はい、できます。(いいえ、できません。) 7. —今日の午後わたしとテレビをみられますか。—はい、見られます。(いいえ、見られません。) 8. —わたしといっしょに本を読めますか。—はい、読めます。(いいえ、読めません。) 9. —うみでおよげますか。—はい、およげます。(いいえ、およげません。) 10. —わたしの家に来られますか。—はい、来られます。(いいえ、来られません。)
練習3 (sample answers) 1. はい、ひけます。 2. はい、とれます。 3. はい、乗れます。 4. いいえ、できません。 5. はい、歌えます。 6. はい、泳げます。 7. いいえ、走れません。 8. はい、話せます。 9. いいえ、行けません。 10. いいえ、来られません。
練習4 ひけます、話せます、読めます、とれます、泳げます、かけます、食べられます

29. Verb Te-Form + います

練習1 —林さんは何をしていますか。—ひるねをしています。—町田さんは何をしていますか。—コーヒーを飲んでいます。/—ブラウンさんとカワムラさんは何をしていますか。—話しています。/—カーティスさんは何をしていますか。—本を読んでいます。/—三村さんは何をしていますか。—テレビを見ています。/—チンさんは何をしていますか。—てがみを書いています。
練習2 1. わたしはブラウンさんを2年前から知っています。 2.カワムラさんは30分前からおふろに入っています。 3. 山口さんの奥さんは3時からデパートに行っています。 4. カーティスさんは去年から日本に来ています。 5. さとみさんは先週からキャンプに出かけています。
練習3 (sample answers) 1. 3つとっています。けいざい学と日本語とドイツ語のクラスをとっています。 2. 1年前から勉強しています。 3. はい、毎日勉強しています。 4. 100知っています。 5. いいえ、持っていません。 6. はい、知っています。 7. いいえ、降っていません。 8. えんぴつを使っています。 9. Tシャツを着ています。 10. すわっています。 11. ユージンに住んでいます。

30. Relative Clauses

練習1 1. ギャンブラー 2. レスラー 3. 学校 4. 図書館 5. スイマー 6. カメラ 7. 余暇 8. 日本語 9. 映画館 10. プール
練習2 1. 父が昨日買ったカメラは高かったです。 2. わたしが毎日およぐプールはうちのそばにあります。 3. 昨日の夜聞いたレコードは町田さんのレコードです。 4. カルチャーセンターでヨガを教えている先生はインドから来ました。 5. わたしがいつも行く近くのレストランは安くて、おいしいです。 6. ブラウンさんが住んでいる中野は静かで、便利です。
練習3 ひるねをしている男の人は林さんです。コーヒーを飲んでいる女の人は町田さんです。カ

ワムラさんと話している女の人はブラウンさんです。本を読んでいる男の人はカーティスさんです。テレビを見ている男の人は三村さんです。てがみを書いている女の人はチンさんです。
練習4 (sample answers) 1. 昨日行った 2. おととい買った 3. 昨日日本語を勉強した 4. ブラウンさんがとった 5. 私がよく行く 6. 私がいちばんよく聞く 7. 日本から来た 8. 昨日行った 9. カワムラさんと話している 10. マラソンをする人
練習5 (sample answers) 1. はい、知っています。 2. いいえ、ありません。 3. はい、あります。 4. はい、あります。 5. はい、あります。 6. いいえ、ありません。 7. はい、知っています。 8. はい、知っています。 9. いいえ、ありません。 10. ダイエットコークです。

31. Describing a Change in State: なります

練習1 1. 大きく 2. 長く 3. 便利に 4. ひまに 5. 上手に 6. 赤く 7. 安く 8. あたたかく 9. 多く 10. 少なく (白く) 11. きれいに 12. 好きに
練習2 1. エアロビクスが好きなので、エアロビクスのインストラクターになりました。 2. 英語が話せるので、英語の先生になりました。 3. 車が好きなので、カー・レーサーになりました。 4. プログラミングができるので、プログラマーになりました。 5. 体が大きくて、強いので、ボディーガードになりました。

CHAPTER 6

32. Expressing Experience: The Verb Ta-Form + ことがある

練習1 (sample answers) 1. —料理をしたことがありますか。—はい、あります。 2. —日本へ行ったことがありますか。—はい、あります。 3. —ゴルフをしたことがありますか。—いいえ、ありません。 4. —日本の音楽を聞いたことがありますか。—はい、あります。 5. —すきやきを食べたことがありますか。—はい、あります。 6. —お金をおとしたことがありますか。—いいえ、ありません。 7. —お金をひろったことがありますか。—はい、あります。
練習2 1. —あのレストランへ行ったことがありますか。—はい、三度あります。 2. —あのコーラを飲んだことがありますか。—はい、何度もあります。 3. —ロシア語を勉強したことがありますか。—はい、一度あります。 4. —スピルバーグの映画を見たことがありますか。—はい、五年前にあります。 5. —日本の食べ物を買ったことがありますか。—はい、二回ぐらいあります。 6. —コンピュータを使ったことがありますか。—はい、一度あります。 7. —山村さんに会ったことがありますか。—三年前に一度あります。 8. —あのプールで泳いだことがありますか。—いいえ、一度もありません。 9. —この町で雪が降ったことがありますか。—いいえ、一度もありません。 10. —町田さんはウェートレスをしたことがありますか。—はい、五年前にあります。
練習3 1. 日本へ行ったことがありますか。 2. フランス語を勉強したことがありますか。 3. すしを食べたことがありますか。 4. 家でパーティーをしたことがありますか。 5. 学校でDをとったことがありますか。 6. へやをそうじしたことがありますか。
練習4 (sample answers) 1. はい、何度もあります。 2. メキシコレストランやフランスレストランへ行ったことがあります。 3. はい、ときどきあります。 4. はい、一度あります。 5. いいえ、ありません。

33. Expressing a Desire: ほしい、ほしがる、〜たい、 and 〜たがる

1. ちょっと休みたいです。 2. 朝早く起きたくないです。おそく起きたいです。 3. フランス語の辞書が買いたいです。 4. スーパーへ行きたくないです。デパートへ行きたいです。 5. 働きたくないです。休みたいです。 6. 町田さんに会いたいです。 7. 映画が見たいです。 8. 林さんと話したいです。 9. 日本語を練習したいです。 10. 今日、宿題がしたくないです。テニスがしたいです。
練習2 1. ブラウンさんはちょっと休みたがっています。 2. ブラウンさんは朝早くおきたがっていません。おそく起きたがっています。 3. ブラウンさんはフランス語の辞書を買いたがっています。 4. ブラウンさんはスーパーへ行きたがっていません。デパートへ行きたがっています。 5. ブラウンさんは働きたがっていません。休みたがっています。 6. ブラウンさんは町田さんに会いたがっています。 7. ブラウンさんは映画を見たがっています。 8. ブラウンさんは林さんと話したがっています。 9. ブラウンさんは日本語を練習したがっています。 10. ブラウンさんは今日、宿題をしたがっていません。テニスをしたがっています。
練習3 1. うみへ行きたがっています。 2. スパゲッティーを食べたがっています。 3. 家族に会いたがっています。 4. えいがに行きたがっています。 5. 日本茶を飲みたがっています。 6. テ

ニスをしたがっています。 7. ジャズを聞きたがっています。 8. スターウォーズを見たがっています。

練習4 (sample answers) 1. じしょ 2. ハイキングに行き 3. 休み 4. 何か食べ 5. てりやきを食べ 6. レコード

練習5 (sample answers) 1. すしが食べたいです。 2. くるまが買いたいです。 3. ゆっくり休みたいです。 4. CDプレーヤーがほしいです。 5. ペルーへ一番行きたいです。 6. アーセニオ・ホールに一番会いたいです。 7. スペイン語です。 8. そうじすることです。

34. Expressing an Opinion: ... と思う

練習1 1. 林さんと話さなかったと思います。 2. その日、そのレストランは休みだったと思います。 3. その人に会ったことがあったと思います。 4. 山口さんの家の台所はとてもきれいだと思います。 5. ブラウンさんの作ったケーキはとてもおいしかったと思います。 6. あの男の人はコックだと思います。 7. さとみさんは料理をしていると思います。

練習2 (sample answers) 1. いいえ、あまり勉強しないと思います。 2. はい、とても上手に話せると思います。 3. いいえ、とてもうるさいと思います。 4. いいえ、料理は下手だと思います。 5. はい、たくさん食べると思います。 6. ピアノをほしがっていると思います。 7. えいがかんへ行ったと思います。

35. 〜すぎる

練習1 1. あつ 2. 食べ 3. 飲み 4. 高 5. 広 6. から 7. 長

練習2 1. このしけんはむずかしすぎます。 2. かんじが多すぎます。 3. はたらきすぎます。 4. このへやは寒すぎます。 5. 音楽がうるさすぎます。 6. このしけんはかんたんすぎます。 7. このセーターは大きすぎます。

36. Quoting Speech: ... と言う

練習1 1. 朝ごはんといいます。 2. やさいといいます。 3.「ようこそ」といいます。 4. (*The name of your school*) といいます。 5. *cuisine* といいます。 6. もしもしといいます。 7. いただきますといいます。 8. ごちそうさまといいます。

練習2 1. コンピュータ 2. きょうかしょ 3. (*the name of your school*) 4. (*the name of your town*) 5. カルネ・アサーダ

練習3 1. —あれは何という映画館ですか。—テアトロシアターという映画館です。 2. あれは何という果物ですか。—キィウィという果物です。 3. —ここは何という町ですか。—中野という町です。—これは何という車ですか。—セリカという車です。 5. あそこは何というレストランですか。—セブンシーズというレストランです。 6. —これは何という教科書ですか。—ようこそという教科書です。

練習4 1. —アコードという車を知っていますか。—ええ、日本の車です。 2. —東京大学という大学をしっていますか。—ええ、ブラウンさんの大学です。 3. —ラッキーマートというスーパーを知っていますか。—ええ、ブラウンさんの近所のスーパーです。 4. —おでんという食べ物を知っていますか。—ええ、日本の食べ物です。 5. —しょうゆという調味料を知っていますか。—ええ、日本の調味料です。

練習5 1. 町田さんはレストランへ行ったと言った。 2. チンさんはわたしに中国語を教えていると言いました。 3. カワムラさんはハンバーガーが好きかと聞きました。 4. テレビのレポーターはハワイはとても暑いと言っています。 5. 林さんは英語が話せないと言った。 6. 山口さんは毎日料理したと言いました。 7. 山本さんは新聞を読んでいないと言いました。 8. カーティスさんは昼ごはんを食べたかと聞いた。 9. ギブソンさんは二十日は土曜日だと言いました。 10. ブラウンさんは雨の日が好きではないといつも言っています。

練習6 (sample answers) 1. 山口さんは「ステーキを食べましょう」と言いました。 2. カーティスさんは「本を読みましょう」と言いました。 3. チンさんは「勉強しましょう」と言いました。 4. 三村さんは「ねむいです」と言いました。 5. 町田さんは「おやすみなさい」と言いました。

37. Expressing Intention: つもり and the Volitional Form of Verbs

練習1 1. 朝早く起きようと思います。 2. 毎朝ジョギングをしようと思います。 3. 朝ごはんを毎日食べようと思います。 4. コーヒーを飲むのをやめようと思います。 5. スーパーで夕ごはんの材料を買おうと思います。

練習2 (sample answers) 1. てんぷらを食べるつもりです。 2. としょかんへ行くつもりです。 3. へやのそうじをするつもりです。 4. はい、日本へ行くつもりです。 5. 毎日スキーをしようと思います。

練習3　すきやきを作るつもりでしたが、肉がなかったので作れませんでした。ぶた肉をかうつもりでしたが、お金がなかったのでかえませんでした。ブラウンさんにでんわするつもりでしたが、わすれました。ハイキングに行くつもりでしたが、雨で行けませんでした。

38. The Te-Form of Verbs + みる、しまう、いく、and くる

練習1 (sample answers)　1. いいえ、わかりません。先生に聞いてみてください。 2. ちょっと飲んでみます。 3. ちょっと会ってみます。 4. すきやきを作ってみてください。 5. 週末に読んでみます。 6. 日曜日に行ってみます。

練習2　2. —カラムラさんはどうしましたか。—もう帰ってしまいました。 2. —昨日買ったアイスクリームはどうしましたか。—もう食べてしまいました。 3. —手紙はどうしましたか。—もう書いてしまいました。 4. —ビデオはどうしましたか。—もう見てしまいました。 5. ウイスキーはどうしましたか。—もう飲んでしまいました。 6. —宿題はどうしましたか。—もうしてしまいました。 7. ナイフとフォークはどうしましたか。—もう洗ってしまいました。 8. —チンさんのバースデー・ケーキはどうしましたか。—もう買ってしまいました。

練習3　1. じゃあ、ちょっと買っていきましょう。 2. じゃあ、セーターを着ていきましょう。 3. じゃあ、昼ごはんを食べていきましょう。 4. じゃあ、走っていきましょう。 5. じゃあ、ちょっと話していきましょう。 6. じゃあ、ちょっと休んでいきましょう。 7. じゃあ、ちょっと聞いていきましょう。 8. じゃあ、ちょっと飲んでいきましょう。

練習4　1. いいえ、食べてきました。 2. ええ、話してきました。 3. ええ、教科書を読んできました。 4. ええ、買ってきました。 5. ええ、走ってきました。 6. ええ、お酒を飲んできました。 7. ええ、3時に帰ってきました。 8. おもしろい映画を見てきました。

39. Expressing Simultaneous Actions: ～ながら

練習　1. ワインを飲みながら、ステーキを食べた。 2. 町を歩きながら、写真をたくさん撮りました。 3. テレビを見ながら、勉強しました。 4. メモを取りながら三村さんの話を聞きました。 5. 昼はアルバイトをしながら、夜は学校へ行っています。

CHAPTER 7

40. Saying When Something Happens: Temporal Clauses Ending in 時

練習1　1. d　2. a　3. f　4. c　5. b　6. e

練習2　1. A: どんな時、買い物に行きますか。B: ひまな時、行きます。 2. A: どんな時、本を読みますか。B: 時間がある時、本を読みます。 3. A: どんな時、コートを着ますか。B: 寒い時、着ます。 4. A: どんな時、図書館へ行きますか。B: 勉強をする時、行きます。 5. A: どんな時、ネクタイをしめますか。B: 仕事へ行く時、しめます。 6. A: どんな時、日本語を話しますか。B: 日本人の友だちと話す時、話します。

練習3　1. 買い物に行く時、いつも友だちと行きます。 2. しずかな時、本を読みます。 3. コンサートへ行った時、プログラムを買います。 4. 日本語を話す時、ゆっくり話してください。 5. 仕事がない時、昼ごろ起きる。 6. ひまな時、ウインドーショッピングをします。 7. 学生の時、デパートでアルバイトをしました。 8. 日本にいた時、このワープロを買った。

練習4 (sample answers)　1. コーラを飲みます。 2. テニスをしました。 3. 5人の学生がいました。 4. はしを使います。 5. はい、使います。 6. スエットシャツを着ます。 7. パーティーへ行った時、お酒を飲みます。 8. えいがを見ます。 9. 前にすわります。 10. デートの時、行きます。

練習5 (sample answers)　1. さびしい時、音楽を聞きます。 2. 雨が降った時、としょかんにいました。 3. 天気がいい時、テニスをします。 4. クラスがない時、パーティーをしました。 5. そのステレオを買った時、うれしかったです。 6. パーティーをする時、スーパーで飲み物を買います。 7. 友だちが家に来た時、すしを作りました。 8. デパートのセールの時、服をたくさん買いました。

練習6 (sample answers)　1. ひまな時、テレビを見ます。 2. 休みの時、映画に行きました。 3. 道がわからない時、おまわりさんにききます。 4. しけんが終わった時、パーティーをします。 5. 日本語のしゅくだいをする時、辞書を使います。 6. くすりを買う時、薬局へ行きます。

41. Indefinite Pronoun の

練習1　1. A: すみません。スカートをください。B: 長いのがいいですか。短いのがいいですか。A: 長いのをおねがいします。 2. A: すみません。テープレコーダーをください。

B: 大きいのがいいですか。小さいのがいいですか。A: 大きいのをおねがいします。 3. A: すみません。アイロンをください。B: 重いのがいいですか。軽いのがいいですか。A: 重いのをおねがいします。 4. A: すみません。ネクタイをください。B: はでなのがいいですか。じみなのがいいですか。A: はでなのをおねがいします。 5. A: すみません。リボンをください。B: 黒いのがいいですか。赤いのがいいですか。A: 黒いのをおねがいします。

練習2 1. でも、この黒いのはわたしには似合いませんね。 2. あついのはありますか。 3. もっと便利なのを探しましょう。 4. 有名なのはありますか。 5. からくないのがあちらにありますから、それを食べましょう。

練習3 1. 先週買ったのはブラウスです。 2. あの店で売っているのはおいしいケーキです 。 3. 私が電話したのはブラウンさんです。 4. 昨日ステーキを食べたのは林さんです。 5. たいへん有名なのはこの本です。 6. とても便利なのは東京の電車です。

42. Making If-Then Statements: The ～たら Conditional

練習1 1. 行ったら 2. 聞いたら 3. 寒かったら 4. 買ったら 5. 消したら 6. 静かだったら 7. たてたら 8. 来たら 9. おもしろかったら

練習2 (sample answers) 1. もし明日しけんがなかったら、学校を休むでしょう。 2. もし日本語が上手だったら、日本のかいしゃではたらくでしょう。 3. もしお金がたくさんあったら、ヨットを買うでしょう。 4. もしステレオを持っていたら、毎日クラシックを聞くでしょう。 5. もし雨が降っていなかったら、ピクニックに行くでしょう。

練習3 (sample answers) 1. マドンナが来たら、いっしょにうたをうたいます。 2. 6時になったら、夕ごはんを食べます。 3. 1万ドルあったら、ラスベガスへ行きます。 4. マイケル・ジャクソンから電話があったら、サイン (autograph) をおねがいします。 5. そのコートが安かったら、買います。 6. フランス語が上手だったら、フランス人とデートします。 7. 春が来たら、ピクニックへ行きます。 8. 車があったら、べんりです。 9. 日本へ行ったら、パチンコをします。

43. Going Somewhere with a Purpose: Using the Particle に to Express Purpose

練習1 1. 三村さんは電話をかけに行きました。 2. ブラウンさんはスキーをしに出かけました。 3. チンさんはカーティスさんと話しに来ました。 4. 山口さんとカワムラさんは映画を見に行きました。 5. 山口さんは昼ごはんを食べに帰りました。 6. 町田さんは服を着替えにもどりました。

練習2 1. —何をしに行きましたか。—泳ぎに行きました。 2. —何をしに行きましたか。—バスケットボールをしに行きました。 3. —何をしに行きましたか。—日本語をれんしゅうしに行きました。 4. —何をしに行きましたか。—としょかんへ (に) 本を読みに行きまし。 5. —何をしに行きましたか。—セーターを買いに行きました。

44. Reporting Hearsay: …そうです

練習1 1. 林さんの話では、ギブソンさんはカナダの出身だそうです。 2. チンさんの話では、このケーキはあそこのお菓子屋で買ったそうです。 3. カワムラさんの話では、そのビールは酒屋で売っているそうです。 4. カーティスさんの話では、あのワープロは高かったそうです。 5. 山口さんの話では、ご主人は若い時、ハンサムだったそうです。 6. 山本さんの話では、高田さんのネクタイはちょっとはでだったそうです。 7. 高田さんの話では、フィルムはデパートでも買えるそうです。

練習2 1. 高田さんの車は古いそうです。 2. チンさんのアパートはあまり便利じゃないそうです。 3. 北海道は雪が降って、とても寒かったそうです。 4. ブラウンさんは京都へ行っていたそうです。 5. ブラウンさんは夏休みは洋品店でアルバイトをすることにしたそうです。

45. Saying Whether or Not Something Is True: …かどうか

練習 1. 来たかどうかわからないから、ブラウンさんに聞いてみます。 2. 降るかどうかわからないから、テレビの天気予報を見てみます。 3. 大きいかどうかわからないから、図書館でしらべてみます。 4. カナダ人かどうかわからないから、ギブソンさんに聞いてみます。 5. 勉強しているかどうかわからないから、見てみます。 6. 行くかどうかわからないから、電話で聞いてみます。 7. 新しいかどうかわからないから、肉屋さんに聞いてみます。

46. Giving Reasons with …し、…し

練習1 1. きれいな色だし、よくにあうし、いいセーターですね。 2. おいしいし、安いし、いいレストランですね。 3. やさしいし、親切だし、いい人ですね。 4. 速いし、便利だし、東京のタクシーはいいですね。 5. わたしの家に近いし、静かだし、この公園によく来ます。

練習2 (sample answers) 1. わたしのアパートはせまいし、大学からとおいし、ふべんです。 2. 町田さんはあたまがいいし、やさしいし、いい人です。 3. この町は車が多いし、木が少ないし、あまり好きではありません。 4. このハンドバッグはかるいし、きれいだし、たいへん好きです。 5. このけいさんきは小さいし、かるいし、べんりです。 6. カーティスさんはハンサムだし、しんせつだし、とてもいい人です。 7. 今日はたくさん食べたし、たくさん飲んだし、楽しい一日でした。

APPENDIX 9: Kanji List

The following are **kanji** presented for active acquisition in *Yookoso!* In **kanji** dictionaries, **kanji** are listed according to their basic components, or radicals. Within each group sharing the same radical, the kanji are further classified in terms of the number of strokes beyond those which make up the radical. For instance, 本, which has five strokes, is listed below the radical 木, which has four strokes. Thus, you can find 本 in the one-stroke section under the radical 木. A more complex example is 楽, which contains nine strokes outside the radical and is therefore found in the nine-stroke section. The following list indicates the number of strokes for each **kanji** and the radical under which it is listed in most kanji dictionaries. The numbers following the radicals are the number of strokes remaining after subtracting the stroke-count of the radical. Note that some characters, such as 木、日、 and 人, are themselves radicals.

Kanji	Total Number of Strokes	Radical	Name of Radical	Number of Strokes Beyond the Radical
CHAPTER 1				
日	4	日	(ひ)	0
本	5	木	(き)	1
学	8	子	(こ)	5
生	5	生	(うまれる)	0
名	6	口	(くち)	3
年	6	干	(たてかん)	3
何	7	人	(にんべん)	5
月	4	月	(つき)	0
人	2	人	(ひと)	0
一	1	一	(いち)	0
二	2	二	(に)	0
三	3	一	(いち)	2
四	5	囗	(くにがまえ)	2
五	4	二	(に)	2
六	4	八	(はち)	2
七	2	一	(いち)	2
八	2	八	(はち)	0
九	2	乙	(おつ)	1
十	2	十	(じゅう)	0
百	6	白	(しろ)	1
先	6	儿	(にんにょう)	4
話	13	言	(ごんべん)	6
語	14	言	(ごんべん)	7
大	3	大	(だい)	0

CHAPTER 2

Kanji	Total Number of Strokes	Radical	Name of Radical	Number of Strokes Beyond the Radical
間	12	門	(もん)	4
半	5	十	(じゅう)	3
上	3	一	(いち)	2
下	3	一	(いち)	2
分	4	刀	(かたな)	2
小	3	小	(しょう)	0
好	6	女	(おんな)	3
町	7	田	(た)	2
左	5	工	(え)	2
右	5	口	(くち)	2
中	4	丨	(ぼう)	3
外	5	夕	(た)	2
前	9	刀	(かたな)	7
後	9	彳	(ぎょうにんべん)	6
時	10	日	(ひ)	6
山	3	山	(やま)	0
口	3	口	(くち)	0
千	3	十	(じゅう)	1
万	3	一	(いち)	2
方	4	方	(ほう)	0
近	7	辶	(しんにょう)	4
遠	13	辶	(しんにょう)	10
有	6	月	(つき)	2

CHAPTER 3

Kanji	Total Number of Strokes	Radical	Name of Radical	Number of Strokes Beyond the Radical
朝	12	月	(つき)	8
明	8	日	(ひ)	4
午	4	十	(じゅう)	2
昼	9	日	(ひ)	5
来	7	木	(き)	3
行	6	行	(いく)	0
聞	14	耳	(みみ)	8
食	9	食	(しょく)	0
出	5	凵	(うけばこ)	3
飲	12	食	(しょく)	4
入	2	入	(いる)	0
休	6	人	(にんべん)	4
夕	3	夕	(た)	0
今	4	人	(ひとやね)	2
週	11	辶	(しんにょう)	8
曜	18	日	(ひ)	14
毎	6	母	(なかれ)	2
回	6	囗	(くにがまえ)	3

Kanji	Total Number of Strokes	Radical	Name of Radical	Number of Strokes Beyond the Radical
見	7	見	(みる)	0
起	10	走	(はしる)	3
読	14	言	(ごんべん)	7
火	4	火	(ひ)	0
水	4	水	(みず)	0
木	4	木	(き)	4
金	8	金	(かね)	0
土	3	土	(つち)	0
会	6	人	(ひと)	4

CHAPTER 4

Kanji	Total Number of Strokes	Radical	Name of Radical	Number of Strokes Beyond the Radical
天	4	大	(だい)	1
気	6	气	(きがまえ)	2
雨	8	雨	(あめ)	0
雪	11	雨	(あめ)	3
度	9	广	(まだれ)	6
風	9	風	(かぜ)	9
台	5	口	(くち)	2
番	12	田	(た)	7
春	9	日	(ひ)	5
夏	10	夂	(すいにょう)	7
秋	9	禾	(のぎへん)	4
冬	5	冫	(にすい)	3
東	8	木	(き)	4
西	6	西	(にし)	0
南	9	十	(じゅう)	7
北	5	ヒ	(ひ)	3
高	10	高	(たかい)	0
多	6	タ	(た)	3
少	4	小	(しょう)	1
強	11	弓	(ゆみ)	8
弱	10	弓	(ゆみ)	7
昨	9	日	(ひ)	5
暑	12	日	(ひ)	8
寒	12	宀	(うかんむり)	9
空	8	宀	(うかんむり)	5

CHAPTER 5

Kanji	Total Number of Strokes	Radical	Name of Radical	Number of Strokes Beyond the Radical
手	4	手	(て)	0
家	10	宀	(うかんむり)	7
男	7	田	(た)	2
女	3	女	(おんな)	0
子	3	子	(こ)	0
母	5	母	(なかれ)	1
父	4	父	(ちち)	0

Kanji	Total Number of Strokes	Radical	Name of Radical	Number of Strokes Beyond the Radical
CHAPTER 5				
兄	5	儿	(にんにょう)	3
弟	7	弓	(ゆみ)	4
姉	8	女	(おんな)	5
妹	8	女	(おんな)	5
作	7	人	(にんべん)	5
族	11	方	(ほう)	7
勉	10	力	(ちから)	8
道	12	辶	(しんにょう)	9
使	8	人	(にんべん)	6
国	8	囗	(くにがまえ)	5
音	9	音	(おと)	0
楽	13	木	(き)	9
全	6	人	(ひとやね)	4
部	11	阝	(おおざと)	8
運	12	辶	(しんにょう)	9
動	11	力	(ちから)	9
CHAPTER 6				
思	9	心	(こころ)	5
終	11	糸	(いと)	5
始	8	女	(おんな)	5
物	8	牛	(うし)	4
肉	6	肉	(にく)	0
事	8	亅	(はねぼう)	7
茶	9	艹	(くさかんむり)	6
酒	10	酉	(ひよみのとり)	3
牛	4	牛	(うし)	0
鳥	11	鳥	(とり)	0
湯	12	水	(みず)	9
野	11	里	(さと)	4
魚	11	魚	(さかな)	0
味	8	口	(くち)	5
悪	11	心	(こころ)	7
料	10	斗	(とます)	6
理	11	玉	(たま)	7
米	6	米	(こめ)	0
品	9	口	(くち)	6
和	8	口	(くち)	5
洋	9	水	(みず)	6
夜	8	夕	(た)	5
言	7	言	(ごんべん)	0
貝	7	貝	(かい)	0

Kanji	Total Number of Strokes	Radical	Name of Radical	Number of Strokes Beyond the Radical
CHAPTER 7				
同	6	口	(くち)	3
長	8	長	(ながい)	0
場	12	土	(つち)	9
市	5	巾	(はば)	2
主	5	丶	(てん)	4
電	13	雨	(あめ)	5
売	7	士	(さむらい)	4
切	4	刀	(かたな)	2
店	8	广	(まだれ)	5
引	4	弓	(ゆみ)	1
白	5	白	(しろ)	0
屋	9	尸	(しかばね)	6
黒	11	黒	(くろ)	0
色	6	色	(いろ)	0
買	12	貝	(かい)	5
青	8	青	(あお)	0
赤	7	赤	(あか)	0
服	8	月	(つき)	4
返	7	辶	(しんにょう)	4
花	7	艹	(くさかんむり)	4
黄	11	黄	(き)	0
員	10	口	(くち)	7
暗	13	日	(ひ)	9
円	4	冂	(どうがまえ)	2

Japanese-English Glossary

This glossary lists all Japanese words presented in this book with the exception of lesser known place names, some proper nouns, conjugated forms, compound words, and foreign loanwords that are very similar to the source language word in pronunciation and meaning.
Entries are arranged in a-i-u-e-o Japanese alphabetical order. As in Japanese dictionaries, each word is presented in hiragana or katakana, followed by the kanji transcription, if appropriate.
Verbs and adjectives are cited in their dictionary form except for a few special cases. The classification is provided for each verb Class 1, 2, or 3.
Nominal verbs are followed by [する]. I-adjectives are unmarked, but na-adjectives are followed by (な).
English translations for nouns are given in the singular plural is an alternate gloss in most cases.
Only the most commonly used polite variants are included.
Finally, remember that these translations are not equivalents but reminders of the meanings you have learned in class. Only real-life context and native usage can be relied on to define the full range of meaning and nuance for each word.
The following abbreviations are used:

adv.	word or phrases that functions as an adverb
C1	Class 1 verb
C2	Class 2 verb
C3	Class 3 verb
coll.	colloquial
conj.	conjunction
ctr.	counter suffix
cop.	copula
dem. adj.	demonstrative adjective
dem. pron.	demonstrative pronoun
dem. adv.	demonstrative adverb
f.	female speech (word used primarily by females)
hbl.	humble
inf.	informal
interj.	interjection
m.	male speech (words used primarily by males)
part.	particle
pl.	plural
p.n.	proper noun
pol.	polite
pron.	pronoun
s.	singular

あ

あんまり (*with negative*) not very much
ああ *interj.* Oh, Ah (exclamation of surprise or pleasure)
ああ *dem. adv.* (in a manner) like that
あい (愛) love
あいいろ (藍色) dark (indigo) blue
あいさつ[する] (挨拶) greeting
あいだ (間) between; XとYの間に between X and Y
アイロン iron (*the appliance*); アイロンをかける to iron
あう (会う) *C1* to meet (*someone for the first time*); to meet with, see (*a person*); Xさんに会う X to meet Mr./Ms. X
あお (青)/あおい (青い) blue; green (less common)
あか (赤)/あかい (赤い) red
あかるい (明るい) bright (*vs.dark*), cheerful (*personality*)
あき (秋) fall, autumn
あきさめ (秋雨) autumn rain
あきる (飽きる) *C2*, to become bored, get tired of
アクセサリー accessory, jewelry
あける (開ける) *C2*, to open Xを開ける to open X
あげる (揚げる) *C2*, to deep fry
あさ (朝) morning
あさごはん (朝ごはん) breakfast
あさって the day after tomorrow
あざやか (鮮かな) vivid (*color*)
あさゆう (朝夕) morning and evening
あじ (味) taste, flavor; 味がいい to taste good; 味がない to have no taste; 味が悪い to taste bad
あした (明日) tomorrow
あじみ (味見)[する] taste test
あじわう (味わう) *C1*, to taste
あそ (阿蘇) *p.n.* Asọ (a town in Kyushu)
あそこ *dem.*, (that place) over there
あそぶ (遊ぶ) *C1*, to play around, to loaf
あたし f. I; あたしたち f., we
あたたかい (暖かい) warm
あたま (頭) head
あたらしい (新しい) new
あちら *dem.*, pol. (that place) over there, that way over there
あつい (厚い) thick (*in dimension*)
あつい (暑い) hot (*weather*)
あつめる (集める) *C2*, to collect, gather; Xを集める to collect X
あとで (後で) later; (verb-ta form) ＋後 after (*having done something*)
あなた s. you; あなたたち *pl.* you
あに (兄) one's own older brother
あね (姉) one's own older sister
あの *dem adj.* that over there (. . . ＋Noun)
あのう uh; excuse me (*when trying to get someone's attention*)
アパート apartment, apartment building
あびる (浴びる) *C2*, シャワーを浴びる to take a shower
あぶらえ (油絵) oil painting
アマ amateur
あまい (甘い) sweet
あまり *adv.* (*with negative*) not very much
あみもの (編み物) knitting, crocheting
あむ (編む) *C1*, to knit, crochet
あめ (雨) rain
あらう (洗う) *C1*, to wash
あらし (嵐) storm
アラビア Arabia
あられ hail
ありがとう Thank you.
ある *C1*, there is/there are (*inanimate things*); Xがある to have X; X exists
あるく (歩く) *C1*, to walk
アルバイター part-time worker
アルバイト part-time job, side job
あれ *dem. pron.* that thing over there
あんぜん (な) (安全) safe

い

いい good
いいえ no
いう (言う) *C1*, to say
いえ (家) house
いか cuttlefish
いかが how about
イギリス England
いく (行く) *C1*, to go
いくつ how much, how many items; how old; いくつか some, several
いくら how much
いけばな(生け花) flower arranging
...いじょう (以上) . . . or more
いじわる (な)(意地悪) mean
いす (椅子) chair
いそがしい (忙しい) busy
いたい (痛い) painful
いたす (致す) *C1, hbl.* equivalent of する to do
いただく *C1, hbl.* to receive from a superior, partake; いただきます I will eat now (*a polite phrase said before eating*, literally *I humbly receive*)
いためる (炒める) *C2*, stir-fry, saute
イタリア Italy
いち (一) one
いちがつ (一月) January
いちご (苺) strawberry
いちど (一度) once, one time; (一度も) (*with negative*) not once, never
いちにちじゅう (一日中) all day long
いちば (市場) market
いちばん (一番) No 1; best; most
いちぶ (一部) part, section
いつ when; いつか *adv.* sometime, someday; いつでも any time; いつも *adv.* always
いつのまにか (いつの間にか) before you know it, before long
いつか (五日) the fifth (day of the month); five days
いっしょに (一緒に) *adv.* together; Xと一緒に with X
いつつ (五つ) five (items)
いと (糸) thread

いとこ　cousin
いなびかり(稲光)　lightning
いぬ(犬)　dog
いふく(衣服)　clothes, clothing
イベント　event
いま(今)　now
いみ(意味)　meaning
いも　yam
いもうと(妹)　one's own younger sister; (妹さん)　younger sister (*respectful*)
いや(な)　disgusting, unpleasant
いる　*C1*, to exist (*animate things*); (*verb te-form*) + いる　to be (*do*)ing
いる(要る)　*C1*, to need; X は Y が要る X needs Y
いれる(入れる)　*C2*, to put (*something*) in; X を Y に入れる　to put X in Y
いろ(色)　color
いろいろ(な)(色々)　various
いんき(な)(陰気)　gloomy
インスタントしょくひん(インスタント食品)　instant food
インドネシア　Indonesia

う

ウール　wool
うえ(上)　on, over, up, top; X の上　the top of X
うえの(上野)　*p.n.* Ueno (an area of Tokyo)
うかがう(伺う)　*C1*, *hbl.* to inquire, ask; to visit; to hear
うけつけ(受付け)　reception (desk, area)
うける(受ける)　*C2*, to receive, accept, undergo; 授業(じゅぎょう)を受ける　take a class
うしろ(後ろ)　behind, back; X の後ろ　behind X
うすい(薄い)　thin; light (*in color*), pale
うそ(嘘)　lie; うそ!　you're kidding
うた(歌)　song
うたう(歌う)　*C1*, to sing
うち　house, (my) home; inside
うつ(打つ)　*C1*, to hit
うつくしい(美しい)　beautiful
うどん　udon (*thick, flat wheat noodles*)
うまれる(生まれる)　*C2*, to be born; . . . 年に生まれる　be born in the year . . .; PLACE で生まれる　be born in PLACE
うみ(海)　ocean, sea
うりだし(売り出し)　a sale
うる(売る)　*C1*, to sell
うるさい　noisy, annoying
うわぎ(上着)　jacket, suitcoat
うんうん　*interj.* I see, I see.; Yes, yes
うんてん[する](運転)　driving
うんどう[する](運動)　exercise

え

え(絵)　picture; えをかく(絵をかく)　to draw a picture; 絵はがき　picture postcard
えいが(映画)　movie; 映画館　movie theater
えいぎょうじかん(営業時間)　business hours
えいご(英語)　English language
えいぶん(英文)　written English
えいよう(栄養)　nutrition
えいようし(栄養士)　nutritionist
ええ　yes; Yes, I'm following you
えき(駅)　(*train, bus, subway*) station;
エスエフ　science fiction
エッフェルとう(エッフェル塔)　*p.n.* Eiffel Tower
えび　shrimp
エプロン　apron
えらぶ(選ぶ)　*C1*, to choose
えん(円)　*ctr.* yen
えんげい(園芸)　gardening
えんげき(演劇)　theatrical play
えんそう[する](演奏)　performance, the playing of (*a musical instrument*);
えんぴつ(鉛筆)　pencil

お

おい(甥)　one's own nephew; おいごさん　nephew (*respectful*)
おいしい　delicious, tasty
おいとこさん　cousin (*respectful*)
おおあめ(大雨)　heavy rain
おおい(多い)　many, numerous
おおきい(大きい)　large, big
おおさか(大阪)　*p.n.* Osaka (*city*)
おおゆき(大雪)　heavy snow
オーストラリア　Australia
オーバー　overcoat
おかあさん(お母さん)　mother (*respectful*)
おかげさまで　thanks to you, thanks for asking
おかし(お菓子)　sweets (cake and confections); おかしや(お菓子屋)　confectionary shop
おかし(な)/おかしい　funny, strange
おかね(お金)　money
おきなわ(沖縄)　*p.n.* Okinawa (*island*)
おきゃくさん(お客さん)　customer, passenger; guest
おきる(起きる)　*C2*, to get up, rise, wake up; X がおきる　X wakes up
おく(億)　*ctr.* hundred million
おくさん(奥さん)　wife (respectful), ma'am
おくりがな(送り仮名)　okurigana (*hiragana* used to write grammatical endings of words written in *Kanji*)
おくる(送る)　*C1*, to send; to send someone off
おくれる(遅れる)　*C2*, to be late; おくれている　is late
おこさん(お子さん)　child (*respectful*)
おじ(伯父 or 叔父)　one's own uncle
おじいさん　grandfather (*respectful*)
おしえる(教える)　*C2*, to teach, to inform
おじさん　uncle (*respectful*)
おしゃべり(な)　talkative
おじょうさん(お嬢さん)　daughter (*respectful*)
おすすめひん(おすすめ品)　recommended item (*at a place of business*)

おそい (遅い)　late, slow
おそらく　perhaps
おだやか (な)　calm (*ocean, personality*); gentle (*breeze*)
おちゃ (お茶)　tea
おちる (落ちる)　*C2*, to drop, fall from a height; X がおちる　X falls or drops
おっと (夫)　husband
おつり (お釣り)　change (*money*)
おでん　oden (*a traditional stew*)
おと (音)　sound
おとうさん (お父さん)　father (*respectful*)
おとうと (弟)　one's own younger brother; おとうとさん (弟さん)　younger brother (*respectful*)
おとこ (男)　man; おとこのかた (男の方)　man (*respectful*); おとこのこ (男の子)　boy; おとこのひと (男の人)　man
おとす (落とす)　*C1*, to drop; X をおとす　drop X
おととい　the day before yesterday
おととし　the year before last
おとな (大人)　adult
おどる (踊る)　*C1*, to dance
おなか　stomach; おなかがすく　to get hungry
おなじ (同じ)　same
おにいさん (お兄さん)　older brother (*respectful*)
おねえさん (お姉さん)　older sister (*respectful*)
おねがい (お願い)　request
おば (伯母 or 叔母)　aunt;
おばあさん　grandmother (*respectful*)
おばさん　aunt (*respectful*)
おはよう　good morning; …ございます　good morning (*respectful*)
おふろ (お風呂)　bath; おふろにはいる (お風呂に入る)　to take a bath
おぼえる (覚える)　*C2*, to remember, memorize
おまごさん (お孫さん)　grandchild (*respectful*)
おまわりさん　*coll.* policeman
おみやげ　souvenir
オムレツ　omelette
おもい (重い)　heavy
おもいだす (思い出す)　*C1*, to remember, to recall
おもう (思う)　*C1*, to think, to have a opinion;　…と思う　I think that . . .
おもしろい　interesting, fun
おもちゃや (おもちゃ屋)　toy store
おやすみなさい　Good night
おやつ　snack
おゆ (お湯)　hot water, boiling water
およぐ (泳ぐ)　*C1*, to swim
オランダ　Holland
おりる (降りる)　*C2*, to get off (*a vehicle*)
オレンジ　orange; オレンジいろ (オレンジ色)　orange color
おろす　*C1*, to withdraw (*money*)
おわる (終わる)　*C1*, to end, finish; X が終わる　X ends; X を終わる　to end X
おわん (お椀)　soup bowl
おんがく (音楽)　music; おんがくかんしょう音楽鑑賞　listening to music
おんな (女)　woman; おんなのかた (女の方)　woman (*respectful*); おんなのこ (女の子)　girl; おんなのひと (女の人)　woman

か

か　*part.* (question marker); 一か (一課)　(counter for lessons)
が　*part. (subject marker)*
が　*conj.* but
カーテン　curtain
〜かい (一階)　(*counter for floors of a building*)
〜かい (一回)　(*counter for frequency*)
かい (貝)　shellfish
かいが (絵画)　painting
かいがい (海外)　abroad, overseas
かいぎ (会議)　meeting, conference
がいこく (外国)　foreign country, abroad
がいこくご (外国語)　foreign language
かいしゃ (会社)　company
かいしゃいん (会社員)　company worker
がいしょく [する] (外食)　dining out
かいもの [する] (買い物)　shopping; …に行く　to go shopping
かいわ (会話)　conversation
かう (買う)　*C1*, to buy
かう (飼う)　*C1*, to keep, raise (*a pet*)
かえす (返す)　*C1*, to return (*something*)
かえる (帰る)　*C1*, to return home, go back
かえる (変える)　*C2*, to change (*something*)
かお (顔)　face
かかく (価格)　price
かがく (化学)　chemistry
かかる　*C1*, to take (*time*); 一時間かかる　to take an hour
かぎ (鍵)　key ; lock; かぎをかける (鍵をかける)　*C2*, to lock
かぎかっこ (かぎ括弧)　Japanese quotation marks「...」
かぎる (限る)　*C1*, to limit
かく (書く)　*C1*, to write
かく (描く)　*C1*, to draw
かぐ (家具)　furniture; かぐや (家具屋)　furniture store
がくせい (学生)　university or college student; がくせいしょう (学生証)　student I.D.
がくねん (学年)　year in school; school year
がくぶ (学部)　academic department
かけいぼ (家計簿)　household recordbook
〜かげつ (一ヶ月)　(counter for months)
かける (掛ける)　*C2*, to multiply; 2 かける 2　two times two
かける　*C2*, to lay something on something else; 電話をかける　make a phone call; 眼鏡をかける　to put on glasses
かさ (傘)　umbrella; かさをさす　to put up an umbrella
かし (華氏)　Fahrenheit
かじ (家事)　housework; household chores
かしこまりました　certainly (*said when agreeing to an order from a superior*)

かす (貸す)　*C1*, to lend; rent out
かぜ (風)　wind かぜがふく (風が吹く)　wind blows
かぜ (風邪)　cold; (風邪をひく)　to catch a cold
かぞく (家族)　family
ガソリン・スタンド　gas station
かた (方)　person (*respectful*)
かたくるしい (堅苦しい)　overly formal
がっか (学科)　academic subject
がっき (楽器)　musical instrument
がっこう (学校)　school (*usually pre-college level*)
かっこういい　handsome, good-looking
かつどう (活動)　activity
かていきょうし (家庭教師)　tutor
かど (角)　corner
かない (家内)　one's own wife
カナダ　Canada
かなものや (金物屋)　hardware store
かのじょ (彼女)　she (彼女たち)/(彼女ら)　they (*female*)
かばん (鞄)　tote bag; briefcase
かぶる　*C1*, to wear; to put on (*the head*)
かべ (壁)　wall
かみ (紙)　paper
かみ (髪)　hair; 髪をとかす　to comb one's hair
かみなり (雷)　thunder
かよう (通う)　*C1*, to frequent; to commute ; X にかよう　to commute to X, to frequent X
かようび (火曜日)　Tuesday
から　from; because
からい (辛い)　hot, spicy; salty
カラオケ　karaoke (*singing to recorded accompaniment*)
からだ (体)　body
からて (空手)　karate
かり (狩り)　hunting
かりる (借りる)　*C2*, to borrow; to rent
かるい (軽い)　lightweight
カルタ　Japanese card game
かれ (彼)　he (彼たち)/(彼ら) they (*masculine*)
カレー　curry
かわいい　cute
かんがえ (考え)　thought, idea
かんがえる (考える)　*C2*, to think about, ponder
かんきり (缶切り)　can opener
かんこく (韓国)　South Korea
かんじ (漢字)　kanji
がんじつ (元日)　New Year's Day
かんじょう[する] (勘定)　bill, check; counting, calculation
かんたん(な)(簡単な)　simple, easy
かんづめ (缶詰)　canned food
かんとう (関東)　*p.n.* Kanto District (*the area around Tokyo and Yokohama*)
がんねん (元年)　the first year of an emperor's reign

き

き (木)　tree, wood
きあつ (気圧)　air pressure
きいろ (黄色)/ きいろい (黄色い)　yellow
きおん (気温)　temperature
きかい (機械)　machine
きがえる (着替える)　*C2*, to change clothes
きぎ (木々)　*pl.* trees
きく (聞く)　*C1*, to listen, hear; to ask; X を聞く listen to X; ask about X; X に聞く　ask a question of X
きけん(な)(危険)　dangerous
きご (季語)　seasonal word
きこう (気候)　climate
きこえる (聞こえる)　*C2*, can be heard; X が聞こえる　X can be heard, can hear X
ぎせいご (擬声語)　onomatopoeia (*describing a sound*)
きせつ (季節)　season
きた (北)　north; きたかぜ (北風)　north wind
ぎたいご (擬態語)　onomatopoeia (*describing action or appearance*)
きたない (汚ない)　dirty, filthy
きつい　tough, tight
きっさてん (喫茶店)　coffee shop
きって (切手)　postage stamp; きってあつめ (切手集め)　stamp collecting
きっと　certainly, surely
きないしょく (機内食)　in-flight meal
きぬ (絹)　silk
きねん[する] (記念)　commemoration, memorial
きのう (昨日)　yesterday
きびしい (厳しい)　strict
きもの (着物)　kimono
きゃく (客)　customer, passenger
キャベツ　cabbage
きゅう (九)　nine
きゅうか (休暇)　day off; vacation
きゅうじつ (休日)　day off
きゅうしゅう (九州)　*p.n.* Kyushu (*one of the four main islands of Japan*)
きゅうじゅう (九十)　ninety
ぎゅうにく (牛肉)　beef
きゅうり　cucumber
きょう (今日)　today
きよう(な)(器用)　skillful
きょういくがく (教育学)　education (*academic subject*)
きょうかい (教会)　church
きょうかしょ (教科書)　textbook
きょうしつ (教室)　classroom
きょうだい (兄弟)　siblings
きょうと (京都)　Kyoto (*city*)
きょうよう (教養)　education, culture, liberal arts; きょうようかもく (教養科目)　general education subject
きょねん (去年)　last year
きらい(な)(嫌い)　disliked, hated; X がきらいです　I dislike X
きり (霧)　fog
ぎりの (義理の)　. . . in-law; 義理の母　mother-in-law
きる (着る)　*C2*, to wear; to put on (*the torse*)
きる (切る)　*C1*, to cut

きれい(な)　attractive, pretty, clean
キロ　kilometer, kilogram
きをつける(気をつける)　be careful; Xに気をつける　be careful of X
きんいろ(金色)　gold-color
ぎんいろ(銀色)　silver-color
きんがく(金額)　price, amount of money
きんき(近畿)　*p.n.* Kinki District (*the area of Japan where Kyoto, Osaka, and Kobe are located*)
きんぎょ(金魚)　goldfish
ぎんこう(銀行)　bank
ぎんざ(銀座)　*p.n.* Ginza (*an area in Tokyo*)
きんじょ(近所)　neighborhood
きんようび(金曜日)　Friday
きんろうかんしゃのひ(勤労感謝の日)　Labor Thanksgiving Day (*November 23*)

く

く(九)　nine
く(区)　ward of a city
くがつ(九月)　September
くすりや(薬屋)　drugstore, pharmacy
くだもの(果物)　fruit; くだものや(果物屋)　fruit store
くだる(下る)　*C1*, to go down
くつ(靴)　shoe; くつや(靴屋)　shoe store
くつした(靴下)　sock, stocking
くに(国)　country, nation
くみあわせる(組み合わせる)　*C2*, to combine; XをYと組み合わせる　combine X with Y
くも(雲)　cloud
くもり(曇り)　cloudy weather
くもる(曇る)　*C1*, to become cloudy
〜くらい、〜ぐらい　about, approximately (*duration*)
くらい(暗い)　dark
クラシック　classical music
クリーニングや(クリーニング屋)　dry cleaner's
クリームいろ(クリーム色)　cream-color
くりかえす(繰り返す)　*C1*, to repeat
くる(来る)　*C3*, to come
くるま(車)　car
くろ(黒)/くろい(黒い)　black

け

けいぐ(敬具)　sincerely (*used in a letter*)
けいざいがく(経済学)　economics (*as a field of study*)
けいさんき(計算機)　calculator
けいしょく(軽食)　light meal, snack
けいろうのひ(敬老の日)　Respect-for-the-Aged Day (*September 15*)
けがわ(毛皮)　fur
けさ(今朝)　this morning
けしき(景色)　scenery
けしゴム(消しゴム)　pencil eraser
けしょうひん(化粧品)　cosmetics; けしょうひんてん 化粧品店　cosmetic store
けち(な)　miserly
ーげっかん(一月間)　(counter for the duration in months)
けっこう(な)(結構)　good, satisfactory; いいえ、けっこうです. No, thank you.
けっこん(する)(結婚)　marriage
げつようび(月曜日)　Monday
けど　but (*short form of* けれども)
けれども　but
ーけん(一軒)　(counter for houses, buildings)
けん(県)　prefecture
げんき(な)(元気)　healthy, energetic
けんきゅうしつ(研究室)　professor's office
げんきん(現金)　cash
けんこうてき(な)(健康的)　healthy, good for one's health
げんごがく(言語学)　linguistics
けんこくきねんのひ(建国記念の日)　National Foundation Day (*February 11*)
けんどう(剣道)　Japanese swordmanship or fencing
けんぽうきねんび(憲法記念日)　Constitution Day (*May 3*)

こ

こ(子)　child
ご(碁)　*go* (a Japanese board game)
ご(五)　five
こい(濃い)　dark (*in color*)
こいびと(恋人)　lover
コインランドリー　laundromat
こう　*adv.* like this
ーごう(一号)　Number . . . (*used to number things that come in a series*)
こうえん(公園)　park
こうがい(郊外)　suburbs
こうがく(工学)　engineering
こうがくぶ(工学部)　Engineering Department
こうきゅう(な)(高級)　first-class, high class
ごうけい(合計)　sum, total
こうこうせい(高校生)　high school student
こうこく(広告)　advertisement
こうさい(する)(交際)　social interaction
こうじちゅう(工事中)　under construction
ーごうしつ(一号室)　Room Number . . .
こうずい(洪水)　flood
こうすいりょう(降水量)　amount of precipitation
こうちゃ(紅茶)　black tea
こうはん(後半)　the latter half
こうばん(交番)　police box
こえる(超える)　*C2*, to go beyond, go over
コーヒー　coffee
ごかぞく(御家族)　family (*respectful*)
ごがつ(五月)　May

ごきょうだい (御兄弟)　siblings (*respectful*)
こくせき (国籍)　nationality
こくばん (黒板)　chalkboard; こくばんけし (黒板消し) chalkboard eraser
こくみん (国民)　citizens, the people
ここ　here
ごご (午後)　afternoon, P.M.
ここのか (九日)　ninth day of the month; nine days
ここのつ (九つ)　nine (*items*)
こさめ (小雨)　light rain
ごじゅう (五十)　fifty
ごしゅじん (御主人)　husband (*respectful*)
こしょう (胡椒)　black pepper
ごしんせき (御親戚)　relative (*respectful*)
ごぜん (午前)　morning, A.M.
ごぜんちゅう (午前中)　during the morning
こたえ (答)　response, answer
こたえる (答える)　*C2*, to respond; しつもんに答える　answer a question
ごちそう (御馳走)　treat; 御馳走様 (さま) でした　*pol.* Thank you for the food (*said after a meal*)
こちら　here; this way; こちらがわ (こちら側)　this side
コック　cook
こっとうひん (骨董品)　antiques
コップ　glass
こと (琴)　koto (Japanese zither)
こと　thing, matter, fact; (*used as a nominalizer*); (dictionary form of verb) + こと　the act of . . ., (do) ing
ことができる　to be able to do . . ., can do . . .
ことし (今年)　this year
ことば (言葉)　word, language
こども (子供)　child; 子供の日　Children's Day (*May 5*)
この　*dem.* this (- *Noun*)
ごはん (御飯)　meal, cooked rice
ごふうふ (御夫婦)　married couple (*respectful*)
ごふくや (呉服屋)　kimono store
こまる　*C1*, to be troubled; to become upset
こむ (混む)　*C1*, to get crowded; X が混んでいる　X is crowded
こめ (米)　rice (uncooked); こめや (米屋)　rice dealer
ごらく (娯楽)　entertainment, pastime
ごりょうしん (御両親)　*pl.* parents (*respectful*)
これ　this thing; これまでに　by now
～ころ、～ごろ (頃)　around, approximately (*point in time*)
ゴロゴロ [する]　to loaf, to idle one's time away
コロンビア　*p.n.* Colombia
こわれる　*C2*, to become broken; X がこわれている　X is broken
こんげつ (今月)　this month
こんしゅう (今週)　this week
コンセント　electrical outlet
コンソメ　consomme
こんど (今度)　this time, this next time
こんにちは　good afternoon
こんばん (今晩)　this evening; こんばんは　Good evening
こんや (今夜)　tonight

さ

さあ　*interj.* Let's begin; Well, I don't know . . .
サークル　circle, club
ザーザー　adv. 雨がザーザーふる　to rain cats and dogs
サービス [する]　something given for free
－さい (－歳)　(*counter for years of age*)
さいきん (最近)　recently
さいこうきおん (最高気温)　highest temperature
さいしょ (最初)　first
さいたま (埼玉)　*p.n.* Saitama (*prefecture*)
さいてき (な) (最適)　most suitable
さいふ (財布)　wallet
ざいりょう (材料)　ingredient
サイン [する]　signature
さがす (探す)　*C1*, to look for; X を探す　to look for X
さかな (魚)　fish; さかなや (魚屋)　fish store, fish monger's; さかなをつる (魚を釣る)　to fish
さかや (酒屋)　liquor store
さく (咲く)　*C1*, to bloom
さくねん (昨年)　last year (*more formal than* きょねん)
さくら (桜)　cherry blossom
さけ (鮭)　salmon
さそう (誘う)　*C1*, to invite
－さつ (－冊)　(*counter for books and other bound volumes*)
サッカー　soccer
ざっし (雑誌)　magazine
さて　well, then
さとう (佐藤)　Satoo (family name)
さとう (砂糖)　sugar
さどう (茶道)　tea ceremony
さびしい (寂しい)　lonely
～さま (～様)　(title) Mr., Mrs., etc. (*more respectful than* ～さん)
さみだれ (五月雨)　early summer rain
さむい (寒い)　cold (*weather*)
さよ (う) なら　Goodbye
さら (皿)　plate, dish
サラリーマン　white collar worker
さわる (触る)　*C1*. to touch; X にさわる　to touch X
～さん　(title) Mr., Mrs., Ms.
さん (三)　three
さんがつ (三月)　March
さんじゅう (三十)　thirty
ざんねん (な) (残念)　regrettable, too bad
さんぽ [する] (散歩)　walk, stroll

し

し (四)　four
し (市)　city (*used after the name of the city*)
し　and furthermore, and besides
－じ (－時)　o'clock
しあい (試合)　game; athletic contest
しいたけ　shiitake mushroom
シーディー　CD(compact disc)
ジーパン　jeans

ジェイアール (JR)　Japan Railways
しお (塩)　salt
しおからい (塩辛い)　salty
しか　except for, only (*negative*); X しかない　There is nothing but X
しかし　but, however (*used at the beginning of a sentence*)
しがつ (四月)　April
じかん (時間)　time (*as a concept*), (*counter for hours*)
じかんわり (時間割)　timetable
しき (四季)　four seasons
しぐれ (時雨)　drizzle
しけん (試験)　examination; …をする　to give a test; …をうける　to take a test
しこく (四国)　*p.n.* Shikoku (*one of the four main islands of Japan*)
じこしょうかい [する] (自己紹介)　self-introduction
しごと [する] (仕事)　job, work
ししゅう [する] (刺しゅう)　embroidery
じしょ (辞書)　dictionary
しずか (な) (静か)　quiet, peaceful
した (下)　below, under, down; X のした　under X
したぎ (下着)　underwear
しち (七)　seven
しちがつ (七月)　July
しちゃくしつ (試着室)　fitting room
シチュー　stew
じっけんしつ (実験室)　laboratory
しつど (湿度)　humidity
しっと [する] (嫉妬)　jealousy
しつもん [する] (質問)　question
しつれい (な) (失礼)　rude; . . . する　to be rude, to take one's leave (*polite*)
じてんしゃ (自転車)　bicycle
シトシト　it drizzles あめがシトシトふる　it drizzles
しなぎれ (品切れ)　out of stock, sold out
しぬ (死ぬ)　*C1*, to die; 死んでいる　is dead
しばらく　*adv.* for the moment, for a long time
しぶい (渋い)　astringent
じぶん (自分)　one's self, self; 自分で　by one's self, on one's own
しま (島)　island
しま (縞)　stripe
しまう　*C1*, (literally: *to put away*); (the - te form of the verb + . . .) do completely, do suddenly, do in a displeasing manner.
しまね (島根)　*p.n.* Shimane (*prefecture*)
じみ (な) (地味)　quiet (*in color*), plain
じむしつ (事務室)　administrative office
しめる (閉める)　*C2*, to close; X を閉める　to close X
しも (霜)　frost
じゃあ　*interj.* well, then
シャープペンシル　mechanical pencil
しゃかいがく (社会学)　sociology
じゃがいも　potato
しゃげき [する] (射撃)　shooting guns
しゃしん (写真)　photography, photograph; しゃしんをとる (写真を撮る)　to take a photo
シャツ　shirt
しゃみせん (三味線)　shamisen (*banjo-like Japanese instrument*)
シャワー　shower
シャンペン　champagne
じゅう (十)　ten
じゅういちがつ (十一月)　November
じゅういちにち (十一日)　the eleventh day of the month; eleven days
じゅうがつ (十月)　October
〜しゅうかん (一週間)　(*counter*) week
じゅうごにち (十五日)　the fifteenth day of the month; fifteen days
じゅうさんにち (十三日)　the thirteenth day of the month; thirteen days
じゅうどう (柔道)　judo
じゅうにがつ (十二月)　December
じゅうににち (十二日)　twelfth day of the month; twelve days
しゅうぶんのひ (秋分の日)　Autumnal Equinox Day (*around September 22*)
しゅうまつ (週末)　weekend
じゅうまん (十万)　one hundred thousand
じゅうよっか (十四日)　the fourteenth day of the month; fourteen days
じゅぎょうりょう (授業料)　tuition
しゅくじつ (祝日)　national holiday
しゅくだい (宿題)　homework
しゅげい (手芸)　handicrafts
しゅじん (主人)　one's own husband; shop owner
しゅっしん (出身)　origin; ロサアンジェルスの出身です　I am from Los Angeles; 東京大学の出身です　I am a graduate of Tokyo University.
しゅっしんち (出身地)　native place
しゅっぱんしゃ (出版社)　publishing company
しゅふ (主婦)　housewife
しゅみ (趣味)　hobby
しゅもく (種目)　event, item
しゅるい (種類)　kind, type
じゅんい (順位)　rank, ranking
じゅんび [する] (準備)　preparation
しゅんぶんのひ (春分の日)　Vernal Equinox (*around March 21*)
しょうかい [する] (紹介)　introduction
しょうぎ (将棋)　shogi (*a Japanese board game*)
しょうしゃ (商社)　trading company
じょうず (な) (上手)　good at, skilled at; X は Y が上手です　X is good at Y
じょうだん (冗談)　joke
しょうてんがい (商店街)　shopping mall, shopping area
ショートパンツ　shorts
じょうねつ (情熱)　passion, enthusiasm
じょうば (乗馬)　horseback riding
しょうひん (商品)　goods, merchandise
じょうぶ (な) (丈夫)　robust, strong, tough
しょうゆ (醤油)　soy sauce
しょうわ (昭和)　Showa Era (1926-1989)
しょくじ (食事)　meal; . . . する　to eat a meal
しょくどう (食堂)　dining hall, informal restaurant

しょくりょうひん (食料品)　foodstuffs, groceries; しょくりょうひんてん (食料品店)　grocery store
じょしがくせい (女子学生)　female student
じょせい (女性)　woman
しょどう (書道)　brush calligraphy
ショパン　Chopin
しらせ (知らせ)　notice, announcement
しりあう (知り合う)　*C1*, to know each other
しる (知る)　*C1*, to find out; 知っている　know (s)
しろ (白)　or しろい (白い)　white
しろくろしゃしん (白黒写真)　black and white photo (graphy)
シンガポール　Singapore
しんかんせん (新幹線)　bullet train
じんこう (人口)　population
じんじゃ (神社)　Shinto shrine
しんじる (信じる)　*C2*, to believe
しんせき (親戚)　relative
しんせつ (な) (親切)　kind
しんぶん (新聞)　newspaper
じんるいがく (人類学)　anthropology

す

す (酢)　vinegar
すいえい (水泳)　swimming
すいさいが (水彩画)　watercolor
すいようび (水曜日)　Wednesday
すうがく (数学)　mathematics
スーパー　supermarket
すき (な) (好き)　liked, favored; X が好きです　I like X
すきやき　sukiyaki
～すぎる (～過ぎる)　*C2*, to do . . . excessively (*conjunctive form of verb* ＋～すぎる)
すぐ (に)　*adv.* immediately, soon
すくない (少ない)　few, scarce
すごい　awesome, terrible, very awful
すこし (少し)　a little, a bit
すごす (過ごす)　*C1*, to spend (*time*), pass (*time*)
すし (寿司)　sushi; すしや (寿司屋)　sushi restaurant
すずしい (涼しい)　cool
スチュワーデス　stewardess
すっかり　totally
ずっと　all the way
すっぱい (酸っぱい)　sour
ストーブ　space heater
スノーブーツ　snow boot
スペイン　Spain
すべて (全て)　all
ズボン　trousers
スマート (な)　slender, fashionable
すまい (住まい)　housing
すみえ (墨絵)　*sumie* ink painting
すみません　excuse me, sorry
すむ (住む)　*C1*, to reside, live; X に住んでいる　lives in X
すもう (相撲)　sumo wrestling
する　*C3*, to do

せ

～せい (～製)　made in . . .; 日本製　made in Japan
せいきゅうしょ (請求書)　bill; invoice
せいじか (政治家)　politician
せいじがく (政治学)　political science
せいじんのひ (成人の日)　Coming-of-Age Day (*January 15*)
せいねんがっぴ (生年月日)　birthdate
せいふく (制服)　uniform
せいぶつがく (生物学)　biology
セーター　sweater
せかいじゅう (世界中)　all over the world
せき (席)　seat
せっし (摂氏)　centigrade, Celsius
せびろ (背広)　men's suit
せまい (狭い)　narrow, not spacious
せわ [する] (世話)　care; X の世話をする　take care of X
せん (千)　thousand
ぜん～ (全～)　all . . .; ぜんてん (全店)　all store (s); ぜんぴん (全品)　all items
せんげつ (先月)　last month
せんこう [する] (専攻)　academic major; X を専攻する　major in X
ぜんさい (前菜)　appetizer
せんしゅ (選手)　athlete, competitor
せんしゅう (先週)　last week
せんせい (先生)　teacher, professor; doctor (*title*)
ぜんぜん (全然)　. . . not at all (*in a negative sentence*)
せんぬき (栓抜き)　bottle opener
ぜんぶ (全部)　all; ぜんぶで (全部で)　in total
せんもんかもく (専門課目)　specialized subject
せんもんてん (専門店)　specialty store

そ

そう　like that; so; そうですね　Well, let me see.
そうじ [する] (掃除)　housecleaning
ソース　prepared sauce (*somewhat like steak sauce*)
…そうだ　they say . . . (plain form of verb + . . .)
一そく (一足)　(*counter for shoes, socks*)
そこ　there (near by)
そして　and then
そちら　there, that way
そつぎょう (卒業)　graduation; 大学を卒業する　graduate from college
そと (外)　outside
その　that (+ Noun); そのあと (その後)　after that
そば　vicinity; X のそば　the vicinity of X
そば　soba, buckwheat noodles
そばや　soba restaurant
そふ (祖父)　one's own grandfather
ソフト [ウエア]　software
そぼ (祖母)　one's own grandmother
そら (空)　sky
そる (剃る)　*C1*, to shave
それ　that thing; それから　and then; それで　therefore, then
そんな　that kind of; そんなに　*adv.* that much, that many

た

だ　*cop.* to be (*plain form of* です)
ーだい(ー台)　(*counter for machines*)
たいいくかん(体育館)　gym
たいいくのひ(体育の日)　Health-Sports Day (*October 10*)
だいがく(大学)　university
だいがくいんせい(大学院生)　graduate student
だいがくせい(大学生)　university student
だいきらい(な)(大嫌い)　hated
たいしょう(大正)　Taisho Era (1912-1926)
だいすき(な)(大好き)　favorite, much liked
たいそう(体操)　gymnastics
だいどころ(台所)　kitchen
タイプ[する]　typing
たいふう(台風)　typhoon
たいへいようがわ(太平洋側)　the Pacific Ocean side
たいへん(な)(大変)　terrible, awful
ダイヤ　diamond
たいよう(太陽)　sun
たいわん(台湾)　Taiwan
たかい(高い)　expensive, high
だから　*conj.* therefore
たくさん　many, a lot
だけ　*part.* only . . .; X だけ　only X
たこ　octopus
たす(足す)　*C1*, to add; 二足す二　Two plus two
だす(出す)　*C1*, to take out, put out; to mail; to send
たつ(立つ)　*C1*, to stand
たっきゅう(卓球)　table tennis, Ping Pong
たてもの(建物)　building
たてる　*C2*, to set up; プランをたてる　to make plans
たのしむ(楽しむ)　*C1*, to enjoy
たのむ(頼む)　*C1*, to request, ask
タフ(な)　strong
たぶん(多分)　perhaps
たべもの(食べ物)　food
たべる(食べる)　*C2*, to eat
たまご(卵)　egg
たまに　once in a while
たまねぎ　onion
だめ(な)　not good, worthless; defective
ためし(試し)　trial, experiment
ためす(試す)　*C1*, to try out
だれ　who; だれか　someone; だれでも　anyone and everyone, everybody; だれも　no one (*with negative verbs*)
だんしがくせい(男子学生)　male student
たんじょうび(誕生日)　birthday
だんせい(男性)　man
たんだい(短大)　junior college
だんだん　gradually

ち

ちいさい(小さい)　small
チェック　check (*pattern*)
ちか(地下)　underground, basement
ちかい(近い)　near, close
ちかい(地階)　underground floor
ちがう(違う)　*C1*, to differ, to be wrong
ちかく(近く)　vicinity
ちかてつ(地下鉄)　subway
ちず(地図)　map
ちち(父)　one's own father
ちば(千葉)　*p.n.* Chiba (*prefecture*)
ちほう(地方)　region, area outside the major metropolitan areas
ちゃいろ(茶色)　or ちゃいろい(茶色い)　brown
ーちゃく(ー着)　(*counter for jackets, clothes*)
ちゃわん(茶碗)　teacup, rice bowl
ちゅうがくせい(中学生)　middle school student
ちゅうかりょうり(中華料理)　Chinese food (*as adapted to Japanese tastes*)
ちゅうごく(中国)　1) Chugoku District (*the western end of the island of Honshu*); 2) China
ちゅうしゃじょう(駐車場)　parking lot
ちゅうしょく(昼食)　lunch
ちゅうぶ(中部)　Chubu District (*the central part of Honshu, including Nagoya and Kanazawa*)
ちゅうもん[する](注文)　order (*a meal or merchandise*)
ちょう(兆)　trillion
ちょうさ[する](調査)　investigation
ちょうじょ(長女)　oldest daughter
ちょうしょく(朝食)　breakfast
ちょうなん(長男)　oldest son
ちょうみりょう(調味料)　seasoning
〜ちょうめ(〜丁目)　district number (*within a city*)
ちょきん[する](貯金)　deposit (*money*)
チョコレート　chocolate
ちょっと　*adv.* a little, a bit

つ

ついたち(一日)　first day of the month
つうきん[する](通勤)　commuting to work
つかう(使う)　*C1*, to use
つかれる(疲れる)　*C2*, to become tired; 疲れている　is tired
つぎ(次)　next
つくえ(机)　desk
つくる(作る)　*C1*, to make; to cook
つくろう(繕う)　*C1*, to mend
つけもの(漬物)　Japanese-style pickled vegetables
つける(付ける)　*C2*, to wear; to put on (*something that attaches*); to attach; to put on
つたえる(伝える)　*C2*, to convey (*a message or idea*)
つづく(続く)　*C1*, to continue; X が続く　X continues
つづける(続ける)　*C2*, to continue; X を続ける　to continue X
つつみがみ(包み紙)　wrapping paper
つつむ(包む)　*C1*, to wrap
つとめる(勤める)　*C2*, to become employed; X に勤める　to become employed at X
つま(妻)　wife

つまらない　boring
つゆ(梅雨)　rainy season (*in June and July*)
つゆ(露)　dew
つよい(強い)　strong
つり(釣り)　fishing
つれていく(連ていく)　to take a person

て

で　te-form of copula
で　*part.* with, at, by means of
ティーシャツ　T-shirt
テーブル　table
でかける(出かける)　*C2*, to go out for a while, leave
てがみ(手紙)　letter
できる　*C2*, to be able to do; to be completed; X は Y ができる　X can do Y
てじな(手品)　juggling
てつがく(哲学)　philosophy
てつだう(手伝う)　*C1*, to help, assist; X のしごとを手伝う　help X work
では　*conj.* Well, then
デパート　department store
てぶくろ(手袋)　glove
でも　but, even so
てら(寺)　Buddhist temple
でる(出る)　*C2*, to leave, go out, appear
テレビ　television
テレビゲーム　video game
てんいん(店員)　store clerk
てんき(天気)　weather
でんき(電気)　electricity, electric light
てんきず(天気図)　weather map
てんきよほう(天気予報)　weather forecast
でんきや(電気屋)　electrical appliance store
でんごん(伝言)　message
でんしゃ(電車)　electric train
てんじょう(天井)　ceiling
てんのう(天皇)　Emperor
てんのうたんじょうび(天皇誕生日)　Emperor's Birthday (*December 23*)
てんぷら(天麩羅)　tempura; (天麩羅屋)　tempura restaurant
でんわ[する](電話)　telephone; でんわばんごう(電話番号)　telephone number

と

と　*part.* and,
と(都)　capital city; 東京都　Tokyo metropolitan area
ーど(一度)　(*counter for number of times*); (*counter for degrees of temperature*)
ドア　door
ドイツ　Germany
トイレ　restroom, bathroom, toilet
ーとう(一頭)　(*counter for large animals*)
どう　*dem. adv.* how; どうか　please, somehow; どうも　indeed
どう(道)　abbreviation of Hokkaido
とうきょう(東京)　*p.n.* Tokyo; 東京都　*p.n.* Tokyo Metropolitan Area
どうして　how, why
どうぞ　please feel free, please go ahead
とうふ(豆腐)　tofu, bean curd
とうほく(東北)　*p.n.* Tohoku District (*in northern Honshu*)
とうめい(な)(透明)　transparent
とお(十)　ten items
とおい(遠い)　far, far away
とおか(十日)　tenth day of the month, ten days
とおり(通り)　avenue
とかす　*C1*, to comb
とき(時)　time; . . . 時　when . . .
ときどき(時々)　sometimes
とくい(な)(得意)　especially skilled or favored (*activity*)
とくぎ(特技)　special talent
どくしょ［する］(読書)　reading for pleasure
どくしん(独身)　single, unmarried
とくに(特に)　especially
とけい(時計)　clock, watch
とけいや(時計屋)　clock shop
どこ　where; どこか　somewhere; どこでも　anywhere, everywhere; どこも　(negative) nowhere
とこや(床屋)　barbershop
とし(年)　age; としした(年下)　younger in age; としうえ(年上)　older in age
どしゃぶり(土砂降り)　downpour (of rain)
としょかん(図書館)　library
としより(年寄)　elderly person
とじる(閉じる)　*C2*, to close; X を閉じる　to close X
どちら　where (*polite*); which (*of the two*); どちらか　either; どちらでも　whichever; どちらのほう　which one; どちらも　both (. . . + *negative*); neither
どっち　(*colloquial form of* どちら)
とても　very
どなた　*pol.* who; どなたか　*pol.* someone; どなたでも　*pol.* anyone; どなたも　*pol.* no one (*negative*)
となり(隣)　next to; nextdoor
どの　*dem. adj.* (. . . + noun) which (*of more than two*)
とぶ(飛ぶ)　*C1*, to fly
とほ(徒歩)　by walking, on foot
ともだち(友だち)　friend
どようび(土曜日)　Saturday
トランプ　card game
とり(鳥)　bird
とりにく(鳥肉)　chicken (*meat*)
とる(取る)　*C1*, to take
とる(撮る)　*C1*, to take (*a photo*)
どれ　*dem. pron.* which thing (*of more than two*); どれか　one of the several; どれでも　any of them; どれも　all of them; (. . . + *negative*) none of them
どんな　*dem. adj.* what kind of

な

なか (中) in, inside; X の中 inside X
ながい (長い) long
ながそで (長袖) long sleeves; long-sleeved
なかなか rather, quite
なかの (中野) *p.n.* Nakano (*an area of Tokyo*)
ながの (長野) *p.n.* Nagano (*prefecture, city*)
なく (泣く) *C1*, to cry
なげる (投げる) *C2*, to throw
なし (梨) pear
なぜ why; なぜか somehow
なつ (夏) summer
など and so on
なな (七) seven
ななじゅう (七十) seventy
ななつ (七つ) seven (items)
なに (何) what; なにいろ (何色) what color; なにか (何か) something; なにご (何語) what language; なにじん (何人) what nationality; なにも (何も) anything, nothing; cf. なん
なのか (七日) the seventh daty of the month; seven days
なべ (鍋) pan, pot
なま (生) raw
なまえ (名前) name
ならう (習う) *C1*, to learn
なる *C1*, to become, turn into; X になる become X
なるほど I see
なん (何) what; なんがつ (何月) what month; なんさい (何歳) how old; なんじ (何時) what time; なんじかん (何時間) how many hours; なんでも (何でも) anything; なんど (何度) how many degree; なんとか (何とか) in some way, somehow; なんども (何度も) many times; なんにち (何日) what day, how many months; なんねん (何年) what year, how many years; なんねんせい (何年生) what year in school; なんぷん (何分) what minute, how many minutes; なんようび (何曜日) what day of the week

に

に (二) two
に *part.* at, in
にあう (似合う) *C1*, to be suited; fit; X に似合う to fit X
におい (臭い) smell, odor
にがい (苦い) bitter
にがつ (二月) February
にがて (な) (苦手) unskilled at and not fond of; weak point
にぎやか (な) lively
にく (肉) meat; にくや (肉屋) butcher shop
にし (西) west
にじゅう (二十) twenty
にじゅうよっか (二十四日) the twenty-fourth day of the month; twenty-four days
にちじょうせいかつ (日常生活) everyday life
にちようび (日曜日) Sunday
にほん (日本) Japan; にほんかいがわ (日本海側) the Japan Sea side; にほんご (日本語) Japanese language; にほんしゅ (日本酒) Japanese sake; にほんぶよう (日本舞踊) Japanese traditional dance
ニュース news
にゅうもん (入門) entry level, introduction
にる (煮る) *C2*, to cook in liquid
にわかあめ (にわか雨) sudden shower
ーにん (ー人) (*counter for people*)
にんき (人気) popularity
にんじん carrot

ぬ

ぬう (縫う) *C1*, to sew
ぬぐ (脱ぐ) *C1*, to take off (*clothes*)

ね

ね Right? Isn't that so?
ねぎる (値切る) *C1*, to bargain, haggle over price
ねこ (猫) cat
ねだん (値段) price
ねぼう [する] (寝坊) oversleeping
ねむり (眠り) sleep
ねむる (眠る) *C1*, to sleep, fall asleep
ねる (寝る) *C1*, to sleep; to go to bed
ねんごう (年号) Imperial era
ーねんせい (ーねんせい) (年生) (*counter for years in school*; 1 年生) first-year student
ねんれい (年齢) age, age group

の

の *part.* (*possessive marker*)
の (Adj. + . . .) one; いいの good one
ノート notebook
のせる *C2*, to put on, to give a ride; X をYにのせる to put X on Y
のどがかわく (咽が乾く) *C1*, to become thirsty
のびる (伸びる) *C2*, to extend, to stretch; X が伸びる X stretches
のべる (述べる) *C2*, to state
のみほうだい (飲み放題) all you can drink
のみもの (飲み物) beverage
のむ (飲む) *C1*, to drink
のり (海苔) a kind of seaweed, laver
のる (乗る) *C1*, to ride, to get on (*a vehicle*); X に乗る to ride or get on X

は

は *part.* (*topic marker* [pronounced] わ)
は (歯) tooth; はをみがく (歯を磨く) to brush one's teeth
はい *interj.* yes
ーはい (ー杯) (*counter for glasses or cups of drinks*)
ーばい (ー倍) (*counter for multiplication*); X が3倍ある to have 3 times as much X
はいいろ (灰色) gray
バイキングりょうり (バイキング料理) all you can eat buffet

はいけい (拝啓)　Dear . . . (*used at the beginning of a letter*)
はいたつ[する] (配達)　delivery
はいる (入る)　*C1*, to enter; X に入る　enter X
はく　*C1*, to wear; to put on (*the feet or legs*)
はくぶつかん (博物館)　museum
はこ (箱)　box
はさみ (鋏)　scissors
はし (箸)　chopsticks
はじ　edge
はじまる (始まる)　*C1*, to start; X が始まる　X starts
はじめに (初めに)　first, first of all
はじめまして　Nice meeting you.
はじめる (始める)　*C2*, to start; X を始める　to start X; 始めましょう　Let's start
ばしょ (場所)　place
はしる (走る)　*C1*, to run
バス　bus
はずす　*C1*, to take off (*glasses*, etc.); to undo (*buttons*, etc.)
バスてい (バス停)　bus stop
はたち (二十歳)　twenty years old
はたらく (働く)　*C1*, to work
はち (八)　eight
はちがつ (八月)　August
はちじゅう (八十)　eighty
パチンコ　pachinko (*Japanese pinball*)
はつおん[する] (発音)　pronunciation
はつか (二十日)　the twentieth day of the month
はで (派手)　gaudy, bright, loud (*in color*)
はなし (話)　story, talk, speech
はなしあう (話し合う)　*C1*, to talk to each other; X は　Y と話し合う　X talks to Y
はなす (話す)　*C1*, to speak, tell, talk
はなみ (花見)　cherry blossom viewing
はなや (花屋)　florist
はは (母)　one's own mother; ははのひ (母の日)　Mother's Day
はめる　*C2*, to put on (*rings, gloves*, etc.)
はやい (早い)　early
はやく (速く)　fast, quick
はらう (払う)　*C1*, to pay
はり (針)　needle
はる (春)　spring
はるがっき (春学期)　spring quarter, spring semester
はるさめ (春雨)　spring rain
はれ (晴れ)　clear weather
はれる (晴れる)　*C2*, to clear up (*weather*)
はん (半)　half
ーばん (ー番)　Number . . .; 一番　Number one
パン　bread
はんがく (半額)　half price
ハンカチ　handkerchief
ばんぐみ (番組)　television or radio program
ばんごう (番号)　assigned number
ばんごはん (晩ごはん)　dinner, supper
ハンサム (な)　handsome
はんそで (半袖)　short sleeves; short-sleeved
ばんち (番地)　block number (*in an address*)
パンツ　underpants
パンティーストッキング　pantyhose
はんぶん (半分)　half
パンや (パン屋)　bakery

ひ

ピーマン　green pepper
ビール　beer
ひがい (被害)　damage; 被害を与(あた)える　*C2*, tr. to cause damage
ひがし (東)　east
ーひき (ー匹)　(*counter for small animals*)
〜びき (引き)　reduced . . .%
ひく (引く)　*C1*, to subtract, pull
ひく (弾く)　*C1*, to play (*a string or keyboard instrument*)
ひくい (低い)　low
ひげ　beard, facial hair
ピザ　pizza
ひさしぶり　after a long time; after a long absence
びじゅつ (美術)　art
びじゅつかん (美術館)　art museum
びじん (美人)　pretty woman
ひだり (左)　left
ひでり (日照り)　drought
ひと (人)　person
ひどい　terrible, severe
ひとつ (一つ)　one (item)
ひとり (一人)　one person; ひとりで (一人で)　by one's self, alone
ひま (な) (暇)　free, not busy
ひゃく (百)　one hundred
ひゃくまん (百万)　one million
びょういん (病院)　hospital
びよういん (美容院)　beauty parlor
びょうき (病気)　illness; sick
ひる (昼)　noon
ビル　building
ひるごはん (昼ごはん)　lunch
ひるま (昼間)　daytime
ひろい (広い)　wide, spacious

ふ

ふ (府)　prefecture (*used for Kyoto and Osaka only*)
ファスナー　zipper
フィルム　photographic film
ふうふ (夫婦)　married couple
ふえる (増える)　*C2*, to increase; X が増える　X increases
ふかめる (深める)　*C2*, to deepen; X を深める　to deepen X
ふく (服)　clothes
ふく (吹く)　*C1*, to blow (*wind*); to play a wind instrument
ふくそう (服装)　clothes, dress, appearance
ふじんふくてん (婦人服店)　women's wear store
ふたつ (二つ)　two (items)
ぶたにく (豚肉)　pork

ふたり (二人)　two people
ふつう (普通)　usual, ordinary
ふつか (二日)　the second day of the month; two days
ぶつりがく (物理学)　physics
ぶどう (葡萄)　grape
ふとる (太る)　*C1*, to get fat; 太っている　is fat
ふとんや (布団屋)　futon store
ふぶき (吹雪)　snowstorm
ふべん (な) (不便)　inconvenient
ふまじめ (な) (不真面目)　not serious, lazy
ふゆ (冬)　winter
ブラジャー　brassiere
ブラジル　Brazil
プラモデル　plastic model
フランス　France
プリン　pudding
ふる (降る)　*C1*, to fall (*used with rain and snow*); 雨が降っている　It's raining.
ふるい (古い)　old
フレンチフライ　French fries
プロ　professional
ーふん (一分)　(*counter for minutes*)
ぶんか (文化)　culture
ぶんがく (文学)　literature
ぶんがくぶ (文学部)　literature department
ぶんかつばらい (分割払い)　installment payment
ぶんかのひ (文化の日)　Culture Day (*November 3*)
ーふんかん (一分間)　(*counter for minutes of duration*)
ぶんぼうぐ (文房具)　stationery
ぶんぼうぐや (文房具屋)　stationery store

へ

へ　*part.* (motion towards) (pronounced え)
ペア　pair
へいきん (平均)　average
へいじつ (平日)　weekday
へいせい (平成)　Heisei Era (1989–present)
へえ　*conj.* Oh (*exclamation of surprise*)
ペキン　Beijing
へた (な) (下手)　bad at, unskilled
べつ (別)　separate; べつに (別に)　Negative *adv.* (not especially)
ベトナム　Vietnam
へや (部屋)　room
へる (減る)　*C1*, to decrease; X が減る　X decreases
へん (な) (変)　strange, weird
べんきょう [する] (勉強)　study
べんとう (弁当)　packed lunch
ペンパル　pen pal
へんぴん [する] (返品)　returning merchandise
べんり (な) (便利)　convenient

ほ

ほう　direction
ほうがく (法学)　study of law
ぼうし (帽子)　cap, hat
ほうちょう (包丁)　cleaver, big cutting knife
ボールペン　ball-point pen
ぼく (僕)　I (*male*); ぼくたち (僕たち)　we (*male*)
ほくせい (北西)　northwest
ほしい (欲しい)　wanted; X がほしいです　I want X
ほしがる (欲しがる)　*C1*, to want; X をほしがる　to want X
ほっかいどう (北海道)　Hokkaido (*island*)
ポツポツ　(*sound of raining in big, scattered drops*)
ほど　as much as; extent
ほとんど　almost; (+ *negative*) rarely
ほん (本)　book
ーほん (一本)　(*counter for long, often cylindrical items*)
ホンコン (香港)　Hong Kong
ぼんさい (盆栽)　bonsai (*dwarf tree*)
ほんしゅう (本州)　Honshu (*island*)
ほんとう (本当)　real, true
ほんや (本屋)　bookstore

ま

まあまあ　so so
マージャン　mah-jongg (*game*)
ーまい (一枚)　(*counter for thin, flat items*)
まい (毎〜)　every; まいあさ (毎朝)　every morning; まいしゅう (毎週)　every week; まいつき (毎月)　every month; まいにち (毎日)　every day; まいばん (毎晩)　every night
〜まいどり (〜枚撮り)　(*counter for the number of exposures on a roll of film*)
まえ (前)　front; X の前　the front of X
まぐろ　tuna
まご (孫)　grandchild
まさか　*interj.* It can't be that . . .; No way!
まじめ (な)　serious
まず　first of all
まずい　not tasty
また　again
まだ　*adv.* still; (+ *negative*) not yet
まち (町)　town
まちがいでんわ (間違い電話)　wrong number
まちがう (間違う)　*C1*, to be mistaken
まつ (待つ)　*C1*, to wait; X を待つ　wait for X
まったく (全く)　totally; (+ *negative*) absolutely not
まで　up to, until
まど (窓)　window
マトン　mutton
まめ (豆)　bean, pea
まもなく (間もなく)　soon, before long
まるい (丸い、円い)　round
まわり (回り)　around; X の回り　the surroundings of X
まん (万)　ten thousand
まんいん (満員)　at full capacity
まんが (漫画)　comic strip, comic book
まんなか (真ん中)　middle
まんねんひつ (万年筆)　fountain pen

み

みえる (見える)　*C2*, be visible, can be seen; X が見える　X is visible
みがく (磨く)　*C1*, to brush, polish; to wipe clean a smooth surface
みかん　mandarin orange
みぎ (右)　right
みじかい (短かい)　short
ミシン　sewing machine
みず (水)　water
みずぎ (水着)　bathing suit, swimwear
みずたま (水玉)　polka dots
みせ (店)　store, shop
みせる (見せる)　*C2*, to show
みそ (味噌)　miso (*fermented soy bean paste*)
みそしる (味噌汁)　miso soup
みぞれ　sleet
みち (道)　street
みっか (三日)　the third day of the month; three days
みつける (見つける)　*C2*, to find, discover; X を見つける　find X
みっつ (三つ)　three (items)
みどり (緑)　green
みどりのひ (緑の日)　Greenery Day (*April 29*)
みな (皆)　all, everyone
みなさん (皆さん)　everyone, all of you
みなみ (南)　south; みなみかぜ (南風)　south wind; みなみがわ (南側)　south side
みぶんしょうめいしょ (身分証明書)　identification card
みりん　sweet cooking sake
みる (見る)　*C2*, to see
みんな (皆)　all, everyone (*variant of* みな)

む

むいか (六日)　the sixth day of the month; six days
むかい (向かい)　across from, facing; X の向い　facing X
むく (向く)　*C1*, to fit, be suited for; X に向いている is suited for X
むこうがわ (向こう側)　the opposite (*of the street, river, etc.*)
むじ (無地)　unpatterned, solid color
むしあつい (むし暑い)　sultry, hot and humid
むす (蒸す)　*C1*, to steam
むずかしい (難しい)　difficult
むすこ (息子)　son
むすこさん (息子さん)　son (*respectful*)
むすめ (娘)　daughter
むすめさん (娘さん)　daughter (*respectful*)
むっつ (六つ)　six (items)
むら (村)　village
むらさき (紫)　purple
むらさめ　passing rain
むり (な) (無理)　impossible
むりょう (無料)　free of charge

め

めい (姪)　niece
めいごさん (姪ごさん)　niece (*respectful*)
めいし (名詞)　name card, business card
めいじ (明治)　Meiji Era (1868 - 1912)
めいわく (な) (迷惑)　nuisance, trouble; 迷惑をかける　cause trouble for someone
メーター　meter (measuring instrument)
メートル　meter (unit of length)
めがね (眼鏡)　eyeglasses
めがねや (眼鏡屋)　glass store, optician's
メキシコ　Mexico
めずらしい (珍しい)　rare, unusual
メロ・ドラマ　soap opera
めん (綿)　cotton fabric
めんせき (面積)　area, size, floor space

も

も　*part.* also
もう　already; (+ *negative*) not anymore
もう　more
もうしこみしょ (申込書)　application form
もうしぶんない (申し分ない)　satisfactory, good enough
もくようび (木曜日)　Thursday
もしもし　*interj.* hello (*on the telephone*)
もちろん　of course
もつ (持つ)　*C1*, to have, own
もっと　more
モデル　fashion model
もどる (戻る)　*C1*, to return; go back; come back; back up
もの　thing, item
もよう (模様)　pattern
もん (門)　gate
もんだい (問題)　problem; question

や

や　*part.* and so on
やおや (八百屋)　vegetable store, green grocer's
やきゅう (野球)　baseball
やく (焼く)　*C1*, to broil, grill, bake
やさい (野菜)　vegetable
やさしい　easy; lenient
やしょく (夜食)　evening snack
やすい (安い)　inexpensive, cheap
やすみ (休み)　time off, rest
やすむ (休む)　*C1*, to rest, to take time off
やっきょく (薬局)　pharmacy, drugstore
やっつ (八つ)　eight (items)
やはり　after all
やま (山)　mountain; やまやま (山々)　mountains
やまのぼり (山登り)　mountain climbing
やめる　*C2*, to stop, quit; X をやめる　quit X

ゆ

ゆうがた (夕方)　evening
ゆうこうに (有効に)　effectively

ゆうごはん(夕ごはん) dinner
ゆうしょく(夕食) dinner, supper
ゆうだち(夕立) evening rain shower
ゆうびんきょく(郵便局) post office
ゆうめい(な)(有名) famous
ゆうめいじん(有名人) celebrity
ゆか(床) floor
ゆき(雪) snow
ゆっくり slowly, leisurely
ゆびわ(指輪) ring
ゆめ(夢) dream
ゆるい loose

よ

よ *part.* (*emphatic sentence-final particle*)
ようか(八日) the eighth day of the month; eight days
ようき(な)(陽気) cheerful, lively
ようし(養子) adopted child
ようじ(用事) errand
ようしょく(洋食) Western cuisine
ようひんてん(洋品店) Western clothing store
ようふう(洋風) Western-style
ようふく(洋服) Western clothes
よか(余暇) free time
よく *adv.* often; well
よこ(横) side
よしゅう[する](予習) preparation for class
よっか(四日) the fourth day of the month; four days
よっつ(四つ) four items
ヨット yacht
よてい(予定) plan
よぶ(呼ぶ) *C1*, to summon, call for
よむ(読む) *C1*, to read
よやく[する](予約) reservation
より more than . . .; X よりきれい prettier than X
よる(夜) night
よろしく please treat me well; pleased to meet you
よわい(弱い) weak
よん(四) four
よんじゅう(四十) forty

ら

ラーメン ramen (*Chinese-style noodles*)
ラーメンや(ラーメン屋) ramen restaurant
らいげつ(来月) next month
らいしゅう(来週) next week
らいにち[する](来日) coming to Japan
らいねん(来年) next year
ラジカセ radio cassette
ラム lamb (*meat*)
ランゲージ・ラボ language lab

り

りくじょうきょうぎ(陸上競技) track and field
リモコン remote control
りゅうがくせい(留学生) foreign student
りょう(寮) dormitory
りょうしゅうしょ(領収書) receipt
りょうしん(両親) parents
りょうり[する](料理) cooking, cuisine
りょくちゃ(緑茶) green tea
りょこう[する](旅行) trip, travel
りりく[する](離陸) (*airplane*) take-off
りんご apple

れ

れい(零) zero
れいぞうこ(冷蔵庫) refrigerator
れいとうしょくひん(冷凍食品) frozen food
れきし(歴史) history
れきしがく(歴史学) the study of history
レジ cash register, cashier
レジャー leisure
レストラン restaurant
レバー liver
レンジ range; cook stove
れんしゅう[する](練習) practice

ろ

ろうにん(浪人) masterless samurai
ろく(六) six
ろくがつ(六月) June
ろくじゅう(六十) sixty
ロシア Russia
ロマンス romance novel

わ

ーわ(一羽) (*counter for birds*)
わ *part.* (sentence-final emphatic used mostly by women)
わあ *interj.* Wow!
ワープロ word processor
ワイシャツ men's dress shirt
わかい(若い) young
わがまま(な) selfish, egoistic
わかる(分る) *C1*, to understand; to be clear; X が分る understand X; X is clear
わしょく(和食) Japanese cuisine
わすれる(忘れる) *C2*, to forget
ワセリン Vaseline
わた(綿) cotton plant; cotton tuft
わたし(私) I
わたしたち(私たち) we
わふく(和服) Japanese-style clothes
わらう(笑う) *C1*, to laugh, smile
〜わり(割) ten percent; 二割 20 percent
わりびき[する](割引) discount
わる(割る) *C1*, to divide, to split open; X を割る to split X
わるい(悪い) bad
ワンピース dress

を

を *part.* (*direct object*)

Index

About the Author

Yasu-Hiko Tohsaku is Associate Professor at the University of California, San Diego, where he is the Director of the Language Program at the Graduate School of International Relations and Pacific Studies and the Coordinator of the Undergraduate Japanese Language Program. He received his Ph.D. in Linguistics from the University of California, San Diego, in 1983. He is the author of numerous articles on second language acquisition and Japanese language pedagogy. In addition, he has been involved with the development of Japanese language teaching videos and computer-assisted language learning programs.

144 © Yutaro Isobe/Camera Tokyo Service; *150* © Charles Gupton/Stock, Boston; *153* © Fujifotos/The Image Works; *168* © Hiroshi Mizofuchi/Camera Tokyo Service; *210* © Geographic Photo/Camera Tokyo Service; *216* © Burbank/The Image Works; *217* © Lou Jones; *225* © Naoki Watanabe/Camera Tokyo Service; *230* © Keiki Haginoya/Camera Tokyo Service; *276* © Fumihiko Murakami/Camera Tokyo Service; *280* © Fujifotos/The Image Works; *285* © Barbara Alper/Stock, Boston; *289* © Charles Gupton/Tony Stone Images; *292* © Sonia Katchian/Photo Shuttle: Japan; *298* © Don Smetzer/Tony Stone Images; *350* © Sonia Katchian/Photo Shuttle: Japan; *353* © Janet Wishnetsky/Comstock; *356* © Cameramann/The Image Works; *414* © Gary Chapman/The Image Bank; *423* © Fujifotos/The Image Works; *470* © Sonia Katchian/Photo Shuttle: Japan; *474* © Cameramann/The Image Works; *475* © Tsutomu Takahashi/Camera Tokyo Service; *486* © Sonia Katchian/Photo Shuttle: Japan.

Realia: *Page 33* Reprinted with permission of Cafe-Terrasse Yókó; *40* Reprinted with permission of Citizen Watch; *100* Teito Rapid Transit Authority; *211 Non-no*, Shueisha; *235* Courtesy of *The Yomiuri Shimbun* and the Japan Meteorological Agency; *316* Reprinted with permission of Lotteria; *341* Community Plaza Shinyuri, Odakyu Department Store; *351* Juujiya Food Center; *365–366* From *Zai-tech Kakeibo 1987*, Shufunotomo-sha; *483* Reprinted with permission of Domino's Pizza.®